IMA
ON

CITY OF GOD
The Coronation

THE DIVINE HISTORY AND LIFE
OF THE
VIRGIN MOTHER OF GOD

MANIFESTED TO MARY OF AGREDA
FOR THE ENCOURAGEMENT OF MEN

Translated from the Original Spanish

BY

FISCAR MARISON

(Rev. Geo. J. Blatter)

Printed in U.S.A.

AVE MARIA INSTITUTE
WASHINGTON, NEW JERSEY 07882
Copyright 1971 by Ave Maria Institute

IMPRIMATUR

Rome City, Ind., Aug. 24, 1912.
The Rev. George J. Blatter,
    Dear Rev. Father:—

My Imprimatur is herewith granted to your English translation of the work entitled "Ciudad de Díos." Wishing you every blessing, I remain

Devotedly in Domino,

H. J. ALERDING, Bishop of Fort Wayne.

MYSTICAL

CITY OF GOD

THE MIRACLE OF HIS OMNIPOTENCE
AND THE ABYSS OF HIS GRACE
THE DIVINE HISTORY AND LIFE OF THE VIRGIN

MOTHER OF GOD

OUR QUEEN AND OUR LADY, MOST HOLY MARY
EXPIATRIX OF THE FAULT OF EVE
AND MEDIATRIX OF GRACE

Manifested in these later ages by that Lady to her handmaid

SISTER MARY OF JESUS

Superioress of the convent of the Immaculate Conception of the town
of Agreda, of the province of Burgos in Spain, under
obedience to the regular observance
of the seraphic father

SAINT FRANCIS

For new enlightenment of the world, for rejoicing
of the Catholic Church, and encouragement of men.

———————

Translation from the Original Authorized Spanish Edition

BY

FISCAR MARISON

Begun on the Feast of the Assumption
1902

REV. GEO. J. BLATTER.

"Dear Sir:

"Twelve years of labor in translation, and many more years of expense and sacrifice, are not too great a price to pay for opening up such a treasure as CIUDAD to the millions of English-speaking people." *Respectfully,*

     FISCAR MARISON, Translator,

       South Chicago, Ill.

CONTENTS

BOOK ONE

INTRODUCTION

CHAPTER I.

CHAPTER II.

CHAPTER III.

CHAPTER IV.

CHAPTER V.

·CHAPTER VI.

CHAPTER VII.

CHAPTER VIII.

CHAPTER IX.

CHAPTER X.

CHAPTER XI.

CHAPTER XII.

CHAPTER XIII.

CONTENTS

CHAPTER XIV.

CHAPTER XV.

CHAPTER XVI.

CHAPTER XVII.

BOOK TWO

CHAPTER I.

CHAPTER II.

CHAPTER III.

CHAPTER IV.

CHAPTER V.

CHAPTER VI.

CHAPTER VII.

CHAPTER VIII.

CHAPTER IX.

CHAPTER X.

CONTENTS

A List of Noted Men in High Stations of Life Who have Praised and Recommended Ciudad de Dios of Agreda

Official approbation of Michael, Bishop of Tarazona, in whose diocese the work was written and first published, given May 6, 1667.

The noted Jesuit Theologian, Andreas Mendo, S. J., at the College of Madrid, on Oct. 29, 1666, at the order of the Bishop, closely examined Ciudad and confesses that no praise can be equal to its merits, which statement is officially endorsed on Nov. 6, 1666, by his superior, Dr. D. Francisco Forteza.

Official approbation of Paulus de Halmale, censor of the Antwerp diocese, June 12, 1686.

Imprimatur and recommendation of Constantius Caldonatius, Vicar General of Trent, Nov. 14, 1708.

High recommendation and approbation of the Ordinary of Augsburg through Johannes Michael Sembler, D. D., specially for the German edition, June 18, 1714, Jo. Casimirus Episc. Myclensis, for the Latin edition April 2,1719, Jan. Jacob. Episcopus Pergamensis.

Diocesan approbation of the French edition in Tournai, May 6, 1858, signed A. R. V. Descamps, Vic. Gen.

Highest recommendation of Ciudad by Fr. Alfons Salizanes, general of the Franciscan Order, Nov. 12, 1668, published in an official letter to Fr. Joseph Ximenes Samaniego.

After fourteen years of closest scrutiny, the Inquisition at Madrid, July 3, 1686, through Antonius Alvarez de la Puente, Bishop and Inquisitor General, permits the free publication of Ciudad, as containing nothing objectionable.

Didacus de Silva, Theologian and General of the

Spanish Benedictines, unstintedly praises Ciudad as ranking among the most excellent writings, Madrid, Dec. 15, 1666.

"The work is its own highest recommendation" words occurring in an official approbation of the Portuguese Jesuits, Lisbon, March 6, 1680, and signed P. Franciscus de Almada, S. J.

More extended praise from Antonius de Moralez, Theologian, ordinis SS. Trinitatis, March 18, 1680.

Official declaration of the University of Salamanca, issued July 4, 1699, that Ciudad in all things harmonizes with orthodox teachings of Catholic Theology, this declaration being signed by the theological faculties of practically all the religious orders, namely the Augustinians, Benedictines, Carmelites, Dominicans, Jesuits, Cistercians, Basilians, Minims, Hieronymites, Premonstratensians, Theatines, the Calced and Discalced Trinitarians, the Calced and Discalced Mercedarians, the Reformed Augustinians and the Canons Regular.

Official approbations of the Universities of Alcala, June 17, 1699.

The University of Granada, in 1698, approves the high encomiums of Ciudad published in a book by Dr. Johannes de Leyba.

The University of Saragossa in the same year, that of Philip Bezerra.

The Academy of Perpignan, in France, through the Ordinary and through Anton de Camps, Jesuit professor there, issues highest recommendations of Ciudad.

Even the University of Paris, the Sorbonne, although many of its faculty were tainted with Jansenism, and therefore adverse to giving proper honor to the Mother of God, nevertheless, according to the records of votes taken and the expressed sentiments of the greater and saner part of its faculty at the time, was constrained unofficially to approve of Ciudad de Dios. As practically all adverse criticism originated from the Sorbonne, above fact should be especially noted.

Another great French University, that of Toulouse, endorsed the publication of Grenier's "Compendium" by issuing an official commendation of Ciudad in highest terms of praise, which document was signed for the faculty by Casemajon, Rabii, and J. Gisbert, S. J., Theologians, on Nov. 25, 1694.

In Volume III, The Transfixion, is given in full the official approbation of the great University of Louvain, to which we refer the reader. The high recommendations contained therein, placing the CITY OF GOD among the greatest books of the world, are repeated in nearly all the above mentioned documents.

It was necessary to confine ourselves merely to the dates and signatures of a few documents, because if these and many others were quoted in full, it would be necessary to add hundreds of pages to this volume. If all the writings of eminent and learned men in Christianity, praising the CITY OF GOD as the most wonderful, the most useful, the most interesting, the most reliable book in the world, were to be printed in connection with this translation, this book would probably have to be extended to one hundred volumes instead of being restricted to four.

Why multiply recommendations?

All adverse criticism you may see written or hear expressed, is absolutely without foundation and mere waste of time in our day. The past three centuries have more closely scrutinized every line of Ciudad to find a flaw than you can ever hope to do. And there was no flaw to be found. *Read and be convinced!*

FISCAR MARISON.

APPROBATIONS

THE first Pope officially to take notice of "Ciudad de Dios" was Pope Innocent XI, who, on July 3, 1686, in response to a series of virulent attacks and machinations of some members of the Sorbonne, known to be Jansenists, issued a breve permitting the publication and reading of the "Ciudad de Dios." Similar decrees were afterward issued by Popes Alexander VIII, Clement IX and Benedict XIII. These decrees were followed by two decrees of the Congregation of Rites, approved by Benedict XIV and Clement XIV, in which the authenticity of "Ciudad de Dios" as extant and written by the Venerable Servant of God, Mary of Jesus, is officially established. The great pope Benedict XIII, when he was archbishop of Benevent, used these revelations as material for a series of sermons on the Blessed Virgin. On Sept. 26, 1713, the bishop of Ceneda, Italy, objecting to the publication of the "City of God," was peremptorily ordered by the Holy Office to withdraw his objections as interfering with the decree of pope Innocent XI for the universal Church.

The process of canonization of Mary of Agreda was promoted by the Spanish bishops and other eminent men of the Church soon after her death in 1666. It has resulted so far in securing her the title of Venerabilis, thus clearing the way to her beatification, for which, let us hope, God will soon raise a promoter among the many pious and eminent men who hold in esteem her writings and have learned of her holy life and of the miracles wrought at her tomb.

The Redemptorist Fathers published a new German translation in 1885, which was approved and highly recommended by the Bishop of Ratisbon in the following terms:

"We take pleasure in giving our episcopal approbation to the annotated translation of the Spanish original "Ciudad de Dios" of Mary of Jesus and recommend this book, which will surely edify all readers and be the occasion of great spiritual blessings."

Ratisbon, September 29, 1885.

✠IGNATIUS, Bishop of Ratisbon.

Notable is the high recommendation of the Prince-Archbishop of Salzburg, Apost. Legate, Primate of Germany, etc.

"According to the decrees of Pope Innocent XI and Clement XI the book known as 'Ciudad de Dios' written by the Venerable Servant of God, Maria de Jesus, may be read by all the faithful."

"A number of episcopal approbations, the recommendations of four renowned universities, namely, of Toulouse, Salamanca, Alcala and Louvain, and of prominent members of different orders, coincide in extolling the above-named work. The learned and pious Cardinal D'Aguirre says that he considers all the studies of fifty years of his previous life as of small consequence in comparison with the doctrines he found in this book, which in all things are in harmony with the Holy Scriptures, the Holy Fathers and Councils of the Church. The Venerable Superior-General of St. Sulpice, Abbé Emery, adds: "Only since I read the revelations of Mary of Agreda do I properly know Jesus and his Holy Mother."

"We therefore do not hesitate—in granting our episcopal approbation to—"Ciudad de Dios"—and wish to recommend it to the faithful and especially to our clergy."

✠Franz Albert,
Archbishop.

Archiepiscopal Chancery, Salzburg.
September 12, 1885.

A more recent official approbation of "Ciudad de Dios" is from the Bishop of Tarazona, prefacing the new edition of 1911-1912.

"We, Dr. James Ozoidi y Udave, by the grace of God and of the Apostolic See, Bishop of Tarazona, Administrator Apostolic of the Diocese of Tudela, etc., etc.

Having charged the priest Don Eduardo Royo, chaplain and confessor at the convent of the Immaculate Conception of Agreda, carefully and exactly to compare the manuscript which is to serve as copy for the printing of the new edition of the "City of God" now about to be published by the religious of the above-named convent, with the authenticated autograph manuscript of that work there preserved,—and having ascertained by a personal revision of a great part of the manuscript that the said priest has diligently and faithfully fulfilled this charge imposed upon him by us:

We now therefore certify that this present edition of 'Ciudad de Dios,' with the exception of a few mere orthographic modifications, is entirely conformable to the autograph of that work as composed and written by the Venerable Mother Mary of Jesus of Agreda.

Tarazona, April 7, 1911.

[Diocesan Seal]   ✠James, Bishop of Tarazona.

Finally follows the official approbation of the Right Reverend Bishop of the Fort Wayne Diocese, where this English translation is published.

Rome City, Ind., Aug. 24, 1912.

The Rev. George J. Blatter,

Dear Rev. Father:—

My Imprimatur is herewith granted to your English translation of the work entitled 'Ciudad de Dios.' Wishing you every blessing, I remain,

Devotedly in Domino,

✠H. J. ALERDING, Bishop of Fort Wayne.

The author has made use of capital letters in the text slightly at variance with common usage, in order to avoid complication and secure greater clearness. The paragraph numbers are those of the newest Spanish edition of "Ciudad de Dios" in 1912. In the abridgment they vary slightly.

City of God is divided into three Parts and eight Books. Part I contains Books 1 and 2. Part II contains Books 3, 4, 5 and 6. Part III contains Books 7 and 8. As circumstances compel a serial publication of the four volumes, the author judged it best to head these divisions as follow:

THE CONCEPTION, Books 1 and 2.

THE INCARNATION, Books 3 and 4.

THE TRANSFIXION, Books 5 and 6.

THE CORONATION, Books 7 and 8.

The Coronation

The heavenly Life of the Queen of Heaven, most
holy Mary, containing the Events of her Life
from the Coming of the Holy Ghost until
the Assumption and Coronation of
the Virgin Mother of God in
Heaven.

INTRODUCTION

1. In navigating a deep and dangerous sea, the navigator is so much the more dangerously beset with its terrors and the attacks of pirates, the farther he has penetrated into its wide expanses. His cares are vastly increased on account of his weakness and want of certainty; for he does not know when or whence danger may come, and he is powerless to avert its coming and unable to resist it when at hand. This is just what is now happening to me since I am engulfed in the immense ocean of the excellence and magnificence of the works of the most holy Mary. And yet it is a sea full of repose and tranquillity, as I know and confess. Nor can the fact, that I have advanced so far upon this sea of grace, and that I have finished the first and second part of her life, give me assurance; for in this work I have, as in a most clear mirror, only so much the more clearly perceived my own incapability and vileness, and the deepest conviction forces itself upon me, that her history is most impenetrable and incomprehensible to all created understanding. Nor are the enemies, the princes of darkness, ever at rest; for, like the most persistent pirates, they continue to afflict and discourage me by false illusions and temptations with a malice and astuteness beyond all calculation. The navigator has no other recourse than to fix his sight upon the north-star, according to which, as his

star of the sea, he must guide and direct his course amid the waves. I am trying to do the same in the midst of these multitudinous and tormenting temptations and fears. Guided by my Star, the most holy Mary, in whom, through obedience, I can ascertain and fix my will upon the will of the Eternal, and being many times afflicted, full of unquietness and fear, I cry out from the bottom of my heart and say: "My Lord and most high God, what shall I do in my doubts? Shall I proceed, or shall I desist, in writing this history? Do thou, O Mother of grace and my Instructress, make known to me thy will and that of thy divine Son."

2. I must confess truly, and as due to the divine condescension, that God has always answered my clamors and has never denied me his paternal kindness in making known his will in many ways. Although this is sufficiently evident in the assistance rendered to me in the writing of the first and second parts, yet besides this proof, there are innumerable other assurances given me by the Lord himself, by his most holy Mother, and his angels, so that evidences have been heaped upon evidences, and testimonies upon testimonies, to counteract my cowardice and fear. What is more, the angels themselves in visible shapes, being the prelates and ministers of the Lord in his holy Church, have pointed out and reiterated the divine commandment, bidding me to believe and execute this commission, and to continue to the end. Nor was there wanting to me the light of infused science, which sweetly and forcefully called, enlightened and moved my heart to the knowledge of the highest perfection, the most immaculate holiness, the most perfect virtue and the most desirable of what can be sought by the will. It has at the same time referred me to all this as enclosed and reserved, like a hidden

manna, in that ark of the covenant, most holy Mary, open for all that wish to approach and taste thereof.

3. Nevertheless, on entering upon the writing of this third part, I was beset by new and harassing contradictions, not less formidable than those experienced in the first two portions of this history. I can say without fear, that I have not composed a sentence or a word, nor have I brought myself to write the least part of it, without experiencing more temptations than the letters of the alphabet of which it is composed. Although the hindrances caused by my own fear would have been sufficient (since I know who I am, and cannot help being cowardly, nor ever can put less confidence in myself than what my own weakness will warrant); yet neither this, nor the magnitude of the undertaking were the real impediments, though these were at first unsuspected. I presented to the Lord the second part, which I had written, in the same way as I had presented the first. Under strict obedience I was compelled to begin this third part, and, by the strength which this virtue gives to all that practice it, I allayed the fear and faintness of my heart in executing what had been assigned to me. But fluctuating between my desire and fear of commencing, I was cast about like a vessel, combated by violent and contrary winds.

4. On the one hand, the Lord bade me proceed in what I had begun, as such was his will; nor, in my continual prayers, did I ever feel impelled to a different course. It is true, for some time I paid no attention to these directions of the Most High and did not manifest them immediately to my superior and to my confessor (not because I wished to conceal them, but in order to act more securely and in order that they might not suspect I followed only my own insight). But the

Lord, who is so even and equable in all his works, inspired them with a new energy in pressing their continual exhortations and commands. Yet on the other hand, the envy and malice of the ancient serpent maligned all that I did or was moved to undertake. He raised up against me tormenting and alluring temptations, by which he sometimes sought to inspire me with his own boundless pride. At others, and very often, he sought to cast me down to deepest dejection and involve me in darkest and most disorderly fears, increasing his efforts as this history progressed, and especially as it was coming to a close. This enemy also availed himself of the judgment of some persons, who justly could claim my respect and who would not further this work. He caused also disturbances among the religious under my charge. It seemed to me that I had no time to spare and was obliged to attend to the welfare of the community, as the most important duty of a superioress. With all these molestations I came to no such interior peace, as is necessary for and befitting the actual enlightenment and intelligence concerning the mysteries to be treated of. For this light cannot be perceived, nor is it properly communicated, amid the spiritual storms of temptation, but will shine only in the peace and serenity of the soul's faculties.

5. Afflicted and harassed by such a variety of temptations, I ceased not in my clamors. On one day in particular I spoke to the Lord: "Highest Lord and Good of my soul, to thy wisdom are not concealed my sighs and my desire to please Thee and to avoid errors in thy service (Ps. 37, 10). Lovingly I lament in thy royal presence; for, either Thou commandest me, O Lord, what I cannot fulfill, or Thou permittest thy and my enemies to hinder by their malice what Thou com-

mandest." The Lord answered my complaint and with some severity, said: "Remember, soul, that thou canst not continue what thou hast begun, nor wilt thou finish the writings of my Mother's life, if thou wilt not become altogether perfect and pleasing in my eyes. For I wish that thou gather within thee the copious fruits of this benefit, and that thou among the first, profit by it in greatest abundance. In order that thou mayest share its fruits as I wish, it is necessary, that all which is earthly in thee and savoring of a daughter of Adam be consumed. Thou must be free from the effects of sin with all its evil inclinations and habits." This answer of the Lord excited in me new solicitudes and the most burning desire of performing all that it implied; namely, not only a common mortification of all the inclinations and passions, but an absolute death of the animal and terrestrial life and its renovation and transformation into a celestial and angelic state of existence.

6. Desiring to apply my powers to what was proposed to me, I examined my inclinations and appetites, I searched the bystreets and corners of my interior and felt a most ardent wish to die to all that is visible and earthly. For some days I suffered in these exercises great affliction and melancholy; for, in proportion to my anxiety, increased also the dangers and occasions of being diverted by attention to creatures. The more I sought to withdraw myself from all my surroundings, so much the more did I find myself bound and oppressed by what I abhorred. Of all this the enemy availed himself for my discouragement, representing such a life as altogether impossible to me. To this affliction was suddenly added another new, strange disorder. I felt in my body a condition so sensitive that the least exertion, even the most insignificant mor-

tification, became more intolerable to me than until then
the most severe penances. Those that I was accustomed
to undergo most willingly, required now the most violent
exertion, and I found myself become so delicate that they
seemed to inflict upon me mortal wounds. To undergo
discipline was an excruciating pain, causing swoons, and
each stroke cut through my very heart. Without exaggeration I say, that merely to touch one hand with the
other forced out my tears, so that I felt great confusion
and grief at being so miserable. In forcing myself to
labor in spite of this infirmity, I found my blood oozing
from my fingernails.

7. I could not account for this new experience, and
in considering it, I impatiently exclaimed: "Ah me!
What misery is this? What change do I feel within
me? The Lord commands me to mortify myself and
die to all creatures, and I feel myself much more alive
to pain and much less mortified." For some days I
suffered in great bitterness and impatience of my soul.
In order to moderate my disturbance, the Most High
consoled me, saying: "My Daughter and Spouse, let not
thy heart be afflicted at the vividness of thy sufferings.
I have sought by this means to distinguish in thee the
effects of sin and to restore thee to a new life and prepare thee for works more exalted and pleasing to Me.
Until thou shalt have attained this state, thou canst not
begin to write what remains of the life of my Mother
and thy Mistress." This answer of the Lord somewhat
encouraged me; for his words are words of life, vivifying
the heart (John 6, 69). Although my troubles and temptations were not abated, I prepared myself for labor and
battle; yet I continued to distrust my weakness and inability and despaired of finding a remedy. I sought
it in the Mother of life, and I resolved to ask for help

in sincerity and constancy. For She is the only and most certain refuge of the needy and affflicted and She has continually heaped her many favors upon me, the most useless creature of the world.

8. I prostrated myself at the feet of the great Lady of heaven and earth, and pouring out my spirit in her presence, I besought Her mercifully to remedy my imperfections and defects. I represented to Her my desire of pleasing Her and her divine Son and again offered myself for her service, even if I should have to pass through fire and torments and shed my blood. The kind Mother answered my supplications by saying: "My daughter, understand well, that these desires, which the Most High again excites in thy heart, are pledges and effects of his love, by which He calls thee to his intimate intercourse and familiarity. It is his most holy will and mine, that thou on thy part correspond to them in order that thou mayest not hinder thy vocation or retard any longer the pleasure of his Majesty in what He requires of thee. During all the writing of my life I exhorted and reminded thee of thy obligations connected with this blessing, namely that thou imprint in thyself the living image of its teachings and of my example according to the graces thou receivest. Thou hast now arrived at the third and last part of this history; and it is time thou raise thyself to a perfect imitation of Me, clothing thyself with new strength and extending thy hand to strong doings (Prov. 31, 17). By such a life and behavior thou wilt be able to begin what still remains to be written; for it must be written in such a way, that thou put in practice the lessons it inculcates. Without such a disposition thou wilt not be able to write it; since it is the will of the Lord, that my history shall be written more in thy heart than on paper,

and that thou feel what thou writest, in order that thou mayest write what thou feelest."

9. "Therefore I desire that thy interior be cleared from all earthly images and inclinations (Ps. 44, 11); so that, having put away and forgotten all visible things, thou mayest center all thy conversation and intercourse upon thy Lord (Phil. 3, 20), upon me, and upon his angels; and let all other things be strange and foreign to thee. In the strength of this virtue and purity, which I require of thee, thou shalt crush the head of the ancient serpent and conquer his opposition to thy writing and laboring. Because thou art so tardy in responding to the wishes of the Lord, in entering upon the path He wishes thee to pursue, and in placing full confidence in his blessed intentions, I tell thee truly: while attending to these empty fears, thou art so tardy in responding to the Lord, in entering upon the path He wishes thee to pursue and in placing full confidence in his blessed intentions, that, precisely on this account, divine Providence has permitted the dragon to be the minister of his justice in punishing thy unbelief and thy want of submission to his will. That same enemy has concocted schemes to draw thee into some faults by setting before thee his deceits in the garb of a good intention and of virtuous ends, and by seeking falsely to persuade thee, that thou art not destined for such high favors and exalted blessings; and, in order that thou mayest not merit them, he has made thee dull and tardy in rendering thanks for them. Thou hast been taken in by the deceit of deeming these works of the Most High due to thee in justice, and not as works of grace; and so thou hast neglected to co-operate to the fullest extent with the divine graces and hast not corresponded to those thou receivest without any merit of thy own. It is time,

my dearest, that thou be assured, and that thou believe
the Lord and me; for I teach thee the highest perfection,
namely the imitation of me. Thus shall be conquered
the pride and cruelty of the demon and his head crushed
by divine power. There is no reason why thou shouldst
impede its effects; but, forgetting all things, consign
thyself lovingly into the hands of my divine Son and
mine; for We desire of thee what is most holy, most
praiseworthy and pleasing in our eyes and estimation."

10. By this instruction of my heavenly Lady, Mother
and Teacher, my soul was replenished with new light
and with the desire of obeying Her in all things. I
renewed my good resolutions, I resolved to raise myself
by the help of divine grace, and I strove to prepare
myself for the fulfillment of the will of the Most High
without resistance. I availed myself of my bodily condition, by which, as mentioned above, my sensibility to
mortification had been so much enlivened and increased.
But the demon abated not in his strife and opposition.
He knew that the enterprise I was to assume was very
arduous and that the state to which the Lord raised
me was a refuge, but one far above human weakness
and earthly dullness. Gladly will I confess this truth
and the slowness caused by my frailty and sluggishness.
I acknowledge, that the Lord has labored with me during
my whole life in order to raise me from the dust and
from the dunghill of my vileness, multiplying his blessings and favors beyond all my comprehension. Moreover He has seconded all these blessings by the aid of
his right hand in order to gain his end. I cannot at
present mention all that He did for me; but at the same
time it seems unjust to pass it over in silence entirely,
since it will show to what misery sin has brought us
and what distance there is between the capacity of

the reasoning creature and the summit of virtue and perfection it can attain. It will also show what it costs to restore man to that capacity.

11. Some years before writing this I was repeatedly favored with an extraordinary blessing at the hands of God. It was a sort of death to all the animal and terrestrial operations, like that of civil death; and this state was followed by another, which was one of new enlightenment and of more exalted operations. But since the soul always remains clothed in mortal and earthly corruption, I continue to feel the heavy weight of the flesh overwhelming and degrading the soul (Wis. 9, 15), unless the Lord renews his wonders and favors me with the assistance of divine grace. On that occasion this renewal was wrought in me through the Mother of piety, who, speaking to me in a vision, said: "Take heed, my daughter, that now thou must begin to live not thy own life, but the life of thy Spouse Christ in thee (Gal. 2, 20); He is to be the life of thy soul, and the soul of thy life. For this purpose I wish to cause in thee the death of thy old life, which has so far operated in thee, and establish in thee the new life, which We ask of thee. Let it then today be known to heaven and earth, that sister Mary of Jesus, my daughter and servant, dies to the world, and that the Most High works this change, in order that this soul may live only to what faith teaches. Just as in natural death all things are left behind; so shall this, my daughter, thus freed, by her last will and testament consign her soul to her Creator and Redeemer and her body to the earth of self-knowledge and patient suffering. Of this soul my divine Son and I shall take charge, in order to fulfill entirely his holy will, if she will obey Us promptly. We will celebrate her exequies with our courtiers, in order to bury her in the bosom of

the divine humanity of the Word, which is the sepulchre of those that die to the world while still in mortal life. From now on she must not live in her own self, nor for herself, after the fashion of Adam; but in all things she is now to manifest in her the life of Christ, who is her life. I shall beseech Him to look kindly upon this deceased one and to receive her soul as his own; to acknowledge her as a stranger and pilgrim, living not on earth, but in the higher and divine regions. I shall instruct the angels to accept her as a companion and to treat and converse with her as if she were freed from mortal flesh."

12. "I command the demons to let alone this dead one, just as they must let alone the other dead, who are not under their jurisdiction and in whom they have no part; for from this day on she shall be more dead to visible things than those who have passed from this world. I conjure men to lose her out of sight and forget her, as they forget the dead, in order that they may thus allow her to remain in peace and tranquillity. And thee I command and exhort, that thou consider thyself as one who has finished life in this world and has entered eternal life in the presence of the Most High. I desire thee to imitate the life of the blessed in faith; since the certainty and assurance of truth is the same for thee as for them. Thy conversation is to be on high (Phil. 3, 20); thy intercourse, with the Lord of all creation and thy Spouse; thy conference shall be with the angels and saints, and thou must rivet thy whole attention upon me, thy Mother and Teacher. For all the rest that is earthly and visible thou must have neither movement of life, nor any activity; no more than a dead body, which shows no feeling of life in response to anything that may happen to it or may be done with it. Neither

must difficulties inquiet thee, nor flattery or pleasures affect thee; thou must not respond to injuries, nor be elated by honors; let neither presumption inflate thee, nor mistrust cast thee down; thou must not give consent to any feeling of concupiscence or anger; because thy model in all these passions must be a dead body, already freed from all of them. Nor must thou have any more dealings with the world than the dead; for the world immediately forgets those whom it has praised in life, and to such an extent, that, though they be father or brother, and the most intimate relatives, it hastens to put them out of sight. All this the deceased permit, without a murmur or a feeling of offense; nor do the dead make any account of the living, much less do they attend to them or to anything they may have left among their survivors."

13. "Having thus died to thyself, it remains for thee to consider thyself as the food of worms, fit only for vilest corruption. Thus shalt thou bury thyself in the earth of thy self-knowledge, in order that thy senses and passions may not presume to give forth their bad odor in the sight of the Lord, nor, like an ill-covered and half-buried corpse, may not presume to give forth its bad odor in the presence of the Lord and of those that have entered the blessed life. Let thy horror of showing any signs of life, or of not being entirely mortified in the sight of thy God and of the saints, be much greater than that caused by unburied bodies among men. The use of thy senses such as sight, hearing, touch and others for the purpose of entertainment or delight, should be a greater surprise and offense to thee, than to see a corpse moving about. By this death thou shalt be prepared and fit to be the only spouse of my divine Son, and my true and most beloved disciple and daughter.

Such is the state which I require of thee, and so high is the wisdom, which I am to teach thee in following my footsteps and in imitating my life, reproducing in thyself, as far as is granted thee, all my virtues. This should be the fruit of recording the wonders and sacraments of my sanctity manifested to thee by the Lord. I wish that they escape not the secrecy of thy bosom and be made known without having moved thee to the perfect fulfillment of the will of my divine Son and of mine, which tends to nothing else than toward thy own highest perfection. Drink then the waters of wisdom from their fountainhead, the Savior: there is no reason why thou shouldst remain void and unsatiated of that, which thou art to administer to others, nor that thou shouldst finish writing this history without deriving the fruits of this blessing. Prepare thy heart then for this death, which I urge upon thee, and thou shalt attain thy wishes and mine."

14. Such were the words of the great Lady of heaven to me on this occasion, and on many others She has repeated this teaching of the salutary and eternal life. Of these teachings I have written much in the chapters of the first and second part, and shall continue to do so in the third part. From all this my sluggishness and ingratitude toward such great benefits is very apparent. For, though this great Queen and her divine Son have so often promised to raise me to a most exalted state and habitation, once I die to the earth and to myself, and though in their divine kindness They now promise it freely and anew; yet I find myself continually backward in virtue and much entangled in the pursuits of a daughter of Adam. This state is a solitude and desert, created for the soul in the midst of the surrounding creatures. In it my soul has no

intercourse with the rest of visible creatures, but enjoys the presence and the communications of the Lord, of his holy Mother and the angels, at the same time permitting all its activity and all its dealings to be governed by the promptings of the divine will for God's greater glory and honor.

15. During the whole course of my life, from earliest childhood, the Most High has exercised me in continual infirmities, sorrows and other molestations of creatures. But with the advance of years He increased also the sufferings of another kind of trial, which made me forget much of those already suffered in the past; it was like a two-edged sword which divided my soul and spirit, as the Apostle says (Heb. 4, 12). This trial was that constant fear, of which I have so often spoken, and for which I have been reprehended in this history. Much of it I felt even from childhood, but it developed and rose to the highest pitch since my entrance into religion, where I applied myself entirely to the spiritual life, and experienced the manifestations of the Lord to my soul. Since that time God has placed me upon this cross, or into this wine-press of the heart, namely: permitting me to remain in the continual dread of not being on the right path, of being deceived, or of having lost the grace and the friendship of God. My difficulties were much augmented by the publicity, which some persons incautiously and to my great grief, gave to my affairs, and by the terrors with which others filled me at my danger. So deeply rooted in my heart was this terror, that it has never ceased, and could never be allayed by the satisfaction and complete assurances of my confessor and superiors, nor by their kind encouragement, nor by their corrections, nor by the many other means they used for this purpose. What

is more, although the angels and the Queen of heaven, and the Lord himself continually reassured and soothed me, and although I feel myself free in their presence; yet, as soon as I issue from this sphere of divine light I am again assailed with incredible violence. This might easily be recognized as the cruel machination of the infernal dragon, if my troubles, afflictions and fears had not the appearance of arising from other sources than the devil. This fiend especially assails me, whenever I am about to open my heart to my confessors, particularly to the superior, who directs me; for nothing does this prince of darkness fear more than the light and the power possessed by the ministers of the Lord.

16. In the bitterness of this sorrow and the most ardent desire of grace and of not losing God, I have lived many years, and the various and numerous happenings amid this constant strife I cannot record. The root of this fear, I believe, was holy, but many of its branches have been fruitless, although the divine wisdom knew how to use them all for his different ends. On this account He permitted the enemy to avail himself of the blessings of the Lord for my affliction. For the inordinate fear, which hinders the good, though it appear to imitate ever so much the good, is evil and of the demon. My afflictions have at times reached such a pass, that I considered it a great gain not to lose the life of my body, and especially that of my soul. But the Lord, whom the winds and the waves obey (Matth. 8, 27) and whom all things serve (Ps. 118, 91), who gives nourishment to every creature in opportune time (Ps. 144, 15), has now in his condescension wished to give peace to my spirit in order that I might enjoy more tranquillity in writing the rest of this history. It is some years ago, that the Lord consoled

me and promised me peace and interior quiet before I should die; informing me at the same time, that the dragon is so furious against me, because he suspects there is little time left him for persecution.

17. In order to set about writing this third part the Lord on a certain day, with singular condescension and complacency, spoke to me as follows: "My dearest Spouse, I wish to alleviate thy pains and moderate thy afflictions; quiet thyself, my dove, and rest securely in the sweetness of my love and of my powerful and kingly word; for I assure thee upon this word, that it is I, who speak to thee and who have selected thy paths according to my pleasure. It is I, that lead thee along these ways; it is I, the same One, that is at the right hand of the eternal Father and present in the sacrament of the holy Eucharist in the species of bread. I give thee this assurance, in order that thou quiet and convince thyself. For I do not wish thee, my dearest, to be my slave, but my daughter and spouse, and I desire thee to enjoy my gifts and delights. Enough of fears and of bitterness hast thou suffered; let peace and tranquillity enter into thy afflicted heart." Such favors and assurances of the Lord, often repeated, one would think, should not be humiliating, but should afford only the greatest joy; but they are of such a kind, that they abase the heart to the lowest dust and fill me with solicitude and anxiety. Those that think different, have little experience and are only slightly capable of the secret operations of the Most High. It is certain, that I have been instructed in many new things interiorly and was much alleviated in the troubles and temptations caused by these disorderly fears. But the Lord is so wise and powerful, that on the one hand He assures, and on the other He stirs up the soul, injecting new fear

of falling and thereby preserving it in the knowledge and humiliation of self.

18. I must acknowledge that by these and other continual favors, the Lord has not so much freed me from fears, as confirmed me in them; for I live in continual dread, lest I show myself ungrateful and fail to correspond by displeasing Him or losing Him; lest I be wanting in the perfect love of Him, who is so good in Himself; and lest I should not deserve to retain the fullest possible love toward Him, or even that which is not possible. Filled with these anxieties, and on account of my great misery, solicitude and many faults, I said on one occasion to the Most High: "My sweetest Love, Lord and Master of my soul, although Thou givest me so many assurances to quiet my troubled heart, how can I do away with my fears amid the dangers of this laborious and dreadful life, full of temptations and persecutions, during which I hold my treasure in a vase more fragile and weak than that of any other creature?" With paternal condescension He responded: "My cherished spouse, I do not wish thee to lose the just fear of offending Me; but it is my will, that thou be not disturbed and grieved in a disorderly manner, nor so as to hinder thee from rising to my exalted and perfect love. Thou hast my Mother for a Teacher and a model, for thy instruction and imitation. I shall assist thee by my grace and support thee with my direction. Tell Me then, what thou askest, or what thou desirest for thy peace and security."

19. With the greatest resignation that I could muster I replied: "Highest Lord and Father, much is that which thou askest, although thy goodness and immense love deserve that I fulfill it all. But I know my weakness and inconstancy, and I shall be satisfied in no other

way than by not offending Thee, neither by the slightest thought, nor by the least movement of my faculties; and I shall rest only when all my actions shall be according to thy pleasure and good will." The Lord answered: "My continual help and favors shall not fail thee, if thou correspond to them. In order that thou mayest do it so much the better, I wish to perform a work, which is in keeping with the love I have for thee. I will connect my immutable Being with thy insignificance by an especial Providence, chaining and binding thee in such a way, that, whenever thou shalt, in the weakness of thy will, do anything less pleasing to Me, thou shalt feel my influence detaining and recalling thee to Me. The effect of this blessing Thou shalt know and feel immediately within thyself, just like a slave, who is bound by chains in order that she may not fly."

20. To the great joy and advantage of my soul the Almighty fulfilled his promise and among many other favors and blessings (which may not be mentioned and which do not concern my purpose), none has been so precious to me as this one. I perceive it not only in great dangers, but in the smallest; and in such a way, that if I neglect or carelessly omit any work or ceremony, although it be no more than to humiliate myself or to kiss the floor on entering the choir to adore the Lord, as is customary in the convent, I at once feel a sweet force, which draws me and calls my attention to the defect, and which, on its part, permits not the least imperfection. If sometimes in my weakness I fall into any, this divine force is at once present, causing in me heart-rending pain. This pain serves as a check to the least disorderly inclination and at the same time as a goad toward seeking immediate remedy for the fault or imperfection committed. As the gifts of the Lord are

without regret (Rom. 11, 29), He has not only bound
me with this mysterious chain, but, in his divine condescension, on a certain day, that of his holy Name and
Circumcision, I perceived that He tripled it, in order to
restrain me and bind me still more forcibly, since a
triple cord, as the wise man says, is difficult to break
(Eccles. 4, 12). All this was necessary on account of
my weakness, in order that I might not be overcome
by the importunate and astute temptations of the ancient
serpent.

21. In the meanwhile these temptations increased so
much, that in spite of the blessings and commandments
of the Lord mentioned above, in spite of the demands
of obedience and of others not to be mentioned here,
I nevertheless hesitated to begin the last part of this
history; for I felt again the fury of the powers of darkness, which tried to overwhelm me. I understood this
and I will explain it by what saint John says in the
twelfth chapter of the Apocalypse: That the great red
dragon shot forth from its maw a river of water against
that heavenly Woman (Apoc. 12, 15), whom he had
pursued from heaven, and that, since he could not touch
or destroy Her, he turned in great rage against the rem-
nants and the seed of that great Lady, against those
who are sealed with the testimony of Jesus Christ (Apoc.
12, 17) in his Church. During the time of which I
am speaking this ancient serpent strained all his wrath
to disquiet me and, as far as he could, force me to
commit some faults, which retarded the purity and perfection of life required of me and necessary for writing
what I was commanded. While this interior battle continued, the feast of the holy Guardian Angel on the first
of March intervened. Reciting matins in the choir I
suddenly felt a noise or great disturbance, so that I

shrank and humiliated myself to the very dust. Then I saw a great multitude of angels, which filled the whole choir, and from their midst proceeded a still greater refulgence or splendor as of a judge, seated upon a tribunal or judgment-seat. I understood at once, that it was the archangel saint Michael. Without delay they intimated to me, that they were sent by the Most High with especial power and authority to arraign me for my negligence and for my faults.

22. I desired to prostrate myself on the earth to acknowledge my transgressions and humbly to weep before those celestial judges, but as I was surrounded by the nuns, I dared not make the presence of the angels known by prostrating myself in body. I did what was possible interiorly, bitterly weeping over my sins. In the meantime I saw the holy angels speaking and conferring with each other, saying: "This creature is useless, slow, and not at all fervent in fulfilling the commands of the Most High and of our Queen. She will not come to a full trust in the blessings and the enlightenments, which she continually receives at our hands. Let us deprive her of all those blessings, since she does not put them to use, nor earnestly strive to be so pure and perfect as the Lord teaches her to be; neither does she proceed to write the life of his most blessed Mother, as He has commanded her so many times. If she does not mend, it is not just that she should receive so many and such great favors and instructions in holiness." Hearing these words I was sadly afflicted at heart and I wept the more. Full of confusion and grief I spoke to the holy angels in the bitterness of my soul and I promised amendment of my faults and obedience unto death to the Lord and to his most holy Mother.

23. At my humiliation and my promises the angelic

spirits relaxed somewhat in their severity and with greater kindness they told me: that, if I would diligently fulfill what I had promised, they would assure me of their continual favor and assistance, admit me as their companion and friend, and hold intercourse with me in the same way as they conversed with each other. I thanked them for their kindness and besought them to present my thanks also before the Most High. They disappeared, warning me, that for the favors they would show me, I must imitate them in purity, committing no fault or imperfection wilfully; and this they intimated as the condition upon which this promise depended.

24. After these and many other happenings, which need not be mentioned, I was left in a state of greater humiliation, as was natural with one who had been so severely reprehended for ingratitude, unworthiness and insensibility toward so many blessings, exhortations and commandments. Full of confusion and sorrow I considered within myself, what little excuse or pretext I had for resisting the divine will, in view of all that I had come to know and in view of its importance to my welfare. I resolved firmly to execute the command or die in the attempt, and I sought for some powerful and tangible means which should rouse and urge me on to combat my want of attention, and which should keep me alert, if possible, against any imperfection in all my operations and movements, so that I might always do what is most holy and pleasing in the eyes of the Lord. I betook myself to my confessor and superior and besought him, in all the sincerity and submission of my heart, to reprehend me severely and force me to be perfect and solicitous in the most exact fulfillment of the divine will and in the execution of what the divine Majesty required of me. Although he was most zealous

and vigilant as one who took the place of God and one who knew his will and my prescribed path; yet he could not always come to my assistance or be present on account of the absentations required by his duties as a religious and as a superior. I resolved therefore also to engage one of the nuns to assist me, asking her to reprehend and advise me often, or warn me and stir me up by threats. All these means and others I sought in the most ardent desire of pleasing the Lord, his most holy Mother and my Teacher, the holy angels, all of whom were of the same mind in regard to my advance in perfection.

25. In the midst of these solicitudes it happened to me one night, that my holy guardian angel showed himself to me as being particularly pleased and said: "The Most High wishes to condescend to thy desires and has appointed me to serve thee as a guide to spur thee on. I shall be thy faithful friend and companion in order to advise thee and rouse thy attention; and thou shalt find me present, just as now, whenever thou shalt turn thy eyes toward me in the desire of pleasing and faithfully serving thy Lord and Spouse. I will teach thee how to praise Him continually and how to alternate with me in canticles. I will manifest to thee new mysteries and treasures of his greatness; I will give thee deeper understandings of his immutable being and divine perfections. And whenever thou art engaged in outward works of obedience or charity, or when, through some negligence, thou turnest to earthly and exterior things, I shall call thee to fly to the Lord; and for this purpose I shall use some words of admonition, which often shall be these: Who is like unto the God, that dwells on high and in the hearts of the humble? At other times I shall call to thy mind the blessings thou hast received from

God and thy duty to his love. At still others, I shall remind thee to look upon Him and raise up to Him thy heart. But to all these warnings thou must be punctual, attentive and obedient."

26. "The Most High also desires me not to conceal to thee any longer a favor, which until now thou hast overlooked among the many conferred upon thee by his most liberal bounty; and for this thou must now begin to thank Him. It is this, that I am one of the thousand angels, who served as a guard to our great Queen in this world, and one of those, who bear the device of his admirable and holy name. Look upon me and thou wilt see it upon my breast." I looked and there recognized the holy name in refulgent splendor, filling my soul with new consolation and jubilee. The holy angel proceeded and said: "He has also commanded me to call thy attention to the fact, that of us thousand angels very rarely any are appointed as guardian angels of souls and whatever souls so far have been committed to our care, have all been of the number of the saints and none of them of the reprobate. Take heed then, O soul, of thy obligation not to interrupt this series; for if in spite of this blessing thou art lost, thy punishment and chastisement shall be of the severest ever inflicted upon the damned and thou shalt be known as the most unhappy and ungrateful of all the daughters of Adam. That thou shouldst be favored by having me as thy guardian, who was one of the guardians of our great Queen, most holy Mary and the Mother of the Creator, was ordained by the most high Providence and in view of thy being chosen to write and imitate the life of his most blessed Mother. I was appointed to instruct thee and assist thee, because I was an eye-witness of her divine works and excellences."

27. "This office of a guide will be fulfilled principally

by the great Lady herself; but I am to furnish thee
with the necessary images in order to elucidate what
the heavenly Mistress shall teach thee, and I am to give
thee other understandings ordained by the Most High,
for the clearer recording of the mysteries manifested to
thee. Thou shalt experience all of them although thou
shalt not always know the connection and the sacraments
hidden under this providential guidance. Thou shalt also
perceive that the Lord himself, making use of this special
providence in thy regard, has commissioned me to compel thee, with sweetest urgency, to imitate the purest
Mary our Queen, and to follow Her and obey Her in her
doctrine. From now on I shall execute this mandate
of the Lord with greater insistence and force. Resolve
then to be most faithful and thankful in regard to these
blessings and seek to scale the highest summits of the
perfection taught thee and asked of thee. Remember,
that even if thou reach the perfection of the highest seraphim, thou shalt still be in great debt to God's copious
and liberal mercy. The new mode of life, which the
Lord asks of thee, is contained and is made clear in the
instructions given to thee by our great Queen and Lady,
and in what thou shalt understand and write in this third
part of her life. Listen to Her with a submissive heart,
thank Her humbly, execute Her doctrine anxiously and
carefully; for if thou do this, thou shalt be fortunate
and eternally blessed."

28. Other things, which the angels told me, need not
be mentioned for my present purpose. But what is contained in this introduction, will manifest partly the providence of the Most High toward me and it will also make
known the high purposes of divine Wisdom in the writing
of this history. These are, that not only I, but all who
desire, may reap the fruits of this blessing, and that

each one for himself may use it as an efficacious means of salvation. It will also become evident, that Christian perfection cannot be attained without great battles with the demon or without incessant labor in overcoming and subjecting the passions and evil inclinations of our depraved human nature. Finally, the heavenly Mother and Instructress, that I might begin to write this third part of her history, in sweetest kindness, said to me: "My eternal blessing, and that of my most holy Son, come over thee, in order that thou mayest write the rest of my life and in order that thou mayest labor and strive after the perfection We desire of thee. Amen."

BOOK ONE

How the divine Right Hand showered upon the Queen of Heaven highest Gifts, in order that She might labor in the holy Church; the Coming of the Holy Ghost; the copious Fruit of the Redemption and the Preaching of the Apostles; the first Persecution of the Church, the Conversion of saint Paul and the arrival of saint James in Spain; the Apparition of the Mother of God in Saragossa, and the Founding of the Pilgrimage of our Lady of the Pillar.

CHAPTER I.

OUR SAVIOR JESUS REMAINS SEATED AT THE RIGHT HAND OF THE ETERNAL FATHER, WHILE THE MOST HOLY MARY DESCENDS FROM HEAVEN TO THE EARTH, IN ORDER THAT, WITH HER ASSISTANCE AND INSTRUCTION, THE NEW CHURCH MIGHT BE FOUNDED.

1. In finishing the second part of this history I showed how our great Queen and Lady, most holy Mary, was privileged by God to be miraculously present in body at two places, in the Cenacle as well as in the empyrean heavens, where She was seated at the right hand of her Son and eternal God (Ps. 44, 10) ; how, in order to make his glorious Ascension more wonderful, the Son of God and of the Virgin, took Her with Him for the purpose of putting Her in possession of the ineffable rewards She had until then merited and to assign Her the place, which, for her past and future merits, He had prepared for Her from all eternity. I said also, that the three Persons of the most blessed Trinity left it to the free

29

choice of the heavenly Mother either to return to the world for the consolation of the first children of the Church and for its foundation, or permanently to establish Herself even then in the most blessed state and remain in the possession of the glory They had conferred upon Her. For, conditional to her choice and in pursuance of the great love They had for this peerless Creature, the will of the divine Persons inclined toward retaining Her in the abyss of their glory and not to restore Her to the banished children of Adam upon earth. In a certain sense justice seemed to demand this; since the world was already redeemed by the Passion and Death of her Son, toward which She had co-operated in all plenitude and perfection. Death had in Her no further claims, not only because She had suffered its pains in that of Christ our Savior (as explained by me in its place); but also because the great Lady never was tributary to death, nor the demon, nor to sin, and therefore was not subject to the common law of the children of Adam (Heb. 9, 27). According to our mode of thinking, the Lord desired that She, without dying like the others, should pass by another kind of transition from the state of pilgrimage to that of comprehension, from mortality to immortality, and that She should not suffer death upon the earth, who, while remaining upon it, had committed no fault to merit death; for the Most High could have passed Her from one state into the other in another way.

2. Against this, however, stood the charity and humility of this admirable and sweetest Mother; for her love urged Her to come to the assistance of her children and to seek the manifestation and exaltation of the name of the Most High in the new evangelical Church. She desired also to gather into the faith many faithful fol-

lowers by her solicitation and intercession and to imitate her children and brethren by dying upon the earth; though, by reason of her sinlessness, She owed no such tribute (Rom. 6, 23). In her vast wisdom and admirable prudence She knew how much more precious it is to merit a reward and crown, than to possess them gratuitously in advance, even if they happen to be those of eternal glory. Her wisdom and humility were not without their present reward; for the eternal Father made known to all the courtiers of heaven, at the same time both his own desires and the choice of most holy Mary for the good of the militant Church and for the succor of the faithful. All the inhabitants of heaven then began to know what is but just that we should know also on earth; namely: that, as we are told by saint John, the eternal Father so loved the world as to give not only his Son for its Redemption (John 3, 16); but also his Daughter, the most holy Mary, sending Her from her glory to build up the Church, which Christ its Artificer had established; and in like manner and for the same purpose the Son delivered up his most loving and beloved Mother, and the Holy Ghost his sweetest Spouse. To this must be added another circumstance enhancing this blessing: namely that it followed closely upon the injuries which Christ our Redeemer received in his Passion and frightful Death, making the world altogether unworthy of this benefit. O infinite love! O immense charity! How evident is it become, that the multitudinous waters of our sins cannot extinguish thee! (Cant. 8, 7).

3. After most holy Mary had remained in heaven for three entire days and had enjoyed in body and soul the glory of the right hand of her Son and true God, She departed with the benediction of the blessed Trinity from the highest empyrean and returned, according to

her desire, to this nether world of the earth. God ordered an innumerable multitude of angels, selected from all the choirs and from the highest seraphim nearest to his throne, to accompany their Queen. She was enveloped in a cloud or globe of the most resplendent light, which served Her as a couch or reliquary and in which She was borne downward by the seraphim. The beauty and exterior splendor in which this heavenly Queen came to the earth can never be compassed by the human mind in mortal life; and it is certain that no living creature could have looked upon Her in merely natural powers without losing its life. On this account it was necessary, that the Most High should hide her refulgence from those that saw Her, until the splendors of her beauty should have moderated. Saint John the Evangelist alone was privileged to see the Queen in the full redundance of the divine glory which She had enjoyed. The immense beauty of this magnificent Queen and Mistress of the heavens, as She descended from the throne of the blessed Trinity, can easily be understood, when we consider how the face of Moses, after having spoken with the Lord and received the law on the mountain, shone with such light that the Israelites could not bear it or look upon his face. We are not informed that the Prophet saw the Divinity face to face; and if he saw It, his vision of God certainly did not approach in the least to that enjoyed by the Mother of God.

4. The great Lady arrived at the Cenacle as a substitute of her divine Son in the new evangelical Church. In the gifts of grace, which She had received for this ministry, She showed such a plenitude and abundance, that She excited the wonder of the angels and the astonishment of the saints; for She was a living image of Christ our Redeemer and Master. Beneath the

globe of light, in which, unseen, She arrived in the Cenacle, She was restored to her natural existence, in so far as to be thenceforward present only in that place. Immediately the Mistress of holy humility prostrated Herself to the ground and abasing Herself to the dust, said: "Most high God and my Lord, behold this vile worm of the earth, acknowledging itself formed from it (Gen. 2, 7), and coming from nothingness to this existence, which I hold through thy most liberal clemency. I acknowledge also, O highest Father, that thy ineffable condescension, without any merits of mine, has raised me from the dust, to the dignity of being the Mother of thy Onlybegotten. From my whole heart I praise and exalt thy immense goodness in so favoring me. In gratitude for such great blessings I offer myself to live and labor anew in this mortal life, according to all the decrees of thy divine will. I consecrate myself as thy faithful servant and as the servant of the children of the Church. All of them I present before thy immense charity and implore Thee from my inmost heart to look upon them as their kindest God and Father. For them I offer up the sacrifice of being deprived of thy glory and peace, and of having chosen of my own free will suffering rather than joy, denying myself the vision of Thee in order to perform what is so pleasing in thy sight."

5. The holy angels that had come with the Queen took leave of Her to return to heaven, congratulating the earth for again possessing as its inhabitant their great Queen and Lady. I wish to mention, that while I wrote of this, the holy princes asked me, why I did not more frequently call Mary the Queen and Mistress of the angels, and they told me not to neglect the use of that title in the balance of this history, since they derived

such great delight therefrom. In order to obey and please them I shall use it many times from now on. But returning to our history, we must take notice, that the heavenly Mother, during the first three days after her descent from heaven, remained much withdrawn from earthly things, still lingering in the overflow of the joy and admirable influences of her triduum of glory in the heavens. Of all mortals the Evangelist saint John alone had cognizance of this mystery; for in a vision he had seen the great Queen of heaven ascend with her divine Son and had also seen Her descend in her glory and graces for the enrichment of the Church. Two days he remained as it were entranced and suspended in admiration at this extraordinary mystery. Knowing that his most holy Mother had descended from on high he desired to speak to Her, but dared not presume.

6. Battling between the urgency of his love and the restraint of his humility, the beloved Apostle hesitated nearly a whole day. Conquered by his filial love, he at last resolved to seek the presence of his heavenly Mother in the Cenacle, and on his way thither, he stopped to argue with himself. "How can I presume to do what I desire, before knowing the will of the Most High and of my Mistress? Yet my Redeemer and Master has given Her to me as a Mother and favored and bound me to Her as a son; hence it is my duty to serve and assist Her. She is not ignorant of my desire, and will not despise it; She is kind and sweet, and will pardon me. I wish to prostrate myself at her feet." Therewith saint John came to a resolve, and he went to the place where the Queen was in prayer with the rest of the faithful. At the instant in which he raised his eyes to look upon Her, he fell down pros-

trate just as he and the other two Apostles had fallen
at seeing the transfigured Lord on mount Tabor (Matth.
17, 2). For the splendors which he now saw in the
countenance of most blessed Mary were very like to
those seen on our Savior Jesus at that time. As the
impression caused by the vision of her descent from
heaven was also still enduring, his human weakness was
so much the more completely overwhelmed and he fell
to the earth, without power of again rising to his feet
for the space of an hour. Nor were the Apostles and
disciples, who were present in the Cenacle, necessarily
astonished at this fall; because, in imitation of their
divine Master, and moved by the example and instructions of the most holy Mary, they were frequently,
during the time they were expecting the Holy Ghost,
lying prostrate and in the form of a cross praying for
the coming of the Paraclete.

7. The kindest Mother then approached the humble
and blessed Apostle, and raised him from his prostrate
position, and, assuming a more natural appearance, fell
herself upon her knees, and said to him: "My master
and son, thou already knowest that I am to be governed
in all my actions by obedience to thee; for thou takest
the place of my divine Son and Master, in order to
command me in all that I am to do. I now ask thee
anew to be solicitous in commanding me, on account of
the consolation I derive from obeying in all things."
Hearing these words, saint John felt great confusion and
perplexity on account of what he had seen and experienced concerning Her, and he once more prostrated
himself before Her, offering himself as her slave and
begging Her to command and govern Him entirely. In
this urgent request saint John persevered for some time,
until, overcome by the humility of our Queen, he sub-

jected himself to her will and was persuaded to yield to Her, agreeing to command Her as She wished. For this was of the greatest profit for his own advancement, and for us a unique and efficacious example, reminding us of our pride and teaching us to crush it. If we acknowledge ourselves devout children of this heavenly Mother and Mistress of humility, we are justly obliged to imitate and follow Her. The vision of the great Queen of the angels in her state of glory was so deeply impressed upon the understanding and the interior faculties of the Evangelist, that the image of it remained within Him during all His life. At the moment when he saw Her descend from heaven, he cried out in great wonder. The intelligence he then received concerning Her he afterwards manifested in the Apocalypse, and especially in the twelfth chapter, as I will explain later on.

INSTRUCTION WHICH THE GREAT QUEEN AND MISTRESS
OF THE ANGELS GAVE ME.

8. My daughter, though I have until now so many times urged thee to detach thyself from all visible and earthly things and to die to thyself and to all that savors of a child of Adam, and though I have fully exhorted and instructed thee in the first and second part of my life already written; yet I now call upon thee anew, with the affection of a kind and loving Mother, and I invite thee in the name of my divine Son, in my own name and in that of the angels, who also love thee so much, that, forgetting all else, thou raise thyself to another life, more exalted and heavenly, approaching that of the eternal felicity. I desire that thou leave entirely the ancient Babylon, thy enemies and all their

false and harassing vanities, and that thou approach the holy and celestial Jerusalem, live in its porches, where thou art to occupy thyself in the true and perfect imitation of my life and thus arrive by the divine grace at the intimate union of my Lord and thy most faithful Spouse. Hear me then, my dearest; with a joyful attention and alacrity of soul follow me fervently, reproducing in thy life the image of what thou writest, and study what works I performed after I came back from the right hand of my divine Son to this world. Meditate upon and penetrate into all my doings, in order that, according to the graces thou receivest, thou mayest continually copy, what thou understandest and writest. Divine favor will not fail thee, for the Most High will not deny it to those, who on their part exert themselves according to their power, and He will not refuse thee his assistance to attain what is pleasing and acceptable to Him, if thou do not by thy negligence make thyself unworthy. Prepare and expand thy heart, inflame thy will, purify thy understanding, and cast out from thy faculties every image and impression of visible creatures. For thus will none of them interfere with thee, nor any of them draw thee into venial sin or imperfections; the Most High will deposit in thee his hidden wisdom and thus thou shalt be prepared and anxious to execute all that is most pleasing in our eyes and enjoined upon thee by Us.

9. From now on thy life is to be like that of one newly called from the grave. Just as such a one is apt to turn to a new life, as if estranged and foreign to all that he loved in his former life, changed in all his desires, reformed and alienated from all his former inclinations; so I desire, that thou, my daughter, be renewed. For thou must live as if thou wert re-endowed

with the highest possible gifts of the soul by the divine
power within thee.   But for these divine operations it
is necessary that thou use thy own efforts and prepare
thy whole heart, so that thou mayest be entirely free
and become a blank tablet as it were, whereon the
Lord, with his own fingers, may write and stamp, as
in soft and yielding wax, the seal of my virtues.   His
Majesty desires thee to be an instrument in his hands
wherewith to operate his own holy and perfect will; and
thou knowest, that an instrument does not offer resistance to the artisan, and if it possesses free will, it uses
it only in order to permit itself to be freely moved.
Now then, my dearest, come, come whither I call thee;
and remember that if it is natural to the highest Good
to bestow favors and communicate Itself to the creatures
at all times, yet in the present age, this Lord and Father
of mercies seeks to manifest more abundantly his liberal
kindness toward mortals. For the times have advanced
toward their end and there are few, who are willing
to dispose themselves for the reception of his divine
gifts.   Do not thou lose such a favorable occasion; follow me, and tread in my footsteps; and since I invite
thee to such a happiness in motherly love and by such
high and perfect doctrine, do not grieve the Holy Ghost
by thy tardiness.

CHAPTER II.

10. It befitted the exalted dignity of saint John as being appointed the son of most holy Mary by Jesus on the Cross, that he should be the secretary of the ineffable sacraments and mysteries of the great Queen, which were kept concealed from other persons. For this reason many of her mysteries were revealed to him before her excursion into heaven, and he was made an eye-witness of the hidden mysteries on the day of the Ascension, when this sacred Eagle saw the divine Sun, Christ (Isaias 30, 26), ascend in seven-fold light, as Isaias said, and with it, the moon Mary shining as the sun, on account of her likeness to Christ. The most fortunate Evangelist saw Her ascend and seated at the right hand of her Son; he saw Her also descend, as I have said, with renewed astonishment; because he recognized the change and renovation at her return to the earth after having experienced the influences of the divine glory and godlike attributes. As is said in the second part, our Savior Jesus had already promised the Apostles, that before going to heaven He would arrange for the stay of his most blessed Mother for the consolation and direction of his holy Church. But the Apostle saint John, during his first joy and wonder at seeing the great Queen seated at the right hand of Christ our Savior,

forgot this promise and, absorbed in the consideration of this unthought of event, he began to fear or get anxious, lest the heavenly Mother should remain in the glory which She enjoyed. Agitated by this uncertainty, saint John, amid the jubilee of his soul, felt also the afflicting pangs of love at the loss; and these lasted until he again remembered the promises of his Master and Savior and saw his most holy Mother descending to the earth.

11. The mysteries of this vision remained impressed upon the memory of saint John, so that neither these, nor all the others revealed to him by the Queen of the angels, ever escaped his mind; and the sacred Evangelist sought to spread the knowledge of them in the holy Church. But the humility of the most prudent Mary our Lady deterred him as long as She lived and persuaded him to keep them hidden within his bosom until the Most High should command otherwise; for it was not opportune to manifest them to the world beforehand. The Apostle obeyed the wishes of the heavenly Mother. Before his death, at the time when God commissioned him to enrich the Church with the hidden treasures of these sacraments, he was instructed by the Holy Ghost to reveal them in deeply metaphorical and enigmatic language, which, as the Church itself confesses, is difficult to understand. It was proper that they should not be open to all, but shut up as the pearl is in nacre or in its shell, or as the gold is hidden in the minerals of the earth. The holy Church, gradually more enlightened and studying them diligently, could draw upon these treasures as necessity required; and in the meanwhile preserve them in deposit within the obscurity, which the holy doctors have met with and acknowledge in the holy Scriptures, and especially in the Apocalypse.

12. In the course of this history I have already spoken

of the providence of the Most High in concealing the
greatness of his most holy Mother in the primitive
Church, (Part II, 413) and I will offer no excuse for
pointing it out anew, because of the admiration it will
cause in those, who now come to know of it. In order to
moderate our doubts (if any should be entertained), we
need only consider what the various saints and doctors
have said anent the providential concealment of the body
and the burial of Moses (Deut. 34, 6). This was ordained
they say, in order that the people of the Jews, so given
to idolatry, might not be led astray into giving adoration
to the body of the Prophet, whom they esteemed so
highly, or that they might not begin to venerate him by
some superstitious and vain cult. For the same reason
they say, that Moses, writing of the creation of the world
and of all creatures, although the angels were the most
noble of all, did not expressly mention their creation, but
only indicated it by the words: "God created light;" because these words can be understood as well of the material light of this visible world, as also, by a hidden
metaphor, of those substantial and spiritual lights, the
holy angels, of whom a more open mention was at that
time not opportune.

13. If the Hebrews were subject to the danger of
idolatry because of the intercourse and vicinity of heath-
enism and because of their blind inclination to attribute
Divinity to men or to whatever seemed great, powerful
or in any way superior; then, if, in the first preaching of
the Gospel and the faith of Christ our Savior, the great
excellences of his most holy Mother had been propounded
to them, the gentiles would have been in still greater
danger of this error. In corroboration of this we have
the saying of Dionysius the Areopagite, who, though
he was such a great philosopher that he had found out the

existence of the true God even by his natural acumen of mind, openly maintained, after he had become a Catholic, that, when he had seen and conversed with the most holy Mary, he would certainly have esteemed and adored Her as a God, if faith had not taught him otherwise. In this danger then would have fallen, much more easily, the ignorant, and they would certainly have confounded the Divinity of Christ the Redeemer, which they were obliged to believe together with the greatness of his most pure Mother, thinking that, since they were propounded at the same time and showed such similarity in holiness, She was a God just as her Son. But this danger vanished after the faith and practice of the Church had taken such deep roots and after it had been so clearly established by the teachings of the holy doctors and by so many miracles wrought by God in testimony of the Redeemer. Enlightened by these testimonies we know that He alone is God and true man, full of truth and grace; and that his Mother is a mere creature, full of grace without possessing the Divinity and next to God above all the rest of creation. In our times then, so enlightened by the divine truths, the Lord knows when and how it is proper to spread the glory of his most holy Mother by opening up the enigmas and secrets of the holy Scriptures wherein He holds them enshrined.

14. The mystery of which I am about to speak, with many others concerning our great Queen, was recorded by the Evangelist in the metaphors of the twenty-first chapter of the Apocalypse; especially introducing the most holy Mary under the type of the holy Jerusalem and describing Her under cover of all the circumstances mentioned in that chapter. Although in the first part I have explained it at length in three chapters, applying it, as it was then given me to understand, to the mystery of the

Immaculate Conception of the blessed Virgin Mother; yet it is necessary now to interpret it in relation to the mystery of the descent of the Queen of angels after the Ascension of the Lord. Let it not be objected that there is a contradiction or repugnance in these different applications; for both of them are legitimately founded on the literal text of the Scriptures, and there can be no doubt, that the divine Wisdom can comprehend in the same and identical words many mysteries and sacraments. As David said: In one word we can include more than one thing, and God certainly included a double meaning in the same words without equivocation or contradiction (Ps. 61, 12). This is one of the sources of the difficulties found in holy Scripture, and one that was necessary in order to make it more pregnant and precious in its meaning and in order that the faithful may study it with greater humility and reverence. That it should be so full of enigmas and metaphors is necessary, since in that style and wording, the sacred mysteries, which would be strained by the more proper terms, can be expressed much more fully.

15. This will be better understood in the mysteries now under consideration, for saint John says that "he saw the holy city of the new Jerusalem, prepared and adorned as a bride, descending from heaven," etc. There is no doubt that this metaphor of a city refers truly to the most holy Mary, and points out her descent after having ascended with her most blessed Son. At the same time it also refers to her descent in the divine mind by her Immaculate Conception, in which She was formed as the new earth and the new heaven, as explained on in the first part. The Evangelist included both these sacraments, when he speaks of this event in the twenty-first chapter. Therefore it will be necessary to explain it in

this new sense, though this will imply a repetition of
the sacred text; but I will explain it more briefly on
account of what I have already said in the first part.
I will now speak in the name of the Evangelist, for the
sake of greater brevity.

16. "And I saw a new heaven and a new earth. For
the first heaven and the first earth was gone, and the
sea is now no more" (Apoc. 21, 1). He calls the most
sacred humanity of the incarnate Word and that of his
heavenly Mother, a new heaven and a new earth: a
heaven, on account of the inhabitation of the Divinity in
humanity, and a new one, on account of the renovation of
mankind. In Christ Jesus our Savior lives the Divinity
(Col. 2, 9), in a oneness of personality following from
the indissoluble substantial union; while in Mary another
kind of union is effected, an extraordinary union of
graces. These heavens are now new; the passible humanity, which the Evangelist had seen wounded and dead
in the sepulchre, he now saw elevated and placed at the
right hand of the eternal Father, crowned with glory and
with the gifts merited by his life and death. He saw
also the Mother, who had given to Christ this passible
nature and had co-operated in the Redemption of the
human race, seated at the right hand of her Son (Ps. 44,
10) and absorbed in the ocean of the inaccessible light of
the Divinity, participating in the glory of her Son as his
Mother and meriting it in justice and on account of her
ineffable works of charity. He called also the earth of
the living a new heaven and a new earth, as it was renewed by the lamp of the Lamb (Apoc. 21, 23), replenished with the spoils of his triumph and newly illumined
by the presence of his Mother; renewed also because as
Sovereigns They had taken possession of their reign
through all the eternities. They renewed it also by hav-

ing afforded its inhabitants the opportunity to see Them
with their own eyes and to partake of their benefits, by
having populated this earth with the new children of
Adam as its citizens and their allies and by having turned
it over to them without any danger of loss. On account
of these different kinds of renewal he said that the first
heaven and the first earth had gone; not only because
the sacred humanity of Christ and that of most holy
Mary, in which He had lived as in the first heaven, had
betaken Themselves to the eternal habitations, bearing
with them also the earth of their human essence; but also
because men themselves from the ancient heaven and
earth of their passible being, had passed to the state of
impassibility. Gone were the rigors of justice, and
blessed rest was attained. The winter of troubles had
fled (Cant. 2, 11) and the eternal springtime of joy and
delight had come. The first earth and heaven of all the
mortals had also vanished; for the celestial Jerusalem
had been barred and locked during five thousand two hundred years, so that none could enter and all the mortals
would have been confined to the old sin-stained earth, if
through the entrance of Christ and his most blessed
Mother these bars and locks had not been shattered and
the divine justice had not been satisfied.

17. In an especial sense the most blessed Mary was a
new heaven and earth and new earth by ascending with
her Son, the Savior Jesus, and by taking possession at his
right hand in the glory of body and soul without having
passed through the death common to all the sons of men.
Although even in her human condition upon earth She
was a heaven, whence She saw the Divinity; but this
condition of the great Lady passed away, to take the place
of another condition, making Her, by an admirable disposition of the divine Providence, a new heaven, in

which God might dwell among all creatures in the highest glory. In this new order of things, in this new heaven, there was no sea; for through Her the bitterness and sorrows of labor had come to an end, if She would have consented to remain from that time on in that most happy state. In regard to the other saints, who in body and soul, or only in the soul, remained in glory, all storms and dangers of the first earth in mortal life now really had an end.

18. The Evangelist proceeds: "And I John saw the holy city, the new Jerusalem, coming down out of heaven from God, prepared as a bride adorned for her husband." I, an unworthy Apostle of Jesus Christ, am the one to whom this hidden sacrament was revealed in order that it might become known to the world: and I saw the Mother of the Incarnate Word, the true mystical city of Jerusalem, the vision of peace, descending from the throne of God himself to the earth, and I saw Her clothed as it were with the Divinity and adorned with a new participation in God's attributes, his wisdom, power, holiness, immutability, and amiability, and resembling his Son in her actions and behavior. She came as an instrument of his Omnipotence and taking the place of God by a new participation. Although She came to the earth in order to labor upon it for the benefit of the faithful and for this purpose deprived Herself voluntarily of the vision of eternal glory, nevertheless the Most High resolved to send Her adorned and furnished with the power of his own arm and to compensate Her for the beatific vision She relinquished. Instead of it She was favored with another sort of vision and participation in his incomprehensible Divinity, suited to her present state of pilgrimage, but yet so divine and exalted, that it exceeds all the thoughts of angels and men. He adorned Her with

gifts limited only by Herself and has prepared Her as a Bride for her Spouse, the incarnate Word, enriching Her so that no grace or excellence was wanting in Her. Nor should her absence from his right hand deprive Her of the presence and intercourse of her Man, who was to remain in Her, as in his proper heaven and throne. Just as the sponge receives and soaks up the fluids into its hollow spaces, so, according to our mode of understanding, this great Lady was filled with influences and communications of the Divinity.

19. The text further states: "And I heard a great voice from the throne, saying: Behold the tabernacle of God with men, and He will dwell with them. And they shall be his people; and God himself with them shall be their God." This voice proceeding from the throne, filled all my mind with sweetness and joy. I understood how the great Lady, before her death, attained possession of the great reward merited as a singular favor and the prerogative due only to Her among all the mortals. None of these, after attaining possession of their glory, had permission or authority to return to life; yet this privilege was conceded to this only Bride for the increase of her glory. She, in full possession of eternal beatitudes and proclaimed by all the courtiers of heaven as their legitimate Queen and Lady, wished of her own free will to descend and become the Servant of her vassals, educating and governing them as her children. On account of this charity She deserved to have all the mortals as her subjects, and to be put in possession of the militant Church, where She was to dwell, over which She was to preside and draw the blessing, the mercy and forgiveness of God; for in her bosom the Lord was sacramentally present during the whole time in which She lived in the primitive Church after her descent from heaven. If

there had been no other reason, her Son would have instituted the most holy Sacrament in the world in order thus to dwell in Her; and through her merits and petitions He remained among men with new graces and benefits; wherefore the Evangelist adds:

20. "And God shall wipe away all tears from their eyes; and death shall be no more, nor mourning, nor crying." This great Lady came as the Mother of grace, of mercy, of joy, and of life. She it is, that fills the world with joy, that dries away the tears brought on by the sin of our mother Eve. She turned mourning into rejoicing, tears into new jubilee, clamors into praise and glory, the death of sin into life for all who seek it. Now the death of sin is at an end, and all the clamors and the pains of the wicked are at an end, if only, before their damnation, they will flee to this sanctuary and there find pardon, mercy and consolation. The first ages, which were not blessed with the presence of Mary, the Queen of the angels, have fled and passed with all the sorrows and sighs of those that sought Her and could not see Her; for now the world possesses Her for a refuge and help, and for a shield of mercy against the divine justice that hangs over the sinner's head.

21. "And He that sat upon the throne, said: Behold I make all things new." This was the voice of the eternal Father, who gave me to understand, how He would make all things new: a new Church, a new Law, new Sacraments. Having conferred upon men such new blessings as to give them his Onlybegotten Son, He added to this blessing by sending them the most holy Mary thus renewed, endowed with such wonderful gifts and power as to enable Her to distribute the treasures of the Redemption, and by placing them altogether into her hands to be scattered broadcast according to her most prudent

will. For this purpose did He send Her from the royal throne, a faithful reproduction of his Son, and, like a faithful copy of the Original, sealed Her, in as far as is possible in a mere creature, with the attributes of the Divinity. Her holiness was also to be copied by the new evangelical Church.

22. "And He said to me: Write, for these words are most faithful and true. And He said to me: It is done. I am Alpha and Omega; the beginning and the end. To him that thirsteth, I will give of the fountain of waters, freely. He that overcometh shall possess these things, and I will be his God; and he shall be my son." The Lord from his throne (says saint John), commanded me to write down this mystery, in order to give witness to the fidelity and truth of his words and of the works of the most holy Mary, into whose hands He has pawned his Omnipotence. And because these sacraments are so exalted and hidden, I announce them in figures and riddles, leaving it to the Lord to manifest them in the world at his own time, and letting all understand, that whatever is possible has been done for the restoration and welfare of mortals. In saying "it is done," God reminds men of their obligations toward Him for sending his Onlybegotten to suffer and die for them and to teach them his doctrine; and for sending his Mother to assist and succor the Church; and for sending the Holy Ghost to promote and enlighten, to strengthen and comfort it with the gifts He had promised. And since the eternal Father had nothing more to give us, He says: "It is done." As if he had said: "All that is possible to my Omnipotence and proper to my equity and bounty, I have given, and the One who is the beginning and end of all that has being. As the beginning, I give it by the omnipotence of my will; and as the end of all, I receive all things, providing

in my wisdom the means by which they attain their last end. These means are all under the control of my most divine Son and his Mother, my chosen and beloved One among the children of Adam. In Her are the pure and living waters of grace, from which all the mortals, who thirst after their eternal salvation, may draw it as from its fount and source (John 7, 37). For them these waters are distributed gratis; since they could not merit them, yet with his own life, my incarnate Son has merited them, and his blessed Mother gains and merits them for those that apply to Her. And whoever shall overcome the hindrances to these waters of grace, that is: Whoever overcomes himself, the world and the demon, shall find Me a liberal, loving and mighty God; he shall possess all my goods and whatever through my Son and his Mother I have prepared for him; for I shall adopt him as my child and as an inheritor of my eternal glory.

23. "But the fearful, and unbelieving, and abominable, and murderers, and whoremongers, and sorcerers, and idolaters, and all liars, they shall have their portion in the pool burning with fire and brimstone, which is the second death." To all the sons of Adam I give my Onlybegotten as a Master, Redeemer, and Brother and his Mother as a Protectrix, Mediatrix and Advocate powerful before Me; and as such I send Her again into the world, that all may understand how much I wish them to avail themselves of her protection. But those that do not overcome the repugnance of their flesh to suffering, or do not believe my testimonies and wonders wrought in their behalf, or those witnessed by my holy Scriptures; and those who, having believed, have entangled themselves in the base impurities of carnal delights, the sorcerers, idolaters, who forsake my true power and Divinity, following the demon; all those that work deceit and malice,

shall have no other inheritance than what they thus choose for themselves. This will be the dreadful fire of hell, which is a pool of burning sulphur, full of darkness and stench, where for each of the damned there shall be different pains and torments according to the abominations committed by each one; but all of them shall be eternal and connected with the loss of the divine and beatific vision enjoyed by the saints. This shall be the second death, from which there shall be no salvation; because those overtaken by it have not availed themselves of the Redemption from the first death of sin through the Redeemer and his blessed Mother in grace. Still describing his vision the Evangelist proceeds:

24. "And there came one of the seven angels, who had the vials full of the seven last plagues, and spoke with me, saying: Come and I will show thee the Bride, the Wife of the Lamb." I saw that this angel and the others were of the highest and closest to the throne of the blessed Trinity; and that they were endowed with special powers to chastise the presumption of men who should commit the above-mentioned sins, after the mystery of the Redemption, the life, teaching and death of the Savior had been proclaimed, and the excellence and power of his most blessed Mother in assisting the sinners had become known. And as, in the course of time, these sacraments, with their miracles and enlightenment, with the example of the saints, and especially that of the apostolic men, of the founders of religious communities, and of the great number of martyrs and confessors, have become more and more manifest: therefore the sins of men in the last ages are more heinous and detestable, their ingratitude toward such blessings is more abominable and worthy of greater punishments. Consequently they rouse so much the greater indignation and wrath of

the divine justice. Thus in the future times (which are the present ones for us), God shall punish men with greater rigor, sending upon them the plagues reserved for the rapidly approaching days of the final judgment. Let the reader refer to paragraph 266 in the first part.

25. "And he took me up in spirit to a great and high mountain; and he showed me the holy city of Jerusalem coming down out of heaven from God." I was raised by the power of God to a high mountain of exalted intelligence and enlightenment concerning the hidden sacraments, and in this state I saw the Bride of the Lamb, his Woman, like the city of Jerusalem; the Bride of the Lamb, on account of her likeness in reciprocal love to Him, who took away the sins of the world (John 1, 29); his Woman, because She accompanied Him inseparably through all his works and wonders, and because for Her He came forth from the bosom of his eternal Father to have his delight with the children of men, who were the brethren of this Bride and, through Her, also his own brethren. I saw Her also as the city of Jerusalem, who enclosed Him within herself and afforded Him a spacious habitation, though He cannot be encompassed by heaven or earth; and because He placed in that City the temple and the propitiatory, where He wished to be sought and propitiated by mankind. And although on earth She humiliated and prostrated Herself beneath the feet of all, as if She had been the least of creatures, I saw Her raised on high to the throne and the right hand of her Onlybegotten, whence She again descended, prosperous and bountiful, to enrich the faithful children of the Church.

CHAPTER III.

26. This holy city of Jerusalem, Mary our Mistress, according to the Evangelist, "Having the glory of God, and the light thereof, was like to a precious stone, as to the jasper stone, even as a crystal." From her very beginning, the soul of the most holy Mary was filled and, as it were, bathed, in new participations of the Divinity, such as was never seen or known of any other creature; for She alone was the aurora sending forth the splendors of the Sun, Christ, true God and man, to whom She was to give birth. And this divine light and clearness went on increasing until She reached the highest state, seated at the right hand of her Son on the very throne of the blessed Trinity and clothed in the variety of all the gifts, graces, virtues, merits and glory beyond all creatures (Ps. 44, 10). When I saw Her in this place of inaccessible light, it seemed to me, that She possessed no other splendor than that of God himself, who seemed to communicate it to Her from the fount and origin of his immutable Being. Through the humanity of his Only-begotten the same light and clearness seemed to be both in the Mother and the Son, each according to their degree; yet in substance seeming one and the same, not found in any of the other blessed, nor in all of them together. In variety She seemed like jasper, in preciousness She was inestimable, and in beauty of body and soul She was like translucent crystal, permeated by the very substance of clearness and light.

53

27. "And it had a wall great and high, having twelve gates, and in the gates twelve angels, and names written thereon, which are the names of the twelve tribes of the children of Israel. On the east, three gates; and on the north, three gates; and on the south, three gates; and on the west, three gates." The wall which defended and enclosed this holy city of most holy Mary, was so great and high as is God himself and all his omnipotence and divine attributes; for all the power and greatness of God, his immense wisdom, were called in requisition to fortify, to secure and defend this great Lady from the enemies that might assault Her. And this invincible defense was redoubled, when She descended to live alone in the world, without the company of her divine Son, and to establish the new Church of the Gospel. For this purpose She held at the disposal of her will, in a new manner, God's own power against all the enemies of the Church, visible and invisible. Since, after the foundation of this new city of Mary, the Most High threw open most liberally all his treasures, and since He wished to call through Her all mortals to the knowledge of Himself and to the eternal happiness, the gentiles, Jews, barbarians, without distinction of nationality or estate: therefore He built this holy City with twelve gates opening up toward all directions of the world. In them He placed the twelve angels, who were to call and invite all the children of Adam; and especially rouse all men to devotion and piety toward their Queen. In these gates are also the names of the twelve tribes of Israel, in order that no one might think himself excluded from the sacred refuge of this heavenly Jerusalem, and in order that all might understand, that most holy Mary holds their names written in her heart and intimately connected with the favors She received of the Most High as the Mother of clemency and mercy, and not of justice.

28. "And the wall of that city had twelve foundations, and in them, the twelve names of the twelve Apostles of the Lamb." When our great Mother and Mistress was at the right hand of her Son and God in the throne of his glory, She offered Herself to come back to the world to plant the Church; thereupon the Lord charged Her especially with the care of the Apostles and wrote their names in the inflamed and pure bosom of that heavenly Instructress, where we would see them written, if that were possible to our mortal eyes. Although at that time there were only eleven names of the Apostles, that of Mathias was selected beforehand to take the place of Judas. And because upon the wisdom and love of this great Lady depended the doctrine, the instruction, the firmness and entire government, by which we twelve Apostles and saint Paul were to found the Church, on this account our names are written in the foundation of this mystical city of Mary; for She is to be the mainstay and the groundwork of the holy Church and of its founders, the Apostles. By her doctrine She taught us, by her wisdom She enlightened, by her charity She inflamed us, by her patience She bore with us, by her meekness She drew us on, by her counsel She governed us, by her advice She prepared us for her work, and by the dispensation of her heavenly powers She delivered us from dangers. To all She rendered assistance as if there were but one that needed it, and each one She helped as if each were a multitude. To us twelve Apostles were these gates opened up more widely than to all the children of Adam. While our Mistress lived, She never failed in protecting each one of us, but remained present with us at all times and places, defending us and protecting us without fail in all our necessities and labors. From this great and powerful Queen, and through Her, we participated and

received all the blessings, graces and gifts of the Most High, in order that we might be fit ministers of the New Testament (II Cor. 3, 6). For these reasons were our names written in the foundations of the walls of this mystical City, the most blessed Mary.

29. "And he that spoke to me, had a measure of a reed of gold, to measure the city and the gates thereof, and the wall. And the city lieth in a foursquare, and the length thereof is as great as the breadth: and he measured the city with the golden reed for twelve thousand furlongs, and the length and the height and the breadth thereof are equal." In order that I might understand the immensity of this holy City of God, the one that spoke to me measured it in my presence. For measurement he had a hollow cane or a reed of gold, which symbolized the deified humanity of the Word, with its gifts, graces and merits; and in which were united the frailty of the human and terrestrial nature with the precious and inestimable essence of God, exalting the humanity and its merits. Although this measure so greatly exceeds that which it was to measure, namely the blessed Mary; yet in all the heavens and the earth nothing else could be found to measure the most holy Mary and her greatness, than her own Son and true God. For all the creatures, human and angelical, were inferior and unsuited to the measurement and exploration of this mystical and divine City. But measured by her Son, She was found commensurate with Him, as a Mother worthy of Him, without failing in anything belonging to this dignity. Her greatness was twelve thousand stadia, equal in all its dimensions; hence it forms a cube, proportionate in all its parts. Such was also the proportion and immensity of the gifts of the great Queen; so that if the saints each received five or two talents, She received in proportion

twelve thousand of each gift, reaching immense magnitude. Though She was already measured thus when She passed into existence by her Immaculate Conception and prepared for the Mothership of God; yet She was measured again on this occasion, when She returned from the right hand of the eternal Son and her dimensions were proportionate to take the place and office of her Son and Redeemer of the world.

30. "And the building of the wall thereof was of jasper stone: but the city itself pure gold, like to clear glass. And the foundations of the walls of the city were adorned with all manner of precious stones." The doings and the outward behavior of most holy Mary, which, like the walls surrounding a city, are visible to all, were of such wondrous beauty and variety, that merely by her example She conquered and attracted the hearts of all that looked upon Her or conversed with Her. By Her sole presence She routed the demons and all his fantastical illusions; and therefore the walls of this City were of jasper. By her conduct and labors, as far as they became known exteriorly, our Queen produced more fruits and wrought greater wonders in the primitive Church, than all the Apostles and saints of that age. The interior of this city was of the finest gold of inexplicable clearness, participated from her own Son and so closely resembling the light of the infinite Being, that it seemed but the reflex of it. And this City was not only of the finest and most precious gold, but it seemed as of the purest and transparent glass; for She was an immaculate mirror of the Divinity, admitting no other image. She was like a crystalline tablet on which was written the evangelical law. In Her it should become known to the whole world; therefore this tablet was of clear glass and not of opaque stone, as that of Moses,

for one people only.   All the foundations in the walls of this great City were of precious stones; for it was founded by the hand of the Most High, who, being rich and powerful, built it without stint or measure, with whatever was most precious, estimable and secure of all his gifts, privileges and favors.   These were typified by the most solid, rich, beautiful and valuable stones known among men.   (Let the tenth chapter of the first book, first part, be consulted.)

31. "And the twelve gates of the city are twelve pearls, one to each: and every several gate was of one several pearl.   And the street of the city was pure gold, as it were transparent glass.   And I saw no temple therein.   For the Lord Almighty is the temple thereof, and the Lamb."   He that comes to this holy city of Mary and enters through faith, hope, veneration, piety and devotion, will find it a precious pearl that will make him fortunate, rich and prosperous in this life and blessed through her intercession in the next.   He will feel no repugnance in entering this City of refuge, because its gates are lovely and desirable, like rich and precious gems. Hence no mortal will have an excuse, if he does not avail himself of the most blessed Mary and of her kindness toward the sinners.   For there is nothing in Her which is not capable of attracting the soul to Her and to eternal salvation.   If the gates then are so beautiful and precious to all that approach them, much more beautiful will be the square of this City; for it is of the purest gold and translucent, which signifies her most ardent love and desire to admit all and enrich them with the treasures of eternal happiness.   For this purpose She manifests Herself to all in the clearest light; and no one will find in Her the darkness of deceit or falsehood.   And because into this holy city of Mary came God himself and in an

especial manner, and the Lamb, her own Son in sacramental form, thus filling and occupying Her: therefore I saw in Her no temple and no propitiatory except the omnipotent God and the Lamb. Nor was it necessary to build a temple in this City for the ceremonious offering of prayers and petitions as in other cities. For God himself and her divine Son were her temple and They were attentive and propitious to all her petitions, prayers, and requests offered for the faithful of the Church.

32. "And the city hath no need of the sun, nor of the moon, to shine in it. For the glory of the Lord hath enlightened it, and the Lamb is the lamp thereof." After our Queen had returned to the world from the right hand of her divine Son, her spirit was enlightened not only in the manner common to the saints, nor only in the manner She had been enlightened before her ascension, but, in recompense for the clear vision and fruition of which She deprived Herself in order to return to the militant Church, another kind of vision, an abstractive and continual vision of the Divinity, was conferred upon Her, and with it was joined another kind of fruition proportionate to it. Hence, in a manner peculiar to Her, She participated in the state of the comprehensors, though She was yet a pilgrim. Besides this privilege She enjoyed also another: that her divine Son in the sacramental species of bread remained continually within her bosom, as in his proper tabernacle: for whenever She received holy Communion, the sacred species were not dissolved until She received them the next time; so that as long as She lived in the world after her descent from heaven, She bore with Her without intermission her divine Son and sacramental God. By a special kind of vision She also saw Him within Herself and conversed with Him without the necessity of seeking his

royal presence anywhere outside of Herself. She bore Him within her bosom and could say with the Spouse: I hold Him and will not let Him go (Cant. 3, 4). Hence there could be no night in this holy City, where grace shone as the moon, nor was there need of any other rays than those of the Sun of justice, since She possessed them in all plenitude, and not only in part, as the rest of the saints.

33. "And the nations shall walk in the light of it: and the kings of the earth shall bring their glory and honor into it." No excuse or justification can the banished children of Eve have, if by the divine light, which Mary gave to the world, they do not walk in the path of true happiness. In order that She might enlighten his Church in the first age, her Son sent Her and made Her known to the first children of his holy Church. In the course of ages He has continued to manifest her holiness and greatness by the wonders performed by this Queen and by innumerable favors and blessings flowing from her hands upon mankind. In these last ages, which are the present, He will spread her glory and make Her known in new splendor, on account of the Church's great need of her intercession and of her help against the world, the demon and the flesh. For these, through men's own fault, as we see even in our day, will assume greater sway and strength to hinder the working of grace in men and to make them more unworthy of glory. Against this new malice of Lucifer and his followers the Lord wishes to oppose the merits and intercession of purest Mary and the light sent into this world by the example of her life. She is to be the refuge and sanctuary of sinners and the straight and secure way, full of splendor for all that wish to walk upon it.

34. If the kings and princes of the earth would walk

in that light and seek their honor and glory in this city of Mary and employ the greatness, power, riches of their states in advancing the honor of her name and that of her most holy Son, then they could rest assured, that being directed by this Northstar, they will be assisted in the exercise of their dignities and will govern their states with great success. In order to renew this confidence in our Catholic princes, professors and defenders of the faith, He discloses all that I now and in the course of this history have been made to understand and record. For this reason the highest King of kings and the Restorer of monarchies has given the most holy Mary the title of Patroness, Protectress and Advocate of these Catholic kingdoms. Through this singular blessing the Most High has resolved to remedy the calamities and difficulties, which the Christians on account of their sins, are to endure and suffer and which in our own times we sorrowfully and tearfully are sustaining. The infernal dragon has poured out his froth and fury against the holy Church, because he sees the carelessness of its heads and members and because he sees so many men in love with vanity and delusive pleasures. The greater part of the guilt and its punishment falls upon those who call themselves Catholic, whose offenses, as being those of children, are more heinous; for they know the will of their heavenly Father, who dwells on high, and yet do not strive to fulfill it more earnestly than the strangers. Though knowing that the kingdom of heaven suffers violence and must be gained by labors, they have nevertheless given themselves over to idleness and pleasure, temporizing with the world and the flesh. This dangerous deceit of the demon, the just Judge punishes by the demon himself, giving him, in his just judgments, the liberty to afflict the holy Church and scourge its children with rigor.

35. But the Father of Mercies, who is in heaven, does not permit the works of his kindness to be entirely undone; and in order to preserve them He offers us the opportune protection of most holy Mary, in order that through her prayers and intercession his divine justice may find some pretext or excuse for the suspension of the rigorous chastisements hanging over us. He wishes to wait and see, whether we shall avail ourselves of the intercession of this great Queen and Lady of Heaven for pacifying the just indignation of her divine Son, and whether we shall amend our lives, by which we make ourselves unworthy of his mercy and provoke his justice. Let not the Catholic princes and the inhabitants of these kingdoms neglect this occasion, wherein the blessed Mary offers the days of salvation and the acceptable time of her protection. Let them exalt the glory and honor of this Queen by devoting themselves entirely to the service of her divine Son and of Her, in thankfulness of the blessing of the Catholic faith, which has been preserved until now so pure in these kingdoms. For both Mother and Son have through this preservation of the faith shown to the world their singular love toward these kingdoms, and they now show it again, by vouchsafing this salutary advice. Let them therefore zealously strive to employ their power and their influence for spreading and exalting the name of Christ and that of most blessed Mary through all the nations. Let them believe, that in order to oblige the Son, there can be no more efficacious means than to exalt his Mother with due reverence and to spread the knowledge and veneration of Her through all the nations of the world.

36. For a still greater proof and testimony of the clemency of the most blessed Mary, the Evangelist adds: "And the gates thereof shall not be shut by day: for

there shall be no night there. And they shall bring the glory and honor of the nations into it." Let no one, even though he has been neglectful and a sinner, an infidel or a pagan, approach the Mother of mercy with diffidence. She who deprived Herself of the glory of the right hand of her Son in order to assist us, cannot shut the portals of kindness to any one that seeks relief with an humble heart. Whether he arrives in the night of sinfulness or in the day of grace, at any hour of his life, he shall be admitted and assisted. If he who calls in the middle of the night at the door of a true friend, will force him, either through his necessity or importunity, to rise and help him with the desired bread, what will not She do, who is so loving a Mother, who calls us and earnestly invites us to the remedy? (Luke 11, 8). She will not wait until we ourselves importune Her; for She hastens to assist. She is eager to respond, most sweet and delightful in her favors, and most liberal in enriching us. She is the leaven of mercy, inducing the Most High to grant it; She is the portal of heaven, opened up for our entering through her intercession and prayers: "There shall not enter into it anything defiled, nor deceitful." She is never roused to indignation or hatred against men; in Her there is no deceit, no fault or defect; She cannot fail in anything that mortals may need for their salvation. We have no excuse or pretext for not going to Her with humble acknowledgment; since She, being pure and spotless Herself, will purify and cleanse also us. She holds the keys to the fountains, from which, as Isaias says, we may draw the waters of the Redeemer; her intercession, in response to our petitions, will turn these keys, so that the waters will gush forth to wash us and to make us worthy of her most blessed company, and that of her divine Son for all the eternities.

INSTRUCTION GIVEN TO ME BY THE GREAT QUEEN AND
MISTRESS OF THE ANGELS.

37. My daughter, I wish to tell thee for thy comfort
and the comfort of my servants, that thou hast written
of these mysteries in these chapters to my great satisfaction and with the approbation of the Most High. He
wishes the world to know what I have done for the
Church in coming back from the empyrean heaven to
assist the faithful, and how much I desire to help the
Catholics who seek my aid in accordance with the commands of God and my own maternal affection. The
saints also, and especially saint John, were particularly
rejoiced, that thou hast made mention of their jubilee at
seeing me ascend with my Son and Lord; for it is time
that the children of the Church should know this and
understand more fully the blessings to which the Omnipotent has raised me. They are thereby to enliven their
hope and make themselves more capable of the favors I
can and will bestow upon them. Let them know that I,
as a loving Mother, am filled with pity at seeing them
so deceived and oppressed by the tyranny of satan, to
whom they have blindly fallen victims. Saint John my
servant has concealed many other sacraments in the
twenty-first and the twelfth chapter of the Apocalypse
concerning the favors shown me by the Almighty. In
the course of this history thou hast revealed those which
the faithful can profitably know at present, and thou shalt
reveal still more.

38. But thou must without delay gather for thyself
the fruits of all thou hast understood and written. First
of all thou must advance in heartfelt love and devotion
toward me, and be convinced that I shall be thy help in
all tribulations, thy constant assistance in all thy works;

that the portals of my mercy are opened up for thee and for all whom thou recommendest to me, if only thou shalt make thyself such as I desire. Therefore I inform thee, my dearest, and urgently remind thee, that, in the same manner as I was fitted out in heaven for returning and engaging in a more perfect activity on this earth, so the Lord desires thee to be renewed in the heaven of thy interior, in the secret and superior parts of thy spirit, in those private exercises by which thou hast created the interior solitude for writing the rest of this life. Understand that all this has not been brought about without special providence of God, which thou wilt easily see in pondering over and recording thy experiences before beginning this third part. Now that thou art left alone and art freed from the government and daily intercourse of this community, I give thee this advice; and there is now especial reason, that with the divine favor thou renew thyself in the imitation of my life and in putting into practice, as far as possible, what thou knowest of me. This is the will of my divine Son, and is in harmony with thy own wishes. Hear then my teaching and gird thyself with fortitude (Prov. 31, 17). Resolve with all the powers of thy will to be attentive, fervent, constant, eager and diligent in seeking to please thy Spouse and Lord. Accustom thyself never to lose Him out of sight, even when thou descendest to intercourse with creatures and engagest in the works of Martha. I shall be thy Teacher. The angels shall stand by thee, so that with them and by means of their enlightenments thou continually praise the Lord. The Most High will lend thee his strength, so that thou mayest fight his battles with his and thy enemies. Do not make thyself unworthy of such great blessings and favors.

CHAPTER IV.

THREE DAYS AFTER THE MOST BLESSED MARY DESCENDED
FROM HEAVEN, SHE MANIFESTS HERSELF AND SPEAKS
IN PERSON TO THE APOSTLES; CHRIST OUR LORD VIS-
ITS HER: OTHER MYSTERIES UNTIL THE COMING OF
THE HOLY GHOST.

39. I again remind those who shall read this history
not to be astonished at the hidden sacraments recorded
of the most blessed Mary therein, nor to hold them unworthy of belief, because they have not been until now
revealed to the world. For, even setting aside the fact
that they are all worthy and befitting this great Queen,
we cannot deny, that, though we have until now no written record of her wonderful doings after the Ascension
of the Lord, yet we must suppose Her to have wrought
many and exceeding great wonders in her office as
Teacher, Protectress and Mother of the new evangelical
Church, which was to be introduced into the world under
her assistance and supervision. And if the Lord reno-
vated Her in all her powers, as was stated, and if He exerted all his Omnipotence through Her, no favor or
blessing, no matter how great, can consistently with the
Catholic truth be disputed as pertaining justly to this
peerless and singular Creature.

40. Mary was three days in heaven enjoying the beatific vision (as I said in the first chapter) and She came
back from her heavenly seat on the day which corresponds to the Sunday after the day of the Ascension,
called in the holy Church the Sunday within the octave

of that feast. She remained in the Cenacle three succeeding days enjoying the after-effects of the beatific
vision. During this time the heavenly splendors, which
still clothed Her, were tempered and only the Evangelist
saint John had full knowledge of the mystery; for it was
not opportune, that it should become known to the rest of
the Apostles at that time, because they were scarcely as
yet capable of such sacraments. Although She remained
in their company, it was necessary that her glory should
be hidden from them. For even the Evangelist, though
he was especially strengthened by grace for the privilege
of looking upon Her with that veil withdrawn, fell prostrate upon the ground as soon as he came into her presence. Nor, on the other hand, was it befitting that the
Lord should suddenly deprive our great Queen of her
refulgence and the other exterior and interior effects of
her admission into the glory of his throne. He ordained
in his infinite wisdom, that the effects of those divine
gifts and favors diminish by degrees and that her virginal body return gradually to the more common visible
state for conversing with the Apostles and the rest of the
faithful of the holy Church.

41. I have also said above, that this miracle of Mary's
admission into heaven does not conflict with what is
written in the Acts of the Apostles, though we there read,
that the Apostles and the holy women persevered unanimously in prayer with Mary, the Mother of Jesus, and
with his brethren after the Lord had ascended into heav-
en (Acts 1, 14). What I have said evidently agrees
with this passage; for saint Luke writes his history according to what he and the Apostles saw in the Cenacle
of Jerusalem, and irrespective of the mystery of which
they were ignorant. The sacred body of Mary was in
two places at the same time. Although the attention and

use of the senses and faculties was more perfect and real
in heaven, nevertheless it could be truly said, that She
was in the company of the Apostles and that She was
seen by all.   Moreover it was true that the most blessed
Mary persevered with them in prayer; for She saw them
from her place in heaven and there She united her
prayers and petitions with those of all the holy refugees
of the Cenacle; She presented them to her divine Son, at
whose right hand She was seated, and obtained for them
perseverance and many other great favors of the Most
High.

42. The three days in which the great Lady enjoyed
the after-effects of glory and while the redundance of
its splendors gradually lessened, She spent in most ardent
and divine sentiments of love, gratitude and ineffable
humility, beyond all the terms or words, which I can find
for manifesting what I have been made to understand of
this sacrament, for they fall far short of the truth.   The
angels and seraphim, who attended upon Her, conferred
in new wonder with each other on these miracles, and
they discussed among themselves, which was the greatest
miracle: that the Most High should raise a mere Creature to such favors and greatness, or that any one, after
having been raised to such heights of grace and glory,
should abase Herself beneath the lowest of creation and
deem Herself the most insignificant of all that is created.
I perceived that the highest seraphim stood, as it were,
with bated breath at beholding the doings of their Queen.
Speaking to each other they said: "If the demons before
their fall had been privileged to behold this example of
humility, it would have been impossible for them to yield
to their pride.   This our great Lady is She, who, without
any defect, without any deficiency, not only in part, but
in all plenitude, has filled up the vast voidness of humil-

ity in all creatures. She alone has worthily conceived the majesty and supereminent greatness of the Creator and the littleness of all creation. She is the One, that knows when and how He must be obeyed and reverenced; and She faithfully acts out her knowledge. Is it possible, that among the thorns sown by sin among the children of Adam the earth should produce such a pure Lily, emitting such fragrance for the delight of the Creator and for mortals? (Cant. 2, 2), that from the desert of the world, void of grace and full of earthliness, such a heavenly Creature, affluent with the delights of the Almighty, should arise? (Cant. 8, 5). Let Him be eternally praised in his wisdom and goodness, who formed such a Creature, so wonderfully appointed for our emulation in holiness and for an example and for the glory of the human kind. And Thou, blessed among women, distinguished and chosen among all creatures, be Thou congratulated, known and praised by all generations! (Luke 1, 48). Mayest Thou enjoy for all eternity the excellence given to Thee by thy Son and Creator! May He find his pleasure and complaisance in Thee on account of the beauty of thy works and gifts; may in Thee be satiated his immense charity for the justification of all men. Thou, for all of them dost render Him satisfaction, and looking upon Thee He shall not repent of having called into existence ungrateful man. If they grieve and irritate Him, Thou appeasest Him and turnest Him to mercy and kindness. We do not wonder that He should favor men so much, since Thou, our Lady and Queen, livest among them and callest them thy people."

43. With these praises and many other hymns the holy angels celebrated the humility and the works of the most blessed Mary after She descended from heaven; and to some of these praises She herself joined her re-

sponses. After dismissing the host of the angels, who had accompanied Her from heaven, and after having remained in seclusion still filled with the splendors of heaven perceived only by saint John, She knew that it was time to deal and converse with the faithful. She therefore left her retirement and, like a loving Mother, began to hold tender intercourse with the Apostles and disciples. With them She offered tearful prayers to her divine Son, including them and all who in future ages were to receive the grace of the holy Catholic faith. From that day also, as long as She lived upon earth, She asked the Lord to hasten the times, when the feasts of the sacred mysteries should be celebrated on earth in the same way as She knew they would be celebrated in heaven. She also asked the Lord to send men of exalted and distinguished holiness for the conversion of sinners, having at the same time a foreknowledge of their sending. In these prayers her burning charity for men rose to such a pitch, that according to the natural course it would have destroyed her life. In order to sustain Her and moderate the force of these desires, her divine Son frequently sent one of his highest seraphim, who should answer Her and promise Her the fulfillment of her desires and petitions, at the same time revealing to Her in what order the divine Providence would arrange all this for the greater advantage of mortals.

44. By the abstractive vision of the Divinity, which, as I have said, She continued to enjoy, the conflagration of love which swept through that purest and chastest of hearts, became so ineffable, that beyond all comparison it exceeded that of the most love-inflamed seraphim next to the throne of the Godhead. If at times She permitted these flames of divine love to abate somewhat, it was in order to contemplate the humanity of her most holy Son;

for no other image of visible things was ever allowed to take up her interior faculties, except when She actually employed her senses in dealing with creatures. At the consciousness and memory of her absent Son She felt some natural tenderness; but this was always a moderate and reasonable one, as She was the most prudent Mother. But as the heart of the Son re-echoed to this love, He permitted Himself to be wounded by the loving desires of his Mother: and the words of the Canticle were literally fulfilled, that the eyes of his beloved Spouse and Mother drew Him down to the earth (Cant. 4, 4).

45. This happened many times, as will be said later on, and it took place the first time during the few days which passed between her descent from heaven and the coming of the Holy Ghost, not more than six days after She again began to converse with the Apostles. Christ our Savior would not permit Himself a longer delay than these few days before He again descended personally to visit and fill Her with new gifts and ineffable consolation. The purest Dove was fainting with love and with those pangs, which She says, cause well ordered charity in the wine-cellar of the King (Cant. 2, 4). The Lord then coming to Her permitted Her to recline upon his breast in the left arm of his humanity, and with the right arm of his Divinity He illumined Her and enriched Her, filled Her anew with vivifying and strengthening influences. Then again were quieted the loving anxieties of this wounded Deer, now drinking to her satisfaction from the fountain of the Savior. She was refreshed and strengthened anew, in order that She might be inflamed still more by the fires of her inextinguishable love. She was made whole by being so much the more deeply wounded; She was healed by a new sickness and vivified by delivering Herself over so much the more completely

to the agonies of her affection; for this kind of sickness neither knows nor admits of any other kind of remedy. When the sweetest Mother by these favors had regained strength and when the presence of the Savior was revealed to her senses, She prostrated Herself before his royal Majesty in order to ask Him humbly for his blessing and to give Him most fervent thanks for the favor of his visit.

46. The most prudent Lady was surprised at this favor not only because it was such a short time since She was deprived of her divine Son, but also because the Lord had not informed Her of the time of his visit, nor had her most profound humility permitted Her to expect such a divine condescension in affording Her relief. As this was the first favor of this kind, She was so much the more abashed and annihilated in her own mind. She spent five hours with the Word enjoying his presence; and none of the Apostles at that time knew of the favor, although they knew, from what they noticed in the countenance and in the bearing of their blessed Lady, that something wonderful was transpiring. None of them, however, on account of their timidity and reverence, presumed to inquire further into the cause. In order to take leave of her divine Son, when She became aware that He wished to return to heaven, She prostrated Herself again to the ground, asking Him for his blessing and for his guidance in correcting any deficiency in her behavior for the time when He should return to visit Her in the future. She asked this favor, because the Lord himself had offered to visit Her sometimes in her loneliness. Moreover, often before his Ascension, She had prostrated Herself at his feet in acknowledgment of her unworthiness and of her want of fervor thanking Him for his favors, as I have narrated in the first part. Al-

though She could accuse Herself of no fault, because as
the Mother of holiness, She never committed any; and
although She could not, as the Mother of wisdom, commit any fault; yet the Lord permitted full sway to her
humility and love in the worthy acknowledgment of her
debt to God as a mere creature. In her most exalted
knowledge and humility all that She did seemed small in
recompense for the supernatural blessings. This inequality She attributed to Herself and although this could not
be called a fault, She wished to acknowledge the inferior-
ity of earthly things in comparison with divine excellence.

47. But among the ineffable mysteries and favors
which She received since the day of the Ascension of her
divine Son our Savior, were those connected with the
worthy preparation of the Apostles and disciples for the
advent of the Holy Ghost. The great Queen well knew
how estimable and divine was to be the blessing which
was held in store for them by the Father of lights; She
considered also the fleshly affection of the Apostles for
the humanity of their Master Jesus. For the purpose of
correcting this defect and perfecting them in all things,
as a tender Mother and powerful Queen, She, on arriving
in heaven with her divine Son, sent some of her angels
to the Cenacle as her messengers in order to intimate to
the faithful her own and her Son's will, that they should
raise themselves above themselves and henceforth live
more by faith and love of God, than in the operations of
their sensual nature; that they should not be borne along
solely by the sight of God's humanity, but that they let it
serve them as a portal and a path to the Divinity, where
they would find adequate satisfaction and repose. Such
advice and exhortation the heavenly Queen ordered the
angel to give to the Apostles. Afterwards, when She
again descended from on high, She consoled them in their

sorrow and soothed them in their dismay, speaking to them for one hour every day and explaining to them the mysteries of the faith taught Her by her divine Son. She did this however not by any formal instruction, but in the manner of a conference, exhorting them also to spend another hour during the day in discussing among themselves the admonitions, promises, doctrine and teachings of their divine Master Jesus and to occupy themselves during some other part of the day in reciting vocally the Our Father and some psalms, while the rest of the time they were to spend in mental prayer. Towards evening they were to partake of bread and fish and then indulge in moderate sleep. Through these prayers and fasts they were to dispose themselves for the advent and reception of the Holy Ghost.

48. The vigilant Mother, empowered by the right hand of her divine Son, took care of that happy family in order to bring all their works up to the highest perfection. After her descent from heaven, She instructed the Apostles, yet She never entered upon this duty without first being requested by saint Peter or saint John. Through her prayers She moved her divine Son to inspire them with these commands, in order that She might obey them as his vicars and priests. Thus all things happened as arranged by the Mother of humility and She obeyed as a handmaid. Laying aside all pretense to her dignity as Queen and Lady, and making no use of her sovereignty and dominion, She obeyed as a servant and conducted Herself as if She were an inferior, and in this spirit She conferred with the Apostles and the other faithful. During those days She explained to them the mystery of the blessed Trinity in terms most exalted and mysterious, yet suited to the understanding of all. She explained also the mystery of the hypostatic union, and

those of the Incarnation, adding many others, which they had already been taught by the Master; telling them at the same time that they would be enlightened by the Holy Ghost for a deeper understanding of all these things.

49. She taught them how to pray mentally, insisting on the excellence and necessity of that kind of prayer; how the principal duty and the most noble occupation of the rational creature was to raise itself, by the understanding and the will, above all that is created to the knowledge and love of God; and that no other object or occupation should ever be preferred or should ever interrupt this duty, so as not to deprive the soul of this supreme benefit, the beginning of eternal life and happiness. She taught them also how to thank the eternal Father for having given us his only Son for our Redeemer and Master, and for the love with which the Lord redeemed us at the cost of his Passion and Death. She exhorted them to give thanks to God for having singled them out as his Apostles, as his companions and as the founders of his holy Church. Such were the exhortations and teachings, with which the heavenly Mother at that time enlightened the hearts of the eleven Apostles and the other disciples and by which She prepared and disposed them for the reception of the Holy Ghost and his divine effects. As She saw into the inmost recesses of their hearts and knew the natural condition and character of each one, She accommodated Herself to the necessities, the bent of mind and the graces of each in order to fill them with joy, consolation and constancy in the practice of virtue. She exhorted them to persevere in humble prostrations and other actions of worship and reverence in adoring the greatness and majesty of the Most High.

50. Every morning and evening She approached the Apostles to receive their benediction, first that of saint Peter, as their chief, then of saint John and of the rest according to their age. At first they all shrank from performing this ceremony, beholding in Her their Queen and the Mother of their Master Jesus. But the most prudent Lady insisted that all should bless Her as ministers and priests of the Most High, explaining to them how the highest reverence and respect was due to them on account of their supreme dignity and office. As this was a contest of humility, it was certain that the Mother of humility would be victorious and the disciples would be overcome and instructed by her example. Besides, the words of Mary were so sweet and persuasive for moving the hearts of those first believers, that She urged them on with a heavenly force and enlightened them to practice the highest perfections of virtue and holiness. Perceiving these wonderful effects upon themselves, they wonderingly commented upon them among each other, saying: "Truly in this pure Creature we have found again the teaching and consoling doctrine, of which we are deprived by the absence of her Son, our Master. Her words and doings, her counsels, her sweet and gentle intercourse, teach us and draw us on in the same way as the conversation of the Lord, when He lived in our midst. Our hearts are inflamed by the teachings and exhortations of this wonderful Being as with those of Jesus our Savior. There is no doubt that He as the omnipotent God, has deposited in the Mother of the Only-begotten his own divine wisdom and grace. We can now dry our tears, since for our instruction and consolation He has given us such a Mother and Mistress, and since He has left with us this living ark of the Testament, wherein He has placed for us his law, his wonderful

staff, and the sweetest manna for our sustenance and comfort" (Heb. 9, 4).

51. If the holy Apostles and the other firstborn children of the Church had recorded in writing what they saw as eye-witnesses of her deeds of eminent wisdom; what they heard and what passed in their intercourse with Her for so long a time, then we might be filled with higher conceptions of the holy and heroic works of the sovereign lady. We would then see that as well in the doctrine which She taught, as in the wonders which She wrought, her most holy Son had communicated to Her a virtue, which although coming from the Lord as from its fountain, yet, in the heavenly Lady, was in a certain manner divine and was distributed from Her as from an aqueduct to all the mortals. The Apostles however had the happiness and good fortune of drinking the waters of the Savior and of the teachings of his purest Mother in their very fount, receiving them in a sensible manner and thus preparing them for their office and ministry in founding the hóly Church and planting the evangelic faith throughout the world.

52. By the treason and death of that unhappy one among all mortals, his episcopacy, as David says, had become vacant and it was necessary to provide some other one worthy of the apostolate (Ps. 108, 8). For it was the will of the Most High, that the number twelve, which had been determined upon by the Master of life as the proper number when He chose his Apostles, should also be their number at the coming of the Holy Ghost. This decree of the Lord was explained to the Apostles by the blessed Mary in one of her instructions; all of them acceded to it and they asked Her as their Mother and Mistress to choose one who should seem worthy and most fit for the apostolate. The heavenly Lady knew

beforehand who was to be chosen; for the names of the twelve, including saint Mathias, were written in her heart, as is said in the third chapter. But in her profound humility and wisdom She judged it right to leave this to saint Peter in order that he might begin to exercise in the new Church the office of pontiff and head, as vicar of Jesus Christ, its Author and Master. She therefore instructed the Apostle to hold this election in the presence of all the disciples and other faithful so that all might see him act as the supreme head of the Church. Saint Peter thereupon arranged it all according to her directions.

53. The proceedings of this first election in the Church are related by saint Luke in the first chapter of the Acts of the Apostles. He says, that in the days intervening between the Ascension of Christ and the coming of the Holy Ghost, the Apostle saint Peter, having called together the one hundred and twenty, who had been present at the Ascension, reminded them that the prophecy of David concerning the treason of Judas in the fortieth psalm must be fulfilled; that Judas, having been chosen as one of the twelve Apostles, had unhappily prevaricated and made himself the leader of those that captured Jesus; that with the price of his treason had been bought the field called Haceldama; that at the end, as unworthy of divine mercy, he had hung himself, had burst in the middle and his entrails had fallen out, as was known to all who lived in Jerusalem; that therefore it was becoming, another should be chosen to the apostolate in his place in order to give testimony to the resurrection of the Savior, in accordance with another prophecy of David (Ps. 108, 8); and that the one to be chosen should be from the number of those who had followed Christ the Master in his preaching ever since his Baptism by saint John.

54. Having thus persuaded all the faithful of the propriety of electing the twelfth Apostle, they left it to saint Peter to determine the manner of this election. The Apostle then ordained, that from the seventy-two disciples two, Joseph, called the just, and Mathias, should be selected. Between these two lots were to be drawn and that one should be assigned to the apostleship, who would draw the proper lot. All approved of this manner of election, which at that time was a very secure way, since the divine power wrought great miracles for the foundation of the Church. They wrote the two names, with the title of Disciple and Apostle of Christ, upon as many cards and placed them in an urn, where they could not be seen. All of them then fell to prayer, asking God to choose the one pleasing to Him, since, as the Lord, He knew the hearts of all (Acts 1, 25). Saint Peter thereupon drew out one of the lots, on which was written the name of Mathias as Apostle and Disciple of Christ; joyfully Mathias was accepted and acknowledged as the legitimate Apostle, and the eleven embraced him. The most holy Mary, who was present at all these proceedings, asked his blessing and, in imitation of Her, all the other faithful did the same. Then all of them continued their prayers and fasting until the coming of the Holy Ghost.

INSTRUCTION WHICH THE QUEEN OF HEAVEN, MOST
BLESSED MARY, GAVE ME.

55. My daughter, thou hast rightly wondered at the hidden and supernal favors, which I received at the hands of my Son, and at the humility and thankfulness, with which I received them; likewise the loving attention which I paid to the necessities of the Apostles and the

faithful of the Church amid all my joy. It is time, my dearest, that thou gather the fruits of this knowledge; for neither canst thou now comprehend more, nor do I desire less of thee than that thou be to me a faithful daughter, who imitates me fervently, and a disciple, who listens to me and follows me with all her heart. Stir up thy faith then in order to be convinced, that I am powerful to confer favors, and trust, that I will enrich thee in unstinted liberality with gifts beyond all thy desires. But at the same time do thou humiliate thyself to the very earth and shrink to the very last place among creatures; for of thyself thou art more useless than the most vile and despicable dust and thou canst call nothing thy own except misery and want. Consider well within thyself how great and exquisite is the kindness and condescension of the Most High in regard to thee, and what kind of thanks thou owest Him. If the one who pays his debts, even entirely, cannot take to himself special credit; then it is just, that thou, who canst not satisfy thy debt, shouldst remain humble, for though thou labor ever so much and according to all thy powers, thou shalt nevertheless remain a debtor. What shall then be thy indebtedness, if thou remain remiss and negligent?

56. In this prudent alertness thou wilt understand, how closely thou must imitate me in living faith, in confident hope and in fervent love, in profound humility and in the worship and reverence due to the infinite greatness of the Lord. I warn thee again of the cunning vigilance of the serpent, who seeks to induce mortals to neglect the veneration and worship due to God and presumptuously to despise this virtue and what it implies. Into the minds of the worldly and of the vicious he instills a most foolish forgetfulness of the Catholic truths, in order that divine faith may not keep alive in them the

fear and veneration of the Most High; and thus he succeeds in making them like to the heathens, who do not know the true God. Others, who strive after virtue and perform some good works, the enemy leads into a dangerous lukewarmness and negligence, wherein they overlook what they are losing on account of their want of fervor. Those that concern themselves more earnestly about perfection, the dragon deceives with a certain coarse over-confidence, so that on account of the favors they receive and on account of the divine mercy which they experience, they begin to consider themselves as special favorites of the Lord, forgetting the humble fear and veneration, which they ought to experience in the presence of Him, before whom, according to the teaching of the holy Church, the powers of heaven tremble. But since I have on other occasion reminded and admonished thee concerning this danger, let my mentioning it here suffice.

57. In this manner I desire that thou be faithful and punctual in the practice of this doctrine, exercising it in all thy exterior actions without affectation or excess, and teaching others by thy own example the holy fear and veneration due from creatures to their Creator. I desire that thou teach and impress this science especially upon thy religious, so that they may not be ignorant of the humility and reverence, with which they are to converse with God. The most efficacious instruction thou canst give, will be thy example in fulfilling all thy obligations; for these works thou must neither conceal, nor ever omit for fear of vanity. This example is due in much greater degree from those that govern others, since it is their duty to exhort, move and accompany their subjects in the holy fear of the Lord, which is done more efficaciously by example than by words. Admonish them

particularly to hold in veneration the priests as the anointed of the Lord. In imitation of me do thou always ask for their blessing, when thou approachest or leavest them. The more thou seest thy own self favored by the divine condescension, so much the more bear in mind the necessities and the afflictions of thy neighbors and the dangers of those in sin, praying for all in great faith and confidence. For, thy love of God cannot be true, if thou art content with enjoying only thyself, and in the meanwhile forgetest thy brethren. Thou must anxiously solicit the highest goods, which thou knowest of and participatest in, for all men, since no one is excluded therefrom and since all need the help and communication of God. In the love of me thou wilt understand, how thou must imitate me in all things.

CHAPTER V.

THE COMING OF THE HOLY GHOST UPON THE APOSTLES
AND THE OTHER FAITHFUL; THE MOST BLESSED MARY
SEES HIM INTUITIVELY; OTHER MOST HIDDEN MYS-
TERIES WHICH HAPPENED ON THAT OCCASION.

58. In the company of the great Queen of heaven,
and encouraged by Her, the twelve Apostles and the rest
of the disciples and faithful joyfully waited for the fulfillment of the promise of the Savior, that He would
send them the Holy Ghost, the Consoler, who should
instruct them and administer unto them all that they
had heard in the teaching of their Lord (John 14, 26).
They were so unanimous and united in charity, that
during all these days none of them had any thought,
affection or inclination contrary to those of the rest.
They were of one heart and soul in thought and action.
Although the election of saint Mathias had occurred,
not the least movement or sign of discord arose among
all those first-born children of the Church; yet this was
a transaction, which is otherwise apt to arouse differences
of opinion in the most excellently disposed; since each
one is apt to follow his own insight and does not easily
yield to the opinion of others. But into this holy congregation no discord found entrance, because they were
united in prayer, in fasting and in the expectation of the
Holy Ghost, who does not seek repose in discordant and
unyielding hearts. In order that it may be inferred, how
powerful was this union in charity, not only for disposing
them toward the reception of the Holy Ghost, but for

overcoming and dispersing the evil spirits, I will say; that the demons, who since the death of the Savior had lain prostrate in hell, felt in themselves a new kind of oppression and terror, resulting from the virtues of those assembled in the Cenacle. Although they could not explain it to themselves, they perceived a new terrifying force, emanating from that place, and when they perceived the effects of the doctrine and example of Christ in the behavior of the disciples, they feared the ruin of their dominion.

59. The Queen of the angels, most holy Mary, in the plenitude of her wisdom and grace, knew the time and predestined hour for the sending of the Holy Ghost upon the apostolic college. When the days of Pentecost were about to be fulfilled (Act 2, 1), (which happened fifty days after the Resurrection of the Lord our Redeemer), the most blessed Mother saw, how in heaven the humanity (John 14, 26) of the Word conferred with the eternal Father concerning the promised sending of the divine Paraclete to the Apostles, and that the time predetermined by his infinite wisdom for planting the faith and all his gifts in his holy Church, was at hand. The Lord also referred to the merits acquired by Him in the flesh through his most holy Life, Passion and Death, to the mysteries wrought by Him for the salvation of the human race and to the fact, that He was the Mediator, Advocate and Intercessor between the eternal Father and men, and that among them lived his sweetest Mother, in whom the divine Persons were so well pleased. He besought his Father also, that, besides bringing grace and the invisible gifts, the Holy Ghost appear in the world in visible form, that so the evangelical law might be honored before all the world; that the Apostles and faithful, who were to spread the divine truth, might be encouraged, and that

the enemies of the Lord, who had in this life persecuted and despised Him unto the death of the Cross, might be filled with terror.

60. This petition of our Redeemer in heaven was supported on earth by most holy Mary in a manner befitting the merciful Mother of the faithful. Prostrate upon the earth in the form of a cross and in profoundest humility, She saw, how in that consistory of the blessed Trinity, the request of the Savior was favorably accepted, and how, to fulfill and execute it, the persons of the Father and the Son, as the Principle from which the Holy Ghost proceeded, decreed the active mission of the Holy Spirit; for to these Two is attributed the sending of the third Person, because He proceeds from Both; and the third Person passively took upon Himself this mission and consented to come into the world. Although all the three divine Persons and their operations spring from the same infinite and eternal will without any inequality; yet the same powers, which in all the Persons are indivisible and equal, have certain operations *ad intra* in each Person, which are not in the others and thus the understanding engenders in the Father, not in the Son, who is engendered; and the will breathes forth in the Father and the Son, and not in the Holy Ghost, who is breathed forth. On account of this reason the Father and the Son, as the active Principle, are said to send the Holy Ghost *ad extra,* while to the Latter is attributed the being sent, as if in a passive manner.

61. On Pentecost morning the blessed Virgin Mary exhorted the Apostles, the disciples and the pious women, numbering about one hundred and twenty, to pray more fervently and renew their hopes, since the hour was at hand in which they were to be visited by the divine Spirit from on high. At the third hour (nine o'clock), when

all of them were gathered around their heavenly Mistress
and engaged in fervent prayer, the air resounded with a
tremendous thunder and the blowing of a violent wind
mixed with the brightness of fire or lightning, all cen-
tering upon the house of the Cenacle. The house was
enveloped in light and the divine fire was poured out
over all of that holy gathering (Acts 2, 2). Over the
head of each of the hundred and twenty persons appeared a tongue of that same fire, in which the Holy
Ghost had come, filling each one with divine influences
and heavenly gifts and causing at one and the same
time the most diverse and contrary effects in the Cenacle
and in the whole of Jerusalem, according to the diversity
of the persons affected.

62. In the most holy Mary these effects were altogether divine, and most wonderful in the sight of all
the heavenly courtiers; for as regard us men, we are
incapable of understanding and explaining them. The
purest Lady was transformed and exalted in God; for
She saw intuitively and clearly the Holy Ghost, and for
a short time enjoyed the beatific vision of the Divinity.
Of his gifts and divine influences She by Herself received
more than all the rest of the saints. Her glory for that
space of time, exceeded that of the angels and of the
blessed. She alone gave to the Lord more glory, praise
and thanksgiving than all the universe for the benefit
of the descent of his Holy Spirit upon his Church and
for his having pledged Himself so many times to send
Him and through Him to govern it to the end of the
world. The blessed Trinity was so pleased with the
conduct of Mary on this occasion, that It considered
Itself fully repaid and compensated for having created
the world; and not only compensated, but God acted
as if He were under a certain obligation for possessing

such a peerless Creature, whom the Father could look upon as his Daughter, the Son as his Mother, and the Holy Ghost as his Spouse; and whom (according to our way of thinking) He was now obliged to visit and enrich after having conferred upon Her such high dignity. In this exalted and blessed Spouse were renewed all the gifts and graces of the Holy Spirit, creating new effects and operations altogether beyond our capacity to understand.

63. The Apostles, as saint Luke says (Acts 2, 2), were also replenished and filled with the Holy Ghost; for they received a wonderful increase of justifying grace of a most exalted degree. The twelve Apostles were confirmed in this sanctifying grace and were never to lose it. In all of them, according to each one's condition, were infused the habits of the seven gifts: Wisdom, Understanding, Science, Piety, Counsel, Fortitude and Fear. In this magnificent blessing, as new as it was admirable in the world, the twelve Apostles were created fit ministers of the new Testament and founders of the evangelical Church for the whole world: for this new grace and blessing communicated to them a divine strength most efficacious and sweet, which inclined them to practice the most heroic virtue and the highest sanctity. Thus strengthened they prayed, they labored willingly and accomplished the most difficult and arduous tasks, engaging in their labors not with sorrow or from necessity, but with the greatest joy and alacrity.

64. In all the rest of the disciples and the faithful, who received the Holy Ghost in the Cenacle, the Most High wrought proportionally and respectively the same effects, except that they were not confirmed in grace like the Apostles. According to the disposition of each the gifts of grace were communicated in greater or less

abundance in view of the ministry they were to hold in the holy Church. The same proportion was maintained in regard to the Apostles; yet saint Peter and saint John were more singularly favored on account of the high offices assigned to them: the one to govern the Church as its head, and the other to attend upon and serve the Queen and Mistress of heaven and of earth, most holy Mary. The sacred text of saint Luke says, that the Holy Ghost filled the whole house in which this happy congregation was gathered (Acts 2, 2), not only because all of them were filled with the Holy Ghost and his admirable gifts, but because the house itself was filled with wonderful light and splendor. This plenitude of wonders and prodigies overflowed and communicated itself also to others outside of the Cenacle; for it caused diverse and various effects of the Holy Spirit among the inhabitants of Jerusalem and its vicinity. All those, who with some piety had compassioned our Savior Jesus in his Passion and Death, deprecating his most bitter torments and reverencing his sacred Person, were interiorly visited with new light and grace, which disposed them afterwards to accept the doctrine of the Apostles. Those that were converted by the first sermon of saint Peter, were to a great extent of the number of those who, by their compassion and sorrow at the death of the Lord, had merited for themselves such a great blessing. Others of the just who were in Jerusalem outside of the Cenacle, also felt great interior consolations, by which they were moved and predisposed by new effects of grace wrought in each one proportionately by the Holy Ghost.

65. Not less wonderful, although more hidden, were some contrary effects produced on that day by the Holy Ghost in Jerusalem. By the dreadful thunders and

violent commotion of the atmosphere and the lightnings accompanying his advent, He disturbed and terrified the enemies of the Lord in that city, each one according to his own malice and perfidy. This chastisement was particularly evident in those who had actively concurred in procuring the death of Christ, and who had signalized themselves in their rabid fury against Him. All these fell to the ground on their faces and remained thus for three hours. Those that had scourged the Lord were suddenly choked in their own blood, which shot forth from their veins in punishment for shedding that of the Master. The audacious servant, who had buffeted the Lord, not only suddenly died, but was hurled into hell body and soul. Others of the Jews, although they did not die, were chastised with intense pains and abominable sicknesses. These disorders, consequent upon shedding the blood of Christ, descended to their posterity and even to this day continue to afflict their children with most horrible impurities. This chastisement became notorious in Jerusalem, although the priests and pharisees diligently sought to cover it up, just as they had tried to conceal the Resurrection of the Savior. As these events, however, were not so important, neither the Apostles nor the Evangelists wrote about them, and in the confusion of the city the multitude soon forgot them.

66. The chastisement and terror extended also to the depths of hell, where the demons felt themselves seized with new confusion and oppression for three days, just as the Jews lay on the earth for three hours. During these three days Lucifer and his demons broke forth in fearful howlings, communicating new terror and confusion of torments to all the damned. O ineffable and powerful Spirit! The holy Church calls Thee the finger of God, because Thou proceedest from the Father and

the Son, as the finger from the arm and the body; but on this occasion it was manifested to me, that Thou holdest the same infinite power with the Father and the Son. Through thy sovereign presence the heaven and the earth are moved by such opposite effects in all its inhabitants at one and the same time; but they are similar to those, that will happen at the last judgment. The saints and the just Thou fillest with thy grace, thy gifts and thy ineffable consolations; and the impious and the proud Thou chastisest and overwhelmest with confusion and pain. Truly I see here fulfilled what Thou sayest through the mouth of David; that Thou art a God of vengeance and workest freely, dealing out retribution to the wicked, in order that they may not glory in their unjust malice nor say in their heart that Thou failest in perception or judgment while reproving and chastising their sins (Ps. 93, 1).

67. Let the insipid of this world then understand, and let the foolish be warned, that the Most High knows the vain thoughts of men; that if He is liberal and most kind to the just, He is also rigid in punishing the impious and the wicked (Ps. 93, 11). It was befitting that the Holy Ghost should show Himself to be the one as well as the other on this occasion; for He proceeded from the incarnate Word, who had assumed human nature for the sake of men, who had died for their salvation, and had suffered ignominies and torments without opening his mouth or seeking retribution for those insults and offenses. In coming down into this world it was just that the Spirit should be zealous for the honor of that same incarnate Word; though He did not punish all his enemies, yet He indicated in the punishment of the most wicked, what all the others deserved, who, in their stubborn perfidy had despised Him, if by the respite

allowed them, they did not return to truth in heartfelt penance. It was also befitting, that the few, who had received the Word and had followed Him as their Master and Redeemer, and those who were to preach his faith and doctrine, be rewarded and furnished with the proper means for establishing the Church and the evangelical law. The Apostle says, that leaving one's father and mother and uniting oneself with a wife (as also Moses had said), is a great sacrament in Christ and the Church (Gen. 2, 24; Ephes. 5, 32), because He descended from the bosom of the Father in order to unite Himself with it in his humanity. Since then Christ came down from heaven in order to be with his spouse, the Church, it follows that the Holy Ghost came down on account of the most holy Mary, who was not less his Spouse than Christ was of the Church, and who was not less beloved by Him than the Church was beloved of Christ.

INSTRUCTION WHICH THE GREAT QUEEN OF HEAVEN AND OUR LADY GAVE ME.

68. My daughter, in small esteem and thankfulness do the children of the Church hold this blessing of the Most High, by which, in addition to sending of his Son as their Master and Redeemer, He sent also the Holy Ghost into his Church. So great was the love, by which He sought to draw them to Himself, that, in order to make them sharers of his divine perfections, He sent them first the Son, who is wisdom (John 3, 16) and afterwards the Holy Ghost, who is love, so that all might be enriched in the manner in which they were capable. The divine Spirit, in coming for the first time upon the Apostles and the others gathered with them, intended it as a pledge and testimony, that He would

confer the same favor on the rest of the children of the Church, of light and of the Gospel, and that He was ready to communicate his gifts to all, if all will dispose themselves toward receiving them. In witness to this truth the Holy Ghost came upon many of the faithful in visible form and with visible effects (Acts 8, 17; 10, 44; 11, 15), because they were truly faithful servants, humble and sincere, pure and ready of heart to receive Him. Also in our times He comes to many just souls, although not with such open manifestations, because it is neither necessary nor proper. The interior effects and gifts are all of the same nature, acting according to the disposition and state of the one who receives them.

69. Blessed is the soul which sighs and aspires after this blessing and seeks to participate in this divine fire, which enkindles, enlightens and consumes all that is terrestrial and carnal, which purifies and raises it up to a new existence, union and participation with God himself. This happiness, as thy true and loving Mother, I desire for thee, my daughter, and in order that thou mayest attain it in its fullness, I again exhort thee to prepare thy heart by seeking to preserve inviolable tranquillity and peace in all that may happen to thee. The divine clemency wishes to raise thee to a habitation very exalted and secure, where the torments of thy spirit shall come to an end and whither the assaults neither of the world nor of hell can reach; where in thy own repose the Lord shall rest and find in thee a worthy dwelling-place and a temple of his glory. Thou shalt not escape the attacks and temptations, directed against thee by the dragon with the most cunning astuteness; but do thou live in continued wariness, lest thou be disturbed or disquieted in the interior of thy soul. Guard thy treasures in secret; enjoy

the delights of the Lord, the sweet effects of his chaste love, the influences of his holy science; for in this regard He has singled thee out from many generations in utmost liberality.

70. Take heed then of thy calling and assure thyself, that the Most High offers thee anew the participation and communication of his divine Spirit and his gifts. Remember however, that when He confers them, He does not take away the freedom of thy will; for He ever leaves the election of good or evil to its free arbitrament. Hence, trusting in the divine favor, thou must efficaciously resolve to imitate me in the works shown to thee of my life and thou must never hinder the effects and the operations of the gifts of the Holy Spirit. In order that thou mayest understand better this my doctrine, I will explain to thee the effects of all his seven gifts.

71. The first one, which is the gift of Wisdom, fills the mind with the knowledge and the delight of divine things and moves the heart to a sincere love toward the practice and exercise of all that is good, all that is best, most perfect and agreeable in the eyes of the Lord. With this impulse thou must concur, yielding thyself entirely to the pleasure of his divine will and despising all that might hinder thee, no matter how pleasant it may seem to thy inclinations or alluring to thy appetite. Wisdom is aided by the second gift, that of Intellect, which gives special light to penetrate profoundly into the object presented to the understanding. With this gift thou must co-operate by diverting and turning aside thy attention and thoughts from all the bastard and foreign objects of knowledge, which the demon either by himself or through other creatures shall present to thy mind in order to distract it and prevent it from penetrating deeply into the truth of divine things. This

kind of distraction greatly embarrasses the mind, for the two kinds of knowledge are incompatible with each other, and whenever the limited faculties of man are divided into their attention to many objects, they enter into them less and attend less, than if all their operations were riveted on one alone. In this is evident the truth of what the Gospel says: that no one can serve two masters (Matth. 6, 24). When the whole attention of the soul has thus been riveted on understanding the good, Fortitude, the third gift, is necessary, in order to execute resolutely all that the understanding has perceived as most holy, perfect and agreeable before the Lord. The difficulties and hindrances in the pursuit of the good are to be overcome by Fortitude, making the creature ready to suffer whatever labor or pain, in order not to be deprived of the true and highest Good it has come to know.

72. But it often happens, that natural ignorance and doubt added to temptation withhold the creature from following out the conclusions and consequences of the divine truth, and thus create hindrances in the execution of what is more perfect. Hence, against the false prudence of the flesh, God furnishes the fourth gift, that of Science, which gives light to distinguish between different kinds of good, teaches the most certain and secure way, and decides upon it, when necessary. To this is joined the gift of Piety, the fifth, which inclines the soul with sweet urgency to all that is truly pleasing and acceptable to the Lord and to what is of real spiritual benefit to the one executing it. It inclines the creatures to these things not through the natural passions, but by holy, perfect and virtuous motives. Then, in order that man may be guided by high prudence, the sixth gift, that of Counsel, supports his understanding, in order that he may act with

precision and without temerity; weighing the means and taking counsel with himself and with others discreetly for gaining honest and holy ends by the selection of the proper means. To all these is added Fear, the last, which guards and sets the seal upon all of them. This gift inclines the heart to fly and avoid all that is imperfect, dangerous or alien to the virtues and perfections of the soul, thus serving as a wall of defense. It is necessary to understand the object and the manner of this holy Fear, lest it grow excessive and cause the creature to fear, where there is no occasion. Such has often happened to thee through the astuteness of the serpent, when, under guise of holy Fear, the devil entangled thee in an inordinate liking for the blessings of the Lord. But by this instruction thou art now informed how thou must exercise in thee the gifts of the Most High and prepare thyself for them. I remind and admonish thee, that this science of holy Fear is the accompaniment of the favors communicated to thee by the Most High, and that it fills the soul with sweetness, peace and tranquillity. It enables the creature properly to estimate and appreciate the gifts, which come from the powerful hand of the Almighty; neither are any of them unimportant, nor does this Fear hinder a proper estimate of these gifts. It induces the soul to give thanks with all its powers and to humiliate itself to the dust. In understanding these truths without error and in suppressing the cowardly fear of slaves, thou shalt be filled with filial Fear, which, as thy guiding star, will help thee to navigate securely in this ocean of tears.

CHAPTER VI.

73. On account of the visible and open signs, by
which the Holy Ghost descended upon the Apostles, the
whole city of Jerusalem with its inhabitants was stirred
to wonder. When the news of the astounding events at
the house of the Cenacle spread about, the multitude of
the people gathered in crowds to know more of the happenings (Acts 2, 6). On that day was being celebrated
one of the paschs or feasts of the Jews; and as well
on this account, as on account of the special dispensation
of heaven, the city was crowded with foreigners and
strangers from all parts of the world. For to them the
Most High wished to manifest the wonders of the first
preaching and spreading of the new law of grace, which
the incarnate Word, our Redeemer and Master, had ordained for the salvation of men.

74. The sacred Apostles, who were filled with charity
by the plenitude of the gifts of the Holy Ghost and who
knew that all Jerusalem was gathering at the doors of
the Cenacle, asked permission of their Mistress and
Queen to go forth and preach to them; in order that
such great graces might not even for a moment fail
to redound to the benefit of souls and to new glory
of their Author. They all left the house of the Cenacle

and, placing themselves before the multitudes, began to preach the mysteries of the faith and of eternal life. Though until then they had been so shy and seclusive, they now stepped forth with unhesitating boldness and poured forth burning words, that like a flashing fire penetrated to the souls of their hearers. All the people were filled with wonder and astonishment at these events, the like of which had never before been heard or seen in the world. They looked at each other and in consternation asked each other, saying: "What is this that we witness? Are not all these that speak Galileeans? How then do we hear them speaking in the language in which we were born? We Jews and Proselytes, Romans, Latins, Greeks, Cretans, Arabs, Parthians, Medes and all the rest of us from different parts of the world, hear them speak and we understand them in our own languages? O greatness of God! How admirable is He in all His works!"

75. This miracle, that all the men of so many different tongues then assembled in Jerusalem should hear the Apostles in their own language, joined to the doctrine which they preached, caused great astonishment. Yet I wish to remark, that though all the Apostles, on account of the plenitude of science and of gifts gratuitously received, were able to speak in the languages of all nations, because that was necessary for the preaching of the Gospel, yet on that occasion they all spoke the language of Palestine. Using only this idiom they were understood by all the different nationalities there present, as if they had spoken in the several idioms. This miracle the Lord wrought at the time in order that they might be understood and believed by those different nations, and in order that saint Peter might not be obliged to repeat in the different languages of those present,

what he preached to them concerning the mysteries of
faith. He preached only once and all heard and understood him, each in his own language, and so it happened
also with the other Apostles. For if each one had spoken
in the language of those who heard them, and which
they knew as their mother tongue, it would have been
necessary for them to repeat what they said at least
seven or eight times according to the different nationalities mentioned by saint Luke (Acts 2, 9). This would
have consumed a longer time than is intimated by the
sacred text, and it would have caused great confusion
and trouble to repeat the same doctrines over and over
again or to speak so many languages on one occasion;
nor would the miracle be so intelligible to us as the
one mentioned.

76. The people who heard the Apostles did not understand the miracle, although they wondered at hearing each
their own idiom. What saint Luke says about their
speaking different languages, must be understood as
meaning, that the Apostles were then and there able to
understand them, as I shall mention later on (Acts 2, 4),
and because on that day, those that came to the Cenacle
understood them all speaking in their own language.
But this miracle and wonderment caused in their hearers
different effects and opinions, according to the dispositions of each one. Those that listened piously received
a deep understanding of the Divinity and of the Redemption of man, now so eloquently and fervently propounded to them. They were moved eagerly to desire
the knowledge of the truth; by the divine light they
were filled with compunction and sorrow for their sins
and with desire of divine mercy and forgiveness. With
tears in their eyes they cried out to the Apostles and
asked what they must do to gain eternal life. Others,

who hardened their hearts, altogether untouched by the divine truths preached by them, became indignant at the Apostles, and instead of yielding to them, called them innovators and adventurers. Many of the Jews, more impious in their perfidy and envy, inveighed against the Apostles, saying they were drunk and insane (Acts 2, 13). Among these were some of those who had again come to their senses after having fallen to the ground at the thunder caused by the coming of the Holy Ghost; for they had risen still more obstinate and rebellious against God.

77. In order to refute their blasphemies saint Peter, as the head of the Church, stepped forth and, speaking in a louder voice, said: "Ye men of Judea, and all ye that dwell in Jerusalem, be this known to you and with your ears receive my words. For these are not drunk as you suppose, seeing it is but the third hour of the day. But this is that which was spoken of by the prophet Joel: 'And it shall come to pass, in the last days, (saith the Lord) I will pour out of my Spirit upon all flesh: and your sons and your daughters shall prophesy, and your young ones shall see visions, and your old men shall dream dreams. And upon my servants indeed, and upon my handmaids I will pour out my Spirit, and they shall prophesy. And I will show wonders in the heaven above, and signs on the earth beneath: blood and fire, and vapor and smoke. The sun shall be turned into darkness, and the moon into blood, before the great and manifest day of the Lord arrives; and it shall come to pass, that whosoever shall call upon the name of the Lord, shall be saved.' Ye men of Israel, hear these words: Jesus of Nazareth, a man approved of God among you, by miracles, and wonders, and signs, which God did by Him in the midst of you, as you also know: This same, being

delivered up by the determinate counsel and foreknowledge of God, you, by the hands of wicked men, have
crucified and slain. He was a holy Man, approved of
God in his virtues, by miracles and prodigies wrought in
the midst of your people, of which you know and are
witnesses. And God has raised Him from the dead,
according to the prophecies of David. For that holy
king could not speak of himself, since you have his
sepulchre in your midst, where lies his body. He spoke
as a prophet of Christ, and we are ourselves witnesses
as having seen Him risen and ascending into heaven by
his own power, to be seated at the right hand of the
Father, as likewise David has prophesied (Os. 15, 8;
Ps. 109, 1). Let the unbelievers understand these words
of truth, which they wish to deny in the perfidy of their
malice; for against them stand the wonders of the Most
High which wrought in us as witnesses to the doctrine
of Christ and to his admirable Resurrection."

78. "Let then the whole house of Israel understand,
and let them be assured, that God hath made this Jesus,
whom you have crucified, his Anointed and the Lord of
all, and that He has raised Him from the dead on the
third day." On hearing these words the hearts of many,
that stood there, were moved to compunction and with
great wailing they asked saint Peter and the rest of the
Apostles, what they should do for their salvation (Acts
2, 37). Thereupon saint Peter said to them: "Do penance and be baptized every one of you in the name of
Jesus Christ, for the remission of sins; and you shall receive the gift of the Holy Ghost. For the promise is
to you, and to your children, and to all that are far off,
whomsoever the Lord our God shall call. Seek therefore now to make use of the remedy, and to save yourselves from this perverse and incredulous generation."

Many other words of life saint Peter and the other
Apostles spoke to them, by which the perfidious Jews
and the other unbelievers were much confounded; and
as no one could answer, they withdrew and left the
Cenacle. But the number of those that received the
true faith of Jesus Christ amounted to about three
thousand (Acts 2, 41). They all attached themselves
to the Apostles and were baptized by them to the great
consternation and fear of all Jerusalem; for the wonders
and prodigies performed by the Apostles filled with
terror and dismay all the unbelievers.

79. The three thousand, who were converted by the
first sermon of saint Peter, were from all the nations
then gathered in Jerusalem, so that forthwith all nations,
without excluding any, might partake of the fruits of
the Redemption, all might be gathered to the Church,
and all might experience the grace of the Holy Spirit;
for the holy Church was to be composed of all nations
and tribes. Many were Jews, who had followed Christ
our Savior with kindly feelings and witnessed his sufferings and Death with compassion, as I said above.
Some also of those, who had concurred in his Passion,
were converted, though these were few, because many
would not alter their disposition; for, if they had done
so, all of them would have been admitted to mercy and
received pardon for their error. After their preaching
the Apostles retired that evening within the Cenacle, in
order to give an account to the Mother of mercy, the
purest Mary. With them also entered a great number
of the new children of the Church, in order that they
might come to know and venerate the Mother of mercy.

80. But the great Queen of the angels was ignorant
of nothing that had happened; for from her retreat
She had heard the preaching of the Apostles and She

knew the secret hearts and thoughts of all the hearers. The tenderest Mother remained prostrate with her face upon the ground during the whole time, tearfully praying for the conversion of all that subjected themselves to the faith of the Savior, and for all the rest, if they should consent to co-operate with the helps and the graces of the Lord. In order to help the Apostles in their great work of beginning to preach, and the bystanders in properly listening to them, the most holy Mary sent many of her accompanying angels with holy inspirations, encouraging the sacred Apostles and giving them strength to inquire and to manifest more explicitly the hidden mysteries of the humanity and Divinity of Christ our Redeemer. The angels fulfilled all the commands of their Queen, while She Herself exercised her own power and gifts according to the circumstances of the occasion. When the Apostles came to Her with those copious first-fruits of their preaching and of the Holy Ghost, She received them with incredible joy and sweetness and with the most loving kindness of a true Mother.

81. The Apostle saint Peter spoke to the recently converted and said to them: "My brethren, and servants of the Most High, this is the Mother of our Redeemer and Master, Jesus Christ, whose faith you have received in acknowledging Him as true God and man. She has given Him the human form, conceiving Him in her womb, and She bore Him, remaining a Virgin before, during and after his birth. Receive Her as your Mother, as your Refuge and Intercessor, for through Her you and we shall receive light, direction, and release from our sins and miseries." At these words of the Apostle and at the sight of most holy Mary these new adherents of the faith were filled with admirable light and consolation; for this privilege of conferring great interior bless-

ings and of giving light to those who looked upon Her with pious veneration, was renewed and extended in Her at the time when She was at the right hand of her divine Son in Heaven. As all of those faithful partook of these blessings in the presence of their Queen, they prostrated themselves at her feet and with tears besought her assistance and blessing. But the humble and prudent Queen evaded this latter, because of the presence of the Apostles, who were priests, and of saint Peter, the Vicar of Christ. Then this Apostle said to Her: "Lady, do not refuse to these faithful what they piously ask for the consolation of their souls." The blessed Mary obeyed the head of the Church and in humble serenity of a Queen She gave her blessing to the newly converted.

82. The love which filled their hearts made them desire to hear from their heavenly Mother some words of consolation; yet their humility and reverence prevented them from asking for this favor. As they perceived how obediently She had yielded to saint Peter, they turned to him and begged him to ask Her not to send them away without some word of encouragement. Saint Peter, though he considered this favor very proper for these souls who had been born again to Christ by his preaching and that of the other Apostles, nevertheless, aware that the Mother of Wisdom knew well what was to be done, presumed to say no more than these words; "Lady, listen to the petitions of thy servants and children." Then the great Lady obeyed and said to the converts: "My dearest brethren in the Lord, give thanks and praise with your whole hearts to the Almighty God, because from among all men He has called and drawn you to the sure path of eternal life in the knowledge of the holy faith you have received. Be firm in your confession of it from all your hearts and in hearing and believing

all that the law of grace contains as preached and ordained by its true Teacher Jesus, my Son and your Redeemer. Be eager to hear and obey his Apostles, who teach and instruct you, so that you may be signed and marked by Baptism in the character of children of the Most High. I offer myself as your handmaid to assist you in all that serves toward your consolation, and I shall ask Him to look upon you as a kind Father and to manifest to you the true joy of his countenance, communicating to you also his grace."

83. By this sweetest of exhortations those new children of the Church were filled with consolation, light, veneration and admiration of what they saw of the Mistress of the world; asking again for her blessing, they for that day left her presence, renewed and replete with the wonderful gifts of the Most High. The Apostles and disciples from that day on continued without intermission their preaching and their miracles, and through the entire octave they instructed not only the three thousand, who had been converted on Pentecost day, but multitudes of others, who day by day accepted the faith. Since they came from all parts of the world, they conversed and spoke with each one in his own language; for as I have said above, they spoke in various languages from that time on. This grace was given not only to the Apostles, although it was more complete and noticeable in them; also the disciples and all the one hundred and twenty, who were in the Cenacle at the time, and also the holy women, who received the Holy Ghost, were thus favored. This was really necessary at the time on account of the great multitudes, who came to the faith. Although all the men and many of the women came to the Apostles, yet many, after having heard them, went to Magdalen and her companions, who catechized, instructed and con-

verted them and others that came at the report of the
miracles they performed. For this gift was also conferred on the women, who, by the imposition of hands,
cured all the sicknesses, gave sight to the blind, tongue to
the mute, motion to the lame, and life to many of the
dead. These and other wonders were principally wrought
by the Apostles, nevertheless both their miracles and
those of the women excited the wonder and astonishment
of all Jerusalem; so that nothing else was talked about
except the prodigies and the preaching of the Apostles
of Jesus, of his disciples, and followers of his doctrine.

84. The fame of these events soon extended beyond
the city; for no one sought a cure in vain. Such miracles were at that time very necessary, not only for the
confirmation of the new law and doctrine of Christ our
Savior, but also because the natural desire of health and
life would stimulate men to seek the welfare of their
body and thus bring them within hearing and influence
of the divine word. Thus they returned cured as well
in body as in soul, which generally happened to those,
who came to the Apostles in their maladies. Hence
the number of the faithful daily increased, and their
fervor in faith and charity was so ardent, that all of
them began to imitate the poverty of Christ, despising
their riches and property and laying all their possessions
at the feet of the Apostles without reserving anything
for themselves as their own (Acts 2, 45). They wished
to possess all things in common and thus free themselves
from the dangers of riches, preferring to live in poverty,
sincerity, humility and continual prayer without any other
care than that of eternal life. All of them considered
themselves as brethren and children of one Father in
heaven (Matth. 23, 9). As faith, hope and charity, and
the sacraments were the common blessing of all, and as

they were all seeking the same grace and eternal life, inequality in other things seemed dangerous to these Christian children of one Father, the inheritors of his goods and professors of his law. It seemed to them inappropriate, that, having such a bond of union in the principal and essential things, some should be rich and others poor, and that temporal things should not be communicated, where each one enjoyed those of grace; for all gifts are from one and the same Father for all of his children.

85. This was the happy beginning and the golden age of the evangelical Church, where the rushing of the stream rejoiced the city of God (Ps. 45, 5) and the current of grace and the gifts of the Holy Ghost fertilized this new paradise recently planted by the hands of the Savior Jesus, while in its midst stood the tree of life, most holy Mary. Then was faith alive, hope firm, charity ardent, sincerity pure, humility true, justice most equitable, when the faithful neither knew avarice nor followed vanity, when they trod under foot vain pomp, were free from covetousness, pride, ambition, which later prevailed among the professors of the faith, who while confessing themselves followers of Christ, denied Him in their works. We are inclined to object, that those were the first-fruits of the Church, of the Spirit (Rom. 8, 23), that the faithful were few; that now the times are different, that in those times the Mother of wisdom and grace lived in the Church, whose presence, prayers and protection, defended and encouraged the faithful to bring forth heroic works of the faith.

86. To this we answer by what will be said in the course of this history, whence it will appear that none other than the faithful have permitted so many vices to creep into the fold of the Church; such as the demon himself, with all his pride and malice, never expected

to see established among Christians. I content myself with saying, that the power and grace of the Holy Spirit were not exhausted in those first-fruits. His influence is always the same and would be just as efficacious with the many to the end of the Church, as it was with a few in its beginnings, if those many were as faithful as those few. It is true that the times have changed; but this change from virtue to vice, from good to evil, consists not in any change of the heavens and the stars, but in a change of men, who have strayed from the straight way of life eternal and walk the way of perdition. I do not speak now of the pagans or of the heretics, who have fallen away not only from the light of true faith, but even from right reason. I speak of the faithful, who pride themselves in being children of light, but content themselves with only the name, and who sometimes use it merely to cloak their vices and to cover up their crimes.

87. It will not be possible in this third part to describe even the least part of the wonderful and great works accomplished by the mighty Queen in the primitive Church; but from those which I will describe, and from her life in this world after the Ascension, much can be inferred. For She did not rest or lose one moment or occasion of conferring some singular favor either upon the whole Church or some of its members. For She consumed Herself either in praying and beseeching her divine Son, without ever experiencing a refusal; or in exhorting, instructing, counseling, and, as Treasurer and Dispenser of the divine favors, distributing graces in diverse manners among the children of the Gospel. Among the hidden mysteries, which were made known to me concerning this power of the blessed Mary, was also this, that in those first ages, during which She lived in the holy Church, the number of the damned was pro-

portionately very small; and that, comparatively, in those
few years a greater number were saved than in many
succeeding ages.

88. I acknowledge, that, if the lapse of time had de-
creased the power, the charity and clemency of that highest Sovereign, the good fortune of those living in that
happy time might cause a holy envy in those living by
the light of faith in our more protracted and less favored
times.   It is true we have not the happiness of seeing
Her, conversing with Her and listening to Her with
our bodily senses; and in this respect those first children
of the Church were more fortunate. But let us all remember, that in the heavenly knowledge and charity of this
most loving Mother we were all present to Her, also during those times (Vol. III., 78); for She saw and
knew us all in the order and succession in which we were
to be born in the Church; and She prayed and interceded
for us no less than for those who lived in her times.   Nor
is She at present less powerful in heaven, than She was
then upon earth; nor less our Mother, than of those
first children; and She held us as her own, just as well
as them.   But alas! that our faith and our fervor and
devotion should be so very different!   Not She has
changed, nor is her love less ardent, nor would we
experience less of her intercession and protection, if in
these troubled times we would hasten to Her with the
same sentiments of humility and fervor, asking for her
prayers and trustfully relying upon Her for help, as was
the case with those devoted Christians in the first beginning.   Without a doubt the whole Catholic Church
would then immediately experience the same assistance
of the Queen throughout the whole world.

89. Let us return to the solicitude of the kindest
Mother for the Apostles and for the recently converted,

attending to the consolation and necessities of all and of each one in particular. She exhorted and animated the Apostles and the ministers of the divine word, fixing their attention upon the prodigious manifestation of the divine power, by which her most holy Son began to plant the faith of his Church; the virtue which the Holy Ghost had communicated to them in order to make them fit ministers; the ever present assistance of the divine right hand. She exhorted them to acknowledge and praise Him as the author of all these wonderful works and to render Him humble thanks for all of them; to follow up in secure confidence their preaching and exhortation, the exaltation of the name of the Lord, in order that He might be known, extolled and loved by all the faithful. She herself practiced what She taught and inculcated, by prostrating and humiliating Herself before the Most High and by breaking forth in canticles of praise and exaltation. These duties She fulfilled with such plenitude, that for none of the converted did She ever omit giving thanks and offering fervent prayers to the eternal Father; all of them remained distinctly present in her mind.

90. Not only did She do all these things for each one of them; but She received all, listened to all, and endeared Herself to them with words of light and life. During those days following upon the coming of the Holy Ghost many conversed with Her in private, opening up their inmost souls, and the same happened also with those who were converted afterwards in Jerusalem. Not that She was ignorant of their secrets; for She knew the hearts of all, their affections, inclinations and conditions, enabling her by this divine knowledge and wisdom to accommodate Herself to the necessities and natural character and to render salutary assistance against the

maladies of each of her clients.   Hence the most blessed
Mother conferred such exquisite blessings and vast favors
to innumerable souls, that they never can be known in
this world.

91. There were many who were privileged to be instructed and catechized in the holy faith by the heavenly
Mother and not one of them was lost; for at that time,
and as long as they lived, She continued to offer special
prayers for them, so that all of them were written in
the book of life.   In order to bind her divine Son She
said to Him: "My Lord and life of my soul! According
to thy will and pleasure have I returned to the world in
order to be the Mother of thy children, my brethren and
the faithful sons of the Church.   Let not my heart be
torn by seeing the fruit of thy priceless blood fail in
any one of these that seek my intercession; and let
them not reap unhappiness from their having availed
themselves of me, the insignificant worm of the earth,
for obtaining thy clemency.   Admit them, my Son, into
the number of thy friends, predestined for thy glory."
To these her prayers the Lord immediately responded,
promising that what She asked would be done.   And I
believe the same happens in our day to all those that
merit her intercession and ask for it with all their hearts;
for if this purest Mother comes to her Son with similar petitions, how can it be imagined, that He shall
deny to Her that little, to whom He has given his own
Self, in order that She might clothe it in human flesh
and nature, and then nurse Him at her own virginal
breast?

92. Many of those new faithful, highly impressed with
her greatness by their conversation with the heavenly
Mistress, returned to present to Her jewels and the rich-
est gifts; especially the women despoiled themselves of

fineries to lay them at her feet. But She would receive or permit none of these gifts. When it seemed to Her appropriate not to refuse entirely, She secretly inspired the minds of the givers to bring them to the Apostles, in order that they might be equitably and justly distributed in charity among the most poor and needy of the faithful. But the humble Mother gratefully acknowledged them as if they had been given to Her. The poor and the sick She received with ineffable kindness, and many of them she cured of inveterate and long-standing infirmities. Through the hands of saint John She supplied many secret wants, never omitting the least point of virtue. As the Apostles and disciples were engaged all day in preaching the faith and in converting those that came, the great Queen busied Herself in preparing their food and attending to their comfort; and at stated times She served the priests on her knees and with incredible humility and reverence asked to kiss their hands. This She observed especially with the Apostles, knowing and beholding their souls confirmed in grace, endowed with all that the Holy Ghost had wrought in them and exalted by their dignity of being the highpriests and the founders of the Church (Eph. 2, 20). Sometimes She saw them clothed in great splendor, which elicited from Her increased reverence and veneration.

INSTRUCTION WHICH THE GREAT QUEEN OF THE ANGELS GAVE ME.

93. My daughter, in what thou hast come to know of the events related in this chapter, thou wilt find a great deal that points to the mystery of the predestination of souls. Be convinced that, since the Redemption was so overflowing and copious, it was sufficient for the

salvation of all men (Rom. 5, 20). The divine truth
was made known to all, whoever heard its preaching or
who saw the effects of the coming of the Godman into
the world. Besides the outward preaching and knowledge of the remedy, all received interior inspirations and
helps in order to seek and accept the means. You are
surprised that, in spite of all this, only three thousand
were converted by the first sermon of the Apostle among
all that great multitude then in Jerusalem. It should
cause a greater surprise that in our times so few are converted to the way of eternal life, as the Gospel is more
widespread, its preaching is frequent, its ministers numerous, the light of the Church clearer and the knowledge of the divine mysteries more definite. With all this
men are blinder, the hearts more hardened, pride more
inflated, avarice more bold, and all the vices are practiced
without fear of God and without consideration.

94. In this most perverse and unhappy state mortals
cannot complain of the most high and equitable providence of the Lord, who offers to all and every one his
fatherly mercy, and points out to them both the way of
life and the way of death; so that if any man hardens
his heart, God can permit it in strictest justice. The reprobate will have none but themselves to blame, if afterwards, when there is no more time, they shall be uselessly
dismayed with what in opportune time they could and
should have known. If in the short and transient life,
which is given to them in order to merit the eternal, they
close their eyes and ears to the truth and to the light, and
if they listen to the demon, giving themselves up to all the
promptings of his malice; if they thus abuse the goodness and clemency of the Lord, what can they then allege
as their excuse? If they do not know how to pardon an
injury and for the slightest offense meditate the direst

vengeance; if, for the sake of increasing their property, they pervert the entire order of reason and of natural brotherhood; if for a passing delight they forget the eternal pains, and if, in addition to all this, they despise the warnings, helps and admonitions sent to them by God to inspire them with the fear of perdition and induce them to avoid it, how shall they afterwards find fault with the divine clemency? Let then mortals, who have sinned against God, undeceive themselves: without penance there shall be no grace, without reform no pardon, without pardon no glory. But just as these are not conceded to those that are unworthy, so they are also never denied to those that are worthy; nor is ever the mercy of God withheld from any one who seeks to obtain it.

95. From all these truths I desire, my daughter, that thou collect for thyself what will be for thy welfare. Let the first be, that thou receive attentively each holy inspiration, each advice or instruction, although it come from the most inferior minister of the Lord, or from whatever creature. Thou must prudently consider, that none comes to thy notice by chance and without divine predisposition; for there is no doubt that the Providence of the Most High ordains all things for thy instruction, and in this light must thou look upon them with humble thanks, trying to find the virtue, which thou canst and shouldst practice in accordance with the reminder and to exercise it in the manner in which thou understandest and knowest it. Do not despise any one of them, though it may seem only a trifle; for by it thou must dispose thyself for other works of greater virtue and merit. Consider secondly, what a damage is wrought in souls by the neglect of so many helps, inspirations, callings and other blessings of the Lord; for their ingratitude vindicates the justice of the Most High in allowing so

many sinners to become hardened in their sins. If this
is such a formidable danger for all men, how much more
will it be a danger for thee, if thou abuse the abundant
graces and favors, which the kindness of the Lord has
showered upon thee in preference to many generations of
men? And since my divine Son ordains all these things
for thy own good and for the good of other souls, I wish,
lastly, that in imitation of me, as has been shown thee,
thou impregnate thy heart with a most sincere determina-
tion to assist all the children of the Church, and all other
men, as far as thou canst, clamoring to the Lord from
thy inmost heart and asking Him to look upon the souls
with mercy for their salvation. And in order that they
may gain this blessing, offer to suffer for them as a
victim if necessary; remembering, that they cost my
divine Son and thy Spouse the shedding of his blood
and his life, and remembering my own labors in the
Church. Do thou continually implore the divine mercy
for the fruit of that Redemption, and this practice I command thee under obedience.

CHAPTER VII.

THE APOSTLES AND DISCIPLES MEET IN ORDER TO SOLVE
SOME DOUBTS, IN PARTICULAR ABOUT THE FORM OF
BAPTISM; THEY ADMINISTER THAT SACRAMENT TO
THE CATECHUMENS; SAINT PETER CELEBRATES THE
FIRST MASS; THE DOINGS OF MARY IN THE MEAN-
WHILE.

96. It is not the object of this history to relate all the
doings of the Apostles in the order followed by saint
Luke, nor to record all that they did after the descent of
the Holy Ghost; for, though the great Queen and Lady
certainly knew all that passed, yet many things happened
where She was not personally present. Of such it is not
necessary to speak here, nor would it be possible to describe the manner in which the heavenly Queen co-
operated in the works of the Apostles and disciples, and
in all else that happened; for in order to do this, there
were need of many large volumes. It is sufficient for my
purpose and for the sequence of this history to select
the salient points of the Acts of the Apostles written by
the Evangelist, and make intelligible much of what he
omits concerning our Queen, and what was not to his
purpose nor proper for him to write at that time.

97. As the Apostles continued their preaching and
wonders in Jerusalem the number of the faithful increased and, as saint Luke says in the fourth chapter of
the Acts, after seven days reached five thousand. All
of them were busy catechising the newcomers in preparation for Baptism, though that work was done principally

by the disciples; for the Apostles were preaching and were conducting some controversies with the pharisees and sadducees. On this seventh day the Queen of Angels, being in the retirement of her oratory and considering how the little flock of her divine Son was increasing, asked the Lord to give light to the Apostles in order that they might begin to institute a government for the better direction of those new children of the faith. Prostrate upon the floor She adored the Lord and said: "Most high and eternal God, as a vile worm of the earth I wish to praise and exalt Thee for the immense love Thou hast manifested for the human race; and because Thou showest the mercy of a Father by calling so many to the knowledge and faith of thy divine Son, glorifying and spreading the honor of thy name through the world. I beseech thy Majesty, O Lord, to enlighten and instruct thy Apostles, my masters, to dispose and order all that concerns the government, amplification and preservation of thy holy Church."

98. Then the most prudent Mother, in the vision of the Divinity She had at that time, perceived that the Lord was very well pleased and answered Her: "Mary my Spouse, what dost thou wish? and for what dost thou ask Me? Thy voice and thy sighs have sounded sweetly in my ears (Cant. 2, 14). Ask what thou wishest, my will is inclined toward thy petitions." The heavenly Mary answered: "My Lord and my God, Master of all my being, my desires and my sighs are not unknown to thy infinite wisdom (Ps. 37, 10). I desire, seek and solicit thy greater pleasure and satisfaction, thy greater glory and the exaltation of thy name in the holy Church. I present to Thee these new children, with whom Thou hast so quickly befruited it and also my desire that they receive holy Baptism, since they have already been in-

structed in the faith. And if it is according to thy will and service, I desire also that the Apostles commence even now to consecrate the body and the blood of thy and my Son, in order that by this new and admirable sacrifice they may give Thee praise and thanks for the blessing of the Redemption and all the favors Thou hast through it conferred upon the world, and also that according to thy will the children of the Church may in it receive the nourishment of eternal life. I am but dust and ashes, the least handmaid of thy faithful, and a woman; and on that account I hesitate in proposing this to thy priests and Apostles. But do Thou inspire, O Lord, the heart of saint Peter, thy Vicar, to ordain what Thou wishest."

99. The Church therefore owes thanks to most holy Mary for this special blessing: that by her most discreet attention and intercession the body and blood of her divine Son was consecrated for the first time after the Ascension and after the coming of the Holy Ghost. It was natural, that through her efforts the bread of life should begin to be distributed among her children (Prov. 31, 14), since She was the richly laden and prosperous vessel, which brought it from heaven. The Lord then answered Her: "My beloved Dove, let what thou wishest, be done. My Apostles, with saint Peter and John, shall speak to thee and thou shalt order through them what thou wishest to be done." Immediately all of the Apostles entered the presence of the great Queen, and She received them as usual by reverently falling on her knees before them and asking their blessing. This Saint Peter, as the head of the Apostles, imparted. He spoke for all of them and represented to Mary, how the newly converted had already been instructed in the mysteries of the Lord's faith; how it was just, that they should receive Baptism, and that they should be marked as the children

of Christ and admitted to the bosom of the Church; he therefore asked the heavenly Mistress to point out the order to be followed as most appropriate and pleasing to the Most High. The most prudent Lady answered: "My master, thou art the head of the Church and the vicar of my divine Son in it; all that shall be ordained by thee in his name, shall be approved of Him and his will with thine shall be mine."

100. Thereupon saint Peter ordained that on the following day (which corresponds to the Sunday of the most holy Trinity), Baptism should be given to those who had been converted during that week; this arrangement of saint Peter was satisfactory to our Queen and to the other Apostles. Immediately there arose a doubt as to what Baptism was to be given to them: the baptism of saint John, or the Baptism of Christ our Savior. To some it seemed that the baptism of saint John, which was that of penance, should be given to them, and that through it they were to enter into the faith and justification of their souls. Others, on the contrary, said, that with the Baptism and the Death of Christ the baptism of saint John had expired, since it had served merely to prepare the souls for the reception of Christ the Redeemer, and that the Baptism of the Lord gives grace sufficient for justifying the souls and for washing off all the sins from those properly disposed; and that it was necessary to introduce it immediately into the Church.

101. This opinion was approved of by saint John and saint Peter, and was confirmed by the most holy Mary. Hence they determined to institute at once the Baptism of Christ our Lord and to confer it on the new converts and the rest who came to the Church. In regard to the material and form of that Baptism there was no doubt among the Apostles; for all of them agreed that the

material should be natural and elementary water, and the form should be: I baptize thee in the name of the Father and of the Son and of the Holy Ghost; because these were the matter and form designated by the Lord our Savior and these words He had made use of in the Baptism He had himself administered. This way of baptizing was observed always from that day on. Wherever in the Acts of the Apostles it is said that they baptized in the name of Jesus, this saying does not refer to the form, but to the Author of the Baptism, namely Jesus, in contradistinction to the author of the other baptism, that of saint John. To baptize in the name of Jesus was the same as to baptize with the Baptism of Jesus; but its form was that which the Lord himself had given and contains the express mention of the three Persons of the most holy Trinity (Math. 28, 19), as the foundation and beginning of all the Catholic truth and faith. The Apostles therefore ordained, that all the catechumens should gather in the house of the Cenacle in order to be baptized; and that the seventy-two disciples should have charge of preparing them for that occasion.

102. Then the great Lady, having asked permission, spoke to that whole congregation and said: "My masters, the Redeemer of the world, the true God and my Son, out of the love which He had for men, offered to the eternal Father the sacrifice of his sacred body and blood, consecrating Himself under the species of bread and wine. Under these appearances He resolved to remain in his Church, in order that its children might have in it the sacrifice and food of eternal life they are to expect hereafter. Through this sacrifice, which embodies the mysteries of the life and death of the Son, the Father is to be placated; and in it and through it, the Church shall give the thanks and praise which it owes to Him as its God

and Benefactor.   You are the priests and ministers, who
alone are to offer it.   It is my desire, if such be your
will, that you begin to offer this unbloody sacrifice and
that you consecrate the body and blood of my divine
Son, in order that we may render fit thanks for the benefit
of his Redemption and of the sending of the Holy Ghost
into the Church; and in order that the faithful, by receiving this Sacrament, may begin to enjoy this bread
of life in all its divine effects.   All those may partake of
the sacred body, who shall have received Baptism and
who seem to be more fit and better prepared; but Baptism is the first requisite for its reception."

103. All the Apostles and disciples conformed to the
wish of the blessed Mary, and they thanked Her for Her
solicitude and her instruction.   It was resolved, that on
the following day, after the Baptism of the catechumens,
the body and blood of Christ should be consecrated, and
that Saint Peter should be the celebrant, since he was the
head of the Church.   The holy Apostle consented.   But
before dismissing them he proposed another difficulty to
the consideration of all, namely, concerning the order to
be observed in receiving and distributing the alms and
the goods of the newly converted.

104. He therefore said: "My dearest brethren, you
already know, that our Redeemer and Master, Jesus, by
his example, his doctrines and commands ordained and
taught the true poverty (Matthew 6, 20) in which we
should live, abhorring and shunning the cares entailed
by riches and possessions, and neither desiring or amass-
ing wealth in this life.   Besides this salutary doctrine we
have before our eyes the recent and formidable example
of the perdition of Judas, who was an Apostle as we ourselves, and who, by his avarice and covetousness, went
astray and has fallen from the dignity of the apostolate

into the abyss of wickedness and eternal damnation. This tremendous danger we must avoid, so that no one may hold in possession or handle money and that all may imitate and follow the strictest poverty of our Captain and Master. I know that all of you desire this, well understanding that in order to preserve us from this contagion the Lord has placed this risk and chastisement before our eyes. Therefore that we all may be free from the hindrances connected with the gifts and alms brought us by the faithful, it is necessary to arrange some form of administration. It is proper that you now determine upon the manner and order to be maintained in the reception and the distribution of the moneys and gifts of the faithful."

105. The whole gathering of the Apostles and disciples were somewhat at a loss to find the proper course to be pursued; and several opinions were proposed. Some of them suggested that a chief stewart be chosen, who should receive all the money and gifts, and who should distribute it according to the necessities of all. But this suggestion was not favored by this gathering of the poor and of the disciples of the Master of poverty, on account of the example of Judas so recently before their eyes. To others it seemed good to make a deposit of all the goods into the hands of a reliable person not belonging to the apostolic college, who should be master of it and apply the profits or rents according to the needs of the faithful; but also this seemed inappropriate, just as other measures also proposed. The great Mistress of humility, the blessed Mary, listened to all without saying a word; as well because She wished to show this reverence to the Apostles, as because no one would have advanced his own opinion, if She had first made known her view. Although She was the Teacher of all, She

always conducted Herself as a disciple anxious to listen and learn. But saint Peter and saint John, perceiving the diversity of opinion among the rest, besought the heavenly Mother to show them the right way in their doubts and to declare what should be most pleasing to her divine Son.

106. She obeyed and speaking to the whole gathering, She said: "My masters and brethren, I was in the school of our true Teacher, my divine Son, from the time when He was conceived in my womb, until He died and ascended into heaven; I have never seen Him touch or handle money, nor accept a gift of much value or price. When, shortly after his birth, He accepted the presents offered to Him by the Kings at their adoration (Matth. 2, 11), it was because of the mysterious signification connected with them and in order that He might not frustrate the pious intentions of those Kings, who were the first-fruits among the heathens. But without delay, while resting on my arms, He ordered me immediately to distribute them among the poor and the temple, as I also did. Many times during his life He told me, that one of the high purposes of his coming into the world was to raise up poverty and to teach it to mortals, who stand in horror of it. In his conversations, his teachings and his most holy life He manifested to me, and made me understand, that the holiness and perfection, which He had come to teach, was to be founded on the most perfect voluntary poverty and the contempt of riches. The more earnestly these were cultivated in the Church, so much greater would be her sanctity in the course of the ages; and this will be evident in the coming times."

107. "Since we are to follow the footsteps of our true Master and practice his teachings, in order that we may found his Church by imitating his example; it is neces-

sary that we all embrace the most strict poverty and
that we honor and revere it as the mother of all virtues
and holiness.   Hence I am of opinion that we all should
detach our hearts from the love of money and riches and
that all of us should refuse to handle it or to accept valuable and precious gifts.   In order that no one may be
defiled by avarice, six or seven persons of approved life
and established virtue might be appointed, who are to
receive the alms and offerings and whatever else the
faithful wish to deposit in their desire to live more securely and to follow Christ my divine Son without the
embarrassment of possessions.   All this must be given in
the form of alms, not in the manner of rents, or income,
or capital.   All of it should be used for supplying the
needs of the community and of our brethren and poor,
the needy and the infirm; and let none of the congregation, nor the Church, consider any of these goods as
belonging to themselves any more than to any of the
brethren.   If the alms thus offered for the sake of God
should not suffice for the maintenance of all, let those
that are appointed for this work ask for more in the
name of God.   Let all of us understand, that our lives
depend upon the most high Providence of my divine Son
and not upon the solicitude for acquiring money, nor
upon increasing our possessions under pretext of providing for our sustenance.   Let us rather have confidence
and if necessary, rely on the beneficence of almsgiving."

108. None of the Apostles nor the other faithful of
that gathering objected to the decision of their Great
Queen and Teacher; but all of them heartily embraced
her doctrine, knowing that She was the only and legitimate disciple of the Lord, and that She was the Teacher
of the Church.   The most prudent Mother, by divine
disposition, would not delegate to one of the Apostles

this instruction and the laying of this solid foundation
of evangelical and Christian perfection in the Church;
because such an arduous task required the authorship and
example of Christ and his most holy Mother.   They
were the Inventors and Institutors of this most noble
poverty and They were the first to honor it by an open
profession of it.   These two Leaders were followed by
the Apostles and by all the children of the primitive
Church.   This kind of poverty flourished afterwards for
many years.   Later on, through human frailty and
through human malice of the enemy, it decayed in some
of the Christians, so that finally it came to be restricted
to the ecclesiastical state.   And because the course of
time made this form of poverty difficult or impossible
also for this state, God raised up the religious communities, where, with some diversity, the primitive poverty
was renewed and kept alive in its entirety or in its main
intent.   Thus it will be preserved in the Church to the
end, securing its privileges to its devotees according to
the degree in which they follow, honor and love this
virtue. None of the states of life approved by the Church
is excluded from its proportionate measure; and none
of those living in those states are excused from striving
after its highest perfection in their own lives.   But as
in the house of God there are many mansions (John 14,
2), so there are also different orders and grades of inhabitants; let each one live up to the poverty which is
in accordance with his state.   But let all of us understand, that the first step in the imitation and following of
Christ is voluntary poverty; and those that pursue it
more closely, can so much the more freely rejoice in
sharing with Christ its advantages and perfections.

109. With the decision of the blessed Mary the meeting of the apostolic college was closed, and six prudent

men were chosen to receive and dispense the alms. The great Lady asked the blessing of the Apostles, who again returned to their work of preparing the catechumens for Baptism on the following day. The Queen, with the assistance of her angels and of the other Marys, proceeded to prepare and adorn the hall, in which her divine Son had celebrated the last Supper; and with her own hands She cleansed it and scrubbed it for his return in the consecration to be performed on the next day. She asked the owner to furnish it in the same way as I have described for the Thursday of the Last Supper and the devout host deferred to her wishes with deepest reverence. She also prepared the unleavened bread and the wine necessary for the consecration, together with the same paten and chalice in which the Savior had consecrated. For the Baptism She provided pure water and the basins for administering it with ease and reverence. Then the loving Mother retired and passed the night in most fervent aspirations, prostrations, thanksgiving and other exercises of exalted prayer; offering to the eternal Father all that She, in her heavenly wisdom, knew would help worthily to prepare Herself and all the rest for the worthy administration of Baptism.

110. Early the next day, which was the octave of the coming of the Holy Ghost, all the faithful and catechumens gathered with the Apostles and disciples in the house of the Cenacle. Saint Peter preached to this gathering instructing them in the nature and excellence of Baptism, the need in which they stood of it and its divine effects, how they would, through it, be made members of the mystical body of the Church, receive an interior character; be regenerated to a new existence as children of God and inheritors of his glory through the remission of sins and sanctifying grace. He exhorted

them to the observance of the divine law, to which they
subjected themselves by their own free will, and to
humble thanksgiving for this benefit and for all the
others, which they received from the hands of the Most
High.   He explained to them also the mysterious and
sacred truth of the holy Eucharist, which was to be celebrated in the consecration of the true body and blood of
Jesus Christ, and he admonished all those especially,
who were to receive holy Communion after their Baptism.

111. Through this sermon all the converts were inspired with additional fervor; for their dispositions were
altogether sincere, the words of the Apostles full of life
and penetration, and the interior grace very abundant.
Then the Apostles themselves began to baptize amid the
most devout and orderly attention of the others.   The
catechumens entered one door of the Cenacle and after
being baptized, they passed out through another, while the
disciples and others of the faithful acted as ushers.   The
most holy Mary was present at the entire ceremony, although keeping to one side of the hall.   She prayed for
all of them and broke forth in canticles of praise.   She
recognized the effects of Baptism in each one, according
to the greater or less degree of virtues infused in their
souls.   She beheld them renewed and washed in the blood
of the Lamb, and their souls restored to a divine purity
and spotlessness.   In witness of these effects, a most clear
light, visible to all that were present, descended upon
each one that was baptized.   By this miracle God wished
to authenticate the first beginnings of this Sacrament in
his holy Church, and to console both those first children
and us, who are made partakers of this blessing without
much adverting to it or giving thanks for it.

112. This administration of Baptism was continued

on that day until all were baptized, although there were about five thousand to receive it. While the baptized were making their thanksgiving for this admirable blessing, the Apostles with all the disciples and the faithful spent some time in prayer. All of them prostrated themselves on the ground adoring the infinite and immutable God, and confessing their own unworthiness of receiving Him in the most august sacrament of the Altar. In this profound humility and adoration they prepared themselves more immediately for Communion. And then they recited the same psalms and prayers which Christ had recited before consecrating, imitating faithfully that sacred function just as they had seen it performed by their divine Master. Saint Peter took in his hands the unleavened bread, and, after raising up his eyes to heaven with admirable devotion, he pronounced over the bread the words of consecration of the most holy body of Christ, as had been done before by the Lord Jesus (II Cor. 11, 24). Immediately the Cenacle was filled with the visible splendor of innumerable angels; and this light converged in a most singular manner on the Queen of heaven and earth and was seen by all these present. Then saint Peter consecrated the chalice and performed all the ceremonies, which Christ had observed with the consecrated body and blood, raising them up for the adoration of all the faithful. The Apostle partook himself of the Sacrament and communicated it to the eleven Apostles as most holy Mary had instructed him. Thereupon, at the hands of saint Peter, the heavenly Mother partook of it, while the celestial spirits there present attended with ineffable reverence. In approaching the altar the great Lady made three profound prostrations, touching the ground with her face.

113. She returned to her place, and it is impossible

to describe in words the effects of this participation of the holy Eucharist in this most exalted of creatures. She was entirely transformed and elevated, completely absorbed in this divine conflagration of the love of her most holy Son, whom She had now received bodily. She remained in a trance, elevated from the floor; but the holy angels shielded Her somewhat from view according to her own wish, in order that the attention of those present might not be unduly attracted by the divine effects apparent in Her. The disciples continued to distribute holy Communion, first to the disciples and then to the others who had been believers before the Ascension. But of the five thousand newly baptized only one thousand received Communion on that day; because not all were entirely prepared or furnished with the insight and attention required for receiving the Lord in this great sacrament and mystery of the Altar. With regard to the manner of Communion in that day, the Apostles observed the distinction of giving to the most holy Mother and the one hundred and twenty, upon whom the Holy Ghost had come, both species, of bread and of wine; but the recently baptized partook only of the species of bread. But this difference was not made because the new faithful were less worthy of the one species than of the other; but because the Apostles knew, that in either one of the species they received the same Object in its entirety, namely the sacramental God; and that there was no precept, and likewise no necessity that each one receive both species. They considered, that there would be great danger of irreverence and other very grave inconveniences to permit the multitude to partake of the species of the blood, while this was not to be feared in the Communion of the few, who then partook of them at that time. I have been made to understand, that, for all those who were not consecrating or celebrating, the practice of communicating only the specie of bread obtained from the very beginning of the Church. Although some, that were not priests, for some time partook of both species; yet, as soon as the Church increased and spread over the whole world, she, being guided by the Holy Ghost, very wisely ordained, that laymen and those not celebrating Mass should communicate only in the specie of the sacred body; and that it was to pertain to those who were celebrating these divine mysteries, to partake of both species. Such is the secure practice of the Roman Catholic Church.

114. All having received holy Communion, saint Peter ended the sacred mysteries by reciting some psalms and prayers, which he and the other Apostles offered up in thanksgiving; for at that time the other rites and ceremonies, which later on were added for the worthy celebration of Mass, as well before as after the Consecration and Communion, had not yet been instituted. In our times the most blessed and wise Roman Church has established all that is contained in the holy Mass as celebrated by the priests of the Lord. The Apostles spent some more time in prayer, and when the day had already declined toward evening they proceeded to other business and to partake of the necessary nourishment. Our great Queen and Lady gave thanks to the Most High for all of them, and the Lord was pleased with her thanksgiving, granting the petitions which his Beloved offered up for the present and the absent in his holy Church.

INSTRUCTION WHICH THE GREAT QUEEN OF THE ANGELS,
THE BLESSED MARY, GAVE ME.

115. My daughter, although in the present life thou canst not penetrate into the mystery of the love which I had and still have for men; yet, in addition to that which thou hast understood, I wish, for thy better information, that thou consider again, how the Lord has given me the title of Mother and Teacher of the Church. With it He infused into my soul an ineffable participation of charity and mercy for the children of Adam. As I was a mere creature and since this blessing was so immense, its effects would have deprived me many times of life, if the divine power had not miraculously sustained me. These effects I felt frequently in my thanksgiving, when souls were received into the Church or were made partakers of the eternal glory; for I alone could know and estimate this happiness in its entirety, and since I realized it, I gave thanks for it to the Almighty with intense fervor and deepest humility. But the occasions in which I was affected most deeply, was when I asked for the conversion of sinners and when any of the faithful fell into eternal perdition. At such and other times, experiencing the extreme opposite of my joys, I suffered much more than the martyrs in all their torments. I exerted myself for each soul with an eminent and supernatural force. For all this the children of Adam stand in debt to me, since I offered up for them so many times my own life. Though at present I am not any more in a condition to offer it for them, yet my love, which seeks their eternal salvation, is not diminished, but is more exalted and perfect.

116. If such was the force of my love of God, when my fellow-men were concerned, thou canst understand what was my love toward the Lord himself, when receiving Him in the blessed Sacrament. I will tell thee a secret concerning what happened when I received holy Communion for the first time from the hands of saint Peter. On this occasion the Most High gave such sway to the violence of my love, that my heart opened up in fact and, as was my desire, permitted the sacramental Lord to enter and take his rest there as in his legitimate throne and tabernacle. From this thou wilt understand, that, if in the glory which I now enjoy I could be sorrowful, one of the reasons for being so would be the dreadful carelessness and presumption with which mortals approach to receive the sacred body and blood of my divine Son; some of them unclean and abominable, others without veneration and respect, and nearly all of them without attention, without appreciation or consideration for the value of that food, which is nothing less than God himself for eternal life or eternal death.

117. Fear then, my daughter, this dreadful danger; weep to see it in so many children of the Church and ask the intervention of the Lord. In pondering over my teachings make thyself worthy to understand profoundly this mystery of love, and when thou art permitted to receive Him, detach and cleanse thy interior from all earthly things, attending only to the fact, that thou art about to receive the infinite and incomprehensible God himself. Surpass thyself in love, in humility, and thanksgiving; since all that thou canst ever do, will be less than is demanded by such an exalted mystery. For thy better preparation, let that which I did on such occasions be thy model and example. I desire especially that thou imitate me interiorly, as in the three bodily

prostrations. Observe also that which thou hast added thyself in order to do reverence to the sacramental flesh and blood as coming from my womb and as having been nourished and grown from my milk. Ever keep up this devotion; for the truth thou hast perceived, that this consecrated body contains part of my own blood and substance, is in fact real. And if in thy love thou wouldst deeply grieve to see the sacred body and blood ignominiously and sacrilegiously trampled under foot; thou shouldst feel the same grief and shed bitter tears at seeing so many children of the Church treat it with irreverence and without any fear or decorum. Weep then over this misfortune; weep, because there are few who weep over it, and weep, because the evident designs of the love of my divine Son are thus frustrated. And in order that thou mayest weep more bitterly, I tell thee, that, just as in the primitive Church there were so many, who were saved by it, now there are countless souls, who damn themselves through it. I do not tell thee what happens in this regard every day; lest, if thou knew it, and have within thee any love, thou shouldst die of grief. This damage is done, because the children of the faith are following darkness, love vanity, covet riches, and nearly all of them seek after vain and deceitful pleasure, which blinds and obscures the understanding and covers up the light with darkness, which knows no distinction between the good and the bad and penetrates not the truths of the evangelical doctrine.

CHAPTER VIII.

118. Until now I have only very slightly touched upon the miracle mentioned in the above heading, and, in order that so great a miracle of the Lord in favor of his most loving Mother may not be without the special mention demanded by our piety, I have reserved it for this chapter. My own limited powers of explanation grieve me; for not only am I ignorant of infinitely more than what I perceive concerning it, but even what I know, I can describe only in most unsatisfactory and inadequate terms and by language falling far short of my conceptions. Nevertheless I dare not pass over in silence the benefits conferred upon our great Queen by the right hand of her divine Son, after She had descended from heaven to take charge of his Church on earth; for if they were great and ineffable before that time, they now increased in eminent variety and exhibited at the same time the infinite power of Him who conferred them, and the immense capacity of that singular and chosen Creature, who received them.

119. To explain this rare and prodigious blessing, that the sacramental body of Christ in the sacred species should be preserved continually in the bosom of Mary, it is not necessary to seek for another cause than that un-

derlying all the other favors with which God distinguished this great Lady, namely: that it was his holy will and according to his infinite wisdom, by which He performs according to measure and weight all that is befitting (Wis. 11, 21). Christian prudence and piety will be content to know as a reason, that God had singled this mere Creature out to be his natural Mother, and that therefore She alone, of all creatures, deserved this distinction. As this miracle of her Mothership was unique and without parallel, it would be shameful ignorance to seek proofs of what the Lord did in Her by comparing it with what He did or ever will do in other souls; since Mary alone rises supereminently above the common order of all. Yet, though all this is true, the Lord nevertheless wishes that by the light of faith and by other enlightenment, we seek the reasons of the propriety and equity, according to which the powerful arm of the Almighty wrought these wonders in his most worthy Mother, so that in them we may know and bless Him in Her and through Her; and so that we may understand, how secure our salvation, all our hope, and our lot are in the hands of that powerful Queen, toward whom her Son has directed all the excess of his love. In accordance with these truths I will explain what has been made known to me of this mystery.

120. The heavenly Mother lived thirty-three years in the company of her Son and true God; and from the time when He was born of her virginal womb She never left Him to the time of his death on the Cross. She nursed Him, served Him, followed Him and imitated Him, conducting Herself always as a Mother, Daughter and Spouse, as a most faithful Servant and Friend; She enjoyed the sight of Him, his conversation, his doctrine and the favors, which, by all these meritorious services,

She attained in this mortal life. Christ ascended into heaven, and the force of love and right reason demanded, that He should take to heaven with Him his most loving Mother, in order that He should not be deprived of Her there, nor She in this world of his presence and company. But the most ardent love which both of Them had for men, dissolved in a manner these bonds of union, inducing our kindest Mother to return to the world in order to establish the Church; and moving the Son to give his consent to her absence from Him during that time. But as the Son of God was powerful enough to recompense Her for this privation to a certain extent, it became for Him an obligation of his love to make such a recompense. And the fulfillment of this obligation would not have been so publicly acknowledged or made so manifest, if He denied his blessed Mother the favor of accompanying Her upon earth, while He remained seated at the glory of the right hand of his Father. Besides, the most ardent love of the blessed Mother, having been accustomed and nourished in the presence of the Lord her Son, would have inflicted upon Her insufferable violence, if for so many years She was to be deprived of that kind of presence of Him, which was possible during her stay in the Church.

121. For all this the Lord our Savior provided by continuing his sacramental presence in the heart of the most fortunate Mother as long as She lived in the Church after his taking his seat in heaven. To a certain extent He abundantly recompensed Her by this sacramental presence for that which She had enjoyed, when He had yet lived with Her in this world; for in those times He often absented Himself in order to attend to the work of our salvation and thus afflicted her heart with anxieties and fears, roused by the works in which He had to engage;

and even when He returned, He could not remain always in her company; and when this was possible, his very presence filled her mind with the terrors of his coming passion and death on the Cross. This sorrow sometimes cast a shadow on the joy of her possessing Him and attending upon Him. But when He was established at the right hand of his eternal Father, having sustained the torment of his Passion, and when this, her same Lord and Son, took his rest sacramentally in her virginal bosom, then the heavenly Mother enjoyed his presence without fear or disturbance. In the Son She continually enjoyed the presence of the entire Trinity by that manner of vision, which I have described before. Thus was fulfilled and realized literally, what this great Queen says in the Canticles: I shall hold Him, and will not leave Him, until I bring Him to the house of my mother the Church. There I will give Him to drink of the spiced wine and of the juice of my pomegranates (Cant. 8, 2).

122. In this blessing the Lord fulfilled his promise made to the Church in his Apostles, that He should be with them to the end of time (Matth. 28, 20). He had already anticipated the fulfillment of this promise even at that time, when He resolved to ascend into heaven, for He had remained sacramentally present in his Mother since the last Supper, as related above. But it would not have been entirely fulfilled after his Ascension, if He had not wrought this new miracle in the Church; for in those first years the Apostles had no temple or proper arrangement for preserving continually the sacred Eucharist, and therefore they always consumed it entirely on the day of its consecration. The most holy Mary alone was the sanctuary and the temple, in which for some years the most blessed Sacrament was preserved, in order that the Church of Christ might not be deprived even for one

moment of the Word made flesh, from the time when He ascended into heaven until the end of the world. Although He was not there present in that Tabernacle for the use of the faithful, yet He was there for their benefit and for other more glorious ends; since the great Queen offered up her prayers and intercessions for all Christians in the temple of her own heart and She adored the sacramental Christ in the name of the whole Church; while by his indwelling in that virginal bosom, Christ was present and united to the mystical body of the faithful. Above all, this great Lady was the cause of that age's being supremely fortunate; for, by thus sheltering within her bosom her sacramental Son and God, just as He is now harbored within the sanctuaries and tabernacles, He was continually adored with highest reverence and piety by the most blessed Mary, and was never offended, as He is now in our churches. In Mary He was satiated with the delights, which He desired to enjoy for the eternal ages among the children of men (Prov. 8, 31), and since all the assistance rendered to the Church was rendered with these delights as an object, the Lord could not have gained this end more fully than by remaining sacramentally present in the heart of his purest Mother. She was the most legitimate sphere of the divinity, and, as it were, the proper element and the focusing point of its proper activity; and all the other creatures outside of the heavenly Mary were in comparison with Her, foreign to it, since this conflagration of divine love, which continues to burn with infinite charity, found no room or element for its flames.

123. From the understanding which has been given me of the mystery of the love of Christ the Lord for his most holy Mother and of the force with which He was drawn toward Her, I would go so far as to say, that if

He had not found this way of remaining with Her in the sacramental species, He would have come down from the right hand of the Father to the world in order to render companionship to his Mother while She sojourned with his Church.   And if it had been necessary that the heavenly mansions and the celestial courtiers should be deprived of the presence of the most sacred humanity from that time, He would have considered that of less importance than to be deprived of the company of his Mother.   It is no exaggeration to say this, when we all must confess, that in the purest Mary the Lord found a correspondence and a degree of love more conformable to his will than in all the blessed combined; and consequently, his own love for Her exceeded his love for all others.   If the Shepherd of the Gospel leaves the ninety-nine sheep in order to go in search of only one that is lost, and if we nevertheless dare not say of Him that He leaves the greater for the less; it should not cause wonder in us that this divine Shepherd should leave all the rest of the saints in order to be in the company of his most sincere Sheep, who clothed Him with her own nature and raised and nourished Him as a Mother. Without a doubt the eyes of his beloved Spouse and Mother would attract Him in swiftest flight from those heights (Cant. 6, 4) to that earth, where He had lived, whither He had before this come for the salvation of the children of Adam, toward whom He was less attracted, yea rather repelled by their sins and by the necessity of suffering for them.   If now He descended to live with his beloved Mother, it would not be to suffer and die; but to enjoy the delights of her company.   Fortunately it was not necessary to rob heaven of his presence; since by descending in sacramental form He could satisfy both his own love and that of his most blessed Mother, in whose heart, as in his couch, this true Solomon could take up his rest without leaving the right hand of his eternal Father (Cant. 3, 7).

124. The manner of operating this miracle was as follows: at the Communion of the most blessed Mary, the sacramental species, instead of entering the portion of the stomach where the natural food is commingled and rarified, and instead of being mixed up or digested with even the little nourishment sometimes taken by the great Lady, halted on their passage and lodged within the heart of Mary, as if in repayment of the blood which it had given up at the Incarnation of the Word and from which was formed the sacred humanity for hypostatical union with the Word, as has been explained in the second part. The participation in the holy Eucharist is called an extension of the Incarnation, and therefore it was proper that the blessed Mother should share in this participation in a new and singular manner, since She also concurred in the Incarnation of the Word in a miraculous and extraordinary manner.

125. The heat of the heart in the perfectly healthy beings is very great, and in man it is certainly not the less on account of his greater excellence and nobility of nature and of his prolonged life and activity; and the providence of nature supplies it with air and ventilation for its refreshment and for moderating that heat, which is the source of all the other animal warmth. Yet, though in the noble constitution of our Queen the ardors of her heart were intense, and though the affections and operations of her inflamed love still more increased them, nevertheless the sacred species, while lodged in her heart, were not changed or consumed. Moreover, although multiplied miracles were required in order to preserve them, they are not to be attributed sparingly in this singular Be-

ing: a Creature, who was altogether a prodigy and a summary of wonders. This favor began at the first Communion and through the preservation of the species continued until the second Communion received at the hands of saint Peter on the octave of Pentecost. Then, as the new species took their place in her heart, the former ones were consumed. By this miraculous exchange, the previous sacramental species continued to yield their place to those She received in her Communions until the end of her life, so that She was never deprived of the presence of her Son and God in sacramental form.

126. Through this privilege, and that of the continual and abstractive vision of the Divinity mentioned before, the most blessed Mary was made so godlike, and her operations and faculties were raised so far above human conception, that it will be impossible to understand them in this mortal life, or to attain of them a proportionate idea as is possible for us concerning other things. Nor can I find words to explain the little which could be made clear to me. After She returned from heaven She was entirely renewed and transformed in regard to the use of her senses; for on the one hand, She was absent from her divine Son, in whom She had worthily employed them, when He was sensibly present; on the other hand, She felt and perceived Him resting in her heart, whereon all her attention was centered. From the day on which She descended She made a new treaty with her eyes and exercised a new dominion and sway over them of not permitting any terrestrial and visible images to enter except those that were necessary for the government of the Church and for the discharge of her duties. She made no use of these images, nor were they necessary to Her, for conversing or meditating interiorly, and they were merely stored in her memory and understanding; her in-

terior meditations and contemplations were actuated by infused images and by the science connected with the abstract vision of the Divinity, after the manner in which the saints know and see in God, or through vision, or knowledge of the creature in themselves. In this manner our Queen understood the will of God in all her works, and She did not make use of her sight in knowing or learning any of these things, although She used her eyes to see where She was going or with whom She was conversing in all the sincerity of heart.

127. The sense of hearing She made use of somewhat more frequently; for it was necessary to listen to the faithful and to the Apostles in what they reported of the state of souls, of the Church, and of its needs and spiritual advancement, in order to answer them, and give them her instruction and counsels. But She governed her sense of hearing so completely, that it was affected by no sound or word, which disagreed in the least with the holiness and perfection of her state, or which were not necessary for the advance of charity toward her fellow-men. Of her sense of smell She made no use for terrestrial odors, or of the common objects of that sense; but by the intervention of the angels She was regaled by the celestial perfumes, which were perceived by Her in praise of the Creator. She experienced a great change also in the sense of taste; for She was made aware, that, after her sojourn in heaven, She could live without earthly nourishment, though that was not commanded Her, but left to her own free will. Therefore She ate very seldom and sparingly, and this only at times, when saint Peter or saint John asked Her, or in order to avoid astonishment in others at not seeing Her eat. But when She thus in obedience or in humility tasted food, She perceived not the common taste or savor of it, so that her

sense reacted not upon it any more than if She had eaten
some apparent or glorified substance. Her touch likewise conformed to this kind of change, for through it
She perceived little of that which She touched and had
in it no sensible delight; but She felt the contact of the
sacramental species in her heart, to which She ordinarily
attended with feelings of admirable sweetness and joy.

128. All these privileges in regard to the senses were
granted Her at her petition; for She consecrated all of
them and her faculties anew to the greater glory of the
Most High and for producing in Her the plenitude of
virtue, holiness and the most eminent perfection. And
though through her whole life, from the first instant of
her Immaculate Conception, She had complied with all
the requirements of a faithful servant (Matth. 25, 20)
and of a prudent dispenser of the plenitude of her graces
and gifts (as appears from the whole course of this history), yet after She ascended to heaven with her Son,
She was perfected in all things and was furnished by the
divine Omnipotence with new faculties of operating.
Though She was yet a pilgrim, since She did not yet enjoy the beatific vision as a comprehensor, nevertheless the
operations of her senses partook of and were rather
similar to those of the saints glorified in body and soul
than to the operations of the other viators. There is no
other way of comparing this state so singular, so blessed
and divine, in which our great Queen and Lady returned
from heaven to govern the holy Church.

129. To this exalted activity of the sensible faculties
corresponded her interior wisdom and knowledge; for
She knew the decrees of the most high Will in all that
She wished and was obliged to do; in what time, in what
manner, in what order and circumstance each work was
to be accomplished; with what words and under what ar-

rangements; so that in this She was not excelled even by the angels, who assist us without ever losing sight of the Lord. The great Queen practiced the virtues with such high wisdom, that She excited their admiration; for they saw that no other mere creature could exceed Her or could arrive at that summit of perfection and holiness, which they saw Her attain. One of the things that filled Her with highest joy was the adoration and reverence exhibited by the supernal spirits to the Lord sacramentally present in her bosom. The same was also shown by the saints, whenever She ascended into heaven bearing her most divine Son with Her in her heart; and this was a sight furnishing new joy and jubilee for all the blessed. The joy of seeing the blessed Sacrament thus honored by the angels was a recompense for the gross negligence of mortals in venerating the sacred body of the Lord. And as such the blessed Lady also offered up the worship and reverence of the celestial spirits, who knew how to estimate this mystery and venerated it without fail or negligence.

130. Sometimes the body of her Son manifested itself to Her openly within Her; at other times with all the beauty of his most holy humanity; at other times, and almost continually, were made known to Her all the miracles contained in the most august Sacrament. All these wonders, and many others, which we cannot understand in this corruptible life, most holy Mary enjoyed, sometimes becoming manifest to Her in themselves, sometimes in the abstractive vision of the Divinity; and with the images of the Divinity were presented to Her also all that She was to do for Herself and for all the Church. What was most consoling to Her, was to perceive the joy and pleasure of her divine Son in remaining sacramentally present in her sincerest heart, which with-

out a doubt (according to what was made known to me) was greater than to be in the company of the saints. O extraordinary, singular and exalted privilege! Thou by Thyself wert more pleasing to the Creator than the high heavens He had made for his habitation (Ps. 113, 16). He who cannot be contained in those illimitable spaces, measured and enclosed Himself in Thee alone, and found a pleasant throne and resting-place, not only in thy virginal womb, but in the immensity of thy capacious love. Thou alone wast a heaven from the first of thy existence, so that God lived in Thee after He gave Thee being and shall rest in Thee in fullest delight through all the ages of his eternity. Let all the nations know Thee; for in Thee they know and praise their true God and Redeemer, since through Thee alone He has visited us and repaired our unfortunate fall (Luke 1, 68).

131. Who of mortals, or even of the angels, can describe the conflagration of love burning in the purest heart of this great Queen so full of wisdom? Who can comprehend the impetus of the river of the Divinity, which inundated and absorbed this City of God? (Ps. 44, 5). What aspirations and acts of virtue did She not enter into while exercising the measureless gifts of grace showered upon Her! What prayers and petitions did She not send forth for the holy Church! What entrancements of love for us did not overwhelm Her! What gifts did She not merit and obtain for us! Only the Author of this prodigy could know them. But let us on our part raise our hopes, enliven our faith, and incite our love in union with this kind Mother; let us solicit her intercession and assistance, since He, who is her Son and our Brother, will deny nothing to Her whom He has so singled out for his love, as I have described, and will describe further on.

INSTRUCTION WHICH THE QUEEN OF THE ANGELS, MOST
HOLY MARY, GAVE ME.

132. My daughter, thou hast so far been well informed of my life and activity, considering that thou art a mere creature. Besides me, there is no other created being, which thou canst better use as thy model and original for thy greater holiness and perfection. But now thou hast entered upon the description of the supreme state of virtue reached by me in mortal life. This favor should oblige thee to renew thy desires and direct all the attention of thy faculties toward the perfect imitation of all that I teach thee. It is time, my dearest, and there is reason, that thou deliver thyself entirely over to my will in what I seek of thee. In order that thou mayest animate thyself to the attainment of this blessing, I wish thee to take notice, that, though the species of the Sacrament are consumed, my divine Son, whenever souls receive Him with reverence and fervor and prepare for Him a pure and ardent heart, remains with them with special graces, by which He assists them, enriches and directs them in return for their hospitality. Few are the souls, who partake of this blessing, because many knowing of it, approach the holy Sacrament without the proper disposition, as if by haphazard or habit, and without being solicitous for the reverence and holy fear due to it. But as thou art now informed of this secret, I desire that, since by the orders of thy superiors thou receivest it every day, thou prepare thyself worthily each time and thus partake of this great blessing.

133. For this end thou must avail thyself of the remembrance of what I did, and by it regulate thy aspirations, thy fervor, thy love, and all that is necessary to prepare thy heart as a temple and habitation of thy

Spouse and highest King. Labor then to collect all thy powers within thyself; before and after receiving observe all that pertains to the fidelity of a Spouse, and especially must thou place a guard over thy eyes and a watch over all thy senses, in order that no profane or foreign image may enter into the temple of the Lord. Keep thy heart entirely pure and unspotted; for when it is impure or preoccupied, the plenitude of divine light and wisdom cannot enter (Wis. 1, 4). All this thou wilt know from what God has shown thee, if thou hast attended to it with an upright purpose. Even supposing that thou canst not exempt thyself from all intercourse with creatures, it is befitting that thou hold thy senses in great subjection, and that thou do not permit them to introduce the image of any sensible thing, by which thou wouldst not be assisted in striving after the most holy and pure of virtue. Separate the precious from the worthless, the truth from deceit. In order that thou mayest imitate me perfectly, I wish that from now on thou attend to the choice thou art to make in all things great or small, so that thou err in none, perverting the order of divine light.

134. Consider attentively the common deception of mortals and the woeful damage they suffer. For in the decisions of their will they ordinarily are moved solely by what they perceive through the senses, and they immediately proceed to act upon their choice without further consideration or counsel. Since the sensible impressions immediately move the animal passions and inclinations, it is evident that men do not act according to right reason, but according to the impulse of passion, excited by the senses and their objects. Hence, he that considers only the injury and pain caused, is straightway moved to vengeance; he that follows only his hankering

after strange property, as soon as he lays his eyes upon
it, is impelled to injustice. In the same manner act so
many unfortunates, who follow the concupiscence of the
eyes, the movements of the flesh, and the pride of life,
because these are the only things offered by the world
and the devil. In their blind deception they follow darkness as their light, taste the bitter as sweet, take deadly
poison for remedy of their souls, and hold that for wisdom which is nothing but diabolical and earthly ignorance. Do thou guard thyself against these pernicious
errors, and never resolve on anything, or govern thyself
by anything that is merely sensible or arising from sensible impressions, nor pursue the advantages held out
through them. In thy actions take counsel first of all
from the interior knowledge and light communicated to
thee by God, in order that thou mayest not go blindly
forward; and He shall always grant thee sufficient
guidance. Immediately seek the advice of thy superiors
and teachers, if thou canst do so before making thy
choice. And if thy superior or teacher is not at hand,
seek counsel of others, even inferiors; for this is more
secure than to follow thy own will, which may be disturbed and blinded by passion. This is the rule to be followed especially in the exterior works, pursuing them
with recollection, with secrecy, and according to the demands of circumstances and fraternal charity as they
occur. In all of them it is necessary not to lose out of
sight the north-star of interior light, while moving in the
profound gulf of the intercourse with creatures, where
there is continual danger of perishing.

CHAPTER IX.

THE MOST HOLY MARY SEES LUCIFER RISING UP TO PER-
SECUTE THE CHURCH: WHAT MEASURES SHE TOOK
TO DEFEND AND PROTECT THE FAITHFUL AGAINST
THIS ENEMY.

135. Elevated to the highest degree of grace and holiness possible in a mere creature, the great Lady of the world saw with eyes of divine knowledge the little flock of the Church increasing day by day. As a most watchful Mother and Shepherdess, from the heights in which She was placed by the right hand of her omnipotent Son, She watched with deepest insight lest any assault or attack from the ravenous wolves of hell threatened the little sheep of her fold; for She well knew their hatred against the new-born children of the Gospel. The watchfulness of the Mother of light served as a wall of defense to this holy family, which the loving Queen had accepted as her own and which She looked upon as the portion and inheritance of her divine Son, selected from the rest of men and chosen by the Most High. For some days the little ship of the Church, governed by this heavenly Commandress, proceeded prosperously onward; being assisted as well by her counsels, her teachings and warnings, as by her incessant prayers and petitions. Not for one moment did She remit her diligence in attending to all that was necessary for consolation of the Apostles and the other faithful.

136. A few days after the coming of the Holy Ghost, while at her prayers, She spoke to the Lord: "My Son,

the God of true love, I know, my Lord, that the little flock of thy Church, of which Thou hast made me the Mother and Defender, is of no less price to Thee than thy own life and blood, by which Thou hast redeemed it from the powers of darkness (Col. 1, 13). It is therefore reasonable that I also offer my life and all my being for the preservation and increase of what is so highly esteemed by Thee. Let me die, my God, if it is necessary for the enhancement of Thy name and for the spread of Thy glory throughout the world. Receive, my Son, the offering of my lips and of my entire will in union with thy own merits. Look kindly upon thy faithful; receive those who hope solely in Thee and give themselves to Thee in faith. Govern thy vicar Peter, that he may rightly direct the sheep Thou hast given him in charge. Watch over all thy Apostles, thy ministers and my masters; meet them with the blessings of thy sweetness, so that we all may execute thy perfect and holy will."

137. The Most High answered the petition of our Queen: "My Spouse and Beloved, I am attentive to thy desires and petitions. But Thou already knowest, that my Church is to follow in my footsteps and my teachings, imitating Me in the way of my suffering and the Cross, which my Apostles and disciples and all my intimate friends and followers are to embrace; for such they cannot be, without this condition of labor and sufferings (Matth. 10, 38). It is also necessary that my Church should bear the ballast of persecutions, by which it will pass securely through the prosperity of the world and its dangers. Such is my high Providence in regard to the faithful and the predestined. Attend therefore, and behold the manner in which this is to be brought about."

138. Immediately the great Queen in a vision saw Lucifer and a great multitude of hellish followers rising

out of the depths of the infernal caverns, where they
had lain oppressed since the time they had been vanquished on mount Calvary and hurled to hell, as I have
described above. She saw that dragon with seven heads
coming up as it were from the depths of the sea, followed
by the rest. Although he came forth very much weakened, in the manner of convalescents, unable, after a long
and grievous sickness, to drag themselves along; yet in
his pride and chagrin he was lashed to implacable fury
and arrogance, having on that occasion experienced that
these passions in him are greater than his power, as Isaias
says (Is. 14, 9). For on the one hand he exhibited the
effects of the crushing defeat which he had undergone in
the victory and triumph of the Savior on the Cross; and
on the other hand he exhibited his wrath and fury, which
now was bursting forth like the fires of a volcano against
the holy Church and her children. Having come upon
the earth, he roamed all over it and reconnoitred; then
he hastened to Jerusalem in order to strain all his rabid
fury in persecuting the sheep of Christ. He began to spy
from afar, gradually approaching and veering around
that fold, which was so humble and yet so formidable to
his arrogant malice.

139. The dragon saw what a multitude had subjected
themselves to the faith, and how many were hourly receiving holy Baptism; how the Apostles continued to
preach and to perform such great miracles for the good
of souls; how the new converts renounced and abhorred
riches; how the holy Church was founded with all the
principles of invincible sanctity. At such astonishing
changes the wrath of the demon increased and his concentrated malice and wrath vented itself in fearful howls.
Lashing himself into fury on account of his being so
powerless against God, and, thirsting to drink up the

pure waters of Jordan (Is. 16, 6), he sought to approach
nearer to the congregation of the faithful; but in this he
could not succeed, because they were all united in perfect
charity. This virtue, together with faith, hope and humility, rose like an unapproachable fortification against
the dragon and his ministers of malice. He roamed
about in the vicinity to find some little sheep, that might
have carelessly strayed from the fold of Christ, in order
to attack and devour it. He schemed and plotted in many
ways to attract some one of them, who should give him an
opportunity of entering the fortress of virtue, by which
all were protected; but everywhere he found his entrance
forestalled and prevented by the vigilance of the Apostles
and the power of grace, and especially by the protection
of most Holy Mary.

140. When the great Mother saw Lucifer and such an
army of demons rising up with malicious wrath against
the evangelical Church, her loving heart was pierced by
a dart of compassion and sorrow; for She knew on the
one hand the weakness and ignorance of men, and on
the other hand the malicious and cunning hatred of the
ancient serpent. In order to restrain and check his pride,
the heavenly Mother turned upon them and said: "Who
is like God, that dwells in the highest? (Ps. 112, 5). O
foolish and vainglorious enemy of the Omnipotent! The
same One who vanquished thee on the Cross and crushed
thy arrogance, redeeming the human race from thy
cruel tyranny, commands thee now; this power annihilates
thee, his wisdom confounds thee, and hurls thee back to
hell. In his name now shall I do this, so as to deprive
thee of the power to hinder the exaltation and glory due
to Him from all men as their God and Redeemer." Then
the solicitous Mother continued her prayers and spoke
to the Lord: "Supreme God and Father, if the power

of thy arm do not restrain and quench the fury, which
I see in the infernal dragon and his hosts, I doubt not
that he will cover the whole face of the earth with the
ruin of its inhabitants.   Be Thou a God of kindness and
mercy to thy creatures: do not permit, O Lord, that this
venomous serpent pour out its poison upon the souls redeemed and washed in the blood of the Lamb (Apoc.
7, 14), thy Son and the true God.   Is it possible, that
the souls themselves should ever deliver themselves over
to such a bloodthirsty beast, their mortal enemy? How is
my heart constrained with fear, lest any of the souls, enriched with the fruit of this blood, fall into such a deplorable misfortune?   O that the wrath of this dragon
might be turned upon me alone, and that thy redeemed
be placed in safety! Let me, eternal Lord, fight the
battles against thy enemies.   Clothe me with thy power
in order that I may humiliate them and crush their pride
and haughtiness."

141.   In virtue of this prayer and the resistance of
the powerful Queen, Lucifer was struck with great fear,
and for the time being he dared not approach any of the
congregation of the faithful.   Yet his fury was not allayed on that account, but he plotted to enlist the scribes
and pharisees, and all of the Jews, whom he perceived
still clinging to their obstinate perfidy.   He betook himself to them and by many suggestions filled them with
envy and hatred against the Apostles and the faithful of
the Church; thus, through the unbelievers, he roused the
persecution, which he could not begin himself. He filled
them with dread, lest by the preaching of the Apostles
and disciples a like or greater damage would arise, than
from the preaching of Jesus the Nazarene. He suggested
to them, how evidently the followers of Christ intended
to spread the glory of his name; how, since they them-

selves had crucified Him as a malefactor, his glory would redound to their dishonor. And, as there were so many disciples and as so many miracles were wrought in his name, how all the people would be drawn toward them; the teachers and the learned in the law would be despised, and lose the accustomed perquisites, as the new believers would donate all their goods to the new teachers; and how inevitably this damage would very soon overtake the teachers of the law, on account of the great multitudes following the Apostles.

142. These malicious suggestions appealed very strongly to the avarice and ambition of the Jews and therefore they accepted them readily as sane and as very conformable to their own desires. Hence arose the many meetings and cabals of the pharisees, sadducees, magistrates, and priests against the Apostles, as mentioned by saint Luke in the Acts. The first occasion arose at the miracle wrought by saint Peter and saint John in healing the paralytic, who had suffered under his malady for forty years from the time of his birth and who was known throughout the city. As this miracle was so evident and remarkable, the inhabitants gathered in great multitudes, all astonished and excited beyond control. Saint Peter preached them a great sermon, proving that they could not be saved except by the name of Jesus, in virtue of which he and saint John had cured this paralytic of forty years standing. In reference to this event the priests held a meeting, in which they called the two Apostles to account. But as the miracle was so notorious and as the people glorified God in it, the iniquitous judges were too much confused to attempt to punish the Apostles, although they commanded them not to preach or teach in the name of Jesus the Nazarene for the future. But saint Peter with invincible courage told them, that

they could not obey this command; because God commanded them the contrary, and it was not right to obey men in opposition to God (Acts 4, 19.) With this warning they were dismissed and the two Apostles immediately repaired to the most holy Queen to report their experience, although She, by a special vision, had been informed of it all. Then they engaged in most exalted prayer, in which the Holy Ghost again came upon all of them with visible signs.

143. A few days afterwards happened the miraculous chastisement of Ananias and Saphira, who, tempted by their avarice, tried to deceive saint Peter. They lied to the Apostle in bringing to him a portion of the price of an inheritance they had sold and secreting the other part. Shortly before, Barnabas, also called Joseph, a levite and a native of Cyprus, had likewise sold his inheritance and brought all the proceeds of it to the Apostles. In order that it might be impressed upon all, that each one should act with the same integrity, Ananias and Saphira were punished, falling dead at the feet of saint Peter one after the other. Through this formidable wonder all in Jerusalem were struck with fear and the Apostles preached with greater freedom. But the magistrates and sadducees were roused to anger and had them seized and cast into the public prison. There they remained but a short time, because the Queen liberated them, as I shall soon relate.

144. I will not pass over in silence the mystery connected with the fall of Ananias and Saphira, his wife. When the great Mistress of heaven and earth perceived, that Lucifer and his demons incited the priests and magistrates against the preaching of the Apostles, and that through his suggestions, they had dragged saint Peter and saint John before their tribunals after the miracle of

the paralytic, this loving Mother feared lest the conversion of other souls might be prevented and therefore,
as her divine Son had enjoined Her, She, with greater
courage than that of Judith, took up their cause as her
own and addressed that cruel tyrant: "Enemy of the
Most High, how dost thou dare, and how shalt thou
be able to rise up against his creatures, when by the
passion and death of my Son and the true God thou art
so completely vanquished, subjected and despoiled of
thy tyrannous empire? What canst thou do, O venomous basilisk, chained and imprisoned in hellish torments
for all eternity by the Almighty? Dost thou not know,
that thou art subjected to his infinite power, and that
thou canst not resist his invincible will? He commands
thee, and I in his name and power command thee, immediately to descend with thy hordes to the depths, from
which thou hast risen to persecute the children of the
Church."

145. The infernal dragon could not resist the mandate
of the powerful Queen; for her divine Son, to the greater
terror of the demons, permitted them all to see Him
sacramentally present in the bosom of the invincible
Mother, as in the throne of his omnipotence and majesty.
This happened also on other occasions, whenever Mary
put Lucifer to confusion, as I shall relate farther on. This
time he hurled himself into the abysses with all that had
accompanied him, and they fell oppressed and annihilated by the divine strength of that peerless Woman. For
some time the demons remained there in consternation
and lashed themselves to fury on account of their woeful
state, which they could not escape, and because they despaired of overcoming this powerful Queen or all those
who should come under her protection. In this furious
dismay Lucifer conferred with his demons and said: "In

what calamity do I see myself plunged! Tell me, what
can I do against this my Enemy, who thus torments and
overwhelms me? She alone battles against me more
strenuously than all the creatures together. Shall I then
give up persecuting Her, in order that She may not succeed in destroying me? Ever have I come forth from
battle with Her vanquished, while She remains victorious.
I must acknowledge, that She is continually diminishing
my powers and that step by step She will succeed in annihilating me, so that I shall be powerless against the
followers of her Son. Yet how am I to suffer such an
unjust oppression? Where is my exalted sovereignty?
Am I then to subject myself to a Woman of a condition
and nature so inferior and vile in comparison with mine?
But I dare not at present battle with Her. Let us seek
to overthrow some of her followers, so that in some
measure my confusion may be allayed and my revenge
satisfied.''

146. The Lord permitted the dragon and his hordes
to return and tempt the faithful for their probation. But
on becoming acquainted with the state of their souls and
the great virtues, with which they were adorned, they
found no approach open, nor any of the faithful that
would listen to their insane deceits and illusions. Yet
on searching the dispositions and natural inclinations of
each one, through which unfortunately they always carry
on their fierce war against us, the demons found that
Ananias and Saphira were attached to money and had
always sought after it with a certain amount of avarice.
Of this weakness they availed themselves for their attack and they suggested to their imagination the ex-
pediency of reserving a part of the price of a heritage,
which they had sold in order to give its proceeds to the
Apostles in thankful acknowledgment of the faith and

Baptism received at their hands. They permitted themselves to be entrapped by this low deceit, because they found it harmonizing with their base inclination, and they sought to deceive saint Peter. The Apostle knew of their sin through a revelation and he chastised them by permitting them both, first Ananias then Saphira, suddenly to fall dead at his feet. Saphira, without knowing what had happened to her husband, shortly afterwards practiced the same deceit and expired in the same way in the presence of the Apostles.

147. Our Queen knew from the very beginning what Lucifer was plotting and that Ananias and Saphira were listening to his wily suggestions. Full of compassion and sorrow the loving Mother prostrated Herself in the divine presence and called out from the bottom of her soul: "Alas, my Son and Lord, that this bloodthirsty dragon should snatch these simple sheep of our flock! How does my heart suffer, O my God, to see the contagion of avarice and deceit infect the souls, who have tasted life and thy blood! If this most cruel enemy scathlessly thus mixes up with them, the evil example of sin will do great damage on account of the weakness of men, and one will follow the other in their fall. I shall lose my life, O Lord, for grief, since I know what an evil sin is in thy eyes, and especially the sin, not of strangers, but of thy children. Do Thou, my Beloved, provide some remedy of this evil, which Thou hast made known to me." The Lord answered Her: "My Beloved Mother, let not thy heart, in which I reside, be afflicted; for I shall draw much good out of this evil for my Church, and it is for this end that my Providence shall permit it. In chastising these sins I shall teach the other faithful, by a visible example, to fear such sins in the Church; and thus shall caution them against the deceit

and the covetousness of money. For the same chastisement, or my anger, impends over all that shall commit the same fault; since my justice shall always remain the same against all that are rebellious to my will as taught by my holy law."

148. With this answer the most holy Mary consoled Herself, although She continued to pity those two ensnared ones, Ananias and Saphira, on account of the divine vengeance about to fall upon them in chastisement. In the meanwhile She offered up most exalted prayers for the rest of the faithful, in order that they might not fall into the snares of satan; and She again turned upon him, to frighten and repel him from irritating the Jews against the Apostles. Prevented by her power he desisted, and the first children of the Church enjoyed much peace and tranquillity. This happiness under the protection of the great Queen and Lady would have continued forever, if men had not thought little of it, giving themselves up to the same and worse deceits than Ananias and Saphira. O that the faithful would fear this example and imitate that of the Apostles!

149. When the Apostles were taken prisoners as related above, they called upon the divine mercy and the protection of their heavenly Queen and Mother; and when She by divine enlightenment became aware of their condition, She prostrated Herself in the form of a cross before the throne of God and made for them the following petition: "My supreme Lord, Creator of the universe! From my whole heart I subject myself to thy divine will, and I know it is according to the dispositions and ordainment of thy infinite wisdom, that the disciples follow Thee as their Master, the true light and guide of thy chosen ones. This I confess, my Son, because Thou camest upon this world in the appearance and habit of

humility, in order to give it credit and destroy pride and in order to teach the way of the cross by patience in labor and in the contempt coming from men. I know also that thy Apostles and disciples must follow this doctrine and establish it in thy Church. But if it is possible, God of my soul, that they at present retain their freedom and their life in order to found the Church, preach thy holy name and bring the world to the true faith, I beseech Thee, my Lord, to permit me to favor thy vicar Peter, and my son, thy beloved disciple John, and all those who by the cunning of Lucifer, are imprisoned. Let not that enemy glory in having now triumphed over thy servants, nor let him raise his head over the other children of the Church. Crush his haughtiness, my Lord, and let him be confounded in thy presence."

150. To her petition the Most High answered: "My Spouse, let what thou desirest be done, for this is also my will. Send thy angels to undo the work of Lucifer, for my power is with thee." With this loving consent the Queen of angels immediately sent one of her guard, of a very high hierarchy, to the prison of the Apostles in order to free them from their fetters and draw them from their dungeon. This was the angel of whom saint Luke speaks in the fifth chapter of the Acts of the Apostles, freeing the Apostles at night at the order of the heavenly Mother; although the Evangelist makes no mention of the secret connected with this miracle. But he was seen by the Apostles, appearing to them full of light and glory and telling them, that he was sent by his Queen to liberate them from prison. He commanded them to preach, as they also did. Besides this angel She sent also others to the magistrates and priests in order to drive away from them Lucifer and his demons, who were irritating and inciting them against the Apos-

tles. They were to inspire them instead with holy
thoughts, and instill into them the fear of injuring these
men or hindering their preaching. The heavenly spirits
obeyed, and they fulfilled their mission so well, that
the venerable Gamaliel delivered himself of the opinion
recorded by saint Luke (Act 5, 34). For when the other
judges were thrown into consternation at the news, that
the Apostles, whom they had cast into prison, were freely
preaching in the temple without its being known through
whom and how they had been freed from the prison,
Gamaliel counseled the priests not to trouble these men,
but to let them continue their preaching; since if this was
the work of God they could not hinder it, and if it was
not, it would soon come to naught of itself. For the
same would happen as what had happened some time
before with the false prophets, Theodas and Judas of
Galilee, who had risen in Jerusalem and Palestine and
who had both perished with all their followers.

151. This counsel was inspired by the holy angels of
the Queen and through their influence the judges acted
upon it, though their own reputation and worldly interest induced them to forbid the Apostles to preach any
more in the name of Jesus of Nazareth. When therefore
they had again brought the Apostles before their tribunal
after their liberation from prison, they dismissed them
with a punishment. The Apostles immediately reported
all their undertakings and experiences to the most blessed
Mary as to their Mother and Teacher; and the most prudent Queen received them with maternal affection and
joy to see them so constant in suffering and so zealous
for the welfare of souls. "Now, my masters," she said,
"you appear to me true imitators and disciples of your
Master, since you suffer affronts and injury for his name
and with a joyous heart help Him to bear the cross. You

become his worthy ministers and assistants in applying the fruit of the blood He has shed for the salvation of men. May his right hand bless you and strengthen you with divine virtue." This she said to them on her knees and kissing their hands; whereupon She ministered to their wants, as described above.

INSTRUCTION WHICH THE GREAT QUEEN OF THE ANGELS, MOST BLESSED MARY, GAVE ME.

152. My daughter, in what thou hast understood and written in this chapter, thou possessest many and important admonitions for thy salvation and for the salvation of the faithful in the Church. First of all thou must meditate upon the solicitude and watchfulness with which I sought after the eternal salvation of all the faithful without overlooking the least of their necessities and dangers. I taught them the truth, prayed incessantly, encouraged them in their labors, urged the Lord to assist them; and above all I defended them from the demons and their cunning and furious wrath. All these blessings I procure for Christians from heaven in our times; and if not all experience them, it is not because I do not solicit them, but because there are very few of the faithful who call to me with all their heart and who dispose themselves toward meriting and reaping the fruit of my maternal love. I would defend them all from the dragon, if all would call upon me and if all would fear his pernicious deceits, by which they are ensnared and entrapped to eternal damnation. In order that all may wake up to this frightful danger, I now give them this new reminder. I assure thee, my daughter, that all those, who damn themselves after the death of my Son and in spite of the benefits and favors procured by my intercession, will suffer greater torments in hell than those who were lost be-

fore his coming and before I was in the world. Thus those who from now on understand these mysteries and despise them to their loss, shall be subject to new and greater punishments.

153. They must also remember in what estimation they should hold their souls, since I did and am doing so much every day for them, after they have been redeemed by the passion and death of my divine Son. This forgetfulness among men is very blameworthy and deserves a fearful chastisement. How unreasonable and how damnable is the conduct of a man, who for a momentary sensible pleasure, which at most must end with life and generally lasts only for a short time, labors so much and still claims to have the faith, while at the same time he takes no account of his immortal soul, and forgets it, as if it ended and were consumed with the visible things? They consider not, that when all comes to an end, the soul begins to suffer or enjoy the eternal and everlasting things. As thou knowest this truth and the perversity of mortals, thou wilt not be astonished at the power of the dragon in our days; for where there is continual combat, he that comes out victorious will gain the strength, which the vanquished loses. This is especially true of the cruel and incessant conflict of the demons, where the souls will gain in strength by victory and the devils will be weakened, as happened when my Son conquered them and I afterwards. But when this serpent finds itself victorious over men, then it will raise its proud head, gain new strength from its weakness and a greater sway, as it does now in the world; for the lovers of its vanity have subjected themselves and are following the standard and the fabulations of the devil. In the midst of this ruin hell has opened its maw and the more it is glutted, the more insatiable becomes its hunger, seeking to bury in its infernal caverns all the rest of mankind.

154. Fear, my dearest, this danger as thou knowest it, and do thou live in a continual watchfulness not to open the gate of thy heart to the wiles of this bloodthirsty beast. Thou hast a warning in Ananias and Saphira, into whose soul the demon entered as soon as he had found out their desire of money and could assault them through this portal. I do not wish thee to strive after anything pertaining to this mortal life; and I wish thee so to suppress and extinguish within thyself all the passions and inclinations of weak nature, that not even the evil spirits, with all their watchfulness, shall find in thee the least disorderly movement of pride, covetousness, vanity, anger or any other passion. This is the science of the saints, and without it no one can live secure in mortal flesh. On account of ignoring it, innumerable souls perish. Do thou learn it diligently, and teach it thy religious, in order that each one may be vigilant over her own self. With it they shall live in true peace and charity without deception; each one, and all of them together, united in the peaceful tranquillity of the divine Spirit and adorned by the exercise of all virtues, will be an impregnable fortress for their enemies. Remind thyself and thy religious of the chastisement of Ananias and Saphira, exhort them to be very solicitous in the observance of their rules and constitutions; for thus shall they merit my protection and special assistance.

CHAPTER X.

THE FAVORS WHICH THE MOST HOLY MARY CONFERRED
UPON THE APOSTLES THROUGH THE MINISTRY OF HER
ANGELS; THE SALVATION OF A WOMAN PROCURED BY
MARY IN THE LAST HOUR, AND WHAT HAPPENED TO
OTHERS THAT DAMNED THEMSELVES.

155. As the new law of grace continued to spread in
Jerusalem so the number of the faithful increased and
the new evangelical Church was augmented day by day
(Acts 5, 14). In like manner did the solicitude and attention of its great Queen and Teacher, Mary, expand
toward the new children engendered by the Apostles
through their preaching. As they were the foundation-
stones of the Church, on which the security of that building was to depend, the most prudent Lady lavished
especial care upon the apostolic college. Her heavenly
solicitude augmented in proportion to the wrath of
Lucifer against the followers of Christ and especially
against the Apostles, as the ministers of eternal salvation
to the other faithful. It will never be possible to describe
or to estimate in this life the blessings and favors conferred by Her upon the Church and upon each of its
mystical members. This happened especially in regard
to the Apostles and disciples; for as has been revealed to
me not a day or hour passed, in which she did not work
for them many wonders. I will relate in this chapter
some of the events, which are very instructive on account
of the secrets of divine Providence therein contained.
From them we can form an estimate of the most vigilant
charity and zeal of the blessed Mary for souls.

156. All the Apostles She loved and served with incredible affection and reverence, both on account of their great holiness and on account of their dignity as priests, as ministers, preachers and founders of the Gospel. During all their stay in Jerusalem She attended upon them, counseled and directed them in the manner noted above. With the increase of the Church they were obliged to go outside of Jerusalem in order to baptize and admit to the faith many of the inhabitants of the neighboring places; but they always returned to the city, because they had purposely delayed separating from each other, or leaving Jerusalem, until they should receive orders to do so. From the Acts we learn that saint Peter went to Lydda and Jaffa, where he raised Tabitha from the dead and performed other miracles, returning again to Jerusalem. Although saint Luke relates these excursions after speaking of the death of saint Stephen (of which I shall treat in the following chapter), yet during these events, many were converted throughout Palestine, and it was necessary, that the Apostles go forth to preach to them and to confirm them in the faith, always returning in order to give an account of their doings to their heavenly Mistress.

157. During all their journeys and preachings the common enemy of all sought to hinder the spread of the divine Word, or its fruit, by rousing the unbelievers to many contradictions and altercations with the Apostles and their listeners or converts; for it seemed to the infernal dragon more easy to assault them, when he saw them removed and far from the protection of their Mistress. So formidable the great Queen of the angels appeared to the hellish hosts, that in spite of the eminent holiness of the Apostles, Lucifer imagined them disarmed and at his mercy, easily approachable to his temptations,

as soon as they left the presence of Mary.   The furious pride of this dragon, as is written in Job (Job 41, 18), esteems the toughest steel as weak straw, and the hardest bronze as a stick of rotten wood.   He fears not the dart nor the sling; but he dreaded the protection of the most blessed Mary, and in tempting the Apostles, he waited until they should have left her presence.

158. But her protection failed them not on that account; for the great Lady, from the watch-tower of her exalted knowledge, reached out in every direction.   Like a most vigilant sentinel She discovered the assaults of Lucifer and hastened to the relief of her sons and ministers of her Lord.   When in her absence She could not speak to the Apostles in any of their afflictions, She immediately sent her holy angels to their assistance in order to encourage, forewarn and console them; and sometimes also to drive away the assaulting demons.   All this the celestial spirits executed promptly in compliance with the orders of their Queen.   At times they would do it secretly by inspirations and interior consolations; at others, and more frequently, they manifested themselves visibly, assuming most beautiful and refulgent bodies and informing the Apostles of what was proper for the occasion, or what had been ordered by their Mistress.   This happened very often on account of their purity and holiness and on account of the necessity of favoring them with such an abundance of consolation and encouragement. In all their difficulties and labors the most loving Mother thus assisted them, besides offering up for them her continual prayers and thanksgiving.   She was the strong Woman, whose domestics were sheltered by double garments; the Mother of the family, who supplied all with nourishment and who by the labors of her hands planted the vineyard of the Lord.

159. With all the other faithful She proportionately exhibited the same care; and although there were many converts in Jerusalem and in Palestine, She remembered them all in thir necessities and tribulations. And She thought not only of the needs of their souls, but of those of the body, and many She cured of most grave sicknesses. Others, whom She knew were not to be cured miraculously, She visited and assisted in person. Of the poor She took a still greater care, with her own hand administering to them food on their beds of sickness, and seeing to their being kept clean, as if She were the servant of all, infirm with the infirm. So great was the humility, the charity and solicitude of the great Queen of the world, that She refused no service or lowliest ministry to the faithful, no matter how humble and insignificant the condition of those applying for her assistance. She filled each one with joy and consolation and lightened all their labors. Those upon whom on account of their absence She could not personally attend, She assisted secretly through her holy angels or by her prayers and petitions.

160. In an especial manner her maternal kindness exhibited itself to those who were in the agony of death; for she attended many of the dying and would not leave them, until they had secured their eternal salvation. For those who went to purgatory She offered up most fervent prayers and performed some works of penance, such as prostrations in the form of a cross, genuflections and other exercises, by which She satisfied for their faults. Then She sent one of her angels in order to draw them from purgatory and present them to her Son in heaven as his own and as the fruits of his blood and Redemption. This happiness the Queen of heaven procured to many souls during her stay upon earth. And, as far as

was made known to me, this favor is not denied in our days to those, who during their earthly life dispose themselves properly for meriting her presence, as I have written in another place.   But, since it would be necessary to extend the scope of this history very much, if I were to describe how the most blessed Mary assisted many in the hour of death, I cannot dilate upon this matter.   I will recount only one incident, in which She freed a girl from the jaws of the infernal dragon.   It is one which is so extraordinary and worthy of the attention of us all, that it would not be right to omit it in this history, or deprive ourselves of the lesson it contains.

161. Among the five thousand who were first converted and who received Baptism in Jerusalem, there was also a young girl of poor and humble parentage.   This young woman, busying herself with her household duties, took ill and for many days She dragged on in her sickness without improvement.   As happens to many other souls, she on that account fell from her first fervor and in her neglect committed some sins endangering her baptismal grace.   Lucifer, who never relaxed in his thirst for the ruin of souls, approached this woman and attacked her with fiercest cruelty, being thus permitted by God to do so for his greater glory and that of his most blessed Mother.   The demon appeared to her in the form of another woman and with much cajolery told her to withdraw from those people, who were preaching the Crucified, and not to believe anything they said, because it was all falsehood; that, if she would not follow this advice, she would be punished by the priests and judges who had crucified the Teacher of that new and counterfeit religion; whereas, if she obeyed, she would live peacefully and free from danger.   The girl answered: "I will do what thou sayest; but what shall I do in regard to

that Lady, whom I have seen with these men and women and who appears to be so kind and peaceful? I desire her good will very much." The demon replied: "This One, whom thou mentionest, is worse than all the rest, and Her thou must shun before all. It is most important, that thou withdraw from her snares."

162. Infested with this deadly poison of the ancient serpent, the soul of this simple dove was brought near to eternal death and her body, instead of being relieved, dropped into more serious illness and was in danger of a premature end. One of the seventy-two disciples, who visited the faithful, was informed of the dangerous illness of the girl; for from her neighbors he heard that one of his sect living in that house, was on the point of expiring. The disciple entered in order to visit her and encourage her according to her necessities. But the sick girl was so ensnared by the demons, that she did not receive him or answer him one word, although he zealously sought to exhort and instruct her; she on the contrary sought to hide and stop her ears in order not to hear him. From these signs the Apostle saw the imminent peril of this soul, although he did not know the cause. Eagerly he hastened to report to the Apostle saint John, who without delay visited the patient, admonishing her and speaking to her words of eternal life, if she would only listen. But she treated him in the same way as the disciple, obstinately resisting the efforts of both. The Apostle saw many legions of devils surrounding the girl, and, though they retired at his approach, they failed not immediately afterward to renew the illusion with which they had filled the unhappy girl.

163. Seeing her obstinacy, the Apostle betook himself in great affliction to the most blessed Mary in order to ask for help. Immediately the great Queen turned her

interior vision upon the sick one and She recognized the
unhappy and dangerous condition, in which the enemy
had drawn that soul. The kind Mother bewailed this
simple sheep, thus deceived by the bloodthirsty infernal
wolf; and prostrate upon the floor She prayed for her
rescue. But the Lord answered not a word to the petition of his blessed Mother; not because her petition
was disagreeable to Him, but for the contrary reason and
because He was pleased with her clamors, pretending
deafness in order to hear them so much the longer; also
in order to teach us how great was the prudence and charity of our Mother on these occasions. The Lord left
Her for this purpose to the common and ordinary state
without favoring Her with a new inspiration in regard to
what She was asking. She however did not cease on that
account, nor did She permit her ardent charity to relax;
for She knew that She was not to be wanting in her office
as Mother on account of the silence of the Lord as long
as She did not know expressly the divine will. Proceeding thus prudently She dispatched one of her angels to
bring aid to that soul by defending it against the devil and
exhorting it by holy inspirations to forsake his deceits
and return to God. The holy angel fulfilled this commission with the speed in which they are wont to obey
the Most High; but, even though he made a diligent use
of all his powers as an angel, he could not overcome the
girl's obstinacy in clinging to her illusions. To such a
state can a soul be reduced by delivering itself over to the
devil.

164. The holy angel returned to his Queen and said:
"My Mistress, I return from the task of assisting this
girl in her mortal danger, as Thou, the Mother of mercy,
hast imposed upon me; but her hardness of heart is such,
that she will not receive or listen to the holy inspirations

I have given her. I have fought against the demons in
her defense, but they resisted, standing on the rights
which this soul has freely yielded and continues to yield
to them. The power of divine justice has not co-operated
with me as I desired in trying to fulfill thy will; and I
cannot, O Lady, give Thee the consolation Thou ex-
pectest." The loving Mother was much afflicted at this
answer; but as She is the Mother of love, of knowledge
and holy hope, She would not yield in what She had
merited for all of us and what She teaches. Retiring
once more to pray for the salvation of that erring soul,
She prostrated Herself upon the ground and said: "My
Lord and God of mercy, behold here this vile wormlet of
the earth; chastise and afflict me, but let me not see this
soul, which was marked as one of the first-fruits of thy
blood and is now deceived by the serpent, become the
spoil of his malice and of his hatred against thy faithful."

165. The most blessed Mary continued for some time
in this petition; but she received no answer from the
Lord, in order that her invincible heart and her charity
toward her neighbor might be put to the proof. The
most prudent Virgin bethought Herself of what had
happened to the prophet Eliseus (IV Kings 4, 34), who
had vainly sent his staff with his servant Giezi to resuscitate the boy and had found that he himself must touch
and stretch himself over his body in order to restore him
to life. Neither the angel nor the Apostle were powerful enough to awaken from sin and from the stupor of
satan that unfortunate girl; therefore the great Lady
resolved to go and heal her in person. This resolve She
recommended to the Lord in her prayer, and, although
She received no answer, She considered that the work itself was a sufficient warranty to proceed. She arose
therefore to leave her room and to walk with saint John

to the dwelling of the sick woman, which was at some distance from the Cenacle. But no sooner had She taken the first steps than the holy angels, at the command of the Lord, approached to bear Her up on the way. As God had not manifested his intention, She asked them, why they thus detained Her; to which they answered: "There is no reason why we should consent to thy walking through the city, when we can bear Thee along with greater propriety." Immediately they placed her upon a throne of resplendent clouds, on which they bore Her along and placed Her in the sick-room. The dying girl, being poor and now speechless, had been forsaken by all and was surrounded only by the demons, who waited to snatch off her soul.

166. But as soon as the Queen of angels made her appearance all the evil spirits vanished like flashes of lightning and as if falling over each other in their dismay. The powerful Queen commanded them to descend into hell and remain there until She should permit them to come forth, and this they were forced to do without the least power of resistance. The kindest Mother then approached the sick woman and taking her by the hand and calling her by her name, spoke sweetest words of life. Instantly a complete change came over the girl, and she began to breathe more freely and recover herself. Then she said to the heavenly Mary: "My Lady, a woman came to me, who persuaded me to believe, that the disciples of Jesus were deceiving me and that I had better immediately separate myself from them and from Thee; otherwise, if I should accept their way of life, I should fall into great misfortune." The Queen answered: "My daughter, she, who seemed to thee a woman, was thy enemy, the devil. I come in the name of the Most High to give thee eternal life; return then to his true faith,

which thou hast received, and confess Him with all thy heart as thy God and Redeemer, who, for thy salvation and that of all the world, has died upon the Cross. Adore and call upon Him, and ask Him for the pardon of thy sins."

167. "All this," the patient answered, "I have believed before; but they told me, it was very bad, and that they would punish me, if I should ever confess it." The heavenly Teacher replied: "My friend, do not fear this deceit; but remember that the chastisement and pains which are really to be feared are those of hell, to which the demons wish to bring thee. Thou art now very near death and thou canst avail thyself of the remedy I now offer thee, if thou wilt only believe me; and thou shalt thus free thyself of the eternal fire, which threatens thee on account of thy mistake." Through this exhortation and the graces procured for this poor woman by Mary, she was moved to abundant tears of compunction and implored the blessed Lady further to assist her in this danger, declaring herself ready to obey all her commands. Then the loving Mother made her openly profess her faith in Jesus Christ and elicit an act of contrition in preparation for confession. At the same time She sent for the Apostles to administer the Sacraments to her. The sick girl, repeating the acts of contrition and love, and invoking Jesus and Mary, who was directing her, happily expired in the arms of her Protectress. The blessed Mary had remained with her two hours, in order to prevent the demons from again renewing their assaults. Her assistance was so effectual, that She not only brought back the young woman to the path of eternal life, but delivered her soul from all guilt and punishment. She sent her immediately to heaven accompanied by some of the twelve angels that bore on their breasts the sign of

the Redemption and palms and crowns in their hands as special guardians of the devotees of the great Queen. Of these angels I have spoken on a former occasion, and it is not necessary to describe them here. I will only remark, that the heavenly Queen chose the angels for different offices in the service of men, in accordance with the graces and virtues, of which they were possessed.

168. After the rescue of that soul, the rest of the angels brought back their Queen, seated on the same cloud, to her oratory. She immediately humiliated Herself, prostrating Herself and adoring the Lord, and giving Him thanks for having snatched that soul from the jaws of the infernal dragon. She composed thereon a hymn of praise in his honor. This wonder was wrought by the wisdom of God, in order that the angels, the saints of heaven, the Apostles and also the demons might know the resistless power of most holy Mary and in order that they might learn, that, as She was the Mistress of all, so not all of them together could equal Her in power; that nothing would ever be denied to her prayers in favor of those who loved Her, served Her or called upon Her. For this fortunate girl, having loved this heavenly Lady, secured salvation through Her; while the demons, oppressed and confounded, were left in despair of ever prevailing against the power of Mary when exerted in favor of her clients. Other lessons might be drawn from this example, which I leave to the prudent meditation of the faithful.

169. The same blessing was not attained by two other converts, who failed to merit the efficacious intercession of the blessed Virgin. Since their fate may serve as a lesson and as a warning, like that of Ananias and Saphira, against the astuteness of Lucifer in tempting and ruining human souls, I shall relate it likewise, as far as

it was made known to me. May the instruction it conveys inculcate the fear of the just judgments of the Most High (Ps. 118, 120). After the miracle just related the demon was permitted to return with his host to the world in order to test the constancy of the faithful; for thus must the just and the predestined gain their crowns. He came forth filled with still greater wrath and began to seek entrance into the hearts of the faithful by searching out the evil inclinations of each one, as he does even now. For experience has given him confidence, that we children of Adam usually follow our inclinations and passions more than the dictates of reason and of virtue. A multitude cannot be perfect in all its components, and as the Church went on increasing in number, so also the fervor of charity began to cool in some, thus affording a greater field for the sowing of his hellish cockle. Among the faithful saint John found two, who were beset with evil inclinations and habits before their conversion and who sought favor and alliance with some of the Jewish princes in the hope of worldly gain and honor. Infected by this covetousness (which always was the root of all evils), they temporized with the powerful and flattered them in order to retain their friendship.

170. On account of these dealings the demon judged them to be weak in their faith and virtue. He thought he might be able to pervert them through the influence of the Jewish priests, upon whom they depended. Following up his plot, the serpent suggested to those priests many ways of reprehending and intimidating the two converts for having accepted the faith in Christ and received Baptism. Yielding to the instigations of satan the priests pressed their threats with great show of authority and severity. As the anger of those in authority is apt to frighten weak subjects, such as these two in their at-

tachment to their own interest happened to be, they proceeded from weakness to apostasy from the faith of Christ in order not to incur the displeasure of those powerful Jews. They moreover still retained a certain unhappy and deceitful confidence in their patrons and therefore soon dropped away from the gathering and the other faithful, ceasing to attend the preaching and the other holy exercises of the converts and thus making apparent their treasonable falling away.

171. The Apostles were much aggrieved at the ruin of these converts and at the scandal, which would be occasioned by such a pernicious example in the beginnings of the Church. They conferred among themselves, whether they should notify the blessed Mary of this event, but they hesitated to cause Her this sorrow and pain. Saint John told them, that the great Lady knew all the affairs of the Church and that therefore also this one could not have escaped her most vigilant attention and charity. Thereupon all went to give Her an account of those two apostates, whom they had already exhorted and tried to lead back to the faith. The loving and prudent Mother saw no occasion for hiding her sorrow at the threatened loss of souls already aggregated to the Church. It was also proper, that the Apostles should learn from the sorrow of the great Lady, how they must esteem the children of the Church and with what zeal they were to preserve them in the faith and bring them to eternal life. Our Queen returned immediately to her chamber and, prostrate on the floor as usual, She poured out a most fervent prayer for the two apostates, shedding copious and bloody tears.

172. In order to lessen somewhat her grief by the knowledge of his hidden judgments, the Lord answered: "My Spouse, chosen among all the creatures, I wish thee

to understand my just decrees concerning those two
souls, for whom thou prayest, and concerning others,
who are to enter my Church.   These two, who have
apostatized from my true faith, might do more harm than
good among the other faithful, if they continue their intercourse with them; for they have very depraved habits
and have become still more hardened in their evil inclinations. Hence in my infinite knowledge I foresee that they
will be reprobates and that it will be better to separate
them from the flock of the faithful and cut them off
from the mystical body of the Church.   Thus they shall
be prevented from infecting others by their contagion.
It has already become necessary, my beloved One, that, in
conformity with my most high Providence, both the predestined and of the foreknown should join my Church:
some, who by their sins shall incur damnation, and others,
who, through my grace, are to save themselves by good
works.   My teachings and my Gospel are to be as the
net, which gathers in all kinds of fish, good and bad, the
wise and the foolish, and the enemy is to sow his cockle
among the pure grain of truth (Matth. 13, 28), in order
that the just may justify themselves so much the more,
and the impure, if so they choose in their malice, may de-
file themselves still more."

173. This was the answer given by the Lord to this
prayer of the most holy Mary.   At the same time He renewed within Her the participation in his knowledge, in
order that She, perceiving the equity of the Most High
in condemning those unworthy of his friendship and
glory, might dilate her afflicted heart. But as the heavenly Mother alone held the measure of the sanctuary in her
most eminent wisdom, knowledge and charity, She alone
also, among all creatures, estimated and pondered fully
what it meant to lose God eternally and to be condemned

to eternal torments in the company of the demons; and so her sorrow was in proportion. We are aware, that the angels and the saints of heaven, who know this mystery in God, cannot feel sorrow or pain, because that would be inappropriate to their happy state. If it would be compatible with their state of glory, their sorrow would be in proportion to the loss caused by the eternal perdition to those, whom they love with perfect charity and whom they desire to have with them in glory.

174. Hence, the sorrow and pain for the perdition of souls, which was impossible to them, the blessed Mary felt in a degree so much the greater as She exceeded them in wisdom and charity. For She was in the state of pilgrimage, in which She could feel this pain; She was endowed with the knowledge of the blessed by which She understood its cause; for when She enjoyed the beatific vision, She saw in the essence of God, his love and infinite goodness for the salvation of men, together with the sorrow which He would have for the perdition of souls, if such sorrow were possible. She knew the horrible character of the demons, their wrath against men, the terrors of the infernal torments and of the endless company of the devils and the damned. As the most holy Mary saw, that these two souls and an almost infinite number of others in the church were to draw upon themselves eternal damnation, what a sorrow, what pains and commiseration were caused in that tender, kind and loving heart at these evils and many others far beyond my power of describing? Many times did She lament such misfortunes and exclaim: "Is it possible, that any soul, of its own free will, should ever deprive itself eternally of seeing the face of God, and should chose rather to look upon so many demons in hell?"

175. The secret of the reprobation of these first apos-

tates the most prudent Queen reserved to Herself without manifesting it to the Apostles. But while she was thus retired in her affliction, saint John the Evangelist entered to visit Her and to inquire as to her wishes and how to serve Her. When he saw Her so afflicted and sorrowful, he was filled with consternation and asked permission to speak, saying: "My Lady and Mother of my Lord Jesus Christ, since our Master died I have never seen on thy countenance such grief and sorrow as now, when thy face and thy eyes are bathed in tears of blood. Tell me, Lady, if possible, the cause of this new affliction, and whether I can alleviate it at the cost of my life." The most blessed Mary answered: "My Son, weep now for this very reason." Saint John conceived that the memory of the Passion had renewed in the loving Mother this bitter grief and under that impression he said: "My Lady, as thy Son and our Redeemer is now glorious and triumphant in heaven at the right hand of the eternal Father, Thou canst moderate thy tears. Although it is not just, that we forget what He suffered for men, yet it is also right that we rejoice in the blessings following upon his Passion and Death."

176. She answered: "It is also just that I weep when I see, that after He died, some are seeking to crucify Him anew by their sins and their apostasy and by the abuse of the fruits of his precious blood; for I know that in his most ardent love for men, He has suffered for the salvation of each one in particular whatever He suffered for all together. I see this immense love so little requited and so many lost who should know Him, that I cannot constrain my sorrow, nor continue to live, unless the Lord preserves my life. O children of Adam, formed according to the image of my Son and Lord, what are you thinking of? Where is your judgment and your

justification for thus incurring the calamity of losing God forever?" Saint John replied: "My Mother and Mistress, if thy sorrow is occasioned by those two apostates, thou must know that among so many there must be unfaithful servants; for even in our apostolate itself was numbered Judas, a disciple in the school of our Redeemer and Teacher." "O John," answered the queen, "if God himself wished the perdition of some souls, I should be able to restrain my sorrow; but, though He permits the damnation of the reprobate since they themselves seek it, this is not the absolute will of the divine goodness; He wishes all to attain salvation, if only they would not of their own free will resist. That not all should be predestined and gain the fruit of the blood shed for them, has cost my Son the sweating of blood. And if even now He could be aggrieved for a soul that damns itself, He would doubtlessly be more aggrieved than if He had again to suffer for it. Hence I, who know this truth and am still living in the flesh, rightfully feel what my Son desires to feel if it were possible." By these and other words of the Mother of mercy saint John was moved to tears and lamentations, in which he joined with Her for a considerable time.

INSTRUCTION WHICH THE QUEEN OF HEAVEN, MOST BLESSED MARY, GAVE ME.

177. My daughter, since in this chapter thou hast particularly learnt of the matchless and bitter sorrow, with which I bewailed the perdition of souls, thou thyself must learn also what thou must do for the salvation of thy own and that of others in order to imitate me in the perfection which I require of thee. No torment, nor death itself, would I have refused, if such had been neces-

sary to save any of the damned, and to save them, I would have esteemed all sufferings a sweet alleviation in my most ardent charity. Hence, if thou dost not die of this kind of sorrow, thou art at least not excused from willingness to suffer all that the Lord sends thee for advancing this cause, or from praying and laboring all in thy power to prevent any sin in thy neighbor; and when thou canst not all at once obtain thy object, or dost not know whether the Lord has heard thee, do not lose confidence, but enliven it and persevere in thy efforts; for such a solicitude can never displease Him, who desires the salvation of all his redeemed more than thou. If nevertheless thou art not heard in thy prayers, make use of the means, which prudence and charity require, and return anew to thy prayers. The Most High is always attracted by this sort of charity for the neighbor and by the love which seeks to hinder sin. He desires not the death of the sinner (Ezech. 33, 11); and, as thou hast written, He does not entertain an absolute and antecedent decree of damning his creatures, but seeks to save them all, if they do not pursue perdition of their own free will. Although He permits this in his justice as being inseparable from the free will of man, it is against his inclination. Do not restrict thyself in these petitions, and in those concerning temporal things, pray that his holy will be done in all that is proper.

178. If I desire that thou labor with such fervor of charity for the salvation of thy brethren, consider what thou must do to save thyself, and in what estimation thou must hold thy own soul, for which an infinite price was offered. I wish to admonish thee as a Mother, that when temptations and passions incline thee toward the commission of any sin, no matter how small, remember the sorrows and the tears which the knowledge of the

sins of men and the desire to prevent them has caused me. Do not thou cause the like in me, my dearest; for although I am now incapable of that pain, yet thou deprivest me of the accidental joy of seeing thee, to whom I condescended to become a Mother and Teacher, really endowed with the perfection taught in my school. If thou art unfaithful in this, thou wilt frustrate my great desire of seeing thee please my divine Son and accomplish his holy will in all its plenitude. By the infused light which thou receivest, do thou ponder how great are any faults thou mayest commit after being so favored and bound in duty to the Lord and to myself. Dangers and temptations will not be wanting to thee during the rest of thy earthly life; but in all of them remember my teaching, my sorrows and my tears, and above all what thou owest to my divine Son, who is so liberal toward thee in applying to thee the fruit of his blood for the purpose of eliciting thy grateful correspondence.

CHAPTER XI.

179. The office of Mother and Teacher of the holy Church, which the Lord had conferred upon most holy Mary, was necessarily accompanied by a knowledge and light proportionate to those high offices. For she was to know all the members of this mystical body which She governed, so that She might apply her teachings and her ministrations according to each one's station, condition and necessity. This blessing our Queen received with the plenitude and abundance of wisdom and knowledge as is clear from all that I am writing. She knew all the faithful that joined the Church, was informed of the natural inclinations, of the degree of virtue and grace they possessed, the merit of their works, their beginning and end. She was ignorant of nothing pertaining to the Church, except when sometimes the Lord concealed from Her some affair, which afterwards was made known to Her at its conclusion. Her knowledge was not barren or profitless, but was inspired with the charity of her divine Son toward all She saw and knew. As She at the same time was aware of the sacraments of divine Providence, She used all her wisdom according to the measure and weight of her interior charity; for She gave neither more nor less than was proper according to the deserts of love and estimation due to each one; and this is a defect which we children of Adam ordinarily incur, even if we think we have used the nicest equity.

180. But the Mother of beautiful love and knowledge did not pervert the order of distributive justice, mixing up her affections; She dispensed it by the light of the Lamb, who enlightened and governed Her, dealing out her heartfelt love to each according to his merits, neither more nor less. Nevertheless She conducted Herself as a most loving Mother, without niggardliness or forgetfulness. But in her exterior manifestations of this love She governed Herself according to other rules of highest prudence, carefully avoiding special predilections in her intercourse with others and the slightest grounds of envy or emulation. For these are very apt to disrupt communities and families, where many eyes are always watching the public proceedings. It is a common and natural passion in men to seek estimation and distinction, especially in the eyes of those who are powerful; and there is scarcely any one, who does not presume on possessing equal merits with all the rest and deserving equal, or even greater favors. This kind of emulation is not wanting even among those who are in the highest position, or have attained high virtue, as is seen in the apostolic college, where, on account of some distinction shown to one, the question of precedence and dignity was immediately raised and broached before the Lord (Matth. 18, 1).

181. In order to prevent and forestall these heartburnings the great Queen was most solicitous to show unbiased and uniform favor to all the members of the Church in public. This conduct was not only worthy of such a Mistress, but most necessary in the beginnings of her government. For the principles upon which her behavior was founded, were to be well established for the guidance of prelates in the future government of the Church. Moreover in those happy beginnings all the

Apostles and disciples, and others of the faithful, excelled in the working of miracles and in divine gifts, while in the latter times many were to signalize themselves in holy science and learning. It was proper to teach all, that neither on account of great gifts, nor for lesser ones, should any one exalt himself in vain presumption, or deem himself worthy of great honors, or of being favored more highly, especially by God or by his most holy Mother, as far as outward appearances are concerned. Let the just be satisfied with being loved by the Lord and favored by his friendship; and whoever is not satisfied with this, will not be benefited by exterior honor and estimation.

182. But the great Queen did not, on account of this restraint, fail in the veneration and honor which She knew to be due to the dignity or office of the Apostles or the other faithful. For just as She taught moderation in all that was to be rendered to each one freely and gratuitously, so She was also an example in all that was due under obligation to each one. Our admirable Queen was so prudent in all her intercourse, that not one of the faithful ever left Her dissatisfied, nor could any one with any show of reason, even if it were only apparent, deny Her esteem and respect; all of them loved and blessed Her, and were filled with joy and gratitude for her loving and maternal kindness. No one ever suspected Her of forsaking Him in his necessity, or denying him her consolation. No one perceived himself to be less esteemed, or that She favored or loved some more than others; nor did She give any one an occasion of making a comparison in this regard. Moreover She did not wish to assign, on her own responsibility, any of the offices or dignities, which were to be filled among the faithful; nor would She use her influence in favor of any one in

this matter. All such appointments She left to the well-seeming and the wishes of the Apostles, and relied upon her secret prayer for guiding them aright.

183. She was led also to this wise disposition of her actions by her profoundest humility. In this She was an example to all, since they knew that She was the Mother of wisdom, who knew all things and could not err in her conduct. She wished to leave this shining example in the Church, in order that no one may presume on his own knowledge, prudence or virtue, especially not in serious matters; but that all may understand, that true insight is conditioned by humility and good counsel, and that, in all matters that are not to be decided merely by private judgment, such private judgment implies presumption. She likewise took into consideration, that to intercede and favor others in temporal matters, has the appearance of superiority, and still more does it expose one to desire thankful returns from those so favored. All these inequalities and defects in the practice of virtue were far removed from the supreme sanctity of our heavenly Queen; and therefore She taught us by her living example the rules of our exterior conduct, which exclude as well the loss of merit as the hindrance of the greatest perfection. Thus in her modesty She never refused to give counsel to the Apostles when they so frequently applied to Her for direction in the exercise of their office and in their undertakings; and the same line of conduct She observed with the other disciples and faithful of the Church, because She conducted Herself in all things according to the plenitude of wisdom and charity.

184. Among the saints who were especially fortunate in meriting the greater love of the Queen of heaven, there was one by the name of Stephen, who belonged to the

seventy-two disciples; for from the very beginning of his following Christ our Savior, She looked upon him with an especial love, placing him first, or among the first, in her estimation. She immediately saw, that this saint was chosen by the Master of life for the defense of his honor and his holy name, and that he was to give up his life for him. Moreover this courageous saint was of a sweet and peaceful disposition; and he was rendered much more amiable and docile to all holiness by the workings of grace. Such dispositions made him very pleasing to the sweetest Mother; and whenever She found any persons naturally of a peaceful and meek character, She was wont to say, that they resembled her divine Son. On this account and on account of many heroic virtues of saint Stephen She loved him tenderly, procured him many blessings, and thanked the Lord for having created, called and chosen such a one for the first-fruits of his martyrs. In consideration of his coming martyrdom, revealed to Her by her divine Son, her heart was filled with additional affection for this great saint.

185. The blessed saint corresponded in most faithful attention and deepest reverence with the benefits conferred upon him by Christ our Savior and his heavenly Mother; for he was not only of a peaceful, but of an humble heart, and those that are so disposed in truth, are thankful for all benefits, even though they may not be so great as those conferred on saint Stephen. He always entertained the highest conceptions concerning the Mother of mercy, and in his high esteem and fervent devotion he continued to seek her favor. He asked information on many mysterious matters; for he was very wise, full of the Holy Spirit and of faith, as is told us by saint Luke. The great Lady answered all his inquiries, encouraged and exhorted him zealously to work for the honor of

Christ. In order to confirm him more in his strong faith, Mary forewarned him of his coming martyrdom and said: "Thou, Stephen, shalt be the first-born of the martyrs, engendered by my divine Son and Lord by the example of his death; thou shalt follow his footsteps, like a privileged disciple his master, and like a courageous soldier his captain; and at the head of the army of martyrs, thou shalt carry his banner of the Cross. Hence it is meet thou arm thyself with fortitude under the shield of faith, and be assured, that the strength of the Most High shall be with thee in the conflict."

186. This warning of the Queen of the angels inflamed the heart of saint Stephen with the desire of martyrdom. As is recorded in the Acts of the Apostles, he was filled with grace and fortitude and wrought great wonders in Jerusalem. Besides the Apostles saint Peter and saint John, no one except he dared to dispute with the Jews. His wisdom and spirit they could not resist, because he preached to them with an intrepid heart, refuted and accused them oftener and more courageously than the other disciples (Acts 6, 9). All this saint Stephen did with burning desire of attaining the martyrdom of which he had been assured by the great Lady. As if he were afraid of any one gaining this crown in advance of him, he offered himself before all others to engage in the disputes with the rabbis and teachers of the law of Moses, so eager was he to defend the honor of Christ, for whom he knew he would lay down his life. The infernal dragon, gradually becoming observant of the ambitions of saint Stephen, directed his malignant attention toward him and strove to hinder his attaining public martyrdom in testimony of the faith of Christ. In order to destroy him, he incited the most incredulous of the Jews to kill saint Stephen in secret. Lucifer was tormented by the virtue

and courage of saint Stephen and he feared lest great things should be accomplished by him alive or in dying for the confirmation of the faith and teachings of his Master. On account of the hatred of the Jews against this disciple, the devils easily persuaded them to make away with him in secret.

187. They attempted it often during the short time, which intervened between the coming of the Holy Ghost and his martyrdom. But the great Mistress of the world, who knew the cunning and malicious attempts of Lucifer and of the Jews, protected the saint from all their assaults, until the proper time for his being stoned to death should have arrived. Three times the Queen sent one of her angels to lead him from a house, in which his enemies had made arrangements to choke him to death. The holy angel, while remaining invisible to the assassins, was seen by saint Stephen, when he was delivered from their hands and carried to the Cenacle into the presence of his Queen. At other times She warned him by the same angel not to go to a certain street or house, where his enemies were lying in ambush; and sometimes She detained him in the Cenacle, because She knew they were waylaying to kill him. They not only surrounded the Cenacle to murder him on his way to his lodging, but they made the same attempts at other houses. For saint Stephen, as I have mentioned, in his ardent zeal hastened about to bring help and consolation to many of the faithful, and not only was without fear in all these mortal dangers, but sought them out and welcomed them. As he did not know how long the Lord would let him wait for this happiness and saw how many times the blessed Mother freed him from dangers, he was wont lovingly to complain to Her, saying: "My Lady and Protectress, when shall the day arrive, in which I shall pay to my God and

Master the debt of my life, by sacrificing it for the honor and glory of his holy name?"

188. To the heavenly Mother these loving complaints of her servant Stephen afforded incomparable joy; and with maternal and sweetest affection She would answer: "My son and most faithful servant of the Lord, the time appointed by his infinite wisdom is drawing near and thy hopes shall not be frustrated. Do thou at present fulfill the rest of thy task in the holy Church, so that thou mayest secure for thyself thy crown; give thanks continually to the Lord, who has it in store for thee." The purity and holiness of saint Stephen were most exalted and perfect, so that the demons could not approach within a great distance of him; and he was much beloved by Christ and his blessed Mother. The Apostles ordained him a deacon. Even before he was martyred, his virtues reached a heroic degree, meriting for him the distinction of being the first one after the Passion to receive the palm of martyrdom. I will add here what was made known to me in explanation of what saint Luke wrote in the sixth chapter of the Acts.

189. A difference arose among the newly converted in Jerusalem. The Greek complained of the Hebrew converts, that in the daily service and work of relief, the widows of the Greeks were not admitted in the same way to office as those of the Jews (Acts 6, 1). Both the ones as well as the others were Israelites, though the Jews born in Greece were called Greeks, and those born in Palestine, Hebrews; and in this distinction was founded the complaint of the Greeks. The daily administration consisted in the distribution of the alms and offerings for the support of the faithful, as has been described in the seventh chapter. This duty had been assigned to six approved men with the consent of all, according to the

direction of the blessed Mary. But as the number of the faithful increased it became necessary to appoint also some widows of a mature age, to help along in the same work of providing for the wants of the faithful, especially of the women and the sick; these widows were to distribute, whatever they received from the six almoners. They were of Hebrew birth, and as the Greek Jews saw, that none of theirs were admitted to this office they complained to the Apostles of this want of confidence in their own widows.

190. In order to compose this difference, the Apostles called together the faithful and spoke to them: "It is not meet, that we should leave the word of God and serve tables. Wherefore, brethren, look ye out among you seven men of good reputation, full of the Holy Ghost and wisdom, whom we may appoint over this business. But we ourselves will give all our time to prayer and to the ministry of the word, while these men may solve your doubts and difficulties in regard to the support of the faithful" (Acts 6, 2). All approved of this expedient, and without regard to nationality they elected the seven men mentioned by saint Luke. The first and principal one was saint Stephen, whose faith and wisdom was universally known. These seven were superintendents over the six first ones and over the widows without excluding the Greeks; for they looked to virtue rather than nationality. It was saint Stephen who by his admirable wisdom and holiness extinguished the resentment of the Greeks and smoothed over their differences with the Hebrews, so that at least during the months in which he lived, all again united like children of Christ in sincere charity without partiality or distinction of persons.

191. But saint Stephen did not on that account neg-

lect preaching or arguing with the unbelieving Jews. As
these Jews could not murder him in secret, nor overcome his wisdom in public, they vented their mortal
hatred in seeking false testimony against him (Acts 6, 1).
They accused him of blasphemy against God and against
Moses, of inveighing continually against the holy temple and the Law, and of asserting that Jesus would destroy as well the one, as the other. As the witnesses
loudly proclaimed their slander and the people were being
roused by their falsehoods, they brought him into the
hall where the priests were gathered as the judges of
these accusations. The presiding judge first took the
deposition of saint Stephen before the court. The saint
took occasion to prove with highest wisdom, that Christ
was the true Messiah promised to them in the holy
Scriptures; and in conclusion he reprehended them for
their unbelief and hardness of heart so strongly, that they
could find no answer and, gnashing their teeth, they
stopped their ears, in order not to be obliged to hear his
words.

192. The Queen of heaven knew of the seizure of
saint Stephen; and, in order to animate him in her name
for the approaching conflict, She immediately sent him
one of her angels, even before He entered into dispute
with the priests. Through the holy angel saint Stephen
sent Her answer, that he went with joy to confess his
Master and with unflinching heart to give his life for
Him, as he had always desired. Through the same messenger, he begged Her, as his kindest Teacher and
Mother, to assist him and, from her retirement, to send
him her blessing, since his not having been able to obtain
her parting benediction was the only regret he felt now,
when he was about to lay down his life according to Her
wishes. These last words of saint Stephen moved the

maternal bosom of Mary to even greater love and esteem than hitherto; and She desired to attend upon him in person, at this hour, when her beloved disciple was to give up his life for the honor and defense of his God and Redeemer. But the blessed Mother hesitated at the difficulties, which would arise in her passing through the streets of Jerusalem at a time of popular excitement and also in finding an opportunity of speaking publicly to saint Stephen.

193. She prostrated Herself in prayer, begging the divine favor for her beloved disciple; and She presented to the Lord her desire of helping him in the last hour. The clemency of the Most High, which is always at the beck of his Spouse and Mother and which was anxious to enhance the death of his faithful disciple and servant Stephen, sent from heaven a multitude of angels, who, with those of her guard, should carry their Queen to the place where the saint then was. And immediately the mandate of the Lord was executed: the angels placed Her upon a refulgent cloud and bore Her to the tribunal, where the highpriest was examining into the charges against saint Stephen. The vision of the Queen of heaven was hidden from all except the saint. He however saw Her before him, supported in the air by the holy angels in a cloud of heavenly splendor and glory. This extraordinary favor inflamed anew the divine love and the ardent zeal of this champion of the honor of God. In addition to the joy of seeing Mary, the splendors of the Queen shone from the countenance of saint Stephen, so that it gleamed with wonderful beauty and light.

194. On account of this unwonted spectacle the Jews listened with great attention to his words, as is evident from the sixth chapter of the Acts of the Apostles. Those that were in that hall looked upon saint Stephen

and saw his countenance shining as that of an angel; and without a doubt he seemed to them more than man. God did not wish to hide that much of the effects of the presence of the great Queen, in order that the perfidious Jews might be so much the more confounded for not accepting the truth preached in such a miraculous way. They did not know the cause of this supernatural beauty of saint Stephen; for they were not worthy to know it, nor was it a proper occasion to make it known, and therefore saint Luke did not speak of it at that time. The most blessed Mary spoke to Stephen words of life and of wonderful consolation; She assisted him with the blessings of sweetness and asked the eternal Father to fill him anew with the Holy Spirit. All happened according to the prayers of the Queen and he manifested his invincible courage and wisdom to the princes of the Jews, proving by the unanswerable testimony of all the ancient Scriptures, from the calling of Abraham to the Kings and Prophets, that Christ was their Messiah and Savior.

195. At the end of this discourse, through the intercession of the Queen and as a reward of the unconquered zeal of saint Stephen, the heavens opened and the Savior appeared to him standing at the right hand of the Father in the act of assisting him in the conflict. Saint Stephen raised his eyes and said: "Behold I see the heavens opened and its glory, and in it I see Jesus at the right hand of God himself" (Acts 7, 55). But the obdurate perfidy of the Jews esteemed these words as blasphemy and they stopped their ears in order not to hear them. As the punishment of blasphemers according to the law, was death by stoning, they passed upon him that sentence. Then they all surrounded him like wolves and dragged him from the city with great haste and noise. At this juncture the blessed Mother gave him her bene-

diction; and speaking to him words of encouragement and endearment, She left him in charge of her angels, whom She ordered to accompany him and to remain with him until they should present his soul to the Most High. Only one of the guardian angels, in company with those that had descended from heaven as her escort to saint Stephen, now returned with Her to the Cenacle.

196. From her retirement the great Lady by an especial vision saw all that happened in the martyrdom of saint Stephen: how they led him forth from the city with great haste and violence, shouting that he was a blasphemer worthy of death; how Saul was among them, more zealous than the rest, guarding the vestments of those who had taken them off to stone saint Stephen; how the shower of stones fell upon the saint and wounded him, some of them remaining fixed in his head and stained by his blood. Great and tender was the compassion of our Queen at such cruel martyrdom; but still greater her joy in seeing saint Stephen meeting it so gloriously. The kindest Mother failed him not in her tearful prayers from her oratory. When the invincible martyr saw himself near to death, he prayed: "Lord receive my spirit!" Then, on his knees, he exclaimed with a loud voice: "Lord lay not this sin to their charge!" (Acts 7, 59). In these prayers he was supported by those of the blessed Mary, who was filled with incredible joy to see the faithful disciple imitating so closely his divine Master by praying for his enemies and persecutors and commending his spirit into the hands of his Creator and Redeemer.

197. Covered with wounds from the shower of stones thrown by the Jews, saint Stephen expired, while they became still more hardened in their perfidy. Immediately the angels of the Queen bore his pure soul to the

presence of God in order to be crowned with eternal honor and glory. Christ our Savior received him with those words of the Gospel: "Friend, ascend higher; come to Me, thou faithful servant; for, since thou hast been faithful in small things and for a short time, I shall reward thee with abundance, and I shall confess thee before my Father as my faithful servant and friend, just as thou hast confessed Me before men." All the Angels, Patriarchs, Prophets and all the Saints were filled with an especial accidental joy on that day and welcomed the invincible martyr as the first fruits of the Passion of the Lord and as the captain of all those that should follow him in martyrdom. This most fortunate soul was placed very high in glory and close to the most sacred humanity of Christ our Savior. The most blessed Mother participated in the joy through a vision granted to Her; and in praise of the Most High, She composed hymns and canticles with her angels. Those that returned after leaving saint Stephen in heaven, gave thanks to Her for the favor shown to the saint in securing him his eternal happiness.

198. Saint Stephen died about nine months after the passion and death of Christ, our Redeemer, on the twenty-sixth of December, the same date on which the Church celebrates his feast. On that day he had completed his thirty-fourth year, which, with the addition of one day, was also the thirty-fourth year of the birth of the Savior. Hence saint Stephen was born one day later than Jesus, being only twelve months older, and his birth and death happened on the same day of the year, as was clearly shown to me. The prayer of the blessed Virgin and of saint Stephen merited the conversion of Saul, as we will see later on. In order that this conversion might be so much the more glorious the Lord

permitted Saul, from that day on, to take upon himself the task of persecuting and destroying the Church of God; for he began to signalize himself above all other Jews in the persecution, which the wrath of the Jews, highly inflamed by the death of saint Stephen, now began to stir up against the new believers. The desciples secured the body of the invincible martyr and buried it with great mourning, because they had now lost such a wise and strong defender of the law of grace. I have dilated upon his history, because I have been shown the great holiness of this first martyr, and because he was such a devout and highly favored disciple of the most holy Mary.

INSTRUCTION WHICH THE GREAT QUEEN OF THE ANGELS GAVE ME.

199. My daughter, the divine mysteries, when they are presented and explained to such men as are accustomed only to the perception of earthly and sensible things, appear to be insignificant, especially if at the same time their souls are not purified from sin and cleared of the darkness of guilt. For the human faculties, which, besides being of limited capacity, are embarrassed by their attention and affection to what is apparent, draw away from the truth, and, being accustomed to obscurity, are dazzled by the light. On this account the earthly and animal men conceive such distorted and low ideas of the wonderful works of the Most High (1 Cor. 2, 14), and also of the works which I do for them day after day. They tread under foot the gems, and they do not distinguish the bread of the children from the gross food of irrational brutes. All that is heavenly and divine seems to them insipid, because they fail to perceive the

savor of the senses; thus they become incapable of attending to the high things and of profiting from the science of life and the understanding contained in them.

200. But the Most High, my dearest, has sought to preserve thee from this danger and has given thee knowledge and light, improving thy senses and faculties, in order that thou, being made capable and enlivened by the force of divine grace, mayest perceive and distinguish without error the mysteries and sacraments, which I manifest to thee. Although I have many times told thee, that in this mortal life, thou shalt never penetrate or value them in their entirety, yet thou canst and thou must, according to thy powers, show thy appreciation of them by learning and imitating my works. From the variety and bitterness of my pains and sorrows, with which my whole life was interwoven, even after I had returned from the right hand of my Son in heaven to the earth, thou wilt understand, that thy own life must be of the same texture, if thou wishest to follow me as my faithful disciple. In the prudent and impartial humility, with which I governed the Apostles and all the faithful, thou hast an example of how thou must proceed in the government of thy subjects, in meekness, in modesty, with humble dignity, and especially without acceptation of persons and without making a distinction in favor of any person in those things that can and ought to be common to all. This facilitates the true charity and humility of those that govern; for if they show these virtues, they will not be so dictatory in their commands, nor so presumptuous in their own opinion, nor will they pervert the order of justice, as is nowadays done with so much damage throughout Christianity. Pride, vanity, self-interest, self-love and the love of their own relations have infected nearly all the course and conduct of government; and

hence all has gone wrong, and all the governments have been filled with injustice and thrown into frightful confusion.

201. In the most ardent zeal, which I had for the honor of my Son and true God and for the preaching and defense of his holy name; in my joy at seeing the divine will fulfilled and at seeing the fruit of the passion and death of Christ spreading with the Church among souls in the favors which I procured for the glorious martyr Stephen as the first who offered his life for that object; in all this, my daughter, thou wilt find great motives for praising the Most High in his divine works, so worthy of veneration and glory; and thou wilt likewise find cause for imitating me, and blessing his immense goodness for the wisdom He gave me, in order to fulfill all his holy will and pleasure.

CHAPTER XII.

202. Saint Luke says, that on the same day on which
saint Stephen was stoned to death, a great persecution
arose against the Church in Jerusalem. He mentions
especially that Saul devastated it, searching through the
whole city for the followers of Christ in order to seize
and denounce them before the magistrates. This he did
to many of the believers, who were arrested, illtreated,
and killed in this persecution. Although it was very
severe on account of the hatred, which the princes and
priests had conceived against the Christians, and on account of the zealous efforts of Saul in his jealous defense of the law of Moses (of which he himself speaks in
the letter to the Galatians 1, 13); yet there was another
cause for this severity, the effects of which they felt,
though they knew not its origin.

203. This secret cause was the dismay of Lucifer and
his demons, who were much disturbed by the death of
saint Stephen and began to stir up and excite themselves
to diabolical wrath against the faithful, especially against
the Queen and Mistress of the Church, the most holy
Mary. For their greater confusion the Lord had permitted them to see, how the angels had carried Her to
saint Stephen. From this instance of her extraordinary

solicitude and from the constancy and wisdom of saint Stephen, Lucifer concluded, that the powerful Queen would do the same with other martyrs, who were to die for Christ; or at least, that She would aid and encourage them to despise torments or death and meet such persecutions with invincible courage. In his diabolical astuteness he had calculated on torments and sorrows as a means of disheartening the faithful and drawing them from the following of Christ; for it seemed to him, that men love their life so much and are so afraid especially of violent death and pain, that they would be deterred and fall away from the faith rather than encounter such a fate. On this expectation the devil continued to set his hopes, though through the ages his own malice deceived him, just as it had deceived him in the first attempt at the death of Christ, the Leader of all the saints.

204. But in this first beginning of the Church the dragon found himself quite disturbed and confused in his eagerness to irritate the Jews against saint Stephen. When he saw the martyr die so gloriously, he called together his demons and said to them: "I am much disturbed by the death of this disciple and by the favors he has received at the hands of this Woman, our Enemy; for if She thus succors the other disciples and followers of her Son, we shall not be able to overcome or mislead any of them by the threat of torments or death. They will on the contrary all be animated by mutual example to suffer and die like their Master and, instead of succeeding in destroying them, we ourselves shall be overcome and humbled; for our greatest torment and the signal triumph, which they can bring over us, will be their dying for the faith, which we wish to wipe out. We shall ruin ourselves by following this course; yet I do not find any other, nor can I discover the proper mode of

fighting against this incarnate God, his Mother and his followers. Is it possible, that men, who cling so much to life, should be so prodigal of it, and, being so sensitive in regard to suffering, should deliver themselves up to torments to imitate their Master? But nevertheless my just wrath will not be placated on this account. I will persuade others to give up their lives in support of my fallacies, just as they do it for God. Nor will all men n.erit the protection of that invincible Woman, or be so courageous as to undergo such inhuman torments as I shall devise. Let us go and excite the Jews our friends, so that they may destroy this people and blot out from the face of the earth the name of their Master."

205. Then Lucifer proceeded to put into execution his accursed designs and with the innumerable multitudes of the demons he approached the princes and magistrates of the Jews and all the rabid unbelievers among the people, filling them with ungoverned fury and envy against the followers of Christ and, by his deceitful suggestions, inflaming them with a false zeal for the law of Moses and the ancient traditions. It was not difficult to sow this cockle in hearts so perfidious and ravaged by sins; they therefore readily embraced the infernal suggestions. Immediately, in many gatherings and conferences, they consulted about putting a sudden end to all the disciples and followers of Christ. Some were for banishing them from Jerusalem; others, from Palestine; and still others, killing them all, so that this sect might be stamped out at once; some of them again were of the opinion, that they should be subjected to rigorous torments, so as to deter others from joining, and that they should be immediately dispossessed of their goods before they should have given all to the Apostles. This persecution was so severe, as saint Luke tells us, that the

seventy-two disciples fled from Jerusalem, scattering through Judea and Samaria, but at the same time they began to preach through all the land with unfaltering courage. The Apostles, with Mary and many of the faithful, remained in Jerusalem although they kept under cover and in fear, hiding themselves from the diligent search, which Saul instituted for their arrest.

206. The most blessed Mary, amid all this trouble, remained watchful, and first of all, after the death of saint Stephen, ordered his body to be secured and buried. She asked those that attended to this duty, to bring Her a cross, which saint Stephen had habitually carried with him. He had made it in imitation of the one which the Lady herself had borne about with Her since the coming of the Holy Ghost. In this She was imitated also by the other faithful. She received the cross of saint Stephen with especial veneration, not only on its own account, but on account of its having been in possession of the martyr. She called him a saint, and requested, that as far as could be, all his blood should be gathered and preserved reverently as of a martyr already glorified. She extolled his holiness and constancy in the presence of the Apostles and many of the faithful, in order to console and encourage them in their tribulation.

207. In order to understand, at least in part, the magnanimity of heart manifested by the Queen in this and the other persecutions during her earthly life, it is necessary to have in mind a summary of her gifts, which were such that the heart of her Man could rely entirely upon Her (Prov. 31, 11) and entrust Her with all the works ad extra of his Omnipotence. For in her manner of operating the most blessed Mary transcended all the powers of mere creatures and approached to that of God, whose especial image She was. No act or thought of men was

hidden from Her; and She penetrated all the schemes and machinations of the demons. She was ignorant of nothing that was to be done through the holy Church. Yet, though all this was in her mind, She was not confused in the disposition of so many different matters; nor did She ever mix up one with the other; nor was She ever flurried in their management; nor tired of the difficulties; nor oppressed by their multitude; nor was She forgetful of the more remote on account of the more proximate affairs; nor was her prudence ever deficient, because it appeared to be immense and without limit. Hence She attended to all as if She had only one affair, and to each matter as if She had nothing else to attend to. Just as the sun, without trouble, without rest and without intermittence, illumines, vivifies and warms all without diminution of itself; so our great Queen, chosen as the Sun of the Church, governed, vivified and encouraged all its children, without excluding any one of them.

208. When She therefore saw the Church disturbed, persecuted and afflicted by the persecution of the demons and of the men instigated by them, She turned upon the originators of this evil and imperiously commanded Lucifer and his ministers to descend into hell, and they fell howling into the abyss without power of resistance; thus they remained bound and imprisoned for eight entire days, until they were again permitted to rise. Thereupon She called the Apostles and with consoling words encouraged them to remain firm and hope for the divine assistance in this tribulation. Strengthened by this exhortation none of them left Jerusalem. The disciples, who on account of their great number could not conceal themselves properly, took leave of their Mother and Mistress and departed from Jerusalem with her benediction. All of them She exhorted and encouraged, admonishing

them not to be disheartened on account of persecutions, nor to give up preaching Christ crucified; and they faithfully continued their preaching in Judea, Samaria and other provinces. In their labors She comforted and assisted them through her holy angels, inspiring them with courage and bearing them to different localities, whenever necessary. The latter according to saint Luke, happened to Philip on the way to Gaza, when he baptized the Aethiopian, the servant of Queen Candace. In order to assist the faithful in the hour of death, She likewise was wont to send her angels, and after death She took care to assist the souls, who went to purgatory.

209. The cares and labors of the Apostles in this persecution were much greater than those of the other faithful; for as the founders and masters of the Church it behooved them to extend their solicitude to all as well in as outside of Jerusalem. Although they were full of knowledge and of the gifts of the Holy Ghost, yet the work was so arduous and the opposition so powerful, that without the counsel and direction of their Mistress they would often have felt dejected and oppressed. On this account they frequently consulted Her, and She called them to the meetings and conferences which she arranged for transacting the necessary business. For She alone fully understood the present affairs and foresaw clearly those of the future. By her orders they went forth to attend upon matters wherever necessary outside of Jerusalem, as when saint Peter and saint John went to Samaria on hearing that it had accepted the word of God (Acts 8, 14). Amid all these occupations of her own and the tribulations of the faithful, whom She loved as her children, the great Lady retained all the serenity and tranquil peace of her spirit, without falling away in the least point from utmost perfection.

210. She so disposed of things, that She could frequently retire; for, although the exterior actions did not hinder her continued prayer, She reserved many secret and special works for times of solitude. She prostrated Herself, humbled Herself to the dust, sighed and wept for the salvation of mortals and bewailed the fall of so many, whom She recognized as reprobates. As She held written in her heart the evangelical law and stamped therein the image of the Church, She deeply pondered within Herself all that concerned it: the trials and tribulations of its members. In Her conferences with the Lord and with Herself, She sought to dispose and order all its affairs with heavenly knowledge and insight according to the holy will of the Most High. At such times She would renew her participation with the essence and the perfections of God to capacitate Her for such a divine work as the governing of his Church. This therefore She did, without failing in anything and with such a fullness of wisdom and holiness, as made Her seem more than a mere creature, though in truth She was one. In all her thoughts, She was most exalted; in wisdom She was beyond comparison; in counsel, most prudent; in her decisions most equitable and clear-sighted; in her works, most holy; in her words, true and sincere; in all goodness, lovable. Toward the weak, She was most kind; toward the humble, sweet and loving; toward the proud, reserved and majestic. Neither did her own excellence inflate Her, nor adversity disturb Her, nor labors cast Her down: in all her activities She was a faithful copy of her divine Son.

211. The most prudent Mother bore in mind, that the disciples, having dispersed to preach the name and faith of Christ the Savior, had as yet no formula or express creed to guide themselves uniformly and without differ-

ences, so that all the faithful might believe one and the same express truths. Moreover She knew that the Apostles would soon have to go forth over the whole world in order to spread and establish the Church through their preaching, and that it was proper that all should be united in their doctrine, upon which was to be founded all the perfection of a Christian life. Therefore the most prudent Mother of wisdom wished to see all the divine mysteries, which the Apostles were to preach and the faithful to believe, reduced to a short formula. For if those truths were moulded into a few articles, they could more conveniently be brought to the mind of all, the whole Church would be united in one belief without any essential difference, and the whole spiritual edifice of the Gospel would thus rest and be built up on the same firm columns of one foundation.

212. In order to prepare for this work, the importance of which She recognized, She presented her wishes to the Lord, who had inspired them, and for more than forty days She persevered in this prayer with fasting, prostrations and other exercises. Thus, in the same way as it was proper for the giving of the written law that Moses, as mediator between God and the people, should fast and pray for forty days on mount Sinai; so also, for the new law of grace (Christ our Savior being its Author and the Mediator between the eternal Father and men), it was proper that the most blessed Mary should mediate between men and her divine Son. The Church was to have this new law written into the hearts, reduced to articles of faith, which should never change and never show any deficiency, because they are divine and indefectible truths. One day, while persevering in these petitions, She spoke to the Lord thus: "Most High Lord and eternal God, Creator and Ruler of all the uni-

verse, in thy ineffable kindness Thou hast begun the magnificent work of thy holy Church. It is not according to thy wisdom to leave imperfect any works of thy divine right hand; raise then to its high perfection this work, which Thou hast so gloriously commenced. Let not the sins of mortals, O my God, hinder Thee, since the blood and death of thy and my Onlybegotten out-clamor their malice; for they do not call out for vengeance, as the blood of Abel (Gen. 4, 11), but ask pardon for all that are guilty. Look upon the new children which the blood of Christ has engendered for Thee, and upon those who are to be engendered in the Church during the future ages. Give then thy holy Spirit to Peter thy vicar, and to the rest of the Apostles, in order that they may arrange into a convenient form the truths, upon which thy Church is to be founded, and in order that its children may know what to believe without differences of opinion."

213. In order to answer in person to these prayers of his Mother, her divine Son descended from heaven with immense glory and spoke to Her: "My beloved Mother, be relieved of thy affectionate anxiety and let thy ardent thirst for my glory and for the increase of the Church be satiated in my presence and converse. It is in my power to fulfill thy desires and thou art the one to oblige Me to do it, since I will deny nothing to thy desires and prayers." During these words the blessed Mary was prostrate on the ground in adoration of the Divinity and humanity of her Son and true God. But the Lord raised Her up and filled Her with ineffable joy and jubilee, by giving Her his benediction and enriching Her with new favors and gifts of his right hand. She remained in this ecstasy of delight enjoying the most exalted and mysterious converse of her Son and Lord, and her

anxiety for the welfare of the Church was appeased; for He promised Her great gifts and favors for the Church.

214. In answer to her prayer for the Apostles, besides promising to assist them in preparing the symbol of the faith, the Lord informed his Mother of the very wording of the propositions or articles, of which the Creed was to be composed. Of all this the most prudent Lady was well capable, as was explained more fully in the second part of this history; but now, when the time had arrived for executing what had been intended so long before, He wished to renew it all in the purest heart of his virgin Mother, in order that the fundamental truths of the Church might flow from the lips of Christ himself. It was also proper to counteract again the humility of the great Lady, so that She might consent to be called by those with whom She yet lived in mortal flesh and who were to preach and believe in this symbol, the Mother of God and a Virgin before and after his birth. For it was not to be expected, that She, who had been chosen by God for her humility in order to work the greatest of his wonders, would be willing of Herself to publish this prerogative; although it was greater to be the Mother and Virgin in the sight of God, than to be so called in the Church of God (Luke 1, 48).

215. Christ our Lord took leave of his blessed Mother and returned to the right hand of the Father. Immediately He inspired saint Peter his vicar and the rest with the desire of setting up a symbol of the universal faith of the Church. Accordingly they sought conference with the heavenly Mistress concerning its opportuneness and the measures to be taken for this purpose. They resolved to fast and persevere in prayer for ten continuous days, in order to receive the inspiration of the Holy Ghost in

this arduous affair. Having completed these ten days, which were also the last ten of the forty, in which the Queen had treated with the Lord about this matter, the twelve Apostles met in the presence of Mary, and saint Peter spoke to'them as follows:

216. "My dear brethren, the divine mercy, in its infinite goodness and through the merits of our Savior and Master Jesus, has favored his holy Church by gloriously multiplying its children, as we have seen and experienced in this short time. For this purpose the Almighty has multiplied miracles and prodigies and daily renews them through our ministry, having chosen us (though unworthy) as the instruments of his divine will in this work and for the glory and honor of his holy name. Together with these favors He has sent us tribulations and persecutions of the devil and of the world, in order that we may imitate our Savior and Captain, and in order that the Church, evenly ballasted, might reach more securely the port of rest and eternal felicity. The disciples have evaded the wrath of the chief priest and spread through the neighboring cities, preaching the faith of Christ our Redeemer and Lord. We must also soon depart and preach throughout the globe, according to the command of the Lord before ascending into heaven (Matth. 28, 19). Just as there is but one Baptism in which men are to receive this faith, so there must be but one doctrine, which the faithful are to believe. Hence it is meet that we, who are as yet gathered harmoniously in the Lord, define the truths and mysteries which we are to propound expressly to all the nations of the world, and thus, without difference of opinions, believe the same doctrines. It is the infallible promise of the Lord, that where two or three shall be gathered in his name, He shall be in their midst (Matth. 18, 20). Confiding in

his word we firmly hope, that He will now assist us with his divine Spirit to understand and define, in his name and by an unchangeable decree, the articles to be established in his holy Church as long as it shall last, to the end of the world."

217. All the Apostles consented to this proposal of saint Peter. Then he celebrated a Mass, in which he gave Communion to the most holy Mary and the Apostles, whereupon they all, including the blessed Mother, prostrated themselves in prayer calling upon the Holy Ghost. After continuing their prayers for some time, they heard the rumbling of thunder, as on the first coming down of the Holy Ghost upon the gathering of the faithful; at the same time the Cenacle was filled with light and splendor and all were enlightened by the Holy Spirit. Then the most blessed Mary asked each of the Apostles to define a mystery, according as the divine Spirit should inspire them. Thereupon saint Peter began, and was followed by the rest in the following order:

1. Saint Peter: I believe in God, the Father almighty, Creator of heaven and earth.

2. Saint Andrew: And in Jesus Christ, his only Son, our Lord.

3 and 4. Saint James the Greater: Who was conceived through operation of the Holy Ghost, born of the Virgin Mary.

5. Saint John: Suffered under Pontius Pilate, was crucified, died and was buried.

6 and 7. Saint Thomas: Descended into hell, arose from the dead on the third day.

8. Saint James the Less: Ascended into heaven, is seated at the right hand of God the Father almighty.

9. Saint Philip: From thence He shall come to judge the living and the dead.

10. Saint Bartholomew: I believe in the Holy Ghost.

11. Saint Matthew: In the holy Catholic Church, the Communion of saints.

12. Saint Simon: Forgiveness of sins.

13. Saint Thaddeus: The resurrection of the flesh.

14. Saint Mathias: Life everlasting. Amen.

218. This symbol, which we ordinarily call the Creed, the Apostles established after the martyrdom of saint Stephen and before the end of the first year after the death of the Savior. Afterwards, in order to refute the Arian and other heresies, the Church, in the councils held on their account, explained more fully the mysteries contained in the Apostles' Creed and composed the one now chanted in the Mass. But in substance both are one and the same and contain the fourteen articles, which are the basis for the catechetical teaching of the Christian faith and which we are all bound to believe in order to be saved. As soon as the Apostles had finished pronouncing this Creed, the Holy Ghost approved of it by permitting a voice to be heard in their midst saying: "You have decided well." Then the great Queen and Lady of heaven with all the Apostles gave thanks to the Most High; and She thanked also them for having merited the assistance of the divine Spirit, so as to be his apt instruments in promoting the glory of the Lord and the good of the Church. In confirmation of her faith and as an example to the faithful, the most prudent Mistress fell at the feet of saint Peter, loudly proclaimed her belief in the Catholic doctrine as contained in the symbol they had just now composed and formulated. This She did for Herself and in the name of all the faithful, saying to saint Peter: "My lord, whom I recognize as the vicar of my most holy Son, in thy hands, I, a vile wormlet, in my name and in the name of all the faithful

of the Church, confess and proclaim all that thou hast
set down as the divine and infallible truth of the Catholic Church; and in it I bless and exalt the Most High,
from whom it proceeds." She kissed the hands of the
vicar of Christ and of the rest of the Apostles. Thus
She was the first one thus openly to profess the Catholic
faith after it had been formulated into articles.

INSTRUCTION WHICH THE GREAT QUEEN OF THE ANGELS, MOST HOLY MARY, GAVE ME.

219. My daughter, besides the mysteries thou hast recorded in this chapter, I wish for thy greater information and consolation, to manifest to thee other secrets of
my activity. After the Apostles had formulated the
Creed, thou must know that I repeated it many times
during the day on my knees and with the profoundest
reverence. And whenever the words "born of the Virgin Mary" occurred, I prostrated myself upon the earth
with such humility, gratitude and praise of the Most
High, as no creature can comprehend. In these acts of
devotion I had present in my mind all the mortals in
order to make up for the irreverence with which they
pronounce these sacred words. Through my intercession the Lord was induced to inspire the Church to repeat so many times the Credo, the Ave Maria, and Pater
Noster in the divine office; to accustom the religious to
humiliate themselves in reciting them, and to genuflect
in the Credo of the Mass at the words: "Et incarnatus
est." Thus the Church, at least partially, seeks to pay the
debt it owes to the Lord for having vouchsafed such
knowledge, and for the mysteries, so worthy of reverence and gratitude, contained in the Creed.

220. Many times the holy angels sang to me the

Credo with wonderful harmony and sweetness, rejoicing my spirit. Sometimes they would sing the Ave Maria, including those words: "Blessed is the fruit of thy womb Jesus." Whenever they pronounced this most holy name, or the name Mary, they made a most profound bow, causing in me new effects of loving humility, abasing me to the very earth at the thought of how far exalted is the being of God above my own terrestrial existence. O my daughter, bear in mind the reverence with which thou shouldst recite the Credo, Pater and Ave, and do not make thyself guilty of the thoughtless rudeness of many of the faithful in this matter. The frequency with which these prayers and divine words are repeated in the Church should not infringe upon the proper reverence due to them. This presumption arises from pronouncing them merely by the lips without meditating upon their meaning. I desire that they be to thee a subject of continuous meditation; and for this purpose the Most High has given thee a taste for studying the catechism; and thou wilt please the Lord and me, if thou carry it with thee and read it many times, as thou hast been accustomed to and as I again charge thee to do from now on. Recommend it also to thy religious, for this kind of knowledge is the jewel which should adorn the spouses of Christ and which all Christians should bear about with them.

221. It should also impress thee, that I was so anxious to see the Creed written as soon as it was necessary for the welfare of the Church. To know what will advance the glory and service of God and benefit one's own conscience, and not to execute it, or at least to make no effort toward it, is a very reprehensible lukewarmness. And it is especially shameful in those men, who, whenever they are in want of any temporal good, brook no delay and clamorously ask God to satisfy their wishes; as for in-

stance, when they fail in health or fear bad crops, or when they dread being deprived of much less necessary, or even superfluous and dangerous things. At the same time, although they recognize their deep obligations to God, they pretend not to understand them, or delay their fulfillment out of negligence and want of love. Do thou guard thyself against and never permit this disorder. Just as I was most anxious in that which pertained to the service of the children of the Church, so do thou be punctual in all that thou perceivest to be the will of God, whether it is for the benefit of thy soul or for the benefit of thy neighbor; and thus thou wilt imitate my example.

CHAPTER XIII.

THE BLESSED MARY SENDS THE CREED TO THE DISCIPLES
AND OTHERS OF THE FAITHFUL; THEY WORK GREAT
WONDERS WITH IT; THE APOSTLES RESOLVE TO PAR-
TITION THE EARTH AMONG THEMSELVES; OTHER DO-
INGS OF THE GREAT QUEEN OF HEAVEN.

222. In the diligence, watchfulness and solicitude, which the most prudent Mother devoted to the government of her family, the Church, She was like a mother and like to the strong woman, of whom Solomon says, that she considered the paths and the ways of her household in order not to eat her bread in idleness (Prov. 31, 27). The great Lady knew and considered them with the plenitude and knowledge; and as She was clothed in the purple of her charity and in the spotless white of her peerless purity, therefore, in the fulness of her insight, She forgot nothing that was needed by her children and domestics, the faithful. As soon as the symbol of the faith was established, She, both with her own hands and with the assistance of the holy angels serving as her secretaries, provided innumerable copies of the Creed, which were sent without delay to all the disciples preaching in different parts of Palestine. She sent several copies to each one for distribution together with a special letter, in which She informed them of the measures taken by the Apostles and of their orders, that it should be accepted and professed by all the faithful.

223. As the disciples were scattered through different cities, some near and others far, She sent the symbol and

letter to those in the neighborhood by some of the faithful, and to those farther off, by her angels. To some of the disciples, in fact to the greater number of them, the angels appeared visibly; while to others they did not appear, but they placed these documents into their hands in an invisible manner, at the same time admirably moving their hearts. As well through these inspirations, as from the letter of the Queen, the disciples knew whence these messages had come. Moreover She exhorted the Apostles to distribute the written Creed in Jerusalem and in other places and to instruct the faithful, how the Lord had sent the Holy Ghost to inspire and approve it in such a signal manner and thereby imposed its veneration upon all. She told them to omit no means of making it well understood, that this was the only, invariable and secure doctrine, which was to be believed, confessed and preached throughout the Church as the sole means of obtaining grace and life everlasting.

224. The written copies of the Creed of the Apostles were distributed in a very few days among the faithful to their incredible benefit and consolation; for in their fervor they received them with highest reverence and devotion. The Holy Ghost, who had ordained this Creed for the security of the Church, immediately began to confirm it by new miracles and prodigies, operating not only through the hands of the Apostles and disciples, but also through many of the believers. Many who received it with special veneration and love, were suddenly enveloped in divine splendor, filled with heavenly science and celestial manifestations of the Holy Ghost. By these miracles others were in their turn moved to a desire of possessing and reverencing these documents. Others restored the sick to health, raised the dead or expelled the demons from the possessed by merely placing the Credo

upon them. Among other marvels it happened one day that a Jew, who was roused to anger at hearing a Christian devoutly reading the Creed and was about to tear it from his hands, fell dead before he could execute his design. From that time on, those that were baptized, being adults, were required to profess the faith according to the apostolic Creed; and while they pronounced it, the Holy Ghost visibly appeared above them.

225. The gift of tongues likewise continued; for the Holy Spirit gave it not only on the day of Pentecost, but to many of the faithful afterwards, who assisted in preaching or in giving instruction to the new believers; and whenever they spoke or preached to many together of different nationalities, they were understood by each nationality, though they spoke only in the Hebrew language. In like manner they were able to speak in other languages, when they happened upon a gathering of people all speaking the same foreign language. Thus was renewed all that had happened at the first coming down of the Holy Ghost. Besides these miracles the Apostles wrought many others, and whenever they laid their hands upon the believers, or confirmed them, the divine Spirit descended. So many miracles and prodigies were dispensed by the hands of the Almighty, that if they were all recorded, they would fill many volumes. Saint Luke in the Acts describes those in particular, which in justice should not be altogether left unnoticed in the Church of God. He adds in a general way, that they were very numerous, and therefore could not be included in his short history.

226. In pondering and writing of these things I was greatly astonished at the liberal bounty of the Almighty in thus often sending the Holy Ghost upon the believers in the primitive Church. In response to my wonder I

was informed of two reasons for this liberality: first, just as the wisdom, goodness and power of God so ardently desired men to participate in his Divinity by sharing with Him his eternal happiness and glory, that He induced the eternal Word to appear in this world in visible and passible flesh, so also the third Person descended many times in visible and appropriate form upon his Church, in order to establish it and confirm it with like and equally secure demonstrations of his omnipotence and love. Secondly, in the beginnings of the Church the merits of the passion and death of Christ, together with the prayers and intercession of his most holy Mother, were in a certain sense more acceptable and therefore (according to our way of understanding) more powerful with the eternal Father. For the children of the Church had not yet interposed the many and grievous sins, which have been committed since then and which have placed such great obstacles to the benefits of the Lord and to his Holy Spirit. Hence He does not now manifest Himself so familiarly to men as in the primitive Church.

227. Already a full year had passed since the death of the Savior, and now the Apostles, by divine impulse, began to consider about going forth to preach the faith throughout the world; for it was time that the name of God be preached also to the heathens and that they be taught the way of eternal salvation. In order to consult the will of God in the assignment of the kingdoms and provinces in which each one was to preach, they, upon the advice of their Queen, resolved to fast and pray for ten successive days. This practice of fasting and praying for ten days, which they had observed immediately after the Ascension in disposing themselves for the coming of the Holy Ghost, they afterwards also retained in pre-

paring themselves for the more important undertakings. Having completed these exercises, the vicar of Christ celebrated Mass and communicated the most blessed Mary and the eleven Apostles, as they had done in preparing the Creed and as is mentioned in the last chapter. After Mass they all persevered with their Queen for some time in most exalted prayer, ardently invoking the assistance of the Holy Ghost for the manifestation of his will in this matter.

228. Having done this, saint Peter spoke to them as follows: "My dearest brethren, let us prostrate ourselves all together before the throne of God and with all our heart and with deepest reverence let us confess our Lord Jesus Christ as the true God, the Lord and Redeemer of the world, professing his holy faith in the Creed which He has given us by the Holy Ghost and our subjection to his divine will." This they did and thereupon uttered aloud with saint Peter the following prayer: "Most high and eternal God, we, vile and insignificant men, worms of the earth, whom the Lord Jesus Christ in his clemency condescended to choose as ministers of his holy doctrine and law and founders of his Church through the whole world, with one heart and soul prostrate ourselves to suffer and die for the confession and spread of the holy faith in the world according to the commands of our Lord and Master Jesus Christ. We wish to be spared no labors, difficulties or tribulations in the performance of this work, even unto death. But distrusting our weakness, we beseech Thee, Lord God most High, send upon us thy divine Spirit to govern and direct our footsteps in the imitation of our Master and to visit us with his strength. Do Thou manifest and instruct us to which kingdoms and provinces each of us shall depart according to thy good pleasure for the preaching of thy holy name."

229. At the ending of this prayer a wonderful light descended upon the Cenacle surrounding them all and a voice was heard saying: "My vicar Peter shall point out the province, which falls to each one. I shall govern and direct him by my light and spirit." The appointments themselves the Holy Ghost left to saint Peter in order to confirm anew his power as head and universal pastor of the Church, and in order that the Apostles might understand, that it was to be founded throughout the world under the direction of saint Peter and his successors, to whom they were to be subject as the vicars of Christ. In this sense the Apostles understood it, and I was given to understand, that such was the will of the Most High. Saint Peter hearing this voice, proceeded to partition out the provinces. He began with himself, and said: "I, my Lord, offer myself to suffer and die in imitation of my Lord and Redeemer, preaching the faith at present in Jerusalem, and afterwards in Pontus, Galatia, Bythinia and Cappadocia, provinces of Asia; and I shall take up my residence at first in Antioch and afterwards in Rome, where I will establish my seat and found the Cathedra of Christ our Redeemer and Master, and where the head of his Church shall have his residence." These words of saint Peter were spoken in obedience to a positive command of the Lord, pointing out the Roman Church as the centre and capital of the universal Church. Without such a command of the Lord, saint Peter would not have decided this difficult and important matter.

230. Saint Peter then continued: "The servant of Christ, our dearest brother Andrew, will follow his Master preaching his faith in the Scythian provinces of Europe, Epirus and Thrace; and from the city of Patras in Achaia he will govern all that province, and the others of his lot, as far as possible."

"The servant of Christ, our dearest brother James the greater, will follow his Master preaching the faith in Judea, in Samaria and in Spain; thence he shall return in order to preach the doctrine of our Lord Jesus Christ in this city of Jerusalem."

"The most dear brother John shall obey the will of our Savior and Master as made known to him from the Cross, discharging the duties of a son toward our great Mother and Mistress. He shall serve Her and assist Her with filial reverence and fidelity; he shall administer to Her the sacred mysteries of the Eucharist and shall also take care of the faithful in Jerusalem during our absence. And when our God and Redeemer shall have taken into heaven his most blessed Mother, he shall follow his Master in the preaching of the faith in Asia Minor, governing the churches there established from the island of Patmos, whither he shall retire on account of persecution."

"The servant of Christ, our dearest brother Thomas, will follow his Master preaching in India, in Persia and among the Parthians, Medes, Hircanians, Brahmans, Bactrians. He shall baptize the three Magi Kings and, as they shall be attracted by the rumor of his preaching and his miracles, he shall instruct them fully in all things according to their expectations."

"The servant of Christ, our dearest brother James, shall follow his Master in his office of pastor and bishop of Jerusalem, where he shall preach to all the Jews and shall assist John in the attendance and service of the great Mother of our Savior."

"The servant of Christ, our dearest brother Philip, shall follow his Master preaching and teaching in the provinces Phrygia and Scythia of Asia, and in the city called Hieropolis in Phrygia."

"The servant of Christ, our dearest brother Bartholomew, shall follow his Master preaching in Lycaonia, part of Cappadocia in Asia; and he shall go to further India and afterwards to Armenia Minor."

"The servant of Christ, our dearest brother Matthew, shall first teach the Hebrews, and then shall follow his Master, preaching in Egypt and Ethiopia."

"The servant of Christ, our dearest brother Simon, shall follow his Master preaching in Babylon, Persia and also in the kingdom of Ethiopia."

"The servant of Christ, our dearest brother Judas Thaddeus, shall follow our Master, preaching in Mesopotamia, and afterwards shall join Simon to preach in Babylon and in Persia."

"The servant of Christ, our dearest brother Mathias, shall follow our Master, preaching his holy faith in the interior of Ethiopia and in Arabia, and afterwards He shall return to Palestine. And may the Spirit of God accompany us all, govern and assist us, so that in all places we fulfill his holy and perfect will, and may He give us his benediction, in whose name I now give it to all."

231. These were the words of saint Peter. When he ceased speaking a loud thunder was heard and the Cenacle was filled with splendor and refulgence in witness of the presence of the Holy Ghost. From the midst of this splendor was heard a sweet and soft voice saying: "Let each one accept his allotment." They prostrated themselves upon the ground and with one voice said: "Most High Lord, thy word and the word of thy vicar we obey with a prompt and joyous heart, and our souls rejoice and are filled with thy sweetness in the abundance of thy wonderful works." This entire and ready obedience of the Apostles to the vicar of Christ our

Savior, since it was the effect of their ardent and loving desire to die for his holy faith, disposed them on that occasion for the grace of once more receiving the Holy Ghost, who confirmed and augmented the favors they had already received. They were filled with a new light and knowledge concerning the peoples and provinces assigned to them by saint Peter, and each one recognized the conditions, nature and customs of the kingdoms singled out for him, being furnished interiorly with the most distinct and abundant information concerning each. The Most High gave them new fortitude to encounter labors; agility for overcoming distances, although in this regard they were afterwards to be frequently assisted by the holy angels; and the fire of divine love, so that they became inflamed like seraphim lifted far beyond the condition and sphere of mere human creatures.

232. The most blessed Queen was present at all these events, and the workings of the divine power in the Apostles and in Herself, were very clear to Her; for on this occasion, She experienced more of the divine influences than all of them together. As She was exalted supereminently above all creatures, so the increase of her gifts was in like proportion, transcending immeasurably those of others. The Most High renewed in the purest spirit of his Mother the infused knowledge concerning all creatures, and especially concerning the kingdoms and nations assigned to the Apostles. She knew all that each one knew, and more than they all together, because She received a personal and individual knowledge of each person to whom the faith of Christ was to be preached; and She was made relatively just as familiar with all the earth and its inhabitants, as She was with Her oratory and all those that entered therein.

233. As I have said above and shall often repeat far-

ther on, the knowledge of Mary was the knowledge of a supreme Mistress, Mother, Governess and Sovereign of the Church, which the Almighty had placed in her hands. She was to take care of all, from the highest to the lowest of the saints, and also of the sinners as the children of Eve. As no one was to receive any blessing or favor from the hands of her Son except through that of his Mother, it was necessary that this most faithful Dispensatrix of grace should know all of her family, whom She was to guard as a Mother, and such a Mother! The great Lady therefore had not only infused images and knowledge of all this, but She actually experienced it according as the disciples and Apostles proceeded in their work of preaching. Before Her lay open all their labors and dangers, and the attacks of the demons against them; the petitions and prayers of these and of all the faithful, so that She might be able to support them with her own, or aid them through her angels or by Herself in person; for in all these different ways did She render her assistance, as we shall see in many events yet to be described.

234. I wish merely to state here, that besides the knowledge derived by our Queen from infused images She had also in God himself another knowledge of things through her abstractive vision, by which She continually saw the Divinity. But there was a difference between these two different kinds of knowledge: since, when she saw in God the labors of the Apostles and of all the faithful of the Church, enjoying at the same time through this vision a certain participation of the eternal beatitude, the most loving Mother was not affected with the sensible sorrow and compassion, which filled Her when perceiving these tribulations themselves through images. In this latter kind of vision She felt and bewailed them with

maternal compassion. In order that this merit might not be wanting in Her, the Lord conferred this second kind of knowledge upon Her for all the time of her pilgrimage here below. Joined with this plenitude of infused species and knowledge, She held also absolute command of her faculties, as I said above, so that She admitted no images or ideas except those that were absolutely necessary for sustaining life, or for some work of charity or perfection. With this adornment and beauty, which was patent to the angels and saints, the heavenly Lady was an object of admiration, inducing them to praise and glorify the Most High for the worthy exercise of all his attributes in Mary, his most holy instrument.

235. On this occasion She offered a most profound prayer for the perseverance and courage of the Apostles in their preaching throughout the world. And the Lord promised Her, that He would guard and assist them to manifest the glory of his name, and that He would at the end worthily reward them for their labors and merits. By this promise most holy Mary was filled with grateful jubilee and She exhorted the Apostles to give themselves up to this work with all their heart, to set out joyfully and confidently for the conversion of the world. Speaking to them many other words of sweetness and life, She congratulated them on her knees in the name of her divine Son for the obedience they had shown, and in her own name, She thanked them for the zeal they had manifested for the honor of the Lord and for the blessings they had brought to souls by their sacrifice. She kissed the hands of each of the Apostles, offering her prayers and her services and asking them for their blessing, which they, as priests of God, gave Her.

236. A few days after the partition of the earth among the Apostles, they began to leave Jerusalem, especially

those that were allotted the provinces of Palestine, and first among them was saint James the greater. Others stayed longer in Jerusalem, because the Lord wished the faith to be preached there more abundantly and the Jews to be called before all others, if they chose to come and accept the invitation to the marriage-feast of the Gospel; for in the blessing of the Redemption this people, although more ungrateful than the heathens, was especially favored. Afterwards all the Apostles gradually departed for the regions assigned to them, according as time and season demanded and as obedience to the divine Spirit, the counsel of the most holy Mary, and the order of saint Peter dictated. But before leaving Jerusalem each one visited the holy places, such as the garden, Calvary, the holy Sepulchre, the place of the Ascension, Bethany and the other memorable spots as far as possible. All of them showed their veneration, moved even to tears and regarding with loving wonder the very earth, which the Savior had touched. Then they visited the Cenacle, reverencing the spot where so many mysteries had taken place. There, again commending themselves to her protection, they took leave of the great Queen of heaven. The blessed Mother dismissed them with words full of sweetness and divine virtue.

237. But admirable was the solicitude and care of the most prudent Lady in showing Herself as the true Mother of the Apostles at their departure. For each of the twelve She made a woven tunic similar to that of Christ our Savior, of a color between brown and ash-gray; and in order to weave these garments She called to aid her holy angels. She furnished each of the Apostles garments of the same kind and like to that formerly worn by their Master Jesus: for She wished that they should imitate Him even in their garments and thereby be known ex-

teriorly as his disciples. The great Lady procured also
twelve crosses of the height and size of each of the
Apostles and gave one to each, so that, as a witness of
their doctrine and for their consolation, they might carry
it along in their wanderings and their preaching. Each
of the Apostles preserved and carried this cross with him
to his death; and as they were so loud in praise of the
Cross, some of the tyrants made use of this very instrument to torment them happily to death.

238. Moreover the devout Mother furnished each
one of them with a small metal case, in which She placed
three of the thorns from the crown of her divine Son,
some pieces of the cloths in which She had wrapped the
infant Savior, and of the linen with which She had
wiped and caught the most precious blood of the Circumcision and Passion of the Lord. All these sacred pledges
She had preserved with the greatest care and veneration,
as the Mother and the Treasure-keeper of heaven. In
order to consign them to the Apostles She called them
together and, with the majesty of a Queen and the tenderness of a Mother, She told them that these remem-
brances, with which She would enrich them on their
departure, were the greatest treasures in her possession;
for in them they would carry with them vivid remem-
brances of her divine Son and the certain assurance,
that the Lord loved them as his children and as ministers
of the Most High. Then She handed them those relics,
which they received with tears of consolation and joy.
They thanked the great Queen for these favors and prostrated themselves in adoration of the sacred relics. Em-
bracing they bade farewell to each other, saint James
being the first to depart and commence his mission.

239. I was given to understand, that the Apostles
preached not only in the countries assigned to them by

saint Peter, but in many other neighboring and more remote regions. This is not difficult to understand; because many times they were carried from one country to
another by the angels, not only in order to preach, but
in order to consult with each other, especially with the
vicar of Christ saint Peter, and still much more frequently were they brought in the presence of their Queen,
whose sympathy and counsel they needed in the arduous
enterprise of planting the faith in so many different
and barbarous nations. If, in order to bring nourishment to Daniel, the angel took Habbacuc to Babylon
(Dan. 14, 35), it is nothing strange, that such miracles
should be performed for the Apostles in order that they
might preach Christ, make known the Divinity, and plant
the universal Church for the salvation of the human
race. Above I have made mention of the angel, who
carried Philip, one of the seventy-two disciples, from the
road of Gaza to Azotus, as related by saint Luke (Acts
8, 40). All these miracles, and innumerable others unknown to us, were necessary to these men, who were to
be sent to so many kingdoms, provinces, and peoples yet
in possession of the devil, full of idolatries, errors and
abominations, which was the condition of the world at
the time the incarnate Word came to save the human
race.

INSTRUCTION GIVEN TO ME BY THE QUEEN OF THE
ANGELS.

240. My daughter, by the lessons contained in this
chapter I wish to draw thee to deplore, with inmost
groaning and sighing and, if possible, with tears of blood,
the difference between the state of the holy Church in
our times and that of those primitive times; how its
purest gold of holiness has been obscured (Thren. 4, 1),

and the ancient beauty in which the Apostles have founded it, is lost; how it has sought foreign and deceitful powders and paints to cover the horrid and distorted ugliness of vice. In order that thou mayest penetrate into this truth, thou must renew in thyself the consideration of the force and eagerness, with which the Divinity seeks to communicate his goodness and perfection to creatures. So great is the impetus of the river of God's goodness overflowing on mankind, that only the free will of man, which He has given to him in order to receive its benefits, can raise a dam against it; and whenever, through this free will, man resists the influence and force of the divine Goodness, he (according to thy mode of understanding), violates and grieves this immense love in its very essence. But if creatures would place no obstacle and permit its operations, the whole soul would be inundated and satiated with participation in its divine essence and attributes. It would raise the fallen from the dust, enrich the indigent children of Adam, place them above all their miseries and seat them with the princes of his glory (I Kings 2, 8).

241. From this, my daughter, thou wilt understand two things unknown to human wisdom. First, how pleasing to the highest Goodness is the service of those who, with an ardent zeal for God's glory, devote their labor and solicitude toward removing the obstacles, which men place to their own justification and the communication of his favors. The satisfaction of the Most High, arising from this work in others, cannot be estimated in this mortal life. On this account the ministry of the Apostles, the prelates, the priests and preachers of the divine word are so highly exalted; for they succeed in office those, who founded the Church and who labored in its preservation and extension; all of them are to be

co-operators and executors of the immense love of God for the souls created to be sharers in his Divinity. Secondly, thou must ponder the greatness and abundance of the gifts and favors, which the infinite power communicates to those souls, who do not hinder his most liberal bounty. The Lord manifested this truth immediately in the beginnings of the evangelical Church, when, to all those who were to enter into it, He showed his bounty by such great prodigies and wonders, frequently sending the Holy Ghost in a visible manner, working miracles in those who accepted the Creed, and showering forth other hidden favors on the faithful.

242. But most of all shone forth his almighty power and munificence in the Apostles and disciples, because in them there was no hindrance to his eternal and holy will and they were true instruments and executors of the divine love, imitators and successors of Christ and followers of truth. Hence they were elevated to an ineffable participation in the attributes of God, especially as regards his science, holiness and power, working for themselves and for the souls such great miracles, as mortal man cannot ever sufficiently extol. After the Apostles, other children were born to the Church, in which, from generation to generation, this divine wisdom and its effects were transplanted (Ps. 44, 17). Leaving aside at present the innumerable martyrs who shed their blood for Christ and gave their lives for the holy faith, consider the founders of religions, the great saints, who flourished in them, the doctors, the bishops, the prelates and apostolical men, through whom the bounty and omnipotence of God was so abundantly manifested. They are so great, that others, who are ministers of God for the welfare of souls, and all the faithful, can have no excuse, even if God does not work similar ones in those He finds fit for his operations.

243. And to the greater confusion of the negligent ministers of the Church in our days, I desire thee to understand, that in his eternal decrees the Most High dispenses his infinite treasures of the souls through the ministry of the prelates, priests, preachers, and teachers of his divine word. As far as his will is concerned, they might all be angelic rather than human in their holiness and perfection; they might enjoy many privileges and exemptions of nature and grace, and thus become fit ministers of the Most High, if only they would not pervert the order of his infinite wisdom and if they lived up to the dignity to which they are called and chosen before all others. This infinite kindness of God is just as great now, as in the first ages of the Church; the inclination of the highest Goodness to enrich souls is not changed, nor can it be; his condescending liberality has not diminished; the love of his Church is always at its height; his mercy is just as much concerned at the miseries of men, which in our times are become innumerable; the clamor of the sheep of Christ is louder than ever; the prelates, priests and ministers are more numerous than heretofore. If this is so, to what is to be attributed the loss of so many souls and the ruin of the Christian people? Why is it, that the infidels not only do not enter the Church, but subject it to so much affliction and sorrow? that the prelates and ministers do not shine before the world, exhibiting the splendors of Christ, as in the ages gone by and in the primitive Church?

244. O my daughter, I invite thee to let thy tears flow over this loss and ruin. Consider how the stones of the sanctuary are scattered about in streets of the city (Thren. 4, 1). See how the priests of the Lord have assimilated themselves to the people (Is. 24, 2), when, on the contrary, they should raise the people to the holi-

ness, which is due to priesthood. The sacerdotal dignity
and the precious vestments of virtue are soiled by contagion with the worldly; the anointed of the Lord, consecrated solely to his worship and intercourse, have lapsed
from their noble and godlike station; they have lost their
beauty in debasing themselves to vile actions, unworthy
of their exalted position among men. They affect vanity;
they indulge greed and avarice; they serve their own interest; they love money, they place their hopes in treasures of silver and gold; they submit to the flatteries and
to the slavery of the worldly and powerful; and, to their
still lower degradation, they subject themselves to the pet-
ty whims of women, and sometimes make themselves participants in their counsels of malice and wickedness.
There is hardly a sheep in the fold of Christ, which rec-
ognizes in them the voice of its Pastor, or finds from
them the nourishment of that redeeming virtue and holiness, which they should show forth. The little ones ask
for bread, and there is none to distribute (Thren. 4, 4).
And if it is dealt out in self-interest or as a compliment,
how can it afford wholesome nourishment to the neces-
sitous and infirm from such leprous hands? How shall
the heavenly Physician confide to such administrators the
medicine of life? Or how can the guilty ones intercede
and mediate mercy for those who are less, or even equally, guilty?

245. These are the reasons why the prelates and priests
of our times do not perform the miracles of the Apostles
and disciples, and of those who in the primitive Church
imitated their lives by an ardent zeal for the honor of the
Lord and the conversion of souls. On this account the
treasures of the blood and death of Christ in the Church
do not bear the same fruits, either in his priests and
ministers, nor in the other mortals; for if they neglect

and forget to make them fruitful in themselves, how can they expect them to flow over on the rest of the human family? On this account the infidels are not converted on learning of the true faith, although they live within sight of the princes of the Church, the ministers and preachers of the Gospel. The Church in our times is richer in temporal goods, rents and possessions; it abounds with learned men, great prelacies, and multiplied dignities. As all these advantages are due to the blood of Christ, they ought all to be used in his honor and service, promoting the conversion of souls, supporting his poor and enhancing the worship and veneration of his holy name.

246. Is this the use made of the temporal riches of the Church? Let the captives answer, whether they are ransomed by the rents of the Church; let the infidels testify, whether they are converted, whether heresies are extirpated at the expense of the ecclesiastical treasures. But the public voice will loudly proclaim, that from these same treasures palaces were built, primogenitures established, the airy nothingness of noble titles bought; and, what is most deplorable, it is known to what profane and vile uses those that succeed in the ecclesiastical office put the treasures of the Church, how they dishonor the High-priest Christ and in their lives depart just as far from the imitation of Christ and the Apostles, as the most profane men of the world. If the preaching of the divine word by these ministers is so dead and without power of vivifying the hearers, it is not the fault of truth or of the holy Scriptures; but it is because of the abuse and of the distorted intentions of those that preach it. They seek to compromise the glory of Christ with their own selfish honor and vain esteem, the spiritual goods, with base acquisition of stipends; and if those

two selfish ends are reached, they care not for other results of their preaching. Therefore they wander away from the pure and sincere doctrine, and sometimes even from the truth, which the sacred authors have recorded in the Scriptures and according to which the holy teachers have explained them; they slime it over with their own ingenious subtleties, seeking to cause rather the pleasure and admiration of their hearers than their advancement. As the divine truths reach the ears of the sinners so adulterated, they impress upon the mind rather the ingenious sophistry of the preacher, than the charity of Christ; they bring with it no force or efficacy for penetrating the hearts, although full of ingenious artifice to delight the ears.

247. Let not the chastisement of these vanities and abuses, and of others unknown to the world, astonish thee, my dearest, and be not surprised, that divine justice has so much forsaken the prelates, ministers and preachers of his word, or that the Catholic Church, having such an exalted position in its beginnings, should now be brought to such low estate. And if there are some priests and ministers, who are not infected with these lamentable vices, the Church owes so much the more to my divine Son in these times, when He is so deeply offended and outraged. With those that are zealous, He is most liberal; but they are few in number, as is evident from the ruin of the Christian people and from the contempt into which the priests and preachers of the Gospel have fallen. For if the number of the perfect and the zealous workers were great, without a doubt sinners would reform and amend their lives; many infidels would be converted; all would look upon and hear with reverence and fear such preachers, priests and prelates, they would respect them for their dignity and holiness, and not for their usurped

authority and outward show, which induces a reverence too much like worldly applause and altogether without fruit. Do not be afraid or abashed for having written all this for they themselves know that it is the truth and thou dost not write of thy own choice, but at my command. Hence bewail such a sad state, and invite heaven and earth to help thee in thy weeping; for there are few who sorrow on account of it, and this is the greatest of all the injuries committed against the Lord by the children of the Church.

CHAPTER XIV.

248. Our mother the Church, governed by the divine
Spirit, celebrates the conversion of saint Paul as one of
the greatest miracles of grace for the consolation of sinners; for, from a virulent and blasphemous persecutor of
the name of Christ, as saint Paul calls himself (1 Tim. 1,
13), he was changed to an Apostle obtaining mercy
through divine grace. As in obtaining it our great Queen
bore such a prominent part, this rare miracle of the Omnipotent must not be passed over in this history. But its
greatness can be better understood if the state of saint
Paul as a persecutor of the Church at the time of his
calling is explained, and when the causes, which induced
him to signalize himself as such a strong champion of the
law of Moses and bitter persecutor of Christ, are known.

249. Saint Paul was distinguished in Judaism for two
reasons. The one was his own character, and the other
was the diligence of the demon in availing himself of his
naturally good qualities. Saint Paul was of a disposition
generous, magnanimous, most noble, kind, active, courageous and constant. He had acquired many of the
moral virtues. He glorified in being a staunch professor
of the law of Moses, and in being studious and learned
in it; although in truth he was ignorant of its essence, as
he himself confesses to Timothy, because all his learning
was human and terrestrial; like many Jews, he knew

237

the law merely from the outside, without its spirit and
without the divine insight, which was necessary to understand it rightly and to penetrate its mysteries.   But as his
ignorance seemed to him real knowledge and as he was
gifted with a retentive memory and keen understanding,
he was a great zealot for the traditions of the rabbis
(Gal. 1, 14).   He judged it an outrage and absurdity,
that (as he thought), a new law, invented by a Man
crucified as a criminal, should be published in opposition
to them and to that law, which was given by God himself
and received by Moses on the mount (Exod. 24). Hence
he conceived a great hatred and contempt for Christ, his
law and his disciples.   Steeped in this error he called into
activity all his moral virtues, (if that can be called virtue
which was devoid of true charity), and prided himself
much in combating the errors of others.   For that is a
common fault with the children of Adam, that they please
themselves in some good work without making the much
more important effort to reform some of their vices.   In
this self-deception lived and acted Saul, deeply convinced that he was zealously promoting the honor of God
in upholding the ancient law of Moses and its divine or-
dainments.   It appeared to him that in acting thus he
was defending God's honor; for he had not really understood this law, which in its ceremonies and figures was
but temporal and not eternal and which was necessarily
to be abrogated by a more wise and powerful Legislator,
as Moses himself foretold (Deut. 18, 15).

250. This indiscreet zeal and vehemence was fanned
by the malice of Lucifer and his ministers, who irritated
and roused him to even greater hatred against the law
of our Savior Jesus Christ.   Many times have I in the
course of this history mentioned the malicious attempts
and infernal schemes of this dragon against the holy

Church. Among them was his anxious search for men, who should serve as apt and efficient instruments and executors of his malice. Lucifer by himself or his demons, although they are able to tempt men singly, are yet unable to raise up their rebellious banners in public or become leaders in any sect or sedition against God, unless it be through the assistance of some human being in leading on the blind and unenlightened. This cruel enemy was infuriated by the happy beginnings of the holy Church; he feared its progress, and burned with envy to see beings of a lower nature than himself raised to the participation of the Divinity and glory, which he himself had lost. He recognized the inclinations of Saul, his habits and the state of his interior, and all seemed to harmonize well with his own designs of destroying the Church of Christ through the willing hands of unbelievers.

251. Lucifer consulted the other demons concerning this wicked plan in a meeting held especially for this purpose. With common accord the dragon and others of the demons resolved ceaselessly to urge on Saul by stirring up his anger against the Apostles and the whole flock of Christ, using suggestions and reasonings adapted to his state of mind; and, in order that he might be the sooner influenced by them, they were to represent his indignation as a virtue to be gloried in. The demons executed this resolve to the letter and without losing any occasion. Although Paul was dissatisfied and opposed to the teaching of our Lord even before his death on the Cross; yet he had not yet declared himself so zealous a defender of the law of Moses and adversary of the Lord. It was only at the death of saint Stephen, that he showed the wrath, which the infernal dragon had roused against the followers of Christ. As that enemy had

found the heart of Saul on that occasion so ready to execute all his malicious suggestions, he became so arrogant in his malice, that it seemed to him he need not desire more, and that this man would offer no resistance to any malice he ever could propose.

252. In his impious presumption Lucifer tried to induce Saul to attempt single-handed the life of all the Apostles, and, with still greater presumption, even the life of the most blessed Mary. To such a point of insanity rose the pride of this most bloodthirsty dragon. But he deceived himself. The disposition of Saul was most noble and generous, and therefore it appeared to him beneath his dignity and honor to stoop to such crimes and act the part of an assassin, when he could, as it seemed to him, destroy the law of Christ by the power of reasoning and open justice. He felt a still greater horror at the thought of killing the most blessed Mother, on account of the regard due to Her as a woman; and because he had seen Her so composed and constant in the labors and in the Passion of Christ. On this account She seemed to him a magnanimous Woman and worthy of veneration. She had indeed won his respect, together with some compassion for her sorrows and afflictions, the magnitude of which had become publicly known. Hence he gave no admittance to the inhuman suggestions of the demon against the life of the most blessed Mary. This compassion for Her hastened not a little the conversion of Saul. Neither did he further entertain the treacherous designs against the apostles, although Lucifer sought to make their assassination appear as a deed worthy of his courageous spirit. Rejecting all these wicked thoughts, he resolved to incite all the Jews to persecute the Church, until it should be destroyed together with the name of Christ.

253. As the dragon and his cohorts could not attain more, they contented themselves with having brought Saul at least to this resolve. The dreadful wrath of these demons against God and his creatures can be estimated from the fact, that on that very day they held another meeting in order to consult how they could preserve the life of this man, whom they had found so well adapted to execute their malice. These deadly enemies well know, that they have no jurisdiction over the lives of men, and that they can neither give nor take life, unless permitted by God on some particular occasion; nevertheless they wished to make themselves the guardians and the physicians of the life and health of Saul as far as their power extended, namely, by keeping active his forethought against whatever was harmful and suggesting the use of what was naturally beneficial to the welfare of life and limb. Yet with all their efforts they were unable to hinder the work of grace, when God so wished it. Far were they from suspecting, that Saul would ever accept the faith of Christ, and that the life, which they were trying to preserve and lengthen, was to redound to their own ruin and torment. Such events are provided by the wisdom of the Most High, in order that the devil, being deceived by his evil counsels, may fall into his own pits and snares, and in order that all his machinations may serve for the fulfillment of the divine and irresistible will.

254. Such were the decrees of the highest Wisdom in order that the conversion of Saul might be more wonderful and glorious. With this intention God permitted Satan, after the death of saint Stephen, to instigate Saul to go to the chief priests with fierce threats against the disciples of Christ, who had left Jerusalem, and to solicit permission for bringing them as prisoners to Jerusalem

from wherever he should find them (Acts 9, 1). For
this enterprise Saul offered his person and possessions,
and even his life; at his own cost and without salary he
made this journey in order that the new Law, preached
by the disciples of the Crucified, might not prevail
against the Law of his ancestors. This offer was readily
favored by the high-priest and his counselors; they immediately gave to Saul the commission he asked, especially to go to Damascus, whither, according to report, some
of the disciples had retired after leaving Jerusalem. He
prepared for the journey, hiring officers of justice and
some soldiers to accompany him. But his by far most
numerous escort were the many legions of demons, who
in order to assist him in this enterprise, came forth from
hell, hoping that with all this show of force and through
Saul, they might be able to make an end of the Church
and entirely devastate it with fire and blood. This was
really the intention of Saul, and the one with which Lucifer and his demons sought to inspire him and his companions. But let us leave him for the present on his
journey to Damascus, anxious to seize all the disciples
of Christ, whom he should find in the synagogues of that
city.

255. Nothing of all this was unknown to the Queen
of heaven; for in addition to her science and vision penetrating to the inmost thoughts of men and demons, the
Apostles were solicitous in keeping Her informed of all
that befell the followers of her Son. Long before this
time She had known that Saul was to be an Apostle of
Christ, a preacher to the gentiles, and a man distinguished
and wonderful in the Church; for of all these things her
Son informed Her, as I said in the second part of this
history. But as She saw the persecution becoming more
violent and the glorious fruits and results of the con-

version of Saul delayed, and as She moreover saw how
the disciples of Christ, who knew nothing of the secret
intentions of the Most High, were afflicted and somewhat discouraged at the fury and persistence of his persecution, the kindest Mother was filled with great sorrow.
Considering, in her heavenly prudence, how important was this affair, She roused Herself to new courage and confidence in her prayers for the welfare of the
Church and the conversion of Saul.   Prostrate in the
presence of her Son, She poured forth the following
prayer:

256. "Most high Lord, Son of the eternal Father, true
God of the true God, engendered of his own and indivisible substance and, by the ineffable condescension of thy
infinite goodness, become my Son and the life of my
soul, how shall I, thy slave, continue to live, if the persecution of the beloved Church Thou hast commended to
my care shall prevail and be not put down by thy almighty power?   How shall my heart behold the fruit
of thy precious blood despised and trodden under foot?
If Thou, my Lord, givest to me the children begotten by
Thee in the Church and if I am to love them and look
upon them as a Mother, how shall I be consoled, when
I see them thus oppressed and destroyed for confessing
thy holy name and loving Thee with a sincere heart?
Thine is the power and the wisdom; and it is not proper
that he should glory against Thee, who is the dragon of
hell, the enemy of thy name, and the slanderer of my
children and thy brethren.   My Son, confound the pride
of this ancient serpent, which in its pride rises up anew
to vent its fury against the simple sheep of thy flock.
Behold how Lucifer has drawn into his deceits Saul,
whom Thou hast chosen and set apart as thy Apostle.   It
is time, O my God, that Thou show thy Omnipotence and

save this soul, through whom and in whom thy name is to be so highly exalted, and so much good to be secured for all the world."

257. The most blessed Lady persevered in this prayer for a long time, offering to suffer and die, if necessary, for the welfare of the holy Church and the conversion of Saul. As in his infinite wisdom her divine Son had foreseen this mediation of his beloved Mother, He descended from Heaven and appeared to Her in person, while She was praying in the retirement of her oratory. He said to Her: "My beloved Mother, in whom I find the fulfillment of all my will and pleasure, what are thy requests? Tell Me what thou wishest?" As usual She prostrated Herself in the presence of her divine Son and adoring Him as the true God, said: "My highest Lord, far in advance dost Thou know the hearts and the thoughts of thy creatures, and my desires are open to thy eyes. My petitions are those of one knowing thy infinite charity for men, of the mother of thy Church, the advocate of sinners and thy slave. If I have received all from Thee without my merit, I cannot fear to be unheard in my desires for thy glory. I ask, O my Son, that Thou look upon the affliction of thy Church and that, like a loving Father, Thou hasten the relief of thy children engendered by thy most precious blood."

258. The Lord delighted in the voice and clamors of his most loving Mother and Spouse; and therefore He asked more particularly, as if ignorant of what She desired Him to grant and what beforehand could not be denied to her great merits and love. In these ruses of love Christ our Lord continued for some time conversing with his sweetest Mother, while She pleaded for the end of persecution and the conversion of Saul. Among other things He said: "My Mother, if in my

mercy I show clemency to Saul, how shall my justice be satisfied, since Saul persists in the deepest unbelief and malice and with all his heart serves my enemies for the destruction of my Church and the blotting out of my name from the face of the earth, thus meriting my wrath and chastisement?" To this argument, which was so conclusive on the side of justice, the Mother of mercy and wisdom was not at a loss for response, and She answered: "My Lord and eternal God, my Son, the turgid floods of guilt in Saul were not sufficient to extinguish the fire of thy divine love, when, as Thou hast thyself manifested to me, Thou didst choose Paul as thy Apostle and as a vase of election, acceptable to thy divine mind and worthy to be written in thy memory. More powerful and efficacious were thy infinite mercies, by which Thou hast founded thy beloved Church, and therefore I do not ask anything, which Thou thyself hast not resolved upon beforehand; but I grieve, my Son, that this soul should proceed to greater length for the ruin and perdition of itself and of others (if it can be like that of others), and that a hindrance should be placed to the glory of thy name, to the joy of the angels and saints, to the consolation of the just, to the confidence afforded to sinners, and to the confusion of thy enemies. Do not then, my Son and Lord, despise the prayers of thy Mother; let thy divine decrees be executed and let me see thy name magnified; for the time and the occasion are opportune and my heart cannot suffer such a blessing to be delayed."

259. During this appeal the charity in the bosom of the most chaste Virgin Queen broke out into such a flame. that without a doubt it would have consumed her natural life, if the Lord had not preserved Her by the miraculous interference of his almighty power. Although in

order to enjoy the delight of the excessive love of this Creature, He permitted his blessed Mother to suffer some sensible pain and, as it were, to fall into a kind of swoon, yet her Son, who according to our way of understanding, could not longer resist the love which wounded his heart, consoled and restored Her by yielding to her prayers. He said: "My Mother, chosen among all creatures, let thy will be done without delay. I will do with Saul as Thou askest, and will so change him, that from this moment he will be a defender of the Church which he persecutes, and a preacher of my name and glory. I shall now proceed to receive him immediately into my friendship and grace."

260. Thereupon Jesus Christ our Lord disappeared from the presence of his most blessed Mother leaving Her still engaged in prayer and furnished with a clear insight into what was to happen. Shortly afterward the Lord appeared to Saul on the road near Damascus, whither, in his ever increasing fury against Jesus, his accelerated journey had already brought him. The Lord showed himself to Saul in a resplendent cloud amid immense glory, and at the same time Saul was flooded with divine light without and within, and his heart and senses were overwhelmed beyond power of resistance (Acts 9, 4). He fell suddenly from his horse to the ground and at the same time he heard a voice from on high saying: "Saul, Saul, why dost thou persecute Me?" Full of fear and consternation he answered: "Who art Thou, Lord?" The voice replied: "I am Jesus whom thou persecutest; it is hard for thee to kick against the goad of my omnipotence." Again Saul answered with greater fear and trembling: "Lord, what dost Thou command and desire to do with me?" The companions of Saul heard these questions and answers, though they did not see the

Savior. They saw the splendor surrounding him and all of them were filled with dread and astonishment at this sudden and unthought of event, and they were for some time dumbfounded.

261. This new wonder, surpassing all that had been seen in the world before, was greater and more far-reaching than what could be taken in by the senses. For Saul was not only prostrated in body, blinded and bereft of his strength so that, if the divine power had not sustained him, he would have immediately expired; but also as to his interior he suffered more of a change than when he passed from nothingness into existence at his conception, farther removed from what he was before than light from darkness, or the highest heaven from the lowest earth; for he was changed from an image of the demon to that of one of the highest and most ardent seraphim. This triumph over Lucifer and his demons had been especially reserved by God for his divine Wisdom and Omnipotence; so that, in virtue of the Passion and Death of Christ this dragon and his malice might be vanquished by the human nature of one man, in whom the effects of grace and Redemption were set in opposition to the sin of Lucifer and all its effects. Thus it happened that in the same short time, in which Lucifer through pride was changed from an angel to a devil, the power of Christ changed Saul from a demon into an angel in grace. In the angelic nature the highest beauty turned into the deepest ugliness; and in the human nature the greatest perversity into the highest moral perfection. Lucifer descended as the enemy of God from heaven to the deepest abyss of the earth, and a man ascended as a friend of God from the earth to the highest heaven.

262. And since this triumph would not have been sufficiently glorious, if the Lord had not given more than

Lucifer had lost, the Omnipotent wished to add in saint Paul an additional triumph to his victory over the demon. For Lucifer, although he fell from that exceedingly high grace which he had received, had never possessed beatific vision, nor had he made himself worthy of it, and hence could not lose what he did not possess. But Paul, immediately on disposing himself for justification and on gaining grace, began to partake of glory and clearly saw the Divinity, though this vision was gradual. O invincible virtue of the divine power! O infinite efficacy of the merits of the life and death of Christ! It was certainly reasonable and just, that if the malice of sin in one instant changed the angel into a demon, that the grace of the Redeemer should be more powerful and abound more than sin (Rom. 5, 20), raising up from it a man, not only to place him into original grace, but into glory. Greater is this wonder than the creation of heaven and earth with all the creatures; greater than to give sight to the blind, health to the sick, life to the dead. Let us congratulate the sinners on the hope inspired by this wonderful justification, since we have for our Restorer, for our Father, and for our Brother the same Lord, who justified Paul; and He is not less powerful nor less holy for us, than for saint Paul.

263. During the time in which Paul lay prostrate upon the earth, he was entirely renewed by sanctifying grace and other infused gifts, restored and illumined proportionately in all his interior faculties, and thus he was prepared to be elevated to the empyrean heaven, which is called the third heaven. He himself confesses, that he did not know whether he was thus elevated in body or only in spirit (I Cor. 12, 4). But there, by more than ordinary vision, though in a transient manner, he saw the Divinity clearly and intuitively. Besides the being of

God and his attributes of infinite perfection, he recognized the mystery of the Incarnation and Redemption, and all the secrets of the law of grace and of the state of the Church. He saw the peerless blessing of his justification and of the prayer of saint Stephen for him; and still more clearly was he made aware of the prayers of the most holy Mary and how his conversion had been hastened through Her; and that, after Christ, her merits had made him acceptable in the sight of God. From that hour on he was filled with gratitude and with deepest veneration and devotion to the great Queen of heaven, whose dignity was now manifest to him and whom he thenceforth acknowledged as his Restorer. At the same time he recognized the office of Apostle to which he was called, and that in it he was to labor and suffer unto death. In conjunction with these mysteries were revealed to him many others, of which he himself says that they are not to be disclosed (II Cor. 7, 4). He offered himself in sacrifice to the will of God in all things, as he showed afterwards in the course of his life. The most blessed Trinity accepted this sacrifice and offering of his lips and in the presence of the whole court of heaven named and designated him as the preacher and teacher of the gentiles, and as a vase of election for carrying through the world the name of the Most High.

264. For the blessed in heaven this day was one of great accidental joy and jubilee, and all of them composed new songs of praise and exaltation of the divine power for such a rare and extraordinary miracle. If at the conversion of any sinner they are filled with joy (Luke 15, 7), with what joy were they not filled at seeing the greatness of the Lord's mercy thus manifested and such an immense blessing conferred upon all the mortals for the glory of his holy Church? Saul came out of his

rapture changed into Paul; and rising from the ground he seemed to be blind and could not see the light of the sun. His companions brought him to Damascus to the house of one of his acquaintances and there to the admiration of all, he remained three days without eating or drinking engaged in earnest prayer. He prostrated himself on the ground and, as he was now in a state to deplore his sins, with deepest sorrow and detestation of his past life, he prayed: "Woe is me, in what darkness and blindness have I lived, and how far have I hastened on the way of eternal perdition. O infinite love! O charity without measure! O infinite sweetness of the eternal bounty! Who, O my Lord and God, has induced Thee to act thus toward me the vile worm of the earth, thy enemy and blasphemer? But who could induce Thee except thyself and the prayers of thy Mother and Spouse? When I in blindness and darkness persecuted Thee, Thou, most kind Lord, camest to meet me. While I was busy shedding the innocent blood which shall always cry out against me, Thou, the God of mercies, didst wash and purify me with thy own and make me a partaker of thy ineffable Divinity. How shall I praise eternally such unheard of mercies? How shall I sufficiently bewail a life so hateful in thy eyes? The heavens and the earth proclaim thy glory. I shall preach thy holy name and shall defend it in the midst of thy enemies." Such and other aspirations saint Paul repeated with matchless sorrow and with acts of the most ardent charity and with the deepest and most humble gratitude.

265. On the third day after the disablement and conversion of Saul the Lord spoke in a vision to one of the disciples, Ananias, living in Damascus (Acts 9, 10). Calling him by name as his servant and friend, the Lord told him to go to the house of a man named Judas in a

certain district of the city and there to find Saul of Tarsus, whom he would find engaged in prayer. At the same time Saul had also a vision, in which he saw and recognized the disciple Ananias coming to him and restoring sight to him by the imposition of hands. But of this vision of Saul, Ananias at that time had no knowledge. Therefore he answered: "Lord, I have information of this man having persecuted thy saints in Jerusalem and caused a great slaughter of them in Jerusalem; and not satisfied with this, he has now come with warrants from the high-priests in order to seize whomever he can find invoking thy holy name. Dost thou then send a simple sheep like myself to go in search of the wolf, that desires to devour it?" The Lord replied: "Go, for the one thou judgest to be my enemy, is for Me a vase of election, in order that he may carry my name through all the nations and kingdoms, and to the children of Israel. And I can, as I shall, assign to him what he is to suffer for my name." And the disciple was at once informed of all that had happened.

266. Relying on this word of the Lord, Ananias obeyed and betook himself at once to the house, in which saint Paul then was. He found him in prayer and said to him: "Brother Saul, our Lord Jesus, who appeared to thee on thy journey, sends me in order that thou mayest receive thy sight and be filled with the Holy Ghost." He received holy Communion at the hands of Ananias and was strengthened and made whole, giving thanks to the Author of all these blessings. Then he partook of some corporal nourishment, of which he had not tasted for three days. He remained for some time in Damascus, conferring and conversing with the disciples in that city. He prostrated himself at their feet asking their pardon and begging them to receive him as their servant

and brother, even as the least and most unworthy of them all. At their approval and counsel he went forth publicly to preach Christ as the Messias and Redeemer of the world and with such fervor, wisdom and zeal, that he brought confusion to the unbelieving Jews in the numerous synagogues of Damascus. All wondered at this unexpected change and, in great astonishment, said: Is not this the man, who in Jerusalem has persecuted with fire and sword all who invoke that name? And has he not come to bring them prisoners to the chief priests of that city? What change then is this, which we see in him?

267. Saint Paul grew stronger each day and with increasing force continued his preaching to the gathering of the Jews and gentiles. Accordingly they schemed to take away his life and then happened, what we shall touch upon later. The miraculous conversion of saint Paul took place one year and one month after the martyrdom of saint Stephen, on the twenty-fifth of January, the same day on which the Church celebrates that feast; and it was in the year thirty-six of the birth of our Lord; because saint Stephen, as is said in chapter the twelfth, died completing his thirty-fourth year and one day of his thirty-fifth; whereas the conversion of saint Paul took place after he had completed one month of the thirty-sixth; and then saint James departed on his missionary journey, as I will say in its place.

268. Let us return to our great Queen and Lady of the angels, who by means of her vision knew all that was happening to Saul; his first and most unhappy state of mind, his fury against the name of Christ, his sudden casting down and its cause, his conversion, and above all his extraordinary and miraculous elevation to the empyrean heaven and vision of God, besides all the rest,

that happened to him in Damascus. This knowledge was not only proper and due to Her, because She was the Mother of the Lord and of his holy Church and the instrument of this great wonder; but also because She alone could properly estimate this miracle, even more so than saint Paul and more than the whole mystical body of the Church; for it was not just, that such an unheard of blessing and such a prodigious work of the Omnipotent should remain without recognition and gratitude among mortals. This the most blessed Mary rendered in all plenitude and She was the first One, who celebrated this solemn event with the acknowledgment due to it from the whole human race. The holy Mother invited all her holy angels and many others from heaven, who, forming into alternate choirs, sang with Her canticles of praise in exaltation of the power, wisdom and liberal mercy of the Almighty toward Paul; and others on the merits of her most holy Son, in virtue of which this conversion, so full of prodigies and miracles, had been wrought. By this thanksgiving and fidelity of most holy Mary the Most High (according to our way of understanding such things), as it were, compensated Himself for having so highly favored the Church in this conversion of saint Paul.

269. But let us not pass over in silence the reflections of the new Apostle concerning what the kindest Mother might think of him now, and must have thought of him as such an enemy and persecutor of her most holy Son and his disciples, intent on the destruction of the Church. The loving conjectures of saint Paul in this matter arose not so much from ignorance, as from his humility and veneration toward the Mother of Jesus. But he did not know that the great Lady was cognizant of all that had happened in connection with him. Although from this

newly acquired knowledge of heavenly things in God he
had recognized Her as his most kind Helper in his conversion and salvation; yet the wickedness of his past life
abashed, humiliated and somewhat frightened him, as
one unworthy of the favor of such a Mother, whose Son
he had persecuted so furiously and blindly. It seemed
to him that for the pardoning of such grave sins an infinite mercy was necessary, and Mary was a mere
creature. On the other hand, he was encouraged by the
thought, that She, in imitation of her Son, had pardoned
his executioners. The disciples also told him, how kind
and sweet She was with sinners and the needy; and then
he was inflamed with the ardent desire of seeing Her
and he resolved in his mind to throw himself at her feet
and to kiss the ground whereon She walked. But immediately he was again overcome by shame at the thought
of appearing before Her, who was the true Mother of
Jesus, still in mortal flesh and so deeply wronged by his
conduct. He discussed within himself, whether he
should not ask Her to punish him, because that would
be some sort of satisfaction; yet again this vengeance
seemed foreign to her gentleness, since She had obtained for him through her prayers such immense mercy.

270. Amid these and other disquieting thoughts the
Lord permitted saint Paul to suffer a harrowing, yet
sweet sorrow; and at last he said to himself: "Take
heart, vile and sinful man, for without a doubt She will
receive and pardon thee, since She has interceded for
thee as the true Mother of Him who died for thy salvation, and She will act as the Mother of such a Son, since
both of Them are all mercy and kindness and will not
despise the contrite and humble heart" (Ps. 50, 19). The
fears and doubts of saint Paul were not hidden from the
heavenly Mother; for She knew all through her exalted

science. She knew also that the Apostle would not find an occasion to see Her for a long time. Moved by her maternal love and compassion, She would not permit this consolation to be postponed to such a distant period. Therefore, in order to bring it to him from Jerusalem, She called one of her angels and said to him: "Heavenly spirit and minister of my Son and Lord, I am moved to compassion at the sorrow and trouble in the humble heart of Paul. I beg thee, my angel, go immediately to Damascus and console and comfort him in his fears. Congratulate him on his good fortune and remind him of the thanks he owes eternally to my Son and Lord for the clemency with which He has drawn him to his friendship and chosen him as his Apostle. Tell him, that never has such mercy been shown to any man as to him. And in my own name tell him, that I shall aid him as a Mother in all his labors and serve him as the Handmaid of all the Apostles and ministers of the name and doctrine of my Son. Give him my blessing in the name of Him, who condescended to assume flesh in my womb and to be nursed at my breast."

271. The holy angel immediately fulfilled the commission of his Queen and quickly appeared to saint Paul, who had remained in continued prayer; for this happened on the day after his Baptism and on the fourth after his conversion. The angel manifested himself in human form, wonderfully beautiful and resplendent, and fulfilled all the orders of Mary. Saint Paul listened to his message with incomparable humility, reverence, and joy of spirit, and thus replied to the angel: "Minister of the omnipotent and eternal God, I, the most vile of men, beseech thee, sweetest heavenly spirit, do thou, according as thou seest me indebted to the condescending mercy of the infinite God, give Him thanks and due praise, for

having so undeservedly marked me with the character and divine light of his children. The more I flew from his immense bounty, the more He followed me and advanced to meet me; when I delivered myself over to death, He gave me life; when I persecuted Him as an enemy, He raised me to his grace and friendship, recompensing the greatest injuries with the most extraordinary blessings. No one ever rendered himself so hateful and abominable as I; yet no one was so freely pardoned and favored (I Tim. 1, 13). He snatched me from the mouth of the lion in order that I might be one of the sheep of his flock. Thou art a witness of it all, my lord; help me to be eternally grateful. And I beseech thee, tell the Mother of mercy and my Lady, that this her unworthy slave lies prostrate at her feet, adoring the ground on which they tread and with a contrite heart asking Her to pardon him for having so daringly sought to destroy the honor and name of her Son and true God. Beseech Her to forget my offense and deal with this blasphemous sinner as the Mother who as a Virgin conceived, brought forth and nursed the Lord, who had given Her life and had chosen Her for this purpose from amongst all creatures. I am deserving of chastisement and retribution for so many sins and I am prepared to suffer all; but I am aware of the clemency of her heart and I shall not declare myself undesirous of her favor and protection. Let Her receive me as a child of the Church which She loves so much. All the days of my life I shall devote myself entirely to its increase and defense and to the service of Her, whom I recognize as my salvation and as the Mother of grace."

272. The holy angel returned with this answer to the most blessed Mary; and although in her wisdom She well knew it, he repeated it to Her, She heard it with an

especial joy and again gave thanks and praise to the Most High for the works of his divine right hand in the new Apostle saint Paul, and for the benefits which would result therefrom to his holy Church and the faithful. Of the confusion and rout of the demons at the conversion of saint Paul, and of many other secrets made known to me concerning the malice of the devils I shall speak, as far as possible, in the next chapter.

INSTRUCTION GIVEN TO ME BY THE QUEEN OF THE ANGELS, MOST HOLY MARY.

273. My daughter, none of the faithful should be ignorant of the fact, that the Most High could have drawn and converted saint Paul without resorting to such miracles of his infinite power. But He made use of them in order to show men, how much his bounty is inclined to pardon them and raise them to his friendship and grace, and in order to teach them, by the example of this great Apostle, how they, on their part, should cooperate and respond to his calls. Many souls the Lord wakes up and urges on by his inspiration and help. Many do respond and justify themselves through the Sacraments of the Church; but not all persevere in their justification and still a fewer number follow it up or strive after perfection: beginning in spirit, they relax, and finish in the flesh. The cause of their want of perseverance in grace and relapse into their sins is their not imitating the spirit of saint Paul at his conversion, when he exclaimed: "Lord, what is it Thou wishest with me, and what shall I do for Thee?" If some of them proclaim this sentiment with their lips, it is not from their whole heart, and they always retain some love of themselves, of honor, of possessions, of sensual pleasure or of some

occasion of sin, and thus they soon again stumble and fall.

274. But the Apostle was a true and living example of one converted by the light of grace, not only because he passed from an extreme of sin into that of wonderful grace and friendship of God; but also because he co-operated to his utmost with the call of God, departing at once and entirely from all his evil dispositions and self-seeking and placing himself entirely at the disposal of the divine will and pleasure. This total denegation of self and surrender to the will of God is contained in those words: "Lord, what dost Thou wish to do with me?" and in it consisted, as far as depended upon him, all his salvation. As he pronounced them with all the sincerity of a contrite and humbled heart, he renounced his own will and delivered himself over to that of the Lord, resolved from that moment forward to permit none of his faculties of mind or sense to serve the animal or sensual life into which he had strayed. He delivered himself over to the service of the Almighty in whatever manner or direction should become known to him as being the divine will, ready to execute it without delay or questioning. And this he immediately set about by entering the city and obeying the command of the Lord given through the disciple Ananias. As the Most High searches the secrets of the human heart, He saw the sincerity, with which saint Paul corresponded to his vocation and yielded to his divine will and disposition. He not only received him with great pleasure, but multiplied exceedingly his graces, gifts and wonderful favors, which even Paul would not have received or ever have merited without this entire submission to the wishes of the Lord.

275. Conformably to these truths, my daughter, I desire thee to execute fully my oft-repeated commands and

exhortations, that thou forget the visible, the apparent and deceitful. Repeat very often, and more with the heart than with the lips those words of saint Paul: "Lord, what dost Thou wish to do with me?" For as soon as thou beginnest to do anything of thy own choice, it will not be true, that thou seekest solely the will of the Lord. The instrument has no motion or action except that imparted to it by the artisan; and if it had its own will, it would be able to resist and act contrary to the will of the one using it. The same holds true between God and the soul: for, if it entertains any desire of its own independently of God, it will militate against the pleasure of the Lord. As He keeps inviolate the liberty of action conceded to man, He will permit it to lead man astray, as soon as he decides for himself without reference to the direction of his Maker.

276. And since it is not proper that the doings of creatures in this mortal life should be miraculously governed by the divine power, God, in order that men might not advance false excuses, has implanted a law into their hearts and also constituted his holy Church, in order that they might know the divine will and regulate their conduct in the fulfilling of it. Moreover, for additional security, He has appointed superiors and ministers in his Church, in order that hearing and obeying them, men might obey the Lord in them. All this security thou, my dearest, possessest in fullness, so that thou shouldst neither admit of any movement, thought, desire of thy own, nor fulfill thy own will in anything independently of the will and direction of him who has charge of thy soul; for him the Lord sends to thee, just as He sent Ananias to saint Paul. Moreover thou art in a particular manner obliged to this obedience, because the Most High looks upon thee with an especial love and grace and

desires to use thee as an instrument in his hands, assists thee, governs thee, and moves thee directly as well as indirectly through me and his holy angels; and all this He continues to do faithfully, as is well known to thee. Consider then, how much reason thou hast to die to thy own desires and live only for the will of God, and that it alone should give life to all thy actions and operations. Cut short therefore all thy reflections and self-reliance and remember, that, even if thou shouldst have the wisdom of the most learned, the counsel of the most prudent, and the natural intelligence of the angels, thou couldst, with all this, know how to execute his will far less perfectly than by resigning and leaving all to his divine pleasure. He alone knows what is suitable to thee and seeks it with an eternal love; He chose thy ways and governs thee in them. Permit thyself to be guided by his divine light, without losing time in doing thy duty; for in this delay lurks the danger of erring, and in my doctrine lie all security and success. Write it in thy heart and fulfill it with all thy strength, in order that thou mayest merit my intercession and, through it, to be brought near to the Most High.

CHAPTER XV.

THE HIDDEN COMBAT OF THE DEMONS AGAINST SOULS;
HOW THE MOST HIGH DEFENDS THEM THROUGH HIS
HOLY ANGELS, THROUGH THE MOST BLESSED VIRGIN,
AND BY HIS OWN POWER; THE CONSULTATION HELD
BY THE HELLISH FOES AGAINST THE QUEEN AND THE
CHURCH AFTER THE CONVERSION OF SAINT PAUL.

277. By the abundant testimony of holy Scriptures
and later, by the teaching of the holy doctors and masters
of the spiritual life, the whole Catholic Church and all
its children are informed of the malice and most vigilant
cruelty of hell against all men in seeking to draw them
to the eternal torments. From the same sources we
know also how the infinite power of God defends us, so
that, if we wish to avail ourselves of his invincible friendship and protection, and if we on our part make ourselves
worthy of the merits of Christ our Savior, we shall walk
securely on the path of eternal salvation. In order to
assure us in this hope and to console us, all the holy
Scriptures, as saint Paul assures us, were written. But
at the same time we must exert ourselves, lest our hopes
be made vain through want of our co-operation. Hence
saint Paul joins one with the other; for, having admonished us to throw all our care upon the Lord who is solicitous for us, he adds immediately: Be sober and
watch, because your adversary the devil goes about like
a roaring lion, seeking whom he may devour.

278. These and other advices of the sacred Scripture
are given both in general and for each one in particular.
And although from them and from continued experience

the children of the Church might arrive at a more definite and particular knowledge of the attacks and persecutions of the devils against all men; yet, because in their earthliness and gross sensuality they are accustomed to attend only to what they perceive by the senses and never lift their thoughts to higher things, they live in a false security, ignoring the inhuman and hidden cruelty with which the devils solicit and draw them to perdition and therein succeed. Men are ignorant also of the divine protection by which they are surrounded and defended; and like ignorant persons, they neither give thanks for this blessing, nor pay any attention to their danger. Woe is to the earth, says saint John in the Apocalypse (Apoc. 12, 12), because satan has come down to you with great indignation of his wrath. This lamenting voice the Evangelist heard in heaven, where, if the saints could feel sorrow, they certainly would feel it for us on account of the hidden war, which our powerful, and mortally enraged enemy wages against men. But although the saints cannot feel sorrow, they pity us for this danger; while we, sunk in a formidable lethargy and forgetfulness, have neither sorrow nor compassion for ourselves. In order to rouse from their torpor those that read this history, I understand, that throughout the course of these revelations I have been enlightened concerning the hidden schemes of malice concocted by the demons against the mysteries of Christ, against the Church and her children. These I have described in many passages, particularly dilating upon some of the secrets of this terrible war against men, which the devils wage in order to draw us to their side. On this present occasion of the conversion of saint Paul, the Lord has shown to me this truth more openly, enabling me to describe and make known the continual combat and strife, which goes on,

unperceived by our senses, between our angels and the
demons, and to make known the manner in which we are
defended by the divine power, either through our angels,
or through the most blessed Mary, or directly by Christ
or the omnipotence of God.

279. Of the altercations and contentions of the holy
angels in defending us against the hellish envy and malice
of the demons the holy Scriptures contain the most clear
testimony, to which, for my purpose, it will suffice merely to refer. Well known is what the holy Apostle Judas
Thaddeus says in his canonical letter: that saint Michael
contended with the devil against his design of making
known the resting-place of the body of Moses, whom the
holy archangel, at the command of God, had buried in a
place concealed from the Jews. Lucifer wished to make
it known, in order to tempt the Jews to fall away from
the lawful worship into idolatry by inducing them to
offer sacrifices at his sepulchre; but saint Michael opposed the attempt of satan to reveal it. The enmity of
Lucifer and his demons against man is as old as their
disobedience against God; and, as said in the first part,
their fury and cruelty, after they had come to know that
the eternal Word was to take flesh and to be born of that
Woman clothed with the sun (Apoc. 12, 1), are proportionate to their rebellious pride against God. Because
the proud angel rejected these decrees of God and would
not bow his neck in obedience, he conceived this hatred
against God and his creatures. As he cannot vent it upon
the Omnipotent, he executes it upon the works of his
right hand. Besides this, possessing the nature of an
angel, he resolves irrevocably and never ceases to strive
after what he has once determined to attain; hence, although changing the means to attain his end, he never
changes his will in regard to persecuting mankind. On

the contrary his hatred has increased and will increase in
proportion to the favors lavished by God upon the just
and upon the holy children of his Church, and in proportion to the victories gained by the seed of that
Woman, his Enemy, in whom God had threatened to
crush his head, while he should be able to do no more
than lie in ambush at her heels (Gen. 3, 15).

280. Moreover, this fiend is a pure spirit and is not
fatigued or ever in need of rest. Therefore he is so vigilant in persecuting us, that he commences the combat
from the very first instant of our existence in the
mother's womb and he does not abate his fury and strife
against the soul until it leaves the body. The saying of
Job is verified: that the life of man on earth is a warfare (Job 7, 1). This battle does not consist merely in
our being born in original sin and therefore subject to
the "fomes peccati" and the disorderly passions inclining
us to evil; but, besides fomenting the continual battle
within our own selves, the demon wages war against us on
his own account, availing himself of all his own astuteness and malice, and, as far as his power goes, of our
own senses, faculties, inclinations and passions. Above
all he seeks to make use of other natural causes to deprive us of salvation together with our life. And if he
does not succeed in this, he misses no chance of causing
us damage or leading us into sin and robbing us of grace,
even from the moment of our conception until that of
our death. Hence so long must last also our defense.

281. All this, especially with the children of the Church,
happens in the following manner. As soon as the demons
suspect that the conception of a human body is to take
place, he first notes the intention of the parents, and
whether they are in the state of grace or not, or whether
they have committed any excess in the act of generation;

he studies also the complexion of the humors of their bodies, for ordinarily these humors influence also those of the body generated. The demons also take note of the particular as well as of the general natural causes and conditions of nature, which unite in bringing about the generation and the organization of the human body. From these different concurring elements of generation, the demons, with their vast experience, judge as much as possible of the complexion or inclinations of the one conceived and they are wont to lay out great plans for future action. If they fear good results, they seek to hinder as much as possible the last generation or infusion of the soul, waylaying the mother with dangers or temptations to bring about an abortion before the creation of the soul, which is ordinarily delayed forty or eighty days. But as soon as they see God create or infuse the soul, the wrath of these dragons exerts itself in furious activity to prevent the creature from issuing to light, and from attaining Baptism, if it is to be born where this Sacrament can easily be administered. For this purpose they suggest and tempt the mothers to many disorders and excesses, whereby the parturition is forced and a premature birth or the death of the child in the womb might be caused; for among Catholics and heretics, who still administer Baptism, the demons content themselves with depriving children of Baptism and thus withholding them in limbo from the vision of God. Among pagans and idolaters they are not so solicitous, because among them damnation is in certain prospect.

282. Against their malign influence the Most High provides defense and protection in various ways. The most common is that of his vast and universal Providence, which insures the proper effects of natural causes in their time, independently of the perversion or hin-

drance of the demons. For this is the limit set to their power. Otherwise, if God would give free scope to their implacable malice, they would overturn the whole world. The goodness of the Creator will not allow this, nor does He wish to deliver over his works or the government of inferior matters, much less that of men, to his sworn and mortal enemies. For the demons, in his scheme of the universe, hold the places merely of vile executioners; and even in this office they do no more than what is commanded or permitted them. If depraved men would not join hands with these enemies, entertaining their deceits and by their sins meriting punishment, all nature would preserve the common order of cause and effect both in general and in particular; and there would be no occasion for such great misfortunes and losses among the faithful, in the diminution of crops, in contagious diseases, in sudden deaths, and in other devastations invented by the devil. All these and many other evils, happening even at the birth of children through vices and disorders, we merit ourselves by uniting with the demons for our own chastisement and by delivering ourselves over to their malice.

283. Besides this general providence of God for the protection of his creatures must be mentioned the particular protection of the angels, whom, according to David, the Most High has commanded to bear us up in their hands, lest we stumble into the slings of satan (Ps. 40, 12); and in another place of holy Scripture, it is said, that He sends his angels to surround us with his defense and free us from evils (Ps. 33, 8). This defense, like the persecution of the devil, commences from the womb in which we receive being, and continues until our souls are presented at the tribunal of God to be adjudged to the state merited by each one. At the moment

in which a human being is conceived, the Lord commands the angels to stand guard over it and its mother. Afterwards, at the right time, He assigns a particular angel as its guardian, as I said in the first part of this history (Part I, 114). From the very beginning the angels enter into violent combat with the demons for the protection of the souls committed to their care. The demons contend that they have jurisdiction over the creature, because it is conceived in sin, a child of malediction, unworthy of grace and divine favor, and a slave of hell. The angel refutes them by maintaining that it was conceived according to the laws of nature, over which hell has no power; that, if it is conceived in sin, it was due to its human nature, by default of the first parents and not of its own free will; and that, even if conceived in sin, God has created it to know, praise and serve Him, and, by virtue of his Passion, to merit eternal glory; and that these high ends are not to be frustrated by the mere will of the demons.

284. These enemies also argue, that in the begetting of the human being its parents had not the proper intention or rightful purpose, that they committed excess and sin in the act of generation. This is the strongest argument which the devils can advance for their right over human creatures yet in the womb; for without a doubt, sins make the child unworthy of divine protection and justly hinder its conception. Yet, although this latter often happens and a number of human beings are conceived without ever seeing the light, ordinarily the holy angels prevent such a sad result. If they are legitimate children, the angels allege, that the parents have received the Sacraments and blessings of the Church; likewise, that they have some virtues, such as having given alms, being kind, having practised some devotions or good

works. The holy angels avail themselves of these things as powerful arms to ward off the devils and defend their charges. · Over illegitimate children the combat waxes more difficult; the enemy exercises a greater right, because in the begetting of such children, wherein God has been so grievously offended, the enemies obtain a greater right and the parents justly deserve rigorous chastisement. Hence, in defending and preserving illegitimate children, God manifests his most liberal mercy in a special manner. The angels base their arguments against the demon on this mercy, and that, after all, the children are the results of natural causes, as I have said above. If the parents have no merits of their own, neither any virtues, but are sullied by sins and vices, then the holy angels refer to the merits found in the forefathers of the child, in its brothers or relations; to the prayers of its friends and acquaintances, and that it is no fault of the child if the parents are sinners or have committed excess in its generation. They also contend, that those children, if they live, may reach a high degree of virtue and holiness, and that the demon has no right to hinder them from arriving at the knowledge and love of their Creator. Sometimes God manifests to them his design of choosing them for some great work in the service of the Church; and then the defense of the angels is most vigilant and powerful; but also the demons exercise greater fury in their persecution, being incited thereto by the greater solicitude of the angels.

285. All these combats, and those we shall yet speak of, are spiritual, for they take place between pure spirits, the angels and the demons, and are conducted by weapons appropriate to the angels and to the Lord. The most effective arms against the malign spirits are the divine truths and mysteries of the Divinity and of the most holy

Trinity, of Christ the Savior, of the hypostatic union, of the Redemption, and of the immense love with which the Lord, as God and man, seeks our eternal salvation; likewise the holiness and purity of most holy Mary, her mysteries and merits. All these sacraments they present in ever new aspects to the view of the demons, so that they are forced to understand and take notice of them through the activity of the holy angels and of God himself. And then happens, what saint James says, that the devils believe and tremble (Jas. 2, 19), for these truths terrify and torment them so much, that in order not to be obliged to take notice of them, they take refuge in deepest hell; and they are so tormented by their horror of the mysteries of Christ, that they are wont to ask God to take away the knowledge and remembrance of the hypostatic union and other great wonders of divine love. Hence the angels in their contentions with them often repeat those words: "Who is like to God? Who is equal to Christ, the true God and man, who died for the human race? Who is to be compared to the most holy Mary, our Queen, who was exempt from all sin, and gave flesh and bodily form to the eternal Word in her womb, a Virgin before and after?"

286. The persecutions of the demons and the defense of the angels continue at the birth of the child. At that hour the mortal hatred of this serpent exceeds itself, especially with those children who might receive Baptism; because he strives to hinder it by any means in his power. Hence the innocence of the infant cries loudly to the Lord in the words of Ezechias: "Lord, I suffer violence, answer Thou for me" (Isaias 38, 14). For it seems, that the angels, after the child has left the shelter of its mother's womb and is unable either to protect itself or to secure from its elders sufficient protection against

so many perils, are filled with great anxiety and thus begin to solicit for it direct interference of God. Hence the care of the elders is very often supplemented by that of the holy angels, shielding the child in its sleep, when alone, and in other situations, in which many children would perish, if they were not protected by their angels. All of us, that attain the happiness of receiving Baptism and Confirmation, possess in these Sacraments a most powerful defense against the attacks of hell; because through them we are marked as children of the holy Church, being regenerated to justification as children of God and heirs of glory. The virtues of faith, hope and charity, and other virtues, adorn and strengthen us to good works, and we participate in the other sacraments and suffrages of the Church, wherein the merits of Christ and his saints, and all the other great blessings are applied to us. If we would avail ourselves of these advantages, we would vanquish the demon, and hell would have no part in any of the children of the Church.

287. But, O sad misfortune, that there should be so few who on arriving at the use of reason do not lose the grace of Baptism and join hands with the demon against their God! In view of this it would seem just, that we should be deprived and cut off from the protection of his Providence and of his holy angels. He however does not act thus: on the contrary, at the time when we begin to be unworthy of it, He meets us with greater kindness in order to manifest in us the riches of his infinite bounty. Words cannot describe what and how great are the astuteness and diligence of the demon in order to ruin man by inducing him to commit some sin, as soon as he comes to the years of discretion and the use of reason. For this they prepare from afar, seeking to accustom them to vicious actions during the years of their infancy; to pre-

sent to their ears and eyes the example of evil conduct
in their parents, their nurses, and older companions; to
make the parents neglectful in counteracting this bad example. For in this tender age, like in soft wax on the
unwritten tablet, all sensible impressions are deeply en-
graved and thus afford the demons an opportunity to
move the inclinations and passions of the children; and
it is well known, that men ordinarily follow these inclinations and passions, unless prevented by special influences. Hence these children, coming to the use of
reason, will follow the bent of the inclinations and passions in regard to sensible pleasures, with which their
imagination and phantasy are filled. As soon as they
fall into some sin, the demon immediately takes possession of their souls, acquiring new right and power
for drawing them into other sins.

288. Not less active is the diligence and care of the
holy angels to prevent such damage and defend us from
the devil. They frequently inspire the parents with holy
thoughts, urging them to watch over the education of
their children, to catechize them in the law of God, to
enjoin upon them pious works and devotions, to withdraw from evil and exercise themselves in the virtues.
The same good thoughts they instil into the children as
they grow up, or according to the light given them by
God as to his intentions with the souls. In conducting
this defense they enter into great disputes with the demons; because those malign spirits allege all the sins of
the parents against the children and likewise the wrong-
ful doings of the children themselves; for if they are
not guilty, the demons claim that their actions are the
result of his own activity and therefore that he has a
right to continue them in their souls. If the child, on
coming to the use of reason, commences to sin, they put

up a great fight to prevent the good angels from withdrawing them from evil. The good angels on their part allege the virtues of the parents and forefathers, and the good actions of the children themselves. Even if it were no more than that of having pronounced the name of Jesus or Mary as taught them by their parents, they bring this as a defense as their having begun to honor the name of their Lord and of their Mother; and likewise, if they practice other devotions, or know the Christian prayers and recite them. Of all this the angels avail themselves as serviceable arms in our defense against the demon; for with each good action we rob the devils of some of the right acquired over us by original sin, and still more by actual sin.

289. As soon as man enters into the use of his reason the battle between the demons and the angels becomes still more bitter; for whenever we commit some sin, the dragon exerts all his powers to deprive us of our lives before we have time to do penance and thus to seal our eternal damnation. In order that we may commit new crimes, he besets all our ways with slings and dangers peculiar to each one's state of life, and he overlooks none of us, although he does not tempt one as dangerously as the other. But if men would see into these secret workings of the demons just as they happen, and if they could perceive the traps and pitfalls, which of their own fault they permit the demon to prepare for them, all would live in trembling and fear, many would change their state of life, or would refuse to enter upon it, others would forsake the positions, offices and dignities, which they now esteem so highly. But in ignorance of their risk, they live on in pernicious security; they do not know enough to understand or believe more than is evident to their senses and therefore they do not fear the hellish

traps and pitfalls set for their ruin. Hence the number of fools is so great, and that of the truly prudent and wise so small; many are called and few are chosen; the wicked and the sinners are countless, while the virtuous and the perfect are very scarce. In proportion as any one multiplies his sins, in that proportion the devil acquires positive rights over his soul, and if he cannot put an end to the life of his victim, he at least seeks to treat him as his vile slave. For he claims, that each day this soul becomes more his own, and that of its own will it so chooses; that therefore it cannot justly be snatched from his hands, nor deserve the assistance which it will not accept; that the merits of Christ should not be applied to it, when it spurns them; that it should not benefit from the intercession of the saints, when it entirely forgets them.

290. By these and other pretenses, which cannot be all mentioned here, the devil tries to cut short the time of penance for those whom he claims as his own. If he does not succeed in this, he tries to block the way of their justification; and his attempts are successful with many souls. But the protection of God and of the holy angels is wanting to none of us and thus we are delivered from dangers of death by innumerable ways; and this is so certain that there is scarcely any one, who could not verify it in the course of his life. They furnish us with ceaseless inspirations and warnings; they make us of all occasions and means available for our admonishment and exhortation. What is still more valuable, they defend us against the rabid fury of the demons and set in motion against them all that the intellect of an angel or of a blessed spirit can devise, and all that their power and their most ardent charity can command for our safety. All this is necessary many times for some souls and at

times for all the souls, who have delivered themselves over to the jurisdiction of the demons and who use their liberty and their faculties only for such temerity. I do not speak of the pagans, the idolaters and heretics. These indeed, the angels likewise defend and inspire to the practice of the moral virtues, which they afterwards use as arguments against the devils; but ordinarily the most they do for them is to protect their lives, in order that God, having allowed them so much time for their conversion, may be justified in his behavior toward them. The angels also labor to prevent them from committing such great sins as the demons incite them to; for the charity of the angels exerts itself, so that at least they may not incur such great punishments, as the malice of the demons seeks to fasten upon them.

291. Within the mystical communion of the Church however are fought the hardest battles between the angels and the demons, according to the different state of souls. All its members they commonly defend with the ordinary weapons furnished them by the sacramental character impressed upon the soul in Baptism, by grace, by virtues, by the performance of good and meritorious works, by devotions to the saints, by the prayers of the just, and by all the good movements Catholics may have during their life. This defense of the just is most powerful; for since they are in grace and friendship of God, the angels obtain a greater right against the demons, and thus they rout them by showing up the holiness and perfection of these souls, which are so formidable to the powers of hell; and therefore this by itself ought to cause us to esteem grace beyond all creation. There are other lukewarm and imperfect souls who fall into sin and occasionally rise again. Against these the demons obtain more power to persecute them with their cruelty. But

the holy angels strenuously exert themselves in their defense, so that, as Isaias tells us (Is. 42, 3) ; the broken reed may not be crushed, and the smoking flax be not entirely extinguished.

292. There are other souls so unhappy and depraved, that during their whole life after their Baptism they have not performed one good work; or if they have ever risen from sin, they have returned to it with such eagerness, that they seemed to have renounced their God, living and acting as if they had no hope of another life, no fear of hell, no repentance for any of their sins. In these souls there is no vitality of grace, no attempt at true virtue, nor have the holy angels any good or available grounds for their defense. The demons cry out: This soul at least is altogether ours, subject to our commands, and has no part in grace. They point out to the good angels all the sins, wickedness and vices of such souls, which of their own free will serve such evil masters. What then passes between the angels and the demons is incredible and indescribable; because the demons exert all their fury to prevent such souls from receiving inspirations and helps. As they cannot resist the divine power, they seek at least with all their power to hinder them from attending or yielding to the call of heaven. With such souls ordinarily it happens, that whenever God himself or through his holy angels sends them a holy inspiration or movement, these demons must first be put to flight and the soul snatched from their midst, lest these birds of prey immediately pounce upon and destroy the holy seed. This defense the angels usually conduct with the words, which I have quoted above: "Who is like unto God, that dwells on high? Who like Christ, at the right hand of the eternal Father? Who is like to the most holy Mary?" together with other sayings,

before which the infernal dragons take flight; sometimes they are thereby hurled back into hell, although, not abating in their fury, they again return to the conflict.

293. The hellish foes also strive with all their force to induce men to multiply their sins, in order that the measure of their sins may so much the sooner be complete and their time of penance and of life may come to an end; for then the demons would be enabled to carry them off to eternal torments. But the angels, who are rejoiced by the repentance of sinners (Luke 8, 12), even though they may not be able to bring them to repentance, labor diligently to do away with occasions of sin and to lessen the number of sins or prevent them altogether. And when, with all their efforts, unknown to mortals, they cannot bring back the souls from sin, they resort to the intercession of the most holy Mother of God, asking Her to be their Mediatrix with the Lord and lend her aid in confounding the demons. In order to move her merciful kindness the sooner, they induce the souls of sinners to practice some special devotion or perform some service in honor of the great Lady. Although it is true, that all good works performed in the state of sin are dead and very weak weapons against the devil, yet they always retain some remote appropriateness, on account of the good end in view; and thus the sinner is less indisposed toward grace than without them. Moreover these good works, when presented by the angels and especially by the heavenly Mother, possess, in the eyes of the Lord, a certain life, or the resemblance of it, altogether different from that given to them by the sinners; and therefore though He does not bind Himself to respond to them He nevertheless does it on account of the One so asking.

294. In these different ways an infinite number of

souls come out of their sinful ways and are snatched from the claws of the dragon; and as there are innumerable souls who fall into such a dreadful state, that they need a powerful aid, the most holy Queen interposes hers, whenever the angels fail in their defense. The demons are fiercely tormented by their own fury whenever they perceive any sinner calling upon or remembering his Queen; since they know by experience how kindly She receives sinners and how readily She makes their cause her own. Without hope or spirit of resistance the devils immediately give themselves up as foiled and vanquished. It often happens, when God desires to bring about some special conversion, that the great Queen herself peremptorily commands the demons to withdraw from that soul and sink into the abyss, and her commands are always obeyed. At other times, without such peremptory orders, God permits them to see the mysteries, the power, and holiness of his Mother, and this new knowledge, filling them with consternation and confusion, puts them to flight. If the souls respond and co-operate with the grace obtained for them by the heavenly Sovereign, they are freed from the attacks of the demons.

295. Yet though the intercession of the great Queen and her power is so formidable to the devils and though the Most High confers no favor upon the Church or upon the souls without Her, there are nevertheless many occasions in which the humanity of the incarnate Word itself battles for us and defends us against Lucifer declaring Himself openly with his Mother in our favor and annihilating and vanquishing the demons. So great is his love for men and for all that pertains to their welfare, that this happens not only when the demons are made to feel directly the virtues of Christ and his

merits through the operation of the Sacraments in the souls, but also when, in other miraculous conversions, He fills them with particular knowledge of one or more mysteries to their confusion and rout. Of such a kind was the conversion of saint Paul, of Mary Magdalen and other saints; or whenever it is necessary to protect some Catholic kingdom, or the Church, from the treachery and malice of hell for their destruction. On such occasions not only his sacred humanity, but even the infinite Divinity, armed with the omnipotence of the Father, advances upon the demoniacal hosts, filling them in the above-mentioned manner with the knowledge of the mysteries and of his Omnipotence, by which He overwhelms them and forestalls them in their real or intended conquests.

296. Whenever the Lord thus interposes such powerful aid the whole infernal reign of confusion is terrorized and stricken down into the hellish abysses for many days, giving forth howls of mournful despair and totally unable to move from their places until the Lord again gives them permission to rise. But as soon as they receive permission, they again issue forth with their former fury for the ruin of souls. Although it may not seem in harmony with their pride and arrogance to enter into a new contest with the One, by whom they have been overthrown and vanquished, nevertheless their jealous fear lest we come to the enjoyment of God and their furious desire to prevent it, again prevail and urge them to continue their persecutions to the end of our lives. I was made to understand, that if God were not so outrageously misused in his mercy, He would often interpose, even miraculously, his divine Omnipotence in our behalf. Especially would He do this in defense of the mystical body of the Church and of some Catholic gov-

ernments, bringing to naught the counsels of hell for the destruction of Christianity in our times. We do not merit this protection of the infinite power, because all are united in rousing the divine wrath and the whole world has joined hands with the infernal fiends, into whose power it has fallen on account of the blind and insane pursuit of evil rampant among men.

297. In the conversion of saint Paul this assistance of the Most High is openly manifest; for He had set him apart even in the womb of his mother, and chosen him as an Apostle and as a vase of election. Although his life before the persecution of the Church was a series of events, which deceived the demons just as he is deceived in many other souls, yet God watched him from the moment of his conception and regulated his natural character and the care of the angels in his defense and protection. Hence the hatred of the devil and their desire of causing his death in the first years of his life increased. As they failed in this, and as they later saw him become a persecutor of the Church, they were solicitous to preserve his life. When the holy angels found themselves powerless to withdraw Paul from the error, to which he had entirely dedicated himself, the powerful Queen entered the combat and made his cause her own. Through Her, Christ and the eternal Father interposed his divine assistance and snatched him from the grasp of the dragon. In one instant at the apparition of the Lord, all the demons that accompanied saint Paul on the way to Damascus, were hurled to the abyss.

298. On that occasion Lucifer and his cohorts felt the lash of the divine Omnipotence; filled with fear and consternation they for some days lay lifeless in the depths of the infernal caverns. But as soon as the Lord took away from their minds the remembrance of the

divine mysteries, they began to breathe forth new wrath. The great dragon called together the rest and spoke to them: "How is it possible to rest, when every day I see new injuries heaped upon me by this incarnate Word and by this Woman, who conceived and bore Him as man? Where is my strength? Where is my power, and of what use is my fury and the triumphs which I gained over Him among mortals ever since God without reason cast me from the heavens to this abyss? It seems, my friends, that the Omnipotent intends to seal up the portals of these infernal regions and open up those of heaven, which would be the destruction of our reign and of all my coveted designs to drag to these torments the rest of mankind. If God, besides having redeemed men, works for them such miracles, if he shows them such love and seeks to draw them to his friendship by such powerful works of his right hand, they will permit themselves to be overcome, even if they have the disposition of wild beasts and hearts of adamant. All will love and serve Him, if they are not more obstinate and rebellious than we ourselves. What soul can be so callous as not to be drawn to this Godman, who with such a tender love seeks its eternal glory? Saul was our friend, a willing instrument of my designs, subject to my will and command, an enemy of the Crucified, and I had destined him for most cruel torments in this hell. In the midst of all this God suddenly snatches him from my hands, and by his divine power raises this insignificant creature of the earth to such high grace and favors, that we, his enemies, are astounded. What has Paul done to deserve such an exceeding good fortune? Was he not in my service offending his God? If God has been so liberal with him, what protection will He not lavish upon other less grievous sinners? And even if He does not convert

them by such great miracles, He will gain them through
Baptism and the other Sacraments, by which they can justify themselves day by day. This example of God's mighty
defense of the Church, at the time when I attempted to
destroy it through Saul, will draw all the world to his
service. Is it possible that I should see vile human kind
raised to the grace and happiness which I have lost, and
that it should occupy the heaven from which I have been
hurled? This thought torments me more furiously than
the fires of hell. I am filled with a powerless rage
against myself for not being able to destroy myself in
my wrath. Would that God himself would do it, instead
of preserving me in these torments. But since this is
not to be, tell me, my vassals, what shall we do against
this so powerful God? Him we cannot injure; but
in those whom he loves so much, we can avenge ourselves,
because in them we can oppose his will. And since
my majesty is most offended and incensed against
this Woman, our Enemy, who gave him human
being. I wish to inaugurate new ways of destroying Her
and avenging ourselves for having robbed us of Saul and
cast us into these Abysses. I shall not rest until I shall
have vanquished Her. For this purpose I resolve to
execute all the plans formed against God and man after
my fall from heaven. Come, all of you, to help me in
my designs and to execute my will."

299. Such were the words of exhortation addressed to
the demons by Lucifer. Some of them answered: "Our
captain and leader, we are ready to obey thee, knowing
how much this Woman, our Foe, oppresses and torments
us; but it is possible that She by Herself without other
aid may resist us, despising all our efforts and attacks,
as we have seen on other occasions, when She showed
Herself altogether our superior in strength. What She

feels most, is to see us attack the followers of her Son; because She loves them and is solicitous about them as a Mother. Let us raise a general persecution against the faithful, for we have at our service the whole of Judaism, now incensed against the new Church of the Crucified; through the priests and pharisees we may succeed in all our attempts against the faithful and thus vent our wrath against this hostile Woman." Lucifer approved of this counsel and showed favors to the demons, who had given it. Thus agreed, they issued forth to destroy the Church by the hands of others, just as they had attempted it through Saul. Thence resulted what I shall relate further on, and also the battle of the most holy Mary against the dragon and his hosts, wherein She gained such great victories for the holy Church. To this battle I referred in the sixth chapter of the first part, and there stated, that I had reserved it for this place. Of it I shall speak in the next chapter.

INSTRUCTION WHICH THE GREAT MISTRESS OF THE
ANGELS GAVE ME.

300. My daughter, by no power of human words wilt thou in this mortal life ever succeed in describing the envy of Lucifer and his demons against men, or the malice, astuteness, deceits and ruses, with which in his wrath he seeks to bring them into sin and later on to the eternal torments. He tries to hinder all good works, and such as are performed he tries to minimize, or to destroy and pervert as to their merits. All the malice of which his own mind is capable, he attempts to inject into the souls. Against these attacks God provides admirable protection if men will only co-operate and correspond on their part. Hence the Apostle admonishes them to walk carefully amid all these dangers and conflicts;

not like the foolish, but as wise, redeeming their time; because the days of mortal life are evil and full of dangers (Ephes. 5, 15). Again he exhorts them to be fixed and constant in good works, because their labor shall not be in vain before the Lord (I Cor 15, 58). The truth of this our enemy knows and dreads, hence he seeks with deepest malice to cause dismay in the souls at the commission of one sin, in order that they may ruin themselves by despair and leave off all good works; for thus would they throw aside the weapons with which the angels can defend them and do battle with the demons. Although these works in the sinner have not the life of charity or of merit for grace or glory yet they are very useful. Sometime it happens, that on account of the habit of doing good the divine clemency furnishes efficacious help for performing these works with greater fervor, or with sorrow for sins and true charity, by which the soul regains justification.

301. By all our good deeds as creatures we open up ways to the blessed for defending us and for asking the divine mercy to look upon us and snatch us from sin. The saints also feel obliged to come to the assistance of those that sincerely invoke them in danger and that show them a special devotion. If the saints in their charity are so inclined to favor men in the dangerous conflicts with the devils, thou must not be surprised, my dearest, that I am so merciful with the sinners who take refuge in my clemency; for I desire their salvation infinitely more than they themselves. Innumerable are those whom I have saved from the infernal dragon because of their devotion to me, even though they have recited only one Ave, or have said only one word in my honor and invocation. So great is my love for them, that if they would call upon me in time and with sincerity, none of

them would perish. But the sinners and the reprobate do no such thing; because the wounds of sin, not being of the body, do not distress them, and the oftener they are committed, the less regret or sorrow do they cause. The second sin is already like wounding a dead body which knows neither fear, nor defense, nor sensation.

302. The result of this torpid insensibility to eternal damnation, and to the deceits of the devils in fastening it upon men, is dreadful. Without knowing upon what they rest their false security, the sinners are asleep and perfectly at ease as to their ruin, when they ought justly to fear and take heed of the swiftly approaching eternal death; or at least seek help by praying to the Lord, or to me, or the saints. But even this, which costs them so little, they do not know how to begin, until the time, in which the conditions of their salvation can be realized, has, for many of them, passed away. If for some of them I still procure salvation in the last agony, this privilege cannot be common to all. Hence are lost so many children of the Church, who in their ingratitude and foolishness despise the many and powerful helps given by the divine clemency in most opportune time. Therefore also it will increase their confusion, when they shall see, that, with the mercy of their God, my own kindest wishes to save them, and the charity of the saints before their eyes, they have robbed God of the glory of their conversion; and not afforded me or to the angels or saints the joy of saving them in answer to their heartfelt invocation.

303. I wish, my daughter, to manifest to thee still another secret. Thou already knowest, that my Son and Lord in the Gospel says: That the angels have joy in heaven whenever any sinner does penance and is converted to the way of life through his justification (Luke

15, 10). The same happens when the just perform works of true virtue and merit new degrees of glory. Now that which happens among the heavenly inhabitants in the conversion of sinners and in the increase of merit of the just, has a counterpart in what happens with the demons at the sins of the just and the deeper falls of sinners; for no sin is committed by men, however small, in which the demons do not take pleasure; and those that attend to the business of tempting mortals immediately give notice to the demons in the eternal dungeons of their successes. There they enjoy them and record them for further use, both in order to press their claims before the divine Judge, and in order that their greater dominion and jurisdiction over sinners according to the measure of the offense may be publicly known. In this manner they show their treacherous hate of men, whenever they succeed in deceiving them into sin by some momentary and apparent pleasure. But the Most High, who is just in all his works, ordained that also the conversion of sinners and the good works of the just should redound to the torment of the envious demons, since they rejoice so much at the perdition of man.

304. This sort of chastisement therefore causes great torments to all the demons; because by it they are not only confounded and oppressed in their mortal hatred of men, but by the victories of the saints and the conversion of sinners they are deprived of a great part of their power over those, whom they have drawn into sin by their plots. The new torments thus caused to them they seek to vent upon the damned in hell; and just as there is new joy in heaven at the penance and good works of sinners, so, for the same reason, there arise new confusion and misfortune in hell at the good works of the just. On such occasions, amid howls of despair, the

demons inflict new accidental torments upon all that live in those dungeons of dismay and horror. Thus heaven and hell are affected at the same time in contrary ways by the conversion and justification of the sinner. Whenever the souls justify themselves through the Sacraments, especially by a truly sorrowful confession, it often happens that the devils for a long time dare not appear before the penitent, nor for many hours even presume to look at him, if he himself does not again encourage them by losing the divine favor and returning again to the dangers and occasions of sin; for then the demons quickly cast off the fear inspired by true penitence and justification.

305. In heaven there can be no sorrow or pain; but if there could be, then the saints would feel it on account of nothing in the world so much as to see the justified souls falling back and losing grace, and the sinner drawing away further or making it impossible for him to regain divine favor. Sin of its own nature is just as powerful to move heaven to sorrow and pain as penance and virtue are to torment hell. Consider then, my dearest, in what dangerous ignorance mortals ordinarily live, depriving heaven of its joy in the justification of souls, hindering the external glory connected therewith, holding up the punishment due to the demons, and affording them on the contrary the joyful triumph of the fall and perdition of men. I desire that thou, as a faithful and prudent handmaid, be guided by thy higher knowledge, labor in compensating these evils. See that thou always approach the sacrament of Confession with fervor, esteem and veneration, and with a heartfelt sorrow for thy sins; for this Sacrament inspires the dragon with great terror and he exerts himself diligently to hinder souls by his deceits, in order to cause them to receive

this Sacrament lukewarmly, out of mere habit, without sorrow, and without proper disposition. He is so eager in this matter not only because he wishes to cause the loss of souls, but also to avoid the fierce torments of being oppressed and confounded in his malignity by the true penance and justification of his escaped victims.

306. Besides all this, my friend, I wish to remind thee, that, although the infernal dragons are indeed the authors and masters of lies and although they deal with men only in order to mislead and ruin them by their deceits, yet these enemies, whenever in their meetings they confer among themselves in regard to misleading men, are forced to admit certain truths, which they know and cannot deny. They understand them, yet they communicate them to men, not in good faith, but obscured and mixed with their own errors and falsehoods for the promotion of their own malicious designs. Since thou hast in this chapter, and in the whole course of this history, laid bare so many of their counsels, meetings and secrets, they are highly enraged against thee; for they flattered themselves, that these secrets and all their machinations would never come to the knowledge of men. Therefore they are furious to take vengeance upon thee; but the Most High will protect thee, if thou call upon Him to crush the head of the dragon. Do thou also beseech the divine clemency, that these advices and instructions may help to undeceive mortals, and by the divine light redound to their benefit. On thy own part do thou seek faithfully to correspond, as being under greater obligations to Him than all others living in the present age. For if, understanding their malice, thou dost not exert thyself to vanquish them with the assistance of the Most High and of his holy angels, thy ingratitude and the triumph of hell will grow in proportion to the favors thou hast received.

CHAPTER XVI.

THE MOST HOLY MARY PERCEIVES THE INTENTIONS OF
THE DEMON TO PERSECUTE THE CHURCH; SHE IM-
PLORES THE DIVINE ASSISTANCE BEFORE THE THRONE
OF THE MOST HIGH IN HEAVEN; SHE FOREWARNS THE
APOSTLES; SAINT JAMES ARRIVES IN SPAIN TO PREACH
THE GOSPEL AND IS VISITED THERE BY THE MOST
BLESSED LADY.

307. When Lucifer and the infernal chiefs, after the
conversion of saint Paul, were plotting vengeance on the
most holy Mary and the children of the Church, as described in the last chapter, they did not apprehend that
the knowledge of this great Queen and Mistress of the
world penetrated into those obscure and profound abysses
of hell and extended to the most hidden secrets of their
evil counsels. Thus deceived, the blood-thirsty dragons
esteemed their victory and the full execution of their
schemes against Her and the disciples of her Son as most
certain. But from her retreat, the blessed Mother with
the clearness of her heavenly science, knew of all their
conferences and understood all the intrigues of these
enemies of the light. She perceived all their aims and
the means which they intended to use; their wrath
against God and against Her, and their mortal hatred
against the Apostles and the rest of the faithful. Although the most prudent Lady was well aware that the
demons could execute none of their fury without the
permission of the Lord, yet, as this conflict in mortal life
is unavoidable and as She knew the weakness of men

and their only too common ignorance of the demoniacal astuteness and malice intent on their perdition, She was filled with great solicitude and sorrow at the unanimous resolve of those jealous enemies for the destruction of the faithful.

308. In addition to this knowledge and to the charity directly drawn from the Lord, She was endowed with another kind of tireless activity, similar to that of the Divinity, which continues without interruption as one pure act. The most diligent Mother was ceaselessly actuated by her love and solicitude for the glory of the Most High and the consolation and protection of her children. At the same time She pondered in her most chaste bosom upon the supernal mysteries, conferring the past with the present, and both with the future, and preparing for it with a more than human discretion and foresight. Her most ardent desire of the salvation of all the faithful and her maternal compassion for their labors and dangers, compelled Her to estimate all their tribulations and perils as her own and, as far as her love was concerned, She desired to suffer them all Herself, if possible, while the rest of the followers of Christ should labor in the Church without molestation, meriting in joyful peace grace and life eternal for themselves and leaving to Her alone all sorrows and tribulations. Although this was not possible according to the equitable providence of God, yet we stand indebted to the most holy Mary for this extraordinary and wonderful token of love, and not unfrequently her anxious and restless love merits for us great blessings, which the Omnipotent concedes in order to satisfy her yearnings for our salvation.

309. She did not know on this occasion, what in particular were the resolves of the hellish foes in their

conference; for She understood only in general, that their fury was directed against Her in an especial manner. Divine Providence concealed from Her some of their designs, in order that the triumph She would gain over hell might afterwards be so much the more glorious. Nor was it necessary to prepare Her for temptations and persecutions, as was conceded to other faithful, whom She so excelled in high and magnanimous spirit, and of whose trials and tribulations She had a clearer knowledge. According to her wont in all affairs, she resorted to prayer, consulting about them with God in pursuance of the example and teaching of the Lord. For this purpose She retired and, prostrating Herself in admirable reverence and fervor upon the ground, thus besought Him:

310. "Most high Lord and eternal God, holy and incomprehensible, behold here prostrate before Thee thy humble handmaid and vile wormlet of the earth, supplicating Thee, eternal Father, through thy onlybegotten Son and my Lord Jesus Christ. Do not despise my petitions and sighs, which from my inmost soul I present to thy immense charity in union with that which, derived from the furnace of thy own love, Thou hast communicated to thy slave. In the name of all thy holy Church, of thy Apostles and thy faithful servants, I present to Thee, O Lord, the sacrifice of the passion and death of thy Onlybegotten; that of his sacramental body, the most acceptable petitions and prayers He offered to Thee during the time of his mortal and passible life, the love with which He assumed flesh for the Redemption of the world in my womb, his imprisonment there and his rearing at my breast; all this I offer in order to be permitted to ask Thee for that which Thou seest in the desire of my heart."

311. During this prayer the great Queen was raised in divine ecstasy, in which She saw her Onlybegotten at the right hand of the eternal Father, asking Him to concede to his most blessed Mother all her petitions and representing to Him, that She was his true Mother, entirely pleasing to the Divinity and worthy of being received and heard in all her prayers. She saw also, that the eternal Father assented and was pleased with his request, and that looking upon Her, He said: "Mary, my daughter, ascend higher." At this bidding of the Most High, an innumerable multitude of angels of different hierarchies descended from heaven, who surrounded Her and raised Her from the earth on which She lay prostrate. They then bore Her up body and soul to the empyrean heaven and placed Her before the throne of the most holy Trinity, which manifested Itself to Her by a most exalted, not intuitive, but imaginary vision. She prostrated Herself before the throne and adored God in the three Persons with the most profound humility and reverence, at the same time thanking her divine Son for having presented her petition to the eternal Father and asking Him again to do so. The divine Lord, at the right hand of his Father, acknowledging Her as his worthy Mother and the Queen of heaven, would not forget the obedience He had shown Her on earth (Luke 2, 51); but, in the presence of all the courtiers of heaven, renewed the acknowledgment of his filial obligations and again presented to the Father the wishes and prayers of his most blessed Mother. And the eternal Father answered in these words:

312. "My Son, in whom my will finds the plenitude of satisfaction, my ears are attentive to clamors of thy Mother and my clemency is inclined toward all her desires and petitions." Then turning to the most blessed

Mary, he said: "My beloved Daughter, chosen from myriads according to my pleasure, thou shalt be the instrument of my Omnipotence and the Treasure of my love. Let thy anxiety rest and tell Me, my Daughter, what thou askest; for, toward thy desires and petitions, which are holy in my eyes, my will inclines." Thus favored the blessed Mary answered. "My eternal Father and most high God, who art the Author and Preserver of the whole world, thy holy Church is the object of my solicitude and prayer. Remember in thy kindness, that it is the work of thy Onlybegotten, who became man and acquired and planted it by his own blood (Act 20, 28). Anew the infernal dragon and all thy enemies, his allies, are raising up against it and are attempting the ruin and perdition of all thy faithful, who are the fruit of the Redemption of thy Son. Confound the evil councils of the ancient serpent and defend thy servants, the Apostles, and the other faithful of the Church. In order that they may be freed from the attacks and fury of these enemies, let them all direct their assaults against me, if possible. I, my Lord, am only one poor creature, and thy servants are many: let them enjoy thy favors and thy peace, by which they advance thy exaltation and glory, and let me suffer the tribulations, which threaten them. Let me battle against thy enemies and Thou, by the power of thy arm, shalt overcome and confound their malice."

313. "My spouse and my Beloved," answered the eternal Father, "thy desires are acceptable in my eyes and I will grant thy petition as far as is possible. I shall defend my servants in what is proper and conducive to my glory, and permit them to suffer in what is necessary for their crown. In order that thou mayest understand the secret of my wisdom, by which these mysteries are

to be fulfilled, I wish to raise thee to my throne, where thy ardent charity merits thee a place in the consistory of our great counsels and in the participation of our divine attributes. Come, my Beloved, and thou shalt understand our secrets for the government of the Church, its increase and progress; and thou shalt follow thy will, which is ours, now about to be manifested to thee." By the force of these most sweet words Mary felt Herself raised to the throne of the Divinity and placed at the right hand of her Son to the admiration and joy of all the blessed, who recognized the voice and the will of the Almighty. And truly it was wonderful and new to all the angels and saints to see a Woman, in mortal flesh, called and elevated to the throne and council of the most blessed Trinity in order to be informed of the mysteries hidden to the rest and enshrined in the bosom of God for the government of the Church.

314. It would seem astounding, if in some city of this world some woman were called to the councils of the government, and still more surprising to introduce her into the select and close circles, where the more difficult the important matters of the whole government are discussed and transacted. Such a course would of right seem hazardous, since Solomon says, that in seeking truth and reason among men he found but one out of a thousand who followed it, and among women not one. On account of their natural frailty, there are so few of them who possess constancy and integrity of judgment, that ordinarily it is presumed in none, and if there are any, they are scarcely capable of managing affairs that are difficult of understanding and require deep insight, unless they are aided by other light beyond the ordinary and natural. This common law did not extend to our great Queen and Lady; for if on the one hand our

mother Eve, in her ignorance, began by destroying the palace of this world built by God, on the other hand the most blessed Mary, who was most wise and the Mother of wisdom, rebuilt it and restored it by her peerless prudence; and therefore She was worthy to enter into the councils of the most holy Trinity where its restoration was to be planned.

315. There She was again asked what favors She requested and desired for Herself and for the whole Church, in particular for the Apostles and disciples of the Lord. The most prudent Mother repeated her most fervent desires for the glory and exaltation of God's holy name, and for restriction of the persecution designed by the enemies of the Lord against the faithful. Although the three Persons of the most holy Trinity well knew all her desires, yet they commanded the great Lady to propose them, in order to elicit their approbation and delight and in order to make Her more capable of new mysteries of their divine Wisdom and the predestination of the elect. To explain what has been shown me of this sacrament, I will say, that, because the will of the most holy Mary was most just, holy, and in all things pleasing and conformable to the most blessed Trinity, it seems (according to our way of understanding such things) God could not will anything contrary to this most pure Lady; for He was bent in the direction of her holiness and was wounded by the hair and eyes of so beloved a Spouse (Cant. 4, 9), and One so singular among all creatures; and since the Father looked upon Her as his Daughter, the Son as his Mother, and the Holy Ghost as his Spouse, and since all Three had entrusted to Her the Church in fullest confidence, therefore the three Persons did not wish to decree the execution of anything without, as it were, consulting the wisdom and the pleasure of the Queen of all Creation.

316. In order that the will of the Most High and of the most blessed Mary might coincide in these decrees, it was necessary that the great Lady should first receive a new measure of science and insight into the most hidden counsels of his providence, by which all the affairs of his creatures are arranged in weight and measure (Wis. 11, 21) and all their means and ends in highest equity and propriety. For this purpose the most holy Mary received on this occasion a most clear insight in all that was to be done and preordained by the divine power in the Church militant. She saw the most hidden reason for all that was to be done; how many and which of the Apostles were to die before She should pass from this life; the labors they were to undertake for the name of the Lord; the reason why all this should be so according to the secret judgments of God, and the predestination of saints; and why they should thus shed their blood for the planting of the Church, just as the Lord and Redeemer had shed his for its foundation in his Passion and Death. She understood also how, through her own compassion and sorrow at seeing the sufferings of the Apostles and followers of Christ, She could compensate Herself for not being allowed to take upon Herself their sufferings as She desired; for this momentary labor could not be spared them, if they were to reach the eternal reward in store for them (II Cor. 4, 17). To afford the great Lady an opportunity for this kind of merit, She was informed of the near death of saint James and the imprisonment of saint Peter, but not of his liberation by an angel. She understood also, that the Lord portioned out to the Apostles and the faithful that kind of suffering or martyrdom, which corresponded with each one's grace and strength of soul.

317. In order to satisfy in all things the most ardent

charity of this purest Mother, the Lord permitted Her
to fight anew all the battles with the dragons of hell and
gain over them victories and triumphs, which the rest of
the mortals shall never attain.   By this means She was
to crush their head and humble their pride, weakening
their forces and breaking their strength, which they were
mustering against the faithful.   God renewed in Her all
his gifts and participations in his divine attributes, and
each of the three Persons gave Her his blessings.   The
holy angels brought Her back to the Cenacle in the
way as they had brought Her to the empyrean heaven.
As soon as She found Herself recovered from her ecstasy, She prostrated Herself with her face upon the
ground in the form of a cross and with most tender
tears and incredible humility thanked the Almighty for
this new blessing conferred upon Her in answer to her
most humble petitions.   For some time She conferred
with her holy angels concerning the mysteries and necessities of the Church in order to attend to its most pressing needs.   It seemed advisable to prepare and encourage
the Apostles for coming trouble, since the common
enemy was to direct his main battle against them.   For
this purpose She spoke to saint Peter, saint John and
the rest in Jerusalem, advising them of many particulars,
that were to happen to them and to the whole Church,
confirming the report of the conversion of saint Paul
and telling them of the zeal, with which he was preaching the name of his Master and Lord.

318. To those Apostles and disciples, who were not
in Jerusalem, She sent angels, in order to notify them of
the conversion of saint Paul and in order to prepare and
encourage them with the same good counsels as those in
Jerusalem. She sent an especial angelic messenger to warn
saint Paul of the intended assaults of the devil and to

animate and confirm him with the hope of divine assistance in his tribulations. Obediently the angels fulfilled all these errands with their accustomed celerity, manifesting themselves in visible forms to the Apostles and disciples. All of them were exceedingly consoled and encouraged by these favors of the most blessed Mary; and each one answered through the same envoys, sending humble acknowledgment and offering themselves to die for the honor of their Redeemer and Master. Saint Paul especially showed his gratitude in his answer; for his desire of seeing and thanking his Protectress urged him to demonstrate his devotion in a more fervent manner. He was at that time in Damascus preaching and disputing in the synagogues, although soon after he went to Arabia to preach; but from there he afterwards came to Damascus a second time, as I shall relate further on.

319. Saint James the great was farther away than any of the others. He was the first one to leave Jerusalem, and, having preached some days in Judea, he departed for Spain. For this journey he embarked at Joppe, which is now called Jaffa, in the year thirty-five in the month of August, called Sextilis, one year and five months after the passion of the Lord, eight months after the martyrdom of saint Stephen and five months before the conversion of saint Paul, all according to what I said in the eleventh and fourteenth chapters of this last part. Sailing from Jaffa, saint James touched at Sardinia and shortly afterwards arrived in Spain, disembarking at the port of Carthagena where he began his preaching. He tarried but a short time in Carthagena, and guided by the Spirit of the Lord, He took his way to Granada, where he was made aware that the harvest was bountiful and the occasion opportune for beginning his labors for his Master; and so it really turned out.

320. Before going farther I will state, that saint James was one of the most intimate and beloved disciples of the great Mistress of the world. Though he was related to Her, as was also saint John, his brother, not much of this predilection could be seen in her exterior conduct, on account of the impartiality of the most prudent Lady, already referred to in chapter the eleventh. With regard to saint John the whole apostolic college knew that the Lord had appointed him as the Son of his most pure Mother; therefore the most prudent Lady was not under such restrictions in regard to exterior tokens of love with saint John as She was with saint James and the other Apostles. But interiorly the blessed Lady loved saint James with special tenderness, as I have already stated in the second part, and She manifested it in extraordinary favors, conferred upon him during his life until his martyrdom. Saint James deserved these favors on account of his special piety and affection toward Mary, distinguishing himself therein from all the rest. He needed the protection of the great Queen, because he was of a generous and magnanimous heart, and of a most fervent spirit, being resistlessly drawn on to offer himself for labors and dangers. Hence he was the first one to go forth preaching the faith and the first of all the Apostles to suffer martyrdom. While on his missionary journeys he was indeed like the lightning flash, like the son of thunder, as he was called and designated by his brethren upon entering into the apostolate (Marc. 3, 17).

321. During his labors in Spain the demons raised up incredible persecutions through the unbelieving Jews. Nor were those of small import which he afterwards met in Italy and Asia Minor, whither he had returned to preach and to suffer his martyrdom. This he underwent in Jerusalem, having in the few years of his apos-

tolate traveled in many distant countries. As it cannot be my purpose to relate all that saint James suffered in his extensive journeys, I will record only what concerns more closely this history. In general I have understood that the great Queen of heaven watched over him with an especial love, for reasons already stated, and that through her angels She defended and rescued him from many and great dangers, consoled him and comforted him many times, sending information and advice, such as he needed more particularly and oftener than the other Apostles during his short life. Many times also Christ our Savior sent angels from heaven to defend his great Apostle and to carry him from one region to another during his missionary travels.

322. During the time of his preaching in these Spanish kingdoms, the great Queen, besides many other tokens of her love, twice favored saint James by a personal visit in order to defend him in his tribulations and dangers. In Saragossa happened one of these visits or apparitions, which is no less certain than celebrated in the world and which cannot be denied without doing violence to a well-known fact, corroborated and witnessed by great miracles and the traditions of sixteen hundred and more years. Of this I will speak in the next chapter. Of the other miraculous visit I do not know whether there is any record in Spain; for it happened not so publicly. As was revealed to me, it took place in Granada, and in the following manner. The Jews had in that city some synagogues, maintained there ever since the time of their first coming from Palestine to Spain; for, on account of the fertility of the soil and the facility of communication with Palestine by sea, they could live there more comfortably. When saint James came to preach in Granada, they were already informed of what concerned

Christ our Redeemer. Although some of them desired
to become acquainted with his doctrine and the grounds
upon which it rested, yet others, the greater number, having been influenced by the devil not to believe, and to
reject his teaching, would not permit his doctrines to be
preached even to the heathens, as being contrary to the
rites of the Jews and of Moses and as endangering
Judaism, if once received by the gentiles. Stirred on by
this diabolical deceit the Jews hindered the faith from
spreading among heathens, who knowing Christ to be a
Jew and seeing his own countrymen and co-religionists
persecuting Him as a false deceiver, hesitated in becoming
his adherents in the beginnings of the Church.

323. When saint James therefore came to preach in
Granada, the Jews commenced their opposition, proclaiming him as an adventurer, a deceiver, the author of false
sects, a legerdemain and enchanter. Saint James brought
twelve disciples with him, in imitation of his Master.
As all of them persisted in preaching, the hatred of the
Jews and of their followers increased, so that they wished
to assassinate the disciples; and they really killed one
of them, who in his ardent zeal had opposed the Jews.
But as the holy Apostle and his disciples not only not
feared death, but courted suffering for the name of
Christ, they continued to preach the faith with still greater
zeal. Having thus labored for many days and converted
many of the infidels of that city and province, the fury
of the Jews rose to a higher pitch. They seized them all
and led them forth bound and fettered beyond the city
walls and there likewise chained their feet, for they
considered them to be magicians and sorcerers who might
otherwise escape. As their enemies made preparations
to decapitate them all immediately, the holy Apostle
ceased not to call upon the Most High and upon his

Virgin Mother, praying as follows: "Most holy Mary, Mother of my Lord the Redeemer Jesus Christ, extend thy favor in this hour to thy humble servant. Pray for me, sweetest and kindest Mother, and for these faithful professors of the faith. If it is the will of the Most High, that we here give our lives for the glory of his holy name, do Thou ask, O Lady, that my soul may be received in his presence. Remember me, most clement Mother, and bless me in the name of Him who chose Thee among all creatures. Receive in sacrifice my resignation to the misfortune of not seeing Thee, if this is to be the last day of my life. O Mary! O Mary!"

324. These last words saint James repeated many times. But from her oratory in the Cenacle, where She was favored by an especially clear vision, the great Queen heard all and saw what was passing with her most beloved apostle saint James. Thus informed She was moved with tenderest compassion at the tribulation of her servant and at his clamors. She felt still more sorrow at being so far away, and, as She knew that nothing is difficult to the divine power, She entertained the loving desire of helping and defending the Apostle in his danger. As She knew moreover that this Apostle was to be the first to shed his blood for her divine Son, her compassion became more vehement. But She did not ask the Lord or the angels to bring Her to the place where saint James then was; because her admirable prudence prevented Her from making such a petition. For She knew that divine Providence would need no such reminder on her part, nor fail in anything that was necessary. In asking such miracles, as long as She lived in the flesh, She exercised highest discretion and restraint always subjecting her desires to the will of the Lord.

325. But her Son and true God, who took notice of

the wishes of such a Mother, knowing that they were holy, just and full of piety, immediately commanded the thousand angels of her guard to assist Her and fulfill the will of their Queen and Lady. They all manifested themselves to Her in human shape and told Her what the Most High had commanded. Without delay they placed Her upon a throne made of a beautiful cloud and carried Her to the field in Spain, where saint James and his companions were awaiting martyrdom in their fetters. Their enemies had already bared their scimitars or swords to strike off their heads. The Apostle alone saw the Queen of heaven in the clouds from which She spoke to him in most endearing terms, saying: "James, my son and dearest friend of my Lord Jesus Christ, be of good heart and be blessed eternally by Him who called and brought thee to his divine light. Rise then, faithful servant of the Most High, and be free of thy bonds." The Apostle, as far as he had been able in his fetters, had prostrated himself upon the ground. At the words of the powerful Queen his fetters and those of his disciples instantly fell and they found themselves free. The Jews, on the contrary, who stood with drawn weapons, all fell to the earth where they remained for some hours deprived of their senses. The demons, who had accompanied them and stirred them on, were hurled to the profound abysses, thus leaving saint James and his disciples at liberty and giving thanks to the Almighty for this blessing. The Apostle most fervently thanked the heavenly Mother with exceeding humility and in the jubilee of his soul. His disciples, although they did not see the Queen or her angels, understood the miracle and were informed by the Apostle of some of the particulars, by which they might be confirmed in faith, hope and devotion toward the most blessed Mary.

326. The heavenly Queen still more extended this favor; for She not only freed saint James from imminent death, but wished all Spain to benefit from his preaching and instruction. From Granada She ordered him to continue his journeys, commanding hundreds of her guardian angels to accompany him and show him the way from one place to another, to defend him and his disciples from all dangers, and finally, after having traversed all the provinces of Spain, to bring him to Saragossa. All this the hundred angels set about doing according to the orders of their Queen, while the rest brought Her back to Jerusalem. In such celestial company and guardianship saint James traveled through all the Spanish realm, more securely than the Israelites through the desert. In Granada he left some of his disciples, who afterwards suffered martyrdom, and with the others and those he afterwards gathered, he continued his missionary tours in many parts of Andalusia. Then he came to Toledo, Portugal Galicia and Asturia. Afterwards, making digressions to different places, he arrived in Rioja, thence, passing through Lograno, he went to Tudela and Saragossa, where happened what I shall relate in the next chapter. During his peregrinations saint James left disciples as bishops in the different cities of Spain, planting the faith and divine worship. So great and prodigious were the miracles he performed in this kingdom, that those of which we know must not appear extraordinary in comparison with those we know nothing of, since these are much more astonishing. The fruit of his preaching in Spain was immense in proportion to the shortness of his stay; and it would be a great error to say or think, that the conversions he made were few, for in all the places reached by him, he established the faith and ordained

many bishops for the government of the children he engendered to Christ in this kingdom.

327. In concluding this chapter I wish to state, that by different means I was made acquainted with the many contrary opinions of ecclesiastical historians concerning the things which I am describing; as for instance, concerning the departure of the Apostles from Jerusalem for the purpose of preaching the faith, the partition among them of the world by lot, the establishing of the Creed, the departure of saint James and his death. About all these and other events, I understand, writers differ very much in assigning the years or dates of their happening and in harmonizing them with the text of the canonical writings. But I have no commission from the Lord to clear up these and other doubts, or decide the controversies. From the very beginning I have said, that the Lord commanded me to write this history without regard to opinions, and without mixing up my certain knowledge with opinions. If what I write follows naturally and does not contradict in any way the sacred text, and at the same time maintains the dignity corresponding to the matter, I cannot undertake to add to the authenticity of this history, and Christian piety will ask for no more. It is also possible that, by proceeding in this manner, some of the differences of historians may be made to harmonize, and to this the well-read and the learned will attend.

INSTRUCTIONS GIVEN TO ME BY THE QUEEN OF HEAVEN, MOST HOLY MARY.

328. My daughter, the miracle of my being raised by the divine power to the sovereign throne of God in order that I might be consulted in the decrees of his divine

wisdom and will, as described by thee in this chapter, is so great and extraordinary, that it exceeds all the capacity of man in this mortal life, and only in eternal glory and in beatific vision men shall recognize this sacrament with a most special joy of accidental glory. As this blessing and wonderful privilege was the effect and the reward of the most ardent charity with which I loved and do love the highest Good, and of the humility by which I considered myself as his slave, and as these virtues truly raised me to the throne of the Divinity and established me there even while yet in mortal flesh, I wish thee to have a more intimate knowledge of this mystery, which without a doubt was one of the most exalted wrought in me by the divine Omnipotence and which excited the greatest wonder in the angels and saints. Thy own admiration I wish thee to turn into a most vigilant care and into a most lively desire of imitating me and in following me in the virtues, by which I merited such favors.

329. Remember then, my dearest, that not only once, but many times was I raised to the throne of the most holy Trinity in mortal flesh during the time which intervened from the descent of the Holy Ghost to my Assumption to eternal glory. In what still remains for thee to write of my life, thou wilt understand many other secrets connected with this privilege. And every time the puissant right hand of the Most High showed me this favor I experienced most copious effects of graces and gifts, according to the different ways of the divine Omnipotence and according to my, as it were, ineffable and boundless capacity of participating in the divine perfections. Sometimes in conferring upon me these favors the eternal Father said to me: "My Daughter and Spouse, thy love and fidelity bind Us to thee more than to any

other creature and fill Us with the plenitude of satisfaction. Ascend to our throne, so that thou mayest be absorbed in the abyss of our Divinity and hold in this Trinity the fourth place, as far as is possible to a mere creature. Take possession of our glory, the treasures of which We place in thy hands. Thine are the heavens, the earth and all the abysses. Enjoy in this mortal life all the privileges of the blessed more fully than all the saints. Let all the nations and creatures, whom We have called into existence, serve thee; let the powers of heaven obey thee, let the supreme seraphim be subject to thee and let all blessings be thine own in our divine consistory. Be thou enlightened as to the great counsels of our wisdom and divine will and do thou take part, in our decrees, since thy will is most equitous and faithful. Penetrate into the reasons for whatever We resolve in justice and holiness; and let thy will and thy motives be one with ours in whatever We provide for our holy Church."

330. In such ineffable condescension the Most High governed my will, that He conformed it entirely to his own and that nothing was done in the Church without my decision, which was to be conformable to that of the Lord himself, since He knew the appropriate reasons and motives for each of the decrees of his eternal counsels. I saw that it was not possible for me according to the common law to suffer all the labors and tribulations of the Church and especially not of the Apostles, as I had desired. This charitable desire, though it was impossible of execution, was not a deviation from the divine will, but was given to me by God as a token and witness of the boundless love with which I loved Him; for it was on account of the love of the Lord toward men, that I desired to take upon myself the labors and

sufferings of all men. And because on my part this love was true and my heart was prepared to fulfill this charity, and as I truly grieved not to be able to suffer for all, therefore it was so acceptable in the eyes of the Lord and He rewarded it as if I had really fulfilled it in deed. Hence arose my compassion for the martyrdom and torments of the Apostles and the others persecuted for Christ; in all of them and with all of them I was afflicted and tormented, and in some measure died their death. Such was the love I had for my faithful children; and, with the exception of suffering), it is the same now, although Christians do not suspect or know how much my charity deserves their gratitude.

331. I received these ineffable blessings from the right hand of my divine Son at the time when I was raised from the world and placed at his side, partaking of his exaltation and glory in the full measure possible to a mere creature. The hidden decrees and sacraments of the infinite Wisdom were first made manifest to the most holy humanity of my Lord, which, being united to the eternal Word, was the admirable medium of the Divinity. Through this humanity in another manner, they were communicated to me; for the union of his humanity with the Word is immediate and substantial and hence it participates intrinsically of the Divinity and of its decrees, in a manner corresponding to the substantial and personal union. I however partook of this favor by another wonderful and unexampled process, considering that I was a mere creature and not having the divine nature; in a manner similar to the most holy humanity and as one, who, next to the Mangod, was closest to the Divinity. Thou canst not at present understand more or penetrate deeper into this mystery. But the blessed understood it, each one according to his degree of heav-

enly science; and all of them understood this conformity and similitude of myself with my divine son,
as well as the difference between me and Him.   All of
this was, and is now, to them a motive for new canticles
of glory and praise of the Omnipotent; for this was one
of the great wonders wrought in me by the powerful
right hand of God.

332. In order that thou mayest increase the force of
thy holy affections and desires as well of nature as of
grace, although they may not be within the possibility
of execution, I will reveal to thee another secret.   It is
this: when I perceived the effects of the Redemption in
the justification of souls by the operation of grace through
contrition, or through Baptism and the other Sacraments,
I conceived such an esteem for them, that I was filled
with a holy emulation and desire to participate in their
effects.   As I had no sins of which I could be cleansed and
justified, I could not partake of their effects in the same
degree as the sinners who received them.   But because I
wept over their sins more than they all, and as I thanked
the Lord for these blessings so liberally conferred upon
them, I gained more graces than were necessary to justify
all the children of Adam.   So much the Most High permitted Himself to be indebted to my works and such was
their merit of grace in the eyes of God.

333. And now, my daughter, consider under what obligations thou art after being informed and enlightened
concerning these great and venerable secrets.   Let not
these talents lie idle, nor waste or despise such great
blessings of the Lord; follow me in perfect imitation
of all my doings manifested to thee.   In order that thou
mayest nourish the flame of divine love, ceaselessly bear
in mind how my most holy Son and I in this mortal life
sighed and ardently yearned for the salvation of all the

children of Adam and wept over the eternal perdition incurred by so many in their deceitful and counterfeit pleasures. In this charitable zeal I wish thee to distinguish thyself very much, as my daughter and disciple, and as a most faithful spouse of my Son, who delivered Himself to the death of the Cross on this very account. For if the force of this love did not take away my life, it was because the Lord miraculously preserved it; and this is the love which placed me upon the throne of God and made me partaker of the counsels of the most blessed Trinity. If thou, my dear, shalt be as diligent and fervent in imitating me and as anxious to obey me, as I expect of thee, I asure thee of a participation in the favors shown to my servant James; I will hasten to thy aid in thy tribulations; I will govern thee, as I have so often promised thee; and more than this, the Most High will be more liberal with thee than all thy highest wishes can ever hope to compass.

CHAPTER XVII.

LUCIFER STIRS UP ANOTHER PERSECUTION AGAINST THE
CHURCH AND AGAINST THE MOST BLESSED MARY; SHE
MAKES IT KNOWN TO SAINT JOHN, AND AT HIS AD-
VICE RESOLVES TO GO TO EPHESUS; HER DIVINE SON
APPEARS TO HER AND COMMANDS HER TO VISIT SAINT
JAMES IN SARAGOSSA; THE EVENTS CONNECTED WITH
THIS VISIT.

334. In the eighth chapter of the Acts of the Apostles
saint Luke narrates the persecution incited by hell against
the Church after the death of saint Stephen. He calls
it a great persecution, because, through the zealous
efforts of saint Paul before his conversion, the infernal
dragon succeeded in raising it to highest pitch. Of this
persecution I have spoken in the twelfth and fourteenth
chapter of this part. But from what I have said there,
it will be understood that this enemy of God did not rest
or consider himself so completely overcome, as not to
venture new battles against the Church and the most
blessed Lady. From what saint Luke himself says in his
twelfth chapter concerning the imprisonment of saint
Peter and James by Herod, it is clear that this persecution began anew after the conversion of saint Paul, not
even considering his express statement, that Herod sent
soldiers to afflict some of the faithful of the Church (Acts
8, 1). In order that what I said and will say may be
better understood, I repeat, that these persecutions were
all plotted and set in motion through the demons, by inciting certain malicious men. And because divine Provi-

dence at times gave the demons this permission, and at others withdrew it, casting them into hell, as at the conversion of saint Paul and at other occasions, it naturally happened, that the primitive Church sometimes enjoyed peace and tranquillity, at other times, when this truce was again broken, it was molested and afflicted; and this is the lot of the Church in all ages.

335. Peace was favorable to the conversion of the faithful, and persecution increased their merit and practice of virtues; and this kind of variation was ordained, and will always be maintained, by the divine Providence. Hence, after the conversion of saint Paul the Church enjoyed some months of peace, namely, from the time when Lucifer and his companions were hurled vanquished into hell until their return to the earth, of which I will speak directly. Of this time of tranquillity saint Luke speaks in the ninth chapter where, after relating the conversion of saint Paul, he says, that the Church had peace throughout Judea, Galilee and Samaria, and that it increased and walked the way of the Lord in consolation of the Spirit. Although the Evangelist mentions this after speaking of the coming of saint Paul to Jerusalem, yet it occurred long before; for saint Paul's coming to Jerusalem happened more than five years after his conversion and saint Luke, in writing his history, mentions this coming of saint Paul to Jerusalem before mentioning his conversion, as is the case with many events in the Evangelists, who were in the habit of anticipating historical facts in order to finish and illustrate their present point; for they did not intend to write the history of all the events, although in the main they did follow the course of events according as they happened.

336. This being understood and following up what I said in the fifteenth chapter concerning the hellish meet-

ing called by Lucifer after the conversion of saint Paul,
I wish to say, that this conference lasted for some time
and the infernal dragon with his demons evolved diverse
schemes and resolved on different measures for the destruction of the Church and for the possible debasement
of the great Queen from her high state of reputed holiness. But the serpent's ignorance about Her was incom-
parably greater than his knowledge. The days of peace
enjoyed by the Church being past, the princes of darkness
issued forth from the abysses in order to execute their
malicious designs fabricated in the infernal dungeons,
and at the head of them all came forth Lucifer. It is
worthy of attention, that so great was the fury and indignation of this blood-thirsty beast against the Church and
the most blessed Mary, that he brought with him from
hell more than two thirds of his demons for this enterprise and without doubt he would have emptied hell of all
its demons, if a part had not been necessary for the
torture of the damned souls. For not only are the
damned ceaselessly burning in the fires lighted by divine
justice, but this dragon never permits the absence of all
the demons to relieve them of the sight and companionship of their tormentors. Though Lucifer is so ravenous
for the destruction of mortals on earth, he is just as
unwilling to grant any relief to the damned in hell, and
therefore he will never entirely empty it of the demons.
Such an impious, cruel and inhuman master the unfortunate sinners on earth continue to serve!

337. The holiness of the blessed Mother, their divine
favor and protection lavished on the faithful as exhibited
in saint Stephen and saint Paul, and all the other events
after the death of the Savior, which all came to the
knowledge of the dragon, had raised his wrath to the
highest and to inconceivable pitch. Therefore he took

up his seat in Jerusalem personally to erect his batteries against the very stronghold of the faith and in order to direct the operation of all the infernal squadrons; for the demons preserve order among themselves only for the purpose of warfare against men, while in all the rest they are full of discord and confusion. The Most High has never permitted full sway to their envy, for in one moment they would overturn and destroy the whole world; but He gave them a limited freedom, in order that by affliction the Church might take deep roots in the blood and the merits of the saints and so that in persecution and torments might be manifested the wisdom and power of the Pilot directing this little ship of the Church. Immediately Lucifer commanded his satellites to scour the whole earth in order to find out where the Apostles and disciples were preaching the name of the Lord. The dragon in Jerusalem sought the localities most remote from the places consecrated by the mysteries and the blood of the Lord; for he and all the demons dreaded these spots and the nearer they approached, the more they felt themselves weakened and oppressed by the divine power. These effects they feel to this day, and will feel to the end of the world. Sorrowful it is indeed, that this sanctuary of the faithful, on account of the sins of men, is now in the hands of pagans; and happy are the few children of the Church who are within its precincts, such as the sons of our great father and restorer of the Church, saint Francis!

338. Through the information brought by his demons Lucifer learnt the condition of the faithful in all the places where the faith of Christ was being preached. He issued new orders for the persecution of Christians, assigning more or less powerful demons according as he thought it necessary against the different Apostles, dis-

ciples or followers of the faith. Others he appointed as messengers to furnish him with accounts of what was happening, or to transmit his orders for conducting the warfare against the Church. Lucifer also pointed out to his demons unbelieving, perfidious, evil-minded and depraved men, whom they were to excite and provoke to envious wrath against the followers of Christ. Among these were Herod and many Jews, who abhored the Crucified and wished to blot out his very name from the land of the living (Jer. 11, 19). They also availed themselves of the gentiles that were most depraved and most given to idolatry. They selected, both from the ones as from the others, the worst and most perfidious to act as helpers and instruments of their malice. In this way they began the persecution of the Church, and they continued in succeeding ages to use similar diabolical arts for the ruin of virtue, of the fruits of the Redemption and the blood of Christ. In the primitive Church the infernal dragon caused great havoc among the faithful, overwhelming them with diverse kinds of tribulation, not recorded or known to us; although we know, that what saint Paul in his epistle to the Hebrews says of the persecution of the ancient saints, was repeated in the saints of the new Testament. In addition to these exterior persecutions the demons afflicted all the just, the Apostles, disciples and believers with hidden temptations, suggestions, illusions and malicious promptings, as he continues to do now with all those who desire to walk in the divine law and follow Christ our Redeemer and Master.

339. But nothing of all this was hidden to the great Mother of wisdom, because in the clearness of her eminent science She perceived all the secrets of hell, that were hidden to the rest of mortals. Although blows and wounds, when they find us prepared, are wont to cause

us less damage, and although the most prudent Virgin was so well fortified against the coming troubles of the holy Church that She could not be surprised by them, yet, as they concerned the Apostles and the faithful whom She loved from her inmost soul, the prospect of these afflictions wounded her most tender heart and filled Her with sorrow in proportion to her almost boundless charity. It would have deprived Her of life many times, if, as I have often said, the Lord had not wonderfully preserved it. And in truth, all just souls, who are perfected in divine love, would be moved at seeing the wrath and fury of such a host of demons, so vigilant and astute, exerted against the few faithful in their needy and frail condition and burdened with so many miseries of their own. In consideration of their danger, the most blessed Mary forgot all that concerned Herself and was ready to undergo any possible suffering for the protection and consolation of her children. She multiplied her sighs and tears, her exertions and prayers, for their safety. Especially the Apostles and disciples She sought to fortify and encourage by renewing her counsels and exhortations. Many times She restrained the demons by her sovereign commands as Queen, and snatched from their claws innumerable souls, whom they were deceiving and perverting, and thus She rescued them from eternal death. At other times She prevented great cruelties intended for the ministers of Christ; for Lucifer sought the life of the Apostles, as he had already done before through Saul. All this happened likewise to the disciples, who were preaching the faith.

340. Though the heavenly Mistress preserved her interior peace and tranquillity and her exterior equanimity and serenity, yet her compassionate anxiety and maternal solicitude failed not to reveal, in

some measure, the sorrow of her heart in her countenance. And as saint John attended upon Her with the watchful devotion of a son, the slight change in her appearance could not remain concealed from the eagle eyes of this seer. He was deeply afflicted, and having in vain battled with his anxiety, he betook himself to the Lord seeking enlightenment and saying: "My Lord and God, Savior of the world, I acknowledge my indebtedness to Thee for having, without my merits and out of pure condescension, given me Her as a Mother, who is thy own; who conceived Thee, bore and nursed Thee at her bosom. Through this blessing I am made rich and prosperous in the possession of the greatest Treasure of heaven and earth. But without thy royal presence thy Mother, my Mistress, is forsaken and alone, and for it neither men nor angels can compensate, much less I, a vile worm and a slave. My God and Savior of the world, I now see Her sorrowful, who gave Thee human form and who is the joy of thy people. I desire to console Her and alleviate her grief, but I find myself incapable of doing it. Reason and love urge me on; but reverence and my frailty prohibits it. Give me, O Lord, light and spirit for doing what will please Thee and serve thy Mother."

341. After this prayer the saint debated with himself for some time, whether he should ask the great Mistress of heaven concerning her sorrow or not. On the one side his love urged him thereto, on the other he was restrained by his holy fear and reverence for Her. Three times he approached the door of Her oratory, and was as many times withheld by his reverence from asking the question. The heavenly Mother knew all that saint John was doing and what passed through his heart. Out of respect for him as a priest and minister of the Lord,

She thereupon rose from her prayer and sought him out saying: "Master, tell me what thou asketh of thy servant." I have already stated, that the Lady called the priests and ministers of her Son "masters." The Evangelist was consoled and encouraged by this advance and with some hesitation answered: "My Lady, my office and desire of serving Thee has caused me to notice thy sorrow and I am troubled at thy suffering, which I am anxious to alleviate."

342. Saint John added no more words; but the Queen knew his desire to be informed of her trouble, and in promptest obedience She fulfilled his wishes as those of her superior, even before he should express them. Most holy Mary turned to the Lord and said: "My God and Son, Thou hast wished thy servant John to take thy place as my companion and attendant, and I have received him as my prelate and superior, whose will and desire, as soon as they become known to me, I wish to obey in order that I, thy humble servant, may live and be governed by thy obedience. Give me permission to tell him of my anxiety according to his wish." She felt at once the fiat of the divine will and falling on her knees at the feet of saint John, She asked his blessing and kissed his hands. Having asked his permission to speak, She said: "My master, lord, the sorrow of my heart is well founded, for the Most High has shown to me the tribulations which are to come over the Church, and the persecutions, which all its children, especially the Apostles, shall suffer. In preparation and for the execution of this wickedness in the world, I have seen the infernal dragon with innumerable hosts of evil spirits issuing forth from the caverns of the abyss, all filled with implacable wrath and fury for the destruction of the Church. This city of Jerusalem will be the first and fore-

most in their assault.   In it one of the Apostles will meet
his death, and others will be imprisoned and afflicted at
the instigation of the demon.   My heart is filled with
compassion and sorrow at the opposition of these enemies
to the exaltation of the holy name of God and to the
salvation of souls."

343. Thus informed the Apostle was likewise aggrieved
and somewhat troubled. But in the strength of divine
grace he answered the Queen saying: "My Mother and
Lady, thy wisdom cannot ignore that the Most High will
draw great fruits for his Church and for his faithful children from these trials and tribulations, and that He will
assist them in their affliction. We Apostles are prepared to
sacrifice our lives for the Lord, who has offered his own
for the whole human race. We have received great
blessings and it is not just that they remain idle and
useless.   When we were little ones in the school of our
Teacher and Lord, we behaved like children.   But since
He has enriched us with the Holy Ghost and enkindled
in us the fire of love, we have lost our cowardice and
desire to walk the way of the Cross, taught us by his
doctrine and example. We know that the Church is
to be established and preserved by the blood of its ministers and children.   Pray Thou for us, my Lady, that
by the divine power and thy protection we gain the
victory over our enemies and that, for the glory of the
Most High, we triumph over all of them.   But if this
city of Jerusalem is to bear the brunt of the persecution,
it seems to me, my Lady, that Thou shouldst not await
it here, lest the fury of hell, by inciting the malice of
men, attempt some indignity to the tabernacle of God."

344. The great Queen and Lady of heaven, full of
love and compassion for the Apostles and all the other
faithful, and spurning all fear, would rather have stayed

in Jerusalem, in order to visit, console and encourage all in their impending tribulation. But this preference, though so holy, She did not make known to saint John; for, as it was the choice of her heart, She preferred to disregard it and yield in humble obedience to the wishes of the Apostle, whom She held as her prelate and superior. In this subjection, giving no direct answer, She thanked the Evangelist for his courageous desire of suffering and dying for Christ; and, as for departing from Jerusalem, She told him to command and dispose as he thought fit; for She would obey him in all as his subject and would ask the Lord to guide him by his divine light according to his glory and pleasure. On getting this consent of the blessed Mother, (affording us such a great example and reprehending so much our disobedience), the Evangelist proposed to go to Ephesus, as the confines of Asia Minor. In suggesting this journey to the most holy Mary, he said: "My Lady and Mother, in order to leave Jerusalem and seek occasion to labor for the exaltation of the name of the Most High, it seems best for us to retire to the city of Ephesus, where Thou canst bring forth the fruits of faith, which are not to be expected in Jerusalem. Would I were one of the angels, who assist at the throne of the blessed Trinity, so as to serve Thee worthily in this journey; but I am only a vile worm of the earth. The Lord however will be with us, and Thou shalt have Him a propitious Helper as thy God and thy Son."

345. Having resolved upon this journey, the necessary notice and advice was yet to be given to the faithful in Jerusalem. The great Lady therefore retired to her oratory and prayed as follows: "Most high and eternal God, this humble handmaid prostrates herself before thy royal presence and from my inmost heart I beseech

Thee to direct and guide me in thy greater pleasure and good will. I will make this journey in obedience to thy servant John, whose will shall be as thy own. It is not just that thy handmaid and Mother, who has been so favored by the right hand, should take any step which is not for the greater glory and exaltation of thy holy name. Attend, O Lord to my desires and prayers, in order that I may act most appropriately and justly." Then the Lord answered Her and said: "My Dove and dearest Spouse, I have ordained this journey for my greater pleasure. Obey John, and go to Ephesus; for there in due time I wish to manifest my clemency to some souls through thy mediation and presence." By this answer of the Lord the most blessed Mary was consoled in the knowledge of the divine will, and She asked the Lord for his blessing and for permission to prepare for her departure at the time set by the Apostle. Full of the fire of charity She was inflamed with the desire of promoting the good of souls in Ephesus, of which the Lord had given Her hopes. I will now relate, how the most blessed Mary, in obedience to her Son's, our Savior's, will, came to Saragossa in Spain to visit saint James, in what year and day this happened, and what took place on this occasion.

346. All the solicitude of our great Mother and Lady was centered upon the increase and spread of the holy Church, the consolation of the Apostles, disciples and the other faithful, and in defending them from the persecutions and assaults prepared by the infernal dragon and his hosts. In her matchless charity, before She departed from Jerusalem to take up her abode in Ephesus, She ordered and arranged many things, both by Herself and through her holy angels, in order, as much as possible, to provide all that seemed proper

for the needs of the Church in her absence; for at that time She had no knowledge of the duration of her sojourn or of her return to Jerusalem. The most effectual service She could render to the faithful was her continual prayer to secure the assistance of the infinite power of her Son for the defense of the Apostles and the faithful against the proud and vaunting schemes of Lucifer's wickedness. The most prudent Mother knew, that among the Apostles James would be the first one to shed his blood for Christ our Savior, and because She loved him in a special manner, as I have stated above, She offered up more particular prayers for him than for the other Apostles.

347. While the heavenly Mother continued in these prayers, on one of the days, the fourth before leaving for Ephesus, She felt in her chastest heart new and sweetest affections, as was usual, when She was about to receive some signal favor. They are called words of the Lord in the language of holy Scriptures. Responding to them as the Mistress of holy science, the most blessed Lady said: "Lord, what dost Thou command me to do? What dost Thou desire of me? Speak, O Lord, for thy handmaid heareth." Repeating these words She saw her divine Son, descending in person to visit Her, seated upon a throne of ineffable majesty and accompanied by innumerable angels of all the heavenly choirs and hierarchies. With all his court the Lord entered the oratory of his most blessed Mother, and the humble and devout Virgin worshipped Him in deepest reverence from the inmost of her purest soul. Then the Lord spoke to her saying: "My most beloved Mother, of whom I have received human being for the salvation of the world, I am attentive to thy petitions and holy desires and they are pleasing to Me. I shall defend my

Apostles and my Church, and I shall be their Father
and Protector, so that it shall not be overcome nor the
gates of hell prevail against it (Matth. 18, 18).   As
thou already knowest, it is necessary for my glory, that
the Apostles labor with my grace, and that at the end
they must follow Me to the cross and to the death I
have suffered for the whole human race.   The first one
who is to imitate Me therein is my faithful servant
James, and I wish that he suffer martyrdom in this clty
of Jerusalem.   In order that he come hither, and for
other purposes of my glory and thine, I desire thee to
visit him in Spain, where he is preaching my name.   I
desire my Mother, that thou go to Saragossa where he
now is, and command him to return to Jerusalem.   But
before he leaves that city, he is to build a temple in
thy name and title, where thou shalt be venerated and
invoked for the welfare of that country, for my glory
and pleasure, and that of the most blessed Trinity."

348. The great Queen of heaven accepted this commission from her divine Son with new jubilee of her
soul.   And with sincerest gratitude She answered: "My
Lord and true God, let thy holy will be done in thy
servant and Mother for all eternity, and let all the
creatures praise Thee for the admirable works of kindness done to thy servants.   I, O Lord, bless and magnify
Thee in them and give humble thanks for them in the
name of the entire Church and in my own name.   Grant
me, my Son, that in the temple Thou commandest to be
built by thy servant James, I may be permitted to promise
the special protection of thy almighty arm, and that this
sacred place shall be part of my inheritance for the use
of all those that call with devotion upon thy holy name
and ask me to intercede for them with thy clemency."

349. Christ our Redeemer answered Her: "My

Mother, in whom I am well pleased, I give thee my royal word, that I shall look with especial clemency and fill with blessings all those who with devotion and humility call upon Me through thy intercession in that temple. In thy hands have I deposited and consigned all my treasures; as my Mother, who holds my place and power, thou canst signalize that place by depositing therein thy riches and promising in it thy favors; for all will be fulfilled according to thy will and pleasure." Again the most blessed Mary thanked her Son and God for this promise. Then, at the command of the Lord, a great number of the angels that accompanied Her formed a royal throne of a most resplendent cloud and placed Her thereon as the Queen and Mistress of all creation. Christ the Savior gave them his blessing and ascended with the rest of the angels to heaven. The purest Mother, borne by the hands of the seraphim and accompanied by her thousand angels and the rest, departed body and soul for Saragossa in Spain. Although this journey could have been made in the shortest moment of time, the Lord ordered the angels to move along singing hymns of praise and jubilee to their Queen in choirs of sweetest harmony.

350. Some of them sang the "Ave Maria," others the "Salve sancta Parens" and "Salve Regina"; others the "Regina coeli laetare," etc., choir answering choir in such harmony and concord of sounds, as no human art could ever attain. The great lady also, with a heart as humble as this favor was exalted, opportunely responded, referring all this glory to the Most High. She repeated many times: "Holy, holy, holy, Lord God Sabaoth (Is. 6, 3), have pity on the poor children of Eve. Thine is the glory, thine the power and majesty. Thou alone art holy, the most High and the Lord of

all the celestial armies and of all creation." The angels then would respond also to these songs of the Virgin, so sweet in the hearing of the Lord. Proceeding in this manner till about midnight, they arrived in Saragossa.

351. The most fortunate Apostle saint James was encamped with his disciples outside of the wall running along the banks of the river Ebro. In order to engage in prayer, he had separated some distance from his companions. Some of his disciples had fallen asleep and others were absorbed in prayer, all of them far from expecting the strange event. The procession of the angels spread out somewhat and sang still louder, so that not only saint James, but also his disciples could hear them from afar. Those that were asleep awoke and all of them were filled with interior sweetness and wonder, with heavenly consolation, which caused them to remain speechless with admiration and to shed tears of joy. They saw in the sky a most brilliant light, brighter than that of the sun; but it was not diffused beyond a certain space and seemed like a large luminous globe. Lost in admiration and joy they stood motionless until called by their teacher. Through the miraculous effects, which they felt within them, the Lord wished to prepare them for what would be manifested to them concerning this great mystery. The holy angels placed the throne of their Queen and Lady within sight of the Apostle, who was still wrapt in most exalted prayer and heard much more plainly the celestial music and saw more of the light than his disciples. The angels bore with them a small column hewn of marble or jasper; and a not very large image of their Queen, made of some other material. This image was carried by the angels with great veneration. During that night, the angels, exerting their skill in fashioning the things of nature, had prepared all this for the occasion.

352. Seated on her throne in the cloud and surrounded by the angelic choirs the Queen of heaven manifested Herself to saint James. In wonderful beauty and refulgence the great Lady far outshone all the angels. The blessed Apostle prostrated himself upon the earth and in deepest reverence venerated the Mother of his Creator and Redeemer. He was shown at the same time the image and the pillar or column in the hands of some of the angels. The loving Queen gave him her blessing in the name of her divine Son and said: "James, servant of the Most High, be thou blest by his right hand: may He raise thee up and show thee the light of his divine countenance." All the angels answered: "Amen." The Queen of heaven continued: "My son James, this place the most high and omnipotent God of heaven has destined to be consecrated by thee upon earth for the erection of a temple and house of prayer, where, under my patronage and name He wishes to be glorified and magnified, where the treasures of his right hand shall be distributed, and all his ancient mercies shall be opened up for the faithful through my intercession, if they ask for them in true faith and sincere piety. In the name of the Almighty I promise them great favors and blessings of sweetness, and my protection and assistance; for this is to be my house and temple, my inheritance and possession. A pledge of this truth and of my promise shall be this column with my image placed upon it. In the temple which thou shalt build for me, it shall remain and be preserved, together with the holy faith, until the end of the world. Thou shalt immediately begin to build this temple of God, and after thou hast completed it, thou shalt depart for Jerusalem; for my divine Son wishes thee to offer the sacrifice of thy life in the same place where He offered his for the salvation of the human race."

353. The great Queen finished speaking and ordered
the holy angels to set up the column, and upon it the
sacred image, in the same place where they now stand;
and the angels fulfilled her command in one moment.
As soon as the column and the image were in place, the
angels and the holy Apostles recognized that spot as a
house and portal of God, as holy ground, consecrated
as a temple to the glory of the Most High and the invocation of his holy Mother.   As witness to this fact they
immediately worshipped and reverenced the Divinity.
Saint James prostrated himself upon the ground and
with the holy angels celebrated with new canticles the
first dedication of a temple instituted in this world under
the name and title of the great Mistress of heaven and
earth.   This was the happy origin of the sanctuary of
our Lady of the Pillar in Saragossa, which is justly
called the angelic chamber, the house of God and of
his purest Mother, worthy of the veneration of the whole
world and a secure pledge and earnest of the favors and
benefits not prevented by our sins.   It seems to me, that
our great patron and Apostle, the second Jacob, gave
a more glorious beginning to this temple, than the first
Jacob to his in Bethel, when he journeyed to Mesopotamia, although in that name and on that rock was
built the temple of Solomon.   There Jacob saw in his
sleep the mystical and figurative representation of the
ladder with the accompanying angels; but here our Jacob
saw the true Stair of Heaven with his bodily eyes, and
accompanied by many more angels.   There the stone
was consecrated as a temple, which was to be destroyed
many times and after some centuries was to cease to
exist; but here, in the firmness of this truly consecrated
pillar, was established the temple, the faith and the worship of the Most High until the end of the world, where

the angels were to ascend with the prayers of the faithful and to descend with incomparable blessings and favors to be distributed to all htose that in this place devoutly call upon and venerate this great Queen and Lady.

354. Our apostle gave most humble thanks to the most blessed Mary and asked Her for the special protection of this Spanish kingdom and particularly of this place consecrated to her devotion and name. The heavenly Mother granted him all his requests; and having again given him her blessing, She was carried back to Jerusalem in the same order by the holy angels. At her petition the Most High charged an angel with the care and defense of this sanctuary, and from that day until now this angel fulfills this office and will continue it as long as the sacred image and column shall remain there. All the faithful Catholics may see with their own eyes the wonderful preservation of this sanctuary, since it has remained intact and uninjured for more than sixteen hundred years* amid all the perfidy of the Jews, the idolatry of the Romans, the heresy of the Arians, and the savage fury of the Moors and pagans; and still greater would the astonishment of Catholics be, if they could know of the plots and schemes which all hell has fabricated in different ages through the hands of these infidel nations for the destruction of this sanctuary. I will not detain myself in relating these events, because it is not necessary and does not belong to my purpose. It is enough to say, that Lucifer has set all these enemies to attack it many times and the guardian angel of this sanctuary has foiled all his attempts.

355. But I wish to mention two points which have been made known to me for record here. First, that in regard to the promises of Jesus Christ and of his most blessed

---

*Now 1900.

Mother, although they seem absolutely to assure the preservation of this temple and sanctuary, yet they contain an implicit condition, as is the case with many other promises of holy Scripture in regard to particular blessings of divine grace. This implicit condition here is, that we on our part conduct ourselves in such a way as not to oblige God to deprive us of this merciful privilege, thus promised and offered to us. Because the Lord, beneath the mysterious decrees of his justice, hides this compelling measure of sins, therefore this condition is not declared or made manifest to us; and moreover, we know from the teachings of holy Church, that his favors and promises are not to be used by us against the Lord and that we must not sin in reliance upon his liberal mercy, since this, more than aught else, will make us unworthy of it. So many and so great may become the sins of these kingdoms and of that devout city of Saragossa, that we justly draw upon ourselves the loss of this wonderful blessing and of the protection of the great Queen and Lady of the angels.

356. The second point which I will touch upon and which is not less worthy of our consideration, is, that Lucifer and his demons, since they know of these facts and of the promises of the Lord, have attempted and are still attempting to introduce into this illustrious city, with a more refined malice than elsewhere, heinous vices and sins, especially such as may offend against the purity of the most blessed Mary. The purpose of the ancient serpent is to bring about two most execrable effects: first, either to induce the inhabitants of that city, if possible, so to offend God, as to cause Him to abolish the sanctuary, thus reaching the end which he could not otherwise attain; or, if that is not possible, at least to hinder souls from showing proper reverence and devo-

tion to the sacred temple and to the great blessings promised through Mary to all her devout supplicants. Lucifer and his demons know very well that the inhabitants of Saragossa and its neighborhood are much more heavily indebted to the great Queen of heaven than many other cities and provinces of Christianity. For it holds within its walls the storehouse and fountainhead of the favors and blessings, to draw which, others must come from afar; therefore if its inhabitants, while possessing these advantages, would lead a more wicked life and consequently treat with contempt this condescending clemency, which no one can ever merit, then certainly their ingratitude to God and his most blessed Mother would provoke a greater indignation and punishment in divine Justice. Joyfully I will confess to all that shall read this history, that I consider myself extremely fortunate in being permitted to write it in a place which is only two days' foot-journey from the city of Saragossa and I look upon that sanctuary with inmost affection of soul, in acknowledgment of the debt, which, as all know, I owe to the great Mistress of the world. I acknowledge also my obligations and my gratitude toward the piety of that city. In return I desire urgently to bring to the remembrance of its inhabitants the sincere and ardent devotion they owe to the most blessed Mary, the favors they can obtain for themselves by it, and the blessings they may lose by forgetfulness and inattention. Let them consider themselves as more favored and indebted than other faithful. Let them esteem their treasure, happily enjoy it, and let them not make the propitiatory of their God a useless and common dwelling, converting it into a court of justice; for the most holy Mary has appointed it as a workhouse or councilhouse of her mercies.

357. The vision of the most blessed Mary having faded away, saint James called his disciples, who were absorbed in the music and in wonder at the brightness, though they did not hear or see anything else. Their great teacher revealed to them as much as was calculated to animate them toward helping to build the temple, with which he had been commissioned; and, with the assistance of the holy angels, before he left Saragossa, completed the little chapel, in which now the image and the column are still preserved. Afterwards the Catholics erected the sumptuous temple and whatever else surrounds and adorns that celebrated sanctuary. The evangelist saint John at the time knew nothing of this excursion of the heavenly Mother to Spain, nor did She tell him about it; for these privileges and favors did not concern the faith of the universal Church, wherefore she kept the secret of them to Herself. Other greater ones however She made known to saint John and the other Evangelists, because they were necessary for the common instruction and faith of the Christians. But when saint James arrived from Spain and saw his brother John in Jerusalem, He related what had happened to him in his preaching-tours through Spain. He told him also of the two visions of the most blessed Mary and of what had happened in Saragossa in connection with the temple he had erected in that city. Through the Evangelist many of the other Apostles and disciples learnt of this miracle, for he afterwards told them of it in Jerusalem in order to confirm them in their faith and devotion to the Mistress of heaven and awaken their confidence in her protection. Hence, those that knew of these favors to saint James, from that time called upon Her in their labors and necessities; and the loving Mother helped some of them often, and all of

them at different times in certain difficulties and dangers.

358. The miraculous appearance of the most blessed Mary in Saragossa took place in the beginning of the fortieth year of the birth of the Lord, during the night of the second of January. Four years, four months and ten days had passed from the time when saint James left Jerusalem on his missionary tour up to this event; for he had left in the year thirty-five, on the twentieth of August, as I mentioned above (No. 319) ; and after the apparition he spent, in building the temple, in returning to Jerusalem and in preaching, one year, two months and twenty-three days. He died on the twenty-fifth of March in the year forty-one. The great Queen of the angels, at the time She appeared to him in Saragossa, was fifty-four years, three months and twenty-four days of age. For immediately on coming back to Jerusalem, She prepared to depart for Ephesus, as I will relate in the next book and chapter; and She left four days afterwards. Thus this temple was dedicated many years before her glorious transition, as will be evident, when I shall mention her age at her death; for from this apparition to her death intervened a longer time than is ordinarily assumed. During all these years She was already publicly venerated in Spain and had temples built in her honor; for in imitation of that in Saragossa others were soon erected, where altars were raised in her honor and solemn veneration.

359. This wonderful distinction without a doubt exalts Spain beyond all that can be said in its praise; since thereby it signalized itself before all nations and kingdoms in the public veneration, reverence and devotion due to the great Queen and Mistress of heaven and earth, and was more zealous to worship and invoke Her even while She was yet living, than other nations were

after her death and transition to heaven. In return for this ancient and universal devotion, the most blessed Mary, as I was given to understand, has enriched these realms more than the other kingdoms of the earth by spreading the public veneration of so many miraculous images, and sanctuaries dedicated in Spain to her honor. By multiplying these favors the heavenly Mother has sought to familiarize intercourse with Her throughout the kingdoms, offering her protection in so many temples and sanctuaries and meeting the devotions of the faithful in so many places throughout the provinces. This should induce us to acknowledge Her as our Mother and Patroness and give us to understand, that the defense and the spreading of her honor through the whole world is a special privilege of this nation.

360. Therefore I pray and humbly beseech all the subjects and inhabitants of Spain, and, in the name of this great Lady, exhort all of them to refresh their memory, enliven their faith, renew and excite their ancient devotion toward the most blessed Mary, and consider themselves more bound and obliged to her service than other nations. Let them hold especially the sanctuary of Saragossa in highest veneration, as excelling all the others and as being the starting-place of the piety and devotion toward this Queen in Spain. And let all those who read this history believe, that the former happiness and greatness of Spain was a gift of the most blessed Mary and a reward for the service rendered to Her by the Spanish people. If we in our days see the glory and happiness of Spain so much diminished, it is the fault of our negligence by which we oblige Her to withdraw her protection. If we desire a remedy for so many calamities, we can obtain it only through this powerful Queen, gaining her favor by new and extraor-

dinary proofs of our devotion. And as the admirable blessing of the Catholic faith and the other benefits I have mentioned, have come to us through our great patron and Apostle saint James, let our devotion and confidence toward him likewise be renewed, in order that the Almighty through his intercession may renew his wonders.

INSTRUCTION WHICH THE QUEEN OF HEAVEN, MOST BLESSED MARY, GAVE ME.

361. My daughter, thou knowest, that not without some mysterious reason I have in the course of this history so many times shown thee the secret machinations and treacherous counsels of hell for the ruin of mankind, and the furious and restless wrath with which Lucifer seeks to encompass it. In this assault hell misses no opening, no occasion, and lets no stone unturned, nor forgets any path, any state or person in laying snares for their fall and in trying to find ways so much the more dangerous and deceitful, the more they find their victims desirous of eternal life and of the friendship of God. Besides these general warnings thou hast often been shown the council-meetings and the plots laid against thee. It is important for all the children of the Church to escape the ignorance in which they live concerning the dangers besetting their eternal salvation; for they do not know or take notice, that their ignorance of these secrets is the chastisement of the sin of Adam, and how, after being enlightened, they again lose it and become more unworthy of it than before through their own sins. Many of the faithful are as oblivious and careless, as if there were no demons to persecute and deceive them; and if they sometimes think of them, it is superficially and lightly, falling immedi-

ately back into their forgetfulness, which for many of them means no less than eternal punishment. If at all times and in all places, in all their works and on all occasions the demons set their snares, it is but just and proper that Christians on their part take not one step without asking divine light to see and avoid the danger. But as the children of Adam are so torpid in regard to this matter, they perform scarcely one work without being assailed by the infernal serpent and infected by his poison. Thus they accumulate sins upon sins, evil upon evil, irritating the divine justice and shutting out mercy.

362. In these dangers I exhort thee, my daughter, that just as the fury and watchfulness of hell against thee is greater, so also, with the divine grace, thy watchfulness be more earnest and continual in order to vanquish those astute enemies. Consider what I did, when I saw the designs of Lucifer to persecute me and the holy Church: I multiplied my prayers, tears, sighs and supplications; and when the demons tried to avail themselves of the help of Herod and the Jews of Jerusalem, although I needed not fear the least for myself in the city and desired to remain there, I nevertheless gave up my desire of staying in order to furnish an example of caution and of obedience by flying from danger and by yielding to the will of saint John. Thou art not strong and art in great danger from creatures; and, what is still more, thou art my disciple, and hast my life and works for thy model. Therefore I desire thee to fly from danger as soon as thou seest it; and if necessary, avoid it at the cost of the greatest sensible pain, always acting under obedience, which thou must look upon as thy guiding-star and as thy support against the danger of a fall. Cautiously examine, whether beneath some

apparent work of piety there lurk not the snares of the demon and see that thou do not suffer evil in doing good to others. Do not trust to thy own judgment, although it may seem good and secure to thee; never hesitate to obey in all things, seeing that I by obedience safely passed through many labors and difficulties.

363. Renew also the loving desire of following my footsteps and of imitating me perfectly, so as to finish what still remains of my history, at the same time writing it in thy heart. Run on the way of humility and obedience after the order of my life and virtues, and if thou obey me (as I have wished and so often asked of thee) I will assist thee as my daughter in thy necessities and tribulations. My divine Son shall execute his designs in regard to thee, as thou hast desired before beginning this work; his promises so often repeated to thee will be fulfilled and thou wilt be blessed by his powerful right hand. Praise and magnify the Most High for the favor shown to my servant James in Saragossa, for the temple there erected before my Assumption into heaven, and for all the wonders concerning it. Remember that this was the first temple of the evangelical law and was most pleasing to the will of the most blessed Trinity.

BOOK TWO

PART III, BOOK VIII.

Describes the Journey of the Most Blessed Mary with Saint John to Ephesus; the Death and Chastisement of Herod; the Destruction of the Temple of Diana; the Return of the Most Blessed Mary from Ephesus to Jerusalem; the Instructions She gave to the Evangelists; the exalted State of Her purest Soul before Her death; Her most blessed Transition, Assumption and Coronation in heaven.

CHAPTER I.

THE MOST BLESSED MARY DEPARTS WITH SAINT JOHN FROM JERUSALEM FOR EPHESUS; SAINT PAUL GOES FROM DAMASCUS TO JERUSALEM; SAINT JAMES ARRIVES THERE; HE VISITS THE GREAT QUEEN IN EPHESUS; REFLECTIONS ON THE MYSTERIOUS HAPPENINGS DURING ALL THESE JOURNEYS.

365. The most blessed Mary, having enriched and blessed Saragossa and the kingdom of Spain by her presence, and her promises of protection, and having established through saint James and her angels the temple as a monument to her sacred name, was borne by the hands of the seraphim back to Jerusalem. As soon as the great Lady of heaven and Queen of the angels had left the cloud-throne, on which She had been borne, and set her foot upon the floor of the Cenacle, She prostrated Herself upon it, humbling Herself to the dust in order to praise the Most High for the favors conferred upon Her, upon saint James and upon the kingdom of Spain in this miraculous journey. At the thought of a temple built in her honor and for her invocation, She, in her ineffable

337

humility, so annihilated Herself in her own estimation, as
seemingly to have entirely forgotten that She was the
Mother of God, a sinless Creature and without measure
superior to all the highest seraphim. She humbled Herself
and gave thanks for these benefits, as if She were a mere
worm of the earth, of less value and guilty of more sins
than all the creatures. This new debt seemed to Her so
great, that She felt obliged to aspire to new and more
exalted degrees of holiness in recompense. This She resolved to do and really accomplished, arriving at a degree
of wisdom and humility beyond all our capacity to
conceive.

366. In these exercises, and in praying with great fervor for the defense and increase of the Church, She spent
the greater part of the four days after her return to Jerusalem. In the meanwhile the evangelist saint John made
preparations for the journey and embarkation for
Ephesus, and on the fourth day, which was the fifth of
January of the year forty, saint John notified Her that it
was time to leave; for there would be a ship and all things
had been arranged for the journey. The great Mistress
of obedience, without answer or delay, knelt down and
asked permission of the Lord to leave the Cenacle and
Jerusalem; and then She proceeded to take leave of the
owner of the house and its inhabitants. It can easily be
imagined, how sorrowful they were at this leave-taking;
for on account of her most sweet conversation, and because of the favors and blessings received at her liberal
hands, all were held captives and prisoners in love and
veneration of Her, whereas now all at once they were to
be deprived of her consoling presence and of this rich
Treasure, the well spring of so many blessings. All of
them offered to follow and accompany Her; but as this
was not opportune, they asked Her to hasten her return

and not to forsake forever this house, which was entirely at her disposal. The heavenly Mother thanked them for these pious and loving wishes by expressing her own humble love, and She somewhat allayed their grief by giving them hope of her return.

367. Then She asked permission of saint John to visit the holy places of our Redemption and there to worship and adore the Lord, who had consecrated them by his presence and his precious blood. With the Apostle She made these sacred stations, exhibiting incredible devotion and tears of reverent love, and saint John, deeply consoled at being permitted to accompany Her, exercised himself in heroic acts of virtue. The most blessed Mother saw at each of the holy places the angels, who had been deputed to guard and defend them; and anew She charged them to resist Lucifer and his demons, lest they destroy or profane by irreverence those sacred spots, as they desired and intended to do through the unbelieving Jews. She told the angels to drive away by holy inspirations the bad thoughts and diabolical suggestions, by which the infernal dragon sought to excite the Jews and other mortals to blot out the memory of Christ our Savior in those holy places, and She charged them with this duty for all the future times, since the wrath of the evil spirits against the places and the works of the Redemption endures through all the ages. The holy angels obeyed their Queen and Mistress in all that She ordained.

368. Having satisfied her piety, She asked saint John on her knees to bless Her for the journey, just as She had been wont to do with her divine Son; for She continued to exercise the same great virtues of obedience and humility toward the beloved disciple, his substitute. Many of the faithful of Jerusalem offered Her money, jewels, vehicles and all things necessary for her journey to the

sea and to Ephesus. The most prudent Lady humbly
showed her appreciation to all, but accepted nothing. For
her journey to the sea She made use of an unpretentious
beast of burden, on which She was carried along as the
Queen of the virtues and of the poor. She recollected the
journeys and pilgrimages She had made with her divine
Son and with her spouse Joseph, and these recollections,
together with the heavenly love, which had induced Her
once more to travel, awakened in her dove-like heart
tender and devout affections. In order to be in all things
most perfect, She excited new acts of resignation to the
divine will in being deprived, for the glory and exaltation
of his name, of the company of her Son and of her spouse,
whose consoling presence She had enjoyed on her former
journeys. She also resigned Herself to the divine will
in regard to leaving the quiet of the Cenacle, the neighborhood of the sacred places, and the intercourse with so
many of the faithful and devout children of the Church,
and praised the Most High, because He had given Her
the beloved disciple as a companion in her banishment.

369. For her greater alleviation and comfort during
this journey all her holy angels on her leaving the Cenacle,
appeared to Her in visible and corporeal forms surrounding Her and protecting Her in their midst. With this
escort of the celestial host and the human company of
saint John She journeyed to the port, where the vessel
was ready to sail for Ephesus. She spent her time in oft-
repeated and sweet colloquies and canticles with the celestial spirits, sounding the praises of the Most High. At
other times She conversed with saint John, who with
admirable reverence was tenderly solicitous to serve Her
in all that occurred and seemed opportune. This solicitude of saint John was met by the heavenly Mother with
incredible humility and gratitude; for these two virtues,

gratitude and humility, made all the favors She received
appear to Her very great, and although all service was
due Her in justice, She nevertheless acknowledged it as
the most voluntary favor.

370. They came to the harbor and immediately embarked in the ship with other passengers. The great
Queen of the world was now for the first time upon the
sea. She saw and comprehended with clearness the vast
Mediterranean and its communication with the great
ocean. She beheld its height and depth, its length and
breadth, its caverns and secret recesses, its sands and
minerals, its ebb and tide, its animals, its whales and fishes
of all sizes, and whatever other portentous animals it
enclosed. She knew how many men had drowned and
perished in voyaging it and She remembered the saying
of Ecclesiasticus: That those who navigate the sea, nar-
rate its dangers (Ecclus 43, 26), and that of David:
Wonderful are the surges and pride of the swollen waves
(Ps. 92, 4). The heavenly Mother could easily know all
this, as well because of an especial dispensation of her
divine Son, as on account of her supreme angelic privilege
and grace, and of her singular participation in the divine
attributes, which resembled those of the most sacred humanity of Christ our Savior. In virtue of these gifts and
privileges, her knowledge extended to all these things not
only as they are in themselves and without deceit, but far
beyond the sphere of angelic knowledge.

371. When this great panorama of creatures, in which
were reflected, as from a most clear mirror, the greatness
and omnipotence of the Creator, was presented to her
faculties filled with heavenly wisdom, her spirit winged
its ardent flight to the very being of God, so wonderfully
reflected in those creatures, and for all of them, and in all
of them, She gave praise and glory and magnificence to

the Most High. With the compassion of a most loving
Mother for those who trusted their lives to the indomitable
fury of the sea in navigating over its waves, She most
fervently besought the Almighty to protect from its
dangers all who should call upon her name and ask for her
intercession. The Lord immediately granted this petition
and promised to favor whoever upon the sea should carry
some image of Her and should sincerely look upon this
Star of the sea, most blessed Mary, for help in its perils.
Accordingly it will be understood, that, if the Catholics
and the faithful encounter ill success and perish in navigation, it is because they ignore the favors to be obtained
from the Queen of the angels, or because on account of
their sins they fail to remember Her in the raging storms,
or fail to seek her favors with sincere faith and devotion;
for neither can the word of the Lord ever fail, nor will
the great Mother ever deny assistance to those endangered
by the perils of the sea.

372. Another wonder also happened; for when the
most blessed Mary saw the sea with the fishes and other
maritime animals, She gave them all her blessing and
commanded them to acknowledge and praise their Creator
in the manner they were capable of. Then it was wonderful to see all the fishes of the sea obeying her command
and with incredible swiftness placing themselves in front
of the ship. None of the species of sea-animals was missing, each being represented by an innumerable multitude.
All of them surrounded the ship and showed their heads
above the water and with unwonted motions and signs
of pleasure for a long time acknowledged Her as the
Queen and Mistress of creatures and showed themselves
grateful to Her for coming upon the waters and visiting
them in their place of habitation. This strange event
astonished all the passengers as something never before

seen. The multitudes of large and small fishes, so crowded and packed together, somewhat impeded the progress of the vessel, and the passengers gazed upon this spectacle and wonderingly discussed it, for they did not know the cause of this miracle. Saint John alone understood it, and for a while he could not restrain his tears of devoted joy. After some time he asked the heavenly Mother to give them her blessing and her permission to depart since they had so promptly obeyed Her when asked to praise the Most High. The sweetest Mother complied, and immediately that army of fishes disappeared and churned the sea into foam by their quick motion. Thereupon the ship pursued its way over the tranquil and serene bosom of the waters, arriving at Ephesus in a few days.

373. When they landed the great Queen continued to work miracles equal to those wrought upon the sea. She cured the sick and the possessed, who, as soon as they came into her presence, were set free. I will not tarry to relate all these wonders; for many books would be necessary and much time to describe all the doings of the most blessed Mary and the favors of heaven, which She dispensed as the instrument and medium of the omnipotence of the Most High. I will record only those, which are necessary for this history and which shall suffice to manifest in some measure the unknown and wonderful works of our great Queen and Lady. In Ephesus lived some Christians, who had come from Jerusalem. There were not many, but on learning of the arrival of the Mother of Christ the Redeemer, they hastened to pay Her a visit and offer their dwellings and their possessions for her use. But the great Queen of virtues, who sought neither ostentation nor temporal commodities, chose for her dwelling the house of a few retired and poor women, who were living by themselves free from intercourse with men. By the in-

tervention of the angels, they lovingly and generously placed their home at the disposition of the Lady. In it they selected a very retired room for the Queen and another for saint John, which these Two occupied during their stay in Ephesus.

374. The most blessed Mary thanked the owners, who were to live with Her. Then She retired to her room and, prostrate upon the ground as was usual in her prayers, She adored the immutable essence of God, offering to sacrifice Herself in his service in this city and saying: "Lord God omnipotent, by the immensity of thy Divinity Thou fillest all the heavens and the earth (Jer. 23, 24). I, thy humble handmaid, desire to fulfill entirely thy holy will, on all occasions, in all places, and at all times, in which thy Providence shall deign to place me; for Thou art my only Good, my being and my life, and toward thy pleasure and satisfaction tend all my thoughts, words and actions." The most prudent Mother perceived that the Lord accepted her prayer and her offering, and that He responded to her desires with divine power, ready to assist and govern Her always.

375. She continued her prayer for the holy Church and laid out her plans for the assistance of all the faithful. She called her angels and sent some of them to aid the Apostles and disciples, whom She knew to be much pressed in the persecutions, raised by the demons through infidel men. In those days saint Paul fled from Damascus before the attacks of the Jews, as he himself mentions in the second epistle to the Corinthians, where he says, that he was let down from the walls of the city in a basket (II Cor. 11, 23). To defend him from these perils and those with which Lucifer threatened him on his way to Jerusalem, the great Queen of angels sent her angels to be his guard and protection; for the wrath and fury of hell was

roused against saint Paul more than against any of the other Apostles. This is the journey the Apostle himself refers to in his letter to the Galatians (Gal. 1, 18), where he says, that after three years he went to Jerusalem to visit saint Peter. These three years are not to be counted from the time of his conversion, but from the time he had returned from Arabia to Damascus. This is to be inferred from the text itself, for after stating that he returned from Arabia to Damascus, he immediately adds, that after three years, he went up to Jerusalem. If those three years are counted from the time before his sojourn in Arabia, the text would occasion much confusion.

376. With greater clearness this may be proved by computing the time of the death of saint Stephen and the journey of the most blessed Virgin to Ephesus. For counting from the day of his Nativity, saint Stephen died at the end of the thirty-fourth year of Christ, but counting them from the day of the Circumcision, as the Church does now, saint Stephen died seven days before the completion of the thirty-four years, being the seven days before the first of January. The conversion of saint Paul happened in the year thirty-six, on the twenty-fifth of January. If he had come to Jerusalem three years afterwards, he would have found there the most holy Mary and saint John, while he himself says, that he had not seen any one of the Apostles there, except saint Peter and saint James the less, who was called Alpheus. If the holy Queen and saint John had at that time been in Jerusalem saint Paul would certainly not have missed seeing them, and he would have mentioned at least saint John; yet he says, that he had not seen him. The explanation is, that saint Paul came to Jerusalem in the year forty, four years after his conversion, and a little less than a month after the most blessed Mary had departed for Ephesus.

Saint Paul had entered the fifth year of his conversion and the other Apostles, except the two he saw, had already left Jerusalem and were preaching the Gospel of Christ, each one in his appointed province.

377. Conformably with this reckoning we must assume, that saint Paul spent the first year after his conversion, or the greater part of it, in journeying to Arabia and preaching the Gospel there; then, the three following years, in Damascus. Hence the evangelist Luke, in the ninth chapter of his Acts of the Apostles, although he says nothing of Paul's journey to Arabia, nevertheless says that for many days after his conversion the Jews of Damascus plotted to take his life, these many days referring to the four years thus passed. Then he adds, that his disciples, aware of the plots of the Jews, on a certain night lowered him in a basket from the city walls and thus despatched him on his journey to Jerusalem. There, although knowing of his miraculous conversion, the Apostles and the new disciples, nevertheless retained a certain fear and suspicion of his not persevering, because he had been such a professed enemy of Christ, our Savior. Hence they at first held themselves aloof from saint Paul, until saint Barnaby spoke to them and introduced him to saint Peter, saint James and other disciples (Acts 26, 27). Saint Paul prostrated himself at the feet of the vicar of Christ, kissed them in acknowledgment of his errors and sins, and begging to be admitted as one of his subjects and as a follower of his Master, whose holy name and faith he desired to preach at the cost of his blood.

378. From the fear and suspicion of saint Peter and James concerning the perseverance of saint Paul we can likewise deduct that he arrived in Jerusalem in the absence of the most blessed Mary and saint John; for he would have presented himself first of all to Her to allay suspicion

against him; and the two Apostles would likewise have first asked Her, whether they could trust saint Paul. All of them would have been set at ease by the most prudent Lady, as She was so solicitous and attentive in consoling and instructing the Apostles, especially saint Peter. But since the great Lady had already left for Ephesus, they had no one to assure them of the constancy of saint Paul, until saint Peter reassured himself of it at seeing him thus prostrate at his feet. Thereupon he was received with great joy of soul by saint Peter and the other disciples. All of them gave humble and fervent thanks to the Most High, and commissioned saint Paul to preach in Jerusalem. This he gladly did, to the astonishment of all the Jews who knew him. As his words were like burning arrows, that penetrated into the hearts of all that heard him, they were struck with terror; and in two days all Jerusalem was roused by the news of his arrival, flocking to see him with their own eyes.

379. Lucifer and his demons were not asleep on this occasion, for they were visited by the Almighty with an increase of torment at the arrival of saint Paul. The divine power, so evident in him, oppressed and paralyzed the infernal dragons. But as their pride and malice shall never be extinguished through all the eternity of their existence (Ps. 73, 23), they were roused to fury, as soon as they recognized this divine virtue as flowing from Paul. Lucifer, with incredible rage, called together many legions of the demons and exhorted them anew to rouse themselves and exert all the forces of their malice for the entire destruction of saint Paul, and not to leave any stone unturned in Jerusalem and in all the world for the attainment of this object. The demons without delay set about this work, exciting Herod and the Jews against the Apostle, and directing their attention to the burning zeal with which he began to preach in Jerusalem.

380. The great Mistress of heaven perceived all this from her retirement in Ephesus; for in addition to the knowledge of all things through her heavenly science, She received information of all that happened to saint Paul from the angels She had sent for his defense. As the most blessed Mother expected the disturbance about to be raised by the malice of Herod and the Jews, especially against saint Paul, and as, on the other hand, She knew the importance of preserving his life for the exaltation of God's name and the spread of the Gospel, the great Queen was filled with new solicitude and regret at being absent from Palestine, where She could have rendered more immediate assistance to the Apostles. Therefore She sought to furnish it so much the more abundantly from Ephesus by multiplying her prayers and petitions, her ceaseless tears and sighs, and by other measures through the hands of her holy angels. In order to allay her anxieties, the Lord, one day in her prayer, assured Her, that He would fulfill her petitions and protect the life of saint Paul in this danger and in these assaults of the devil. And so He did: for one day saint Paul, while praying in the temple, was raised to an ecstatic rapture and filled with most exalted enlightenment and understanding, wherein the Lord commanded him immediately to leave Jerusalem and save his life from the hatred of the unbelieving Jews.

381. Hence saint Paul sojourned in Jerusalem at that time not more than fifteen days, as he himself says in his epistle to Galatians (Gal. 1, 18). After some years he returned thither from Miletus and Ephesus and was taken prisoner, and he refers to this ecstasy in the temple and to the command of the Lord to leave Jerusalem in the twenty-second chapter of the Acts. Of this vision and command he informed saint Peter, as the head of the apostolic college; and after consultation concerning his mortal

danger, he was secretly sent to Caesarea and Tarsus with
orders to preach indiscriminately to the gentiles, which he
did. The most blessed Mary was the instrument and
Mediatrix of all these miraculous favors. It was through
Her that her Divine Son operated them, and from Her,
God received the proper thanks for the graces distributed
to the whole Church.

382. Having thus been reassured in regard to the life
of saint Paul, the most blessed Mother entertained the
hope that through the assistance of divine Providence
She might save the life of her cousin James, who was
very dear to Her and who was still in Saragossa, protected by the hundred angels She had appointed for his
guardians and companions at Granada. These holy angels
frequently went back and forth, bringing the petitions of
the Apostles to the most blessed Mary and her counsels
back to him. In this way saint James learned of the sojourn of the great Queen in Ephesus. When he had
brought the chapel or small temple of the Pillar in Saragossa to a sufficient state of completion, he consigned it
to the care of the bishop and the disciples appointed by him
here as in other cities in Spain. Some months after the
apparition of the Queen, he departed from Saragossa,
continuing to preach through different provinces. Having
come to Catalonia, he embarked for Italy, where without
much delay, he pursued his journey overland always
preaching until he again embarked for Asia, and ardently
desiring to see there the most blessed Mary, his Mistress
and Protectress.

383. Saint James happily attained his object and
reached Ephesus. There he prostrated himself at the feet
of the Mother of his Creator, shedding copious tears of
joy and veneration. From his inmost heart he thanked
Her for the peerless favors obtained at her hands from

the Most High during his travels and his preaching in Spain, and especially for her having visited him and conferred such blessings upon him during her visits. The heavenly Mother, as Mistress of humility, immediately raised him from the ground and said to him: "My Master, remember thou art the anointed of the Lord and his minister, and that I am an humble wormlet." With these words the great Lady fell on her knees and asked the blessing of saint James as a priest of the Most High. He remained for some days in Ephesus in the company of the most blessed Mary and of his brother John, to whom he gave an account of all that had happened to him in Spain. With the most prudent Mother during those days he held most exalted colloquies and conferences, of which it will suffice to record the following.

384. In order to prepare saint James for his leave-taking the blessed Mary one day said to him: "James, my son, these will be the last few days of thy life. Thou knowest how deeply I love thee in the Lord, and how I desire to raise thee to his intimate love and eternal friendship, for which He has created thee, redeemed and called thee. In the few days that still remain of thy life, I desire to demonstrate to thee my love and I offer thee all that by the divine grace I can do for thee as a true Mother." To this exceedingly great favor saint James responded with deepest veneration: "My Mistress and Mother of my God and Redeemer, from the bottom of my soul I thank Thee for this new benefit, possible only to thy unbounded charity. My Lady, I beseech Thee, give me thy blessing that I may suffer martyrdom for thy Son, my true God and Savior. If it is his will and for his glory, I beseech Thee from my soul, not to forsake me in the sacrifice of my life, but that I may see Thee with my own eyes in my passage and that Thou offer me as an acceptable victim in his divine presence."

385. The most holy Mary promised to present his petition to the Lord and that She would fulfill it, if the divine will and condescension should so permit. Thus inspiring him with the hope of her assistance and with other consolations of eternal life, She comforted the Apostle and strengthened him for his expected martyrdom. Among other words She spoke to him also as follows: "My son James, what torments or suffering shall ever seem great at the prospect of entering the eternal joys of the Lord? The most bitter shall seem sweet and the most terrible, welcome and desirable to him who knows the infinite and highest Good, which he shall possess in return for a momentary sorrow (II Cor. 4, 17). I congratulate thee, my master, for thy most happy lot and that thou art so soon to leave the tribulations of this mortal life in order to enjoy the infinite Good as a comprehensor in the gladness of his divine countenance. In this my heart is lightened that thou art so shortly to obtain what my soul desires for thee; and that thou givest thy temporal life for the unending possession of eternal rest. I give thee the blessing of the Father, of the Son and of the Holy Ghost, in order that all the three Persons, in the oneness of their essence, assist thee in tribulation and lead thee to the desired end; and my own blessing shall be with thee in thy glorious martyrdom."

386. The great Queen added other words of admirable wisdom and highest consolation in parting from saint James. She asked him, in her name and in the name of all the creatures to praise God, and to intercede for the holy Church, as soon as He should come to the vision of the blessed Trinity. Saint James offered to do all She desired and again asked her favor and protection in the hour of his martyrdom. This She once more promised, and taking leave of Her, saint James said: "My Mistress,

blessed among women, thy life and intercession is the prop
on which the holy Church, now and during the ages in
which it is to exist, shall rest securely in the midst of the
persecutions and temptations of the enemies of the Lord.
Thy charity shall be to Thee the instrument of thy martyrdom. Keep in mind always, as our sweetest Mother, the
kingdom of Spain, where the holy Church and the faith
of thy divine Son and Redeemer has now been planted.
Receive it under thy special protection and preserve in it
thy sacred temple and the faith, which I unworthily have
preached; and give me thy holy blessing." The most
holy Mary promised to fulfill his petition and desires, and
She parted from him, bestowing upon him her reiterated
blessing.

387. Saint James took leave also of his brother saint
John, who shed abundant tears, not so much of sorrow as
of joy, on account of the happy lot of the elder brother,
since he was to be the first of the Apostles to attain eternal
happiness and the palm of martyrdom. Thereupon saint
James journeyed without much delay to Jerusalem, where
he preached for some days before he died, as I shall show
in the next chapter. The great Lady of the world remained
in Ephesus, attentive to all that happened to saint James
and all the other Apostles, without losing them from her
interior vision or intermitting her prayers for them and
for all the faithful of the Church. At the thought of the
martyrdom of saint James for the name of Christ, such
conflagrations of love and desires of giving her life for
the Lord welled up in the purest heart of Mary, that She
merited, many times over, the crowns gained by the Apostle and by all others together; for with each one of the
martyrs She suffered many martyrdoms of love, more
excruciating to her chaste and burning heart than the
torments of sword and fire to the bodies of the martyrs.

388. My daughter, in the events of this chapter thou
wilt find much guidance for a perfect life. Consider then,
that just as God is the beginning and origin of all the being and faculties of creatures, so also, according to right
reason, He is to be their sole last end; for if man has received all without meriting it, then he likewise owes all to
Him who has given it gratis; and if men have received
all in order to produce results, then all the results belong
to the Creator and not to the creatures. This truth, which
I understood fully and pondered in my heart, urged me
to prostrate myself and lower myself to the very dust in
adoring the immutable being of God. I reflected how I
was created out of nothing, formed of earth, and in the
presence of God I annihilated myself, acknowledging Him
as the Creator, to whom I owed my life, being and motion
(Acts 17, 28), and protesting that without Him I was
nothing, and that all was due to Him as the one beginning
and end of all creation. In the light of this truth, all that
I did and suffered seemed little; and although I ceased
not to do good, I continually longed and sighed to do and
suffer still more. Never was my heart satisfied, because
I still found myself a debtor, getting poorer and ever
more indebted. This state of mind is very well founded
in right reason and still more on faith, and this debt is
manifest and common to all men, if they would only direct
their attention toward it. But amid the universal forgetfulness of men I wish, my daughter, that thou solicitously
imitate me in the practices and exercises described to thee,
and especially that thou humble thyself to the dust and
abase thyself in proportion as the Most High raises thee
up by the favors and blessings of his right hand. The ex-

ample of my humility thou wilt see clearly evident in the special favors, as for instance, when He commanded a temple to be built, in which I was to be honored and invoked even during my mortal life. This and other favors humbled me beyond all human imagination. Therefore, if I thus humbled myself after performing such great things, consider how much more thou must do it in response to such great liberality of the Lord toward thee and after such niggardly correspondence on thy part.

389. I wish also, my daughter, that thou imitate me in being very careful to practice poverty of spirit concerning the use of necessities and comforts, offered thee by thy sister-nuns or by thy well-wishers. Choose and accept only the most poor and most ordinary, the most undesirable and humble things for thy use; for otherwise thou canst not imitate me in the spirit, in which without ostentation I refused all comforts and good things of this life offered to me by the faithful of Jerusalem, and of which I accepted only what was absolutely necessary during my sojourn in Ephesus. In the exercise of this virtue is contained much that will make human beings happy, while the deceived and blind worldlings please themselves in pursuing what is entirely opposed to this virtue and truth.

390. Seek also to guard thyself from another very common mistake: namely that by which men, instead of acknowledging that all the goods of body and soul belong to the Lord, nevertheless appropriate all of them to themselves and consider them so much their own, that they not only refuse to offer them freely to their Creator, but even, if at any time they must part with them, lament and are aggrieved over their loss, as if they had been injured or as if God had treated them unjustly. With such a disorderly affection parents are wont to love their children, and children their parents, married men their wives,

and wives their husbands, and all of them, their possessions, honor, health and other temporal goods, while many
souls thus love even the spiritual goods; and they go so
far in this disorderly love, that they have no measure in
their sorrow, when they lose them. Though it be impossible to recover them, they live in unrest and dejection,
passing from the disorder of their sensible affection to the
disorder of their reason and to unjust complaint. Hence
they dare not only condemn the rulings of divine Providence and lose the merit of sacrificing what is the Lord's,
but they wish to have it understood, that they esteem the
possession of these transitory goods as their highest aim,
and that, if they were permitted, they would live many
ages content with these apparent and perishing things.

391. None of the children of Adam can have a love
greater, or one equal to that, with which I loved my divine
Son and my spouse saint Joseph; yet this love was so
well ordered while I lived in their company, that I willingly sacrificed their conversation and intercourse during
all the time in which I was deprived of their presence.
This conformity and resignation I desire thee to imitate,
whenever something is wanting to thee, which thou
shouldst love in God; for outside of God thou art permitted to love nothing. The anxious desire of seeing the
supreme Good and of loving God eternally and forever
in heaven must alone be perpetual in thee. For this happiness thou must sigh in tears from thy inmost heart; for
it thou must gladly suffer all the hardships and afflictions
of this mortal life. Thou must live in these aspirations
in such a way, that from now on in trying to make thyself
worthy of God thou be anxious to suffer all that thou
hearest or understandest as having been suffered by the
saints. But remember these desires of suffering and these
aspirations and attempts to see God are to be of such a

kind, that thy suffering becomes real through thy sorrow
at not being able actually to encounter actual torments and
at not being found worthy of bearing all the martyrdom
thou thus desirest. In thy flights of desire to arrive at the
beatific vision thou must permit no other lower motive
to intermingle, such as the relief afforded by the joy of
God's vision against the hardships of this life; for to
desire the vision of the highest Good, is not love of God,
but love of self and of one's own comfort, and cannot
merit reward in the eyes of the all-penetrating and all-
weighing omnipotent God. But if thou do all these
things sincerely and in all perfection, as a faithful servant
and spouse of my divine Son, desiring to see Him in order
to love Him, praise Him, and never to offend Him
eternally, and if thou covet all labors and sufferings only
for these ends, believe me and assure thyself, that thou
wilt draw Us to thee and that thou wilt arrive at the kind
of love thou continually desirest; since precisely for this
purpose, We are so liberal with thee.

CHAPTER II.

392. Our great apostle saint James came to Jerusalem at a time when that whole city was very much incensed against the disciples and followers of Christ our Lord. This new fury the demons had secretly roused by stirring up the zeal of the Jews for the old Law and their jealousy against the new evangelical Law. The immediate cause of these movements was the preaching of saint Paul, who, although he remained not more than fifteen days in Jerusalem, nevertheless in that short time, by the divine power, had converted many and excited the wonder and admiration of all the people. Although the unbelieving Jews felt relieved somewhat by the news of his having left Jerusalem, yet they were again thrown into consternation by the speedy arrival of saint James, who showed no less zeal and heavenly wisdom in proclaiming the name of Christ our Redeemer. Lucifer, who was not ignorant of his coming, availed himself of it as a new means of exciting the spleen and rousing the wrath of the highpriests, priests and scribes. Saint James began to preach most fervently the name of the Crucified, his mysterious Death and Resurrection. In the first few days he converted to the faith some of the Jews, among whom were especially Hermogenes and Philetus, both of them magicians and sorcerers, who had a pact with the devil. Hermogenes was deeply versed in magic and Philetus was

his disciple; the Jews wanted to engage the services of these two in order either to overcome saint James in dispute, or if that was impossible, to take away his life by their magic arts.

393. This wickedness the devils had intended to execute through the instrumentality of the unbelieving Jews; for they themselves could not come near saint James on account of the terrors of the divine grace emanating from the Apostle. Philetus first began the dispute with saint James, so that, if he should gain no advantage, Hermogenes, as the more skillful master in the magic art, might enter the combat. Philetus brought forth his sophistical and false arguments, but the holy Apostle spoke with such wisdom and force, that all his sophism yielded as the darkness before the light: Philetus was overcome and converted to the truth of Christ, becoming from that time on a defender of the Apostle, and his doctrine. But fearing the diabolical arts of his master Hermogenes, he sought the protection of saint James. The holy Apostle gave him a piece of cloth or linen, which he had received from Mary, and with this relic Philetus protected himself against the power of Hermogenes for some days, until the latter himself entered the dispute.

394. Although Hermogenes feared saint James, he could not evade the meeting, because he had pledged himself to the Jews to enter the discussion and convince saint James. Accordingly he tried to enforce his errors by more cogent arguments than his disciple. But all that he could do was unavailing against the heavenly force and wisdom of the Apostle, which was like an impetuous torrent. He brought Hermogenes to silence and obliged him to confess his belief in the mysteries of the faith of Christ, just as he had done with Philetus: both of them accepted the faith and doctrine preached by the Apostle. The demons were roused to fury against Hermogenes and, through the power they had acquired over him, began to maltreat him on account of his conversion. As he learned how Philetus

had defended himself by the relic obtained from the Apostle, he sought a like favor against his enemies. Saint James gave him the scarf he had used in his travels and with it Hermogenes put to flight the demons and made them powerless to approach or afflict him further.

395. These conversions and others made by saint James in Jerusalem were hastened by the tearful sighs and prayers of the great Queen in her retreat at Ephesus, where (as I have often said) She knew by vision all that was done by the Apostles and the other faithful of the Church; and particularly what happened with the beloved Apostle James for whom She was especially solicitous as being so near his martyrdom. Hermogenes and Philetus persevered for some time in the faith of Christ; but afterwards they fell away and lost it in Asia, as is evident from the second epistle to Timothy, where saint Paul says that Figelus, or Philetus, and Hermogenes had left him. Although the seed of the faith had sprung up in the hearts of these men, it took no sufficient root to resist the temptations of the demon, whom they had served and familiarly entertained for so long a time. The evil and perverse inclinations of their vices still remained and again prevailed, withdrawing them from the faith they had accepted.

396. When the Jews, through the conviction and conversion of Philetus and Hermogenes, saw their hopes frustrated, they were filled with new anger against the apostle saint James and they determined to put an end to his life. For this purpose they bribed Democritus and Lysias, centurions of the Roman militia, to furnish them with soldiers for the arrest of the Apostle. In order to hide their treachery they were to raise a feigned quarrel or disturbance on a certain day during his preaching and thus get him within their power. The execution of this wicked design was left to Abiator, the high-priest of that year, and to Josias, a scribe of the same mind as the high-priest. As they had planned, so they executed their scheme; for, while the saint was preaching to the people

about the mystery of the Redemption, proving it to them with admirable wisdom from the testimonies of the ancient writings and moving his audience to tears of compunction, the priest and the scribe were roused to diabolical fury. Giving the signal to the Roman soldiers, the priest sent Josias to throw a rope around the neck of saint James and fell upon him, proclaiming him a disturber of the people and the author of a new religion in opposition to the Roman empire.

397. Democritus and Lysias thereupon rushed up with their soldiers and brought the Apostle bound to Herod, the son of Archelaus, whose malice had been roused interiorly through the astuteness of Lucifer and exteriorly by the evil-minded and hateful Jews. Thus doubly incited, Herod began against the disciples of the Lord, whom he abhorred, the persecution mentioned by saint Luke in the twelfth chapter of the Acts and sent his soldiers to afflict and imprison them. He instantly commanded saint James to be beheaded, as the Jews had asked. Incredible was the joy of the holy Apostle at being seized and bound like his Master and at seeing himself conducted to the place, where he was to pass from this mortal life to the eternal through martyrdom, as he had been informed by the Queen of heaven. He offered most humble thanks for this benefit and publicly reiterated the open profession of his faith in Christ our Lord. Remembering the petition he had made in Ephesus, that She be present at his death, he called upon Her from his inmost Soul.

398. The most holy Mary from her oratory heard these prayers of her beloved Apostle and cousin; for She was attentive to all that happened to him and She helped and favored him with her own efficacious petitions. During this her prayer, She saw a great multitude of angels and heavenly spirits of all hierarchies descending from heaven, part of them surrounding the Apostle in Jerusalem as he was led to the place of execution, while numerous others approached their Queen at

Ephesus. Presently one of them addressed Her saying: "Empress of heaven and our Lady, the most high Lord and God bids you immediately to hasten to Jerusalem to console his great servant James, to assist him in his death and to grant all his loving and holy desires." This favor the most blessed Mary joyfully and gratefully acknowledged. She praised the Most High for the protection granted to those who trust in his mercy and put their lives in his hands. In the meanwhile the Apostle was led to execution and on the way thereto he wrought great miracles upon the sick and ailing and on some possessed by the demons. There were a great number of them, because the rumor of his execution by Herod had spread about and many of the unfortunates hastened to receive his last ministrations and counsels. All that applied were healed by the great Apostle.

399. In the meanwhile the holy angels placed their Queen and Mistress upon a most refulgent throne, as they had done on other occasions, and on it bore Her to Jerusalem and to the place of the execution of saint James. The holy Apostle fell upon his knees in order to offer his life to the Most High in sacrifice, and when he raised his eyes toward heaven, he saw in the air near him the Queen of heaven, whom he had been invoking in his heart. He beheld Her clothed in divine splendors and great beauty, surrounded by multitudes of the angels. At this heavenly spectacle the soul of James was moved to new jubilee and his heart was seized with the ardors of a divine love. He wished to proclaim the most blessed Mary as the Mother of God and the Mistress of all creation. But one of the sovereign spirits restrained him in this fervent desire and said: "James, servant of our Creator, restrain within thy own bosom these precious sentiments and do not manifest to the Jews the presence and assistance of our Queen; for they are not worthy or capable of knowing Her, but instead of reverencing Her will only harden themselves in their hatred." Thus advised the Apostle forebore and

moving his lips in silence, he spoke to the heavenly Queen as follows:

400. "Mother of my Lord Jesus Christ, my Mistress and Protectress, Thou consolation of the afflicted and refuge of the needy, in this hour bestow upon me, my Lady, thy so much desired blessing. Offer for me to thy Son and Redeemer of the world, the sacrifice of my life, since I am burning with desire to be a holocaust for the glory of his name. Let today thy most pure and spotless hands be the altar of my sacrifice, in order that it may become acceptable in the eyes of Him, who died for me upon the cross. Into thy hands, and through them into the hands of my Creator, I commend my spirit." Having said these words, and keeping his eyes fixed upon the most holy Mary, who spoke to his heart, the holy Apostle was beheaded by the executioner. The great Lady and Queen of the world (O wonderful condescension!) received the soul of her beloved Apostle and placing it at her side on the throne, ascended with it to the empyrean heavens and presented it to her divine Son. As the most blessed Mary entered the heavenly court with this offering, She caused new joy and accidental glory to all the heavenly inhabitants and was received with songs of praise. The Most High received the soul of James and placed it in eminent glory among the princes of his people. The most blessed Mary, prostrate before the throne of the Almighty, composed a song of praise and thanksgiving for the triumphal martyrdom first gained by one of his Apostles. On this occasion the great Lady did not see the Divinity by intuitive vision, but by an abstractive one, such as I have described before this. But the blessed Trinity filled Her with new blessings and favors for Herself and for the holy Church, for which She had made great preparations. All the saints likewise blessed her and then the holy angels brought Her back to her oratory in Ephesus, where in the meanwhile an angel had impersonated Her. On arriving the heavenly Mother of virtues prostrated Her-

self as usual in order to give thanks to the Most High for all that had happened.

401. The disciples of saint James during the following night secured his sacred body and secretly brought it to Jaffa, where by divine disposition they embarked with it for Galicia in Spain. The heavenly Lady sent an angel to guide and accompany them to the port, where according to the divine will they were to disembark. Although they did not see the angel, they felt his protection during the whole voyage and often in a miraculous manner. Thus Spain, just as it owed its first instruction in the faith so deeply rooted in the hearts of its people, to the protection lavished by most holy Mary upon the Apostle, now also owes to Her the possession of his sacred body for its consolation and defense. Saint James died in the year forty-one of our Lord, on the twenty-fifth of March, five years and seven months after his setting out to preach in Spain. According to this count and that which I gave above, the martyrdom of saint James happened seven full years after the death of our Savior Jesus Christ.

402. That his martyrdom was at the end of March is clear from the twelfth chapter of the Acts, where saint Luke says, that because of the rejoicings of the Jews in the death of saint James, Herod imprisoned also saint Peter with the intention of beheading him after the feast of the Pasch, which was that of the paschal lamb, or of unleavened bread. This the Jews celebrated on the fourteenth of the moon of March. From this passage it appears that the seizure of saint Peter was during this Pasch or very near it; and that the death of James had preceded it a few days, the fourteenth of the moon of March in the year forty-one, according to our present computation of the years and months, occurred in the last days of March. Accordingly the death of saint James happened on the twenty-fifth, before the fourteenth of the moon, and soon thereupon took place the imprisonment of Peter and the Pasch of the Jews. The holy Church does not celebrate the feast of saint James on the day of his death, because

it falls on the same day as the Incarnation and ordinarily also in the time of the Lord's passion. It was therefore transferred to the twenty-fifth of July, which is the day on which the body of the Apostle was brought to Spain.

403. The death of saint James and the haste of Herod in inflicting it, greatly increased the most impious cruelty of the Jews; for in the savage brutality of the wicked king they saw a valuable means of pursuing their vengeance against the followers of Christ the Lord. Lucifer and his demons were of like opinion; they, by their suggestions, and the Jews, by their insistent flatteries, persuaded him to seize upon saint Peter, which he readily did in order to gain the good will of the Jews for his own temporal ends. The demons stood in great awe of the vicar of Christ on account of the power emanating from him against them; and therefore they secretly sought to hasten his imprisonment. Saint Peter, bound with many chains, lay in the dungeon awaiting his execution after the holidays of the Pasch. (Acts 12, 4). Although the undaunted heart of the Apostle was as free from anxiety or solicitude as if he had been at liberty, yet the whole body of the Church of Jerusalem was in consternation, and all the disciples and the faithful were greatly afflicted at the news that Herod was to execute him without delay. In their affliction they multiplied their prayers and petitions to the Lord for the preservation of saint Peter, whose death threatened the whole Church with great havoc and tribulation. They invoked also the protection and powerful intercession of the most blessed Mary, from whom they all expected deliverance.

404. The dangerous crisis impending over the Church was not unknown to the heavenly Mother, for, from her retreat in Ephesus, by her clearest interior vision of all things, She saw all things that passed in Jerusalem. She likewise increased her ardent requests, her sighs, prostrations and bloody tears, supplicating the Lord for the liberation of saint Peter and the protection of the holy Church. These prayers of the blessed Mother penetrated

the heavens and wounded the heart of her Son Jesus, our Savior. In response the Lord descended in person to her oratory, where She was lying prostrate with her virginal face upon the ground mingling with the dust. The sovereign King entered and raised Her lovingly from the ground, saying: "My Mother, moderate thy sorrow and ask whatever thou wishest; for I shall grant it all and thou shalt find grace in my eyes to obtain it."

405. By the presence and loving caresses of her Son the heavenly Mother was reanimated and filled with glad consolation; for the tribulations of the Church were the sole cause of her martyrdom, and to see saint Peter in prison condemned to death, and the dangers thus threatening the primitive Church, afflicted Her more than can be conceived. She renewed her petition in the presence of Christ the Redeemer, and said: "Lord and true God, my Son, Thou knowest the tribulations of thy holy Church and her clamors sound in thy ears, while they penetrate to the inmost of my afflicted heart. Thy enemies are resolved to take away the life of her Pastor, thy vicar; and if Thou, my Lord permit it now, they will scatter thy little flock and the infernal wolves will triumph over thy name in seeing their wishes fulfilled. Issue then, my Lord God and life of my soul, thy sovereign command over this sea of tribulation, and the winds and waves, that batter this little ship, shall be quieted and I shall live. Protect thy vicar and confound thy enemies. And if it is to thy glory and according to thy will let these tribulations come over me, so that I may suffer for thy faithful children and be the aid of thy right arm I may battle with the invisible enemies in the defense of thy holy Church."

406. Her divine Son answered: "I desire that thou act according to thy wishes, using the powers I have given Thee: do or undo whatever is necessary for the

welfare of my Church, and Thou mayest be sure, that all
the fury of the demons will be turned toward Thee." She
thanked him for this new favor and offered to undertake
the battles of the Lord for his faithful, saying: "Most
High Lord, hope and life of my soul, prepared is the heart
and spirit of thy servant to labor for the souls bought
with thy blood and life. Although I am but useless dust, I
know Thee to be infinite in power and wisdom; with the
favor of thy assistance I fear not the infernal dragon. As
Thou wishest me to dispose and act in thy name for the
welfare of the Church, I now command Lucifer and all
his ministers of wickedness, who are disturbing the
Church, to descend to the abyss and there be silenced
until it shall please thy Providence to permit their return
to the earth." This command of the Queen of the world
in Ephesus was so powerful, that at the very moment
of her issuing it, all the demons in Jerusalem were pre-
cipitated into hell, the whole multitude descending into
the eternal caverns without power of resisting the divine
force exerted through the most blessed Mary.

407. Lucifer and his companions knew that this chastisement proceeded from our Queen, whom they called
their enemy because they dared not pronounce her name.
They remained in hell, confounded and dismayed as on
other occasions, until they were permitted to rise in order
to battle against Mary, as will be related further on.
During that time they consulted anew about the means
of attaining this end. Having obtained this triumph over
the demons the most blessed Mary bethought Herself of
overcoming likewise the opposition of Herod and the
Jews, and therefore She said to her divine Son: "Now,
my Son and Lord, if it is thy will, let one of thy holy
angels be sent to deliver thy servant Peter from prison."
Christ our Lord approved of her wish and, at the orders

of both these Sovereigns, one of the heavenly spirits there present hastened to liberate saint Peter from his prison in Jerusalem.

408. The angel executed these orders very swiftly. Coming to the dungeon, he found saint Peter fastened with two chains, guarded by two soldiers at his side and by a number of other soldiers at the entrance of the prison. The Pasch had already been celebrated and it was the night before he was to be executed according to the sentence passed upon him. But the Apostle was so little disturbed that he was sleeping with as much unconcern as his guards (Acts 12, 6). When the angel arrived, he was obliged to wake him by force and while saint Peter was still drowsy, said to him: "Arise quickly; put on thy girdle and thy shoes, take thy mantle and follow me." Saint Peter found himself free of the chains and, without understanding what was happening to him and ignorant of what this vision could mean, followed the angel. Having conducted him through some streets, the angel told him, that the Almighty had freed him from prison through the intercession of his most blessed Mother, and thereupon disappeared. Saint Peter, coming to himself understood the mystery and gave thanks to the Lord for this favor.

409. Saint Peter thought it best first to give an account of his liberation and consult with James the Less and others of the faithful, before seeking safety in flight. Hastening his steps he came to the house of Mary, the mother of John, who was also called Mark. This was the house of the Cenacle, where many of the disciples had gathered in their affliction. Saint Peter called to them from the street, and a servant-maid, by the name of Rhode, descended to see who was calling. As she recognized the voice of Peter, she left him standing at the door outside and fled excitedly to the disciples, telling them that it was

Peter. They thought it some foolish misunderstanding of
the servant; but she maintained, that it was Peter; so they,
far from guessing the liberation of Peter, concluded that
it might be his angel. During these questions and answers
saint Peter was in the street clamoring at the door, until
they opened it and with incredible joy and gladness saw
the holy Apostle and head of the Church freed from the
sorrows of prison and death. He gave them an account of
all that had happened to him through aid of the angel,
in order that they might in strict secrecy notify saint James
and all his brethren. Foreseeing that Herod would search
for him with great diligence, they unanimously decided
that he leave Jerusalem that very night and not return,
lest he should be taken in some future search. Saint Peter
therefore fled, and Herod, having instituted a search in
vain, chastised the guards, and was roused to new fury
against the disciples. But on account of his pride and
impious designs, God cut short his activity by a severe
punishment, of which I shall speak in the following
chapter.

INSTRUCTION WHICH THE QUEEN OF THE ANGELS GAVE
ME.

410. My daughter, thy astonishment at the singular
favor conferred by me on my servant James at his death,
affords me an occasion to tell thee of a privilege confirmed
to me by the Almighty at the time when I bore the soul of
the Apostle to heaven. Although I have already on other
occasions revealed to thee something of this secret, thou
shalt now understand it more fully in order to increase thy
filial devotion toward me. When I brought to heaven the
happy soul of James, the eternal Father spoke to me in
the hearing of all the blessed: "My Daughter and Dove,
chosen for my acceptation from all the creatures, let my

courtiers, angels and saints understand that, for the exaltation of my holy name, for thy glory and for the benefit of mortals, I now give thee my royal word, that if men, in the hour of their death invoke thee and call upon thee with affection in imitation of my servant James, soliciting thy intercession with me, I will bend to them in clemency and look upon them with eyes of fatherly mercy; I will defend and guard them against the dangers of that last hour; I will ward off the cruel enemies that seek the perdition of souls in that hour; I will furnish them through thee with great helps for resisting these enemies and gaining grace, if they wish to avail themselves of this help; and thou shalt present to Me their souls to be rewarded by my liberal hands."

411. For this privilege the whole triumphant Church, and I with it, sang hymns of thanks and praise to the Most High. Although the angels have the office of presenting the souls when they issue from the captivity of mortal life, to the tribunal of the just Judge, yet I have this same privilege in a more exalted degree than is granted to any other creature by the Omnipotent; for I possess it by another title and by a particular and supereminent right. Many times I make use of this privilege and I have done so with some of the Apostles. Since I see thee desirous of knowing how thou canst obtain from me this favor so precious to the soul, I answer thy pious wish by exhorting thee to take care lest thou make thyself unworthy by ingratitude and forgetfulness; and before all, to gain for thyself that inviolate purity, which I expect of thee and of the other souls. For the great love which I owe and cherish toward God, obliges me, with sincerest affection and charity to demand of all men the observance of his holy law and the preservation of their friendship and grace with God. This thou must prefer before thy life and be willing to die rather than offend thy God and highest Good.

412. I wish that thou set about obeying me, act out my instructions, and work with all thy might to imitate what thou seest and writest of me; that thou permit no intermission in thy love, nor forget for one moment the heartfelt affection thou owest to the liberal mercy of thy Lord; that thou be thankful for all his blessings and to me, since thy obligations are far beyond the power of fulfillment by thee in this mortal life. Be faithful in thy correspondence, fervent in thy devotion, ready to do what is most holy and perfect. Let thy heart expand and do not narrow it in pusillanimity, following the instigations of the devil. Extend thy hand to strong and powerful deeds, filled with confidence in the Lord; be not oppressed by adversities, thus impeding the will of the Lord in thee, and the high ends of his glory. Retain vivid faith and hope, even in the greatest assaults and temptations. In all this let the example of my servants James and Peter assist thee, and the certain knowledge of possessing through me the happy security of those who live under the protection of the Most High. In this confidence and in devotion to me James obtained the singular favor I showed him in his martyrdom; trusting in me he undertook immense labors in order to reach that crown. In this confidence saint Peter remained so tranquil and content in his prison-chains, nor lost for a moment the serenity of his soul. Thus he merited at the same time, that my divine Son and myself should plan his liberation. Of such favors the children of darkness make themselves unworthy, because they build all their hopes on that which is visible and on their diabolical earthly astuteness. Raise up thy heart, my daughter, and withdraw it from these deceits; aspire to that which is most pure and holy, since with thee shall be the arm of the Almighty, who wrought such great wonders in Me.

CHAPTER III.

413. In the rational creature love produces on the heart effects similar to those of the force of gravity on the stone. The stone tends to move whithersoever its own weight draws it, that is to its centre of attraction; love is the weight of the heart, drawing it to its centre, namely, to that which it loves. If at any time the heart is diverted by necessity or inadvertence, love will immediately make it recoil like a liberated spring returning again to its normal position. This weight or sway of love in a manner seems to take away the liberty of the heart, in so far as it becomes subject and subservient to what it loves, and prevents the will from commanding any other course of action than that sought and ordered by the urgency of this love. The happiness or unhappiness of a creature arises from the good or evil use it makes of love, for what man loves that he makes his master; if this master is evil and vile, so will also the man be tyrannized and degraded; if good, then will he be ennobled and made happy, and so much the more, the more noble and excellent the good is, that he loves. By these principles I hope to be able to explain in part, what has been made known to me concerning the exalted state in which the most holy Mary lived never having dropped from it but rising higher

and higher from the first instant of her Conception without interruption or relaxation, until She entered the state of a comprehensor in the beatific vision.

414. If all the love of the holy angels and of men could be united in one person, it would be less than that of the most holy Mary; yet, if we could unite the love of all the other creatures into one whole, it is certain that such a conflagration of love would result, that, without being infinite, it would seem so to us, on account of its surpassing all our comprehension. If then the charity of our great Queen exceeded all this, only the infinite Wisdom could measure the love of this Creature and estimate the intensity, with which it inclined and tended toward the Divinity. We however can at least understand that in this chastest, purest and most inflamed heart there could be no other mastery or sway, no other movement or liberty, except that of loving supremely the highest Good; and this in such an exalted degree, that with our limited capacity we can much sooner believe than understand it, confess than penetrate it. This charity of the most pure Virgin filled Her at the same time with the most ardent desires of seeing the face of God, who was absent, and assisting the holy Church, which was present to Her. Thus She was consumed by two opposite tendencies; but She governed them with such wisdom, that there arose from them no conflict within Her, nor did She give Herself up to the one to the neglect of the other; but She attended to both, exciting wonder in all the saints and fullest complacency in the Lord of the saints.

415. In this exalted and eminent state of holiness the most holy Mary often consulted within her heart about the condition of the primitive Church left in her charge; and how She could exert Herself for its peace and progress. In these aspirations the liberation of saint Peter,

which made it possible for him to continue the government of the faithful, and also the casting forth of Lucifer and his demons from Jerusalem, which freed the faithful from their tyranny and allowed them some respite, afforded the most holy Mary some relief and consolation in her anxiety. The divine Wisdom, which dispenses labors and consolations with weight and measure (Wis. 11, 21), ordained that the most blessed Mother should at that time have a very intimate knowledge of the evil disposition of Herod. She perceived the abominable ugliness of that most unfortunate soul brought on by his boundless vices and oft-repeated crimes, which had roused the wrath of the just and almighty Judge. She knew how greatly Herod and the Jews were enraged against Jesus and his disciples after the escape of saint Peter. She saw, also, how the seed of rage, sown by the demons in the hearts of Herod and the Jews, had grown, and how furious their hatred against Jesus our Redeemer and his disciples had become; how the iniquitous ruler had conceived the purpose of exterminating all the faithful within the confines of Judea and Galilee and how he would employ in this work all his forces and means. Although the most blessed Mary was aware of this design of Herod, She was not informed at that time of his horrid death. But as She knew his power and the depravity of his soul, She was horrified at his evil state, and deeply grieved at his wrath against the followers of the faith.

416. In her anxieties and in her reliance upon the divine help our Queen labored incessantly in prayers and tears, travailing in her clamors as I have shown on other occasions. Ever governed by her most exalted prudence, She spoke to one of the highest angels of her guard, saying: "Minister of the Most High and creature of his hands, my solicitude for the holy Church strongly urges

me to seek its welfare and progress. I beseech thee to ascend to the throne of the Most High, represent to Him my affliction; ask Him in my name, that I may be permitted to suffer instead of his faithful servants and that Herod be prevented from executing his designs for the destruction of the Church." Immediately the angel betook himself to the Lord with this message, while the Queen of heaven, like another Esther, remained in prayer for the liberty and salvation of her people and of Herself. (Eph. 4, 16). The heavenly ambassador was sent back by the blessed Trinity with the answer: "Princess of heaven, the Lord of hosts says, that Thou art the Mother, the Mistress and the Governess of the Church, and that Thou holdest his power while Thou art upon earth; and He desires Thee, as the Queen and Mistress of the heaven and earth, to execute sentence upon Herod."

417. In her humility the most blessed Virgin was somewhat disturbed by this answer, and urged by her charity, She replied to the angel: "Am I then to pronounce sentence against a creature who is the image of the Lord? Since I came forth from his hands I have known many reprobates among men and I have never called for vengeance against them; but as far as I was concerned, always desired their salvation if possible, and never hastened their punishment. Return to the Lord, angel, and tell Him that my tribunal and power is inferior to and dependent upon his, and that I cannot sentence any one to death without consulting my Superior; and if it is possible to bring Herod to the way of Salvation, I am willing to suffer all the travails of the world according to the disposition of his divine Providence in order that this soul may not be lost." The angel hastened back with this second message of his Queen and having presented it before the throne of the most blessed Trinity, was sent back to

Her with the following answer: "Our Mistress and Queen, the Most High says, that Herod is of the number of the foreknown, since he is so obstinate in his malice, that he will take no admonition or instruction; he will not co-operate with the helps given to him; nor will he avail himself of the fruits of the Redemption, nor of the intercession of the saints, nor of thy own efforts, O Queen and Lady, in his behalf."

418. For the third time the most holy Mary despatched the heavenly prince with still another message to the Most High, saying: "If it must be that Herod die in order to hinder him from persecuting the Church, do thou, O angel, represent to the Almighty, how in the infinite condescension of his charity, He has granted me in mortal life to be the Refuge of the children of Adam, the Advocate and Intercessor of sinners; that my tribunal should be that of kindness and clemency for the refuge and assistance of all that seek my intercession; and that all should leave it with the assurance of pardon in the name of my divine Son. If then I am to be a loving Mother to men, who are the creatures of his hands and the price of his life-blood, how can I now be a severe judge against one of them? Never was I charged with dealing out justice, always mercy, to which all my heart inclines; and now it is troubled by this conflict of love with obedience to rigorous justice. Present anew, O angel, this my anxiety to the Lord, and learn whether it is not his pleasure that Herod die without my condemning him."

419. The holy messenger ascended for the third time and the most blessed Trinity listened to his message with the plenitude of pleasure and complacency at the pitying love of his Spouse. Returning, the angel thus informed the loving Mistress: "Our Queen, Mother of our Creator and my Lady, the almighty Majesty says that thy mercy

is for those mortals who wish to avail themselves of thy powerful intercession, not for those who despise and abhor it like Herod; that Thou art the Mistress of the Church invested with all the divine power, and that therefore it is meet Thou use it as is opportune: that Herod must die; but it shall be through thy sentence and according to thy order." The most blessed Mary answered: "Just is the Lord and equitable are his judgments (Ps. 118, 137). Many times would I suffer death to rescue this soul of Herod, if he himself would not by his own free will make himself unworthy of mercy and choose perdition. He is a work of the Most High (Job. 10, 8), formed according to his image and likeness (Gen. 1, 27); he was redeemed by the blood of the Lamb, which taketh away the sins of the world (Apoc. 1, 5). But I set aside all this and, considering only his having become an obstinate enemy of God, unworthy of his eternal friendship, by the most equitable justice of God, I condemn him to the death he has merited, in order that he may not incur greater torments by executing the evil he has planned."

420. This wonder the Lord wrought for the glory of his most blessed Mother and in witness of his having constituted Her as the Mistress of all creatures with supreme power to act as their Sovereign like her divine Son. I cannot explain this mystery better than in the words of the Lord in the fifth chapter of saint John, where He says of Himself: "The son cannot do anything that the Father does not; but He does the same, because the Father loves Him; and if the Father raises the dead, the son also raises whom he pleases, and the Father has given to the Son to judge all, in order that just as all honor the Father, they may also honor the Son; for no one can honor the Father without honoring the Son." And immediately He adds: that He has

given Him the power of judging, because He is the Son of man, which He is through his most blessed mother. On account of the likeness of the heavenly Mother to her Son (of which I have often spoken) the relation or proportion of the Mother with the Son in this power of judgment must be transferred to the Mother in the same manner as that of the Son from the Father. Mary is the Mother of mercy and clemency to all the children of Adam that call upon Her; but in addition to this the Almighty wishes it to be understood that She possesses full power of judging all men and that all should honor Her, just as they honor her Son and true God. As his true Mother He has given Her the same power with him in the degree and proportion due to Her as his Mother and a mere creature.

421. Making use of this power the great Lady sent the angel to Cæsarea, where Herod then was, to take away his life as the minister of divine justice. The angel executed the sentence without delay. The evangelist saint Luke says, that the angel of the Lord struck Herod and, eaten up by worms, the unhappy man died the temporal and eternal death. The wound of this stroke was interior and from it sprang the corruption and the worms that so miserably finished him. From the same text it appears that, after having beheaded saint James and after saint Peter had escaped, Herod descended to Cæsarea in order to compose some differences that had arisen between him and the inhabitants of Sidon and Tyre (Acts 12, 23). Within a few days, vested in the royal purple and seated upon a throne, he harangued the people with great show of words. The people, full of vain flattery, proclaimed him as a victor and as a god; and Herod, in foolish vanity, was pleased with this adulation of the people. Because he had not given honor

to God, but usurped to himself divine honor in vain pride, as saint Luke says, the angel of the Lord struck him. Although this was his last crime, which filled the measure of his iniquity, he merited the chastisement not only for this, but for so many other crimes committed by him in persecuting the Apostles, mocking the Lord our Savior (Luke 23, 11), beheading the Baptist (Mark 6, 27), committing adultery with his sister-in-law Herodias, and for many other abominations.

422. Immediately the angel returned to Ephesus and gave an account of the execution of the sentence against Herod. The merciful Mother wept over the loss of this soul; but praised the judgments of the Lord and gave him thanks for the benefit, which the Church would derive from his chastisement; for, as saint Luke says (Acts 12, 24), the Church grew and increased by the word of God. This was true not only in Galilee and Judea, where the persecutor Herod was removed, but, through saint John and the help of the most holy Mother, the Church was taking root in Ephesus. The science of the blessed Apostle was full as that of the cherubim, and the love of his heart was inflamed like that of the seraphim; and he had with him as his Mother and Teacher, the Mistress of wisdom and grace. On account of these precious advantages the Evangelist could undertake great and wonderful works for the foundation of the law of grace, not only in Ephesus, but in all neighboring regions of Asia and in the borderlands of Europe.

423. Arriving at Ephesus the Evangelist began to preach in the city, baptizing those whom he converted to the faith of Christ our Savior and confirming the faith by great miracles and prodigies, such as had never been witnessed by those gentiles. Since the Greek schools in those countries turned out many philosophers and men

learned in what, notwithstanding the admixture of many errors, could be called human sciences, the blessed Apostle convincingly taught them the true science, making use not only of miracles and signs, but of argumentation for the credibility of the Christian faith. All his catechumens he immediately sent to the most holy Mary and She instructed many; as She knew the interior inclinations of all, She spoke to the heart of each one and filled it with heavenly light. She wrought prodigies and miracles for the benefit of the unfortunate, curing the possessed and the infirm, succored the poor and the needy and, by the labor of her own hands, gave assistance to the sick in the infirmaries, attending upon them in person. In her house the kindest Queen had a supply of clothes for the most poor and forsaken of her fellowmen. She helped many in the hour of their death, gaining these souls in their last agony and bringing them safely through all the assaults of the demon to their Creator. So many souls did She draw to the path of truth and life eternal, and so numerous were the wonders She wrought for this end, that they could not be recorded in many books; for no day passed in which She did not increase the possessions of the Lord by the copious and abundant fruit of souls.

424. On account of the growth of the primitive Church through the holiness, solicitude and labors of the Queen of Heaven, the demons were filled with confusion and furious disappointment. Although they rejoiced in the condemnation of all souls because it swelled the numbers of the damned in hell yet they were grievously put out at the death of Herod; for on account of his obstinacy they had expected from him no amendment of his vile and abominable life and therefore had considered him a powerful instrument for the persecution of

the followers of Christ our Lord. The divine Providence permitted Lucifer and the other infernal dragons to emerge from the depths of hell, whither they had been cast forth from Jerusalem by the most blessed Mother, as I have related in the last chapter. After having spent their time in hell in planning and preparing temptations for their conflict with the invincible Queen of the angels, Lucifer resolved to make complaint against Her to the Lord himself, as he had done against holy Job (Job 1, 9) ; although he now did it with greater wrath. With this intent, before issuing from the abyss, he spoke to his ministers as follows:

425. "If we do not vanquish this Woman, our Enemy, I fear that without a doubt She will destroy my sovereignty; for we all find in Her a strength more than human, which annihilates and oppresses us, whenever and in whatsoever manner She pleases to exercise it. This is what makes Her intolerable to me; for if She were God, who is offended by my high aspirations and hostility and who has infinite power to destroy us, I would not feel so much confusion at being overcome; but this Woman, though She is the Mother of God, of the incarnate Word, is not God; She is a mere creature of a nature inferior to ours. I shall not further endure to be treated by Her in such an imperious manner and be ruined by her opposition to me. Let us all go forth to destroy Her and let us make our complaint to the Omnipotent as we have now concluded to do." In reliance upon his pretended rights the dragon executed his resolve; for he alleged, that God, instead of leaving Her in her humble condition exposed to the persecutions and temptations of the demons, had by his graces and gifts unjustly raised this Woman above him, though She was but dust of the earth while he was an

angel of such superior essence. But I must remark, that these hellish foes did not present themselves before the Lord so as to see Him, being entirely incapable thereof; but through their knowledge and belief in the supernatural mysteries, which is conceded to them in a curtailed yet by them unavoidable measure, they are permitted to speak to God. This is what is meant, when they are mentioned as being in the presence of God to make complaint or to have converse with Him.

426. The Almighty gave Lucifer permission to go forth in battle against the most blessed Mother; but the conditions asked by Satan were unjust, and therefore many of them were not conceded. The divine Wisdom furnished those weapons, which were appropriate to each combatant, in order that the victory of his Mother might be so much the more glorious and crush the head of this ancient and poisonous serpent (Gen 3, 15). This battle was mysterious, no less than its triumphant issue, as we shall see in the following chapters; moreover its mysterious character is plainly evident in the twelfth chapter of the Apocalypse and from the other mysteries of which I have spoken in my explanations of the first part of this history (Part 1, No. 94). I wish only to state here, that the divine Providence foreordained all this, not only for the greater glory of his most holy Mother and for the exaltation of the divine power and wisdom, but also in order to bring relief to the Church from the persecutions roused against it by the demons; and also to bind Himself with some show of justice to the bestowal of the infinite favors and blessings which the most holy Mary alone and no other souls could ever merit for the whole Church. The Lord continually works in this manner in his Church: preparing and fortifying some chosen souls, against which, as members and parts of his holy Church, the

dragon may exert all his wrath and fury. If they overcome him by the help of divine grace, their victories
redound to the benefit of the whole mystical body of the
faithful and the enemy loses some of his right and power
over them.

INSTRUCTION WHICH THE GREAT QUEEN OF THE ANGELS,
MOST HOLY MARY, GAVE ME.

427. My daughter, when in the course of this history
I so often call thy attention to the lamentable state of
the world and to that of the holy Church in which thou
livest, and when I so often express my maternal solicitude that thou imitate me, remember, my dearest, that I
have great reasons for obliging thee to lament with me
and for wishing thee to weep over that which I bewailed
in my mortal life; and which would afflict me in my present state, if in it I were capable of sorrow. I assure
thee, soul, thou hast reached times, in which thou
oughtest to shed tears of blood because of the calamities
coming over the children of Adam. Since thou canst
not at one and the same time attain a full knowledge
of them all, I remind thee of what from my place in
heaven I see going on in the whole world among the believers of the holy faith. Turn then thy eyes upon those
multitudes and behold the greater part of the children
of Adam in the darkness and errors of unbelief, rushing
without hope of salvation to eternal perdition. Behold
also the children of the faith and of the Church, how
heedless and forgetful of this damage they continue to
be, so that there are none who seem to deplore it. For in
contempt of their own salvation, they care not about
that of others and, their faith being dead and their love
extinct, they sorrow not for the loss of souls created by
God and redeemed by the blood of the incarnate Word.

428. All are the children of the eternal Father who is in heaven (Matth 23, 9) and all are obliged to have a care of their brethren according to each one's condition. This obligation rests more especially upon the children of the Church, who can live up to it by their prayers and supplications. But this duty lies still more directly upon those who have influence, upon those who are nourished by the Christian faith, and who enjoy more of the benefits of the liberal hand of the Almighty. Those who through the law of Christ are favored with temporal advantages and who make use of them for the service and the delights of the flesh, are they who, as the powerful, are to be more powerfully tormented (Matth 23, 9). If the pastors and the chiefs of the house of the Lord seek only a life of ease, without caring to engage in true earnest labor, they will make themselves accountable for the ruin of the flock of Christ and for the carnage brought on by the infernal wolves. O my daughter, into what a lamentable state has the Christian people been cast by the powerful, by the pastors, and by the wicked ministers, whom God has given them in his secret judgments! O what confusion and chastisements await them! Before the tribunal of the just Judge they will have no excuse; since the Catholic truth undeceives them, their conscience loudly protests, while they wilfully remain deaf to all warnings.

429. The cause of God remains neglected and without a champion; his possessions, which are the souls, are left without increase; all as it were look but to their own interest and preservation, each one according to his own diabolical cunning and according to his state of life. Truth is obscured, flattery raises its voice, avarice is unbridled, the blood of Christ is trodden under foot, the fruits of the Redemption are held in contempt; no one

wishes to risk his own comfort or interest in order to
save what has cost the Savior his blood and life. Even
the friends of God are influenced by the evils; for they do
not make use of their charity and its holy liberty as they
ought; and most of them allow themselves to be overcome by their cowardice and content themselves with
working for themselves alone, forsaking the common
cause of the souls of others. Hence thou mayest understand, my daughter, that now, after the evangelical
Church has been established by my divine Son and fertilized by his own blood, those unhappy times have come,
of which the Lord himself complains through his holy
Prophets, saying: what the palmerworm hath left the
locust has eaten, and what the locust left the bruchus
consumed, and the residue is destroyed by the mildew;
(Joel 1, 4) and in order to gather some fruits from his
vineyard, the Lord goes about like the gleaner after the
vintage, who seeks some remaining grape, or some olive,
which is not dried up, or carried away by the demons
(Is. 24, 13).

430. Tell me now, my daughter, how is it possible, if
thou still hast a true love for my divine Son and for me,
that thou find consolation or rest in thy heart at the sight
of the loss of souls, which He redeemed by his blood and
I have sought with blood-mingled tears? Even today,
if I could shed them, I would begin to do so with new
weeping and compassion; and since it is not possible for
me now to weep over the dangers threatening the Church,
I wish that thou do it and that thou spurn consolation in
a misfortune so calamitous and so worthy of lament.
Weep bitterly then, and lose not the merit of such a
sorrow; and let it be so deep, that thou findst no relief
except in affliction for the sake of the Lord whom thou
lovest. Think of what I did, in order to stave off the

damnation of Herod and to prevent it for those who wish
to avail themselves of my intercession.   In the beatific
vision I pray without ceasing for the salvation of my
clients.   Let not the labors and tribulations sent to thee
by my divine Son intimidate thee from helping they brethren and acquiring them for the possession of Christ
Amidst the injuries done to Him by the children of
Adam, do thou labor to recompense them in some measure by the purity of thy soul, which I desire shall be
rather that of an angel than of an earthborn woman.
Fight the battles of the Lord against his enemies and in
his name and mine, crush their head, reign over their
pride and cast them into hell.   Do thou also counsel the
ministers of Christ with whom thou conversest, to use
their power in doing the same, to defend the souls in
lively faith and, in them, the honor and glory of the
Lord; for thus shall they repress and vanquish them
with divine power.

CHAPTER IV.

THE MOST BLESSED MARY DESTROYS THE TEMPLE OF DIANA
IN EPHESUS; HER ANGELS BRING HER TO THE EMPY-
REAN HEAVENS, WHERE THE LORD PREPARES HER FOR
THE BATTLE AND VICTORY OVER THE INFERNAL
DRAGON; THIS CONFLICT BEGINS WITH TEMPTATIONS
TO PRIDE.

431. Most celebrated is the history of the city of
Ephesus, situated on the western confines of Asia; for
many renowned events of past ages made that city famous
and illustrious throughout the globe. But its greatest
privilege and excellence consists in having entertained
and harbored within its walls the supreme Queen of
heaven and earth for the space of some months, the
number of which I will state later on. This privilege
was a most fortunate one for Ephesus; since the other
things which are mentioned for its renown made it truly
unhappy and infamous, because through them the prince
of darkness had permanently set up his throne in that
city. But as our great Lady and Mother of grace found
Herself hospitably entertained and thus considered Herself under obligation to its inhabitants, who received Her
liberally and offered her gifts, it naturally followed, that
She, in accordance with her most perfectly ordered and
burning charity deeming Herself brought nearer to these
her benefactors, should repay their hospitality with greater blessings. For if She was liberal to all, even strangers,
She would certainly be much more free with her gifts
and favors to the inhabitants of Ephesus. Her own

gratitude moved Her to this, since She considered Herself indebted to the whole commonwealth. She offered up for it special prayers, asking her divine Son to pour out over its inhabitants his blessings and as a kind Father to, illumine and bring it to the knowledge of the true faith.

432. The Lady received answer that, as the Mistress and Queen of the whole Church, She was free to do as She pleased; that, however, She should take notice of the obstacles, which this city placed in the way of the divine clemency by its ancient and still existing abominations; that its inhabitants had thereby locked the gates of mercy and merited the rigors of justice, which would have already been executed upon them, if the Lord had not ordained Her to live among them just at the time, when their wickedness had reached the highest point and called the loudest for punishment. Together with this answer the most blessed Mother perceived, that the divine Justice, as it were, asked her permission and consent to the destruction of that idolatrous people of Ephesus and its neighborhood. At this answer and what it implied the kind heart of the sweetest Mother was much afflicted; but her immense charity was not intimidated, and multiplying her prayers, She answered the Lord:

433. "Most High, just and merciful King! I know well that the rigor of thy justice will be executed, if thy mercy is excluded; but for thy mercy any motive found by thy wisdom is sufficient, although small may be the inducement presented on the part of sinners. Consider therefore, O Lord, how this city has afforded me a dwelling according to thy will and how its inhabitants have helped me and offered me and thy servant John their goods. Temper thy rigor, my God, and let it be exercised on me, for I am willing to suffer for the salvation of

these unfortunates. Thou, O Allpowerful, whose infinite goodness and mercy forever conquers in good or evil, canst take away the obstacle, which prevents their profiting of thy blessings; let not my eyes behold the destruction of so many souls, the works of thy hands, purchased by thy blood." The Lord replied: "My Mother, I desire that thou see for thyself the cause of my just indignation and how much these men, for whom thou pleadest, have merited it. Attend, and thou shalt see." And immediately, by a most clear vision, She saw what follows.

434. She perceived that many centuries before the incarnation of the Word in her virginal womb, among the many councils held by Lucifer for the destruction of men, one was held in which he thus spoke to his demons: "From the delights of my former state in heaven, from the prophecies made by God to man and from the favors shown to many of his friends, I conjecture how much God shall be beholden to men and women for abstaining from certain vices, which I desire to maintain upon the world. These vices are especially those connected with the delights of the flesh and with the pleasures of possession or avarice; in these He seeks to induce them to renounce even what is allowed. In order that they may be so induced, He shall furnish them with many helps, so that they may be chaste and poor of their own accord, and subject their free will to that of others. If through these virtues they overcome us, they will merit great reward before God, as I have spied out in some who were chaste, poor and obedient. My plans will be seriously frustrated, if we do not take measures to counteract this damage and seek to compensate for it in all the ways open to our astuteness. I take into consideration also, that, if the divine Word is to assume human flesh, as I

have been given to understand, He will be very chaste and pure, and that He will teach chastity to others, not only men, but women, who, though they are weaker, yet usually are more tenacious. If they, whom I overcame in the first woman, shall thus vanquish me, it will be so much the more tormenting to me. Besides all this, the Scriptures of the ancients speak much of the favors, which men shall enjoy through the incarnate Word. For the human nature of the Son of God is to enrich and raise up earthborn men by his power."

435. "In order to oppose all this" Lucifer continued, "I desire your counsel and your diligent help; and we must begin even now to hinder men from attaining such great benefits." Thus the hateful plotting of hell against evangelical perfection was far in advance of its profession in the religious orders. This matter was thoroughly considered by the demons and the result of their deliberations was, that a great many demons should be appointed as heads of hellish legions, who were to tempt those desirous of living a life of chastity, poverty and obedience. In derision of chastity especially, they were to institute a sort of false and apparent state of virginity, in which counterfeit and hypocritical virgins were to consecrate themselves to Lucifer and all the demons. The enemies hoped thereby to gain over these persons to themselves not only for their own triumph, but also to cast discredit upon the chaste life of religious orders, which they presumed would be instituted by the incarnate Word and his Mother in the world. In order that this false religion might be propagated so much the better in the world, they resolved to found it upon worldly abundance and on whatever is most pleasing to nature, as in reality it was; for in secret those interested agreed to live licentiously under the name of chastity in honor of false gods.

436. But immediately the question arose, whether this religion was to be for men or for women. Some of the demons wanted it to be for men only, in order that through their greater constancy those religious orders might be more permanent; others again thought that men are not so easily deceived as women, since they reason more deeply and could more easily detect error; while there was not so much of this risk in women, who were of weak judgment, ready to believe earnestly in what they like and have once settled upon, and inclined to persevere in their error. This argument prevailed and was approved by Lucifer, although he did not entirely exclude men; for he judged, that some would be found, who would embrace the fallacy on account of the influence they would thereby gain over others. This could be expected especially if the demons would help along by nourishing their fear of losing the estimation of their fellowmen and by astutely making use of public opinion to keep alive the fallacies in those who would engage in this service.

437. Following up their infernal schemes the demons set about instituting a counterfeit and false religious order or congregation of virgins; for Lucifer said to the other demons: "Although it would be a great pleasure to me to have real virgins consecrated and dedicated to my worship and adoration in the same way as God wishes them for Himself; yet chastity and purity of the body so offends me, that I cannot endure this virtue, even if practiced entirely in honor of my greatness. Therefore we must see to it, that these virgins be the object of our basest attempts. If any of them should remain chaste in body, we shall fill her with bad thoughts and desires, so that in reality none of them will be chaste, though they may strive to contain themselves out of vain pride;

and as they are to be impure in their thoughts, we will seek to maintain them in the vainglorious conceit of their virginity."

438. In order to start these false religious orders the demons scoured through the whole earth, and it seemed to them, that among all the nations, certain women called Amazons were best suited for the execution of their devilish plans. These Amazons had come from Scythia to Asia Minor where they now lived. They were warlike, covering up by their arrogance and pride the weakness of their sex. By force of arms they had possessed themselves of extended provinces, and had constituted Ephesus as the centre of their power. For a long time they governed themselves, disdaining subjection to men and life in their company, for such a life, they in their presumptuous pride, called slavery or servitude. Since much is said of them in histories, though with many contradictions, I will not dilate upon this matter. For my purpose it is sufficient to state, that, since these Amazons were proud, vainglorious and averse to men, Lucifer found them predisposed toward his counterfeit virginity. He filled them with vain hopes of gaining great veneration and renown in the world by being known as pledged to virginity and stirred them with the desire of becoming famous and admired of men and perhaps of one of them reaching the position and worship of a goddess. In their unbridled desire of this worldy honor they gathered around them many Amazons, both true and counterfeit virgins, and instituted their spurious congregation of virgins at Ephesus, the place of their origin.

439. In a short time these more than foolish virgins grew very numerous and through the instigations of the demons were much admired and applauded by the world. Among them one signalized herself and became very cele-

brated for her beauty, nobility, high intellect, chastity and other allurements. She was called Diana and the fame and admiration of her became widespread. The veneration of her and the multitude of her companions were the occasion of the building of the renowned temple of Ephesus, which the world estimated as one of its marvels and which took many years to construct. As Diana gradually gained the worship and title of goddess among the blind multitude, this rich and sumptuous temple was finally dedicated to her, and was called the temple of Diana. In imitation of it and under the same title, many others were built in other parts of the world. In order to spread the renown of this counterfeit virgin during her lifetime in Ephesus, the demon communicated with her and filled her with diabolical illusions; many times he surrounded her with a false splendor and manifested to her secrets to be promulgated. He taught her also some ceremonies and forms of worship similar to those of the people of God; by which she and the people might worship the devil. The rest of the virgins venerated her as a goddess; which was also done by the other heathens, who were as prodigal as they were blind in attributing divinity to all that seemed to them wonderful.

440. These diabolical frauds had thus been established when the neighboring kings defeated the Amazons and assumed the government of Ephesus. They preserved this temple of Ephesus as something sacred and divine, and they permitted the continuance of that gathering of foolish virgins. Although some man of the people burned this temple, the city and the government authorities rebuilt it, being especially helped by the contributions of women. This was a little more or less than thirty years before the Redemption of the human race. Hence at the time when the most blessed Mother was in Ephesus not

the old temple stood, but the second one, built later. In this temple the virgins occupied different apartments. But as, during the time of the Incarnation and death of Christ, idolatry was so firmly established in the world, those diabolical women not only had not improved in their customs, but deteriorated, and nearly all of them held abominable intercourse with the demons. In connection therewith they committed other most loathsome crimes and deceived the world by their humbugging prophecies, by which the devil filled both them and their dupes with their insanities.

441. This and much more did the most blessed Mary behold around Her in Ephesus and on account of it She was struck with a sorrow certainly mortal, if She had not been preserved by the Lord. But having seen that Lucifer had appropriated the statute of Diana as a seat or throne of his wickedness, She prostrated Herself upon the ground before her divine Son and said: "Lord God Most High, worthy of all reverence and praise! It is proper that these abominations, which have lasted for so many ages, should cease. My heart cannot bear to see that an unhappy and abominable woman receive the worship due to the true God, such as Thou alone as the Infinite deservest; nor can I endure to see the name of chastity so profaned and prostituted in honor of the demons. Thy infinite condescension has made me the guide and the mother of virgins, as a most noble part of thy Church, the most precious fruit of thy Redemption, most pleasing to Thee. The title of chastity must be consecrated to Thee in the souls, which shall be my children, and I cannot consent to leave it any longer to these adulterous women. I make complaint against Lucifer and against hell, for their presumption in unjustly appropriating such a right. I beseech Thee, my Son, to chastise them

by rescuing these souls from his tyranny and conferring on them the liberty of thy faith and true light."

442. The Lord answered: "My Mother, I grant thy petition, for it is not just that, even were it only in name, this virtue of chastity, which was so ennobled in Thee and is so pleasing to Me, should be ascribed to my enemies. But many of those counterfeit virgins are foreknown as reprobates on account of their abominations and their obstinacy, and all of them will not embrace the way of eternal life. Some few of them will accept the faith, which shall be taught them." At this juncture saint John came to the oratory of the most blessed Mother; but he did not then know of the mystery She was then engaged in, nor of the presence of her divine Son. But the true Mother of the humble wished to join to her prayers those of his beloved disciple. She therefore secretly asked permission of her Son to speak to him and said to him: "John, my Son, my heart is grieved on acount of the abominable crimes committed against the Most High in the temple of Diana and my soul desires to see them ended and atoned." The holy Apostle answered: "My Lady, I have seen something of what passes in that abominable place. I cannot restrain my sorrow and my tears, that the demon should be there venerated and worshipped as is due to God alone; and no one can put a stop to such great evils, unless Thou, my Mother, wilt take this matter in hand."

443. The most blessed Mary then ordered the Apostle to join Her in prayer for a remedy of these evils. Saint John betook himself to his chamber, while the most blessed Lady remained with the Savior in hers. Prostrate before the Lord and shedding copious tears, She resumed her prayers and petitions. She persevered therein with most burning fervor and as it were in agonizing sorrow.

Appealing to her divine Son for comfort and consolation, She received the following response to her petitions and prayers: "My Mother and my Dove, let what thou askest be done without delay; give thy orders and commands according to thy heart's wishes as the powerful Mistress." By this favor the love of the most blessed Virgin was inflamed with zeal for the honor of the Divinity. As Queen She imperiously commanded all the demons in the temple of Diana to descend immediately to the depths of hell and to leave the place, which they had infested as their own for so many years. Many legions of them inhabited that temple, deceiving men by their superstitions and profaning the souls; but in the shortest twinkling of an eye, in virtue of the powerful command of the Queen, most holy Mary, all of them were hurled into hell. So great was the terror by which She struck them down, that as soon as She opened her lips to pronounce the first word they waited not for the second; for they were then already in hell and the swiftness of an angel, proper to them as pure spirits, seemed to them tardy in their flight from the Mother of the Omnipotent.

444. They were unable to leave the abyssmal caverns until, as I shall soon relate, they received permission to come forth with the great dragon to do battle with the Queen of heaven; and in hell itself they sought the localities farthest removed from the place where She was upon earth. I must remark, that by these triumphs the most holy Mary so vanquished the demon, that he could not return to reassume the same position or jurisdiction in those places of which he was dispossessed. But this infernal serpent was and is so venomous, that new heads grow upon him where the former are cut off, continually evolving new schemes of malice and wickedness against God and his Church. Following up her victory

the great Mistress of the world, with the consent of Christ our Savior, immediately ordered one of her holy angels to repair to the temple of Diana and destroy it without leaving a stone upon a stone. Of all the women that dwelt there he was to save only nine designated by Her, while all the rest should die and be buried in the ruins of the building. These were reprobates, whose souls, before they could increase their punishment by more sins, should be buried in hell with the demons, whom they had obeyed and worshipped.

445. The angel of the Lord executed the mandate of his Queen and Mistress, and in the shortest space of time the rich and famous temple of Diana, the establishment of which had consumed many ages, was shattered to the dust: so sudden was the destruction and ruin of it, that it roused the astonishment and fear of the inhabitants of Ephesus. He saved the nine women designated by the most holy Mary in pursuance of the command of Christ our Savior; for these alone accepted the faith, as I shall relate. All the others perished in the ruins, not leaving even a remembrance of themselves. Although the inhabitants of Ephesus instituted an inquiry, they could find no one upon whom to put the blame, as they had been able to do in the burning of the first temple when, for the sake of the fame attached to his crime, the incendiary delivered himself up of his own accord. The evangelist saint John took occasion from this event to preach with still greater fervor the divine truth and to free the Ephesians from the deceits and errors of the demons. The Evangelist joined the Queen of heaven in giving thanks to the Most High for this triumph over Lucifer and over idolatry.

446. But it is necessary here to explain, that this event must not be connected with that mentioned in the nine-

teenth chapter of the Acts of the Apostles concerning the temple of Diana, which saint Luke relates, that a renowned artificer of Ephesus, called Demetrius, who manufactured silver images of the goddess Diana, conspired with others, who were interested in his art or trade, against saint Paul; for the Apostle preached all through Asia, that those were no gods, which were manufactured by the hands of men. On account of this new doctrine Demetrius persuaded his associates, that saint Paul was not only ruining their trade, but causing the temple of Diana, so greatly venerated in Asia and the whole world, to be despised. This conspiracy roused the artisans, and they, the whole city, so that the cry went up: "Great is the Diana of the Ephesians," bringing on what saint Luke relates in that chapter. In order to make intelligible what I have said above, I will add, that this temple, of which saint Luke speaks, was another, less costly and more ordinary temple, which the Ephesians began to build after the most blessed Virgin had returned to Jerusalem. When saint Paul came to preach in Ephesus this temple had already been completed. From what saint Luke says, we can gather how deeply ingrown idolatry and the cult of Diana was in the Ephesians and in the whole of Asia. This was natural not only on account of the length of the time in which this error had held sway, but also because that city had made itself illustrious and famous throughout the world by the worship of Diana and by its great temple. The inhabitants of Ephesus having been delivered from this deceit and vanity by the Blessed Virgin, and their city being the seat and source of this worldwide superstition, imagined that they could not live without their goddess or without their building temples in her honor. So ingrained was the ignorance of the true God among the heathens, that many Apostles and

many years were required for making known the truth
and rooting out the cockle of idolatry, especially among
the Romans and the Greeks, who esteemed themselves the
most wise and civilized of all the nations of the earth.

447. Having destroyed the temple of Diana the most
holy Mary conceived still greater desires of laboring for
the exaltation of the name of Christ and for the spread
of the holy Church, in order that the triumph gained over
the enemies might bring its proper fruit. While She was
thus multiplying her prayers and petitions for this purpose, it happened one day that the holy angels manifested
themselves to Her in visible forms and said to Her:
"Our Queen and Mistress, the great God of celestial
hosts commands us to bring Thee to heaven before his
royal throne to which He calls Thee." The most holy
Mother answered: "Behold here the handmaid of the
Lord; let his holy will be done in me." Then the angels
received Her on a throne of light, such as I have described
on other occasions, and bore Her to the empyrean heavens
and to the presence of the most holy Trinity, which manifested Itself not by an intuitive, but by an abstractive vision. She prostrated Herself before the sovereign throne,
adored the immutable being of God in profound humility and reverence. Then the eternal Father spoke
to Her and said: "My Daughter and meekest Dove, the
cries of thy inflamed heart for the exaltation of my holy
name have come to my ears, and thy petitions for the holy
Church are acceptable in my eyes, inclining me to mercy
and clemency. In response to thy love I wish to renew
in thee my power, in order that thou mayest defend my
honor and glory, triumph over my enemies and their
ancient pride, bind and crush their necks, and in order
that through thy victories thou mayest assist my Church
and acquire new blessings and favors for its members,
thy brethren."

448. The most holy Mary replied: "Behold, O Lord, I am the least of thy creatures; my heart is prepared for all that shall be thy pleasure and for all that shall promote the exaltation of thy ineffable name and thy greater glory; let thy divine will be done in me." The eternal Father added: "Let all my courtiers of heaven understand, that I appoint Mary as the chief and leader of all my hosts, and as the conqueror of all my enemies gloriously to triumph over them." The other two divine Persons, the Son and the Holy Ghost, added their approval; and all the blessed with the angels answered: "Thy holy will be done, O Lord, in heaven and on earth." Thereupon the Lord ordered eighteen of the highest seraphim to adorn, strengthen, and arm their Queen for battle against the infernal dragon. On that occasion were mysteriously fulfilled the promise in the book of Wisdom: that the Lord armed the creatures for vengeance upon his enemies, and the other sayings there recorded (Wis. 5, 18). Six of the seraphim first came forward to adorn the most blessed Lady with a sort of light as with an impenetrable armor, which at the same time manifested the holiness and justice of the Queen, so invincible and impenetrable to the demons, that in an ineffable manner She was made godlike in strength. For this wonder the seraphim and the saints gave thanks to God.

449. Immediately another six of the seraphim approached and, in obedience to the command of the Lord, they furnished Her with another new enlightenment. It was a sort of reflection of the Divinity in her countenance, unbearable to the sight of the demons. In virtue of this gift, the enemies, although, as we shall see, they came to tempt Her, could not look upon her godlike face, not being deemed worthy of this privilege by the Lord. Then came also the last six seraphim and at the command

of the Lord they furnished Her with offensive weapons, since She was to take upon Herself the defense of the Divinity and its honor.   In pursuance of their divine commission the angels added to all the faculties of the great Lady new qualities of divine virtue, corresponding to the gifts with which the Most High had endowed Her. In virtue of this privilege the great Mistress received the power to impede, restrain and counteract at her will the most secret schemes and attempts of all the demons, so that all of them became subject to the will and mandate of the most holy Mary, without liberty to hinder her decrees; and of this power She availed Herself frequently in favor of the faithful and of her clients.   All these special powers, and whatever they implied, the three divine Persons confirmed, each One separately conferring upon her gifts corresponding to his divine attributes and bidding Her return to the Church and by them triumph over the enemies of the Lord.

450. In parting the three divine Persons gave their blessing to the most blessed Mary and She adored Them in deepest reverence.   Then the angels, full of wonder at the works of the Most High, brought Her back to her oratory, exclaiming: "Who is She, that so godlike, rich and prosperous, descends from the highest heaven to the world to defend the honor of God's name?   How well appointed and how beautiful does She advance to battle for the Lord?   O Queen, O most exalted Lady, proceed prosperous in thy beauty, go forth and reign over all the creatures, and let all of them praise and magnify Thee; because He has shown Himself so liberal and powerful in thy blessings.   Holy, holy, holy is the Lord God Sabbaoth, the Lord of the celestial hosts (Is. 6, 3) and in Thee shall bless Him all the generations of men." Arriving at her oratory the most blessed Mary gave

humblest thanks to the Almighty, prostrating Herself to the dust as She was wont to do on such occasions.

451. The most prudent Mary conferred within Herself for some time, in order to prepare for her conflict with the demons. While thus meditating She saw issuing upon the earth, as from the abyss, a fearful red dragon with seven heads, from each of which came forth the smoke and fire of vast wrath and fury, while many other demons followed him in similar shapes. This vision was so horrible that no other living being could have looked upon it without losing its life; and it was indeed necessary, that the most blessed Mary should be forewarned and made so invincible in order to enter into battle with these blood-thirsty beasts of hell. They gathered around the great Queen in furious howlings and began to vaunt their threats, saying; "Come, come let us destroy this our enemy; we have the permission of the Almighty to tempt Her and make war upon Her. This time we shall make an end of Her, we shall take vengeance for the injuries She has continually inflicted on us and for the destruction of our temple of Diana. Let us destroy Her likewise; She is but a Woman, a mere Creature, whereas we are knowing, astute and powerful spirits; we need not fear this earthly creature."

452. That entire host of infernal dragons advanced upon the invincible Queen, Lucifer leading them on and challenging Her to battle. As the most deadly poison of this serpent is his pride, by which he usually instills his vices for the destruction of innumerable souls, it seemed to him proper to begin with this vice, outwardly concealing it in accordance with the state of sancity, which he attributed to the most holy Mary. For this purpose the dragon and his followers transformed themselves into angels of light and thus manifested themselves to

Her, imagining that She had not yet seen and recognized them as demons and dragons of hell. They began with praise and flattery saying: "Powerful art Thou, Mary, great and valorous among women; all the world honors and celebrates Thee for the virtues it sees in Thee and for the prodigies and wonders Thou performest through them. Thou art worthy of glory, since no one equals Thee in holiness. We know this better than all the rest, and therefore we proclaim it and sing to Thee in festive joy at thy doings." By these counterfeit acknowledgments Lucifer sought to excite in the mind of the humble Queen, haughty thoughts of pride and presumption. But instead of moving or persuading Her to any pleasure or consent in them, he drew forth in Her living darts of pain, that transfixed her sincerest heart. Not all the torments of the martyrs were to Her so painful as these diabolical flatteries. In order to confound them, She excited acts of humility, annihilating Herself and debasing Herself in such an admirable and resistless a manner, that hell could not bear it nor remain longer in her presence; for the Lord had ordained that Lucifer and his ministers should recognize and feel these acts of humility. All the devils fled with dreadful howls, saying: "Let us away to the abyss, for less painful to us is the confusion of that place than the humility of this invincible Woman." They left Her, and the most prudent Lady gave thanks to the Almighty for this first victory.

INSTRUCTION WHICH THE GREAT QUEEN AND LADY OF HEAVEN GAVE ME.

453. My daughter, the pride of the demon includes a desire which the devil himself knows is absurd: namely, his desire that the saints serve and obey him as god, and

thus make him like to God in this respect. But the fulfillment of this desire is impossible, since it implies in
itself a contradiction. The essence of holiness consists in
the creature's conforming itself to the divine will, loving
God above all things in obedience, whereas sin consists
in deviating from this rule by the love of some other
object and obedience to the demon. But the uprightness
of true virtue is so conformable to reason, that even
the devil cannot ignore it. On this account he seeks, if
possible, to cause the good to fall in order to satisfy his
wrath and envy at not being able to draw them to his
service, and satiate his intense desire of preventing the
glory of God in his saints, which he cannot appropriate
for himself. Hence also his violent efforts to fell to
the earth some cedar of Lebanon in sanctity and to enslave
those who have been the servants of the Most High.
With this in view he exerts all his ingenuity and care, and
often he seeks to induce his devotees to practice some of
the moral virtues, even if only in appearance, as is done
by hypocrites and as we have seen in the virgins of Diana.
He hopes thereby to have his share in what God loves
and desires, and to sully and pervert what the Lord
wishes to use as a channel for his purity.

454. Remember, my daughter, that the byways, snares
and schemes of this serpent for the fall of the just are
so numerous, that without the special favor of the Most
High the souls could never know them, much less overcome them or escape his treacherous plots. In order to
deserve this protection of the Lord, God wishes the
creature on its part never to relax in vigilance, nor trust
in its own strength, nor ever be remiss in asking and desiring this help; for without it, man can do nothing and
will soon perish. What especially draws down the divine
clemency is fervor of the heart and promptness in divine

worship, and above all, persevering obedience and humility, which give stability and fortitude against the
assaults of the enemy, I wish to impress upon thy mind,
not for thy discouragement, but for thy advice and warning, that the works of the just, to which this serpent does
not impart some of its poison, are very rare. For usually
he tries with utmost subtlety to excite some terrestrial
passion or inclination, by which he secretly deflects or
perverts the intentions, preventing man from acting purely for God and for the legitimate ends of true virtue.
Since the cockle of some foreign affection, either in part
or the whole, is thus sown with the wheat, it is difficult
to detect, unless souls strip themselves of all earthly inclinations and examine their works in the divine light.

455. Thou art well warned, my daughter, against this
peril and against the ceaseless efforts of the demons,
which are more violent against thee than against other
souls. Let not thy vigilance be less than his, and do
not trust in the mere appearance of good intention in
thy works; for, though appearances must always be
good and upright, yet this is not sufficient, nor can the
creature always discern them. The demon often deceives
the soul under the cloak of a good intention, proposing
some apparently or remotely good end, in order to lead
them into proximate danger; and thus it happens, that,
enmeshed in this danger, the men never attain the good
which drew them into action. At other times he prevents the soul, under cloak of this good intention, from
examining into circumstances, which vitiate the act by
imprudence in the performance. Then again, under the
outwardly good intention, are often hidden the earthly
passions and inclinations, which dominate the heart.
Hence, amid so many dangers, thou canst find safety
only in scrutinizing thy actions by the light which the

Lord infuses into the superior part of thy soul; by it thou wilt know how to distinguish the good from the evil, the truth from the falsehood, the bitter from the sweet, passions from right reason (Jer. 15, 19). Then the divine light in thee will not be obscured by darkness, the eye will be single and will purify the body of thy actions (Matth. 6, 22), and thou wilt be entirely and in all things pleasing to thy Lord and to Me.

CHAPTER V.

THE MOST HOLY MARY, CALLED BY THE APOSTLE SAINT
PETER, RETURNS FROM EPHESUS; SHE CONTINUES HER
BATTLE WITH THE DEMONS; IS OVERTAKEN BY GREAT
STORMS AT SEA; SOME OTHER INTERVENING MYSTER-
IES.

456. After the death of the unhappy Herod the primitive Church of Jerusalem enjoyed some measure of quiet
and tranquillity for a considerable time. The great Lady
of the world merited this favor through her maternal
solicitude and care. During this time saint Barnaby and
saint Paul preached with wonderful success in the cities
of Asia Minor, Antioch, Lystra, Perge and others, as
is related by saint Luke in the thirteenth and fourteenth
chapter of the Acts of the Apostles and in connection with
the miracles and prodigies performed by saint Paul in
those cities and provinces. The apostle saint Peter, after
his liberation from prison, fled from Jerusalem and retired to another part of Asia not under the jurisdiction
of Herod. From that place he governed the faithful
accruing to the Church in Asia and those that were
in Palestine. All of them acknowledged and obeyed
him as the Vicar of Jesus Christ and head of the Church,
believing that all he ordained and enacted upon earth
was confirmed in heaven. With this firm faith they
came to him with all their doubts and difficulties as to
their supreme pontiff. Among other matters they asked
him to decide the questions raised by some of the Jews
concerning the doings and teachings of saint Paul and

Barnaby as well in Jerusalem as in Antioch, in opposition to the circumcision and the law of Moses, as I will relate later on and as is recorded by saint Luke in the fifteenth chapter of the Acts of the Apostles.

457. On this occasion the Apostles and disciples of Jerusalem begged saint Peter to return to the holy city in order to settle these controversies and establish order, so that the preaching of the faith might not be hindered; for since the death of Herod the Jews had no one to assist them in their persecutions, and therefore the Church enjoyed greater peace and tranquillity in Jerusalem. On the same grounds they also asked him to request the holy Mother of Jesus to come to that city; for all the faithful longed for Her with loving hearts, expected to be consoled in the Lord and hoped for the prosperity of all the affairs of the Church through her presence. On account of these appeals saint Peter resolved to return at once to Jerusalem, and before setting out, he wrote the following letter to the most holy Queen.

458. Letter of Saint Peter to most holy Mary.

"To Mary, the Virgin, Mother of God:

Peter, the Apostle of Jesus Christ, thy servant and the servant of the servants of God."

"Lady, among the faithful some doubts and differences have arisen concerning the doctrine of thy Son and our Redeemer, whether the ancient law of Moses is to be observed in conjunction with his teachings. They wish to know from us what is proper, and that we state to them what we heard from the mouth of the divine Teacher. In order to consult with my brethren, the Apostles, I am now setting out for Jerusalem and, for the consolation of all and by thy love for the Church, we beseech Thee likewise to come to that city, where, since the death of Herod, the Jews are more peaceful and the faithful more at ease. The multitude of the followers of Christ desire to see Thee and console themselves in thy presence. When we shall have arrived at Jerusalem, we shall notify the other cities, and with thy assistance will be established what shall be conducive to the interests of the holy faith and to the excellence of the law of grace."

459. This was the tenor and contents of the letter. The Apostles usually observed the same method, addressing first the person or persons to whom they were writing, then mentioning the writer, or inversely, as is apparent in the letters of saint Paul, and of saint Peter and of the other Apostles. To call the Queen Mother of God was agreed among the Apostles after they had composed the creed; and in speaking of Her they used indiscriminately the term of Virgin or Mother, because it was very important that all the faithful of the Church should accept the doctrine of the virginity and maternity of the great Lady. Some of the other faithful called Her Mary of Jesus, or Mary of Jesus, the Nazarene. Others less significantly called Her Mary, the daughter of Joachim and Anne. Such were the titles given to our Queen by the faithful in their conversation. The holy Church, preferring the names given Her by the Apostles, calls Her Virgin and Mother of God, and to these it has added other titles, still more illustrious and mysterious. A messenger brought the letter of saint Peter to the heavenly Lady, and in giving it to Her, he mentioned that it was from the Apostle. She received it on her knees, in reverence for the Vicar of Christ, and kissed it; but She would not open it, because saint John was absent preaching in the city. As soon as the Evangelist returned, She as usual asked his benediction on her knees, and handed him the letter, telling him that it was from saint Peter, the supreme high-priest. Saint John asked her what it

contained; but the Mistress of all virtues answered: "Do thou, my master, first read it and then tell me what it contains." This the Evangelist proceeded to do.

460. I cannot restrain my wonder and confusion at the humility and obedience of the most holy Mary in a matter of so small moment; for only her heavenly prudence could inspire Her, the Mother of God, with the thought, that it would be more humble and submissive not to read this letter of the Vicar of Christ except in the presence and under the obedience of the one to whose guidance She had submitted Herself as her superior. Her example reproves and stigmatizes the presumption of inferiors, who try to find excuses and pretenses for evading the humility and obedience due to their superiors. But the most holy Mary was a model and a teacher of holiness in all things, great or small. Having read the letter to Her, he asked Her, what She thought best to write to the Vicar of Christ. But also in this She did not wish to give any appearance of her being his equal or superior, preferring to obey; and therefore She answered: "My son and master, do thou arrange whatever shall be proper; for I, as thy servant, will obey." The Evangelist replied, that it seemed to him best to obey saint Peter and return immediately to Jerusalem. "It is right and proper to obey the head of the Church," answered the purest lady; "let us prepare even now for our departure."

461. Thus resolved, saint John went out to seek passage for Palestine and to prepare whatever was necessary for a speedy departure. In the meanwhile, at the request of the Evangelist, most blessed Mary called together the women who were her acquaintances and disciples in Ephesus, in order to take leave of them and instruct them in what they must do to persevere in their

holy faith. There were seventy-three of them, many
of them virgins, among whom were also the nine saved
from the ruins of the temple of Diana. These and many
others Mary herself had converted and catechized in the
faith; and She had formed of them a community in the
house of their hostesses. Through this congregation of
women the heavenly Lady had begun to atone for the
sins and abominations, perpetrated in the temple of
Diana for so many ages, and She established the observance of chastity in community life in that very city of
Ephesus where the devil had profaned it. Of all this,
these women had been informed, though they did not
know that She had destroyed the temple of Ephesus; for
this remained a secret, in order that neither the Jews
should find a pretext, nor the heathens be stirred to
anger against the gentle Mother by their insane love of
Diana. The Lord provided that the ruin of the temple
should be looked upon as an accident and be soon forgotten, so that profane authors wrote nothing about it,
though they had written much concerning the burning
of the first temple.

462. The most blessed Mary, in her desire to console
them for her absence spoke to these disciples in
sweetest words. She left them a paper, in which She had
written with her own hand: "My daughters, the will
of the Almighty calls me back to Jerusalem. In my absence keep in mind the doctrine, which you have received
from me and which I heard from the mouth of the Redeemer of the world. Look upon Him always as your
Lord and Master and as the Spouse of your souls, serving Him and loving Him with all your heart. Remember
the commandments of his holy law, in which you shall
be instructed by his ministers and priests, reverence and
obey them in humility, without ever accepting other

teachers, who are not disciples of Christ my divine Son, or followers of his doctrine. I shall always see that his ministers assist and protect you, and I shall never forget you or cease to commend you to the Lord. In my place will remain Mary, the elder: obey her in all things with great respect, and she will care for you with the same love and solicitude as I have done. You will observe inviolate retirement and recollection in this house, and no man shall ever enter it; and if it is necessary to speak to anyone, it shall be in the portal, in the presence of three of your number. Your prayers shall be uninterrupted and in private, reciting and singing those I have left you written in my chamber. Observe silence and meekness and treat your neighbors as you would be treated yourselves. Speak always the truth and be ever mindful of Christ crucified in all your thoughts, words and actions. Adore Him and confess Him as the Creator and Redeemer of the world; and in his name I give you his blessing, and I ask Him to live in your hearts."

463. These and other exhortations the most blessed Mother left for the congregation, which She had dedicated to her Son and true God. The one She had appointed their superior was one of the pious women, who had offered Her hospitality and who owned the house. This woman was well able to govern, for she had had much intercourse with the Queen and had been well informed concerning the law of God and its mysteries. She was called Mary the elder, because the most holy Mother had given her own name to many others in Baptism, communicating, as the Wise man says, without envy the excellence of her name (Wis. 7, 13); as this one was the first thus baptized in Ephesus, She was called Mary the elder, to distinguish her from the later ones. The most blessed Mary left them also in writing, the

Our Father, the Creed and the ten Commandments together with other prayers, which they were to recite vocally. To encourage them in these and other exercises She also left them a large cross made quickly at her request by the hands of the angels and set up in her oratory. Besides all this, as a kind Mother, and in order to bind them to Her still more, She distributed the things in her possession, which, though of trifling human value, were nevertheless rich and inestimable to them as being pledges and proofs of her maternal love.

464. Moved to great pity because, having engendered them in Christ, She was now obliged to relinquish them as orphans, She took leave of them. They all prostrated themselves at her feet with great wailing and abundant tears; for now they were to lose in one moment the consolation, the refuge and the joy of their heart. But on account of the continued solicitude of the most blessed Mother for her devout congregation all the seventy-three afterwards persevered in the fear of God and the faith of Christ our Lord. Yet the demon raised up violent persecutions against them and against the inhabitants of Ephesus. Foreseeing this the prudent Queen fervently prayed for them before leaving and asked her divine Son to guard and preserve them, and to appoint some angels for the defense of this small flock. All this the Lord granted Her according to her wish; and She afterwards often consoled them by sending exhortations from Jerusalem and by charging the disciples and Apostles at Ephesus to watch over these virgins and retired women. The great Lady continued this loving care during her whole life.

465. When the day of departure arrived, the Humblest of the humble asked saint John for his blessing and with it they betook themselves to the ship, having re-

mained in Ephesus two years and a half. On leaving their dwelling all her thousand angels manifested themselves in visible human forms, but all of them were armed for battle and formed into squadrons. This unwonted sight gave Her to understand, that She was to be prepared to continue her conflict with the great dragon and his allies. Before reaching the sea She saw a great multitude of the infernal legions meeting Her in various dreadful and terrific shapes; in the midst of them came a dragon with seven heads, so horrible and huge as to exceed the size of a large ship, and so fierce and abominable as to cause torment by its mere presence. Against these formidable hosts the invincible Queen fortified Herself by the most firm faith and fervent love, repeating the words of Psalms and the sayings from the mouth of her most holy Son. She ordered her holy angels to assist Her, for those terrific shapes naturally inspired Her with some human dread and horror. The Evangelist knew nothing of this conflict until the heavenly Lady afterwards informed him and gave him an insight into it.

466. Our blessed Lady embarked with the saint, and the ship's sails were set. But it had proceeded only a short distance from the port, when those dragons of hell, making use of the permission given them, stirred up the sea by a tempest such as had not been seen before that time nor until now; for the Almighty wished to exalt the power of his arm and the holiness of Mary and therefore He permitted such liberty to the malice and powers of the demons in this battle. The waves rose with terrific roarings, piling themselves upon the winds and apparently even upon the very clouds, forming with them mountains of water and foam, as if they were preparing for an onset to break the bounds of the abysses that imprisoned the ocean (Ps. 13, 9). The ship was

lashed and battered to and fro, and it seemed a miracle that it was not shattered to splinters at each shock. Sometimes it was hurled up into the clouds, at others sent to plow up the sand of the ocean's abysses; often its sails and masts were buried in the foaming waves. During some of the onsets of this unspeakably furious hurricane the ship was held in the air by the angels in order to save it from some of the vaster billows, which would inevitably have overhelmed and sent it to the bottom.

467. The mariners and passengers perceived the effects of this assistance, but remained ignorant of the cause; in their distress they were beside themselves, bewailing their ruin, which they deemed inevitable. The demons added to their terror; for, assuming human shapes, they loudly called upon the mariners as if from neighboring ships sent to their aid and urged them to forsake their ship and save themselves in the others. For though all the vessels suffered in this storm, yet the wrath of the demons and their power of doing harm was confined principally to the ship on which our Lady sailed and the distress and peril of the other vessels was not so great. The malicious designs of the demons were known only to the most blessed Virgin and not to the sailors, and therefore they believed these voices as of true passengers and sailors. Thus deceived they at times gave up caring for their own ship and left it to the fury of the sea, expecting to save themselves on one of the other ships. But the angels supplied their place directing and steering it when the sailors gave it up in despair to the destruction of the waves.

468. In the midst of this confusion and distress the most holy Mary preserved her tranquillity, serenely borne up by the ocean of her magnanimity and virtue, but at the same time practicing all the virtues by acts heroic in proportion to the exigencies of the occasion and the

dictates of her wisdom. As during this tempestuous voyage She personally experienced the dangers of navigation, which She had understood on her former voyage by divine inspiration, She was moved to new compassion for all voyagers at sea and renewed her former prayers and petitions. The most prudent Virgin also admired the indomitable forces of the sea and was led to consider the wrath of divine justice, so well represented by this insensible creature. And passing from these considerations to that of the sins of mortals, who drew it upon themselves from the Almighty, She entered into the most ardent prayers for the conversion of the world and the increase of the Church. For this She offered up the hardships of this voyage; since notwithstanding the tranquillity of her soul, She suffered much bodily inconvenience and still greater affliction at the thought that all her fellow-voyagers were made to suffer this persecution and tribulation of the demons on her account.

469. A large share of this suffering fell to the evangelist saint John on account of his deep solicitude for his true Mother and Mistress of the world. To this was added his own actual suffering. All was so much the more dreadful to him, because at that time he did not know what was passing in the interior of the most blessed Virgin. He sought a few times to console Her and console himself by assisting and comforting Her. Although the voyage from Ephesus to Palestine usually lasted only about six days, this one lasted fifteen, of which fourteen were tempestuous. One day saint John was very much disheartened at the continuance of this measureless hardship and, no longer able to restrain himself, said "My Lady, what is this? Are we to perish at sea? Beseech thy divine Son to look upon us with the eyes of a Father and to defend us in this tribulation." The blessed

Mother answered him: "Do not be disturbed, my son; for we must now fight the battles of the Lord and overcome his enemies by fortitude and patience." I shall beg of Him that no one who is with us shall perish, and that He sleep not, who watches over Israel (Ps. 70, 4); the strong ones of his court assist us and defend us; let us suffer for Him who placed Himself upon the Cross for the salvation of all." At these words saint John recovered the necessary courage.

470. Lucifer and his demons with increasing fury threatened the powerful Queen by telling Her that She would perish in this sea and not escape alive. But these and other threats were but spent arrows and the most prudent Mother despised them, not even listening to them, or looking upon the demons, or speaking to them a single word. They themselves on the other hand could not bear even to glance at her face on account of the virtue of the Most High shining from it. And the more they strove to overcome this virtue, the weaker they became and the more were they tormented by those offensive weapons, with which the Lord had clothed his most holy Mother. But in all of this lengthened conflict He concealed from her his purpose and also his countenance, never showing Himself to Her in visions as had been usual.

471. But at the end of fourteen days of this stormy voyage her divine Son deigned to descend and visit Her in person. He appeared upon the sea and saying: "My dearest Mother, I am with thee in tribulation." This vision and the words of the Lord, ineffably consoling on all occasions, were especially consoling to the most blessed Mother in this extremity; because help is more welcome in necessity. She adored her Son and God and answered: "My God and only Good of my soul, whom the winds

and the sea obey (Matth. 8, 27), behold, my Son, our
affliction: let not the works of thy hands perish." The
Lord said to Her: "My Mother and my Dove, from
thee have I received human form; therefore I desire that
all my creatures obey thy orders; command them as the
Mistress of all, for they are subject to thy will." The
most prudent Mother had desired the Lord to command
the waves, as He had done in the storm on the sea of
Galilee; but the occasion was different, since at that
time there was no one else but He to command the winds
and the sea. The heavenly Mary therefore obeyed and,
in the name of her divine Son, She first commanded
Lucifer and his hosts instantly to leave the Mediterranean
and cease to harass it. Immediately they fled in the
direction of Palestine; for She had not commanded them
to hell, not wishing to put an end to the battle. The
enemies having retired, She commanded the waters and
the winds to subside. They immediately obeyed, becoming tranquil and serene in the shortest space of time to
the great astonishment of the passengers, who knew not
the cause of this sudden change. Christ the Lord took
leave of his Mother, having filled her with benedictions
and joy and told Her to disembark on the next day. Thus
it also happened; for on the fifteenth day after their embarkation, they arrived happily at port and left the ship.
Our Queen and Mistress gave thanks to the Almighty for
these benefits and offered Him songs of thanksgiving
and praise for having saved Her from the dreadful
dangers. In this also the Evangelist joined, and the
blessed Mother thanked him for having accompanied Her
in her hardships. She asked his blessing and then they
both set out for Jerusalem.

472. The holy angels accompanied their Queen and
Lady in battle array as I have said; for also the demons

were awaiting her arrival resolved to continue the conflict as soon as She had reached the shore. With incredible fury they led on the assault by suggesting various temptations against all the virtues; but all their darts fell back upon themselves; they could make no breach in this tower of David, of which the Spouse says, that it is furnished with the thousand shields and all the arms of the strong, (Cant. 4, 4), and that it is fortified by towers of silver. Before entering her house in Jerusalem the great Lady, in her piety and devotion, yearned to visit the sacred spots consecrated by our Redemption, which was also the last thing She had done on leaving the city; but as saint Peter, at whose call She had come, was waiting, and as She knew the proper order to be maintained in all the virtues, She preferred obedience to her private devotions. Accordingly She betook Herself directly to the house of the Cenacle, where saint Peter then stayed, and falling on her knees before him, She asked for his blessing and begged his pardon for not having complied sooner with his command. She sought his hand in order to kiss it as that of the high-priest; but She did not lay the blame for her delay on the storm, nor did She mention any other circumstance in excuse. Only from the accounts furnished to him afterwards by saint John, did saint Peter learn of the hardships encountered on the voyage. The Vicar of our Savior and all the disciples and faithful of Jerusalem received their Teacher and Mistress with indescribable joy, reverence and love, and they prostrated themselves at her feet, thanking Her for having come to fill them with gladness and consolation and live where they could see and serve Her.

INSTRUCTION WHICH THE QUEEN OF HEAVEN, MOST HOLY
MARY, GAVE ME.

473. My Daughter, I desire that thou continually renew the remembrance of what I have told thee of these
sacred mysteries of my life; for it is not my will that
thou be only an insensible instrument for manifesting
them to the Church, but rather that thou be the one, who
before and above all others shall draw fruit from this
new blessing by practicing my teachings and following
my example. For this purpose has the Lord called thee,
and for it have I chosen thee as my daughter and disciple. Since thou hast duly noticed my act of humility
in not opening the letter of saint Peter without consent
of my son John, I wish to dilate further upon the lesson
contained in this instance. I desire thee to notice that
in those two virtues, humility and obedience, which are
the foundation of Christain perfection, there is nothing
small, and all that pertains to them is most pleasing to
the Most High and draws down the most abundant reward of his generous mercy and justice.

474. Consider then, my dearest, that, just as in the
present condition of man nothing is more contrary to his
nature than the subjection of one's will to that of another, so nothing is more necessary than this subjection
for the bending of that stiff-necked pride, which the
demon seeks to stir up in all the children of Adam. Hence
the enemies labor sleeplessly to induce men to follow their
own judgment and will. Thereby the devils gain many
triumphs and lead many souls into diverse roads of destruction; for in all states and conditions of life the
demon seeks to instill this poison into mortals, secretly

soliciting them to follow their own judgment and refuse to obey the laws and the will of their superiors, but rather to despise and rebel against it, perverting the order of divine Providence for the well-ordering of all things. And because men overthrow this government of the Lord, the world is filled with confusion and darkness, created things are thrown out of order and subjected to opposite force without regard or attention to God and his laws.

475. But though all this damage is odious in the eyes of the supreme Governor and Lord, yet it is especially displeasing to Him in religious, who, being bound by the vows of religion, seek to widen these restrictions or altogether free themselves from their obligations. I am not now speaking of those who transgress their rules in open daring or break their vows in small or in great things; this is nothing else than a dreadful temerity entailing eternal damnation. But, in order that they may not incur such a danger. I wish to exhort those who seek their salvation in religion, to guard themselves against entertaining opinions or explanations for relaxing the obedience due to their superiors in the name of God, or against trying to determine what liberties they might take without committing sin by infringing on obedience and their other vows or against studying whether they may not act according to their own judgment in certain matters great or small. Such disquisitions are never made for the better observance of vows, but always in order to stifle the remorse of conscience in breaking them. I remind them, that the demons seek to induce them to swallow these poisonous gnats, in order that, little by little, after being accustomed to those that seem insignificant, they may arrive at swallowing the camels of the more serious sins. Those that continually hover about

the entrances to mortal sins, will, to say the least, make themselves liable to a strict inquiry by the Judge and thus receive the smallest reward. For they have studied all their lives to give to the Lord the least in their power to oblige Him.

476. These attempts to explain away the binding force of the love of God, tending to remodel it according to the inclinations of the flesh, are very abominable to my divine Son and to myself; for it is a sign of great disaffection to obey the divine law out of necessity, making it apparent, that only the fear of punishment urges one on, and not love toward Him who commands, and that nothing would be done, if no punishment were in store. Many times, in the effort to avoid humiliation at the hands of the immediate superior, the subject appeals to the higher authority and thus asks for exemptions from those who have only a general information and cannot know or understand his particular needs or danger. It cannot be denied, that this is still a kind of obedience; but it is also certain, that it is a shift for greater liberty, diminishes the reward and incurs danger; since without doubt it is more meritorious to obey and subject oneself to the inferior authority, to those in a lower condition, and to those less favorably disposed to one's own views and inclinations. I learned no such doctrines in the school of my divine Son, nor did I show them in practice; for all things I sought the permission of those I held as superiors, never being without them as thou hast seen. Even for opening and reading the letter of saint Peter, the head of the Church, I waited to find out the will of his inferior, who was my more immediate superior.

477. My daughter, I do not wish thee to follow the teachings of those who seek liberty and license in fol-

lowing their own inclinations; but I choose thee and conjure thee to imitate me and walk the secure path of perfection. Hankering after dispensations and exemptions perverts the christian and the religious life. At all times thou must live in humble and obedient subjection, and thou must not hold thyself excused therefrom on account of being a superior, for thou hast thy confessors and superiors. If sometimes in their absence thou canst not act in obedience, ask counsel and obey one of thy subjects. For thee, all of them should be as superiors; and let not this seem strange to thee; since thou art the least of the human born and shouldst consider thyself so, humiliating thyself beneath them all in order to be my true follower, my disciple and daughter. Besides this thou must punctually tell me thy faults twice a day and ask my permission for all that thou art to do during each day, confessing also every day the sins thou committest. I shall exhort thee, and command thee what is proper, both through myself and through my ministers of the Lord; and thou must not shrink to tell many others of thy ordinary faults, in order that in all things and before all men thou humiliate thyself in the eyes of the Lord and in mine. This science, hidden to the world and the flesh, I desire thee to learn and impart to thy nuns. In teaching thee this lesson I wish to reward thee for thy labor in writing my life; for by these instructions in so important a doctrine I wish to impress thee, that, if thou wishest to imitate me as thou shouldst, thou must communicate or speak with no one, nor undertake anything, nor write letters, nor move about, nor allow any thoughts (if possible), except in obedience to me and to those who govern thee. The worldly and carnal men call these virtues impertinent and vain observances; but their ignorant pride will have its punishment when, in the presence of the Judge, truths will be revealed; then will be seen who were the ignorant and the wise, and those will be rewarded, who as true servants have been faithful as well in small as in greater things (Matth. 25, 21); when there is no remedy left, the foolish ones will know the damage done by their carnal prudence.

478. As thou wert moved to a certain envy on learning that I myself governed that congregation of women at Ephesus, I now advise thee to have no such feeling. Remember that thou and thy nuns have chosen me for your Superior and special Patroness in order that I might govern you as your Queen and Lady; and I desire them to know, that I have accepted this office and have constituted myself in it forever on condition, that they be perfect in their vocation and very faithful to their Lord, my divine Son, to whom I have assigned them as his spouses. Remind them often of this, so that they watch over themselves and retire from the world, despising it with all their hearts; that as my daughters they do not degenerate, living in recollection and peace; that they follow and execute the doctrines which I have given thee in this history for thee and for them and that they hold it in high veneration, gratefully writing it in their hearts. For in having presented to them my life for the rule and government of their souls, as it is now written by thy hands, I am fulfilling my office as Mother and Superior, in order that as subjects and as daughters they may tread in my footsteps, imitate my virtues and correspond with me in faithful love.

479. Another important lesson canst thou draw from this chapter, namely: those that do not obey willingly, when any adverse circumstance turns up in what is commanded, will immediately be cast down, afflicted and

disturbed, and, in order to justify their impatience, they
will blame the one that commands, and complain about
him either to his superiors or to others, as if he that
commands were responsible for the untoward accidents
happening to the inferior, or as if he had it in his power
to direct the government of the whole world according to the wishes of his subject. Indeed, many times
God, in reward for complete submission, raises hindrances
in order that the one who obeys may increase his merit
and crown, at other times he punishes those who show
any repugnance in obeying by withholding full success;
and all these accidents can in nowise be blamed upon
the superior, who commands. The Lord simply said:
He who hears you, and who obeys you, hears and obeys
Me (Luke 10, 16). The labor connected with obedience
always redounds to the benefit of those who obey; if
they do not profit by their obedience, it is no fault of
the one that commands. I made no complaints against
saint Peter for asking me to come from Ephesus to
Jerusalem, although I suffered so much on the voyage;
but I asked him pardon for not having fulfilled his command more expeditiously. Never show any grievance
or sign of being displeased toward thy superiors, for
this is a very ugly spirit and such liberty will destroy
all the merit of thy obedience. Look upon them with
reverence, as taking the place of Christ, and thy merit
will be abundant; follow my footsteps, my example and
my doctrine, and thou wilt be perfect in all things.

CHAPTER VI.

THE VISIT OF THE MOST BLESSED MARY TO THE HOLY
PLACES; SHE GAINS MYSTERIOUS TRIUMPHS OVER THE
DEMONS; SHE SEES THE DIVINITY IN HEAVEN BY A
BEATIFIC VISION; THE APOSTLES CONVOKE A COUNCIL;
THE HIDDEN MYSTERIES CONNECTED WITH ALL THESE
EVENTS.

480. All our efforts are gloriously insufficient to describe the plenitude of perfection of all the doings of the most blessed Mary; for unfailingly are we overcome by the grandeur of even the smallest virtue (if indeed there be any of them small) when we come to consider the matter upon which She wrought them. But our efforts, shall always be full of blessings for us, if, without presumptuously attempting to fathom this ocean of grace, we humble ourselves to glorify and exalt in Her the Creator and to discover more and more in what we can imitate Her. I shall esteem myself very fortunate, if by making known the favors conferred by God upon our great Queen, I can show to the children of the Church something of what is so far above that for which I cannot find adequate and appropriate terms to describe; for in all that I can say, I shall still speak as one that is dull, stuttering and without fervor of devotion. Wonderful are the events which have been manifested to me for the purpose of being recorded in this and the following chapters.

481. After the most blessed Mary had complied obediently with the will of saint Peter, as I have related in the

preceding chapter, She thought it proper to satisfy her
piety in visiting the sacred spots of our Redemption. She
performed all her works of mercy with such prudence, that
She omitted none, assigning to each one its place in order
that no circumstance necessary to bring it to perfection
might be wanting. Applying her heavenly wisdom She first
performed that which was greater and foremost in order,
then what seemed of less importance; but, as well the
one as the other, with all the attention of her soul in
the measure as each required. She left the Cenacle to
visit the sacred places and was accompanied by all her
holy angels, as well as followed up by Lucifer and his
legions for further conflict. These dragons, forming in
battle array and presenting the most fearful shapes,
uttered their threats and suggested their temptations.
But as soon as the great Lady approached any of the
holy places to perform her devotions, the demons fell
back, repelled by divine power; they also felt themselves
crushed by the hidden virtue communicated to these
holy places through the Redemption of Christ. Lucifer,
urged on by the temerity of his pride, attempted to come
nearer; for, relying upon his permission to tempt and
persecute the great Lady, he was anxious, if possible,
to gain some victory over Her in the very places where
he had been so signally vanquished; or at least to hinder
Her from showing the veneration and worship required.

482. But the Most High ordained, that the power of
his arm against Lucifer and his demons should be shown
through this very Queen, and that her exercises, which
he tried to disturb, should be the sword with which he was
to be overcome and cut down. And thus it happened;
for the devotion and piety with which the heavenly
Mother worshipped her divine Son and with which She
renewed the grateful remembrance of the Passion, caused

such terror to the demons, that they could not tolerate it and they felt a force so oppressive and tormenting proceeding from Her, that they were obliged to recede still farther from the invincible Queen. They broke out into fearful roarings, audible to Her alone, and they exclaimed: "Let us fly from this Woman, our Enemy, who so confounds and oppresses us by her virtues. We seek to blot out the remembrance and the veneration of these places, in which men were redeemed and in which we were despoiled of our dominion; and this Woman, being a mere creature, hinders our designs and renews the triumphs gained by her Son upon the Cross."

483. The most holy Mary made all the stations of the holy places in company of her angels; and having arrived on mount Olivet, where her Son ascended into heaven, the Lord himself, in effable beauty and glory, descended from his throne to visit and console his most pure Mother. He manifested Himself to Her with the affection and bounty of a Son, yet as the infinite and powerful God. He so filled Her with his Divinity and elevated Her above the terrestrial, that for a long time She was separated from visible things; and though She ceased not to attend to external works, She performed them with a greater constraint upon Herself, being completely spiritualized and transformed into her Divine Son. Through her divine Son She perceived that these favors were part of her reward for her humility and obedience toward saint Peter and in attending upon his commands in preference not only to her devotion, but also her convenience. He also promised Her anew his assistance in her battle against the demons and in immediate fulfillment of this promise, the Lord ordained that Lucifer and his hosts should then and there become convinced of a power in Her such as they had not experienced before.

484. The Queen returned to the Cenacle and as the demons again sought to renew their temptations, they rebounded like inflated rubber balls, when thrown swiftly at a stone wall. These vainglorious hosts were hurled back upon themselves with greater force than that with which they had assaulted the most holy Mary. They broke out in still more furious howlings and, driven to confess certain truths by their own dismay, they said: "O we unhappy ones, who are obliged to look upon such happiness of the human nature! What great excellence and dignity man has now attained in this pure Creature! How ungrateful shall men be, and how foolish, if they do not profit by the blessings bestowed upon them in this Daughter of Adam! She is truly its salvation and our destruction. Great things her Son does with Her; but She is not unworthy of them. A cruel punishment is this, that we must confess all these truths. O would that God conceal from us this Woman, who adds such torments to our envy! How shall we vanquish Her, if the mere sight of Her is insufferable to us? Let us console ourselves in the fact, that men lose so much of what this Woman merits for them, and that they foolishly despise Her. In them shall we avenge our injuries, through them we shall exercise our fury, filling them with illusions and errors; for if they but pay attention to her example, all of them would profit by this Woman and follow her virtues. But this is not enough to console me (added Lucifer) for this Woman, his Mother, can please God more than all the sins we can lead men into shall displease Him; and even if this were not so my position does not permit me to remain indifferent at seeing human nature so highly exalted in a mere weak Woman. This wrong is unbearable: let us return to persecute Her; let us give vent to the fury of our envy

even in spite of torment: and though we all suffer by it, let our pride be not dismayed, for possibly some triumph may yet be gained over this our Enemy."

485. The most blessed Mary knew of and heard all these wrathful threats; but as the Queen of virtues She despised them all. Without the least sign of disturbance in her countenance She retired to her oratory in order prudently to confer with Herself concerning the mysteries of this conflict and concerning the difficult business now before the Church in seeking to end circumcision and the ancient law. In this the Queen of the angels labored for a few days, engaged during her retirement in continual prayers, petitions, tears and prostrations. In her own affairs She also asked the Lord to stretch out his almighty arm against Lucifer and grant Her the victory over him and the demons. Although the great Lady knew Him to be on her side and that He would not leave Her in tribulation, She ceased not her prayers and She acted on her part as if She had been the weakest of creatures in the time of temptation. She taught us what we ourselves should do in temptation, since we are so subject to them and so apt to be overcome. She prayed for the holy Church, asking the Lord to grant to it his evangelical law, pure, unsullied, without wrinkle, and unhampered by the ancient ceremonies.

486. This petition the most blessed Mary urged with the most burning fervor; for She knew that Lucifer and all hell sought through the Jews to unite circumcision with Baptism and the rites of Moses with the truths of the Gospel. The admission of these fallacies would help to maintain the Jews in their stubborn adhesion to the old Law during the coming ages. One of the fruits and triumphs of the great Lady in her battle with the dragon was, that circumcision was immediately rejected by the

council of which I shall speak; and from that time on the pure grain of evangelical truth was separated from the dried and barren stubble of the mosaic ceremonies, as it is to this day in our holy mother the Church. All this the most blessed Mary procured through her merits and her prayers. She knew, in the meanwhile, that saint Paul and saint Barnaby were hastening from Antioch to Jerusalem in order to confer with saint Peter and, as related by saint Luke in the fifteenth chapter of the Acts of the Apostles, solve the difficulties raised by the Jews.

487. Saint Paul and saint Barnaby were aware of the return of the Queen of heaven when they came to Jerusalem. In his ardent desire of seeing Her saint Paul with saint Barnaby, at once sought her presence, and they cast themselves at her feet, shedding abundant tears of joy. Not less was the joy of the heavenly Mother at meeting these Apostles, toward whom She bore an especial love in the Lord on account of their zealous labors for the exaltation of God's name and the spread of the faith. The Mistress of the humble desired them to present themselves first to saint Peter and the rest, and last to Her, judging Herself to be the least of all creatures. But they, preserving the proper order in their reverence and love, thought that none should be preferred to Her who was the Mother of God, the Mistress of all creation and the beginning of all our happiness. The great Lady prostrated Herself before saint Paul and Barnaby, kissed their hands and asked for their blessing. On this occasion saint Paul was favored with a wonderful ecstatic abstraction, in which were revealed to him great mysteries and prerogatives of this mystical City of God, the Blessed Mary, and he saw Her as it were completely invested with the Divinity.

488. Through this vision saint Paul was filled with admiration and with incomparable love and veneration for the heavenly Mary. Somewhat recovering himself, he said to Her: "Mother of all piety and clemency, pardon this vile and sinful man for having persecuted thy divine Son, my Lord, and his holy Church." The Virgin Mother answered and said: "Paul, servant of the Most High, if He who created and redeemed thee, deigned to call thee to his friendship and made thee a vessel of election, how can I, his slave, refuse to pardon thee? (Acts 9, 15). My soul magnifies and exalts Him, because He wished to manifest Himself so powerful, liberal and holy in thee." Saint Paul thanked the heavenly Mother for the benefit of his conversion and for the other favors conferred upon him by Her in saving him from so many dangers. The same also saint Barnaby did, and both again asked for her protection and help, which the most holy Mother promised.

489. Saint Peter, as the head of the Church, had called upon the Apostles and disciples then in and around Jerusalem, and convoked them to a meeting in the presence of the Mistress of the world. In order that the most prudent Virgin, in her profound humility, might not absent Herself from this council, saint Peter had interposed his authority as Vicar of Christ. All of them being gathered, saint Peter said: "My brethren and children in Christ our Savior, it was necessary that we meet in order to solve the difficulties and decide upon the affairs, which our most beloved brethren Paul and Barnaby have brought to our notice, and to determine other matters touching the increase of the holy faith. For this it is proper that we engage in prayer to obtain the assistance of the Holy Ghost and we shall persevere therein for ten days as is our custom. On the first and

on the last day we shall celebrate the sacrifice of the Mass, by which we shall dispose our hearts to receive the divine light." All of them approved of this arrangement. In order to celebrate the first Mass on the next day the Queen prepared the hall of the Cenacle, cleaning and decorating it with her own hands and holding all things in readiness for the Communion of Herself together with the Apostles and disciples during those Masses. Saint Peter alone celebrated, observing all those rites and ceremonies which I have described, when speaking of the Masses on other occasions.

490. The other Apostles and disciples communicated at the hands of saint Peter; then the most blessed Mary, taking the last place. Many angels descended to the Cenacle. All those present saw them and at the time of the consecration the Cenacle was filled with a wonderful light and fragrance, through which the Lord wrought wonderful effects in their souls. Having celebrated the first Mass, they agreed upon certain hours, in which they were to persevere together in prayer, as far as they could without neglecting the necessary ministry of souls. The great Lady retired to a place, where She remained alone and motionless for those ten days without eating or speaking to any one. During that time She experienced such hidden mysteries as to move the angels to astonishment; and I find myself unable to describe what has been manifested to me concerning them. I will briefly indicate a small part of these mysteries, for to state all is impossible. The heavenly Mother having received holy Communion on the first of the ten days and retired to pray alone, at the command of the Lord, was immediately raised up by her angels and others there present to the empyrean heavens. Since She was taken up body and soul, one of the angels took her shape in

order that the Apostles in the Cenacle might not become aware of her absence. They bore Her up with the splendor and magnificence described by me on other occasions, and on this occasion it was even greater on account of the designs of the Lord. When Mary arrived in a region of the air far removed from the earth, the almighty Lord commanded Lucifer and all his hellish hosts to come into the presence of the Queen into those higher regions. Immediately all of them came before Her and She saw them and knew them all just as they were and the condition they were in. The sight was somewhat painful to her, because the demons are so abominable and disgusting; but She was armed with divine virtue, so that She could not be harmed by this horrible and execrable sight. Not so the demons; for the Lord gave them to understand by an especial insight the greatness and superiority of that Woman, whom they were persecuting as their Enemy. They were made to perceive how foolishly presumptuous they had been in their attempts against Her. To their still greater terror they saw that She carried in her bosom the sacramental Christ and that the whole Divinity held Her as it were enveloped in its Omnipotence for their humiliation, overthrow and destruction.

491. The demons moreover heard a voice proceeding from the Deity itself, saying: "With this shield of my powerful arm, invincible and strong, I shall always defend my Church. This Woman shall crush the head of the ancient serpent (Gen. 3, 15), and shall forever triumph over its haughty pride for the glory of my holy name." All these and other mysteries of the most holy Mary the demons perceived and understood while they were gathered around Her in dismay. So great was the despair and crushing pain which they felt,

that they, with loudest clamors, said: "May the power of the Almighty cast us immediately into hell, and let it not keep us in the presence of this Woman, who torments us more than the fire. O invincible and strong Woman! Recede from us, since we ourselves cannot fly from thy presence, where we are bound by the chains of the Almighty. Why dost Thou also torment us before our time? (Matth. 8, 29). Thou alone of all human nature art the instrument of the Omnipotent against us; and through Thee men can acquire the eternal blessings we have lost. Those that have sunk into despair of ever seeing God eternally, are now rewarded for the accredited good works of their Redeemer by the vision of Thee, which in our hate is to us a torment and chastisement. Release us, almighty Lord and God; let this new punishment, in which Thou renewest that of our fall from heaven, cease; for in it Thou executest the punishment Thou hast threatened us with in this wonder of thy powerful arms."

492. During these and other lamentations of despair the demons were held spellbound in the presence of the Queen for a long time, and although thy made the most violent efforts to fly, they were not permitted to do it as fast as their fury urged them on. In order that the terror of the most holy Mary might strike them so much the deeper and become the more notorious, the Lord ordained, that She herself should use her authority as Mistress and Queen in permitting them to leave. At the instant in which She did this, all of them cast themselves, with all the swiftness in their power, from the upper regions into the abyss. They gave forth dreadful howls, terrorizing all the damned souls with new punishments, and, full of dismay and torments in not being able to deny their defeat, they proclaimed in their

presence the power of the Almighty and of his holy Mother. Having won this triumph the most serene Empress proceeded on her way to the empyrean heaven, where She was received with new and admirable jubilee, remaining there for twenty-four hours.

493. She prostrated Herself before the throne of the most blessed Trinity and adored It in the unity of its undivided nature and majesty. She prayed for the Church, in order that the Apostles might understand and resolve what was proper for the establishment of the evangelical law and the termination of the law of Moses. In answer to these petitions She heard a voice from the throne, by which the three divine Persons, One after the Other and each One for Himself, promised to assist the Apostles and disciples in declaring and establishing the divine truth, assuring Her, that the Father would direct its establishment by his Omnipotence, the Son, as head of the Church, assist it by his Wisdom, and the Holy Ghost, as its Spouse, by his Love and his enlightening gifts. Then the heavenly Mother saw, that the most holy humanity of her Son presented to the Father the prayers and petitions, which She Herself had offered for the Church, and how, approving of them, He proposed the reasons why they should be fulfilled, in order that the faith of the Gospel and his entire holy law might be established in the world in accordance with the decrees of the divine will and mind.

494. Immediately, in execution of this will and proposal of Christ our Savior, the Lady saw issuing forth from the Divinity and immutable essence of God the form of a temple or Church, beautiful, clear and resplendent as if built of diamond or of sparkling crystal, adorned with many enamels and reliefs to enhance its beauty. The angels and saints saw it and in astonish-

ment exclaimed: "Holy, holy, holy and powerful art Thou, Lord, in thy works" (Apoc. 4, 8). This Church or temple the most blessed Trinity placed in the hands of the most holy humanity of Christ, and, in a manner which cannot be described in words, He united it with Himself. Thereupon He turned it over to the most holy Mother and as soon as Mary received it, She was filled with new splendor. She annihilated Herself within Herself and then saw the Divinity, clearly and intuitively, by eminent and beatific vision.

495. The great Queen remained in this joy for many hours, truly introduced into the cellar of fermented wine spoken of in the Canticles (Canticle 8, 2). Since what She experienced and received there surpasses all created thought or capacity, it suffices here to say, that anew was ordered in Her love (Cant. 2, 4) and directed with new fervor toward the Church consigned to Her under the above symbol. Enriched by these favors, She was borne back by the angels to the Cenacle, having in her hands the mystical temple She had received from her divine Son. She remained in prayer during the other nine days without motion and without interrupting the acts, in which She had been left by the beatific vision. They fall not within human thought, and can much less be indicated by human words. Among other things which She did, was to distribute the treasures of the Redemption among the children of the Church. Commencing with the Apostles and going through the different ages, She applied them separately to the just and the saints, according to the secret disposition of eternal predestination. The execution of these decrees her divine Son had consigned to the most holy Mary, giving Her dominion over the whole Church and the dispensation of all the graces, that each one earns

through the merits of the Redemption. Regarding a mystery so exalted and hidden, I cannot say more than this.

496. On the last of the ten days saint Peter celebrated the other Mass and all received holy Communion as in the first. Then, all being gathered in the name of the Lord, they invoked the Holy Ghost and began to consult about the solution of the difficulties that had arisen in the Church. Saint Peter, as the head and the highpriest, spoke first, then saint Paul and Barnaby, and saint James the Less, as is related by saint Luke in the fifteenth chapter of the Acts. The first decision of this council was, that the exact law of the circumcision and the law of Moses should not be imposed upon the baptized; since eternal salvation was given through Baptism and faith in Christ. Although saint Luke principally mentions only this decision, yet there were others, which defined certain matters concerning the government and the ceremonies of the Church, in order to stop some abuses introduced by the indiscreet piety of some of the faithful. This is held to be the first council of the Apostles, although they had also gathered to establish the Credo and other things as mentioned before. However, at that only the Apostles had convened, whereas now also those disciples took part, who could come. Also the manner of conferring and of resolving was different, being a formal decision, as is clear from the words of saint Luke: "It has seemed good to the Holy Ghost and to us," etc. (Luke 15, 28).

497. Couched in these terms the decision of the council was sent by letter to the faithful and to the churches of Antioch, Syria and Cilicia; and they remitted these letters through the hands of saint Paul and Barnaby and of other disciples. In order that the approbation of

the Lord might not be wanting, it happened, that, both
in the Cenacle at coming to their decision, and in Antioch when the letters were read before the faithful, the
Holy Ghost descended in visible fire, so that all the faithful were consoled and confirmed in the Catholic truth.
The most holy Mary gave thanks to the Lord for the
blessings thus bestowed upon the Church.   She immediately despatched saint Paul and Barnaby with the rest
and for their consolation She gave them as relics part
of the clothes of Christ our Lord and some objects She
had still left of the Passion.   Offering them her protection and prayers, She sent them filled with new consolation and spiritual force upon the labors still awaiting
them.   During all these days of the council, on account
of the terror with which most holy Mary had inspired
him, Lucifer and his ministers could not come near the
Cenacle; yet they prowled about in the distance, without
being able to execute any of their malice against its
members.   Happy age, and fortunate congregation!

498. Since, in spite of his continual prowling about
the Queen and his roarings as of a hungry lion, Lucifer
saw that he could gain no advantage himself, he engaged
some sorceresses, with whom he had made an express
pact, and persuaded them to attempt the life of Mary
by magic means.   These unhappy dupes tried it in several ways; but their enchantments were of no avail.
Many times, when they purposely placed themselves in
the way of the Queen, they were struck dumb and motionless.   The most blessed Mary, in her boundless charity, labored much to undeceive and convert them by kind
words and deeds; but of the four, who were thus sent
on by the demon, only one was converted and received
Baptism.   And thus all his attempts came to naught,
Lucifer was so confused and enraged, that he would

many times have given up tempting the most blessed Mary, if his unquenchable pride had permitted him. The Lord almighty ordained all this, in order that the victories and triumphs of his Mother might be more glorious, as we shall see in the following chapter.

INSTRUCTION WHICH THE QUEEN OF THE ANGELS, MOST HOLY MARY, GAVE ME.

499. My daughter, in the constancy and invincible fortitude with which I vanquished the demons, thou hast one of the most urgent motives for persevering in grace and acquiring great crowns. The human nature and that of the angels (even though they be devils) are subject to contrary and opposite conditions; for the spiritual nature is indefatigable, and that of mortals weak and so prone to fatigue, that it soon tires and succumbs in labor. As soon as it finds any difficulty in the practice of virtue it is discouraged and turns back; what it pursues with pleasure on one day, it contemns the next; what seemed agreeable today, it finds hard tomorrow; now it wishes, then again it does not wish; sometimes it is fervent, sometimes lukewarm. But the demon is never fatigued or weakened in his efforts at tempting souls. The Almighty, however, is not wanting in his providence; for He limits and restrains the power of the demons, so that they cannot pass the measure set for them, nor exert all their indefatigable powers for the persecution of souls. On the other hand He supports the weakness of men, giving them grace and strength to resist and overcome their enemies on the prescribed battleground.

500. Hence the inconstancy of souls in virtuously maintaining their position during temptation and in not bearing with fortitude and patience the inconveniences

of doing good and fighting against the demons, is not
excusable. The bent of passion, drawing man toward
the sensible and pleasurable, suddenly presents itself
across the path of duty and the demons, with diabolical
astuteness, seek to exaggerate the hardship and disagree-
ableness of mortification, representing it as dangerous
to health and life. Thus he deludes innumerable souls
to precipitate themselves from one abyss to another. In
this thou hast before thy eyes, my daughter, a very common aberration of the worldly-minded, but which is very
abominable in the sight of the Lord and myself. Hence
it is, that many men are weak, wavering and indisposed
toward the practice of virtue or penitential mortification
for their sins. And the very ones who are so weak in
doing good, are strong in doing evil. In the service of
the devil they are constant and are ready to undergo
much more difficult and arduous tasks in sinning, than
the law of God commands for the practice of virtue.
They show themselves tardy and imbecile in the work of
saving their souls, eager and strong to load upon themselves eternal damnation.

501. This damage also those who profess a life of
perfection are wont in part to incur, if they unduly
consider the hardships attached to such a life. Drawn
into this deception, they either hinder their advance in
perfection or afford the devil many victories in temptation. In order that thou, my daughter, mayest not incur
this danger, thou shouldst consider the fortitude and
constancy with which I resisted Lucifer and all hell, and
the magnanimity with which I despised his illusions and
temptations, not permitting myself to be disturbed, or
to pay any attention to them; for this is the best way
to overcome his haughty pride. Nor was I ever led by
temptation to remissness in my labors or in my exercises;

but I augmented them, together with my prayers, petitions and tears, as is necessary in the time of battle with those enemies. Hence I exhort thee to do the same in eager watchfulness; because thy temptations are not of the ordinary kind, but are directed against thee in highest malice and astuteness. Of this I have warned thee many times and this experience teaches thee.

502. Since thou hast noticed the great terror caused to the demons at perceiving the sacramental Lord resting in my bosom, I wish to call thy attention to two things. First, that for the overthrow of hell and for causing fear in the demons, all the holy Sacraments of the Church are most powerful means; but above all the holy sacrament of the Eucharist. This was one of the hidden purposes of the Lord my Son, in the institution of this sovereign mystery and of the other Sacraments. If in our time men do not ordinarily feel these powerful effects, it is because in the frequency of the reception of the Sacraments much of the veneration and estimation in receiving them has been lost. But do not doubt, that souls who frequent them with devotion and piety, are formidable to the demons and that they exercise great power and dominion over them in the same way as thou hast seen and described it of me. The explanation of this fact is: that this divine fire, in the pure souls, finds itself as it were in its own element. In me it was active to the limit of possibility in a mere creature, and therefore I inspired such terror to the demons.

503. In further proof of what I said, I wish secondly to inform thee, that these blessings were not to have an end with me; for in proportion God has wrought the same effects in other souls. In our own times it has happened that, in order to vanquish the demon, God showed and opposed to him a soul bearing within it the

sacramental species and thereby so humiliated and annihilated the dragon, that for many days he dared not
approach this soul and begged the Omnipotent not to be
shown any soul bearing within it holy Communion.   On
another occasion Lucifer, in conjunction with some heretics and other bad Christians, schemed to do severe harm
to these Spanish kingdoms; and if God had not cut them
short through this same person, the whole of Spain would
now be lost and in the hands of the enemies.   The divine
clemency interfered for its defense by showing this person to the devil and his ministers after Communion.   In
their terrors the demons dropped their malicious designs
for the immediate destruction of all Spain.   I will not
tell thee who this person was; for it is not necessary,
and I reveal this secret to thee for no other purpose than
to show how favorably the Almighty looks upon a soul
which tries to merit its favors and worthily receives Him
in holy Communion; and how He manifested Himself
liberal and powerful not only to me, on account of my
dignity and sanctity of Mother, but how He wishes also
in other souls to be known and glorified as relieving the
needs of the Church according to time and occasion.

504. From this thou wilt understand, that, in the same
proportion as the demons fear the souls that worthily
receive holy Communion and other fortifying Sacraments, so they exert all their powers to cause those souls
to fall and to hinder them from accumulating all this
strength of the Lord against them.   Labor then against
these tireless and astute enemies and seek to imitate me
in fortitude.   I desire also that thou hold in great veneration the councils of the Church and all such gatherings, and whatever is resolved and established by them;
for the Holy Ghost assists at these councils and He fulfills his promise, that He will be with those who gather

together in his name (Matth. 8, 20). Hence what is thus ordained and commanded must be obeyed. Although in our times no visible signs of the assistance of the Holy Ghost occur in such councils, yet He does not fail to govern them invisibly; for signs and wonders are not any more so necessary as in the first beginnings of the Church. Such as are necessary are not withheld by the Lord. For all these blessings exalt and praise his liberal kindness and mercy, and especially for those which He conferred on me during my mortal life.

CHAPTER VII.

505. In order to understand better the mysteries to be described in this chapter, it is necessary to presuppose what I have written in the eighth, ninth and tenth chapter, of the first book, of the first part, where I explained the twelfth chapter of the Apocalypse in so far as it was made known to me at that time. Not only there, but during the whole course of this heavenly history, have I referred to the present chapters of this third part for a description of the battles of the most holy Mary with Lucifer and the demons, the triumphs She gained, and the state in which She was left by the Almighty after these battles for the rest of her earthly life. Of all these sacred mysteries the evangelist saint John had a knowledge and he describes them in his Apocalypse (as I have stated at other times), especially in the twelfth and twenty-first chapters. On these two chapters I must discourse in this history for two reasons.

506. First, the secrets contained in them are so exalted and magnificent, that they can never be adequately explained or manifested; especially as the Evangelist, considering it as the sacrament of the King and Queen, has enveloped them in such enigmatical and metaphorical language, as can be interpreted only through divine revelation when and how the Lord shall please; and in

this the Evangelist followed the express commands of the most holy Mary. Secondly, the proud rebellion of Lucifer, although in general opposing the supreme will and orders of the Most High and omnipotent God, was especially directed against Christ our Lord and his Mother, to whose superiority and excellence the apostate angels do not wish to subject themselves. Also the first rebellion and war waged with saint Michael in heaven was in protest against their authority; but at that time they could not war with the incarnate Word and with his Virgin Mother in person, but only against the mysterious sign or representation of that mysterious Woman, which they saw placed in the heavens as a prophetic symbol of all the mysteries of the Incarnation to be enacted in her womb. When the time came for the execution of all these sacraments and for the Incarnation of the Word in her womb, it was proper that this battle of the demons should be renewed and that Christ and Mary should triumph over them in person. For this the Lord, as well in heaven as afterwards in paradise, had threatened them with this enmity between the Woman and the serpent, and between the seed of the Woman and the serpent, in order that She might crush his head.

507. All this was fulfilled to the letter in Christ and in Mary; for of our great Highpriest and Savior saint Paul says, that He was tempted in all things like we ourselves and for our example, but without sin; and the same can be said of the most holy Mary. Lucifer had permission to tempt Them after his fall from heaven, as I have said in the tenth chapter of the first Part. And because this battle with the most holy Mary was to be a counterpart of the first one in heaven and was to be for the demons the fulfillment of the threat and menace contained in her image, it was described and

enveloped in the same enigmatical words. Having sufficiently explained about the first battle, I must now
speak of what happened in the second. Although Lucifer
and his demons had already been punished in their
first rebellion by the eternal loss of the beatific vision
and hurled into hell, they were now punished anew in
this second battle by additional accidental torments corresponding to their evil desires and attempts against the
most blessed Mary. The explanation thereof is, that
the natural faculties of a creature draw satisfaction and
contentment from their attaining what they strive after
and this in proportion to the vehemence with which they
have striven; and on the other hand, pain and disappointment in not attaining their object, or in experiencing
opposite results. Now, the demons since their fall had
desired nothing more vehemently than to see that One
fall from grace, who was to be the medium of grace
for the children of Adam. Hence it was an inconceivable torment for the infernal dragons to find themselves
vanquished and foiled in the desperate desires and hopes
entertained by them for so many ages.

508. The heavenly Mother on the other hand, on
account of the same and many other reasons, in the
overthrow of the ancient serpent gained a most joyful
triumph. For the conclusion of this battle, moreover,
and for the state which She was then to enjoy during
the rest of her life, her divine Son held in readiness so
many and such great blessings, as surpass all human and
angelic capacity. In order to say something of what I
have been made to understand, the reader must remember, that, on account of our limited powers and capacity,
we are constrained to use for the most exalted mysteries
the same terms and words as we use for the more ordinary ones. Yet in what I am to speak of now, there is

infinite latitude and extent of mystery, within which the Almighty can raise the creature from one state, which seems to us the highest, to one much more exalted, and from this again to a higher and more excellent state. For, such a creature as Mary, after being destined and confirmed in this world of graces, gifts and favors, and after reaching (as She really did) all that is not God's essence, must at last embrace within itself a vastness of excellence so great, that, of its own Self, it constitutes a new hierarchy, greater and more exalted than all the rest of the creatures angelic and human.

509. Having premised all this, I will proceed to tell as well as I can, what happened to Lucifer until his final overthrow through the most holy Mary and her Son our Savior. The dragon and his demons were not yet entirely subdued by the triumphs related in the last chapter, when they were hurled down from the upper air into the abyss by the great Lady; nor by their ill-success with the sorceresses in Jerusalem. But, fearing in his malice that he should have little time left for his temptations and persecutions, the enemy, in his implacable malice, wished to make up for the shortness of time by an increase of fury and temerity. Hence he sought out other men, who, having been especially instructed by him in magic and witchcraft, were still greater sorcerers. To these Lucifer gave special and minute directions how to take away the life of Her whom they held as their enemy. These ministers of evil attempted to fulfill their commission many times, making use of very powerful and pernicious charms. But none of them could in any way harm either the life or the health of the most blessed Mary; for the effects of sin exerted no influence over Her who was sinless and who, moreover, for other reasons, was exempt and superior to all natural causes. Seeing this and find-

ing his most deeply laid plans frustrated, the dragon visited those sorcerers with fierce and cruel punishments; for the Lord permitted this, because they had merited chastisement for their temerity and in order that they might know, what kind of master they served.

510. Full of this new fury Lucifer convened all the princes of darkness and reminded them of the many reasons they had since their fall from heaven, for straining all their forces and their whole malice in order to cast down this Woman, their Enemy; since they now clearly recognized in Her the One shown to them at that time. They all agreed with him and resolved to unite and assault Her alone, presuming that on some occasion or another they would find Her less prepared and bereft of her defense. Mary being alone in her oratory, they at once seized this opportunity and, emptying hell for this enterprise, they advanced upon Her in united multitudes. This battle was the greatest ever fought by a mere creature, from the first one in the empyrean heaven to the end of the world; and it was very much like that first one. In order to estimate the fury of Lucifer and his demons, in coming to where the most blessed Mary then was, one must consider their torments, as well in perceiving the divine power emanating from Her as in remembering how often they had been oppressed and vanquished by Her. But their wrath and envy conquered even these torments and drove them, in spite of their pains, to throw themselves as it were upon the bristling pikes and swords to avenge themselves upon the heavenly Lady; for, not to make such an attempt, was a greater torment than any other.

511. The first assault of the demons was directed principally upon the exterior senses of Mary, consisting in terrific howlings and confused clamors. Arraying their

hosts in the air, they produced such a fearful noise and trembling, that the machinery of the whole world seemed on the point of destruction. To make all this appear more real, they assumed diverse visible shapes, some of horrid and different kinds of demons, other of angels of light. In these shapes they pretended to begin a darksome and formidable contest or battle, seemingly without cause and so that only the confused and terrible noise could be heard. Thus they sought to produce fear or disturbance in the soul of the most blessed Lady. And truly they would have excited terror in any other, even the most holy creature, if left to the ordinary resources of grace, and no one could have encountered them without losing life; for this onset lasted for twelve whole hours.

512. But our great Queen and Lady remained immovable and serene, as tranquil as if She heard or saw nothing of all this; She was disturbed or altered in no wise, showed no change in her countenance, no traces of sorrow during the whole of this infernal uproar. Then the demons proceeded to other temptations directed against the internal faculties of the invincible Mother, pouring out their diabolical malice more than I can describe; for all that devilish multitude exhausted the full measure of their hellish astuteness in concocting their false revelations, lights and suggestions, their promises and threats in attempting to infect each of her virtues by temptations to the contrary vice. I will not stop to enumerate in particular these temptations, as it is neither necessary nor convenient. But our Lady and Queen overcame them all, since in opposition to the vices She performed acts of the contrary virtues, which reached an excellence fully in proportion to the impulse and force of her then acquired state of grace, gifts and perfection.

513. As one who was experiencing the strength of hellish malice and who knows the necessity of divine assistance, She prayed on that occasion for all that are afflicted and tempted by the demon. The Lord granted Her the power of extending her protection to all those who are tempted and who invoke her intercession. The demons persevered in this battle until no kind of malice was left unattempted against the most pure Mother. Then She on her part called upon the divine justice, asking God to rise up and judge his cause (as David says Ps. 73, 22), that his enemies might be dispersed and those who abhorred his presence be put to flight. To fulfill his judgment the incarnate Word descended from heaven to her retirement in the Cenacle, appearing to his Virgin Mother as her sweetest and loving Son, and to the enemies as the severe Judge on the throne of his supreme majesty. He was accompanied by innumerable angels, by the ancient saints, Adam and Eve and many patriarchs and prophets, and saint Joachim and Anne. All these presented and manifested themselves to the most blessed Mary in her oratory.

514. Prostrating Herself as usual in deepest veneration and worship, the great Lady adored her Son and true God. The demons did not see the Lord, though they were made aware of his royal presence and tried to fly from the imminent punishment. But the divine power detained them, fettering them in the manner in which their spirit nature permitted; and the ends of their fetters or chains the Lord placed into the hands of his most blessed Mother.

515. Then a voice issued from the throne saying: "Today comes upon you the wrath of the Almighty, and the first sentence, fulminated against the ancient serpent from on high and afterwards in paradise, shall be ex-

ecuted: a Woman descended from Adam and Eve shall crush its head (Gen. 3, 15), because in your disobedience and pride, you have despised the humanity of the Word in the virginal womb." Immediately the most holy Mary was raised from the earth by the hands of six seraphim nearest to the throne of God and, enveloped in a refulgent cloud, was placed at the side of the throne of her divine Son. From his own essence and Divinity issued an ineffable and supereminent splendor, which enveloped and surrounded Her like the globe of the sun. Beneath her feet appeared also the moon, indicating that She was to subject to Her all that was inferior, earthly and variable, symbolized by the concavity of the moon. Over her head was placed a diadem or crown of twelve stars, as an emblem of the divine perfections communicated to Her to the fullest extent possible in a mere creature. She was also shown as pregnant, not only of the concept of God in her mind, but also of the corresponding love. She gave forth a voice as if of the sorrows of the birth of what She had conceived, in order that all creatures might participate in it; and they rejected it, although She desired it with tears and groans (Apoc. 12, 1).

516. This sign, in all the grandeur in which it had been conceived in the divine mind, was shown in heaven to Lucifer, who was present as the great, red dragon with seven heads crowned with seven diadems and ten horns. In this horrid shape he represented himself as the author of the seven capital sins, who attempted to crown these sins with his invented heresies as diadems and who armed by his astuteness and strength as with ten horns, had sought to overthrow the divine law contained in the ten commandments. In like manner he had encircled with his tail and drawn to hell with him a third part of the stars of heaven; (Apoc. 12, 4); not only in seducing the

myriads of angels, who followed him in disobedience, but also in casting from heaven of the Church many of the believers, who seemed to have risen above the stars either in dignity or sanctity.

517. In such a fearful and horrid shape stood Lucifer, and with him, in many other and various, all of them abominable, shapes, stood his fellow-demons, arranged in battle array around Mary, who was about to bring forth in spiritual birth the perpetual existence and enrichment of the holy Church. And the dragon, in furious envy, that this Woman should be so powerful in establishing and spreading this Church, and that She should, by her merits, example and intercession, enrich it with so many graces and raise so many myriads of men to their predestined eternal happiness, stood in readiness to devour if possible, what She was to bring forth and to destroy this new Church. In spite of the envy of the dragon She brought forth a man-child, who was to govern all the nations with a strong rod of iron. This man-child was the most righteous and strong spirit of the Church, which in the righteousness of Christ our God holds sway over all the nations in justice; and likewise it signified all the apostolic men, who in the same righteous spirit are to judge (Matth. 19, 28) with the iron rod of divine justice. All this it was that most holy Mary brought forth, not only because She gave birth to Christ, but also because through her merits and diligence She brought forth the Church in holiness and rectitude, nourished it during the time She lived in it, and even now and forever preserves it in the manly spirit, in which it was born, maintaining the uprightness of the Catholic truth, against which the gates of hell shall not prevail (Matth. 16, 18).

518. Then, says saint John, this man-child was taken

up to the throne of God and the Woman fled to her destined place in the desert in order that She might there be nourished one thousand two-hundred and sixty days. This signifies, that all the legitimate offspring of the heavenly Mother, as well that which is the fruit of the general spirit of holiness in the Church, as also the particular souls which She engendered and engenders as her proper spiritual children, shall arrive at the throne where is her natural Offspring, Christ, in whom and for whom She engenders and raises her children. But the solitude to which the most blessed Mary was carried was a most exalted and mysterious state, to which She was raised after her battle and of which I shall say something presently. It is called a solitude, because She alone of all creatures was in that state, and none other could ever reach or attain it. In it She was without the company of creatures; and She was moreover left alone by the dragon, who more than any one else was ignorant of this mystery, and could not any more tempt or persecute Her in person. There the Lord nourished Her one thousand two hundred and sixty days, which was the time She lived in this state before passing to another.

519. All this was darkly known and intimated to Lucifer and his demons before this heavenly Woman and living Sign was hidden away from their sight. The knowledge of her destiny took away the confidence, which, for more than five thousand years, had inspired the dragon with the hope of being able to vanquish Her who was the Mother of the incarnate Word. Hence the despair and torment of Lucifer and his demons can to a certain extent be imagined; especially as they now saw themselves overcome and held bound by the very Woman, whom they had with such insane fury sought to cast

down from grace and deprive of the merits and fruits of the Church. The dragon in agonizing efforts to escape, said: "O Woman, give me leave to hurl myself into hell, for I cannot bear thy presence, nor will I ever venture to come before Thee as long as Thou livest upon this world. Thou hast conquered, O Woman, Thou hast conquered, and I acknowledge thy power in Him who has made Thee his Mother. Omnipotent God, chastise us Thyself, since we cannot resist Thee; but do not send thy punishments through a Woman of a nature so inferior to ours. Her charity consumes us, her humility crushes us, and She is in all things a living manifestation of thy mercy for men. This is a torment surpassing many others. Assist me, ye demons! But alas, what can our united efforts avail against this Woman, since all our power cannot ever deliver us from her presence until She herself casts us forth? O foolish children of Adam, who follow me, forsaking life for the sake of death, truth or falsehood? What absurdity and insanity is yours, (so in despair I must confess), since you have in your midst and belonging to your own nature the incarnate Word and this Woman? Greater is your ingratitude than mine and this Woman forces me to confess the truths, which I abhor with all my heart. Cursed be my resolve to persecute this Daughter of Adam, who so torments and crushes me!"

520. While the dragon thus gave vent to his despair, the prince of the heavenly hosts saint Michael appeared in order to defend the cause of the incarnate Word and his most blessed Mother; and by the arms of the understanding they began another battle with the dragon and his followers (Apoc. 12, 7). Saint Michael and his angels hurled at them the convincing arguments of old, reproaching them with their pride and disobedience in

heaven and with their temerity in persecuting and tempting the incarnate Word and his Mother, and contending with those in whom they had no part or right whatever, since they could accuse Them of no sin, injustice or imperfection. Saint Michael justified the works of the divine justice, declaring them most righteous and unblamable chastisements for the disobedience and apostasy of Lucifer and the demons. Anew they anathematised them and confirmed the sentence of their damnation, confessing the Almighty as holy and just in all his works. The demon and his angels on the other hand likewise tried to defend their rebellion and the audacity of their pride; but all their reasonings were false, vain, and full of diabolical presumption and error.

521. A silence ensued in the altercation and the Lord of hosts spoke to the most holy Mary: "My Mother and my Beloved, chosen from the creatures by my eternal wisdom for my habitation and holy temple! Thou hast given Me human form and restored the human race; Thou hast followed Me, imitated Me and merited the graces and gifts communicated to Thee above all my creatures and Thou hast never permitted them to be unprofitable in Thee. Be Thou the worthy object of my infinite love, the protection of my Church, its Queen, Mistress and Governess. To Thee is commissioned my power, and, as the almighty God, I place it in thy most faithful disposal. In virtue of it do Thou command the infernal dragon, that as long as Thou shalt live in the Church, he shall not sow the seed of error and heresy which he holds in readiness; cut off his hardened neck, crush his head; for during the days of thy life I desire that the Church shall derive this advantage from thy presence."

522. The most holy Mary executed this command of the Lord and as Queen and Mistress enjoined the infer-

nal dragons to become mute and powerless to spread their
false doctrines among the faithful, and that, as long as
She was to live upon earth, none of them presume to
deceive mortals by their heretical tenets and doctrines.
And so it happened; for although the demon, in his
wrath and vengeance, had intended to pour out this poison
in the Church, the Lord, for the sake of his love of the
heavenly Mother, hindered it during her lifetime. After
her glorious Transition, permission was given to the
demon to spread his heresies because the sins of men
subjected them to the just judgments of the Lord.

523. Thereupon, (as saint John says), the great dragon, the ancient serpent called satan and devil, was cast
forth and with his demons banished from the presence
of the Queen. Their chains were lengthened and they
fell upon the earth, where they were permitted to remain. The voice of the archangel was heard in the
Cenacle, saying: "Now is come the salvation, and the
strength, and the kingdom of our God, and the power
of Christ; because the accuser of our brethren is cast
forth, who accused them before our God day and night.
And they overcame him by the blood of the Lamb, and
by the word of the testimony, and they loved not their
lives unto death. Therefore rejoice, O heaven, and you
that dwell therein. Woe to the earth and to the sea, because the devil is come down unto you, having great
wrath, knowing that he hath but a short time" (Apoc.
12, 10). By these words the angel proclaimed, that in
virtue of the victories and triumphs of the most blessed
Mary, united to those of her Son and Savior, the reign
of God, his Church, and the effects of the Redemption
of man were assured to the just. All this he called the
salvation, the strength and power of Christ. And as,
without doubt, if the most blessed Mother had not over-

come the infernal dragon, this impious and powerful enemy would have hindered the effects of the Redemption; therefore this voice of the angel resounded victoriously at the conclusion of the battle and at his casting forth unto the earth and the sea. He congratulated the saints, because now the head and the plottings of the demon, by which he slandered men, were crushed, and the angel calls them brethren because of their relationship with the angels through the soul, through grace and glory.

524. The calumnies, by which the devil persecuted and accused the mortals were the illusions and deceits by which he expected to pervert the beginnings of the evangelical Church, and his appeals to the justice of God, alleging that men, through their ingratitude and wickedness and by their having taken away the life of Christ the Savior, did not merit Redemption or mercy, but deserved to be punished by leaving them to their own sinfulness and to the darkness of eternal damnation. Against all these accusations, however, Mary, as our most sweet and kind Mother, rose up in our defense, meriting for us faith and its spread, the abundance of mercies and gifts accruing to us from the death of her Son, all of which the sins of those that crucified Him and the others, that would not receive Him, have indeed failed to deserve. The angel, by his prediction of woe, warns the inhabitants of the earth to be prepared for the serpent, which now descended to them in such great wrath; for without a doubt this dragon knows, that he has little time for wrecking his fury upon men, since he has learned of the mysteries of Redemption, the power of most holy Mary, the abundance of grace and wonderful favors in the primitive Church. From all these facts he suspects, that the end of the world is at hand, or that

all men will follow Christ our Lord and avail themselves of the intercession of his Mother to gain eternal life. Alas, that men themselves should be more foolish and ungrateful than even the demon himself dared to think!

525. In further explanation of these mysteries, the Evangelist states, that when the dragon saw himself cast upon the earth, he attempted to persecute the mysterious Woman, who had brought forth the man-child. But to Her were given two wings as of a great eagle, in order that She might fly into the solitude or desert, where She was nourished for a time, and for two times, and for the half of a time, hidden away from the sight of the serpent. And therefore the serpent cast forth after the Woman a great river to overwhelm Her if possible. By these words the wrath of Lucifer against God, his Mother and the Church are more definitely declared; for, as far as this dragon is concerned, he never permits his envy to slumber, his pride to weaken, or his malice to sleep in tempting anew this Queen as long as he has power and permission. But they were taken from him in regard to the Queen; and hence it is said, that two wings were given to Her for flying into the desert, where She is nourished during the stated times. These wings were the divine power of ascending to the vision of the Deity given to Mary and of descending to distribute the treasures of grace to men, as we shall describe in the next chapter.

526. From that time on the serpent had no more power to tempt Mary in person, wherefore it is said that her solitude or desert is removed from the sight of the demon. The times and the time and half of a time are three years and a half, which contain the thousand two hundred and sixty, less a few days, as mentioned before. In this state, and in others yet to be spoken of, the most

blessed Mary spent the rest of her mortal life. But since the dragon was forced to give up tempting Her, he shot forth the blood of his venomous malice after the heavenly Woman; for after her victory he sought astutely to tempt the faithful and to persecute them through aid of the Jews and gentiles; and especially after her glorious Transition into heaven did he loosen the flood of his heresies and false schisms locked up within himself. The threats which he uttered after her victory, referred to the war he intended to wage against men in order to avenge himself upon Her; for, being now unable to vent his rage upon the person of the Queen, he resolved to continue it against those, whom the Lady loved so much.

527. Hence saint John says that the dragon proceeded to make war upon the others, who are of her generation and seed, who observe the law of God, and have the testimony of Christ. And the dragon stood upon the sands of the sea, namely; he relied upon the countless infidels, idolators, Jews and pagans, through whom he has made and does make war upon the holy Church, besides secretly waging the war of temptation against the faithful. But the solid and firm set earth, which is the immutability of the Church, and the imperishable Catholic truth helps the mysterious Woman; because She opens her mouth and swallows and absorbs the flood poured out against Her by the serpent. And so it happened in reality, since the holy Church, which is the organ and the mouthpiece of the Holy Ghost, has condemned and overthrown all the errors, the false sects and doctrines by her definitions, by holy Scriptures, by the decrees of her councils, by the teachings of her doctors, instructors and preachers of the Gospel.

528. All these mysteries and many others the Evangelist intimates and describes under the image of this battle

and triumph of most holy Mary. In order to end the conflict, though Lucifer was already cast from heaven and given over, fettered in chains, into the hands of the victorious Queen, the great Lady perceived it to be the will of the Lord her divine Son, that She hurl him and his hosts into the infernal caverns. Fortified and strengthened by God, She released them and commanded them immediately to depart into hell. As soon as She pronounced the word, all the demons fell into the most distant caverns of hell, where they remained for some time giving forth terrible and despairing howls. Then the holy angels sang new hymns to the incarnate Word on account of his victories and those of his invincible Mother. The first parents, Adam and Eve, gave thanks to God, because He chose this their Daughter for his Mother and thus repaired the ruin they had caused to their posterity; the Patriarchs, because their great expectations and prophecies were so happily and gloriously fulfilled; saint Joachim, saint Anne and saint Joseph, with still greater jubilee, glorified the Almighty for their Daughter and Spouse; and all of them together sang the glory and praise of the Most High, so holy and admirable in his counsels. The most blessed Mary prostrated Herself before the royal throne and adored the incarnate Word, offering Herself anew to labor for the Church, and asking his blessing, which She received with admirable effects. She asked also her parents and her Spouse for their blessing, recommending the holy Church and all the faithful to their prayers. Thereupon the whole celestial gathering took their leave and returned to heaven.

529. My daughter, with the rebellion of Lucifer and his demons in heaven have commenced the battles between the kingdom of light and that of darkness, between Jerusalem and Babylon; and these battles will not cease to the end of the world. The Captain and Head of the children of light is the incarnate Word, as the Author of holiness and grace; and Lucifer, as the author of sin and perdition, has constituted himself as the leader of the children of darkness. Each one of these chieftains defends his followers and seeks to increase his reign and the number of his adherents. Christ seeks to draw men to Himself by the truths of his divine faith, by the favors and gifts of his grace, by the holiness of his virtues, by his consolations in labors and by the certain hope of his promised happiness, commanding his angels to accompany, to console and defend them until they should be able to bring them to heaven; Lucifer, on the other hand, gains his followers by lies, deceits and treachery, by the allurements of ignominious and abominable vices, by darkness and confusion; he treats them in this life like a tyrant, afflicting them relentlessly and depriving them of all consolation; while in the next life he holds in readiness for them eternal and horrible torments, which he himself and through his demons shall inflict upon them with inhuman cruelty as long as God is God.

530. But alas! in spite of this truth, so infallible and so well known to mortals, in spite of the infinite difference of the recompense, how few, my daughter, are the soldiers that follow Christ, as their legitimate Lord, as

their King, their Chief, and their model; and how numerous are those that band with Lucifer, who gives them no existence, no life, who affords them no nourishment, nor any return; who deserves nothing nor in any way obliges them, as was and is the case with the Author of life and grace, my divine Son? So great is the ingratitude of men, so foolish their infidelity, so unhappy their blindness. Merely because God has given men freedom of will, either to follow their Master or not, to show themselves thankful or not, they side with Lucifer and serve him freely, permit him to enter the house of God and his temple, that he may tyrannically confuse and profane it and draw after him the greater part of the world to his eternal torments.

531. This conflict will last to the end, because the Prince of eternity, on account of his infinite goodness, will not cease to defend the souls He created and redeemed by his blood. But not only He himself battles with the dragon, nor only through his angels; for it redounds to the greater glory and exaltation of his name, if He overcomes the enemies and confounds their pride through the human creatures, in whom they seek to avenge themselves upon the Lord. I, being a mere creature, next to my Son, the true God, was the Leader and Sovereign in these battles. Although through his Passion and Death, He vanquished the demons, who had become very haughty by the dominion of sin inaugurated among men by Adam; yet, after He, and I in his name, had triumphed over the enemies and through our victories established the Church in such high perfection and holiness, the Church would have persevered and Lucifer would have remained crushed (as I said before), if the ingratitude and the forgetfulness of men had not impelled him anew toward the perdition and ruin of the whole globe.

532. Nevertheless my divine Son did not forsake the Church, which He had acquired by his blood, nor have I, as its Mother and Protectress, forsaken it; and We continue to look within it for some souls to defend the glory and honor of God and fight the battles against hell for the confusion and crushing of the demons. Hence I wish thee to dispose thyself by divine grace for this battle and not to wonder at the strength of the demon, nor to be downcast at thy misery and poverty. Thou knowest that the wrath of Lucifer against me was greater than against any of the creatures, and greater than against all of them together; but by the power of the Lord I vanquished him gloriously, and thou, in the same power, canst resist him in thy smaller temptations. Although thou mayest be weak and wanting in what is required, I wish thee to understand, that my divine Son acts now as a king who is short of subjects and soldiers and will admit any one who wishes to serve in his army. Encourage thyself then to conquer satan in present matters, for then the Lord will afterwards arm thee for greater battles. I tell thee, that the Church would not be entangled in its present difficulties, if a number of the souls belonging to it had taken it upon themselves to defend the cause and honor of God; but the Church stands very much alone and forsaken by the children, whom it nourished at its own bosom.

CHAPTER VIII.

533. In the measure in which the mysteries of the infinite and eternal Wisdom were being fulfilled, so the great Lady was raised in the sphere of holiness beyond all human thought above the rest of the creatures. As her triumphs over the infernal dragon were gained under the conditions and circumstances I have described, and resulted in the rewards I have mentioned; and as all these events of her life were the sequel of the mysteries of the Incarnation and Redemption and of all the rest, in which She had associated with her divine Son, it is impossible that our lowly human faculties should even faintly comprehend the effects of these mysteries upon the purest heart of the heavenly Mother. She conferred within Herself upon these works of the Lord and weighed them by the scales of her most exalted wisdom. The devouring flame of her celestial love grew into a conflagration, which excited the astonishment of all the angels and courtiers of heaven; and her natural powers of life could not have withstood the impetuous onsets of her desire to annihilate Herself entirely in the essence of the Divinity, if they had not been sustained by miraculous influence. At the same time She was drawn toward men by her most sweet and maternal charity; for they all depended upon Her, just as the plants upon the sun

that vivifies and nourishes them. She therefore lived in a state of violent longing to unite both the objects of her love in her bosom.

534. In such a state the most blessed Mother found Herself after the victories over the dragon. Notwithstanding her having, through the whole course of her life from its first instant, at all times done what was most pure, most holy and exalted, without ever being embarrassed by her travels, labors and cares in the service of her divine Son; yet at this juncture there arose as it were a contest in her heart between her love of God and of the souls. In all her works of charity She felt the force of her aspirations drawing Her to the higher and new gifts and workings of grace. On the one hand She was impelled to withdraw Herself from all the sensible things in order to wing her flight to the continual and supreme union with the Divinity, and, in imitation of comprehensors and especially of the state of her divine Son on earth, free Herself from all hindrance of creatures in order to enjoy all that He enjoyed outside of what belonged to Him in virtue of the hypostatic union. This latter was indeed not possible in the blessed Mother; yet the height of her sanctity and love seemed to demand all that was next below the state of comprehensors. On the other hand She was drawn by her love of the Church to hasten the relief of the faithful in all the necessities; for without thus being engaged in these duties of a Mother of the family, She could scarcely rest satisfied with the favors and delights of the Most High. As each of these activities of Martha required time, She continued to study how She might adjust her life so as to be wanting neither in the active nor the contemplative life.

535. The Most High permitted this sort of solicitude

to arise in his most blessed Mother in order that the favor of her new state, held in readiness for Her by his omnipotence, might come to Her so much the more opportunely. Therefore He spoke to Her and said: "My Spouse and my Beloved, the anxious aspirations of thy most ardent love have wounded my heart and by the power of my right hand I wish to operate in thee what I have done to none of the creatures, nor ever shall do; for thou art chosen as none other of my creatures for my delights. For thee alone have I prepared a state and condition, in which I shall nourish thee with my Divinity as one of the blessed, yet in a different manner; in it thou shalt continually enjoy my sight and my embraces, my peace and tranquillity, without being embarrassed by created things or by thy condition as a pilgrim. In this habitation thou shalt wing thy flight freely and without bonds through the infinite regions required by thy love; and from it thou shalt also fly to the aid of the holy Church, of which thou art Mother. Charged with my treasures, thou shalt distribute them among thy brethren according to thy pleasure in their necessities and labors, so that through thee they all may be relieved."

536. This is the favor which I pointed out in the last chapter and which the Evangelist clothes in these words: "And the Woman fled into the wilderness, where She had a place prepared by God, that there they should feed Her a thousand two hundred and sixty days," and a little farther on: "And there were given to the Woman two wings of a great eagle, that She might fly into the desert unto her place, where She was nourished" (Apoc. 12, 14). It is not easy to make myself understood regarding this mystery; for it contains many supernatural effects, which have no counterpart in any other creature and are wonders reserved by God exclusively to the

faculties of the most blessed Mary; and since faith teaches us, that we cannot measure or comprehend the power of the Almighty, it is proper to confess, that He can operate in Her much more than we can understand and that we need only deny such excellence in Her, as would imply an evident and manifest contradiction.   In that which has been shown me for the purpose of recording it in this history, supposing that I understand it, I do not see any contradiction in the way I see it; although the proper terms for recording it fail me in what I write.

537. I say then, that after Mary our Leader and Mistress had triumphed in her battles over the dragon and his demons, God raised Her to a state in which He manifested to Her the Divinity, not by an intuitive vision like that of the blessed, but by another clear vision through created species, which in this history I have always called abstractive vision; because it depends not upon the actual presence of the object seen, nor moves the understanding by the object itself; but by other species, which present the object as it is in itself, although absent; namely in the same manner as God can show me the city of Rome as it is in itself by infusing into my mind all the images and likenesses of that city.   This kind of vision of the Divinity the most blessed Virgin had enjoyed before during her life, as I have often demonstrated in this history.   Although it was thus not altogether new to Her, since She enjoyed abstractive vision at the moment of her Conception (as said at the time), yet it was new now in two respects.   First, from this time on it was permanent and continual, enduring till her death and till She passed into the beatific vision; while before that time it had been occasional and passing. Secondly, from this time it continued to increase in intensity day by day, and thus reached a degree more

exalted, more admirable and excellent than before, and beyond all created thought and measure.

538. For this purpose all her faculties were touched by the fire of the sanctuary, causing new effects of the Divinity, illuminating and exalting Her above Herself; for this state was to be a participation of that held by the comprehensors and the blessed, yet at the same time different from theirs. Hence it is important to note wherein it was like and wherein it was unlike to theirs. The likeness consisted in Her seeing the same object of the Divinity and the same attributes which they enjoyed by secure possession, only She understood them more deeply than they. The differences consisted in three points: first the blessed see God face to face and by intuitive vision, whereas the most blessed Mary saw Him by an abstractive vision as described; secondly, the beatific vision of the saints in the Fatherland and their essential fruition, in which the glory of the understanding and the will consists, cannot increase; whereas the abstractive vision of Mary in her pilgrimage had no limit or restriction, but her knowledge of the infinite attributes and the divine essence increased day by day; and for this were given to Her two wings of an eagle, by which She was to soar continually in this limitless ocean of the Divinity, comprehending ever more and more of its infinity.

539. The third difference was, that the saints can neither suffer nor merit, this being incompatible with their state; whereas our Queen could well accumulate suffering and merit in her state of vision, as being still a wayfarer. And without this possibility this state would not have been so great and valuable in her eyes, nor for the Church; for the meritorious works of so great a Lady, in this state of so great grace and holiness, were of the

most inestimable value and price to all men. She presented a new and wonderful spectacle to the angels and saints, a sort of portrait of her divine Son; for as the Queen and Mistress She had the power to dispense and distribute the treasures of grace, and at the same time, to add to them by her own ineffable merits. And though She was not a comprehensor, as the saints in heaven; yet in her state of pilgrimage She held a place so near to Christ and so like to his on earth, that, if compared with Him, She was indeed a pilgrim in body and soul; but if compared to the other pilgrims on earth, She seemed a comprehensor and one of the blessed.

540. This her state required that all the armory of her senses and other faculties should be of another order and capable of operations proportionate to her condition. Hence the manner of her activity experienced an entire change, and in the following way: all the species or impressions of creatures, which through her senses had acted upon her understanding, were now at an end or blotted out from her mind; though, as I have said above in this third part (No. 126), the great Lady had not admitted any images or species except only those that were necessary for the exercise of charity and other virtues. Now even these, in as far as they were terrestrial and in as far as they partook of the sensitive in entering her understanding, the Lord abolished, purging and distilling them of all that they yet contained of their origin in the senses. In place of the images and impressions, which thenceforward She could receive through the natural activity of her sensitive and intellectual faculties, the Lord infused into her mind other species, more pure and immaterial, and by means of these her perception and understanding was raised to a more exalted level.

541. This wonder will present no difficulty to the understanding of the learned. In order to explain myself more thoroughly, I wish to say, that, when we call to action the five bodily senses by which we hear, see and taste, we receive certain impressions of the objects presented to them; these impressions are passed on to another interior and corporeal faculty, called the general or common sense, the imaginative, or estimative phantasy, in which all the impressions of the exterior senses are united and perceived or felt and are deposited and kept in reserve, as in a storehouse of the five senses. Up to this point our perception is like that of the animals, although with some difference. After these impressions of the common sense or phantasy have thus been stored within us, who are rational animals, our mind, by means of the natural workings of its faculties, co-operates with them and enables the intellect to become active, distilling from them other spiritual or immaterial images; and by means of these spiritual images, which it produces within itself, it naturally comes to know and understand what first entered through the senses. Hence philosophers say, that, in understanding our mind speculates upon the phantasy in order to draw from it the images of what it is to understand according to the natural routine of our acting faculties. This routine is maintained, because the soul is united to the body and depends upon it in its operations.

542. But in the most blessed Mary, after entering the new state, this mode of procedure was not entirely preserved; for the Lord had miraculously supplied for her intellect another mode of action, independent of the phantasy and the general sense. In place of the species, which her understanding was naturally to draw from the impressions of exterior objects through the senses, He had

infused into Her other kinds of images, which represented exterior objects in a more exalted manner; whereas those which She acquired by the senses, remained in
the storehouse of the phantasy without being used by the
active understanding, which was instead furnished with
and illustrated by the supernatural species. These her
understanding made use of in its activity, while at the
same time those received and stored in the general
phantasy served Her for the feeling of pain and sensible
afflictions. Thus in this temple of the most blessed Mary
was fulfilled what happened in its figure long before: the
stones were shaped and wrought outside the temple,
whereas within, the strokes of the hammer or other
noise were not heard (III Reg. VI 7); likewise the
animals were killed and sacrificed upon the altar outside
the precincts of the sanctuary (Ex. 40, 27); and in it
were offered only the holocaust of the incense and spices
burned in the sacred fire.

543. Through the workings of this miracle in our
great Queen and Lady the stones of her virtues for her
adornment were hewn and polished in the lower sensitive
faculties of her soul, while in the forehall of the common
senses were offered up the hardships, sorrows and pains,
which She bore for the faithful in her labors for the
Church. But in the holy of holies of her intellect and her
will were offered up only the perfume of her contemplation and vision of the Divinity and the fire of her incomparable love. For this purpose the species of the senses,
representing objects in a more earthly manner and with
the turmoil natural to them, were not appropriate. Therefore the divine power excluded them altogether and
replaced them with other images of the same objects,
infused, supernatural and purer, capable of nourishing
the abstractive contemplation of the Divinity and more

appropriate to her knowledge of God, whom She unceasingly looked upon and loved in the inviolable peace, tranquillity and serenity of her soul.

544. These infused species in the most blessed Mary were founded upon the essence of God himself, because they represented all things to her understanding in the same way as a mirror represents objects to our eyes and make themselves known to us without obliging us to inspect them directly.   In this manner She was aware in all things of whatever was for the good of the children of the Church; of what She was to do for them in their labors and difficulties and of the manner in which She was to promote the fulfillment of the divine will in heaven and on earth.   Favored by this kind of vision, She was enabled to make her petitions in such a way as to have them all granted by the Lord.   From this kind of insight the Lord exempted in Her the works which She was to perform in obedience to the commands of saint Peter and saint John, and sometimes requested by some of the other Apostles.   The heavenly Mother herself had asked for this exemption, because She did not wish to interrupt her practice of obedience, which She loved so much; and also because She wished to make it plain, that through obedience the will of God is known with such certainty, that the obedient person needs no other means or byways of finding the will of God than this obedience to the commands of superiors; for this is without a doubt what God wishes and commands, and therefore is right.

545. For all her other doings then (except what pertained to obedience and holy Communion), the understanding of the most blessed Mary did not depend upon her intercourse with sensible creatures, nor on the images of the senses.   But of all of them She remained inde-

pendent and undisturbed, enjoying the abstractive vision of the Divinity without interruption, either awake or asleep, working or at rest, without need of forethought or reasoning about what was most perfect, or more agreeable to the Lord, about the necessities of the Church, or the time and manner coming to its aid. All this was present to her mind in the vision of the Divinity, just like to the blessed through the beatific vision. And just as the least important of the knowledge of the blessed is that concerning the creatures; so also (besides what our great Queen knew concerning the state of the Church, its government and of all the souls), the principal object of her knowledge were the incomprehensible mysteries of the Divinity, which She comprehended more deeply than the highest seraphim and saints. With this heavenly bread and nourishment She was sustained in that solitude prepared for Her by the Lord. In it She was solicitous for the Church without being disturbed, busily employed without inquietude, attentive without distraction, and in all things She was full of God within and without, clothed with the purest gold of the Divinity, immersed and absorbed in this incomprehensible sea. Yet at the same time She was attentive to all her children and their welfare, finding no rest except in the ministrations of her maternal charity.

546. This was the reason why the two wings of an eagle were given to Her; for by them She raised Herself to the solitude where the thoughts of neither angels or men could ever soar; and by them She descended from that unattainable height and flew to the aid of mortals, not haltingly, but with the lightest and swiftest flight. O prodigy of the omnipotence of God! O unheard of miracle, which so clearly manifests his infinite greatness! Our understanding fails us, our comprehension is

suspended and our powers are exhausted in the contemplation of such a hidden sacrament. Happy, golden ages of the beginnings of the Church, when it held such treasures within it, and fortunate we, if we could in our own unhappy times, as far as is possible and as far as our necessities and miseries require, see these signs and wonders renewed through his most blessed Mother!

547. The happiness of that age, and the manner in which the most holy Mother used her powers, will be better understood, if we adduce some practical instances of the assistance rendered by Her to the souls. One was that of a man living in Jerusalem and well known in the city, because he held a prominent position and was endowed with more than an ordinary mind and some moral virtues. As for the rest, he was a zealous upholder of the ancient law like saint Paul, and a bitter opponent of the teachings and the law of Christ the Savior. The blessed Mary knew this in the Lord, and through her intercession God had prepared the way for his conversion. On account of his good standing in the opinion of others, the blessed Lady desired very much to convert and save him. This She asked of the Most High with ardent love and fervor, and the Lord granted Her the request. Before the most blessed Mother entered the new state of being, She had applied her great prudence and insight to find means of converting this soul; but now this kind of study was no longer necessary; for She needed only to attend to the Lord, where, at her request, all that She had to do for his conversion was made clearly manifest.

548. She saw that this man was to come to Her through the preaching of saint John and that She need only tell saint John to preach where this Jew would hear him. The Evangelist obeyed her orders; and at the

same time the guardian angel of that man inspired him with the desire of seeing the Mother of the Crucified, whom all praised as a loving, modest and pious Woman. The Jew did not at that time foresee any spiritual good possibly to result from this visit, because he had not the divine light for such knowledge; but without proposing to himself any such ends, he desired to visit the great Lady out of calculating curiosity, merely in order to see who this Woman, so much spoken of by others, might be. But when he came into the presence of most holy Mary and looked upon Her, while with heavenly prudence She spoke to him, He was entirely changed into a new man. He immediately prostrated himself at the feet of the great Queen, confessing Christ as the Savior of the world and asking to be baptized. He received Baptism then and there at the hands of saint John, and while the words of Baptism were pronounced, the Holy Ghost came in visible form upon this man, who thenceforward was distinguished for his holy life. The heavenly Mother sang a hymn of thanksgiving for this great and wonderful favor.

549. Another inhabitant of Jerusalem, deceived by her cousin versed in witchcraft, apostatized from the faith. As the blessed Lady knew all things in the Lord, She was aware of her fall. In great affliction the Lady applied Herself to tearful prayers and exercises of atonement for the return of this woman, for She knew that such wilful falling away in those who have once given themselves to the pursuit of eternal life, always makes a return much more difficult. The prayers of the most blessed Mother readily paved the way for the salvation of this soul deceived by the serpent. Immediately the Queen saw that this Woman should be warned and exhorted by saint John, in order to bring her to a sense

of her evil deed. Saint John spoke to her, she listened and confessed her sin to him, thus being restored to grace. The blessed Mary afterwards exhorted her to persevere and resist the demon.

550. Lucifer and his demons dared not disturb the Church in Jerusalem during the presence of the Queen, whom they feared to approach; for her power filled them with fear and drove them to flight. Instead they sought to make conquests among the baptized of those ports of Asia where saint Paul and the other Apostles were preaching; they succeeded in perverting some to apostasy and to cause disturbance or hindrance in the preaching of the Gospel. The most zealous Princess knew of the machinations of the dragon and asked the Lord for assistance, if it should be proper under the circumstances. She received answer, that She might act as the Mother, as the Queen and Mistress of all creation, and that She had found grace in the eyes of the Most High. Thus encouraged from on high She clothed Herself with invincible strength; and like the faithful spouse, who rises from the couch, leaves the bridal chamber and the throne of her bridegroom, and arms herself to defend him against his assailants: so the valorous Lady, armed with divine power, rose up against the dragon, snatched the prey from his maw, wounding him by the power of her virtues, and commanding him again to sink into the abyss. And as She commanded, so it was fulfilled. Many other innumerable wonders, wrought by our Queen, could be cited; but these will suffice to indicate the state in which She then was constituted and the way in which She operated therein.

551. For greater perspicuity and in connection with the reckonings given before, it remains to mention the year in which the most blessed Lady received this favor

(Nos. 376, 465, 495, 435). When She betook Herself from Jerusalem to Ephesus, She had attained the age of fifty-four years, three months and twenty-six days; and her voyage took place in year forty of the birth of Christ, on the sixth of January. She remained in Ephesus two and a half years, returning in the year forty-two on the sixth of July; and in the year fifty-six and ten months of her age. The first council mentioned above was held by the Apostles two months after the Queen returned from Ephesus; so that during that council the most blessed Mary completed her fifty-seventh year. Then succeeded the battles and triumphs and her elevation to the exalted state herein described, in the beginning of her fifty-eighth year, and in the year of our Lord the Savior, forty-two and nine months. This state lasted twelve hundred and sixty days mentioned by saint John in the twelfth chapter, and then She passed to another, which I shall describe farther on.

INSTRUCTION WHICH THE QUEEN OF HEAVEN, MOST BLESSED MARY, GAVE ME.

552. My daughter, none of the mortals have any excuse for not ordering their lives in imitation of the life of my divine Son and of my own; for We were an example and model for all. No one can be without blame, if in his own state he is not perfect, having before his eyes the incarnate God, who became the Teacher of holiness for all states of life. Some souls, however, are by the divine will chosen and set apart from the common order, in order that they may enjoy more of the fruit of his blood, imitate more perfectly his life and mine, and cause his divine goodness, omnipotence and mercy to shine forth more resplendently. Whenever these chosen souls

faithfully and fervently correspond with the Lord, only worldly ignorance will wonder, that He should show Himself so liberal in exerting his power to overwhelm them with favors and blessings beyond all human conception. Whoever places such wonders of his beneficence in doubt, will only hinder the glory God seeks in his works. Such unbelievers attempt to measure them by the restricted and curtailed capacity of the human mind, which in them is usually depraved and obscured by their own sins.

553. And if the chosen souls themselves are so gross as to doubt his benefits, or do not dispose themselves to receive and use them prudently, or with the esteem and appreciation due to the operations of God: then, no doubt, they offend his Majesty much more than others, to whom no such blessings or talents are vouchsafed. The Lord does not wish the bread of the children to be cast to the dogs (Matth. 15, 26); nor his pearls to those who tread them under foot or despise them (Matth. 7, 7); for these blessings of special grace are the reserves of his highest Providence, and the capital of the price of the Redemption. Reflect then, my dearest, that such faults are committed by those souls, who are diffident in arduous or adverse events, or who shrink from the Lord, or hinder Him, when they are singled out as the instruments of his power for his service. Their sin is still more reprehensible, when they refuse to confess Christ in all such works for fear of the difficulties connected with them and of the gossip of the world concerning such new undertakings; when they act in such a manner, that they serve God and do his will only when it coincides with their own; or if they practice virtue only when it is accompanied by such and such conveniences; or love only when it does not disturb their tranquillity; or if they believe or

acknowledge benefits only when sweetened by caresses. As soon as adversity or labor is to be encountered for the sake of God, they at once give way to discontent, sorrow, discouragement and impatience, by which they frustrate the designs of the Lord and make themselves incapable of perfection in virtue.

554. All this arises from a deficiency of prudence, knowledge and true love, which prevents these souls from looking to their own and their neighbor's advance. For they look to themselves, rather than to God; and are governed more by selflove, than divine love and charity. Tacitly they are guilty of great presumption, since they attempt to direct God's will and even to reprehend it, professing their readiness for great labors in his service under such and such conditions and their inability under other conditions. They are unwilling to risk their credit and their comfort, even for the common good and for the glory of God. They think that, as they do not openly proclaim their refusal, they do not make themselves guilty of this temerity; yet it is the devil, who conceals it from them, in order that they may incur guilt.

555. In order that thou, my daughter, mayest not fall into this monstrous sin, thou shouldst discreetly ponder what I give thee to understand and record, and how much I desire thee to imitate me. I could not fall into such sins, yet in continual watchfulness I prayed to the Lord to govern me in all my actions according to his will and pleasure only, and I gave myself no liberty of doing anything that was not according to his greater pleasure. Hence I sought for myself the forgetfulness and the retirement from all creatures. Thou art subject to sin, and thou knowest how many snares the dragon, by himself and through the creatures, has laid in order to lead thee into it: hence thou hast good reason for

ceaselessly beseeching the Almighty to govern thee in all thy actions, and for closing the portals of thy senses in such a way as to exclude from thy interior every image or figure of mundane and earthly things. Renounce therefore thy free will into the hands of thy God and yield it to every pleasure of the Lord and mine. In what thou must necessarily transact with creatures for the fulfillment of the divine law and of charity, admit no image except what is unavoidable; and immediately ask, that the remembrance of what is not necessary be blotted out of thy mind. Concerning all thy works, words and thoughts consult with God, with thy angels and with me, for we are always with thee; consult also with thy confessor wherever possible. All that thou dost or resolvest without this consultation, hold in suspicion and as dangerous, and only by comparing it with my teachings, thou canst ascertain, whether it agrees or disagrees with the will of God.

556. Above all never lose sight of the essence of God; for the light of faith which thou hast received, is to serve especially for this purpose. Since this is to be thy last end, I wish that even in mortal life thou attain this vision as far as is possible to thee with the divine grace. It is indeed time that thou cast out those vain fears and suggestions, by which the enemy has sought to hinder and detain thee from giving constant credit to the blessings and favors of the Lord. Begin to be prudent and strong in this confident faith and deliver thyself entirely to the pleasure of his Majesty, in order that He may do with thee and in thee what shall be best for his service.

CHAPTER IX.

THE BEGINNINGS OF THE GOSPELS WRITTEN BY THE EVANGELISTS; THE PART WHICH THE MOST BLESSED MARY HAD IN THEIR COMPOSITION; SHE APPEARS TO SAINT PETER IN ANTIOCH AND IN ROME: SIMILAR FAVORS SHOWN TO OTHER APOSTLES.

557. I have described, as far as I was permitted, the exalted state of the great Queen and Lady after the first council of the Apostles, and also her victories over the infernal dragon and his demons. Although the wonderful works which She accomplished during these times and at all times, cannot be recorded in a history, nor even summed up, I was nevertheless given special light for the purpose of describing the beginnings of the Gospels and the call of the Evangelists to undertake their writing, the part which Mary bore in their being written, her solicitous care for the absent Apostles, and the miracles She wrought for them. In the second part, and on many occasions I have stated, that the heavenly Mother had a positive knowledge of all the mysteries of grace, of the Gospels and other holy writings, which were to serve for the confirmation of the new Law. In this knowledge She was confirmed many times, especially on the day of her ascension with her divine Son into heaven. From that day on, without forgetting anything, She often prostrated Herself in prayer before the Lord, asking Him to send his divine light upon the Apostles and holy writers and to order them to write, when the opportune time should have come.

558. Afterwards, when the Queen returned from heaven and was put in charge of the Church (as related in the sixth chapter of this book), the Lord made known to Her that the time for beginning to write the holy Gospels had arrived and that She should make her arrangements for this purpose as the Mistress and Instructress of the Church. But in her profound humility and discretion She obtained the consent of the Lord, that this should be attended to by saint Peter, his vicar and the head of the Church; and that he should be specially assisted by divine enlightenment for a matter of such importance. All this was granted by the Most High; and when the Apostles met in the council mentioned by saint Luke in the fifteenth chapter of the Acts, after they had settled the doubts about circumcision, as I described in the sixth chapter, saint Peter proposed to them all the necessity of recording in writing the mysteries of the life of Christ our Savior and Teacher, so that they might be preached to all the faithful in the Church without variation or difference, thus doing away with the old Law and establish the new.

559. Saint Peter had already consulted with the Mother of wisdom; and all the council having approved of his proposal, they called upon the Holy Ghost to point out the Apostles and disciples who should write the life of the Savior. Immediately a light was seen descending upon saint Peter and a voice was heard saying: "The highpriest and head of the Church shall assign four for recording the works and the teachings of the Savior of the world." Saint Peter and all present prostrated themselves, giving thanks to the Lord for this favor. When all of them had again risen, saint Peter spoke: "Matthew, our beloved brother, shall immediately begin to write his Gospel in the name of the Father, the Son and the Holy

Ghost. Mark shall be the second, who shall likewise write the Gospel in the name of the Father, the Son and the Holy Ghost. Luke shall write the third, in the name of the Father, the Son and the Holy Ghost. Our most beloved brother John shall be the fourth and last to write the mysteries of our Savior and Teacher in the name of the Father, the Son and the Holy Ghost." This decision the Lord confirmed by permitting the heavenly light to remain until these words were repeated and formally accepted by all those appointed.

560. Within a few days saint Matthew set about writing the first Gospel. While praying in a retired room of the Cenacle and asking to be enlightened for the inception of his history, the most blessed Mary appeared to him seated on a throne of great majesty and splendor, the doors of the room still remaining closed. The great Lady told him to arise, which he did, asking for her benediction. Then She spoke to him and said: "Matthew, my servant, the Almighty sends me with his blessing, in order that with it thou begin the writing of the Gospel which thou hast the good fortune to be entrusted with. In this thou shalt have the assistance of the Holy Ghost and I shall beg it for thee with all my heart. But concerning myself it is not proper, that thou write anything except what is absolutely necessary for manifesting the Incarnation and other mysteries of the Word made man, and for establishing his faith in the world as the foundation of his Church. This faith being established, the Almighty will find other persons, who, when the times arrive in which it shall become necessary, shall reveal to the faithful the mysteries and blessings wrought by his powerful arm in me." Saint Matthew signified his willingness to obey the mandate of the Queen; and while he conferred with Her about composing his Gospel, the

Holy Ghost came down upon him in visible form; and in the presence of the Lady He began to write the words as they are still extant in his Gospel. The blessed Mary then left him and saint Matthew proceeded in his history, finishing it in Judea. He wrote it in the Hebrew language in the year forty-two of our Lord.

561. The Evangelist Mark wrote his gospel four years later, in the forty-sixth year after the birth of Christ. He likewise wrote it in Hebrew and while in Palestine. Before commencing he asked his guardian angel to notify the Queen of heaven of his intention and to implore her assistance for obtaining the divine enlightenment for what he was about to write. The kind Mother heard his prayer and immediately the Lord commanded the angels to carry Her with the usual splendor and ceremony to the Evangelist, who was still in prayer. The great Queen appeared to him seated on a most beautiful and resplendent throne. Prostrating himself before Her, he said: "Mother of the Savior of the world and Mistress of all creation, I am unworthy of this favor, though I am a servant of thy divine Son and of Thyself." The heavenly Mother answered: "The Most High, whom thou servest and lovest, sends me to assure thee, that thy prayers are heard and that his holy Spirit shall direct thee in the writing of the Gospel, with which He has charged thee." Then She told him not to write of the mysteries pertaining to Her, just as She had asked of saint Matthew. Immediately the Holy Ghost, in visible and most refulgent shape, descended upon saint Mark, enveloping him in light and filling him with interior enlightenment; and in the presence of the Queen he began to write his Gospel. At that time the Princess of heaven was sixty-one years of age. Saint Jerome says, that saint Mark wrote his short Gospel in Rome, at the

instance of the faithful residing there; but I wish to call attention to the fact, that this was a translation or copy of the one he had written in Palestine; for the Christians in Rome possessed neither his nor any other Gospel, and therefore he set about writing one in the Roman or Latin language.

562. Two years afterwards, in the year forty-eight and of the Virgin the sixty-third, saint Luke wrote his Gospel in the Greek language. To him also, as to the others, Mary appeared when he was about to begin it. Having represented to the heavenly Mother, that, in order to manifest the Incarnation and life of her divine Son, it was necessary to touch upon the manner of the actual conception of the Word made man and upon other things concerning her dignity as the natural Mother of Christ, and having received orders from Her to pass over in silence the other mysteries and wonders connected with her dignity as Mother of God, saint Luke obtained her permission to write somewhat more freely of the heavenly Mary in his Gospel. The Holy Ghost descended upon him and in the presence of the great Queen he began to write his Gospel, drawing his information principally from direct inspiration of her Majesty. Saint Luke continued a most devoted servant of the Lady and never permitted the image of the sweetest Mother seated on the throne of majesty, as he had seen Her on this occasion, to be effaced from his mind. Thenceforward he lived continually in her presence. Saint Luke was in Achaia, when this apparition happened to him, and there also he wrote his Gospel.

563. The last of the four Evangelists who wrote the Gospels, was the apostle saint John in the year fifty-eight of the Lord. He wrote his in the Greek language, during his stay in Asia Minor after the glorious transi-

tion and assumption of the most blessed Mary. His Gospel was directed against the heresies and errors, which, (as indicated above), the devil immediately after the transition of the Virgin Mother began to sow for undermining the faith in the Incarnation of the divine Word. For as Lucifer had been humiliated and vanquished by this mystery, he at once directed the onslaught of heresy against it. For this reason the evangelist saint John writes so sublimely and adduces so many arguments for the true and undoubted Divinity of Christ our Savior, far surpassing the other Evangelists in this regard.

564. Although when the Evangelist was about to begin his Gospel the most blessed Mary was already in heaven, She descended in person, resplendent with ineffable glory and majesty and surrounded by thousands of angels of all choirs and hierarchies. Appearing to saint John She said: "John, my son and servant of the Most High, now is the proper time for writing the life and mysteries of my divine Son, so that all mortals may know Him as the Son of the eternal Father, as true God and at the same time as true man. But it is not yet the opportune time for recording the mysteries and secrets which thou knowest of me; nor shall they as yet be manifested to a world so accustomed to idolatry, lest Lucifer abuse them for disturbing those who are to receive the faith in their Redeemer and in the blessed Trinity. The Holy Ghost will assist thee and I desire thee to begin writing in my presence." The Evangelist worshipped the great Queen of heaven and was filled with the divine Spirit as the others had been. Assisted by the kind Mother, he immediately set about writing his Gospel. Before She departed to the right hand of her divine Son, She gave him her benediction and prom-

ised him her protection for all the rest of his life. Such
were the beginnings of the sacred Gospels, all of them
having been commenced with the assistance and by the
intervention of the most blessed Mary, giving the Church
to understand, that all these benefits have been vouchsafed at her hands. After having thus anticipated the history of the Evangelists, in order to account for the beginnings of the Gospels, we shall now return to our narrative.

565. In proportion as the most blessed Lady after the
council of the Apostles was exalted by her divine knowledge and the abstractive vision of God, so her care and
solicitude for the welfare of the Church increased; for
the faith was now spreading out over the earth day by
day. As a true Mother and Teacher, She lavished her
special attention upon the Apostles, whose names and
whose welfare She bore written in her heart. All of them,
except saint John and saint James the less, immediately
after the termination of the council, left Jerusalem for
the field of their labors, and the kindest Mother was
deeply concerned at the thought of the hardships and
difficulties connected with their preaching. She looked
upon them with tender pity in their peregrinations, and
held them in highest veneration on account of their
holiness and dignity as priests, as Apostles of her divine
Son, founders of the Church, preachers of his doctrine,
and as the elect of the divine Wisdom chosen for such
high ministries to the glory of the Most High. It was
truly necessary that the most blessed Lady and Mistress,
in order to attend to and take care of so many matters
throughout the holy Church, should be raised to the state
which She now held: for in any lower condition She
could not have so easily and properly attended to so many
duties and at the same time maintain that interior tranquillity and peace, which her soul enjoyed.

566. Besides her own knowledge and solicitude for the whole Church, the most holy Mother again charged her angels to take care of all the Apostles and disciples, to console them in all their tribulations and to haste to their aid in all their difficulties. For by the subtlety of their spiritual nature they could attend to all this without losing sight of the face of God and enjoying beatific vision. She thus charged them because it was so important to establish the Church and because they were the ministers of the Most High and the works of his hands. She told them also to inform Her of all that the Apostles and disciples were doing, and especially when they were in need of any clothing; for to this matter the watchful Mother wished to attend in particular, in order that they might go about clothed in a uniform manner, such as they wore when they departed from Jerusalem. By this prudent foresight, the Apostles showed no difference in their garments as long as the great Lady was alive; but all of them wore clothes of the same form and color, similar to that worn by her divine Son. Assisted by the holy angels, She wove with her own hand the tunics for this purpose and sent them through the angels to the Apostles on their journeys. In thus making it possible for them to wear vestments similar to those which had been worn by Christ our Savior, the great Mother provided that even in their exterior appearance the Apostles preached his doctrines and his most holy life. In regard to the other necessities of life, such as food, She left them to begging and to the labor of their hands, or to the alms which were offered to them.

567. At the orders of the Queen the angels frequently assisted the Apostles in their travels and tribulations and in the persecutions as well of the gentiles and the Jews, as of the demons, who continually excited evil-

minded men against the preachers of the Gospel. The angels often visited them in visible shapes, conversing with them and consoling them in the name of the most blessed Mary. At other times they performed the same office interiorly without manifesting themselves; sometimes they freed them from prison; sometimes they warned them of dangers and snares; sometimes they accompanied them on their way or carried them from one place to another where they were to preach, or informed them of what they were to do according to the circumstances peculiar to certain places or peoples. Of all these things they also kept their blessed Lady informed; for She took care of all of them and labored with them more than all of them together. It is not possible to enumerate the cares, solicitudes and diligent doings of this kindest Mother; for not a day or a night passed, in which She did not perform many miracles for the Apostles and for the Church. Besides all this She wrote to them many times, animating them with heavenly exhortations and doctrines, and filling them with consolation and strength.

568. But what is more wonderful: She not only communed with them by means of her angels and by letters, but She appeared to them Herself, whenever they called upon Her or when they were in some tribulation or necessity. Although (besides appearing to the Evangelists, concerning which I have already spoken), She appeared to many of the Apostles, I will here speak only of her apparitions to saint Peter, who, as head of the Church, stood in greater need of the counsels and assistance of the most blessed Mary. Hence to him She sent her angels more frequently, and the saint sent those, which were assigned to him as pontiff of the Church, and he wrote to Her and communicated with Her oftener

than the other Apostles.   Soon after the council of Jerusalem saint Peter was journeying to Asia Minor and came to Antioch, where he first established his pontifical see.   On account of the difficulties which he met in the execution of his design, the vicar of Christ was downcast and afflicted, and the most blessed Mary well knew of it and how much he stood in need of her favor.   In order to confer it upon him in the manner suited to the importance of the occasion, She had her holy angels bring Her to saint Peter, and appeared to him, seated on a throne of majesty as at other times.   The Apostle, seeing Her before him so resplendent, prostrated himself before Her with wonted fervor, and bathed in tears, said to Her: "Whence this favor to me, a sinner, that the Mother of my Redeemer should come to where I am?"   The heavenly Teacher of the humble descended from her throne, and, moderating the splendors which surrounded Her, knelt before the highpriest of the Church and asked his blessing.   With none of the other Apostles, but only with saint Peter did She observe this conduct in her apparitions to them; although except at these apparitions, when She conversed with them in the natural way, She was wont to ask their blessing on her knees.

569. But because saint Peter was the vicar of Christ and the head of the Church She descended from her royal throne and showed him reverence, acting as one of the members of the Church yet in mortal flesh. Speaking familiarly with the holy Apostle She conferred with him upon the weighty matters then under consideration. One of them was the advisability of beginning to celebrate some of the feasts of the Lord. After they had resolved on the course to be taken, the holy angels took Her back from Antioch to Jerusalem.

Later on, when saint Peter, in obedience to the orders of the Savior, had gone to Rome with the intention of transferring the apostolic see to that city, the blessed Lady appeared once more to saint Peter. There it was ordained that in the Roman Church should thenceforth be celebrated the feast of the Nativity of her divine Son, of the Passion, and of the institution of most holy Sacrament in the manner as it is now done on Holy Thursday or Maundy Thursday. Later on, after many years, was established also the feast of Corpus Christi to be celebrated on the first Thursday after the octave of Pentecost, as is still the rule. But the first feast of the blessed Sacrament on Holy Thursday, was instituted by saint Peter, as also the feast of the Resurrection, the Sundays, the Ascension, with the paschal and other observances of the Roman Church to the present day; and all of these were instituted by the order and according to the counsel of the most blessed Mary. After these doings saint Peter went to Spain, visiting some of the churches founded by saint James and establishing others before returning to Rome.

570. On another occasion, before (though very near), the glorious transition of the heavenly Mother, saint Peter being likewise at Rome, a dispute arose among the Christians, which greatly distressed and afflicted both him and all those concerned. The Apostles remembered the favors he had received in his tribulations at the hands of the great Queen and grieved very much that he should now be deprived of her counsel and assistance. He therefore besought the angels of his guard and those given him as assistants in his office of highpriest, to manifest his troubles and necessity to the blessed Mother in order to obtain help in his difficulties by her powerful intercession with her Son. The Queen, who knew the

fervor and humility of saint Peter, failed not in responding to his wishes.   She commanded the angels of the
Apostle to bring him to Jerusalem, where She then was.
They immediately executed her command and brought
saint Peter to the Cenacle and the presence of his Queen.
This singular favor inflamed the fervent affections of the
Apostle, and he prostrated himself before the most
blessed Mary, full of joy and tears to see the prayer of
his heart fulfilled.   The great Lady commanded him to
arise, and She, instead, fell on her face saying: "My
master, give thy servant thy blessing as vicar of Christ
our Lord my Son."   Saint Peter obeyed and gave
Her his blessing.   Then they gave thanks to the Lord
for having fulfilled their wishes; and although the humble
Mistress of virtues was not unaware of the tribulations
of saint Peter and of the faithful of Rome, She listened
to his account of what had happened.

571. The most blessed Mary advised him of all that
he needed to know and do in order to allay the trouble
and restore peace in the church of Rome.   She spoke
with such wisdom, that, although he had had a high
concept of her prudence, he was carried beside himself
in his admiration and joy of what he heard and experienced of it on this occasion, and he gave humble
thanks for this new favor.   Having thus informed him
of many things for establishing the Church in Rome, She
asked his blessing and took leave of him.   The angels
brought him back to Rome, while, as was her wont, the
most blessed Mary remained prostrate upon the ground
in the form of a cross, asking the Lord to quiet this disturbance.   Her prayer was heard; for on coming back
to Rome, saint Peter found matters in a better state, and
soon the consuls permitted the faithful freely to follow
the law of Christ.   From these miracles, which I have

adduced, some insight is afforded in the doings of Mary in the government of the Apostles and of the Church. For if all were to be recorded, more volumes would be required than I am now writing lines. Hence I refrain from enlarging upon them, in order that in the rest of this history I may describe the wonderful and unheard-of favors, which the Lord conferred upon the most holy Mary in the last years of her life; although at the same time I confess, that I can give only some stray hints of what I have seen, in order that Christian piety may be led to the contemplation and praise of the Omnipotent, the Author of these venerable sacraments.

INSTRUCTION WHICH THE QUEEN OF THE ANGELS GAVE ME.

572. My dearest daughter, at other times I have spoken to thee of a complaint, which I have against the children of the Church, and especially against the women, in whom the fault is greater. In my sight it is abominable, because it is so much opposed to my own conduct in life. I repeat it here, in order that thou mayest imitate me and keep away from what the foolish women and daughters of Belial are guilty of: namely, treating the priests of the Most High without reverence, esteem, or respect. This fault increases day by day in the Church, and therefore I renew this warning already several times recorded. Tell me, my daughter, what must be thought of the fact, that priests, the anointed of the Lord, appointed to represent Christ and to consecrate his body and blood, are serving vile, impure, and earthly women? That they should stand uncovered and do reverence to a proud and miserable woman, only because

she is rich and they are poor? I ask, has the poor priest less dignity than the rich? Or do riches confer a greater or equal dignity, power and excellence, than the one given to priests and ministers by my divine Son? The angels have no regard for the rich on account of their possessions, but they respect priests for their exalted dignity. Hence, how could such an abuse and perversity creep into the Church, that the anointed of the Lord should be outraged and despised by the faithful, who know and confess them to be sanctified by Christ himself?

573. It is true that the priests themselves are very guilty and reprehensible when they, disregarding their dignity, enslave themselves to the service of other men, and much more, of women. But if priests have some excuse in their poverty, the rich have none in their pride, that they should, on account of the poverty of the priests, oblige them to be servants, when in reality they are masters. This monstrosity is very abominable to the saints and very disagreeable in my eyes on account of the veneration I had for the priests. Great was my dignity as Mother of God; yet I often prostrated myself at their feet and considered it a great happiness to kiss the ground on which they trod. But the blindness of the world has obscured the sacerdotal dignity and confounded the precious with the vile (Jer. 15, 19); it has lowered the priests to the position of the common people by its laws and disorderly customs (Is. 25, 2), making use of the one as well as the other for their degradation; and the same minister who now at the altar offers the tremendous sacrifice of the sacred body and blood, afterwards leaves it to serve and subject himself to the service even of women, who by nature and by the condition are so inferior, and sometimes are made even more unworthy by their sins.

574. I wish then, my daughter, that thou seek to make up for this fault and abuse among the children of the Church as far as possible. I give thee to understand, that even from my throne in heaven I look with veneration and respect upon the priests who are on earth. Thou must always regard them with the same veneration, as if they were at the altar, or holding the most blessed Sacrament in their hands or at their breast; and even the ornaments and all their vestments thou shouldst hold in great veneration, just as I with reverence provided garments for the Apostles. Then, besides what thou hast understood and written concerning the divine Scriptures, thou must gage thy esteem for these writings by what they contain and enclose, and by the means which the Almighty took to incite the Evangelists to write them. As well in the Gospels as in the rest of holy writings the Holy Ghost himself lent his assistance, in order that the Church might be rich and prosperous in the abundance of doctrine, of science and light concerning the mysteries and operations of the Lord. To the supreme pontiff of Rome thou must render highest obedience and veneration before all other men; and when thou hearest him mentioned, show reverence by inclining thy head as if thou heardst the name of my divine son or my own named in thy presence; for on earth he takes the place of Christ, and when I lived in the world, I showed my reverence whenever the name of saint Peter was pronounced. In order that thou mayest practice my doctrine and find grace in the eyes of the Most High, whom all these works please very much and who considers none of them small if done for his love, I wish that thou be very attentive and a most faithful follower of my footsteps.

CHAPTER X.

575. Without ever failing in her attention to the exterior government of the Church (as I have until now made plain), the most blessed Mary in secret practiced other exercises and good works, by which She merited innumerable gifts and blessings from the Most High, as well for the common benefit of all the faithful, as for myriads of particular souls in furtherance of their salvation. As far as I can in these last chapters, I shall, for our instruction and admiration and for the glory of the most blessed Mother, write of these hidden and unknown works. First of all I will state, that notwithstanding the many privileges which the great Queen of heaven enjoyed, She constantly kept present in her memory the doings and the mysteries of the life of her divine Son; for besides the abstractive vision, by which She in these last years continually saw the Divinity and knew all things, the Lord had from her Conception conceded to Her the privilege of never forgetting what once She had known or understood; for in this regard She enjoyed the privilege of an angel, as I have stated in the first part.

576. I also stated in the second part, in writing of the Passion, that the blessed Mother felt in her body and purest soul all the pains and torments of our Savior

Jesus, so that none of them were hidden to Her or without the corresponding suffering in her own self. All the images or impressions of the Passion remained imprinted in her interior just as She had received them; for She had made this request of her Lord. These were not blotted out, as were the other sensible images, through the vision of the Divinity; rather they were made more vivid, in order that She might miraculously rejoice in her compassion and at the same time suffer those sorrows, for this was her desire during the time She was still to live in mortal flesh and to this exercise She directed her natural will-power. As exquisite as her favors and privileges were (according to what I have always maintained in my discourse), they nevertheless were all pledges and tokens of the reciprocal love of her divine Son, who, in our way of speaking, could not contain Himself or refrain from dealing with his Mother as the God of love, as the Omnipotent, infinitely rich in mercies. But the most blessed Virgin did not ask for them or seek them; for her sole desire was to be crucified with Christ, to continue within Herself his sorrows, renew his Passion, and without this it seemed to her useless and idle to live in passible flesh.

577. Hence She ordered all her occupations in such a manner, that She might at all times preserve in her heart the image of her divine Son, afflicted, outraged, wounded and disfigured by the torments of his Passion, and within Herself She beheld this image as in a most clear mirror. She heard the injuries, outrages, affronts and blasphemies against Him, with all the circumstances of time and place, and She beheld the whole Passion as in one living and penetrating vista. Throughout the day this sorrowful vision excited Her to most heroic acts of virtue and stirred her sorrow and compassion;

but her most prudent love did not content itself with
these exercises. During stated hours and times She
engaged in other exercises with her holy angels, especially
with those I have mentioned in the first part as bearing
the tokens or the escutcheons of the instruments of the
Passion. These in the first place, and then the other
angels, She engaged as assistants in the following exercises.

578. For each kind of the wounds and sufferings of
Christ our Savior She recited special prayers and salu-
tations, in order to give them special adoration and worship. For each of the contemptuous and insulting words
of the Jews and his other enemies, which had been
spoken either in envy or in fury or vengeance, for each
of the blasphemies uttered, She composed special hymns
of veneration and honor to make up for their attempts
at diminishing it. For the insulting gestures, mock-
eries and personal injuries, She practiced most profound
humiliations, genuflections and prostrations, and in this
manner She sought continually to make up for the affronts and injuries heaped upon her divine Son in his
life and his passion; and thus She confessed his Divinity,
his humanity, his holiness, his miracles, his works and
his doctrines. For all She gave Him glory and magnificence; and in all the holy angels joined Her, and corresponded with Her full of admiration of such wisdom,
fidelity and love united in a mere creature.

579. Even if the most blessed Mother during her
whole life had engaged in no other occupation than these
exercises, She would have accomplished and merited
more than all the saints in all that they have done or suffered for God. By the force of love her sorrow in
these exercises was equal to martyrdom many times
over; and many times would She have died in them, if

the divine power had not sustained her life for still greater merit and glory. And if, as is true, She in her immense charity offered all these works for the Church, let us consider how much we are in her debt as faithful children for thus increasing the treasures of help, which She left at the disposal of us unfortunate children of Eve. And in order that our meditation may not be half-hearted and lukewarm, I will say, that the effects of her contemplations were often astounding; many times She wept tears of blood, which covered her whole face; at other times in her agony She was not only bathed in perspiration, but in a bloody sweat, running from Her even to the ground. What is more, sometimes her heart was wrenched from its natural position by the violence of her grief; and when She was in such extremes, her divine Son came from heaven, furnishing Her with new strength and life to soothe her sorrow and heal the wounds caused by love of Him, and in order that by such assistance and comfort, She might continue the exercises of her compassion.

580. The Lord however wished Her to lay aside these sorrowful sentiments and affections on the days in which She commemorated the mystery of his Resurrection, as I will speak of later on, in order that there might be maintained the proper relation between cause and effect. For some of these sorrows were incompatible with the favors overflowing in their effects upon the body, yet excluding pain. But She never lost sight of his sufferings and therefore felt other effects of her compassion by uniting with her joys, the gratitude for what the Lord endured. Thus in the sweetness of all the favors of the Lord his Passion entered as a mixture of bitterness. She obtained also the consent of the evangelist saint John to remain retired in her oratory for

celebrating the death and burial of her divine Son on
the Friday of each week.   On those days saint John remained in the Cenacle to receive those who called upon
Her and allowed none to disturb Her; and whenever he
could not attend to this duty, it was performed by some
other disciple.   The most blessed Mary retired for this
exercise at five o'clock on Thursday and did not reappear
until toward noon of Sunday.   In order that during
these three days no important matter pertaining to the
government of the Church might be neglected, the great
Lady appointed one of her angels to take her shape and
briefly despatch what would suffer no delay, so provi-
dent and attentive was She in all affairs of charity touching her children and domestics.

581.   To describe or comprehend what happened with
our heavenly Mother during the exercises of these three
days can never be within our capacity; the Lord alone,
who was the Author of them, shall one day manifest it
to us in the light of the saints.   Also what I myself
have come to know of it, I am unable to describe; I will
only say that beginning with the washing of the feet, the
most blessed Mary commemorated all the mysteries up
to that of the Resurrection; and in each hour and moment
She renewed in Herself all the movements, actions,
works and sufferings as they had happened in her divine
Son.   She repeated the same prayers and petitions as
He himself had made and as we have seen described in
their place.   Anew the most pure Mother felt in her
virginal body all the pains endured by Christ our Savior.
She carried the Cross and placed Herself upon it.   In
short, I will say, that as long as She lived, the whole
passion of her divine Son was renewed in Her week for
week.   Through this exercise the great Queen gained
great favors and blessings for those who devoutly bear

in mind the Lord's passion; and hence the powerful
Queen has promised to all such souls, especial assistance
and participation in the treasures of the Passion; for
She desired from her inmost heart, that the Church
should continue and preserve its commemoration. In
virtue of her wishes and prayers the Lord ordained, that
afterwards many persons in the holy Church should
follow these exercises of the Passion, imitating his most
blessed Mother, who was the first one to teach and practice such an exalted profession.

582. In these exercises the great Queen sought especially to celebrate the institution of the most blessed
Sacrament by new hymns of praise, of thanksgiving
and fervent love. She was solicitous to invite for this
purpose her own angels and many others from the empyrean heaven, in order to assist and accompany Her
in these praises of the Lord. It was a wonder worthy
of his Omnipotence, that the Most High should send
from heaven multitudes of angels to view this prodigy
of Christ's remaining sacramentally present in her heart
from one Communion to the other and to incite them to
give glory and praise for the wonderful effects of his
sacramental presence in this Creature, whom they beheld
more pure and more holy than the angels and seraphim
and the like of which they had not seen or would ever
see in all the rest of creation.

583. It was not less wonderful to them (just as it
ought to be to us) to see, that though the great Queen
was worthy of preserving within Herself the sacred
species as in a tabernacle, She was so solicitous in preparing Herself anew by the most fervid exercises and
devotions every time She was again to receive holy
Communion; and this She did nearly every day except on
those in which She remained in her oratory. She first

offered up for this purpose her weekly exercises of the
Passion; and besides this, whenever She retired at night-
fall before the day of Communion, She began other exercises, such as prostrations in the form of a cross, genuflections, prayers, and adorations of the immutable essence of God. She asked permission of the Lord to
speak to Him and to permit Her, in spite of her earthly
lowliness, to partake of his Son in the holy Sacrament;
She appealed to his infinite bounty and to his love
toward the Church in thus remaining sacramentally present, as a reason that She should be favored with this
blessing. She offered to Him his own Passion and
Death, the worthiness with which He had communicated
Himself, the union of his human nature with the divine,
all his works from the moment of his conception in the
virginal womb, all the virtue of the angelic nature and
its works, of all the just in past, present and future times.

584. Then she made most intense acts of humility,
professing Herself but dust and ashes in comparison
with the infinite being of God, to which the highest creatures are so inferior and unequal. In the contemplation
of what She was to receive sacramentally, She was so
affected and so deeply moved, that it is impossible to
describe it in words; for She raised Herself and
transcended above the choirs of seraphim and cherubim;
and as, in her own estimation, She considered Herself
the lowest of all creatures, She called upon her guardian
angels and upon all the other angels, asking them, with
incomparable humility, to supplicate the Lord to dispose
and prepare Her for receiving Him worthily, since She
was but an inferior and earthly creature. The holy angels, obeying Her in joyful admiration, assisted and
accompanied Her in these petitions, in which She persevered for the greater part of the night preceding her
Communion.

585. As the wisdom of the great Queen, although in itself finite, is for us incomprehensible, we can never worthily understand to what height rose her virtues and works of love on these occasions. But they were often of such a kind as to oblige the Lord to respond by a personal visit, in which He gave Her to understand with what pleasure He came to dwell sacramentally in her heart and to renew in Her the pledges of his infinite love. When the hour of her Communion arrived, She first heard the Mass usually celebrated by the Evangelist. In these Masses, although the Epistles and Gospels, being not yet written, were not read, the consecration was always the same as now, and to it were added other rites and ceremonies with many psalms and orations. At the end of Mass the heavenly Mother approached, making three most profound genuflections; all inflamed with love She received her Son in the Sacrament, welcoming in her purest bosom and heart that same God, to whom She had given the most sacred humanity in her virginal womb. Having communicated, She retired, and, unless some very urgent need of her fellowmen demanded otherwise, remained alone for three hours. During these hours the Evangelist was often privileged to see rays of light darting forth from Her as from the sun.

586. The prudent Mother also provided that for the celebration of the unbloody sacrifice of the Mass the Apostles and priests be clothed in ornate and mysterious vestments, different from those they wore in ordinary life. Accordingly, with her own hands, She provided ornaments and sacerdotal vestments for its celebration, thus originating the ceremonious observances in the Church. Although these vestments were not quite of the same form as nowadays; yet they were not materially different in appearance from those which in the course

of time came into use in the Roman Church. The material was more alike; for She made them of linen and rich silks, purchased with the alms and presents made to Her. Whenever She worked at these vestments, sewing or fitting them, She remained on her knees or on her feet, and She would not entrust them to other sacristans than the angels, who assisted and helped Her in all these things; likewise She kept these ornaments and all that pertained to the service of the altar in incredible order and cleanliness; and from such hands as hers, all came forth with a celestial fragrance, which enkindled the spirit of the ministers.

587. From many kingdoms and provinces, where the Apostles were preaching, numbers of converts came to Jerusalem in order to visit and converse with the Mother of the Redeemer of the world, at the same time offering rich gifts. Among others, four sovereign princes, who were royal governors of provinces, visited Her and brought many valuable presents, which they placed at her disposal for her own use and for the Apostles and disciples. The great Lady answered that She was poor like her Son, and that the Apostles likewise were poor in imitation of their Master; that hence these riches were not appropriate to the life they professed. They begged Her to console them by accepting their gifts for the poor or for the divine worship. On account of their persistent requests She received part of what they offered, and from the rich silks She made some ornaments for the altar; the rest She distributed among the indigent and the infirmaries. For She was accustomed to visit such places and often served and washed the poor with her own hands, performing such services, as well as distributing the alms, on her knees. Wherever it was possible She consoled the needy and assisted the sick

in their last agony. Nor did She ever rest from works of charity, either actually engaging in them, or pleading and praying for others in her retirement.

588. She gave salutary advice to those princes or kings at their visit, admonishing them and instructing them in regard to the good government of their provinces. She charged them to watch over the equitable administration of justice without acceptation of persons; to consider themselves mortal men as all the rest, to fear the supreme Judge, by whom all are to be judged according to their own works; and above all, to further the exaltation of the name of Christ, the propagation and security of the holy faith, in which alone the governments and reigns can be firmly established. For without faith, government is but a lamentable and disastrous slavery of the demons, which is permitted by the hidden judgments of God for the punishment of both those that govern and that are governed. The fortunate princes promised faithfully to execute all her instructions and they afterwards remained in communication with the heavenly Queen through letters and other intercourse. The same benefit in its degree resulted to all that visited Her; for all of them left her presence more ardent in virtue, full of light, joy and consolation unspeakable. Many who were as yet unbelievers, on seeing Her, loudly professed their belief in the true God; for they were unable to restrain the interior forces awakened by the presence of their most blessed Mother.

589. And such effects must not be held as surprising, since the great Lady was entirely transformed into a most efficacious instrument of the power of God and of his grace among men. Not only her words, so full of wisdom, roused the admiration and convinced the minds by communicating new light; but on her lips was dif-

fused heavenly grace for communicating it and in her countenance shone the sweetness and beauty of heaven, while her own quiet majesty and modesty, grave yet pleasing, together with the hidden virtue (like that ascribed to her divine Son in the Gospel), attracted and refreshed the hearts (Luke 6, 19). Some remained speechless in admiration, some broke forth in tears, others in exclamations of wonder and praise, confessing that great is the God of the Christians, who had formed such a Creature. Truly could they testify to what some saints said to Her: that Mary was a divine prodigy of virtue. Let Her be eternally known and praised through all the generations as the true Mother of God, who made Her so attractive to human eyes, such a sweet Mother to the sinners, so amiable to angels and men.

590. During these last years the Queen ate or slept very little; and this little only, because saint John asked Her to rest for at least a small portion of the night. But this sleep was only a slight suspension of the senses, lasting no longer than a half hour, during which, in the manner above described, She lost not the vision of the Divinity. Her food was a few mouthfuls of ordinary bread and sometimes a little fish, taken at the instance of the Evangelist and in order to keep him company; for in this, as in other privileges, saint John was thus fortunate, not only eating with Her from the same table, but having the food prepared for him by the great Queen and administered to him as from a mother to her son, and moreover being obeyed by Her as a priest and a substitute of Christ. Very well could the great Queen get along without even this sleep or nourishment, which seemed more a ceremony than the sustenance of life; but She partook of them not from necessity, but in order to practice obedience and humility and thus pay some

tribute to human nature; for in all things She was most prudent.

INSTRUCTION WHICH MARY THE MOST BLESSED QUEEN OF THE ANGELS, GAVE ME.

591. My daughter, through the whole course of my life is evident how gratefully I kept in mind the works of the Redemption, the passion and death of my divine Son, especially after I had actually seen Him sacrificed on the Cross for the salvation of men. But in this chapter particularly have I wished to draw thy attention to the care and the continual exercises, by which I renewed in me not only the remembrance, but the sufferings of the Passion. I desire that the knowledge of this cause men to feel reproach and confusion at their monstrous forgetfulness of the incomprehensible benefit of the Redemption. O what a shameful, what a horrible and dangerous ingratitude of men is this! Forgetfulness is a clear proof of contempt, for one does not forget so easily, what one holds dear. What reason or excuse then can there be, that men forget the eternal blessings they have received? That they should despise the love, with which the eternal Father has delivered over to death his only begotten Son? The charity and patience with which his and my Son accepted it for them (John 3, 16.) The insensible earth responds to the efforts of those that cultivate it; wild beasts become tame and domesticated in return for benefits. Men among themselves are beholden to their benefactors; and when such thankful feelings are not forthcoming, they resent it, condemn it, and call it a great offense.

592. What is the reason then, that only toward their God and Redeemer they should be ungrateful and forget what He suffered in order to rescue them from eternal

damnation? And in view of this very evil return, they complain of not receiving his assistance as they desire. In order that they may understand what fearful guilt they load upon themselves by their ingratitude, I will remind thee, my daughter, that Lucifer and his demons, seeing so many souls oblivious of the sufferings of Christ, draw the following conclusions and say of such souls: "This soul does not remember or hold in esteem the benefit of God's Redemption and we are certain of gaining it over to our side; for the soul that is so foolish as not to remember such a blessing, will certainly not detect our wiles. Let us proceed to tempt and destroy it, since it is deprived of its strongest defense." Having in their large experience found their reasoning on this point to be almost infallible, they zealously seek to blot out the memory of the passion and death of Christ and to excite a contempt for the preaching or discoursing about it among men; and they have succeeded to a great extent, causing dreadful damage to souls. On the other hand they are wary and fearful of tempting those who have accustomed themselves to the meditation and the remembrance of the sufferings of Christ; for from this source they feel issuing against them a force and influence, which often prevents them from approaching those who thus piously cherish the memory of the Passion.

593. I desire thee then, my dearest, not to detach from thy bosom and heart this bouquet of myrrh (Cant. 1, 12) and to imitate me closely in the contemplation and the exercises of the Passion. For thus must thou keep alive the memory of the sufferings of my divine Son and satisfy for the injuries and blasphemies inflicted upon his divine Person by his enemies who crucified Him. Seek thou, as long as thou shalt be upon earth, to compensate for the ingratitude and forgetfulness of mortals.

And in order to do it as I desire, never let thy remembrance of Christ crucified, afflicted and blasphemed be extinguished. Persevere in thy exercises, never omiting them except in obedience or in a just cause; for if thou imitate me in this I shall make thee a participant in the effects I myself felt.

594. In order to dispose thyself day by day for holy Communion thou shouldst apply whatever thou performest in these exercises; imitate also the other works and practices, which thou hast come to know of me. If I, the Mother of Him whom I was to receive, deemed myself unworthy of Communion and by so many means sought the purity necessary for such a Sacrament, consider what thou must do, so poor and subject to so many miseries and imperfections! Purify the temple of thy interior, scrutinizing it by the divine light and adorning it with great virtues, since it is the eternal God, whom thou art to receive; One, of whom nobody but Himself is worthy. Invoke the intercession of the angels and saints to obtain grace from the Lord. Above all I exhort thee to call upon me and ask me to help thee; for thou must know, that I am the special Advocate and Protectress of those, who desire to arrive at great purity for receiving holy Communion. Whenever they invoke me for this purpose, I present myself before the throne of the Most High, and, as one well knowing the disposition required for harboring God himself, I ask his favor and grace for those who are about to receive Him in the holy Sacrament. I have not lost in heaven the solicitude and zeal, which I exhibited upon earth. Having asked me, proceed to ask also the intercession of the angels, for they also are very anxious to see souls approach the holy Eucharist with great devotion and purity.

CHAPTER XI.

595. In the eighth chapter I have stated that the Queen of heaven for a thousand, two hundred and sixty days was nourished and maintained in the condition and state described by the Evangelist, as described in the twelfth chapter of the Apocalypse. That number of days made up more or less three and a half years, and brought the most blessed Mary to the sixtieth year of her life plus two months and a few days and the forty-fifth of the Lord. Just as the stone falls the more swiftly the closer it approaches to its centre of gravity, so, in proportion as the great Queen and Mistress of all the creatures advanced toward the end of her most holy life, the more swift became also the flight of her purest spirit and the impulse of her desires to arrive at the centre of her eternal rest and repose. From the moment of her Immaculate Conception She had issued forth like a vast river from the ocean of Divinity, where She was conceived in the eternal ages; and by the inundations of gifts, graces, favors, virtues, merits and holiness, She was now grown in greatness beyond the limited sphere of all creation. The impetuous floods of her wisdom and love resistlessly rushed back to unite themselves with the ocean of the Infinite; for thence She had isued only in order to shed forth over and over again her maternal clemency upon the Church (Eccles. 1, 7).

596. In these last years of her life the great Queen had already, by the violence of her love, begun to suffer a sort of ceaseless martyrdom. Without a doubt it is true in the spiritual order, what philosophers claim in the corporal: that the nearer a moving object approaches its centre of attraction, the more powerfully is it drawn to that centre; and the most blessed Mary had now approached so closely to the infinite and highest Good, that She was divided from It, as is said in the Canticles (Cant. 2, 9), only by the grating or partition of mortality. This did not any more suffice to impede the reciprocal vision and love, and between Them was only the vast force of love, impatient of all hindrances, to complete the union, so that all other desires were swallowed up by the one immense desire of overcoming and doing away with these hindrances. Such was the desire of her divine Son, held back only by his reluctance to deprive his Church of such a Teacher; such was also the desire of the most holy Mother, who, although She restrained Herself from asking for the natural death, could not restrain the forces of her love and thus felt the violence of the constraint of mortal life and of the fetters hindering her flight.

597. Yet as long as the conditions predetermined by the eternal Wisdom had not arrived, She continued to suffer the pains of that love, which is strong as death (Cant. 8, 6). Through them She called upon her Beloved, who came from his retreat from the mountains to dwell in the village of the plains (Cant. 7, 11), to view the flowers and the fragrant fruits of his vineyard. By the darts of her eyes and of her desires She wounded the heart of her Beloved and drew Him from the heights into her presence. Hence it happened once, in the time of which I am going to speak, that the ardors of love

in the most blessed Mother grew to such proportions, that She could truly be said to be languishing with love (Cant. 2, 5); for without being affected by the infirmities of our earthly passions, She languished on account of the impetus of her loving heart drawn toward the Lord, in order that just as He was the cause of her ailment, He might also be its glorious medicine and cure. Her holy angels full of admiration of the effects of their Queen's impetuous love, spoke to Her angelic words in order to soothe her ardors by inspiring her with hope of secure possession. But these remedies allayed not the flame, but rather enkindled it; and the great Lady answered only by conjuring them to tell her Beloved, that She was languishing with love. To Him they brought her message and presented to Him the tokens She desired. On this occasion, and on others of this last part of her life, (as I wish especially to state), were fulfilled in Her, the only and worthy Spouse, the hidden mysteries of the Canticle of Solomon, and so it came, that the supreme princes of heaven, who were present in visible form, were obliged to support Her in their arms on account of the pains of love that overcame Her.

598. Then her divine Son came down from heaven, seated on a throne of glory and surrounded by myriads of angels, who gave Him praise and magnificence. Coming to the most blessed Lady He refreshed and comforted Her in her pains, and said to Her: "My Mother, most beloved and chosen for our delight, the clamors and sighs of thy loving soul have wounded my heart. Come my Dove, come to my celestial fatherland, where thy sorrow shall be turned to delight, thy tears into gladness, and where thou shalt rest from thy sufferings." Immediately the holy angels, at his command, placed the Queen at the side of the Lord, her divine Son, and with celestial music

they all ascended to the empyrean heaven. Mary fell in adoration at the throne of the most holy Trinity. The sacred humanity of Christ kept Her at his side, causing new accidental joy to all the courtiers of heaven and, according to our mode of speaking, exciting anew the attention of all the saints, He presented Her and spoke to the eternal Father, saying:

599. "My Father and eternal God, this is the Woman, that gave Me my human form in her virginal womb, that nourished Me at her breast and sustained labors for Me, that shared in my hardships and co-operated with Me in the works of the Redemption. This is She, who was always most faithful and fulfilled our will acording to our entire pleasure; She, pure and immaculate as my Mother, through her own works, has reached the summit of sanctity according to the measure of the gifts We have communicated to Her; and when She had merited her reward and could have enjoyed it forever, She deprived Herself of it for our glory and returned to attend to the establishment, the government, and instruction of the Church militant; and We, in order that She might live in it for the succor of the faithful, deferred her eternal rest, which She has merited over and over again. In the highest bounty and equity of our Providence it is just, that my Mother should be remunerated for her works of love beyond all other creatures; and toward Her the common law of the other mortals should not apply. If I have merited for all infinite merits and boundless graces, it is proper that my Mother should partake of them above all the others who are so inferior; for She in her conduct corresponds to our liberality and puts no hindrance or obstacle to our infinite power of communicating our treasures and participating them as the Queen and Mistress of all that is created."

600. To these words of the most sacred humanity of Christ the eternal Father replied: "My most beloved Son, in whom I have the plenitude of my pleasure and complacency (Matth. 17, 5): Thou art the First-born and the Head of all the predestined (Rom. 8, 29) and in thy hands I have placed all things (John 3, 35) in order that Thou mayest judge with equity all the nations and generations, and all my creatures (John 5, 22). Distribute my infinite treasures and communicate them as Thou desirest to thy Beloved, who clothed Thee in passible flesh; reward Her according to her dignity and merit, which are so pleasing in our eyes."

601. In accordance with the pleasure of the eternal Father Christ our Savior decreed and as it were pledged Himself to his most blessed Mother, in the presence of all the saints, that from henceforth, as long as She should live in mortal flesh, She should, on every Sunday after finishing her exercises of the Passion, be brought by the holy angels to the empyrean heaven and there, in the presence of the Most High, celebrate in body and soul the joys of the Resurrection. The Lord also decreed, that in her daily Communion He should manifest to Her his most sacred humanity united to the Divinity in a new and wonderful manner, different from that in which She had enjoyed it until that day; so that this might serve as a pledge and foretaste of the glory, which He had reserved for his most holy Mother in eternity. All the blessed understood how just were these manifestations of his glory and greatness in his holy Mother, how well they corresponded to the dignity and holiness of the great Queen, and how well they were merited by her full response to the divine operations in Her. All of them sang new canticles of praise and glory to the Lord, who was so holy, just and wonderful in all these works.

602. Then Christ our God turned to his purest Mother and said: "My most loving Mother, I shall remain with Thee always as long as thy mortal life shall last; and I shall be with Thee in a new manner, so wonderful, as neither men nor angels have known until now. In my presence thou shalt not feel lonely, and where I am, there shall be my reign, in Me shalt Thou rest from thy anxieties; I shall be thy recompense in the narrowed space of thy exile; for Thee the fetters of thy mortal body shall not be irksome and soon shalt Thou be free of them. Until that day comes, I shall be the end of thy afflictions, and I shall release the barriers still opposing thy loving desires. In all this do I give Thee my royal promise." While these promises and favors were lavished upon Her the most Holy Mary was immersed in her ineffable humility, praising, magnifying and thanking the Omnipotent for his beneficent liberality and annihilating Herself in her own estimation. Such a spectacle can neither be described nor understood in this life. For here was to be seen the infinite God freely proclaiming his Mother worthy of assuming the highest place in the estimation of his infinite wisdom, while She, in rivalry with the infinite Power, humiliated Herself, abased and annihilated Herself, though meriting the exaltation She received.

603. Besides all this She was enlightened and renewed in all her faculties, (in the manner explained elsewhere), for the beatific vision. When She was thus prepared, the veil fell, and for some hours, wrapt in the intuitive vision of God, She enjoyed the essential fruition and glory in a manner far above that of the saints. She drank the waters of life from their own fount; She satiated her most burning desires; She reached her centre and rested from that swift motion, which She was again to resume as soon as She was to return from her vision.

After this vision She gave thanks to the most blessed Trinity and again interceded for the Church. Then, entirely refreshed and comforted, the holy angels brought Her back to her oratory. There, as described on other occasions, her body had remained in visible form, in order that She might not be missed by the faithful. On leaving the cloud, in which She had been borne from heaven, She prostrated Herself as usual upon the ground and humiliated Herself for all these favors and benefits more deeply than all the children of Adam ever humiliated themselves for all their sins and miseries. From that time on, as long as She lived, the promise of the Savior in regard to Her was fulfilled; and on all Sundays, after She had done with the exercises of the Passion, at the hour of the Resurrection, all her angels raised Her in a cloud-throne to the empyrean heaven, where Christ, her most Holy Son, came forth to meet Her and unite Her with Himself. The Divinity did not always manifest Itself intuitively; but aside of this, the effects and participation of this visit were glorious beyond human capacity to comprehend. On these occasions the angels were wont to sing that hymn: "Regina Cœli lætare, alleluia;" and these were days of solemn festivity for all the saints, especially for saint Joseph, saint Joachim and Anne, and those more closely connected with Her, as well as for her guardian angels. At these visits She consulted with the Lord about the arduous affairs of the Church, pray for it, particularly for the Apostles, and return to the earth laden with riches like that ship of the merchant, of which Solomon speaks in the thirty-first chapter of the Proverbs.

604. This privilege, although it was a special grace of the Most High, nevertheless was due to the most blessed Mary on two accounts. First because, for the

sake of watching over the Church, She voluntarily deprived Herself of the joys of the beatific vision, and therefore, by the ardors of her love and of seeing God, many times suffered the agonies of death. Hence, in order to preserve her life it was very proper, that She should sometimes enjoy the divine presence; and whatever was possible and proper, was due to the Mother from her Son. Secondly, in renewing every week the memory of the passion of her divine Son, She as it were suffered it on her own Person and died with the Lord: consequently, it was proper that She should rise with Him. As He however was already glorified in heaven, it was reasonable that She should, through his presence, be made a participant in the joy of his Resurrection, and thus reap the fruits of the sorrows and tears She had sown (Ps. 125, 5).

605. With regard to the second privilege, which the Lord promised her, namely, daily Communion, I advert that, up to the time of which I am speaking, the great Queen omitted holy Communion on some days; as for instance during the journey to Ephesus, during some absences of saint John, and on other occasions. Her profound humility induced Her to submit to these omissions, resigning Herself without complaint in obedience to the Apostles; for in all things the great Lady was the model and Mistress of perfection, teaching us self denial also in such things as appear most holy and proper. But the Lord, who seeks his rest in humble souls and above all desired to rest and live in the heart of his Mother for the purpose of frequently renewing his wonders, ordained that from this time on, She should communicate every day for the rest of her life. This will of the Most High, Mary perceived in heaven; but, being most prudent in all her actions, She resolved to wait until it could be

executed in obedience to saint John; for She did all
things as an humble inferior and as a subject of those
by whom She was to be governed in such things.

606. Therefore She did not herself tell saint John of
what She had recognized as the will of God. But it happened one day that the Evangelist was very much taken
up with preaching and he let the hour for Communion
pass. She spoke to her holy angels, asking their advice;
and they answered, that the command of her divine Son
ought to be fulfilled, and that they would inform saint
John and intimate to him this order of his Master. Then
one of the angels manifested himself to saint John where
he was preaching and said: "John, the Most High wishes
that his Mother, our Queen, receive Him sacramentally
every day during her life upon the earth." Thus reminded,
the Evangelist immediately returned to the Cenacle,
where the most blessed Mary was waiting for holy Communion, and said: "My Mother and Lady, the angel
has told me of the command of the Lord, that I administer
his sacramental body to Thee each day without exception." The most blessed Mother answered: "And thou,
Sir: what dost thou command in regard to this?" Saint
John replied: "That the command of thy Son, my Lord,
be fulfilled." And the Queen said: "Behold me ready
to obey in all things as thy servant." From that day on
She received holy Communion every day without exception to the end of her life. Fridays and Saturdays, the
days of her exercises, were not excepted; while on Sundays, instead of holy Communion, She was raised to
the empyrean heavens.

607. At the moment when She received in her heart
the sacramental species, the sacred humanity of Christ
manifested itself through them in the form He had when
He instituted the blessed Sacrament. Although the

Divinity did not manifest Itself in any other than by the abstractive vision now habitual to Her, yet the humanity manifested Itself to Her glorious, much more resplendent and wonderful than at the Transfiguration on mount Tabor. This vision She enjoyed for three consecutive hours after receiving holy Communion, and its effects upon Her were such as cannot be described in words. This was the second reward offered to Her by her divine Son to recompense Her somewhat for the eternal glory, which He had delayed at her own desire. Besides this there was another reason for this wonder: the Lord wished to recompense Himself and counteract beforehand the ingratitude, the lukewarmness and evil disposition, with which the children of Adam were to receive and handle the sacred mystery of the Eucharist during the ages of the Church. If the most blessed Mary had not made up for these shortcomings of creatures, the Lord would have earned no sufficient thanks from his creatures, nor could He have been satisfied with the returns made by men for the institution of this Sacrament.

INSTRUCTION WHICH THE GREAT QUEEN OF THE ANGELS GAVE ME.

608. My daughter, when mortals, having run the short course of their lives, come to the end at which God expects them to merit eternal life, then will they also by their own experience, see the finish of all their errors and deceits. Then the just will see in what consisted their real salvation and happiness, and the reprobate, wherein lay their lamentable and everlasting perdition. O how happy, my daughter, is the man, who during the short instant of his life seeks to anticipate the divine science, which he is so soon to possess by experience! This is

the true wisdom, not to wait for the end until knowing that end, but look to the end in the beginning of the course, and enter upon it, not with so many doubts whether we shall attain the end, but with some security of attaining it. Consider then, with what sentiments those must be animated, who, at the beginning of a race, see a great prize, which they can attain by pressing on their course for a time with great diligence (I Cor. 9, 24). Certainly they will set out with all speed, without turning aside or permitting themselves to be detained by any cause whatsoever. And if they press not on or if they cease to look to the prize at the end of their course, they will be held either as foolish, or as ignorant of what they were losing.

609. Such is mortal life of men, a short course, the end of which shall bring to the runner either eternal glory or everlasting torment as a reward or punishment. All men are born to run this race by the use of their reason and free will; and no one, much less the children of the Church, can plead ignorance as an excuse. Hence, where is the judgment and good sense of those in the Catholic faith? Why does vanity still retain its hold upon them? Why do they ensnare themselves in the love of what is only apparent and deceitful? Why do they ignore the end to which they shall come so soon? Why will they not understand what there awaits them? Do they perhaps not know that they are born but to die (Ps. 138, 49), that life is but momentary, death infallibly certain, the reward or punishment unavoidable and eternal? (II Cor. 4, 17). What can the lovers of this world answer to these questions? Those that consume all of their short life (for even the longest lives are very short), in accumulating honors, or riches, in wasting their strength and powers in the enjoyment of corruptible and most vile pleasures?

610. Alas, my friend, consider how false and treacherous is the world in which thou art born and which thy eyes behold. In it I desire thee to show thyself as my disciple, my follower, a child of my desires, and a fruit of my prayers. Forget it entirely with a heartfelt abhorrence: do not lose sight of the end toward which thou runnest so swiftly, the purpose for which thy Creator formed thee out of nothing; sigh for it continually, and direct toward it thy anxious solicitude; do not permit thyself to be drawn away by the fleeting, vain and deceitful things of the world; let the divine love alone dwell in thee and engage all thy forces; for that is not a true love, which permits any part of them to be diverted to other things, or which does not free them and mortify them entirely from passing things, and subject them to the one great end. Let this love be in thee strong as death (Cant. 8, 6), so that thou mayest be renewed entirely as I desire. Do not hinder the will of my divine Son in all that He wishes to accomplish in thee, and be assured of his fidelity, which rewards a hundredfold (Matth. 19, 29). Keep in mind with humble veneration what He has until now wrought in thee; and I exhort thee and admonish thee to experience in thee anew his truths, as I have commanded thee. For all this continue thy exercises with new solicitude in finishing this history. And give thanks to the Lord for the great and inestimable benefits of his having ordered and disposed thy superiors to permit thee to receive Him daily in holy Communion. Preparing thyself for it in imitation of me, continue also the petitions I have recommended and enjoined upon thee.

CHAPTER XII.

611. All the offices and titles of honor, which the most
blessed Mary held in the Church, that of Queen, Mistress,
Mother, Governess and Teacher, and all the rest, were
given to her by the Omnipotent not as empty and fruitless
names, but were accompanied by the superabundant plenitude of grace which is proper and which the Almighty
can communicate to each. This plenitude consisted in
this, that as Queen She knew all that concerned her reign
and its extent; as Mistress She knew the measure of her
power; as Mother She knew all the children and de-
pendents of her household, without excepting anyone
through all the ages of the Church until the end; as
Governess She knew all that were subject to Her; and as
Teacher, She possessed the wisdom and science through
which the holy Church, by her intercession, was to be
instructed and guided, while enjoying the presence and
the influence of the Holy Ghost until the end of the
world.

612. Hence our great Queen had a clear knowledge
not only of all the saints that preceded or followed Her
in the Church, of their lives, their works, their deaths, and
rewards in heaven; but also of all the rites, ceremonies,
decisions, and festivities of the Church in course of the
ages, and of all the reasons, motives, necessities and

opportunities, in and for which they were established with the assistance of the Holy Ghost. For He gives us our spiritual nourishment in proper time for the glory of the Lord and the increase of the holy Church. As I have spoken of this matter in the course of this history, especially in the second part, I need not repeat it here. From her full knowledge and her corresponding holiness, there arose within the heavenly Instructress a certain thankful eagerness, to introduce into the Church militant the worship, veneration and festivities observed by the holy angels in the triumphant Jerusalem, and thus imitate, as far as was possible, what She had so often seen done in heaven for the praise and glory of the Most High.

613. In this more than seraphic spirit She commenced to practice by Herself many of the ceremonies, rites and exercises, which were afterwards introduced in the Church; and these She also inculcated and impressed upon the Apostles, in order that they might introduce them as far as the circumstances then allowed. She not only invented the exercises of the Passion, of which I have spoken above, but many other customs and ceremonies, which were later on received in the churches, in the congregations and religions. For whatever She knew as pertaining to the worship of the Lord or the practice of virtue, She performed, and in her wisdom She was ignorant of nothing that ought to be known. Among these exercises and rites was the celebration of the feasts of the Lord and of Herself, in order to renew the memory of the benefits for which She stood indebted, as well the benefits relating in general to the human race, as those especially referring to Herself, striving thus to give thanks and adoration for all. Although She had spent her whole life in this pursuit without relaxation or forgetfulness, yet, when She entered upon this new mysterious

phase of her life, She prepared to signalize these feast days by celebrating them with exercises founded on a deeper insight. As I will speak of the other festivals in the following chapters, I will describe here only how She celebrated her Immaculate Conception and Nativity, the first mysteries of her life. These commemorations or feasts She had begun to celebrate since the Incarnation of the Word; but She celebrated them more particularly after the Ascension, and especially in these last years of her life.

614. On the eighth day of December of each year She celebrated her Immaculate Conception with a jubilee and gratitude beyond all human words; for this privilege was for the great Queen of the highest importance and value. She imagined Herself altogether incapable of ever acknowledging it with sufficient gratitude. She commenced her exercises on the evening before and spent the whole night in admirable devotions, shedding tears of joy, humiliating Herself, prostrating Herself, and singing the praises of the Lord. She deeply reflected, that She was formed of the same earth and descended from Adam according to the common order of nature; that She was preserved and exempted from the weight of the same guilt and conceived with such a plenitude of graces and gifts only because She was set apart and snatched from the rest by the Almighty. She invited her own angels to help Her to return proper thanks, and in union with them She alternated new songs of praise. Then She asked the same favor of the rest of the angels and saints in heaven; but during all this time the divine love so inflamed Her, that the Lord was obliged to strengthen Her, lest all her natural forces be consumed and death ensue.

615. After She had spent the whole night in these ex-

ercises, Christ descended from heaven and the angels raised Her to his royal throne in heaven, where the celebration of the feast was continued with new glory and to the accidental joy of the courtiers of the heavenly Jerusalem. There the blessed Mother prostrated Herself and adored the most holy Trinity, again giving thanks for the benefit of her immunity from sin and her Immaculate Conception. Then She again took her place at the right hand of Christ her Son and the Lord himself as it were acknowledged the goodness of the eternal Father in having given Him a Mother so worthy and so full of grace, exempt from the common guilt of Adam. Anew the three divine Persons confirmed upon Her this privilege, as it were ratifying and approving it and pleasing Themselves in thus having distinguished Her among all the creatures. In order to give repeated testimony to this truth, a voice proceeded from the throne in the name of the Father, saying: "Beautiful are thy footsteps, O prince's Daughter, conceived without sin." Another in the name of the Son, said: "Altogether pure and without contact of guilt is my Mother, who gave Me human form to redeem men." And in the name of the Spirit: "All fair art thou, my Spouse, all fair art thou and without stain of the universal guilt."

616. In between these voices were heard the choirs of all the angels and saints, singing in sweetest harmony: "Most holy Mary, conceived without original sin." To all these honors the most prudent Mother answered by thanksgiving, worship and praise of the Most High, rendered with such profound humility that it passed all angelic understanding. In order to conclude the solemnity She was raised to the intuitive and beatific vision of the most holy Trinity; and after enjoying this glory for some hours, She was brought back by the angels to the Cenacle.

This was the manner in which her Immaculate Conception was solemnized after the Ascension of her divine Son. Now this feast is celebrated in a different manner, as I will describe in another book, which I have orders to write concerning the holy Jerusalem, the Church triumphant, if the Lord shall concede this grace to me. This feast and others She began to celebrate from the time of the Incarnation; for finding Herself to be the Mother of God She wished to commemorate the blessings She had received in virtue of this dignity, and therefore in this latter part of her life, She requited them in company with Her holy angels by rendering her worshipful thanksgiving to the Son of God, who had thus favored Her. The other exercises She performed in her oratory on returning from heaven, and they were of the same kind as I have often referred to on occasions of special favors from God; for all of them ever increased Her admirable humility.

617. The feast of her Nativity She celebrated on the eighth of September, on which She was born. She began on the evening before with the same prostrations and canticles as at the feast of her Conception. She gave thanks for having been born to life into the light of this world, and for the favor of having been raised to heaven in the hour of her birth to look upon the Divinity intuitively, as I have narrated in the first part of this history. She resolved anew to spend her whole life in fulfilling the pleasure of the Lord, acknowledging that for this purpose alone it was given to Her. Though in the first beginning and entrance of her life She had advanced in merit as far as the highest saints and seraphim, She resolved now, in its latter part, to begin to labor anew as if She were just beginning the practice of virtue. She asked the Lord to lend Her his assistance,

govern Her in all her actions and lead Her to the highest
end proposed for his glory.

618. As for the rest concerning this feast, although She
was not raised to heaven as on the day of her Conception,
yet her divine Son came down from there with many
choirs of the angels, with the Patriarchs and Prophets,
and with saint Joachim, saint Anne, and saint Joseph.
With this company Christ our Savior descended in order
to celebrate the birthday of his most blessed Mother upon
earth. And this purest of creatures, in the presence of
that celestial company, adored the Lord with wonderful
reverence and worship, and again expressed her thankful
acknowledgment for having been placed upon the earth
and for the benefits connected therewith. Then the angels
imitated Her and sang: "Nativitas tua, Dei Genetrix
Virgo," etc., signifying: Thy birth, O Mother of God,
announced to all the universe a great joy; for of Thee
was born the Sun of justice, Christ our God. The Patriarchs and Prophets sang their hymns of glory and thanksgiving; Adam and Eve also, because in Her was born the
Restorer of their ruin; her parents and her spouse, because they had been blessed with such a Daughter and
Spouse. Then the Lord himself raised the heavenly
Mother from the ground on which She lay prostrate, and
placed Her at his right hand; and straightway new mysteries of the Divinity were manifested to Her. This
vision, although not intuitive but abstractive, afforded
Her a still deeper insight and participation in the Divinity.

619. By these ineffable favors She was transformed,
inflamed and spiritualized to the likeness of her divine
Son in a new and special manner, as if for a new beginning. On these occasions the Evangelist saint John merited some measure of participation in the feast, for he heard

some of the music of the angels and he was privileged to say Mass while the Lord and the angels were present in the oratory, and to communicate the great Queen while Jesus her Son, whom She was receiving sacramentally, was Himself at her side. These spectacles were the source of new joy to the saints, who served at the same time as witnesses to this Communion, more worthy than any ever was seen since Christ lived, or shall ever be seen upon earth. At the moment of Communion her divine Son remained with the great Lady in the sacramental form, while He himself, in his glorious and natural form, ascended to heaven. O hidden marvels of the divine Omnipotence! If the Lord shows Himself wonderful in all his saints, (Ps. 67, 36), how wonderful will He not have been with his exalted Mother, whom He loved above all, and for whom He had reserved the great and special manifestations of his wisdom and power? Let all the creatures confess Him and give Him glory, virtue and magnificence.

INSTRUCTION WHICH THE QUEEN OF THE ANGELS, MOST BLESSED MARY, GAVE ME.

620. My daughter, first of all I wish to enlighten thee concerning certain doubts of thy heart regarding the exalted and extraordinary mysteries of this history. Two misgivings have disturbed thy interior: first, whether thou who knowest thyself to be such an insignificant, useless and ignorant woman, art a fit instrument for recording these mysteries; whether it would not be better to let some other person, more learned and perfect in virtue, write them and thus give them more authority; since thou art the least of all, the most useless and ignorant. Secondly, whether these mysteries, which are so extraordinary and

never heard of, especially the frequent beatific and intuitive visions of the Divinity during my life, shall ever
find credit among those who read of them. To thy first
doubt I answer, that in truth thou art the least and most
useless of all; since thou hast heard it from the mouth
of the Lord and I confirm it. But remember that belief
in this history and in all that it contains, does not depend on the instrument, but on its Author, who is the
highest truth, and upon the contents of thy writing; and
in this regard not even the highest seraph could add
thereto, nor canst thou diminish or omit anything.

621. That an angel should write this history is not
befitting; and if he should, the unbelievers and the sluggish of heart will nevertheless find occasion to slander
him. It is necessary that the instrument be a human
person; but it was not proper that this person be the
most learned or wise; for then this work might be
ascribed to his knowledge and thus occasion the danger
of having the divine light esteemed no higher, or even
lower, than human knowledge, or it might be attributed
entirely to human forethought and industry. It is more
to the glory of God, that this person should be a woman,
who can rely neither on her own knowledge, nor her own
industry. I likewise take special pleasure and honor
from the fact that thou art this instrument; because
thou (and all others) wilt know, that there is nothing
of thy own in this history and that thou must not
attribute more to thyself than to the pen with which
thou writest, since thou art but the instrument in the
hands of the Lord and the repeater of my words. And,
as thou art such, so insignificant and sinful, thou wilt not
be disturbed in seeing mortals refuse to believe; since,
in disbelieving what thou writest, they will not do any
wrong to thee, but by their unbelief fail in proper rever-

ence for my words. Although thy faults and short-comings are many, they can all be neutralized by the charity and kindness of the Lord, who has not looked for any other instrument of this work, but has raised thee from the dust and manifested in thee his liberal power. He has communicated his doctrine by one in whom the power of his truth would appear more plainly; and hence I desire that thou follow it up in thy conduct and reach the perfection thou desirest.

622. In answer to the second misgiving and anxiety, whether the greatness of these mysteries will not prevent belief in what thou writest, I have said many things in the course of this history. Those that take care to attain a worthy concept and appreciation of me, will find no difficulty in believing me; for they will understand the relation and proportion of my privileges to the dignity of Mother of God. They will understand that God's works are perfect; and if any one begins to doubt in these matters, it is certain that he does not know what God is, or what I am. If God has shown Himself so powerful and liberal in the other saints, that many in the Church are held to have seen the Divinity in mortal life, and certainly have seen it, how, or on what grounds can that be denied to me, what is conceded to so many others inferior to me? All that my divine Son merited and did for them, was ordained for his glory, and secondarily in my honor; the end must be held in higher esteem and valuation than the means: hence greater was the divine love, which inclined God to favor me than all the rest, whom He has benefited for my sake. There is no reason for surprise in stating that what He has done sometimes for them, He has done many times for Her, whom He has chosen as his Mother.

623. Let the pious and the prudent keep in mind what

has been taught in the Church, that the measure of the favors I received from the hands of my divine Son, is his Omnipotence and my capacity; for He has conceded to me all the favors which He could confer, and which I was capable of receiving. These graces were in me not barren, but always fruitful to the fullest extent in which it was possible in a creature. The divine Master himself was my Son, powerful to operate as far as the creature placed no obstacle; since I placed no such obstacle, how can any one dare to limit his works of love toward me his Mother, whom He himself had made worthy of his benefits and favors above all the rest of his saints, not one of whom deprived himself, like I have, of his fruition, even an hour, for the sake of helping his Church? And if what He did for me seem much, I desire thee and all the rest to understand, that all his favors were grounded upon and included in the one privilege of my being conceived without sin; for it was a greater favor to make me worthy of his glory, when I could not merit it, than to show me his glory when I had merited it and had placed no hindrance.

624. By these considerations thy doubts will be solved; and as for the rest, let that be my concern, and let it be thine, to follow and imitate me; for as far as thou art concerned, this is the purpose of all thou understandest and writest. This should be thy solicitude, that thou omit the practice of no virtue made known to thee. I wish that thou also attend to what the other saints have done in following my divine Son and me; for thou dost not owe less than they to his mercy, and with none have I been more kind and liberal. In my school I wish thee to learn the love, the gratitude and humility of a true disciple of mine; for I desire thee to distinguish thyself and advance thyself exceedingly. All my festivals thou

shouldst celebrate with a sincere devotion and invite the saints and angels to assist thee therein; especially the feast of the Immaculate Conception, in which I was so highly favored by the divine power and from which I derived so much joy. In these times, more than formerly, I am solicitous of seeing it acknowledged by men and of their praising the Most High for this extraordinary miracle. On the day of thy own birth into the world thou shouldst render special thanks to the Lord in imitation of me and perform some extra work in his service. Above all thou shouldst resolve thenceforth to amend thy life and to commence to labor in this anew. And all the mortals, instead of spending the anniversary of their birth in demonstration of vain earthly joy, should make similar resolutions.

CHAPTER XIII.

625. Gratitude for the benefits received at the hands of
the Lord is a virtue so noble, that by means of it we may
preserve our intercourse and correspondence with God
himself: He, as rich, generous and powerful conferring
upon us his gifts; we, as poor, humble and aware of our
needs, returning for them our thanks. It is natural that
he who gives liberally and generously should be content
with the thanks of him who, as the needy one, is receiving the benefit; and this thankfulness is a short, easy and
delightful return, which satisfies the liberal giver and
induces him to continue his liberality. If this ordinarily
happens among men of generous and magnanimous
heart, how much more in the dealings of God with men;
for we are misery and poverty itself, while He is rich,
most liberal, and if we could imagine any constraint in
Him, it would be that of receiving and not that of giving.
As this great Lord is so wise, just and equitous, He will
never reject us on account of our poverty, but only on
account of our ingratitude. He desires to give us plenti-
fully, but at the same time He wishes us to be grateful,
rendering Him the glory, honor and praise contained in
gratitude. Such a return for small benefits, obliges Him
to confer other greater ones; if we are grateful for all,
He multiplies them. However it is only the humble that
secure them, since they are at the same time thankful.

533

626. The great Teacher of this science was the most blessed Mary; for, though She alone had received the plenitude of highest blessings possible to be communicated to a mere creature by the Almighty, She forgot none of them, nor ever ceased to acknowledge them by the most perfect thankfulness within the powers of a creature. For each one of the gifts of nature or grace, none of which She failed to recognize and acknowledge, She composed special songs of praise and thanksgiving and instituted admirable exercises in special commemoration and acknowledgment. In view of this She had assigned the days of the whole year, and special hours of each day, in which She sought to renew the memory of these graces and give thanks for them. But in the midst of all these observances and solicitudes She forgot not those of the government of the Church, the instruction of the Apostles and disciples, the counsel and advice to be given to the innumerable persons, who came to Her; for She denied Herself to no one who came, nor failed to respond to the needs of any of the faithful.

627. Hence, if due thankfulness obliges God so much and inclines Him to renew and increase his blessings, what human thought can ever conceive how much his beneficence was called into action by the gratitude shown by his most prudent Mother for his many and exalted blessings and rendered to Him with all the fullness of humble love and praise due to each? All we other children of Adam in comparison with Her are slow, ungrateful and so dull of heart, that the little we do (if we do anything at all), does not appear worthy of consideration; but the great things, which the faithful and thankful Queen performed, seemed little to Her, and even when She did all in her power, She held Herself to be remiss and failing in diligence. In another place I said that

the activity of the most blessed Mary resembled that of
God himself, who is a pure act, operative by his very
being or essence, which cannot cease in its infinite activity. Of this quality and excellence of the Divinity our
great Queen had acquired a certain ineffable participation, so that She seemed in Herself to be one continued
and untiring act. If grace is impatient of rest in others,
no one must be surprised, if in Mary, in whom grace
was without measure and, according to our way of
thinking, without known limits, it should partake in such
an exalted degree of God and his activity.

628. I cannot show or elucidate this mystery better
than by referring to the admiration it caused in the
angels, who were witnesses of it. Many times it happened, in their wonder at what they saw in their Queen
and Lady, that they spoke to Her or to each other: "Powerful, great and admirable is God in this Creature more
than in all his works. Vastly does human nature in Her
rise above us. Eternally be blessed and magnified thy
Maker, O Mary; Thou art the ornament and beauty of
all the human race. Thou stirrest to holy emulation all
the angelic spirits, and to admiration all the inhabitants
of heaven. Thou art the wonder of God's omnipotence
and of the power of his right hand, the summary of the
works of the incarnate Word, the exact copy of his perfections, the reproduction of all his actions, assimilating
Thyself entirely to the One Thou hast given form in thy
womb. Thou art a worthy Teacher of the militant
Church, the special glory of the triumphant, the honor of
our people, the restorer of thy own. Let all the nations
know thy virtue and greatness, and let all generations
praise and bless Thee. Amen."

629. With these heavenly princes the most blessed
Mary celebrated the memory of God's blessings and gifts.

She invited them to accompany Her in rendering proper
thanks, not only because of her most ardent and fervent
love, which, on account of the insatiable thirst caused
by the fire of her charity, demanded such a return as of
justice; but also because of her profound humility,
which caused Her to acknowledge her obligations beyond
all other creatures.   Hence She asked all creation to
help Her in paying her debt, although no one but She
could ever pay it worthily.   Filled with this wisdom, She
drew down to her oratory on earth the court of the supreme King and changed the world into a new heaven.

630. On the anniversary of her Presentation in the
temple in commemorating this benefit, She commenced
the evening before and spent the whole night in exercises
of thanksgiving as described for the feast of her Conception and Nativity.   She acknowledged the blessing of
having been called to his temple by the Lord, and to
the house of prayer at such an early age, and of having
received so many favors while residing there.   But the
most remarkable feature of her celebration was, that the
great Mistress of virtue, full of divine wisdom, renewed in her memory the teachings and instructions
given to Her in the temple by the priest and her teacher
at that early age.   With the same loving solicitude She
preserved in her memory the teachings of her holy parents Joachim and Anne, and those of the Apostles.   All
of them She rehearsed and practiced with greater and
greater perfection according as the advancing years of
her life demanded.   Although the teaching of her divine Son were eminently sufficient for all her doings; yet
She recalled those received from all the others; She permitted Herself no cessation in the practice of humility
and obedience, nor ever overlooked the least point or permitted any of the ingenious secrets of these virtues to

be obscured and remain idle. O how highly did She esteem the sayings of the wise! "Lean not upon thy own prudence; be not wise in thy own conceit" (Prov. 3, 5, 7). "Despise not the discourse and the teaching of the presbyters, and live always according to their sayings" (Eccli. 8, 9). "Do not enter into high speculation with yourselves, but conform to the lowly" (Rom. 12, 16).

631. In celebrating this feast the great Lady felt some certain natural regret for the quiet retirement of the temple in her youth, notwithstanding that She had so promptly obeyed the Lord in forsaking it and in resigning Herself to the exalted ends for which He had withdrawn Her. But He did not fail to requite Her by some special favors on this feast. On this day the Lord descended from heaven in great magnificence and in the company of the angels as on other occasions, and addressing his most blessed Mother in her oratory, He said: "My Mother and Dove, come to Me, thy God and thy Son. I wish to afford thee a temple and a habitation more exalted, more secure and godlike, one that is within my own being: come, my most Beloved, to thy legitimate dwelling." At these most sweet words the seraphim raised their Queen from the ground, where She always lay prostrate at his visits until He bade Her rise, and with heavenly music placed Her at the right hand of the Lord. She perceived or felt Herself at once filled with the Divinity as a temple with his glory, and bathed, surrounded and contained as a fish is in the sea, experiencing by this union or contact with the Divinity new and unspeakable effects. For She thereby attained a possession of the Divinity, which I cannot describe and which afforded the heavenly Mother a great delight and joy, additional to that of seeing God face to face.

632. This great favor the prudent Mother called "My exalted refuge and dwelling," and the feast itself She called "The feast of the Being of God"; and She composed wonderful canticles to express its significance and give thanks. At the end of this day She thanked the Almighty for having created the ancient Patriarchs and Prophets, including all from Adam to her natural parents in whom her lineage ended. She thankfully rehearsed all the gifts of grace and nature conferred upon them by the divine power, and for all their prophecies, and for what is recorded of them in the holy Scriptures. Then She turned to her parents Joachim and Anne, and thanked them for having presented Her so young to God in the temple. At the same time, as they were now enjoying the beatific vision in the heavenly Jerusalem, She besought them to thank God in her stead and to ask Him to teach Her how to be thankful and to be governed by Him in all her doings. Above all, She besought them to give thanks to the omnipotent Lord for having exempted Her from original sin and chosen Her as his Mother. These two blessings She always considered inseparable.

633. The feast days of saint Joachim and saint Anne She celebrated almost with the same ceremonies as that of her Presentation. Both of those saints descended with the Lord to her oratory with an innumerable multitude of angels; with them She gave thanks to God for having provided Her with parents so holy and conformable to the divine will, and for the glory which He had conferred upon them. In acknowledgment of all these works of the Lord She composed new hymns with the angels, which they sang to sweet and harmonious music. Besides this, another marvel took place on these festal days of her parents: the angels of the Queen and others who came from on high, divided into choirs, some ex-

plaining to the Queen the attributes or perfections of the Divinity and others those of the incarnate Word. This colloquy afforded Her incomparable joy and new incentive to her loving and inflamed affections. Saint Joachim and Anne derived therefrom also a great additional delight. Before they returned to heaven the great Lady asked their blessing and then remained prostrate upon the ground in thanksgiving for these favors.

634. On the feast of her most chaste and holy spouse Joseph She celebrated her espousal, in which the Lord had given her a most faithful companion to conceal the mysteries of the Incarnation of the Word and to execute with such high wisdom the secret works of the Redemption of man. As all these dealings and eternal counsels of the Most High were recorded in the purest heart of Mary, and as She held them in so worthy contemplation, She commemorated them with ineffable joy and thanksgiving. On this feast, saint Joseph came in the splendor of glory and with myriads of angels, in order to solemnize the feast with joyful music and to sing the new hymns and canticles, which the heavenly Mother composed in thanksgiving for the blessings received by her holy spouse and Herself at the hands of the Most High.

635. After having consumed many hours in this celebration She spent others of that day in conversing with her glorious spouse about the perfection and attributes of God; for in the absence of her Lord the most loving Mother delighted most in such discourses and conferences. On taking leave from her holy spouse, She begged him to pray for Her in the presence of the Divinity and to praise Him in her name. She recommended to his prayers also the necessities of the holy Church and of the Apostles. Then, after asking his blessing, She

continued her acts of humility and thanksgiving as usual, while the glorious saint Joseph returned to heaven. But I wish here to mention two things: first, that on these festivals, while her Son lived upon earth and happened to be present, He was accustomed to show Himself transfigured as He was on Tabor. This favor He showed Her many times, and mostly on these occasions; for by them He repaid Her in a measure for Her devotion and humility and renewed the divine effects consequent upon these marvels. Secondly, that in order to celebrate these favors and blessings, the great Queen, besides what has already been mentioned, added other observances worthy of her piety and of our attention. Namely, on the days spoken of and on others of which I shall speak directly, She gave food to many of the poor, preparing the victuals Herself and serving them with her own hands and on her own knees. For this purpose She directed the Evangelist to gather the most needy and destitute, which he faithfully did according to her orders. Moreover She had more costly food prepared to be sent to the poor sick in the infirmaries whom She could not gather around Her, and afterwards She went in person to console and heal them by her presence. This was the manner in which the most blessed Mary celebrated the festivals and which She taught the faithful to imitate, showing them how to be thankful for all things as far as possible, both by making sacrifices and by good works.

INSTRUCTION WHICH THE QUEEN OF THE ANGELS, MOST BLESSED MARY, GAVE ME.

636. My daughter, the sin of ingratitude is one of the most heinous committed by men against God and by it they make themselves most unworthy and abominable

in the sight of God and the saints. For both God and the saints have a kind of horror of this vile conduct in men. Yet in spite of its pernicious effects, there is none which men, each one in particular, commit more frequently and thoughtlessly. It is true that in order to lessen the debt accumulating by their most ungrateful and universal forgetfulness of his benefits, God requires from his Church a certain recompense for this want of thankfulness in her children and in mankind. For in recognition of his blessings, the Church as such offers up so many prayers and sacrifices of praise and glory as we see ordained in her. But as the favors and graces of his liberal and watchful Providence are not only for the common good of the faithful, but to the advantage of each mortal in particular, the debt of gratitude is not paid by this general thanksgiving of the Church; each one for himself owes thanks for what he receives from the divine liberality.

637. How many are there among the mortals, who during the whole course of their lives have not excited one sincere act of thanksgiving for the gift of life, for its preservation, for health, food, honors, possessions and all the other temporal and natural goods! Others there are, who, if at any time they give thanks for these benefits, do it not because they truly love God, the Giver, but because they love themselves and delight in these temporal and earthly blessings and in the possession of them. This kind of vain deceit discovers itself in two ways: first, in seeking these earthly and transitory goods, men are full of dissatisfaction, haste and discomfort, and they scarcely can think of, ask for, or desire other more spiritual things, loving only what is apparent and passing. Although many times their being deprived of health, honor, possessions and other things is a blessing

of God, which prevents in them a blind and disorderly
attachment to such matters; yet they think it a misfortune and, as it were, an injury, and they allow their
heart continually to verge on destruction by trespassing
upon what is finite and perishable.

638. Secondly, this deceit is known by the forgetfulness of spiritual benefits in the blind pursuit of what is
transitory, so that men neither recognize or acknowledge
what is beyond. This fault among the children of the
Church is most vile and dreadful, since, without any obligation on the part of God and without any of their
merit, the divine mercy seeks to draw them to the secure
path of eternal life, signally applying to them the merits
of the passion and death of my divine Son. Every one
who is now in a state of holiness in the Church, could
have been born in other times and ages, before God came
into the world; moreover he could have been born among
pagans, idolaters, heretics or other infidels, where his
eternal damnation would be unavoidable. Without their
merit God called such persons to his holy faith, giving
them knowledge of the certain truth; justifying them
in Baptism, putting at their disposal the Sacraments, the
ministers, the teachings and enlightenments of eternal
life. He placed them upon the sure path, granted them
his assistance, pardoned them their sins, raised them
from their falls, waited for their repentance, invited them
by his mercy, and rewarded them with a liberal hand.
He defended them through his holy angels, gave them
Himself as a pledge and as a nourishment of eternal life;
and thus He accumulated so many blessings upon them,
that they are without measure or number, and that not
a day nor an hour passes without increasing their indebtedness.

639. Tell me then, daughter, what thanks are due to

his so liberal and fatherly kindness? And how many men deserve to experience it? The greatest blessing of all is that in punishment for this ingratitude the portals of his mercy have not been closed, and the fountains of his goodness have not dried up; for it is infinite. The root of this most dreadful ingratitude in men is the boundless desire and covetousness for the temporal, apparent and transitory goods. From this insatiable thirst grows their unthankfulness; for as they hanker so much after the temporal goods, they undervalue what they receive and give thanks neither for them nor for the spiritual goods; and thus they are most ungrateful as well for the ones as the others. In addition to this unbearable foolishness they are guilty of a still greater one, namely, they ask God not for what is necessary to them, but for things which are injurious and will bring about their eternal perdition. Among men it is considered mean to ask a favor from the one they have offended; and still more outrageous to ask a favor for the purpose of committing a still greater offense. What must we then say of a vile earthly being, an enemy of God, when he petitions his Creator for life, health, honor, possessions and other things, for which he will never give thanks, and which he does not intend to use for any other purpose than to offend the divine Giver?

640. If, in addition to this, such men never thank God for having created them, redeemed them, called them, borne them with patience and justified them, prepared for them the same glory which He enjoys: and if, while expecting this glory, they do not even ask for the grace of acknowledging and repenting of their sins, they certainly show nothing but the utmost temerity and presumption. I assure thee, my dearest, that this so frequent ingratitude toward God is one of the most certain

signs of reprobation in those who are guilty of such forgetfulness and carelessness. It is also a bad sign, when
the just Judge confers temporal blessings upon those
who ask for them in forgetfulness of the blessings of the
Redemption and Justification; for all such, oblivious of
the means of their eternal salvation, demand but the instruments of their death, and to yield to their demands
is no blessing, but a chastisement of their blindness.

641. All these evils I manifest to thee in order that
thou mayest fear them and avoid their causes. But remember that thy gratitude must not be of the ordinary
or common kind; for the blessings thou hast received
go far beyond thy knowledge and power of appreciation.
Do not allow thyself to be deceived into shrinking from
proper acknowledgment of graces on the plea of humility. Thou knowest the efforts of the demon to make
thee forget the works and the favors of the Lord by
drawing thy attention toward thy faults and miseries
and making thee believe that the blessings of truth, which
thou hast received, are incompatible with these thy shortcomings. Begin in earnest to cast off this deception and
know, that the more thou ascribest the goods thou receivest from his bounty to Him alone, the more dost thou
annihilate and humiliate thyself; and that the more thou
owest to Him, the less able thou art to pay thy debts,
since thou canst not pay even for the least of his favors.
To be convinced of this truth is not presumption, but
prudence; and not to acknowledge this indebtedness is
not humility, but most reprehensible foolishness; for
thou canst not be thankful for what thou dost not know;
nor will thy love be stirred to action readily without
being incited by the blessings and favors of God. Thou
art full of fear of losing the grace and friendship of the
Lord; and with good reason dost thou fear, if thou dost

not make them fruitful; for He has done as much for thee, as would suffice to justify many souls. But to have a prudent fear of losing his grace is quite a different thing from doubting it for the purpose of escaping acknowledgment for it; and this is the kind of doubt into which the enemy labors to cast thee, seeking to substitute a stubborn incredulity for holy fear of God, by clothing it in the mantle of a good intention and humility. Thy fear must exert itself in watching over thy treasure and in striving to imitate me with the purity of an angel and practicing all the teachings which I give thee in this history for this very purpose.

CHAPTER XIV.

642. As the most holy Mary was so faithful in smaller things, there can be no doubt that She was faithful in the greater. If She was solicitous and diligent in giving thanks for the minor blessings, certainly She would render the full measure of thanks for the more important benefits conferred by the Most High upon Her and all the human race. Among these the Incarnation of the eternal Word in the womb of the most blessed and pure Mother takes the first place; for this was the most excellent work and the greatest grace possible to God's infinite power and wisdom in his dealings with men. The joining of the divine essence with the human being in the person of the Word through hypostatic union was the beginning of all the gifts and blessings of the Omnipotent conferred upon the human as well as upon the angelic nature. This truth is more intelligible, when we take into consideration what faith teaches: that the divine Wisdom foresaw in eternity the ingratitude of the reprobate and their abuse and waste of the wonderful blessing of the Incarnation of the true God, by which He became the Teacher, Redeemer and model of all the mortals.

643. Hence the infinite Wisdom marvelously provided, that among men there should be some One, who could

compensate this injustice and, by worthy thanksgiving, be the means of placating and satisfying Him as far as is possible on the part of human nature. This was done in the first place by the sacred humanity of our Redeemer and Master, Jesus, who is our Mediator with the eternal Father, reconciling to Him the whole human race (I Tim. 2, 5), satisfying for its shortcomings and paying its debts by the superabundance of his merits. However, as this Lord was true God and man, human nature apparently remained a debtor to Him, unless some one among mere creatures could repay the Redeemer in as far as with the divine grace it was possible to man. This return was made by his own Mother and our Queen; since She alone was the secretary of the great counsel and the archive of his mysteries and sacraments. She was the only one who knew, weighed and thankfully acknowledged it in the measure to be expected from a human being not united personally with the Divinity. She alone supplied a recompense for all the shortcomings and imperfections, and for the total want of gratitude in the children of Adam. She alone knew how and was able to appease and satisfy her divine Son for the unjust behavior of all the mortals in not having received Him as their Redeemer and Master, as the true God made man for the salvation of all.

644. The incomprehensible and sacred mystery of the Incarnation the great Queen kept so constantly present in her memory, that She never forgot it even for one instant. At the same time She was ever conscious of the ignorance of this blessing in so many of the children of Adam; and in order to give thanks for it in her own name and in the name of all, She practiced many genuflections, prostrations and other acts of adoration, repeating continually in diverse variations the following

prayer: "My Lord and highest God, in thy royal presence I prostrate myself and present myself before Thee in my own name and in that of the human race, I bless and magnify Thee, I confess and adore Thee in the mystery of the hypostatic union of the human and divine nature of the eternal Word. If the unfortunate children of Adam are ignorant of this blessing, and if those that know of it fail in giving worthy thanks for it, remember, our kindest Lord and Father, that they live in the weak flesh, so full of darkness and passions, and that they cannot come to Thee, if Thou in thy loving condescension dost not draw them on (John 6, 44). Pardon, my God, the shortcomings of their weak nature and condition. I, thy slave and vile wormlet of the earth, with all the courtiers of thy glory, give Thee thanks for myself and for each one of the mortals in acknowledgment of this blessing. And I beseech Thee, O my Son and Lord, from the bottom of my soul, to take up this cause of thy brethren and obtain for them the forgiveness of thy eternal Father. Favor with thy immense clemency these unfortunates conceived in sin, who do not recognize their own misfortune, and do not know what they are doing nor what they should do. I beg for thy people and for my own; for as far as Thou art man we are all of thy nature, which do not Thou despise; and in as far as Thou art God, Thou givest infinite value to thy works. Let them be the worthy return and thanksgiving for satisfying our debt, since Thou alone canst pay what we have received and what we owe to the eternal Father for sending Thee from heaven to earth as the Savior of the poor and Rescuer of the captives (Luke 4, 18). Give life to the dead, enrich the poor, enlighten the blind (Matth. 11, 5); Thou art our salvation, our happiness and our restoration."

645. This prayer and others like it were of ordinary occurrence in the life of the great Queen of the world. But to her continuous and daily thanksgiving She added other exercises to celebrate the exalted mystery of the Incarnation, especially on the anniversaries of the days in which the divine Word assumed flesh in her purest womb; and on these days She was more favored by the Lord than on others. This feast for Her lasted not only for one day, but for nine, comprising the nine days before the feast of the Annunciation, or the twenty-fifth of March, during which She had prepared Herself for this sacrament, as described in the beginning of the second part of this history. I have there recorded in nine chapters the marvels which preceded the Incarnation and by which the heavenly Mother was to be worthily prepared for the conception of the incarnate Word in her sacred and virginal womb. It is necessary here to refer to them and recall them briefly in order to describe the manner in which She celebrated and renewed her thanksgiving for this highest of marvels and blessings.

646. She commenced the solemnity on the sixteenth of March in the evening and during the next nine days until the twenty-fifth of March, She remained in retirement without eating or sleeping. Saint John the evangelist was the only one who came to Her, and only in order to minister to Her holy Communion during the nine days. The Almighty renewed all the favors and blessings which He had conferred upon Mary during those days immediately preceding the Incarnation; with this difference however, that her Son and our Redeemer now added new ones; for as He was already born of Her, He took it upon Himself to assist, regale and favor his most loving and worthy Mother in this feast. On

the first six days of this novena, after the blessed Mother had passed some hours of the night in her accustomed exercises, the incarnate Word descended from heaven refulgent in glory and majesty and accompanied by myriads of angels; with them He entered the oratory and showed Himself to his most blessed Mother.

647. The most pious and prudent Mother adored her Son and true God with the humility, veneration and worship, such as She alone in her wisdom knew how to render. Then by the ministry of the holy angels She was raised from the earth and placed on the throne at the right hand of her Son the Lord. There She felt within Herself an intimate and ineffable union with the humanity and Divinity, by which She was transformed and filled with glory and new divine influences unspeakable to man. In this condition and state the Lord renewed in Her the marvels of the nine days before the Incarnation in the order in which they had then occurred. And to these He added other favors and admirable effects, conformable to the state attained since then both by Himself and his blessed Mother. Although the habitual science of all things was always preserved in Her, yet on such occasions Her knowledge was enhanced by a new intelligence and divine light, which enabled Her to apply and exercise her knowledge with greater insight and with more powerful effect.

648. On the first of these nine days were shown Her all the works performed by God on the first day of the creation of the world; the order and mode of their creation; the heaven, the earth and the abysses, with their length, breadth and depth; the light and the darkness, their separation and all the conditions, changes and qualities of these material and visible things. Of the invisible things She saw the creation of the angels, all their spe-

cies and perfections, their perseverance in grace, the strife between the obedient and the disobedient, the fall of the apostates and the confirmation of the others in grace, and all the other mysteries, which Moses includes in the works of the first day (Gen. 1, 1). She recognized likewise the intentions of the Almighty in the creation of these and other things: namely to communicate and manifest his Divinity, so that all the angels and men, according to their faculties, might know and praise Him in them. And lest the renewal of this knowledge be fruitless in the most prudent Mother, Her divine Son said to Her: "My Mother and my Dove! I gave thee knowledge of all these works of my infinite power, in order to manifest to thee my greatness before assuming flesh in thy virginal womb, and I renew it in thee now, in order to confirm in thee thy possession and dominion over the angels, the heavens, the earth, the light, and the darkness, all of which shall serve and obey thee as my Mother; and in order to afford thee an occasion worthily to thank and praise the eternal Father for the blessings of creation, which men do not know how to appreciate."

649. The great Queen faithfully responded to this will of the Lord and satisfied for the indebtedness of mankind in its entirety, giving thanks in her own name and in that of all men for these incomparable blessings. In these exercises, and in other mysterious ones, She passed the day until the Lord returned to heaven. On the second day at midnight the Lord again descended in the same manner and recalled in the heavenly Mother the knowledge of the works of the second day of the creation: how in the midst of the waters was formed the firmament, dividing the one from the other, the number of the heavens, their harmonious arrangement, nature and qualities, their greatness and beauty. All this

She knew with infallible certainty, just as they came into being, without admixture of mere opinions; She knew also what were the views of the learned and of authors. On the third day was refreshed in Her the knowledge of what is indicated in the Scriptures for the third day of creation; that the Lord congregated the waters upon the earth and formed the sea and the dry land; and how the dry land, upon the command of its Creator, immediately produced plants, herbs, trees and other things for its beauty and adornment. She knew the nature and qualities of all these plants and the manner in which they are useful or hurtful to man. On the fourth day She recognized particularly the formation of the sun, the moon and the stars of heaven, their material, their form, properties, influences and all their movements, dividing the time into seasons, days and years (Gen. 1, 14). On the fifth day was manifested to Her the creation and generation of the birds of the air, of the fishes of the sea, how in the beginning they were formed of the waters, and how these animals afterwards are reproduced and propagated; how many were the species, the conditions and faculties of the animals of the land and the sea. On the sixth day She received new enlightenment and insight into the creation of man, as the terminus of all the material creatures; and in understanding his exquisite and harmonious nature as a recapitulation of all the rest of the world of creatures, She comprehended also the mystery of the Incarnation, which was the end and purpose of his creation, and She possessed the other secrets of the divine Wisdom hidden in this and the other works, testifying to his infinite greatness and majesty.

650. On each of these days the great Queen composed a special hymn of praise to the Creator for the works

performed on the corresponding day of creation and for the mysteries made known to Her. Then She prayed for all men, especially for the faithful, asking for their reconciliation to God and their enlightenment concerning the Divinity and his works, in order that they might thereby be helped to know, love and praise the Almighty. And as She was aware of the ignorance of so many unbelievers, who would not come to the knowledge and belief of the true faith, and as She considered the ingratitude and sluggishness of so many believers, who know of these works of the Most High, the most blessed Mother performed heroic and admirable works in compensation for these defects of the children of Adam. Because She so faithfully responded, her divine Son raised Her to a new participation in the gifts of his Divinity and attributes, accumulating upon Her all that the rest of mortals lost by their most ungrateful forgetfulness. Over all the works of that day He confirmed upon Her anew full possession and dominion, in order that all might acknowledge Her and serve Her as the Mother of their Creator, and as the supreme Queen over all creatures in heaven and earth.

651. On the seventh day these divine favors were still further increased and enhanced, although her divine Son did not descend from heaven in the last three days; but instead She herself was raised up to Him, in correspondence with what had happened on the three days before the Incarnation. Accordingly at midnight, at the command of the most high Lord, the angels carried Her up to the empyrean heaven, where, while She was adoring the immutable being of God, the supreme seraphim clothed Her in a vestment more pure and white than the snow and more refulgent than the sun. They girded Her with a girdle of jewels so rich and beautiful that

there are none in nature for comparison; each one shone more brilliantly than the globe of the sun, yea of many suns combined. Then they added bracelets and necklaces, and other adornments befitting Her whom they adorned; and all these adornments the seraphim brought from the throne of the most blessed Trinity, each of them in its own way signifying a new participation and communication of the Divinity. And not only these adornments signified a new participation and communication of the divine perfections in their Queen, but also the seraphim, those six that adorned Her, likewise represented mysteries contained in their ministry.

652. To these succeeded six other seraphim who, in another manner, adorned the Queen, as it were, retouching her faculties and giving them subtlety, beauty and grace unspeakable in human words. And still other six seraphim furnished the celestial light by which her understanding and will was made capable of the beatific vision and fruition. Having thus adorned and beautified the great Queen, all of the eighteen seraphim raised Her to the throne of the most blessed Trinity and placed Her at the right hand of the Onlybegotten, our Savior. There She was asked what was her petition and desire. And the true Esther answered: "I ask mercy for my people, O Lord (Esther 7, 3); and in their name and mine I desire and long to thank thy almighty clemency for giving human form to the eternal Word in my womb for their salvation." To these petitions and prayers She added others of incomparable love and wisdom, supplicating for the whole human race and especially for the holy Church.

653. Then her divine Son spoke to the eternal Father and said: "I confess and praise Thee, my Father, and I offer to Thee this creature, the daughter of Adam, pleas-

ing in thy eyes as the one chosen for my Mother from all the creatures and as a testimony to our infinite attributes. She alone knows worthily and fully to estimate and thankfully to acknowledge the favor I have shown to men in vesting Myself in their nature for the purpose of teaching them the way of eternal life and saving them from death. We have chosen Her in order that She might appease our indignation at the ingratitude and small return We receive from mortals. She makes up for what the others are either unable or unwilling to give; and We cannot despise the prayers which our Beloved offers for them in the plenitude of her holiness and entirely to our pleasure."

654. All these marvels were repeated on each of the last three days of the novena; and on the last, which was the twenty-fifth of March, at the hour of the Incarnation, the Divinity manifested Itself to Her intuitively and with a greater glory than to all the blessed. The saints received an addition to their accidental joy on all those days; but the last was one of greater festivity and of extraordinary jubilee for the whole of Jerusalem triumphant. The favors received by the most blessed Mother on that day far exceed all human thought; for all her privileges, graces and gifts were on that day ratified and increased by the Almighty in an ineffable manner. As She was still a Pilgrim and knew all the conditions of the holy Church in the present and the future ages, She asked and merited great blessings for all times; to say it more briefly, She obtained all the blessings which the divine power wrought for men from the beginning and shall work unto the end of the world.

655. On all these feasts celebrated by the great Queen, She obtained the conversion of innumerable souls, which at that time and at succeeding times were to come to

the Catholic faith. On this feast of the Incarnation, however, this privilege was made still more extensive; for on these days She merited for many kingdoms, provinces and nations the blessings and favors they have received in being called to the holy Church. Those that have persevered more faithfully in the Church are so much the greater debtors to the petitions and merits of the heavenly Mother. But it has especially been shown me, that on the day on which She celebrated the Incarnation, She liberated all the souls from purgatory; and that from heaven, where this favor was granted to the Queen of all creation and the Mother of the Redeemer, She sent the angels to bring them to Her in order that She might offer them as the fruit of the Incarnation to the eternal Father. For in that mystery He had sent his Onlybegotten Son to regain for Him the souls from the tyranny of their enemies. For all these souls Mary composed new canticles of praise, and in the jubilee of having thus augmented the heavenly court of heaven She returned to the earth, where She continued her thanksgiving with her accustomed humility. This miracle is not at all incredible, for it is not strange that on the day on which the most holy Mary was raised to the immense dignity of Mother of God and Mistress of all creation, all the treasures of the Divinity should be opened to the children of Adam, her brethren and her children; for on that same day the Divinity itself was poured out on Her, entering her womb and uniting Itself hypostatically with the substance derived from Her. She alone in her wisdom could worthily appreciate this blessing special to Her and for the common good of all.

656. The solemnity of the birth of Christ her Son She celebrated in still another manner. On the evening before She commenced with the exercises, hymns and

other devotions as for the other feasts; and at the hour
of the Birth, her divine Son descended with myriads
of angels and in glorious majesty as on other occasions.
He was accompanied also by the patriarchs saint Joachim,
saint Anne, saint Joseph and saint Elisabeth, the mother
of the Baptist, as well as other saints. Then the angel
at the command of the Lord raised Her from the ground
and placed Her at his divine right hand amid celestial
harmony, rehearsing the hymn of glory as on the day
of Nativity and other canticles, which the Lady herself
had composed in honor of this mystery and in praise of
God's infinite perfections. After having united with
them in these praises for a long time, the heavenly
Mother, with the permission of her Son, descended from
the throne and prostrated Herself anew at his feet. In
this posture She adored Him in the name of all the
human race and thanked Him for his having been born
into the world for their salvation. In addition to this
thanksgiving She prayed most fervently for all men,
especially for the children of the Church, urging the
weakness of human nature, its need of grace and divine
help for raising itself and for meriting eternal life. As
an argument She alleged the mercy of the Lord in being
born for their salvation, the poverty of his Birth, the
labors and hardships it entailed, how He was nursed at
her breast and cherished by Her as his Mother, and
how many were the other works connected with these
mysteries. This prayer was accepted by her Son, our
Savior; and in the presence of all the angels and saints
that accompanied Him, He acknowledged his obligation
to listen to the charitable pleadings of his most blessed
Mother for her people. Again He confirmed Her as
Mistress and Dispenser of all his treasures of grace and
commissioned Her to apply and distribute them to men

according to her pleasure.   This the most prudent Lady
proceeded to do with admirable wisdom and to the immense benefit of the Church.   At the close of this solemnity of the birth of Christ She begged all the saints to
praise the Lord for the mystery of His birth in her
name and for all the other mortals.   She then asked
the blessing of her divine Son, who in giving it, returned
to heaven.

INSTRUCTION WHICH THE GREAT LADY OF THE ANGELS, MOST HOLY MARY, GAVE ME.

657. My daughter and disciple, I desire that thy admiration in writing of the mysteries of my life and holiness induce thee to praise the Omnipotent for his liberality
toward Me; and thy confidence in my powerful intercession and protection should raise thee above thyself.
But if thou art astonished that my divine Son should
thus add grace upon grace and gifts upon gifts, and that
He should visit me so frequently and raise me to his
presence in heaven, remember what thou hast already
recorded concerning my depriving myself of the beatific
vision for the sake of governing the Church.   And even
if this charity had not merited this recompense during
my mortal life, He was ready, on account of my being
his Mother and He my Son, to work such wonders with
me as are beyond created thought and were due to no
other creature.   The dignity of Mother of God so far
exceeds the sphere of all the other creatures, that it would
be base ignorance on the part of men to deny me favors
greater than those bestowed upon other saints.   Taking
human flesh of my substance carried with it such an obligation in the eternal Word, that (according to thy
mode of understanding) God himself could not meet

it, without a return adequate to his Omnipotence and corresponding fully to my capacity of receiving. This power of God is infinite and inexhaustible, and will always remain so; but that which God communicates, is finite and limited. I, too, am a mere created being, and in comparison with the being of God, all created beings are nothing.

658. In addition to this, on my part, I placed no obstacle, but deserved the unlimited and unrestrained liberality of the Omnipotent in all his gifts, graces and favors as far as they could be communicated to a creature. As these, notwithstanding their wonderful greatness, were always finite and the power and essence of God is always infinite and without limit, it can easily be understood how I could accumulate grace upon grace and blessings upon blessings. And not only was I capable of thus receiving, but it was equitable that I should thus receive, in order that I might correspond with entire perfection to his marvelous work of making me the Mother of God; for none of his works remain imperfect or defective. Since this dignity of being made the Mother of God contains all graces as in their origin and fount, therefore, as soon as men know me to be Mother of God, they implicitly also know, as in their cause, the perfections due to such excellence in dignity. It was left to the devotion, piety and good will of the faithful to earn the regard of my divine Son and my protection, by searching properly into my holiness and gifts and by recording and confessing them in evidence of their devotion and my dignity. For this purpose, special knowledge and enlightenment has been given to many saints, to authors and writers, besides special revelations to others concerning some favors and privileges conceded to me by the Almighty.

659. As nevertheless many of the mortals, even the zealous ones, have been timid in this matter, and others, in their want of piety, unduly sluggish, my divine Son has, in his fatherly condescension and at the time most opportune for his holy Church, manifested to them these hidden mysteries, without depending upon human insight and knowledge, but upon the enlightenment of his own truth, in order that they might gather new joy and hope from the knowledge of my privileges, and give to the Almighty new glory and praise for the blessings coming from me and from the works of the Redemption.

660. I wish, my daughter, that thou consider thyself more under this obligation than all the rest of men, since I have chosen thee for my special disciple and daughter, in order that, by the writing of my life, thy heart may be raised to a more ardent and anxious desire to imitate and follow me. The lesson of this chapter for thee should be, that thou follow me in the ineffable thanksgiving for the blessed Mystery of the Incarnation of the Word in my womb. Write in thy heart this marvel of the Omnipotent, in order never to forget it, and signalize especially the days corresponding to the mysteries which thou hast there described. In them and in my name I desire that thou celebrate this festivity with great fervor and joy of thy soul, thanking God in the name of all mortals for his having become incarnate in me for their salvation; and also praising Him for having raised me to the dignity of being his Mother. And remember that nothing ever caused so much astonishment in the saints and angels, who have a knowledge of the infinite essence of God, than to see Him united to the human nature; and, although they continue to understand more and more of this mystery, there will always remain more to find out through all the ages.

661. In order that thou mayest properly renew and celebrate these benefits of the Incarnation and Nativity of my divine Son, thou must try to acquire humility and purity as of an angel; for by these virtues thy thanksgiving will be pleasing to the Lord and by them thou wilt in a measure give some return for his having made Himself of thy nature. Ponder deeply how heavy are the sins of men who, while having Christ as their Brother, fall from such excellence and neglect their obligations. Consider thyself as a portrait or image of the Godman, and that any kind of sin is equivalent to thy despising it and blotting it out of thy soul. This new dignity to which human nature was raised is much forgotten by the children of Adam and they refuse to forsake their old habits and miseries in order to put on Christ (Rom. 13, 14). But thou, my daughter, forget the house of thy father and thy people (Ps. 44, 11), and seek to renew thyself with the beauty of thy Savior, in order that thou mayest be pleasing in the eyes of the supreme King.

CHAPTER XV.

OTHER FEASTDAYS CELEBRATED BY THE MOST BLESSED
MARY IN MEMORY OF THE CIRCUMCISION, THE ADORA-
TION OF THE KINGS, HER PURIFICATION, THE BAP-
TISM OF THE LORD, HIS FAST, THE INSTITUTION OF
BLESSED SACRAMENT, HIS PASSION AND RESURREC-
TION.

662. In renewing the memory of the mysteries of the
life and death of Christ the Savior, our great Queen
sought not only to give worthy thanks for Herself and
for the whole of the human race, in order, as the Teacher
of all holiness and wisdom, to lead the Church to this
holy science of gratitude; but besides fulfilling this debt
of thanks, She also sought to draw down God's infinite
bounty and merciful clemency to meet the weakness and
misery of the human kind. The most prudent Mother
knew that her divine Son and the eternal Father were
much repelled by the sins of mortals, and that at the
tribunal of his mercy they had no other claim than the
infinite charity by which God had lovingly reconciled
them to Him though they were sinners and his enemies
(Rom. 5, 8). As Christ our Savior had accomplished
this reconciliation by his works and the mysteries of
his life and death, the heavenly Lady thought these very
days, on which the works of Christ had been performed,
most convenient and proper for multiplying her prayers
to the Omnipotent, beseeching Him to show his love
for love's sake to call them to his faith and friendship,
and to justify them for no other reason than because

He had himself merited and gained for them justification and life everlasting.

663. Never will either men or angels fully know what a debt the world owes to the maternal piety of this great Lady and Queen. The many favors which She received at the hands of the Almighty each time She was admitted to beatific vision in her mortal flesh, were blessings not only for Her, but also for us; for on those occasions her divine knowledge and charity reached the highest possible degree in a created being and in the same degree did She desire the glory of the Most High in the salvation of the rational creatures. As She was yet in the state of a pilgrim and thus could merit and gain their salvation, her loving anxieties lest souls lose the enjoyment of God overflowed all bounds in her purest heart. Hence She suffered a martyrdom prolonged through her whole life and it would have consumed her vital forces each hour and each instant, if the power of God had not prevented it; for the thought that so many souls should damn themselves and be eternally deprived of the vision and enjoyment of God, and, in addition to this, that they should suffer the eternal torments of hell, without further hope of the remedy which they had despised, was really a martyrdom to Her.

664. This lamentable misfortune caused an immense sorrow to the sweetest Mother, because She alone recognized and weighed it fully in her wisdom. She was filled with a corresponding charity, and would have suffered without any relief, if She had been left only to the influences of her love and merely to the consideration of what the Lord had done and suffered for rescuing men from eternal damnation. But the Lord foresaw and provided against this deadly sorrow in his most faithful Mother; therefore He at times miraculously preserved

her life; at others He withdrew her mind from it by diverse enlightenments; at others again He revealed to Her the secrets of the eternal predestination, in order that her heart might be quieted by seeing into the equity of his divine Justice. All these and other measures were applied by Christ the Savior in order that his most blessed Mother might not die at the sight of the sins and the eternal damnation of the reprobate. And if this unhappy and calamitous fate of sinners as foreseen by the heavenly Lady, could so afflict her purest heart, and if it could so move her divine Son, that He subjected Himself for their salvation to the sufferings and death of the Cross, what words can describe the blind foolishness of those men, who so senselessly rush upon their irreparable and never sufficiently to be dreaded ruin of their souls?

665. But the manner in which our Savior and Master Jesus alleviated the sorrows of his beloved Mother, was by listening to her petitions and prayers for mortals, by showing his appreciation of her love, by offering Her his treasures and infinite merits, by constituting Her his principal almoner, and by consigning into Her hands the free and loving distribution of all the treasures of his mercy and grace, and thus bring succor to the souls whom in her deep science She knew to be in greatest need thereof. These promises of the Lord to his most blessed Mother, as well as the solicitude and prayers of the loving Queen, were of ordinary and constant occurrence; and they were still more notable on the festivals commemorating the mysteries of her divine Son. For the day of the Circumcision She commenced her exercises at the same hour as at the other feasts; and the incarnate Word descended to her oratory with the same majesty and accompanied by the angels and the

saints. As this mystery consisted in his beginning to
shed his blood for men and in his subjecting Himself to
the law of sinners as if He were one of them, the acts
of his most pure Mother in commemoration of that great
condescension and clemency were ineffable.

666. The great Mother humiliated Herself to the lowest depths; She lovingly compassioned the sufferings of
the Child-God in such a tender age; She thanked Him
for this blessing conferred upon all the children of
Adam; She bewailed the universal forgetfulness and
want of appreciation of the blood shed for the rescue
of all. And, as if ashamed in the presence of her divine
Son for not having paid her debts, She offered her own
life and her own blood in satisfaction and in imitation
of her Master's example. She spent that whole day in
sweet converse and colloquy reiterating her desires and
petitions. Yet, though the Lord accepted her offerings,
it was not befitting to let Her actually pay all the sacrifices of her inflamed love. Therefore She added other
inventions of her charity toward the mortals. She besought her divine Son to divide his gifts, caresses and
favors among all the children of men; She begged that
She alone be singled out to suffer for his love; that all
should share in the reward, all should taste the sweetness of the divine Spirit, that all might be induced to
enter the path of eternal life, and none be lost in eternal
death, since their God himself became man and suffered
for the very purpose of drawing all men to Himself
(John 12, 32). Then She offered to the eternal Father
the blood, which his Son shed in the Circumcision and his
humility in allowing Himself to be circumcised in his
sinlessness. After She had thus exercised acts of incomparable perfection and adored Him as true God and
man, her divine Son gave Her his blessing and returned
to the right hand of the eternal Father in heaven.

667. To prepare for the feast of the Magi She began her devotions some days before, in order as it were to get ready some presents to offer to the incarnate Word. The principal offering of the Queen were the souls brought to a state of grace and called by Her the gold. For this purpose to obtain this gift of gold She availed Herself of the services of the holy angels, ordering them to lead numerous souls to the knowledge and belief of the true God by special and powerful inspirations. This result was brought about by their ministry and much more by her own prayers and petitions, so that She drew many from sin, brought others to the faith and to Baptism, and snatched others from the talons of the infernal dragon at the hour of death. To this gift She then added the gift of myrrh, which were her prostrations in the form of a cross, her humiliations, and other exercises of penance, by which She prepared Herself so as to present her own Self as myrrh before her God. Her third offering was the incense of her inflamed and soaring love, her words and ejaculations, and other promptings of her affection, so full of wisdom and sweetness.

668. In order to receive these offerings, her divine Son, on the day and hour of the mystery, descended with innumerable angels and saints. In their presence, and inviting all the courtiers of heaven to assist, She made her offering accompanying it with wonderful adoration, worship and love; and with the offering She combined a fervent prayer for all the mortals. Then She was taken up to the throne of her Son and true God and made to share the glory of his sacred humanity in an ineffable manner. She was divinely united with it and as it were transfigured by its splendors and translucency. A few times, in order to moderate the conflagration of her love, the Lord himself embraced Her and permitted Her to

recline upon his arms. These favors are such as cannot be described in words; for the Omnipotent sought each day to exhaust upon Her the treasures of his blessings, old and new (Matth. 13, 52).

669. After receiving these favors, She descended from the throne and supplicated the Lord for mercy upon mankind. She concluded her petitions by a canticle of praise in the name of all and She asked the saints to accompany Her in all this. On this day also a wonderful thing happened; namely, at the end of this feast She asked all the Patriarchs and Saints present to intercede for Her with the Almighty, that He might assist and govern Her in all his works. For this purpose She went from one to the other repeating her request and as if humbly kissing their hands. Her divine Son, ineffably pleased, permitted Her to exercise her humility also before her parents, and before the Patriarchs and Prophets related to Her. But this demonstration of her humility was not extended to the angels, because they were her ministers and not in the same relations with Her as her holy forebears. These heavenly spirits attended upon Her in another way, namely serving Her in these exercises.

670. Then the Queen celebrated the Baptism of Christ our Lord with magnificent thanksgiving for his submitting to be baptized Himself and thus establishing this Sacrament. After offering her prayers for the Church She withdrew to fast for the forty following days in order to commemorate the fast of the Lord and of Herself after his Baptism, as I have recorded in its place. During these forty days She did not sleep, or eat, or leave her retreat, unless some great necessity of the Church demanded her presence. Her only intercourse was with saint John when receiving holy Communion, or when She was obliged to despatch some business for the

government of the Church. The beloved disciple was also more solicitous in his attendance upon Her, absenting himself rarely from the Cenacle. He relieved the numerous persons who sought help in their necessities, and he cured the sick by applying some article, which had been used by the powerful Queen. Many possessed by demons also came, and some of them were freed before arriving; for the demons dared not linger within the bodies of those that approached the dwelling of most holy Mary. Others of the demons cast themselves into the abyss as soon as the possessed were touched by the cloak, or the veil, or some other article belonging to the Queen. If any of the demons still resisted, the Evangelist called the blessed Lady, at whose presence they fled without waiting for further commands.

671. It would be necessary to write many books, if all the miracles and works of the great Queen during these forty days were to be recorded; for, if She did not sleep, or eat, or rest, who can estimate what She in her great solicitude and activity accomplished during so long a time? It is enough to know, that She applied and offered up all for the increase of the Church, the justification of souls, the conversion of the world, and to assist the Apostles and disciples preaching the Gospel throughout the earth. At the end of this Lent her divine Son regaled Her with a banquet similar to the one brought by the angels to Him at the end of his fast, as I have described in its place. Only this one was more splendid, since at it was present the glorified Savior, full of majesty and accompanied by myriads of angels, some of them serving, others singing in divine and celestial harmonies; and the Lord himself furnished what was eaten by his most blessed Mother. This day was very delightful to Her, more on account of the presence of her divine Son and

his tokens of love, than on account of the exquisite nectars and mannas of heaven. In thanksgiving She prostrated Herself and asked his benediction, adoring the Lord; and He, having given it to Her, returned to the celestial regions. During all these apparitions of the Lord Christ, the pious Mother performed great and heroic acts of humility, submission and veneration, kissing the feet of her Son, acknowledging Herself unworthy of those favors, and asking for new graces in order to serve Him better in the future.

672. Possibly there may be those, who in their human prudence, will consider as rather frequent these apparitions of the Lord, which I have described for so many occasions. But those who think so, will have to show what is the measure of the holiness of the Mistress of grace and virtue and the reciprocal love of such a Mother and Son, and they will be obliged to tell us how far these favors exceed the measure due to the circumstances. They forget, that both faith and reason convince us, that this measure goes far beyond all human estimate. As for myself, the light in which I see these things excludes all doubt, and moreover it should suffice for any one to consider, that each day, each hour and moment, Christ our Savior descends from heaven, wherever in all the world a priest legitimately consecrates the sacred Host in the Mass. I say, that He descends not only by a bodily motion, but by the change of bread and wine into his sacred body and blood. Though this descent happens in a different manner, which I will not gainsay or dispute; yet the holy Catholic faith teaches me, that the same Christ is actually present and remains in the consecrated host. This wonder the Lord performs thus frequently for men and for their welfare, notwithstanding that there are so many unworthy ones, and some even

among those who consecrate. If any one can induce Him to continue this favor, it is no one else than the most blessed Mary, for whom He will do it and for whom He has principally begun to do it, as I have explained elsewhere. Hence it is not astonishing that He should have visited Her personally so many times; since She alone was able and knew how to merit it not only for Herself, but for all the rest of us.

673. After the fast the great Lady celebrated the feast of her Purification and the Presentation of the infant God in the temple. In order that She might make this offering and that God might accept it, the most blessed Trinity appeared in her oratory with his heavenly court. To prepare Her for offering up the incarnate Word, the angels vested and adorned Her with the same garments and jewels, as I have described for the feast of the Incarnation. Then she offered up a comprehensive prayer, in which She supplicated for the whole human race and especially for the Church. The reward for this prayer and for the humility, with which She subjected Herself to the law of the purification as well as for her other exercises, was a new increase of grace, new gifts and favors for Herself, and for others great helps and blessings.

674. The memory of the Passion, the institution of the blessed Sacrament, and of the Resurrection She celebrated not only every week, as described above, but also on the anniversaries of their happening. Each year She observed their commemoration in the manner as is now done in the Church in the Holy Week. Besides the exercises of each week She added many others; and on Good Friday, at the hour in which Christ was crucified, She placed Herself upon a cross and there remained for three hours. She renewed all the prayers of the Lord, with all

the sorrows and mysteries of that day. But on the following Sunday, which corresponds to the Resurrection, She was raised by the holy angels to the empyrean heavens where during that day She enjoyed the beatific vision, while on the ordinary Sundays her vision of the Godhead was abstractive.

INSTRUCTION WHICH THE QUEEN OF THE ANGELS GAVE ME.

675. My daughter, the divine Spirit, whose wisdom and prudence governs the holy Church, through my intercession has ordained, that in it so many different feasts should be celebrated, not only in order that proper thanks should be given to the Creator and Redeemer for the works of the Redemption, of my life, and of the saints, and that the blessings, which never can be properly repaid, may not be forgotten by mankind; but also in order that these solemnities might afford men an opportunity of attending to holy exercises and of recollecting themselves interiorly by withdrawing from the solicitudes of temporal affairs; and in order that they might, by the exercise of virtue and the good use of the Sacraments, repair the losses sustained by their distractions, imitate the virtues and the lives of the saints, solicit my intercession, merit the forgiveness of their sins and gain the graces and favors held in readiness by the divine mercy in these mysteries.

676. This is the spirit of the holy Church, by which She desires to govern and nourish her children as a devoted mother. And I, who am Mother of them all, sought to attract and bind them to the secure path of their salvation. But the insinuations of the infernal serpent have always (and especially in the unhappy

times in which thou livest) tended to pervert these holy ends of the Lord and mine, and when he cannot pervert the order of the holy Church, he exerts himself to prevent the greater part of the faithful from being benefited by her institutions and strives to induce many to convert them into greater guilt for their condemnation. And the same demon will stand as their accuser at the tribunal of the divine justice; for on the days of greatest solemnity and festivity men not only fail to enter into the spirit of the Church by employing them in works of virtue and in worship of their God; but just on those days they commit the most grievous sins, as is ordinarily the case with carnal and worldly men. Certainly most outrageous and reprehensible is the common forgetfulness and contempt of this duty in the children of the Church, when they profane the sacred and holy days by spending them in diversion and play, in excessive and disorderly eating and drinking, irritating the justice of the Almighty instead of appeasing Him, in succumbing to their invisible enemies instead of vanquishing them, and in permitting them to triumph in their pride and malice.

677. Do thou, my daughter, bewail this damage, since I cannot bewail it now in the same way as I have done it in mortal life; and exert thyself to assist thy brethren in overcoming this widespread carelessness. And although the life of the religious should differ from that of seculars so as to have no distinction of days and to apply every day for the divine worship, for prayer and holy exercises, as thou shouldst teach thy subjects; yet I desire thee to celebrate with them the feasts of the Lord and mine by a more careful preparation and purity of conscience. I wish thee to fill all thy days and thy nights with works holy and pleasing in the sight of the Lord; but on the festivals thou shouldst add other interior and

exterior exercises. Excite the fervor of thy heart,
recollect thyself, and if it seems to thee that thou art
doing much, labor still more earnestly to make certain
thy vocation and election (II Pet. 1, 10), nor ever omit
any exercise out of negligence. Consider that the days
are evil (Ephes. 5, 6), and that life disappears like a
dream (Ps. 143, 4). Live very carefully in order that
thou mayest not be found without merit, holy deeds and
perfect works. To each hour assign its legitimate occupation, as thou hast seen me do it, and as I have many
times admonished and taught thee.

678. For this purpose I exhort thee to live attentive to
the divine inspirations and amid all the other blessings
not to forget those contained in such enlightenments. Let
thy care be such, that no virtuous act or greater perfection, which is possible to thee and comes to thy notice,
remain unexecuted.   I assure thee, my dearest, that
through their negligence and forgetfulness mortals lose
immense treasures of grace and glory. All the perfection
that I knew of my divine Son when I lived with Him, I
imitated, and whatever the Holy Ghost pointed out to
me as being most perfect, I executed as thou hast seen.
This anxious solicitude was as natural to me as to
breathe; and through it I induced my divine Son to show
me so many favors and visit me so often during my
mortal life.

679. I desire likewise that, in order that thou and thy
religious may imitate me in my retirement and solicitude,
thou establish the manner in which the customary retreat
is to be conducted; and that those who make it should
live retired during the days appointed for it in holy obedience.   Thou knowest from experience, what fruit is
gathered in these retreats, since in it thou hast written
nearly the whole of my life; and in this solitude the Lord

visited thee with greater blessings and favors for the betterment of thy own life and the conquering of thy enemies. In order that thy religious may understand how they must conduct themselves in the exercises of the retreat for their greater profit and advancement, I wish that thou write for them a special treatise, in which thou wilt assign all their occupations to certain hours and times. These should be arranged in such a way, that the one who is in retreat does not miss the community exercises; for conformity to them is an obligation superseding all the particular ones. As for the rest, those in retreat should observe perfect silence and go about veiled, in order that they may be known as making the retreat and not spoken to by any of the others. Let none be deprived of this benefit on account of their office and let their duties be assigned to others in obedience. Ask enlightenment of the Lord for writing this treatise, and I shall assist thee to understand more thoroughly my practices in retirement, in order that thou mayest teach it to the others.

CHAPTER XVI.

680. In each one of the works and mysteries of our
great Queen and Lady are found new secrets to penetrate
and new reasons for wonder and praise; but I am running short of new words to make known what I see. From
what I have been made to understand concerning the
love of Christ our Lord for his purest Mother and most
worthy Spouse, it seems to me, that for the sake of this
love, the Lord would have resigned his throne of glory
and the company of the saints to be with his most beloved Mother, if other reasons had not demanded his
presence in heaven and that of the Virgin upon earth
during the time of her separation and bodily absence.
But let no one say that this high opinion of the excellence
of the Queen derogates from that of her divine Son or
the saints; for the Divinity of the Father and the Holy
Ghost was in Christ in its highest individual unity; the
three Persons exist in each one in an inseparable manner,
and the Person of the Word cannot exist without the
Father and the Holy Ghost. It is certain, that the company of the angels was less than that of his most holy
Mother in the eyes of her divine Son; that is, considering
the force of reciprocal love between Christ and his purest
Mother. But for other reasons it was befitting, that the

Lord, after accomplishing the Redemption of man, should return to the right hand of the Father, and that his most blessed Mother should remain in the Church, so that, through her industry and merits, the efficacy of the Redemption should be proved and that She should bring forth to light the fruit of the passion and death of her divine Son.

681. With ineffable and mysterious providence Christ our Savior arranged his works, showing in them his divine wisdom, magnificence and glory, confiding entirely in this strong Woman, as described by Solomon (Prov. 31, 11). And his confidence was not frustrated, since the most prudent Mother, by uniting her own solicitude and merits with his passion and blood, purchased for her Son the field in which She planted the vines of the Church. These were the souls of the faithful, propagated in the Church on earth, and of the predestined, in whom the Church was to be transplanted to the triumphant Jerusalem forever and forever. If it was befitting the glory of the Most High, that all this great work should be entrusted to Mary, in order that our Savior Jesus might enter into the glory of his Father after his glorious Resurrection, then it was also no more than just that, as far as was possible, He should keep up his intercourse with his most blessed Mother, whom He had left in the world and whom He loved without measure. To this He was held not only by his own love toward his Mother, but by her state and the task imposed upon Her during her sojourn on earth, where the grace, the means, the favors and blessings must necessarily be in proportion with the origin and the end of those hidden mysteries. All these requirements were gloriously fulfilled by the frequent visits of the Son to his Mother and by her being raised to the throne of his glory. Thus, neither would

the invincible Queen be totally deprived of her court, nor
would the courtiers for so many years be deprived of the
delightful sight of their Queen and Lady. Hence as
this delight was possible, it was proper that all those concerned should also enjoy it.

682. One of the days (in addition to those already
mentioned) on which the celestial wonders were renewed, was that on which She celebrated each year the
Ascension of her divine Son. This day was a great festival for Her and for all heaven. She prepared for it
during forty days from the day on which She solemnized
the Resurrection of her Son. During all this time She
renewed the memory of the favors and blessings She
had received from her divine Son, and of the glorious
company of the ancient Patriarchs and Saints delivered
from limbo; and of all that had transpired day after day
during those forty days, giving thanks in new hymns
and devotions, as if they were again transpiring before
Her; for all these events were indelibly impressed upon
her memory. I will not enter upon the particulars of what
She did during those times, because I have written about
them sufficiently in the last chapters of the second part.
I will say only, that during this preparation our great
Queen received incomparable favors and experienced new
influences of the Divinity, by which She was made ever
more and more godlike and prepared for the extraordinary favors She was to receive on the feast itself.

683. On the mysterious day on which our Savior Jesus
ascended into heaven, He came down in person to the
oratory of his most blessed Mother, accompanied by innumerable angels and by the Patriarchs and Saints He had
taken up with Him to heaven. The great Lady awaited
his visit, prostrate upon the ground as usual and annihilated in the utmost self-debasement of her ineffable

humility; yet, at the same time, being elevated above all
human and angelic thought to the highest pinnacle of love
possible to a mere creature. Then her divine Son manifested Himself amidst the choirs of saints, and renewing
in Her the sweetness of his blessings, He commanded the
angels to raise Her from the dust and place Her at his
right hand. Executing this command, the seraphim
placed Her, who had given Him human existence, on the
throne of the Lord. Thereupon He asked Her, what
was her request and her desire. To this the most blessed
Mary answered: "My Son and eternal God, I desire the
glory and exaltation of thy holy name; in it I wish to
render Thee thanks for the whole human race, and
acknowledge the blessings of having on this day, through
thy almighty power, raised our nature to eternal glory
and felicity. I beg that all men may know, praise and
magnify thy Divinity and most sacred humanity."

684. The Lord answered: "My Mother and Dove,
chosen from amongst all creatures for my habitation,
come with Me to my celestial country, where thy desires
shall be fulfilled, thy petitions granted, and where Thou
mayest enjoy the solemnity of this day, not among the
mortal children of Adam, but among my courtiers and
among my inhabitants of heaven." Immediately that
whole celestial procession traversed the regions of the
air, as had happened on the day of the Ascension, and,
the Virgin Mother always remaining at the right hand of
her Son, reached the empyrean heavens. But on arriving at the highest place, the whole celestial company
arranged themselves in choirs, and not only they and all
heaven, but the Holy of the holy Himself, were so to
say, wrapped in a new kind of silence and attention. Then
the Queen asked permission of the Lord to descend from
the throne and, prostrate before the footstool of the most

blessed Trinity, sang an admirable song of praise, in which She included the mysteries of the Incarnation and Redemption with all the triumphs and victories of her divine Son up to his glorious Ascension to the right hand of his eternal Father.

685. The Most High manifested his pleasure and complacence at this hymn of praise and all the saints responded with songs of glory, extolling the Omnipotent in this wonderful Creature and being filled with new joy by the presence and exaltation of their Queen. Then, at the command of the Most High, the angels again placed Her at the right hand of her divine Son, and having as on other occasions, been illumined and adorned for the purpose, She looked upon the Divinity in glorious and intuitive vision. In this beatific vision the Queen spent part of the day and during it, the Lord again confirmed upon Her the possession of that place, which from all eternity He had destined for Her and which was mentioned on the day of the Ascension. For our greater admiration and obligation I advert, that each year on that day the Lord himself asked Her, whether She would prefer to remain in that eternal joy forever, or return again to the earth for the benefit of the Church. The decision being thus left entirely in her hands, She answered: that if it was the will of the Almighty, She would return to labor for men, who were the fruit of the Redemption and of the death of the Son of God.

686. This answer so full of resignation, repeated each year, was just as often accepted by the most holy Trinity to the wonder of all the blessed. Thus, not only once, but many times, did the heavenly Mother deprive Herself of the beatific vision, descending for a new period of time to the world in order to direct the Church and enrich it with her incomparable merits. And since the

proper appreciation of these merits can never be reached by our curtailed faculties, it will be no blemish in this history not to attempt an estimate of them and defer it until we shall reach the vision of God. But the rewards corresponding to these sacrifices were reserved for Her according to the divine pleasure, in order that afterwards, in the possession of the beatific vision, She might as much as possible be like to the most sacred humanity of her Son and worthily take her place on the throne at his right hand. As a sequence to these happenings in heaven, the great Queen added her prayers for the exaltation of God's name, for the propagation of the Church, for the conversion of the world and the victories over the devil; and all her petitions were granted, and successively executed in their time and will be executed in all the ages of the Church. These favors would be greater, if the sinners of the world would not hinder them and make mortals unworthy of receiving them. Thereupon the angels brought back their Queen to her oratory in the Cenacle amid celestial music and harmony, and She prostrated Herself in deepest humility to give thanks for these new favors. I wish to mention, that the evangelist saint John had some knowledge of these mysteries and participated in some of their effects; for he usually saw the Queen so refulgent with heavenly light, that he could not look upon her face. As the great Mistress of humility always humbled Herself to the very ground and often asked his consent kneeling at his feet, he was often seized by a reverential fear and disquiet in the presence of the Lady, though it was always mixed with a wonderful joy and incitement to holiness.

687. The great Queen availed Herself of the effects and blessings of the festivity of the Ascension in order to celebrate more solemnly the coming of the Holy Ghost,

and by means of them She prepared Herself for it during the nine days that intervene. She continued without intermission her holy exercises, exciting the most ardent desires for the renewal of the gifts of the divine Spirit in Her. When the day arrived these desires were fulfilled with manifestations of an almighty power; for at the same hour in which He had descended the first time upon the apostolic college in the Cenacle, He descended each year upon the Mother of Jesus, the Spouse and the temple of the Holy Ghost; and although this coming was not less solemn than the first, for He came in the form of visible fire of a wonderful brightness and with a mysterious noise, yet these signs were not manifest to all, as had happened at the first coming. At that first time this was necessary, but afterwards it was not proper that any one except the most blessed Mary, and to a certain extent, saint John, should know of this miracle. Myriads of angels attended upon Her at such times singing the canticles of the Lord in sweetest harmony; and the Holy Ghost entirely inflamed and renewed Her with superabundant gifts and increase of the blessings She already possessed. Then the great Lady gave humble thanks not only for this favor, but because He had filled the Apostles with wisdom and charismatic gifts, to make them worthy ministers of the Lord and founders of his holy Church, and because through his coming He had sealed the works of the human Redemption. In a prolonged prayer She then asked the divine Spirit to continue the influences of his grace and wisdom through the present and the future ages, and not to suspend it on account of the sins and unworthiness of men at any time. All these petitions the Holy Ghost granted to his only Spouse, and the holy Church is now reaping the fruit of them and shall enjoy them until the end of the world.

688. To these mysterious celebrations of the feas s of
the Lord and of Herself, the great Queen, in the course
of the year, added others for her especial jubilee and
devotion: namely, one in honor of the holy angels, and one
in that of the saints. In order to celebrate the excellences
and holiness of the angelic nature She prepared herself
for some days by exercises such as mentioned for some of
the other feasts, adding new songs of glory and praise
and retracing in them the work of the creation of the
angels, and especially their justification and glorification
with all the mysteries and secrets known to Her of all
of them and of each one in particular. When the day
She had assigned for this feast arrived, She invited them
all. Many thousands of the celestial choirs and orders
descended and manifested themselves in wonderful beauty
and glory in her oratory. Then, forming two choirs, one
of which was our Queen and the other all the supernal
spirits, the Lady and the angels sang songs of celestial
harmony in alternate verses during that entire day. If it
were possible to make known to the world the mysterious
canticles composed on those days by the most blessed
Lady and the angels, they would no doubt be reckoned
among the great miracles of the Lord and astonish all
the mortals. I cannot find words nor time to describe
what I have come to know concerning this mystery; for
they began by praising the essence of God in Himself, and
in all his perfections and attributes known to them. Then
the Queen proceeded to bless and magnify Him for having manifested his Majesty, Wisdom and Omnipotence in
the creation of so many and beautiful spiritual beings;
for having favored them with so many gifts of nature
and grace, and appointed them as ministers and executors
of his will in the government of men and of all the lower
and visible creation. The angels on their part responded

by due and thankful acknowledgment of their obligation, and all of them sang to the Almighty wonderful songs of praise for having created and chosen for his Mother a Virgin so pure, so holy, so worthy of his greatest gifts and given Her command and dominion over all, in order that they might proclaim and honor Her as the worthy Mother of God and Restoratrix of the human race.

689. In this manner the supernal spirits rehearsed the great prerogatives of their Queen and blessed God in Her; while She recounted those of the angels for the same purpose. Hence, this day was one of admirable joy and jubilee to the Queen, and of accidental joy to the angels, especially to the thousand of her ordinary guard; for they participated in the glory given to their Lady and Queen. As neither on the one side, nor on the other, there was the obstacle of ignorance, nor any want of the appreciation of the mysteries rehearsed, this interchange of heavenly songs was full of incomparable reverence. And such it shall also be for us, when we shall experience it in the Lord.

690. The other festival in the course of the year was that of the Saints. For this also She prepared Herself with many prayers and exercises of devotion as on other festivals. All the Patriarchs, Prophets and the rest of the Saints, also those who had died after the Resurrection, came from heaven in order to celebrate with their Reparatrix this joyful day. She composed new canticles of thanksgiving for the glory of the saints and efficacy of the death of her divine Son. Great was the jubilee of the Queen on this occasion, because She knew the secret of their predestination, and because, in spite of the dangers of mortal life, they had now attained secure and eternal felicity. For this blessing She extolled the Lord and Father of mercies and rehearsed in her thanksgiving the

favors, graces and benefits, which each of the saints had received at his hands. She asked them to intercede for the holy Church, and for all those who were fighting its battles and were still encountering the danger of losing the crown. After this She remembered also and gave thanks for the victories and triumphs She herself had attained through the divine power over the demons. Finally She added new canticles of humble and fervent thanksgiving for Herself, and for all the souls to be snatched from the powers of darkness.

691. It is a subject of astonishment to men, as it was to the angels, that a mere Creature in mortal flesh should accomplish so many incessant wonders, which would have appeared impossible to multitudes of souls united together, even if they had been as ardent as the highest seraphim; but our great Queen certainly participated in something of the omnipotence of God, which made easy for Her what for other creatures would have been impossible. In these last years of her most holy life her activity increased to such an extent, that there was no cessation or relaxation in her operations so as to exceed all our powers of comprehension; for She was not any more hindered by the mortality and weight of human nature, but operated like the indefatigable spirits, and more than all of them together; and She had become one devouring flame and conflagration of immense activity. To her divine virtues all her days seemed short, all occasions few, and all her exercises limited; since her divine love continually tended to exceed all bounds of what She was doing, though that was without limit. In comparison with what her activity was in reality, all I have said is little or nothing: I am bound to confess and assert my deficiency in this regard, because I see an abyss or distance as it were infinite between what has been

shown to me and what I am capable of understanding in
this life. And if I cannot form an idea of what has been
manifested to me, how shall I speak of that which I saw
not, since I have no gage except my own ignorance? Let
us beware lest we make ourselves unworthy of the light,
which awaits us in heaven for seeing all in God; for this
reward and joy by themselves, even if we receive no
other, should make us willing to endure all the labor,
pains and torments of the martyrs to the end of the
world. We would be richly repaid by the delight of understanding the dignity and excellence of most holy
Mary, seated at the right hand of her Son and true God
and raised above all the angels and saints of heaven.

INSTRUCTION WHICH THE GREAT QUEEN OF THE ANGELS GAVE ME.

692. My daughter, in the measure as thou advancest
in the history of my works and life, I desire that thou
also advance in the perfect following and imitation of
me. This desire increases in me in proportion to the
growth of thy enlightenment and admiration of what
thou seest and writest. It is now time that thou make up
for what thou hast so far missed and that thou wing the
flight of thy spirit to the heights, to which the Almighty
calls thee and to which I invite thee. Fill thy works with
all perfection and sanctity; remember that the opposition
of thy enemies, the devil, the world and the flesh is most
hateful and cruel; and that thou canst not overcome so
many difficulties and temptations, if thou do not enkindle
thy heart with the most ardent fervor and the emulation
invincibly to repel and crush the poisonous serpent, which,
with diabolical astuteness, avails itself of many deceits,
either to cause thy fall or to detain thee in thy course,

prevent thee from gaining thy end, and make thee unfit for the state chosen for thee by the Lord.

693. Thou must not ignore, my daughter, that the demon keeps a constant minute watch over the least carelessness, forgetfulness or inadvertence of souls, and that he is constantly prowling around and lying in ambush to avail himself of every negligence for tempting the incautious to sin and misleading them by means of their passions before they have a chance to know the full extent of the wound he tries to inflict. When afterwards they come to know it and desire to rise from their fall, they feel still greater difficulty and need much more abundant graces and efforts to resist the evil than before they fell. In guilt the soul weakens in virtue, the enemy acquires more influence, and the passions tend to become indomitable and invincible; hence many fall, but not so many rise from their sins. The remedy against these dangers is to live in continual and unremitting anxiousness to merit the divine grace, in ceaseless striving to do the more perfect, not giving the enemy any chance to find the soul off its guard or unoccupied with some exercise or work of virtue. Thereby the weight of the lower human nature will be lightened, the passions and bad inclinations will be crushed, the demon intimidated, the soul will be raised up and will gain strength against the flesh and dominion over the inferior and sensitive faculties, subjecting them to the divine will.

694. In all this thou wilt have a living example in my works, of which thou now writest and which thou hast seen manifested in such great light in order that thou mayest not forget them. Attend then, my dearest, to all that thou seest in this clear mirror; and if thou knowest and confessest me as thy Teacher and thy Mother and as the Mistress of all holiness and true perfection, do not

delay in imitating me and following me. It is not possible that either thou or any other creature arrive at the perfection and excellence of my works, nor does the Lord bind any one to that; but with his divine grace thou canst fill thy life with works of virtue and holiness, and spend in them all thy time and all thy faculties; so that, adding exercise to exercise, prayer to prayer, petition to petition, virtue to virtue, thou let no time, no day, no hour of thy life be bare of good works learned of me. For this purpose I joined other works with those necessary for the government of the Church, and celebrated the festivals in the manner and with the preparations thou hast come to know and describe. As soon as one was solemnized, I began to prepare me for another, so that not for one moment was my life void of works holy and pleasing in the sight of the Lord. All the children of the Church, if they wish, can imitate me and thou shouldst do it more zealously than the others. This is the purpose for which the Holy Ghost ordained the solemnities and commemorations of my divine Son and of myself and of the saints recurring in the holy Church.

695. As I have exhorted thee many times, I wish that thou distinguish thyself by their devout celebration, especially by the celebration of the mysteries of the Divinity and humanity of my divine Son, those of my life and of my glory. Then I desire in thee a special devotion to the angels, as well on account of their great excellence, holiness, beauty and ministry, as also on account of the great favors and blessings thou hast received through these celestial spirits. I desire that thou assimilate thyself to them in purity of thy soul, in the exaltedness of thy thought, in the fervor of thy love, and in living as if thou hadst neither an earthly body nor its passions. They are to be thy friends and companions in thy pil-

grimage, in order that they may be such also in the Fatherland. With them thou shouldst now maintain conversation and familiar intercourse, in which they will show thee the attributes and the tokens of thy Spouse, give thee certain knowledge of his perfections, lead thee to the straight ways of justice and of peace, defend thee from the demon, warn thee of his deceits. In the continued teaching of these spirits and ministers of the Most High thou shalt hear the laws of divine love. Hear and obey them exactly.

CHAPTER XVII.

696. In writing of what still remains of the history of
our Lady, of our only and heavenly Phœnix, the most
blessed Mary, it is no more than right that our hearts be
filled with tenderness and our eyes with tears at the sweet
and touching marvels of the last years of her life. I
should wish to exhort the devout faithful not to read of
them nor consider them as past and absent, since the
powerful virtue of faith can make these truths present
to the mind; and if we look upon them with the proper
piety and Christian devotion, without a doubt we shall
gather the sweetest fruit, and our hearts shall feel the
effects and rejoice in the good, which our eyes cannot see.

697. The most holy Mary had arrived at the age of
sixty-seven years without having tarried in her career,
ceased in her flight, mitigated the flame of her love, or
lessened the increase of her merits from the first instant
of her Conception. As all this had continued to grow
in each moment of her life, the ineffable gifts, benefits and
favors of the Lord had made Her entirely godlike and
spiritual; the affectionate ardors and desires of her most
chaste heart did not allow Her any rest outside the centre
of her love; the bounds of the flesh were most violently
irksome; the overwhelming attraction of the Divinity to
unite Itself with Her with eternal and most close bonds,

(according to our mode of speaking) had attained the summit of power in Her; and the earth itself, made unworthy by the sins of mortals to contain the Treasure of heaven, could no longer bear the strain of withholding Her from her true Lord. The eternal Father desired his only and true Daughter; the Son his beloved and most loving Mother; and the Holy Ghost the embraces of his most beautiful Spouse. The angels longed for their Queen, the saints for their great Lady; and all the heavens mutely awaited the presence of their Empress who should fill them with glory, with her beauty and delight. All that could be alleged in favor of Her still remaining in the world and in the Church, was the need of such a Mother and Mistress, and the love, which God himself had for the miserable children of Adam.

698. But as some term and end was to be placed to the earthly career of our Queen, the divine consistory (according to our mode of understanding), conferred upon the manner of glorifying the most blessed Mother and established the kind of loving reward due to Her for having so copiously fulfilled all the designs of the divine mercy among the children of Adam during the many years in which She had been the Foundress and Teacher of his holy Church. The Almighty therefore resolved to delight and console Her by giving Her definite notice of the term still remaining of her life and revealing to Her the day and hour of the longed for end of her earthly banishment. For this purpose the most blessed Trinity despatched the archangel Gabriel with many others of the celestial hierarchies, who should announce to the Queen when and how her mortal life should come to an end and pass over into the eternal.

699. The holy prince descended with the rest to the Cenacle in Jerusalem and entered the oratory of the great

Lady, where they found Her prostrate on the ground in the form of a cross, asking mercy for sinners. But hearing the sound of their music and perceiving them present, She rose to her knees in order to hear the message and show respect to the ambassador of heaven and his companions, who in white and refulgent garments surrounded Her with wonderful delight and reverence. All of them had come with crowns and palms in their hands, each one with a different one; but all of them represented the diverse premiums and rewards of inestimable beauty and value to be conferred upon their great Queen and Lady. Gabriel saluted Her with the Ave Maria, and added thereto: "Our Empress and Lady, the Omnipotent and the Holy of the holy sends us from his heavenly court to announce to Thee in his name the most happy end of thy pilgrimage and banishment upon earth in mortal life. Soon, O Lady, is that day and hour approaching, in which, according to thy longing desires, Thou shalt pass through natural death to the possession of the eternal and immortal life, which awaits Thee in the glory and at the right hand of thy divine Son, our God. Exactly three years from today Thou shalt be taken up and received into the everlasting joy of the Lord, where all its inhabitants await Thee, longing for thy presence."

700. The most holy Mary heard this message with ineffable jubilee of her purest and most loving spirit, and, prostrating Herself again upon the earth, She answered in the same words as at the incarnation of the Word: "Ecce ancilla Domini, fiat mihi secundum verbum tuum." "Behold the handmaid of the Lord, be it done according to thy word" (Luke 1, 38). Then She asked the holy angels and ministers of the Most High to help Her give thanks for this welcome and joyful news. The blessed Mother alternately with the seraphim and other angels,

sang the responses of a canticle that lasted for two hours. Although by their nature and supernatural gifts the angelic spirits are so subtle, wise and excellent, they were nevertheless excelled in all this by their Queen and Lady, as vassals are by their sovereign; for in Her, grace and wisdom abounded as in a Teacher, in them, only as in disciples. Having finished this canticle and humiliating Herself anew, She charged the supernal spirits to beseech the Lord to prepare Her for her passage from mortal to eternal life, and to ask all the other angels and saints in heaven to pray for the same favor. They offered to obey Her in all things, and therewith saint Gabriel took leave and returned with all his company to the empyrean heaven.

701. The great Queen and Lady of all the universe remained alone in her oratory, and amid tears of humble joy prostrated Herself upon the earth, embraced it as the common mother of us all, saying: "Earth, I give thee thanks as I ought, because without my merit thou hast sustained me sixty-seven years. Thou art a creature of the Most High and by his will thou hast sustained me until now. I ask thee now to help me during the rest of my dwelling upon thee, so that, just as I have been created of thee and upon thee, I may through thee and from thee be raised to the blessed vision of my Maker." She addressed also other creatures, saying: "Ye heavens, planets, stars and elements, created by the powerful hands of my Beloved, faithful witnesses and proclaimers of his greatness and beauty, you also I thank for the preservation of my life; help me then from today on, that, with the divine favor, I may begin anew to perfect my life during the time left of my career, in order that I may show myself thankful to my and your Creator."

702. The third anniversary of the day following this

message, according to the prediction of the archangel was to be the day of the glorious Transition of the most blessed Mary. But from the very hour in which She received the announcement, She became so inflamed with the fires of divine love and so multiplied her exercises of devotion, that it seemed as if She wished to make up for any relaxation or negligence in her fervor up to that time. The traveler hastens his footsteps when a great part of his way is still before him as the day declines; the laborer or the merchant redoubles his exertions, when evening overtakes him before the completion of his task. But our great Queen hastened on in her heroic efforts, not for fear of the approaching night or the risks of journeying in the dark, but urged on by the loving desires of the eternal light and in order to enter more rich and prosperous into everlasting joys of the Lord. She immediately wrote to the Apostles and disciples to encourage them in their labors for the conversion of the world, and thereafter, during those three years, more frequently than before, repeated her injunctions. She used still greater diligence in exhorting and confirming the faithful living near Her by her personal intercourse. Although She kept her own secret, yet her behavior was that of one who begins to take her departure and desires to leave her friends rich and prosperous, filled with celestial benedictions.

703. But in regard to the evangelist saint John She had reason to take a different course; for She regarded him as her son, who attended upon Her and assisted Her in a special manner. Hence it seemed good to the most blessed Lady to inform him of the message regarding her death. After some days therefore and after having asked his permission and blessing, She said to him: "Thou dost already know, my son and master, that among the

creatures of the Most High, I am the most indebted of all
and under the greatest obligations to submit to his holy
will.   If all other creatures are subject to Him, certainly
in me ought to be fulfilled entirely all his pleasure for
time and eternity; and thou, my son, shouldst help me in
this fulfillment, as one who knows by how many titles I
belong body and soul to my God and Lord.   In his condescending mercy He has revealed to me, that the end of
my mortal life is near; and that from the day on which
I have been thus informed, there remain only three more
years of banishment until my passage into eternal life.
I beseech thee, my son, to aid me during this short space
of time, in order that I labor in giving thanks to the
Most High and render Him some return for the immense
blessings I have received of his most liberal love. I beseech
thee from the bottom of my heart, pray for me."

704. These words of the most blessed Mother tore the
heart of saint John, and, unable to restrain his sorrow and
his tears, he answered: "My Mother and my Lady, thy
will and that of the Most High I am bound to obey in
whatever Thou commandest, although my merits are far
below what they ought to be and what I desired.   But do
Thou, most loving Lady and Mother, help thy poor child,
who is to be left an orphan, deprived of thy most desirable company."   Saint John could add no more, because
of the sighs and tears pressed from him by his sorrow.
Although the loving Queen encouraged and consoled
him by sweet and efficacious words; yet on that day the
heart of the Apostle was as pierced by a dart of pain and
sorrow, which struck him down and caused him to wither,
like the flowers in their bloom, which, when at evening
they are about to be deprived of the sun and, after having followed and been rejoiced in its light in its course
during the day, sadden and close up at evening.   Lest

he should lose his life in this affliction, the most blessed Mother came to the relief of saint John by her loving promises, assuring him, that She would be his Mother and Advocate with her divine Son. He informed saint James the less, who, as bishop of Jerusalem and according to the orders of saint Peter mentioned above, assisted saint John in the service of the Empress of the world. From that time on the two Apostles, mindful of what was coming, were still more solicitous in their attendance upon their Queen and Lady. This was especially true of the Evangelist, who would not leave her presence.

705. During the course of these three last years of the life of our Queen and Lady the divine power permitted a certain hidden and sweet force to throw all nature into mourning and sorrow at the prospective death of Her, who by her life beautified and perfected all creation. The holy Apostles, although they were scattered over the earth, began to feel new anxiety and misgivings regarding the time when they should be deprived of their Mistress and her help; for already the divine light intimated to them, that this event could not be far off. The others of the faithful living in Jerusalem and in the country around, began secretly to feel that their treasure and joy should not be theirs much longer. The heavens, the stars and planets lost much of their brightness and beauty, like the day at the approach of night. The birds of the air fell into singular demonstrations of sorrow during these last years. A great multitude of them ordinarily gathered where the most blessed Mary happened to be. Surrounding her oratory in unusual flight and motions, they uttered, instead of their natural songs, sorrowful notes, as if they were lamenting and groaning in their grief, until the Lady herself ordered them again to praise their Creator in their natural and musical tones. Of

this miracle saint John was often a witness, joining them in their lamentations. A few days before the Transition of the heavenly Mother innumerable hosts of the little birds gathered, laying their heads and beaks upon the ground, picking at their breasts in groans, like some one taking farewell forever and asking the last benediction.

706. Not only the birds of the air indulged in this sorrow, but also the brute beasts of the earth; for when one day, according to her custom, the Queen of heaven went to visit the holy places of the Redemption and arrived on mount Calvary many wild beasts came from the surrounding mountains to wait for Her. Some of them prostrated themselves upon the ground, others bowed their necks, and all of them uttered sorrowful sounds and thus for some hours manifested their grief at the impending departure of Her, whom they recognized as the Lady and the honor of all creation. The most wonderful sign of this general mourning among the creatures was that the light of the sun, the moon and the stars was diminished and on the day of her Transition they were eclipsed as at the death of the Redeemer of the world. Although many of the wise and thoughtful men noticed these unwonted changes in the celestial orbs, all were ignorant of the cause, and could only express their astonishment. But the Apostles and disciples, who, as I shall relate further on, were present at her most sweet and happy death, knew then that all these signs were tokens of sorrow in insensible nature. The unintelligent things of creation justly anticipated their mourning for the loss of their Queen, while intelligent human nature failed to weep over the departure of its Sovereign, its legitimate Mistress, its true beauty and adorning glory. In the former alone seemed to be fulfilled the prophecy of Zacharias: that in that day the earth shall weep, and

the families of the house of God, each one for itself, and
that this mourning shall be as for the death of the first-
born, over which all are accustomed to weep. This mourning which the prophet predicts for the Onlybegotten of
the eternal Father, was due in proportion also to the
death of the most pure Lady, as the first-born Daughter
of grace and of life. And just as the faithful vassals and
servants clothe themselves in mourning not only at the
death of their prince or their Queen, but also at the
prospect of their danger or of their loss; so the irrational
creatures anticipated the feeling and the tokens of their
sorrow, at the approach of the Transition of the most
holy Mary.

707. The Evangelist before all others shared in their
sorrow and in a special manner and more deeply than all
the rest felt this impending loss, without being able to
conceal it or dissemble it from the more familiar inmates
of the house. Two daughters of the master of the house,
who were much in attendance upon the Queen of the
world, and some other very devout persons, chanced to
see him shedding many tears in his sorrow. As they
knew the peaceful and tranquil disposition of the saint,
they conjectured that this unusual emotion was caused
by some very weighty event; and in their kind solicitude
they a few times urged him to tell them the cause of this
unusual sorrow in order to relieve him if possible. The
holy Apostle suppressed his grief and for a long time
concealed its cause. But not without divine dispensation
he finally yielded to their importunities and told them
that the happy Transition of their Mother and Lady was
approaching, for these were the titles the Evangelist applied to the most blessed Mary in her absence. Hence,
some time before it really took place, this impending loss
of the Church became known to some of the more fa-

miliar acquaintances of the Queen; for none of those that came to know of it, could restrain their tears and sorrow at this irreparable loss. Thenceforward they multiplied their intercourse and their petitions with the blessed Mother, throwing themselves at her feet, kissing the spots where her sacred feet had trod, asking Her to bless them and take them with Her, and not to forget them in the glory of the Lord, whither She was about to carry away with Her the hearts of all her servants.

708. It was a great mercy and providence of the Lord, that many faithful of the primitive Church were thus timely forewarned of the death of their Queen; for He does not send labors and evils to his people without first manifesting them to his servants, as is said by the prophet Amos (Amos 3, 7). Although this loss could not be spared to the faithful of that age, the divine clemency ordained, that in as far as was possible the primitive Church should find a compensation for the loss of its Mother and Mistress, and that its tears and sorrow should be the means of obliging Her, during the space of time which still remained of her life, to favor and enrich them with the treasures of divine grace, which as the Mistress of them all She could confer upon them in her departure, as for their consolation She really did. For the maternal bosom of the blessed Lady in this extremity was moved by the tears of the faithful, and during those last days of her life, She obtained from her divine Son for them and for all the Church new mercies and blessings of the Divinity. In order not to deprive the Church of these new favors, the Lord did not wish to take away from them unwarned his blessed Mother, in whom they trusted for help, consolation, joy, relief in necessities, lightening of their labors, counsel in their doubts, succor in their afflictions and all kinds of blessings.

709. At no time and on no occasion were those ever disappointed who trusted in the great Mother. She relieved and helped all that did not resist her loving and clement advances. But during the last two years of her life, no one could count or estimate the wonders of beneficence She wrought upon the mortals of all classes that flocked in multitudes around Her. All the sick that presented themselves before Her She healed in body and soul; She converted many to the evangelical truth; She drew innumerable souls from sin to the state of grace. She relieved the great miseries of the poor, dispensing what She possessed or what was offered to Her as gifts, and succoring many others by miraculous means. She confirmed all in the fear of God, in faith and obedience to the Church; and, as Mistress and only Treasurer of the riches of the Divinity, of the life and death of her divine Son, She wished to throw open all her riches of liberal mercy before her death, in order to enrich all her children in the holy Church; and above all She consoled them and encouraged them by her promise, that She would continue to this day to favor us at the right hand of her divine Son.

INSTRUCTION WHICH THE GREAT QUEEN OF THE ANGELS GAVE ME.

710. My daughter, in order to understand the jubilee caused in me by the announcement of the end of my mortal life men must consider the desire and force of the love that urged me on to reach and see God in the glory He had prepared for me from all eternity. This mystery entirely exceeds human capacity; and what the children of the Church are able to understand of it for their consolation, they do not seek to merit or make themselves

capable of; for they do not apply the interior light, or purify their consciences for its proper reception. On thee my divine Son and I have liberally conferred this and other mercies; and I assure thee, my dearest, that happy are the eyes which see what thou hast seen, and the ears which hear what thou hast heard. Guard thy treasure, and do not lose it. Labor with all thy power to gain the fruit of this knowledge and of my teaching. I desire of thee that part of this fruit shall be to dispose thyself from this hour for thy death in imitation of me; since, having the certainty of its coming, any space of time should seem short to thee for completing this business of eternal loss or gain. No rational creature was so certain of eternal reward as I; yet, notwithstanding this certainty, I received notice of my death three years in advance, and thou hast seen, how nevertheless I disposed myself and prepared myself for the hour of death with the holy fear proper to a mortal and earth-born creature. In this I acted as a creature subject to death and as the Teacher of the Church, giving an example to the rest of the faithful of what they are to do as mortals and as more in want of such preparation for avoiding eternal damnation.

711. Among the absurd fallacies introduced by the demon into the world none is greater or more pernicious than the forgetfulness of the hour of death and of what is to happen at the court of the rigorous Judge. Consider, my daughter, that through this portal sin entered into the world; for the serpent sought to convince the first woman principally, that she would not die and need not think of that matter (Gen. 3, 4). Thus continually deceived, there are uncountable fools who live without thought of death and who die forgetful of the unhappy lot that awaits them. In order that thou mayest

not be seized by this human perversity, begin to convince thyself now that thou must die irrevocably; that thou hast received much and paid little; that the account shall be so much the more rigorous, as the Judge has been more liberal in the gifts and talents lavished upon thee in thy sphere. I do not ask of thee more, and also not less, than what thou owest to thy Spouse and to thy Lord, which is always to operate the best in all places, times and occasions, without permitting any forgetfulness, intermission or carelessness.

712. If in thy weakness thou incurrest the guilt of some omission or negligence, let not the sun go down or the day pass without having sorrowed for it, or confessed it, if thou canst, as if it were for the last account. Proposing amendment, even of the slightest fault, commence to work with new fervor and solicitude, like one from whom the time is slipping away for accomplishing such an arduous and laborious task as the gaining of the eternal glory and felicity and the avoiding of everlasting death and punishment. This is to be the continual occupation of all thy spiritual and sensitive faculties, in order that thou make thy hope certain and joyful (II Cor. 1, 7); in order that thou mayest not labor in vain (Phil. 2, 16), nor run on into the uncertain (I Cor. 9, 26), like those who content themselves with some good works which they mix up with many reprehensible and detestable crimes. These cannot walk in security and joy of interior hope; since their own conscience assails them and saddens them, unless they are lost in forgetfulness and in the foolish delights of the flesh. In order to fill all thy works with perfection continue the exercises I have shown thee, and also those thou art accustomed to in preparation for death, and all the prayers, prostrations and aspirations thou usually practicest. Then re-

ceive the spiritual Viaticum as if for departure from the earth to the other life, taking leave and forgetting all that thou hast in this life. Enkindle thy heart with the desire of seeing thy God, and rise up to his presence, where is to be thy future habitation and thy present conversation (Phil. 3, 20).

CHAPTER XVIII.

713. I find myself indeed poor in words now, when I am to speak of the activity of the most blessed Mary's love during the last days of her life, of the impetuous flights of her spirit, of her desires and incomparable yearnings to reach the close embraces of the Divinity. I find no similitude in all nature; and if anything could serve for a comparison, it might perhaps be the element of fire, on account of its correspondence with love. Admirable is the activity and the force of that element above all others, none is more impatient of bounds; for it will either die in confinement, or burst its bonds in order to rise up unconstrained to its proper sphere. If it finds itself imprisoned in the earth, it will tear up the surface, break in two the mountains and shatter the rocks, hurling them with irresistible violence aside until its fury is spent. And, as experience teaches, though its prison be of bronze as in the cannon, if it does not burst it, it at least forces an opening for itself with terrific violence and sends forth the metal ball on its course of destruction. Such is the activity of this insensible creature.

714. But if in the heart of the most holy Mary the fire of divine love was concentrated to one point (I cannot explain myself by other words), then clearly the

603

effects corresponded to their cause; and the effects of fire are not more wonderful in the order of nature, than the effects of her love in the order of grace, and of such immense grace. Our great Queen was always a pilgrim in the world and the only Phœnix upon earth; but when She was ready to depart for heaven and assured of the happy end of her pilgrimage, although her blessed body still lingered upon earth, the flame of her most pure love, with irresistible flight, pressed upward to her proper sphere, that is, the Divinity. She could not withhold or constrain the impetus of her heart, nor seemed to be master of her interior activities, or hold dominion over them; for She had yielded all her liberty to the sway of love and to her desire of possessing the highest Good, in whom She lived transformed and forgetful of earthly mortality. Her love did not burst the narrow prison walls of natural life because it was preserved more by a miracle than by natural forces; nor did it bear up with it her mortal body, because it had not yet arrived at its destined ending, although the activity of her spirit and of her love was sufficient to ravish it from earth. But in this sweet and unquenchable contest of love the operations of nature were suspended, so that this godlike soul seemed to receive its life only from the divine love; and in order to preserve the natural life, a continuous miracle was necessary, requiring the intervention of some supernatural activity for encountering death at each instant and sustaining her natural existence.

715. It happened many times during these last days, that in order to abate somewhat the excesses of her love and in order to prevent her bosom from being forced asunder, She broke the silence of her retreat and spoke to the Lord: "My sweetest Love, highest Good and Treasure of my soul, draw me now after the sweetness

of thy ointments, which Thou hast permitted thy hand-maid and mother to taste in this world (Cant. 1, 3). My will always found its rest entirely in Thee, the highest Truth and my true Good; never have I known any other love than the love of Thee! O my only hope and glory! Let not my course be prolonged, let not the beginning of that much desired freedom be postponed! (Ps. 141, 8). Solve now the chains of that mortal existence, which still detains me! Let the term of my life be fulfilled, let that end come toward which I tended from the first instant in which I received my being from Thee. My dwelling among the inhabitants of Cedar has been prolonged (Ps. 119, 5); but all the powers of my soul and all its facul-ties look toward the Sun which gives it life, follow the fixed North-star that leads them on, and faint away in longing for the Good they are awaiting. O ye supernal spirits, by the most exalted condition of your spiritual and angelic nature, by the happiness, which you enjoy in the never-failing beauty of my Beloved, I beseech you to have pity on me, my friends. Do ye pity this stranger among the children of Adam, captive in the bonds of mortal flesh. Present to my and your Lord the cause of my sorrow, of which He is not ignorant (Cant. 5, 8); tell Him that for his sake I embrace suffering in my ban-ishment, and that I so desire it; but I cannot desire to live in my own self; and if I am to live in Him in order to preserve my life, how can I live in the absence of this, my life? Love it is, which gives my life and at the same time deprives me of it. Life cannot live without love; hence, how can I live without the Life, which alone I love? In this sweet violence I am perishing; tell me if possible of the qualities of my Beloved, for amid such aromatic flowers the swoonings of my impatient love shall find recovery!" (Cant. 2, 5).

716. With such and other still more fervent aspirations the most blessed Mother assuaged the fires of her spirit, that She excited the wonder of the holy angels who attended upon Her and served Her. And as they, by means of their high intelligence and heavenly science, were able to understand these excesses, they on one occasion answered Her as follows: "Our Queen and Lady, if Thou wishest again to hear us speak of the tokens of thy Beloved that we know of, consider that He is beauty itself and that He contains within Himself all the perfections beyond all desire. He is amiable without defect, delightful beyond comparison, pleasing without the least flaw. In wisdom He is inestimable, in goodness without measure, in power boundless, in greatness immeasurable, in essence infinite, in majesty inaccessible, and all his perfections are infinite. In his judgments He is terrible (Ps. 65, 5), his counsels inscrutable (Rom. 11, 33), in his justice most equitable (Ps. 118, 137), in his thoughts unsearchable, in his words most true, in his works holy (Ps. 144, 13), rich in mercies (Ephes. 2, 4). Space cannot overreach Him, narrowness cannot confine Him, sorrow cannot disturb Him, joy cannot cause any change in Him; nor does He ever fail in his wisdom, or change in his will (Jas. 1, 17); abundance cannot overwhelm, or want come near Him, memory adds nothing, forgetfulness takes away nothing from his knowledge; what was, is not past for Him, and what is to come, never happens to Him; the beginning gave no origin to his being, and time will bring to Him no end. Without being caused, He causes all things (Eccli. 18, 1), and He has not need of anything, but all things need participation in Him; He preserves them without labor, He governs them without confusion. Those who follow Him walk not in darkness (John 8, 12), those who know

Him are happy, who love and extol Him, are blessed; for He exalts his friends, and at last glorifies them by his eternal vision and intercourse (John 17, 3). This, O Lady, is the Good which Thou lovest and whose embraces Thou shalt shortly enjoy without intermission through all his eternities." Thus spoke the holy angels.

717. Such colloquies took place frequently between the great Queen and her ministers. But just as the thirst of one laboring under a burning fever is not allayed by small drops of water, but rather increased, so also these incitements of love did not quench the divine flame in that loving Mother, because they rather opened up new sources of loving anguish. During the last days of her life She not only enjoyed the favors mentioned above, namely those of the feast days and the Sundays, and many other favors impossible to enumerate, but in order to sustain and nourish Her in her anguishes of love, her divine Son visited Her more frequently than before. During these visits He recreated Her and comforted Her with wonderful favors and caresses, assuring Her again and again that her banishment would now be short, that He would bear Her up to his right hand, where She would be placed on her royal throne by the Father and the Holy Ghost and be absorbed in the abyss of the Divinity. Thus was She to be the source of new joy to the saints, all of whom were awaiting and desiring to see Her. On these occasions the loving Mother multiplied her petitions and prayers for the holy Church, for the Apostles and disciples, and all the ministers, who in coming ages were to serve in the preaching of the Gospel and the conversion of the world, and for all the mortals who were to accept its teachings and to come to the knowledge of the divine truth.

718. Among the wonders which the Lord wrought

with the most blessed Mother during these last years, there was one, which was manifest not only to the Evangelist, but to many of the faithful. This was, that when the blessed Lady received holy Communion, She shone for some hours with a clearness so wonderful, that She seemed transfigured and gifted with glory. This was caused by the sacred body of her Son, who, as I have before stated, showed Himself to Her in a transfigured and more glorious state than on mount Tabor. All that then beheld Her were filled with a joy and with effects so divine that they could be indeed felt but not described.

719. The devout Queen resolved to take leave of the holy places before her departure into heaven, and having obtained the consent of saint John She left the house with him and with the thousand angels of her guard. Although these sovereign princes had always served and accompanied Her in all her errands, occupations and journeys, without having absented themselves for one moment since the instant of her birth; yet on this occasion they manifested themselves to Her with greater beauty and refulgence, as if they felt special joy in seeing themselves already at the beginning of her last journey into heaven. The heavenly Princess, setting aside human occupations in order to enter upon her journey to the real and true fatherland, visited all the memorable places of our Redemption, marking each with the sweet abundance of her tears, recalling the sorrowful memories of what her Son there suffered, and fervently renewing its effects by most fervent acts of love, clamors and petitions for all the faithful, who should devoutly and reverently visit these holy places during the future ages of the Church. On Calvary She remained a longer time, asking of her divine Son the full effects of his redeeming

Death for all the multitudes of souls there snatched from destruction. The ardor of her ineffable charity during this prayer rose to such a pitch, that it would have destroyed her life, if it had not been sustained by divine power.

720. Thereupon her divine Son descended in person from heaven and appeared to her on this place of his death. Answering her petitions He said: "My Mother and my Dove, Coadjutrix in the work of human Redemption, thy petitions have come to my hearing and have touched my heart. I promise Thee that I shall be most liberal with men, and I shall dispense to them continually the helps of my graces and favors, in order that with their own free will they may merit the glory earned for them by my blood, if they do not of their own accord despise this happiness. In heaven thou shalt be their Mediatrix and Advocate; and all those that shall obtain thy intercession I shall fill with my treasures and infinite mercies." This promise therefore was renewed by the Lord on the very place on which He had redeemed us. The most blessed Virgin, prostrate at his feet, gave Him thanks and there begged Him by his precious and bloody Death, to give Her his last benediction. The Lord gave it, ratified all his royal promises, and then returned to the right hand of his eternal Father. Comforted in her loving anguish, the most blessed Mary pursued her devotions, kissed and worshipped the ground on Calvary, saying: "Holy earth and consecrated spot, from heaven shall I look upon thee with reverence, bathed in that light, which manifests all in its fount and origin and from whence came forth the divine Word to enrich thee in his immortal flesh." Then She again charged the holy angels to assist Her in the custody of those sacred places, to inspire with holy thoughts all the

faithful who should visit them with devotion, so that they might know and esteem properly the admirable blessing of the Redemption wrought thereon. She charged them also with the defense of those sanctuaries; and if the temerity and the crimes of men had not demerited this favor, without a doubt the holy angels would have warded off the profanations of the heathens and the infidels. Even as it is, they defend them in many ways to the present day.

721. The Queen asked also the angels of the sanctuaries and the Evangelist to give Her their blessing in this last leave-taking; and therewith She returned to her oratory shedding tears of tenderest affection for what She loved so much upon earth. There She prostrated Herself with her face upon the earth and poured forth another long and most fervent prayer for the Church; and She persevered in it, until in an abstractive vision of the Divinity, the Lord had given Her assurance that He had heard and conceded her petitions at the throne of his mercy. In order to give the last touch of holiness to her works, She asked permission of the Lord to take leave of the holy Church, saying: "Exalted and most high God, Redeemer of the world, head of the saints and the predestined, Justifier and Glorifier of souls, I am a child of the holy Church, planted and acquired by thy blood. Give me, O Lord, permission to take leave of such a loving Mother, and of all my brethren, thy children, belonging to it." She was made aware of the consent of the Lord and therefore turned to the mystical body of the Church, addressing it in sweet tears as follows:

722. "Holy Catholic Church, which in the coming ages shall be called the Roman, my mother and Mistress, true treasure of my soul, thou hast been the only consolation

of my banishment; the refuge and ease of my labors; my recreation, my joy and my hope; thou hast sustained me in my course; in thee have I lived as a pilgrim to the Fatherland; and thou hast nourished me after I had received in thee my existence in grace through thy head, Christ Jesus, my Son and my Lord. In thee are the treasures and the riches of his infinite merits; thou shalt be for his faithful children the secure way to the promised land, and thou shalt safeguard them on their dangerous and difficult pilgrimage. Thou shalt be the mistress of the nations to whom all owe reverence; in thee are the rich and inestimable jewels of the anxieties, labors, affronts, hardships, torments, of the cross and of death, which are all consecrated by those of my Lord, thy Progenitor, thy Master, thy Chief, and are reserved for his more distinguished servants and his dearest friends. Thou hast adorned and enriched me with thy jewels in order that I might enter in the nuptials of the Spouse; thou hast made me wealthy, prosperous and happy, and thou containest within thee thy Author in the most holy Sacrament. My happy Mother, Church militant, rich art thou and abundant in treasures! For thee have I always reserved my heart and my solicitude; but now is the time come to part from thee and leave thy sweet companionship, in order to reach the end of my course. Make me partaker of thy great goods; bathe me copiously in the sacred liquor of the blood of the Lamb, preserved in thee as a powerful means of sanctifying many worlds. At the cost of my life a thousand times would I bring to thee all the nations and tribes of mortals, that they might enjoy thy treasures. My beloved Church, my honor and my glory, I am about to leave thee in mortal life; but in the eternal life I will find thee joyful in an existence which includes all good.

From that place I shall look upon thee with love, and pray always for thy increase, thy prosperity and thy progress."

723. This was the parting of the most blessed Mary from the mystical body of the holy Roman Catholic Church, the mother of the faithful, in order that all who should hear of Her, might know by her sweet tears and endearments, in what veneration, love and esteem She held that holy Church. After thus taking leave, the great Mistress, as the Mother of Wisdom, prepared to make her testament and last Will. When She manifested this most prudent wish to the Lord, He deigned to approve of it by his own royal presence. For this purpose, with myriads of attending angels, the three Persons of the most blessed Trinity descended to the oratory of their Daughter and Spouse, and when the Queen had adored the infinite Being of God, She heard a voice speaking to Her: "Our chosen Spouse, make thy last will as thou desirest, for We shall confirm it and execute it entirely by our infinite power." The most prudent Mother remained for some time lost in the profoundness of her humility, seeking to know first the will of the Most High before She should manifest her own. The Lord responded to her modest desires and the person of the Father said to Her: "My Daughter, thy will shall be pleasing and acceptable to Me; for thou art not wanting in the merits of good works in parting from this mortal life, that I should not satisfy thy desires." The same encouragement was given to Her by the Son and the Holy Ghost. Therewith the most blessed Mary made her will in this form:

724. "Highest Lord and eternal God, I, a vile wormlet of the earth, confess and adore Thee with all the reverence of my inmost soul as the Father, the Son and the

Holy Ghost, three Persons distinct in one undivided and eternal essence, one substance, one in infinite majesty of attributes and perfection. I confess Thee as the one true Creator and Preserver of all that has being. In thy kingly presence I declare and say, that my last will is this: Of the goods of mortal life and of the world in which I live, I possess none that I can leave; for never have I possessed or loved anything beside Thee, who art my good and all my possession. To the heavens, the stars and planets, to the elements and all creatures in them I give thanks, because according to thy will they have sustained me without my merit, and lovingly I desire and ask them to serve and praise Thee in the offices and ministries assigned to them, and that they continue to sustain and benefit my brethren and fellowmen. In order that they may do it so much the better, I renounce and assign to mankind the possession, and as far as possible, the dominion of them, which thy Majesty has given me over these irrational creatures, so that they may now serve and sustain my fellowmen. Two tunics and a cloak, which served to cover me, I leave to John for his disposal, since I hold him as a son. My body I ask the earth to receive again for thy service, since it is the common mother and serves Thee as thy creature; my soul, despoiled of its body and of all visible things, O my God, I resign into thy hands, in order that it may love and magnify Thee through all thy eternities. My merits and all the treasures, which with thy grace through my works and exertions I have acquired, I leave to the holy Church, my mother and my mistress, as my residuary heiress, and with thy permission I there deposit them, wishing them to be much greater. And I desire that before all else they redound to the exaltation of thy holy name and procure the fulfillment of thy will on earth as it is done in heaven, and that all the nations come to the knowledge, love and veneration of Thee, the true God."

725. "In the second place I offer these merits for my masters the Apostles and priests, of the present and of the future ages, so that in view of them thy ineffable clemency may make them apt ministers, worthy of their office and state, filled with wisdom, virtue and holiness, by which they may edify and sanctify the souls redeemed by thy blood. In the third place I offer them for the spiritual good of my devoted servants, who invoke and call upon me, in order that they may receive thy protection and grace, and afterwards eternal life. In the fourth place I desire that my services and labors may move Thee to mercy toward all the sinning children of Adam, in order that they may withdraw from their sinful state. From this hour on I propose and desire to continue my prayers for them in thy divine presence, as long as the world shall last. This, Lord and my God, is my last will, always subject to thy own." At the conclusion of this testament of the Queen, the most blessed Trinity approved and confirmed it; and Christ the Redeemer, as if authorizing it all, witnessed it by writing in the heart of his Mother these words: "Let it be done as thou wishest and ordainest."

726. If all we children of Adam, and especially we who are born in the law of grace, had no other obligation toward the most blessed Mary than this of having been constituted heirs of her immense merits and of all that is mentioned in this short and mysterious testament, we could never repay our debt, even if in return we should offer our lives and endure all the sufferings of the most courageous martyrs and saints. I do not compare them with the infinite merits and treasures left by

Christ our Savior in the Church, because that is not possible. But what excuse or pretense have the reprobate, who avail themselves neither of the one nor the other? All of them they despise, forget and squander. What torment and despair will be theirs, when they unavailingly come to know that they have lost forever such great blessings and treasures for a momentary delight? Let them confess the justice and equity with which they are chastised and cast off by the Lord and his loving Mother, whom they despised in such foolish temerity.

727. When the great Queen had made her testament, She gave thanks to the Almighty and asked permission to add another petition, saying: "Most clement Lord and Father of mercies, if it is according to thy pleasure, my soul desires that at its departure be present the Apostles, my masters and thy anointed, together with the other disciples, in order that they pray for me and bless me at my transition from this to the eternal life." To this her divine Son answered: "My most beloved Mother, the Apostles are already on the way to come to thee, and those that are near shall shortly arrive, while those that are far off shall be carried by my angels; because, for my and thy greater glory it is my will that all assist at thy glorious departure for the eternal mansions, so that thou and they may be consoled." For this new favor the most blessed Mary gave thanks prostrate upon the ground, and therewith the three divine Persons returned to the empyrean heavens.

INSTRUCTION WHICH THE QUEEN OF THE ANGELS, MOST HOLY MARY, GAVE ME.

728. My daughter, since thou admirest my esteem and love for the holy Church, I wish to assist thy affection in conceiving new appreciation and love for it. Thou canst

not in thy mortal flesh understand what passed in my soul in contemplating the holy Church. In addition to what thou hast understood already, thou wilt see more, if thou consider what moved my heart; namely, the loving works of my divine Son in the interest of the holy Church; they should be thy meditation day and night; for in what He did for the Church, thou wilt be able to estimate his love toward it. In order to be its Head and the Chief of the predestined in this world and forever (Col. 1, 18; Rom. 8, 29), He descended from the bosom of the eternal Father and assumed flesh in my womb. In order to regain his children (Luke 19, 10), lost through the first sin of Adam, He took passible and mortal flesh. In order to leave the example of his un-blemished life and his true and salutary doctrine (I Pet. 2, 21), He lived and conversed with men thirty-three years (Baruch 3, 38). In order to redeem them ef-fectually and merit for them infinite blessings of grace and glory, which they themselves could not merit, He suffered most cruelly, shed his blood accepting a most painful and frightful death on the Cross (Phil. 2, 8). In order that from his sacred body after its death might spring mysteriously his Church, He permitted it to be torn by the lance (John 19, 34).

729. Since the eternal Father was so well pleased with his Life, Passion and Death, the Redeemer instituted in his Church the sacrifice of his body and blood (Luke 22, 19), in which his memory should live and which the faith-ful might offer as a satisfaction and peace-offering to the divine Justice. At the same time through it He wished to remain perpetually present in his Church as a Sacrament for the spiritual nourishment of its chil-dren and as a fountain of grace, a viaticum and certain pledge of eternal life. In addition to this He sent upon

his holy Church the Holy Ghost, to fill it with his gifts and his wisdom, promising that He should guide and govern it always without error free from uncertainty and danger (John 15, 26). He enriched it with all the merits of his Life, Passion and Death, applying them by means of the Sacraments, furnishing all that was necessary for men from their birth to their death for cleansing them from their sins, for persevering in grace, for defending themselves against the demons and vanquishing them by the arms of his Church, for crushing their own natural passions; and at the same time He instituted fit and apt ministers for securing to his faithful all these blessings. In the Church militant He communicates familiarly with all the holy souls; He makes them participants in his hidden and secret favors; He works wonders and miracles for them, and when it is for his glory, assumes their works; He hears their prayers for themselves or for others, thus maintaining the communion of saints.

730. He left in it also other fountains of light and truth, the holy Gospels and writings dictated by the Holy Ghost, the decisions of the sacred councils, the assured and ancient traditions. He sends at opportune times holy doctors full of wisdom; He furnishes teachers and learned men, preachers and ministers in abundance. He spreads the renown of the Church through his wonderful saints; beautifies it with a variety of religious orders, wherein the perfect and apostolic life is professed and preserved; He governs it by many prelates and dignitaries. In order that all may proceed in harmony, He placed over it a supreme head, the Roman Pontiff, his vicar, with the plenitude of highest and divine authority, as the head of this mystical and most beautiful body. He defends and protects him to the end of the world against all the powers of the earth and the infernal

abysses (Matth. 16, 18). Among all these blessings bestowed and still to be bestowed upon his beloved Church, not the least one was, that he left me in it after his wonderful Ascension in order that it might be spread and governed by my merits and my presence. From that time on and forever I hold this Church as my possession; for the Most High has consigned it to me as a gift and has commanded me to take care of it as its Mother and Mistress.

731. These, my dearest, are the greatest reasons and motives for my past and present love of the holy Church, here made known to thee; and I desire that they rouse and enkindle thy heart to an ardent performance of all that pertains to thee as my disciple, as my daughter and that of the holy Church. Love it, respect and esteem it from thy whole heart, enjoy its treasures, gather in the riches of heaven, deposited together with its Author, in his Church. Seek to unite it with thee and to unite thyself with it; for in it thou findest thy refuge and thy salvation, consolement in thy labors, hope in thy banishment, light and truth to guide thee in the darkness of this world. For this holy Church I desire thee to labor during all the rest of thy life; since this is the purpose for which thou hast been called into existence; thus shalt thou imitate and follow me in my tireless solicitude for the Church on earth; this is thy greatest good fortune, for which thou owest eternal gratitude. I wish thee, my daughter, to be mindful of the fact, that with this desire and intent I have applied to thee a great portion of the treasures of the Church for the writing of my life; and the Lord has chosen thee as an instrument and as secretary of its mysteries and hidden sacraments for purposes of his greater glory. Do not conceive, that by having labored somewhat in this work, that thou hast made even

a partial return, absolving thee of thy obligations; but rather feel thyself more deeply pledged and obliged to put in practice the doctrine thou hast recorded; and as long as thou refusest to do so, thou wilt remain poor, unrelieved of thy indebtedness, and subject to a rigorous account for all thou hast received. Now is the time to work, so that thou mayest find thyself prepared, at leisure, and disengaged to receive the Spouse at the hour of death. Look upon my freedom and detachment from all earthly things: govern thyself by it, and let not the oil of light and of love fail thee (Matth. 25, 3), in order that thou mayest enter the nuptials of the Spouse through the open gates of his infinite mercy and clemency.

CHAPTER XIX.

THE GLORIOUS AND HAPPY TRANSITION OF THE MOST
HOLY MARY. HOW THE APOSTLES AND DISCIPLES
ARRIVED PREVIOUSLY IN JERUSALEM AND WERE PRES-
ENT AT HER DEATH.

732. And now, according to the decree of the divine
will, the day was approaching in which the true and living Ark of the covenant was to be placed in the temple
of the celestial Jerusalem, with a greater glory and higher
jubilee than its prophetic figure was installed by Solomon in the sanctuary beneath the wings of the cherubim
(III King 8, 8). Three days before the most happy
Transition of the great Lady the Apostles and disciples
were gathered in Jerusalem and in the Cenacle. The first
one to arrive was saint Peter, who was transported
from Rome by the hands of an angel. At that place the
angel appeared to him and told him that the passing
away of the most blessed Mary was imminent and that
the Lord commanded him to go to Jerusalem in order to
be present at that event. Thereupon the angel took him
up and brought him from Italy to the Cenacle. Thither
the Queen of the world had retired, somewhat weakened
in body by the force of her divine love; for since She
was so near to her end, She was subjected more completely to love's effects.

733. The great Lady came to the entrance of her ora-
tory in order to receive the vicar of Christ our Savior.
Kneeling at his feet She asked his blessing and said:
"I give thanks and praise to the Almighty, that He has

brought to me the holy Father for assisting me in the hour of my death." Then came saint Paul, to whom the Queen showed the same reverence with similar tokens of her pleasure at seeing him. The Apostles saluted Her as the Mother of God, as their Queen and as Mistress of all creation; but with a sorrow equal to their reverence, because they knew that they had come to witness her passing away. After these Apostles came the others and the disciples still living. Three days after, they were all assembled in the Cenacle. The heavenly Mother received them all with profound humility, reverence and love, asking each one to bless Her. All of them complied, and saluted Her with admirable reverence. By orders of the Lady given to saint John, and with the assistance of saint James the less, they were all hospitably entertained and accommodated.

734. Some of the Apostles who had been transported by the angels and informed by them of the purpose of their coming, were seized with tenderest grief and shed abundant tears at the thought of losing their only protection and consolation. Others were as yet ignorant of their approaching loss, especially the disciples, who had not been positively informed by the angels, but were moved by interior inspirations and a sweet and forcible intimation of God's will to come to Jerusalem. They immediately conferred with saint Peter, desirous of knowing the occasion of their meeting; for all of them were convinced, that if there had been no special occasion, the Lord would not have urged them so strongly to come. The apostle saint Peter, as the head of the Church, called them all together in order to tell them of the cause of their coming, and spoke to the assembly: "My dearest children and brethren, the Lord has called and brought us to Jerusalem from remote regions not

without a cause most urgent and sorrowful to us. The Most High wishes now to raise up to the throne of eternal glory his most blessed Mother, our Mistress, our consolation and protection. His divine decree is that we all be present at her most happy and glorious Transition. When our Master and Redeemer ascended to the right hand of his Father, although He left us orphaned of his most delightful presence, we still retained his most blessed Mother. As our light now leaves us, what shall we do? What help or hope have we to encourage us on our pilgrimage? I find none except the hope that we all shall follow Her in due time."

735. Saint Peter could speak no farther, because uncontrollable tears and sighs interrupted him. Neither could the rest of the Apostles answer for a long time, during which, amid copious and tenderest tears, they gave vent to the groans of their inmost heart. After some time the vicar of Christ recovered himself and added: "My children, let us seek the presence of our Mother and Lady. Let us spend the time left of her life in her company and ask Her to bless us." They all betook themselves to the oratory of the great Queen and found Her kneeling upon a couch, on which She was wont to recline for a short rest. They saw Her full of beauty and celestial light, surrounded by the thousand angels of her guard.

736. The natural condition and appearance of her sacred and virginal body were the same as at her thirty-third year; for, as I have already stated, from that age onward it experienced no change. It was not affected by the passing years, showing no signs of age, no wrinkles in her face or body, nor giving signs of weakening or fading, as in other children of Adam, who gradually fall away and drop from the natural perfection of early

man or womanhood. This unchangeableness was the privilege of the most blessed Mary alone, as well because it consorted with the stability of her purest soul, as because it was the natural consequence of her immunity from the sin of Adam, the effects of which in this regard touched neither her sacred body nor her purest soul. The Apostles and disciples, and some of the other faithful, occupied her chamber, all of them preserving the utmost order in her presence. Saint Peter and saint John placed themselves at the head of the couch. The great Lady looked upon them all with her accustomed modesty and reverence and spoke to them as follows: "My dearest children, give permission to your servant to speak in your presence and to disclose my humble desires." Saint Peter answered that all listened with attention and would obey Her in all things; and he begged Her to seat Herself upon the couch, while speaking to them. It seemed to saint Peter that She was exhausted from kneeling so long and that She had taken that position in order to pray to the Lord, and that in speaking to them, it was proper She should be seated as their Queen.

737. But She, who was the Teacher of humility and obedience unto death, practiced both these virtues in that hour. She answered that She would obey in asking of them their blessing, and besought them to afford Her this consolation. With the permission of saint Peter She left the couch and, kneeling before the Apostle, said to him: "My lord, I beseech thee, as the universal pastor and head of the holy Church, to give me thy blessing in thy own and in its name. Pardon me thy handmaid for the smallness of the service I have rendered in my life. Grant that John dispose of my vestments, the two tunics, giving them to the two poor maidens, who have always

obliged me by their charity." She then prostrated Herself and kissed the feet of saint Peter as the vicar of Christ, by her abundant tears eliciting not less the admiration than the tears of the Apostle and of all the bystanders. From saint Peter She went to saint John, and kneeling likewise at his feet, said: "Pardon, my son and my master, my not having fulfilled toward thee the duties of a Mother as I ought and as the Lord had commanded me, when from the Cross He appointed thee as my son and me as thy mother (John 19, 27). I humbly and from my heart thank thee for the kindness which thou hast shown me as a son. Give me thy benediction for entering into the vision and company of Him who created me."

738. The sweetest Mother proceeded in her leave-taking, speaking to each of the Apostles in particular and to some of the disciples; and then to all the assembly together; for there were a great number. She rose to her feet and addressed them all, saying: "Dearest children and my masters, always have I kept you in my soul and written in my heart. I have loved you with that tender love and charity, which was given to me by my divine Son, whom I have seen in you, his chosen friends. In obedience to his holy and eternal will, I now go to the eternal mansions, where I promise you as a Mother I will look upon you by the clearest light of the Divinity, the vision of which my soul hopes and desires in security. I commend unto you my mother, the Church, the exaltation of the name of the Most High, the spread of the evangelical law, the honor and veneration for the words of my divine Son, the memory of his Passion and Death, the practice of his doctrine. My children, love the Church, and love one another with that bond of charity, which your Master has always inculcated upon you

(John 13, 34). To thee, Peter, holy Pontiff, I commend my son John and all the rest."

739. The words of the most blessed Mary, like arrows of a divine fire, penetrated the hearts of all the Apostles and hearers, and as She ceased speaking, all of them were dissolved in streams of tears and, seized with irreparable sorrow, cast themselves upon the ground with sighs and groans sufficient to move to compassion the very earth. All of them wept, and with them wept also the sweetest Mary, who could not resist this bitter and well-founded sorrow of her children. After some time She spoke to them again, and asked them to pray with Her and for Her in silence, which they did. During this quietness the incarnate Word descended from heaven on a throne of ineffable glory, accompanied by all the saints and innumerable angels, and the house of the Cenacle was filled with glory. The most blessed Mary adored the Lord and kissed his feet. Prostrate before Him She made the last and most profound act of faith and humility in her mortal life. On this occasion the most pure Creature, the Queen of the heavens, shrank within Herself and lowered Herself to the earth more profoundly than all men together ever have or ever will humiliate themselves for all their sins. Her divine Son gave Her his blessing and in the presence of the courtiers of heaven spoke to Her these words: "My dearest Mother, whom I have chosen for my dwelling-place, the hour is come in which thou art to pass from the life of this death and of the world into the glory of my Father and mine, where thou shalt possess the throne prepared for thee at my right hand and enjoy it through all eternity. And since, by my power and as my Mother, I have caused thee to enter the world free and exempt from sin, therefore also death shall have no right or

permission to touch thee at thy exit from this world. If thou wishest not to pass through it, come with Me now to partake of my glory, which thou hast merited."

740. The most prudent Mother prostrated Herself at the feet of her Son and with a joyous countenance answered: "My Son and my Lord, I beseech Thee let thy mother and thy servant enter into eternal life by the common portal of natural death, like the other children of Adam. Thou, who art my true God, hast suffered death without being obliged to do so; it is proper that, as I have followed Thee in life, so I follow Thee also in death." Christ the Savior approved of the decision and the sacrifice of his most blessed Mother, and consented to its fulfillment. Then all the angels began to sing in celestial harmony some of the verses of the Canticles of Solomon and other new ones. Although only saint John and some of the Apostles were enlightened as to the presence of Christ the Savior, yet the others felt in their interior its divine and powerful effects; but the music was heard as well by the Apostles and disciples, as by many others of the faithful there present. A divine fragrance also spread about, which penetrated even to the street. The house of the Cenacle was filled with a wonderful effulgence, visible to all, and the Lord ordained that multitudes of the people of Jerusalem gathered in the streets as witnesses to this new miracle.

741. When the angels began their music, the most blessed Mary reclined back upon her couch or bed. Her tunic was folded about her sacred body, her hands were joined and her eyes fixed upon her divine Son, and She was entirely inflamed with the fire of divine love. And as the angels intoned those verses of the second chapter of the Canticles: "Surge, propera, amica mea," that is to say: "Arise, haste, my beloved, my dove, my beau-

titul one, and come, the winter has passed," etc., She pronounced those words of her Son on the Cross: "Into thy hands, O Lord, I commend my spirit." Then She closed her virginal eyes and expired. The sickness which took away her life was love, without any other weakness or accidental intervention of whatever kind. She died at the moment when the divine power suspended the assistance, which until then had counteracted the sensible ardors of her burning love of God. As soon as this miraculous assistance was withdrawn, the fire of her love consumed the life-humors of her heart and thus caused the cessation of her earthly existence.

742. Then this most pure Soul passed from her virginal body to be placed in boundless glory, on the throne at the right hand of her divine Son. Immediately the music of the angels seemed to withdraw to the upper air; for that whole procession of angels and saints accompanied the King and Queen to the empyrean heavens. The sacred body of the most blessed Mary, which had been the temple and sanctuary of God in life, continued to shine with an effulgent light and breathed forth such a wonderful and unheard of fragrance, that all the bystanders were filled with interior and exterior sweetness. The thousand angels of her guard remained to watch over the inestimable treasure of her virginal body. The Apostles and disciples, amid the tears and the joy of the wonders they had seen, were absorbed in admiration for some time, and then sang many hymns and psalms in honor of the most blessed Mary now departed. This glorious Transition of the great Queen took place in the hour in which her divine Son had died, at three o'clock on a Friday, the thirteenth day of August, she being seventy years of age, less the twenty-six days intervening between the thirteenth of August, on which

She died, and the eighth of September, the day of her birth. The heavenly Mother had survived the death of Christ the Savior twenty-one years, four months and nineteen days; and his virginal birth, fifty-five years. This reckoning can be easily made in the following manner: when Christ our Savior was born, his virginal Mother was fifteen years, three months and seventeen days of age. The Lord lived thirty-three years and three months; so that at the time of his sacred Passion the most blessed Lady was forty-eight years, six months and seventeen days old; adding to these another twenty-one years, four months and nineteen days, we ascertain her age as seventy years, less twenty-five or twenty-six days.*

743. Great wonders and prodigies happened at the precious death of the Queen; for the sun was eclipsed (as I said above in No. 706) and its light was hidden in sorrow for some hours. Many birds of different kinds gathered around the Cenacle, and by their sorrowful clamors and groans for a while caused the bystanders themselves to weep. All Jerusalem was in commotion, and many of the inhabitants collected in astonished crowds, confessing loudly the power of God and the greatness of his works. Others were astounded and as if beside themselves. The Apostles and disciples with others of the faithful broke forth in tears and sighs. Many sick persons came who all were cured. The souls in purgatory were released. But the greatest miracle was that three persons, a man in Jerusalem and two women living in the immediate neighborhood of the Cenacle, died in sin and impenitent in that same hour, subject to eternal damnation; but

---

*In figures as follows:

Birth of Christ, 15 years, 3 months, 17 days.
Death of Christ, 33 years, 3 months, .. days.

48 years, 6 months, 17 days.
Death of Mary, 21 years, 4 months, 19 days.
Age at death, 69 years, 11 months, 5 or 6 days.

when their cause came before the tribunal of Christ, his sweetest Mother interceded for them and they were restored to life. They so mended their conduct, that afterwards they died in grace and were saved. This privilege was not extended to others that died on that day in the world, but was restricted to those three who happened to die in that hour in Jerusalem. What festivities were celebrated on that occasion in heaven I will describe in another chapter, lest heavenly things be mixed up with the sacred things of earth.

INSTRUCTION WHICH THE GREAT QUEEN OF HEAVEN, MOST HOLY MARY, GAVE ME.

744. My daughter, besides what thou hast understood and written of my glorious Transition, I wish to inform thee of another privilege, which was conceded to me by my divine Son in that hour. Thou hast already recorded, that the Lord offered me the choice of entering into beatific vision either with or without passing through the portals of death. If I had preferred not to die, the Most High would have conceded this favor, because sin had no part in me, and hence also not its punishment, which is death. Thus it would also have been with my divine Son, and with a greater right, if He had not taken upon Himself the satisfaction of the divine justice for men through his Passion and Death. Hence I chose death freely in order to imitate and follow Him, as also I did during his grievous passion. Since I had seen my Son and true God die, I would not have satisfied the love I owe Him, if I had refused death, and I would have left a great gap in my conformity to and my imitation of my Lord the Godman, whereas He wished me to bear a great likeness to Him in his most

sacred humanity. As I would thereafter never be able
to make up for such a defect, my soul would not enjoy
the plenitude of the delight of having died as did my
Lord and God.

745. Hence my choosing to die was so pleasing to
Him, and my prudent love therein obliged Him to such
an extent, that in return He immediately conceded to me
a singular favor for the benefit of the children of the
Church and conformable to my wishes. It was this, that
all those devoted to me, who should call upon me at the
hour of death, constituting me as their Advocate in memory of my happy Transition and of my desiring to imitate Him in death, shall be under my special protection
in that hour, shall have me as a defense against the
demons, as a help and protection, and shall be presented
by me before the tribunal of his mercy and there experience my intercession. In consequence the Lord gave me
a new power and commission and He promised to confer
great helps of his grace for a good death and for a purer
life on all those who in veneration of this mystery of my
precious death, should invoke my aid. Hence I desire
thee, my beloved daughter, from this day on to keep in
thy inmost heart a devout and loving memory of this
mystery, and to bless, praise, and magnify the Omnipotent, because He wrought such sacred miracles for me
and for the mortals. By this solicitude thou wilt oblige
the Lord and me to come to thy aid in that last hour.

746. And since death follows upon life and ordinarily
corresponds with it, therefore the surest pledge of a good
death is a good life; a life in which the heart is freed
and detached from earthly love. For this it is, which in
that last hour afflicts and oppresses the soul and which
is like a heavy chain restraining its liberty and preventing it from rising above the things loved in this world.

O my daughter! How greatly do mortals misunderstand this truth, and how far they err from it in their actions! The Lord gives them life in order that they may free themselves from the effects of original sin, so as to be unhampered by them at the hour of their death; and the ignorant and miserable children of Adam spend all their life in loading upon themselves new burdens and fetters, so that they die captives of their passions and in the tyranny of their hellish foes. I had no share in original sin and none of its effects had any power over my faculties; nevertheless I lived in the greatest constraint, in poverty and detached from earthly things, most perfect and holy; and this holy freedom I did indeed experience at the hour of my death. Consider then, my daughter, and be mindful of this living example; free thy heart more and more each day, so that with advancing years thou mayest find thyself more free, more detached and averted from visible things, and so that when the Spouse shall call thee to his nuptials, thou wilt not need to seek in vain the required freedom and prudence.

CHAPTER XX.

THE BURIAL OF THE SACRED BODY OF THE MOST BLESSED MARY, AND WHAT HAPPENED THEREAT.

747. In order that the Apostles, the disciples, and many others of the faithful might not be too deeply oppressed by sorrow, and in order that some of them might not die of grief caused by the passing away of the most blessed Mary, it was necessary that the divine power, by an especial providence, furnish them with consolation and dilate their heart for new influences in their incomparable affliction. For the feeling, that their loss was irretrievable in the present life, could not be repressed; the privation of such a Treasure could never find a recompense; and as the most sweet, loving and amiable intercourse and conversation of their great Queen had ravished the heart of each one, the ceasing of her protection and company left them as it were without the breath of life. But the Lord, who well knew how to estimate the just cause of their sorrow, secretly upheld them by his encouragements and so they set about the fitting burial of the sacred body and whatever the occasion demanded.

748. Accordingly the holy Apostles, on whom this duty specially devolved, held a conference concerning the burial of the most sacred body of their Queen and Lady. They selected for that purpose a new sepulchre, which had been prepared mysteriously by the providence of her divine Son. As they remembered, that, according to the custom of the Jews at burial, the deified body of their

632

Master had been anointed with precious ointments and spices and wrapped in the sacred burial cloths; they thought not of doing otherwise with the virginal body of his most holy Mother. Accordingly they called the two maidens, who had assisted the Queen during her life and who had been designated as the heiresses of her tunics, and instructed them to anoint the body of the Mother of God with highest reverence and modesty and wrap it in the winding-sheets before it should be placed in the casket. With great reverence and fear the two maidens entered the room, where the body of the blessed Lady lay upon its couch; but the refulgence issuing from it barred and blinded them in such a manner that they could neither see nor touch the body, nor even ascertain in what particular place it rested.

749. In fear and reverence still greater than on their entrance, the maidens left the room; and in great excitement and wonder they told the Apostles what had happened. They, not without divine inspiration, came to the conclusion, that this sacred Ark of the covenant was not to be touched or handled in the common way. Then saint Peter and saint John entered the oratory and perceived the effulgence, and at the same time they heard the celestial music of the angels, who were singing: "Hail Mary, full of grace, the Lord is with thee." Others responded: "A Virgin before childbirth, in childbirth and after childbirth." From that time on many of the faithful expressed their devotion toward the most blessed Mary in these words of praise; and from them they were handed down to be repeated by us with the approbation of the holy Church. The two holy Apostles, saint Peter and saint John, were for a time lost in admiration at what they saw and heard of their Queen; and in order to decide what to do, they sank on their knees, beseech-

ing the Lord to make it known. Then they heard a voice saying: "Let not the sacred body be either uncovered or touched."

750. Having thus been informed of the will of God, they brought a bier, and, the effulgence having diminished somewhat, they approached the couch and with their own hands reverently took hold of the tunic at the two ends. Thus, without changing its posture, they raised the sacred and virginal Treasure and placed it on the bier in the same position as it had occupied on the couch. They could easily do this, because they felt no more weight than that of the tunic. On this bier the former effulgence of the body moderated still more, and all of them, by disposition of the Lord and for the consolation of all those present, could now perceive and study the beauty of that virginal countenance and of her hands. As for the rest, the omnipotence of God protected this his heavenly dwelling, so that neither in life nor in death any one should behold any other part except what is common in ordinary conversation, namely, her most inspiring countenance, by which She had been known, and her hands, by which She had labored.

751. So great was the care and solicitude for his most blessed Mother, that in this particular He used not so much precaution in regard to his own body, as that of the most pure Virgin. In her Immaculate Conception He made Her like to Himself; likewise at her birth, in as far as it did not take place in the common and natural manner of other men. He preserved Her also from impure temptations and thoughts. But, as He was man and the Redeemer of the world through his Passion and Death, He permitted with his own body, what He would not allow with Hers, as that of a woman, and therefore He kept her virginal body entirely concealed; in fact

the most pure Lady during her life had Herself asked that no one should be permitted to look upon it in death; which petition He fulfilled.   Then the Apostles consulted further about her burial.   Their decision becoming known among the multitudes of the faithful in Jerusalem, they brought many candles to be lighted at the bier, and it happened that all the lights burned through that day and the two following days without any of the candles being consumed or wasted in any shape or manner.

752. In order that this and many other miracles wrought by the power of God on this occasion might become better known to the world, the Lord himself inspired all the inhabitants of Jerusalem to be present at the burial of his most blessed Mother, so that there was scarcely any person in Jerusalem, even of the Jews or the gentiles, who were not attracted by the novelty of this spectacle.   The Apostles took upon their shoulders the sacred body and the tabernacle of God and, as priests of the evangelical law, bore the Propitiatory of the divine oracles and blessings in orderly procession from the Cenacle in the city to the valley of Josaphat. This was the visible accompaniment of the dwellers of Jerusalem.   But besides this there was another invisible multitude, that of the courtiers of heaven.   It was composed of the thousand angels of the Queen, continuing their celestial songs, which were heard by the Apostles and disciples and many others, and which sweetly continued for three days.   In addition to these many other spirits had descended from heaven, namely, many thousands or legions of angels with the ancient Patriarchs and Prophets, among whom were saint Joachim, saint Anne, saint Joseph, saint Elisabeth and the Baptist and numerous other saints, who were sent by our Savior Jesus to assist at the exequies and burial of his most blessed Mother.

753. In the midst of this celestial and earthly accompaniment, visible and invisible, the Apostles bore along the sacred body, and on the way happened great miracles, which would take much time to relate. In particular all the sick, of which there were many of the different kinds, were entirely cured. Many of the possessed were freed from the demons; for the evil spirits did not dare to wait until the sacred body came near the persons thus afflicted. Greater still were the miracles of conversions wrought among many Jews and gentiles, for on this occasion were opened up the treasures of divine mercy, so that many souls came to the knowledge of Christ our Savior and loudly confessed Him as the true God and Redeemer, demanding Baptism. Many days thereafter the Apostles and disciples labored hard in catechizing and baptising those, who on that day had been converted to the holy faith. The Apostles in carrying the sacred body felt wonderful effects of divine light and consolation, in which the disciples shared according to their measure. All the multitudes of the people were seized with astonishment at the fragrance diffused about, the sweet music and the other prodigies. They proclaimed God great and powerful in this Creature and in testimony of their acknowledgment, they struck their breasts in sorrow and compunction.

754. When the procession came to the holy sepulchre in the valley of Josaphat, the same two Apostles, saint Peter and saint John, who had laid the celestial Treasure from the couch onto the bier, with joyful reverence placed it in the sepulchre and covered it with a linen cloth, the hands of the angels performing more of these last rites than the hands of the Apostles. They closed up the sepulchre with a large stone, according to custom at other burials. The celestial courtiers returned to heaven, while

the thousand angels of the Queen continued their watch, guarding the sacred body and keeping up the music as at her burial. The concourse of the people lessened and the holy Apostles and disciples, dissolved in tender tears, returned to the Cenacle. During a whole year the exquisite fragrance exhaled by the body of the Queen was noticeable throughout the Cenacle, and in her oratory, for many years. This sanctuary remained a place of refuge for all those that were burdened with labor and difficulties; all found miraculous assistance, as well in sickness as in hardships and necessities of other kind. After these miracles had continued for some years in Jerusalem, the sins of Jerusalem and of its inhabitants drew upon this city, among other punishments, that of being deprived of this inestimable blessing.

755. Having again gathered in the Cenacle, the Apostles came to the conclusion that some of them and of the disciples should watch at the sepulchre of their Queen as long as they should hear the celestial music, for all of them were wondering when the end of that miracle should be. Accordingly some of them attended to the affairs of the Church in catechizing and baptizing the new converts; and others immediately returned to the sepulchre, while all of them paid frequent visits to it during the next three days. Saint Peter and saint John, however, were more zealous in their attendance, coming only a few times to the Cenacle and immediately returning to where was laid the treasure of their heart. Nor were the irrational creatures missing at the exequies of the Mistress of the universe; for as the sacred body arrived near the grave, innumerable large and small birds gathered in the air, and many animals and wild beasts rushed from the mountains toward the sepulchre, the ones singing sorrowfully the others emitting groans and doleful sounds

and all of them showing grief in their movements as if
mourning over the common loss.   Only a few unbelieving
Jews, more hardened than the rocks and more impious
than the wild beasts failed to show sorrow at the death
of their Restoratrix, as they had failed to do also at the
death of their Redeemer and Master.

INSTRUCTION WHICH THE QUEEN OF HEAVEN, MOST HOLY MARY, GAVE ME.

756. My daughter, in commemorating my natural
death and my burial, I wish that thou also die and be
buried to all worldly things, and this is to be the fruit
and the principal result of thy having known and written
my life.   Many times in the course of thy writing have
I manifested to thee this as my desire and intimated it
to thee as my will, lest thou waste this singular favor
shown to thee by the Lord and by me.   It is a foul offense
in any Christian, if, after dying to sin and after being
reborn in Christ by Baptism, knowing that the Lord
died for him, he returns again to the same faults; and
this will be a still greater wickedness in those souls, who
are called by special grace to be the most dear friends of
the Lord, as is the case with those, who for that very
purpose dedicate and consecrate themselves to his closer
service in religion, each one according to his condition
and state.

757. In these souls the vices of the world cause horror
in heaven itself, because the pride, the presumption, the
haughtiness, the want of mortification, the anger, the
covetousness, the conscious impurities and other wickedness in such souls force the Lord and the saints to withdraw from the sight of their monstrous distortion and
rouse them to greater wrath and offense than the same
sins in other souls.   Therefore the Lord repudiates many

who unrighteously bear the name of being his spouses and leaves them to their own bad counsels, because they have so disloyally broken the fidelity promised to God and to me in their vocation and profession. But if all souls must fear this terrible infidelity, consider well, my daughter, what abhorrence especially thou wouldst deserve in the sight of God, if thou wert guilty of such disloyalty. It is time that thou die to the visible things, and that thy body be buried in thy self-knowledge and self-abasement, while thy soul sink into the being of God. The days of thy life in this world are coming to a close; and I shall be the judge to execute the sentence of thy separation from life and from the world: thou needst not any more be seen with those who live in it, nor they with thee. The writing of my life should be for thee the seal of thy death to the world, as I have so often exhorted thee and as thou hast repeatedly and expressly promised me, with heartfelt tears.

758. I wish this to be the proof of my doctrine and of its efficacy; do not permit it to be discredited in thee to my dishonor, but let heaven and earth perceive the force of its truth and of my example in thy works. For this thou must depend neither upon thy understanding nor upon thy will, and still less upon thy inclinations and passions, because all this for thee has come to a finish. Thy law must be the will of the Lord and my own, and the dictates of obedience. And in order that thou mayest never mistake what is in them the most holy, the most perfect and God-pleasing, the Lord has provided for thy direction in all things, lavishing upon thee his own care, mine, and that of the holy angels. Do not allege ignorance, pusillanimity, or weakness, nor much less, fear. Weigh thy obligation, estimate thy indebtedness, attend to the continual light; operate with the grace thou re-

ceivest, so that amid all these benefits there be no cross so heavy, no death so bitter, as shall not be deemed by thee very light and acceptable. In this consists all thy good, and in it is to be thy delight; since, if thou dost not succeed in dying to all things, besides that thy path will be sown with thorns, thou shalt not reach the perfection thou desirest, nor the state to which the Lord calls thee.

759. If the world will not forget thee, do thou forget it; if it will not leave thee alone, remember that thou hast forsaken it, and that I have separated thee from it. If it follow thee, fly; if it flatter thee, despise it; if it contemn thee, suffer it; and if it seek thee, let it not find thee except in so far as will be to the glory of the Most High. But as regards all the rest, thou must not any more bear it in mind, than the living remember the dead. Forget it just as the dead forget the living, and I desire that thou have no more intercourse with this world, than the dead have with the living. It will not seem extraordinary to thee, that in the beginning, in the middle and at the end of this history I repeat so often this doctrine, if thou ponder what depends upon thy practicing it. Consider, my dearest, what persecutions the devil has roused against thee in secret through the world and its inhabitants under different pretexts and appearances. If God has permitted them for the purpose of trying thee and for the exercise of his grace, it is proper, that, as far as thou are concerned, thou take it as a lesson and a warning. Remember that great is the treasure which thou carriest in a fragile vessel (II Cor. 2, 7), and that all hell conspires and rises up against thee. Thou livest in mortal flesh, surrounded and assailed by astute enemies. Be a Spouse of Christ my divine Son, and I shall be thy Mother and Instructress. Recognize, then, thy need and thy weakness, and correspond with me as a dearest daughter, as an obedient and perfect disciple in all things.

CHAPTER XXI.

760. Of the glory and felicity of the saints in the
beatific vision saint Paul says with Isaias (I Cor. 2, 9;
Is. 64, 4), that neither have mortal eyes seen, nor ears
heard, nor can it enter into the heart of man what
God has prepared for those who love Him and who hope
in Him. In accordance with this Catholic truth, we
should not wonder at what is related of saint Augustine,
the great light of the Church, that, in setting out to write
a book on the glory of the blessed, he was visited by
his friend, saint Jerome, who had just died and entered
into the glory of the Lord, and was admonished by his
visitor, that he would not be able to compass his design;
since no tongue or pen of man could describe the least
part of the blessings enjoyed by the saints in the beatific
vision. Such is the testimony of saint Jerome; and if
through holy Scriptures we had no other information
than that this glory is eternal, it would be beyond all our
comprehension. For, however much of our intellect may
expand, it will never comprehend eternity; and as this
is infinite and boundless, it is inexhaustible and incomprehensible, how much soever it may be known and loved.
Just as God, the Infinite and the Almighty, created all
things, without being thereby exhausted, and even if He

641

had created endless worlds ever anew, would remain still infinite and immutable; so also, although seen and enjoyed by countless saints, He will remain an infinite source of new knowledge and love; for in creation and in glory all creatures participate in Him only to a limited extent, each according to its condition, while He in Himself is without limitation or end.

761. If on this account the glory even of the least of the saints is eneffable, what shall we say of the glory of the most blessed Mary, since among the saints She is the most holy and She by Herself is more like to her Son than all the saints together, and since her grace and glory exceed those of all the rest, as those of an empress or sovereign over her vassals? This truth can and should be believed; but in mortal life it cannot be understood, or the least part of it be explained; for the inadequacy and deficiency of our words and expressions rather tend to obscure than to set forth its greatness. Let us in this life apply our labor, not in seeking to comprehend it, but in seeking to merit its manifestation in glory, where we shall experience more or less of this happiness according to our works.

762. Our Redeemer Jesus entered heaven conducting the purest soul of his Mother at his right hand. She alone of all the mortals deserved exemption from particular judgment; hence for Her there was none; no account was asked or demanded of Her for what She had received; for such was the promise that had been given to Her, when She was exempted from the common guilt and chosen as the Queen privileged above the laws of the children of Adam. For the same reason, instead of being judged with the rest, She shall be seated at the right hand of the Judge to judge with Him all the creatures. If in the first instant of her Conception She was the brightest

Aurora, effulgent with the rays of the sun of the Divinity beyond all the brightness of the most exalted seraphim, and if afterwards She was still further illumined by the contact of the hypostatic Word, who derived his humanity from her purest substance, it necessarily follows that She should be his Companion for all eternity, possessing such a likeness to Him, that none greater can be possible between a Godman and a creature. In this light the Redeemer himself presented Her before the throne of the Divinity; and speaking to the eternal Father in the presence of all the blessed, who were ravished at this wonder, the most sacred humanity uttered these words: "Eternal Father, my most beloved Mother, thy beloved Daughter and the cherished Spouse of the Holy Ghost, now comes to take possession of the crown and glory, which We have prepared as a reward for her merit. She is the one who was born as the rose among thorns, untouched, pure and beautiful, worthy of being embraced by Us and of being placed upon a throne to which none of our creatures can ever attain, and to which those conceived in sin cannot aspire. This is our chosen and our only One, distinguished above all else, to whom We communicated our grace and our perfections beyond the measure accorded to other creatures; in whom We have deposited the treasure of our incomprehensible Divinity and its gifts; who most faithfully preserved and made fruitful the talents, which We gave Her; who never swerved from our will, and who found grace and pleasure in our eyes. My Father, most equitous is the tribunal of our justice and mercy, and in it the services of our friends are repaid in the most superabundant manner. It is right that to my Mother be given the reward of a Mother; and if during her whole life and in all her works She was as like to Me as is possible for a creature to be, let Her also be as like to Me in glory and on the throne of our Majesty, so that where holiness is in essence, there it may also be found in its highest participation."

763. This decree of the incarnate Word was approved by the Father and the Holy Ghost. The most holy soul of Mary was immediately raised to the right hand of her Son and true God, and placed on the royal throne of the most holy Trinity, which neither men, nor angels nor the seraphim themselves attain, and will not attain for all eternity. This is the most exalted and supereminent privilege of our Queen and Lady, that She is seated on the throne with the three divine Persons and holds her place as Empress, while all the rest are set as servants and ministers to the highest King. To the eminence and majesty of that position, inaccessible to all other creatures, correspond her gifts of glory, comprehension, vision and fruition; because She enjoys, above all and more than all, that infinite Object, which the other blessed enjoy in an endless variety of degrees. She knows, penetrates and understands much deeper the eternal Being and its infinite attributes; She lovingly delights in its mysteries and most hidden secrets, more than all the rest of the blessed. Although between the glory of the divine Persons and that of the most holy Mary there is an infinite distance; for the light of the Divinity, as says the Apostle (I Tim. 6, 16), is inaccessible and in it alone dwells immortality and glory by essence; and though also the most holy soul of Christ without measure exceeds in its gifts those of his Mother; yet the great Queen surpasses inaccessibly all the saints in glory and has a likeness to that of Christ, which cannot be understood in this life, nor ever described.

764. Just as little can be explained the extra joy, which the blessed experienced on that day in singing the new songs of praise to the Omnipotent and in celebrating the

glory of his Daughter, Mother and Spouse; for in Her He had exalted all the works of his right hand. Although to the Lord himself could come no new or essential glory, because He possessed and possesses it immutably infinite through all eternity; yet the exterior manifestations of his pleasure and satisfaction at the fulfillment of his eternal decrees were greater on that day, and from the throne a voice, as if of the eternal Father resounded, saying: "In the glory of our beloved and most loving Daughter all the pleasure of our holy will is fulfilled to our entire satisfaction. To all the creatures We have given existence, creating them out of nothing, in order that they may participate in our infinite goods and treasures according to the inclination and pleasure of our immense bounty. The very ones who were made capable of our grace and glory, have abused this blessing. Our cherished Daughter alone had no part in the disobedience and prevarication of the rest, and She has earned what the unworthy children of perdition have despised; and our heart has not been disappointed in Her at any time or moment. To Her belong the rewards, which according to our conditional decree We had prepared for the disobedient angels and for their followers among men, if they had been faithful to their grace and vocation. She has recompensed Us for their falling away by her subjection and obedience; She has pleased Us in all her operations and has merited a seat on the throne of our Majesty."

765. On the third day after the most pure soul of Mary had taken possession of this glory never to leave it, the Lord manifested to the saints his divine will, that She should return to the world, resuscitate her sacred body and unite Herself with it, so that She might in body and soul be again raised to the right hand of her divine Son without waiting for the general resurrection of the dead.

The appropriateness of this favor, its accordance with the others received by the most blessed Queen and with her supereminent dignity, the saints could not but see; since even to mortals it is so credible, that even if the Church had not certified it, we would judge those impious and foolish, who would dare deny it. But the blessed saw it with greater clearness, together with the determined time and hour as manifested to them in God himself. When the time for this wonder had arrived, Christ our Savior himself descended from heaven bringing with Him at his right hand the soul of his most blessed Mother and accompanied by many legions of the Angels, the Patriarchs and ancient Prophets. They came to the sepulchre in the valley of Josaphat, and all being gathered in sight of the virginal temple, the Lord spoke the following words to the saints.

766. "My Mother was conceived without stain of sin, in order that from Her virginal substance I might stainlessly clothe Myself in the humanity in which I came to the world and redeemed it from sin. My flesh is her flesh; She co-operated with Me in the works of the Redemption; hence I must raise Her, just as I rose from the dead, and this shall be at the same time and hour. For I wish to make Her like Me in all things." All the ancient saints of the human race then gave thanks for this new favor in songs of praise and glory to the Lord. Those that especially distinguished themselves in their thanksgiving were our first parents Adam and Eve, saint Anne, saint Joachim and saint Joseph, as being the more close partakers in this miracle of his Omnipotence. Then the purest soul of the Queen, at the command of the Lord, entered the virginal body, reanimated it and raised it up, giving it a new life of immortality and glory and communicating to it the four gifts of clearness, impassibility,

agility and subtlety, corresponding to those of the soul and overflowing from it into the body.

767. Endowed with these gifts the most blessed Mary issued from the tomb in body and soul, without raising the stone cover and without disturbing the position of the tunic and the mantle that had enveloped her sacred body. Since it is impossible to describe her beauty and refulgent glory, I will not make the attempt. It is sufficient to say, that just as the heavenly Mother had given to her divine Son in her womb the form of man, pure, unstained and sinless, for the Redemption of the world, so in return the Lord, in this resurrection and new regeneration, gave to Her a glory and beauty similar to his own. In this mysterious and divine interchange each One did what was possible: most holy Mary engendered Christ, assimilating Him as much as possible to Herself, and Christ resuscitated Her, communicating to Her of his glory as far as She was capable as a creature.

768. Then from the sepulchre was started a most solemn procession, moving with celestial music through the regions of the air and toward the empyrean heaven. This happened in the hour immediately after midnight, in which also the Lord had risen from the grave; and therefore not all of the Apostles were witness of this prodigy, but only some of them, who were present and watching at the sepulchre. The saints and angels entered heaven in the order in which they had started; and in the last place came Christ our Savior and at his right hand the Queen, clothed in the gold of variety (as David says Ps. 44, 10), and so beautiful that She was the admiration of the heavenly court. All of them turned toward Her to look upon Her and bless Her with new jubilee and songs of praise. Thus were heard those mysterious eulogies recorded by Solomon: Come, daughters of Sion, to see

your Queen, who is praised by the morning stars and celebrated by the sons of the Most High. Who is She that comes from the desert, like a column of all the aromatic perfumes? Who is She, that rises like the aurora, more beautiful than the moon, elect as the sun, terrible as many serried armies? Who is She that comes up from the desert resting upon her Beloved and spreading forth abundant delights? (Cant. 3, 6-9; 8, 5). Who is She in whom the Deity itself finds so much pleasure and delight above all other creatures and whom He exalts above them all in the heavens! O novelty worthy of the infinite Wisdom! O prodigy of his Omnipotence, which so magnifies and exalts Her!

769. Amid this glory the most blessed Mary arrived body and soul at the throne of the most blessed Trinity. And the three divine Persons received Her on it with an embrace eternally undissoluble. The eternal Father said to Her: "Ascend higher, my Daughter and my Dove." The incarnate Word spoke: "My Mother, of whom I have received human being and full return of my work in thy perfect imitation, receive now from my hand the reward thou hast merited." The Holy Ghost said: "My most beloved Spouse, enter into the eternal joy, which corresponds to the most faithful love; do Thou now enjoy thy love without solicitude; for past is the winter of suffering for Thou hast arrived at our eternal embraces." There the most blessed Mary was absorbed in the contemplation of the three divine Persons and as it were overwhelmed in the boundless ocean and abyss of the Divinity, while the saints were filled with wonder and new accidental delight. Since, at the occasion of this work of the Omnipotent happened other wonders, I shall speak of them as far as possible in the following chapter.

INSTRUCTION WHICH THE QUEEN OF HEAVEN, MOST HOLY
MARY, GAVE ME.

770. My daughter, lamentable and inexcusable is the ignorance of men in so knowingly forgetting the eternal glory, which God has prepared for those who dispose themselves to merit it. I wish that thou bitterly bewail and deplore this pernicious forgetfulness; for there is no doubt, that whoever wilfully forgets the eternal glory and happiness is in evident danger of losing it. No one is free from this guilt, not only because men do not apply much labor or effort in seeking and retaining the remembrance of this happiness; but they labor with all their powers in things that make them forget the end for which they were created. Undoubtedly this forgetfulness arises from their entangling themselves in the pride of life, the covetousness of the eyes, and the desires of the flesh (John 2, 16); for employing therein all the forces and faculties of their soul during the whole time of their life, they have no leisure, care or attention for the thoughts of eternal felicity. Let men acknowledge and confess, whether this recollection costs them more labor than to follow their blind passions, seeking after honors, possessions or the transitory pleasures, all of which have an end with this life, and which, after much striving and labor, many men do not, and can never attain.

771. How much easier is it for mortals to avoid such perversity, especially for the children of the Church, since they have at hand the easy means of faith and hope for attaining the truth! Even if to gain eternal happiness were as difficult to obtain as honors and riches and other apparent advantages, it would be very foolish to labor as much for the false as for the true advantages for eternal

punishment as for eternal glory. This abominable foolishness thou wilt perceive and bewail with tears, my daughter, if thou wilt consider the world in which thou livest: how it is disturbed by wars and discords; how many unhappy ones it contains, who seek death in exchange for a short and vain honor, vengeance and other most vile advantages, while they do not think or care for eternal life than irrational animals. It would be a blessing for them if like animals they could end altogether with the temporal death; but as the most of them act against justice, and others, who still seek to be just, live in forgetfulness of their end, the ones as well as the others incur the eternal death.

772. This is a sorrow beyond all sorrows, and a misfortune without equal and without remedy. Afflict thyself, lament and grieve without consolation over this ruin of so many souls bought by the blood of my divine Son. I assure thee, my dearest, that, if men would not make themselves so unworthy of it, my charity would urge me, in the celestial glory where thou knowest me to be, to send forth a voice through the whole world exclaiming: "Mortal and deceived men, what are you doing? For what purpose are you living? Do you realize what it is to see God face to face, and to participate in his eternal glory and share his company? Of what are you thinking? Who has thus disturbed and fascinated your judgment? What will you seek, if once you have lost this true blessing and happiness, since there is no other? The labor is short, the reward is infinite glory, and the punishment is eternal."

773. In connection with this sorrow, which I am trying to excite in thee, seek to labor assiduously in order to evade the danger. A living example thou hast in my life, which was a continual suffering such as thou hast

known; but when I came to my reward all of it seemed as nothing, and I forgot it as if it had not occurred. Resolve, my dear, to follow me in my labor; and though thy labor seem to exceed that of all the mortals, look upon it as most insignificant; let nothing seem to thee difficult or hard, or bitter, even to passing through fire and sword. Extend thy hand to great things, and shield thy domestics, the senses, with double vestments (Prov. 31, 19, 21), against hardships and sufferings to the utmost of their powers. At the same time I wish thee to be free from another error, that of men who say: let us secure salvation: greater or less glory does not matter; we shall all be together in that life. By this false principle, my daughter, eternal life is not made secure, but rather put at hazard; since it arises from great foolishness and want of divine love. Who seeks to make such a bargain with God, offends Him, and tempts Him to permit such souls to live in continued danger of perdition. Human weakness always tends to do less good than it desires to do; and when this desire is small, then it will execute very little, and hence risks losing all.

774. He who contents himself with the mediocre or lowest in virtue, always leaves in his will and in his inclinations an opening for earthly affections and love of the passing things. Such an opening is contrary to divine love and therefore unavoidably causes the loss of the latter and the ascendency of the former. When the creature resolves to love God from all its heart and with all its powers, as He commands, God overlooks its human defects and shortcomings, and is pleased with their resolve to reap the highest rewards. But to despise them or wilfully undervalue them shows not the love of children or of true friends, but the base fear of slaves, who are content to live and be let alone. If the saints could

return to merit some additional degree of glory by suffering all torments to the day of judgment, they would doubtlessly return; because they have a true and perfect knowledge of the value of the reward and they love God with a perfect charity. It is not proper that this privilege be granted to the saints; but it was conceded to me, as thou hast recorded in this history; and my example confirms this truth. It also reproves the foolishness of those, who, in order to avoid suffering and the cross of Christ, are looking for a curtailed reward, one which is contrary to the inclination of God's goodness and contrary to his desire of seeing souls multiply their merits and gain copious rewards in the eternal felicity.

CHAPTER XXII.

MOST HOLY MARY IS CROWNED AS QUEEN OF HEAVEN AND OF ALL CREATURES; ALL HER GREAT PRIVILEGES IN FAVOR OF MANKIND ARE AGAIN CONFIRMED UPON HER.

775. When Christ Jesus the Savior took leave of his disciples in order to enter upon his suffering, He told them not to be disturbed in their hearts on account of the things He had told them; because in the house of his Father, which is eternal happiness, there are many mansions. He further assured them, that there was room and reward for all, although the merits and their good works be diverse and that no one should be disturbed in his peace and hope, though he should see others more favored or advanced; because in the house of God there are many grades and many dwellings, in which each one shall be content with what shall belong to him without envy; for this is one of the great blessings of that eternal felicity. I have said that most blessed Mary was assigned to the supreme position and state on the throne of the most blessed Trinity. Many times have I expressed myself in these terms in order to point out great sacraments and similar terms are used by the saints and by the sacred scriptures themselves (Apoc. 1, 4; 3, 21). Although no other argument is really necessary, nevertheless, for those who have not such a deep insight, I will say that God, as He is the purest Spirit and at the same time infinite, immense, incomprehensible, has no need of a material throne or seat; for He fills all creation and is present in all creatures; He is comprehended or circumscribed by none, but

He himself comprehends and encompasses all things. The saints do not see God with corporal eyes, but with those of the soul; but as they see Him in some certain location (in order to adapt ourselves to our terrestrial and material ways of thinking and speaking) we say that He is upon the royal throne of the most blessed Trinity, though in reality He has his glory within Himself and communicates it to his saints. But I do not wish to deny, that the most sacred humanity of Christ our Savior and of his most blessed Mother holds a place supereminent over all the saints; and that among the blessed, who are in heaven with body and soul, there will be some kind of order in their relative position nearer or farther from Christ our Lord and the Queen; but here is not the place to inquire into the manner into which this arrangement shall be made in heaven.

776. We call that the throne of the Divinity, from which God manifests Himself to the saints as the principal cause of their glory and as the infinite, eternal God, independent of all things and on whose will all creatures depend, from which He manifests Himself as the Lord, as the King, as the Judge and Master of all that is in existence. This dignity Christ the Redeemer possesses, in as far as He is God, essentially, and as far as He is man, through the hypostatic union, by which He communicates his Godhead to the humanity. Hence in heaven He is the King, the Lord and supreme Judge; and the saints, though their glory exceeds all human calculation, are as servants and inferiors of this inaccessible Majesty. In this the most holy Mary participates in a degree next inferior and in a manner otherwise ineffable and proportionate to a mere creature so closely related to the God-man; and therefore She assists forever at the right hand of her Son as Queen (Ps. 44, 10), Lady and Mistress of

all creation, her dominion extending as far as that of her divine Son, although in a different manner.

777. After placing the most blessed Mary on this exalted and supereminent throne, the Lord declared to the courtiers of heaven all the privileges She should enjoy in virtue of this participation in his majesty. The Person of the eternal Father, as the first principle of all things, speaking to the angels and saints, said to them: "Our Daughter Mary was chosen according to our pleasure from amongst all creatures, the first one to delight Us, and who never fell from the title and position of a true Daughter, such as We had given Her in our divine mind; She has a claim on our dominion, which We shall recognize by crowning Her as the legitimate and peerless Lady and Sovereign." The incarnate Word said: "To my true and natural Mother belong all the creatures which were created and redeemed my Me; and of all things over which I am King, She too shall be the legitimate and supreme Queen." The Holy Ghost said: "Since She is called my beloved and chosen Spouse, She deserves to be crowned as Queen for all eternity."

778. Having thus spoken the three divine Persons placed upon the head of the most blessed Mary a crown of such new splendor and value, that the like has been seen neither before nor after by any mere creature. At the same time a voice sounded from the throne saying: "My Beloved, chosen among the creatures, our kingdom is Thine; Thou shalt be the Lady and the Sovereign of the seraphim, of all the ministering spirits, the angels and of the entire universe of creatures. Attend, proceed and govern prosperously over them, for in our supreme consistory We give Thee power, majesty and sovereignty. Being filled with grace beyond all the rest, Thou hast humiliated Thyself in thy own estimation to the lowest

place; receive now the supreme dignity deserved by Thee and, as a participation in our Divinity, the dominion over all the creatures of our Omnipotence. From thy royal throne to the centre of the earth Thou shalt reign; and by the power We now give Thee Thou shalt subject hell with all its demons and inhabitants. Let all of them fear Thee as the supreme Empress and Mistress of those caverns and dwelling-places of our enemies. In thy hands and at thy pleasure We place the influences and forces of the heavens, the moisture of the clouds, the growths of the earth; and of all of them do Thou distribute according to thy will, and our own will shall be at thy disposal for the execution of thy wishes. Thou shalt be the Empress and Mistress of the militant Church, its Protectress, its Advocate, its Mother and Teacher. Thou shalt be the special Patroness of the Catholic countries; and whenever they, or the faithful, or any of the children of Adam call upon Thee from their heart, serve or oblige Thee, Thou shalt relieve and help them in their labors and necessities. Thou shalt be the Friend, the Defender and the Chieftainess of all the just and of our friends; all of them Thou shalt comfort, console and fill with blessings according to their devotion to Thee. In view of all this We make Thee the Depositary of our riches, the Treasurer of our goods; we place into thy hands the helps and blessings of our grace for distribution; nothing do We wish to be given to the world, which does not pass through thy hands; and nothing do We deny, which Thou wishest to concede to men. Grace shall be diffused in thy lips for obtaining all that Thou wishest and ordainest in heaven and on earth, and everywhere shall angels and men obey Thee; because whatever is ours shall be thine, just as Thou hast always been ours; and Thou shalt reign with Us forever."

779. In the execution of this decree and privilege conceded to the Mistress of the world, the Almighty commanded all the courtiers of heaven, angels and men, to show Her obedience and recognize Her as their Queen and Lady.   There was another mystery concealed in this wonder, namely, it was a recompense for the worship and veneration, which, as is clear from this history, the most blessed Mary, notwithstanding that She was the Mother of God, full of grace and holiness above the angels and saints, had bestowed upon the saints during her mortal pilgrimage.   Although during the time when they were comprehensors and She yet a pilgrim, it was for her greater merit, that She should humble Herself beneath them all according to the ordainment of the Lord; yet now, when She was in possession of the kingdom, it was just, that She should be venerated, worshipped and extolled by them as her inferiors and vassals.   This they also did in that most blessed state, in which all things are reduced to their proper proportion and order.   Both the angelic spirits and the blessed souls, while rendering their adoration to the Lord with fear and worshipful reverence, rendered a like homage in its proportion to his most blessed Mother; and the saints who were there in their bodies prostrated themselves and gave bodily signs of their worship.   All these demonstrations at the coronation of the Empress of heaven redounded wonderfully to her glory, to the new joy and jubilee of the saints and to the pleasure of the most blessed Trinity.   Altogether festive was this day, and it produced new accidental glory in all the heavens.   Those that partook more especially therein were her most fortunate spouse saint Joseph, saint Joachim and Anne and all the other relatives of the Queen, together with the thousand angels of her guard.

780. Within the glorious body of the Queen, over her heart, was visible to the saints a small globe or monstrance of singular beauty and splendor, which particularly roused and rouses their admiration and joy. It was there in testimony and reward of her having afforded to the sacramental Word an acceptable resting-place and sanctuary, and of her having received holy Communion so worthily, purely and holily, without any defect or imperfection, and with a devotion, love and reverence attained by none other of the saints. In regard to the other rewards and crowns corresponding to her peerless works and virtues, nothing that can be said could give any idea; and therefore I refer it to the beatific vision, where each one shall perceive them in proportion as his doings and his devotion shall have merited. In the foregoing chapter I mentioned that the Transition of our Queen happened on the thirteenth of August, while her Resurrection, Assumption and Coronation happened on Sunday the fifteenth, on the day in which it is celebrated in the Church. Her sacred body remained in the sepulchre thirty-six hours, just as the body of her divine Son; for her Transition and her Resurrection took place in the same hours of the day. According to the computation given above, I advert that this miracle happened in the year of our Lord fifty-five, which had advanced as many days as intervene between the Nativity of the Lord and the fifteenth of August.

781. We have left the great Lady at the right hand of her divine Son, reigning through all the ages of eternity. We now return to the Apostles and disciples, who in flowing tears surrounded the sepulchre of Mary in the valley of Josaphat. Saint Peter and saint John, who had been the most constant in their attendance, noticed that the celestial music had ceased; for they failed

to hear it on the third day. Partly enlightened by the Holy Ghost, they conjectured that the most pure Mother had arisen and had entered heaven, body and soul, like her divine Son. They conferred about this matter and came to the conclusion that so it must be; and saint Peter, as the head of the Church, decided that such a wonderful fact should be ascertained as far as possible and made known to those who had witnessed her death and burial. For this purpose, on the same day, he called together the Apostles, disciples and the other faithful at the sepulchre. He told them of his reasons for the conjecture now in the mind of all and the reasons for manifesting the truth of this wonder to the Church, namely, that it should be reverenced in the coming ages and would redound to the glory of the Lord and of his most blessed Mother. All approved of the decision of the vicar of Christ and at his order immediately removed the stone, which closed the sepulchre. This being done, they saw the grave despoiled of the sacred body of the Queen of heaven and the tunic in the same position as when it had covered her, showing that it must have passed through the tunic and the stone of the sepulchre without disturbing any part of them. Saint Peter took out the tunic and the mantle and, with all the others, venerated it, as they were now certain of the Resurrection and Assumption of the blessed Mother into heaven. In mixed joy and sorrow they wept sweet tears at this prodigy and sang psalms and hymns of praise and glory to the Lord and his most blessed Mother.

782. In their affectionate wonder all of them remained looking at the sepulchre, spellbound, until the angel of the Lord descended and manifested himself to them, saying: "Ye men of Galilee, why are you astounded and tarry here? Your and our Queen now lives body

and soul in heaven and reigns in it forever with Christ. She sends me to confirm you in this truth, and in her name I tell you that She recommends to you anew the Church, the conversion of souls, and the spread of the Gospel. She desires to tell you that you now return to your ministry, with which you were charged, and that from her throne She will take care of you." At this message the Apostles were consoled; they experienced her protection in their wanderings, and much more in the hour of their martyrdom; for to each of them did She appear in that hour to present their souls to the Lord. Other particulars concerning the Transition and Resurrection of the most blessed Mary were not made known to me for record here; nor have I during the whole course of this heavenly history had any choice of saying except what was made known to me and what I was commanded to write.

INSTRUCTION WHICH THE QUEEN OF HEAVEN, MOST HOLY MARY, GAVE ME.

783. My daughter, if anything could lessen the enjoyment of the highest felicity and glory which I possess, and if, in it, I could be capable of any sorrow, without a doubt I would be grieved to see the holy Church and the rest of the world in its present state of labor, notwithstanding that men know me to be their Mother, Advocate and Protectress in heaven, ready to guide and assist them to eternal life. In this state of affairs, when the Almighty has granted me so many privileges as his Mother and when there are so many sources of help placed in my hands solely for the benefit of mortals and belonging to me as the Mother of clemency, it is a great cause of sorrow to me to see mortals force me to remain

idle, and that, for want of calling upon me, so many souls should be lost. But if I cannot experience grief now, I may justly complain of men, that they load themselves with eternal damnation and refuse me the glory of saving their souls.

784. How much my intercession and the power I have in heaven is worth has never been hidden in the Church, for I have demonstrated my ability to save all by so many thousands of miracles, prodigies and favors operated in behalf of those devoted to me. With those who have called upon me in their needs I have always shown myself liberal, and the Lord has shown himself liberal to them on my account. Yet, though many are the souls whom I have helped, they are few in comparison with those, whom I could and am willing to help. The world and the centuries are far advanced; while mortals are tardy in turning toward the knowledge of God; the children of the Church are involving themselves in the snares of satan; sinners multiply and crimes increase, because charity is getting cold even after God became incarnate and has taught the world by his life and doctrine, redeemed it by his Passion and Death, established his evangelical law for the guidance of his creatures, illustrated them by so many miracles, enlightenments, blessings, favors in the Church and in its saints. In addition to all this God has in his goodness opened up his mercies through me and my intercession, constituting me as Mother, Advocate, Protectress and Helper of all men, and, though I am most punctual and liberal in fulfilling all these offices, the result is inadequate. After all, since the crimes of men merit the chastisements, which threaten them and which they begin to feel, and since, under these circumstances, the malice of men has already reached the highest possible point, what wonder is it that divine Justice be irritated?

785. All this, my daughter, is true; but my kind and clement love exceeds all this malice, detains justice and still inclines the infinite Goodness toward men. The Most High still wishes to give liberally of his infinite treasures and resolves to favor those who know how to gain my intercession before God. This is the secure way and the powerful means of advancing the Church, of improving the Catholic reigns, of spreading the faith, of furthering the welfare of families and of states, of bringing the souls to grace and to the friendship of God. In this work, my daughter, I have desired thee to labor and assist according to thy power with the divine grace. Thy labor shall consist not only in having written my life, but in imitating it by following the counsels and salutary teachings, which thou hast so abundantly received, both in what thou hast written and in other favors and blessings of the Almighty. Consider well, my dearest, thy strict obligation of serving me as thy only Mother, as thy legitimate and true Teacher and Superior, who favors thee with all these and many other condescensions. Thou hast likewise often renewed and ratified the vows of thy profession into my hands, and hast therein promised me especial obedience. Remember the promises thou hast so often given to the Lord and his angels. Many times We have manifested to thee our will, that thou live and act as one of them, and that thou, in carnal flesh, participate in the condition and activity of an angel; that thy conversation and intercourse be with those purest spirits; and just as they converse with each other, and just as the higher enlighten and illumine the lower, so they will enlighten and instruct thee in the perfections of thy Beloved and in the exercise of all virtues, especially of the mistress of all of them, charity, by which thou mayest be inflamed in the love of

thy sweet Master and of thy fellowmen. To this state thou must aspire with all thy powers, in order that the Most High may find thee apt for the fulfillment of his most holy will and of all his wishes. May his powerful right hand give thee his eternal benediction, show thee the joy of his countenance and grant thee peace; see that thou do not make thyself unworthy.

CHAPTER XXIII.

AN OFFERING OF PRAISE AND THANKSGIVING MADE BY ME, SISTER MARY OF JESUS, THE LEAST OF THE MORTALS, TO THE LORD AND TO HIS MOST HOLY MOTHER, FOR HAVING BEEN CHOSEN TO WRITE THIS HEAVENLY HISTORY UNDER THE DIRECTION OF THE QUEEN AND MISTRESS OF HEAVEN.

786. I confess Thee, God eternal, Lord of heaven, earth, Father, Son and Holy Ghost, the one and true God, one substance and majesty in the Trinity of Persons; since, not having received aught from anybody that Thou shouldst repay him (Rom. 11, 35), solely through thy ineffable condescension and clemency, Thou revealest thy mysteries and sacraments to thy little ones (Matth. 11, 25); and since Thou dost it in immense bounty and infinite wisdom, pleasing Thyself and doing all things aright. In thy works Thou magnifiest thy holy name, exaltest thy Omnipotence, showest thy greatness, scatterest thy mercies and establishest thy glory, which is due to Thee as the holy, the wise, the powerful, the kind, the liberal God, the sole beginning and Author of all that is good. None is so holy as Thou, none so powerful, none so exalted, who raisest the poor from the dust and from nothingness, and enrichest the needy (Ps. 112, 7). Thine are, O Most high God, the ends and the poles of the earth; Thou givest life and givest death; Thou humblest and castest down to the abyss the proud; Thou raisest up the humble according to thy pleasure; Thou enrichest and impoverishest, in order that in thy pres-

ence no flesh may boast, nor the strongest presume upon his strength, nor the weakest fear or distrust his weakness and his lowliness.

787. I confess Thee, true Lord, as the King and Savior of the world, Jesus Christ. I confess and praise thy holy name, and give glory to Thee, who conferrest wisdom. I confess Thee, Queen of heaven, most holy Mary, worthy Mother of my Lord Jesus Christ, beginning of our salvation, Depositary of the treasures of his grace, living temple of the Divinity, Restoratrix of the general ruin of the human race, new joy of the saints, glory of the works of the Almighty and singular instrument of his omnipotence. I confess Thee as the sweetest Mother of mercy, refuge of the unfortunate, Protectress of the poor and of the afflicted. All that the angelic spirits and the saints proclaim of Thee and in Thee and through Thee, I also confess, and I join them in whatever glory and praise they render in Thee and through Thee to the Divinity, blessing, magnifying and confessing and believing with them all things concerning Thee. O sovereign Mistress of all creation, through thy powerful intercession alone and because Thou hast looked upon me with eyes of mercy, thy divine Son has turned toward me in his clemency and as a Father, not disdaining for thy sake to choose me, the vile wormlet of the earth and the least of his creatures, to manifest his venerable secrets and mysteries. The multitudinous waters of my faults, ingratitudes, and miseries could not extinguish his immense charity; and my torpidity and sluggishness could not dry up or choke the flow of his divine light and wisdom.

788. I confess, O kindest Mother, before heaven and earth, that I have striven with myself and with thy enemies, and that my interior was sadly troubled in hesi-

tating between my unworthiness and my desire of wisdom. I stretched forth my hands and bewailed my insipidity; I led on my heart and I encountered knowledge, and with knowledge I came into the possession of peace; and when I encountered and loved it, I found it a goodly possession and I was not confounded. The sweet and strong force of wisdom wrought within me; it manifested to me the most hidden things and the knowledge most uncertain. I placed before my eyes Thee, the beautiful image of the Divinity and Mystical City of his habitation, in order that through the darksome night of this mortal life Thou mightest be my guiding star, and light me as the Moon of the immense Light, in order that I might follow Thee as my Leader, love Thee as a Mother, obey Thee as a Mistress, hear Thee as my Teacher, and that I might see myself as in an immaculate mirror and reach highest perfection by having before me thy ineffable example, virtues and works.

789. But who could ever have bent the divine Majesty to so vile a slave, if not Thou, O powerful Queen, who art the greatness of love, the vastness of clemency, the source of mercy, the prodigy of grace, and who has filled up the abysses of the guilt of all the children of Adam? Thine, O lady, is the credit and the glory for all that I have written, not only because it records thy most holy and admirable life, but because Thou hast given it a beginning, hast furthered it, and brought it to a close; and if Thou hadst not been its Author and Controller, it could never have entered into the thoughts of man. Let then all thanks and credit be thine; because Thou alone canst give a worthy return to thy divine Son and our Redeemer for this new and peerless blessing. That Thou make such a return, I can only ask Thee in the name of the whole Church and in my own name. And

this I desire now to do, O Mother and Queen of the virtues. Humbled in thy presence deeper than to the dust, I confess that I have received this and other blessings as favors, which I could never merit. Only what Thou hast taught and commanded, have I written; I was but the mute instrument of thy tongue, moved and governed by thy wisdom. Perfect Thou this work of thy hands, not only for the appropriate glory and praise of the Most High, but add to it what is wanting, in order that I may practice thy doctrine, follow thy footsteps, obey thy commands, and run after the odor of thy ointment, which is the sweetness and fragrance of thy virtues diffused with ineffable kindness through this history.

790. I acknowledge myself, O Empress of heaven, as the most unworthy, the most indebted of all the children of the holy Church. In order that the monstrosity of my ingratitude may not become apparent in the Church, before the Almighty and before Thee, I propose, offer, and seek to make known my renunciation of all that is visible and earthly; I again subject my liberty to the divine will and to thy own, engaging myself not to use my free will, except for God's glory and pleasure. I beseech Thee, the Blessed among all creatures, that, just as by the clemency of the Lord and thy own I hold the title of his spouse, and of thy daughter and disciple, and as thy Son, my Lord, has so often deigned to confirm these titles, Thou permit me not, O purest Lady, to fall short of these titles. Thy protection and assistance failed me not in the writing of thy wonderful life; help me now to put in practice thy teachings, wherein eternal life consists. Thou wishest and commandest me to imitate Thee; stamp and engrave upon my soul thy living image. Thou hast sown in my earthly heart the holy seed: guard it, cherish it, O Mother, sweet Mistress, that it may bring forth

fruit a hundredfold; that it may not be snatched away by the birds of prey, the dragon and his demons; for of their wrath I have been warned in every word I have written of Thee, my Lady. Guide me unto the end, command me as my Queen, instruct me as my Teacher, correct me as my Mother. Receive as thanksgiving for all this thy own life and the high pleasure which Thou hast afforded to the most blessed Trinity, as the perfection of his marvels. Let the angels and saints praise Thee, let all nations and generations know Thee; let all creatures, in Thee and through Thee, eternally bless their Creator and let my soul and all my faculties magnify Thee.

791. This heavenly history (as I have adverted throughout the course of it) I have written in obedience to the commands of my superiors and confessors, who have had the guidance of my soul. They have assured me that I would fulfill the will of God through obedience in writing it, and that I should obey the most blessed Mother, who for many years has commanded me to write it; and although I have always subjected all of it to the criticism and to the will of my superiors, withholding not a single word from their scrutiny: I nevertheless submit it again to their better judgment. Above all do I submit it to the amendment and correction of the holy Roman Catholic Church, to whose censure and teaching, as her daughter, I protest I will be subject, ready to believe and hold all that this same holy Church, our Mother, approves and believes, and ready to reject all that she rejects; for in obedience to her I wish to live and to die. Amen.

THE END.